Performing Literature

PERFORMING LITERATURE

An Introduction to Oral Interpretation

BEVERLY WHITAKER LONG
University of North Carolina
Chapel Hill

MARY FRANCES HOPKINS
Louisiana State University
Baton Rouge

PRENTICE-HALL, INC., ENGLEWOOD CLIFFS, NEW JERSEY 07632

Library of Congress Cataloging in Publication Data

LONG, BEVERLY WHITAKER
    Performing literature.

    Bibliography: p. 452
    Includes index.
    1. Oral interpretation.   2. Literature, Modern—20th
century.   I. HopKins, Mary Frances.   II. Title.
PN4145.L573   808.5′4   81-8607
ISBN 0-13-657171-9   AACR2

Editorial supervision and interior design by Serena Hoffman
Cover design by Janet Schmid
Manufacturing buyer: Edmund W. Leone

*Credits for quoted material appear on pp. 459–466, which are to be
considered a continuation of the copyright page.*

© 1982 by Prentice-Hall, Inc., Englewood Cliffs, N.J. 07632

PRINTED IN THE UNITED STATES OF AMERICA
10 9 8 7 6 5 4 3 2 1

ISBN 0-13-657171-9

PRENTICE-HALL INTERNATIONAL, INC., *London*
PRENTICE-HALL OF AUSTRALIA PTY. LIMITED, *Sydney*
PRENTICE-HALL OF CANADA, LTD., *Toronto*
PRENTICE-HALL OF INDIA PRIVATE LIMITED, *New Delhi*
PRENTICE-HALL OF JAPAN, INC., *Tokyo*
PRENTICE-HALL OF SOUTHEAST ASIA PTE. LTD., *Singapore*
WHITEHALL BOOKS LIMITED, *Wellington, New Zealand*

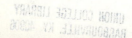

To

BILL LONG and **JACK HOPKINS**

Contents

ANTHOLOGY II

CHAPTER III
PERFORMING THE DRAMATIC SPEAKER
117

The Author   The Speaker   The Performer   Some Practical Advice
Freedom and Boundaries

WORKSHOP III

ANTHOLOGY III

CHAPTER IV
PERFORMING THE SPEAKER'S DRAMA
237

Appearance   Word Choice   Images   Figurative Language   Ellipse
Meter   Sound Patterns   Abstract Form   Free Verse   Plot
Time   Total Form

WORKSHOP IV

ANTHOLOGY IV

CHAPTER V
AFTERWORD
355

WORKSHOP V

ANTHOLOGY V

SELECTED BIBLIOGRAPHY
452

APPENDIX A
ADVANCED ASSIGNMENTS
456

APPENDIX B
SOURCES FOR AUDIO & VIDEO RECORDINGS
OF PERFORMED LITERATURE
458

ACKNOWLEDGMENTS
459

INDEX
467

To the Student

Performing Literature introduces college students to the study of literature through performance. All literary texts are produced by performers (people as authors—or even machines); they contain performers (speakers, personae, characters, narrators); and they offer the possibility of performing to and with others (silent and oral readers, individuals and groups, varieties of audiences).

The dictionary describes *performing* as "executing," "fulfilling," "completing," "furnishing," "finishing." In each case, the plain-speaking synonym is simply "doing." And why this "doing" of literature? The reason lies in the interest of knowing, or better still, *knowing/feeling the experiences expressed in literary texts.* Such a thesis claims that performance, central to the whole literary process, is more fully realized if the reader actually "tries on" what the literature tells about by performing it. If a long-range objective is needed, we can borrow one from Walter Ong: "realizing in a specially intense way one's identity (in a sense) with someone who (in another sense) one is not, remains one of the most human things man can do."[1] The potential liberalizing effect of this "realizing in a specially intense way" may not be scientifically measurable; however, it is a firmly held belief for most teachers and students of liberal and performing arts, and such a belief is the philosophical basis of this book.

[1] Walter J. Ong, S. J., *The Barbarian Within* (New York: Macmillan, 1962), p. 54.
Although we try to avoid sexist language in our own discussion, we have not altered it in quoted material.

As a method of studying literature, performing is potentially (1) revelatory to the performer; (2) revelatory to the listeners; (3) physically, vocally, and psychologically engaging; (4) a synthesizing process; and (5) within the capacities of all of us.

Performing is potentially *revelatory to the performer*. We make discoveries on all levels. Words we thought we understood may not make sense to us when we try to make them our own. Motivations may become both clearer and more complex. Structures subtle in our silent reading may emerge more sharply. Even passages we took to be serious may reveal their humor when performed.

Performing is *revelatory to the listeners.* The performance offers an instance of the text to those who may not already know it. In addition, the shared oral experience is likely to reveal insights to the audience that they overlooked, or enhance those they may not have appreciated fully in their own silent reading.

Performing is *physically, vocally, and psychologically engaging*. Performance demands full participation of the performer. Silent reading is a more passive activity, not only physically and vocally, but also mentally and emotionally. When we read silently, we usually read more quickly without attending to the text fully, often passing over words we don't immediately recognize or incidents that interest us less. Performance can make specific all words, attitudes and tone shifts, thus engaging our whole being.

Performing is a *synthesizing process*. At a given moment, performance forces us to evoke all of our experience with a text—our research into the meanings and significance of its words, our intellectual and emotional understanding of the speaker and the action in the text, and our physical and vocal experience of the sounds.

Performing is *within the capacities of all of us*. Performance is possible for us and accessible to us because everyone has cultivated the necessary skills and sensibilities to some extent. In some way, we all "perform" all the time.

Each chapter begins with a discussion of literature and performance, followed by a workshop and an anthology. The discussions draw upon various sources that deal with theories of literature and performance, ideas for training performers and preparing for performance, suggestions for performing generally and for performing specific texts.

In the workshops, the principles evolved in the discussion are applied to one or more literary texts. This part contains no prescriptions for conventional platform behavior—only descriptions of what is, or may be, occurring in the text and some of the many possibilities of what could happen in performance. In short, no rules apply uniformly when particular texts, performers, and situations converge.

Each chapter concludes with an anthology of twentieth-century poetry, prose fiction, nonfiction, and drama—literature to which college students should be able to respond with some ease. Literature from earlier periods is excluded, not because it cannot or should not be studied through performance; quite the contrary is true. However, such literature is likely to be readily available. The selections included here are more contemporary and possibly serve as a comfortable starting place for studying literature through performance.

The literary texts, varying in length from short poems to complete short stories and plays, are representative of various countries, ethnic groups, minorities, social and political philosophies, styles, and writers' attitudes and purposes. For comparative discussion, most of the anthology sections contain at least two works by some authors and at least two on the same general theme.

In the interest of having the class study the same literature, your professor may ask that you perform only selections included in the book or on handouts. Familiar with the same literary texts, you and your classroom audience can be mutually helpful. Listeners can let performers know to what extent aspects of the text were demonstrated in performance. For an audience, the excitement of hearing unfamiliar literature often lies in novelty and surprise; but the excitement of listening to literature you have already read lies in fulfilled or extended expectations and meaningful discoveries. In this latter situation, the class functions as a loosely organized team engaged in exploring and illuminating literature together; its leader is the performer.

While the *public* performance of literature can be challenging and gratifying for the performer and a rich experience for the audience, the aim in this book is to treat performance as *a way of studying literature in the classroom*. If you were preparing a public performance, you would, no doubt, spend a considerable amount of time searching for material appropriate to your audience's interests and expectation, to the performing space, and to your own skills and abilities. In the classroom, however, your overriding concern is *to show the literature in as much fullness as possible;* it follows that practically any literary text can be studied profitably through performance. When your performance "rings true," you will interest and satisfy your classroom audience.

Another distinction between classroom performance and what is done for public occasions lies in adapting or cutting. Although adapting is a common practice in public programs, it is not recommended in the classroom until you have acquired a full enough understanding of literary structure to avoid distorting or destroying when you adapt. If a selection is too long to meet the time limits, you may want to perform only a section, say, the opening or closing, and alert your audience to what you're doing. Even if you are performing only a few paragraphs from a long selection, you will want to be familiar with the whole literary text.

Louise Rosenblatt, a noted English educator, claims that a written piece of literature is a *text,* and that a *poem* (or any imaginative literature) exists only when a *transaction occurs between reader and text.*[2] The print on the page thus becomes an

experience in literature only when a person or persons make connection with it. The reader must constitute the poem, make it happen, by actively engaging in a relationship with the text. As you study literature through performance, you learn more about that transaction, make it fuller and richer. And you enable the members of the audience to engage in the transaction, increasing the pleasure for all concerned.

Later in life, your performances may range from reading to your children to acting in a Broadway theater. On any occasion, including your own private performance, it is essential to understand the nature of performance and the nature of literature. The process of exploring the self and the literary text and the process of bringing the two together are basic to any performing you will do.

[2]Louise M. Rosenblatt, *The Reader, The Text, The Poem: The Transactional Theory of the Literary Work* (Carbondale: Southern Illinois University, 1978).

ACKNOWLEDGMENTS

To Francine Merritt for introducing us to the interpretation of literature.

To Fabian Gudas for his insights into literary criticism.

To Gresdna Doty and Lee Hudson for their perceptions about performance.

To Don Geiger, whose influence on this book is apparent.

To John Bittner, Steve Dalphin, Hilda Medlin, Brian Walker and Serena Hoffman for various forms of support.

To Carolyn Gray, Paul Gray, Lee Hudson, and Phillis Rienstra Jeffrey for their contributions to Chapter V.

We also wish to express our thanks to the various reviewers who saw rough drafts of the manuscript: Bruce B. Manchester, George Mason University; Larry L. Barker, Auburn University; Robin Vagenas, University of Delaware; Suzanne Bennett, The University of North Dakota; Robert Overstreet, Auburn University; Barbara Kaster, Bowdoin College; Dennis Klinzing, West Chester State College; Richard Haas, The University of Michigan; Leland H. Roloff, Northwestern University; Jill O'Brien, DePaul University; Martha Nell Hardy, The University of North Carolina at Chapel Hill; Gresdna Doty, Louisiana State University; Frances Lea McCurdy; D. Thomas Porter, SUNY at Buffalo; Barbara Becker, Louisiana State University; Stacy Cox, University of North Carolina at Chapel Hill; Linda Craven, University of North Carolina at Chapel Hill; Carole Tallant, University of North Carolina at Wilmington; Sherry Perlmutter, University of North Carolina at Chapel Hill

BEVERLY WHITAKER LONG
MARY FRANCES HOPKINS

Performing Literature

*Acting a role, realizing in a specially intense way one's identity
(in a sense) with someone who (in another sense) one is not,
remains one of the most human things a man can do.*

Walter J. Ong

To Look at Any Thing

*To look at any thing,
If you would know that thing,
You must look at it long:
To look at this green and say
"I have seen spring in these
Woods," will not do—you must
Be the thing you see:
You must be the dark snakes of
Stems and ferny plumes of leaves,
You must enter in
To the small silences between
The leaves,
You must take your time
And touch the very peace
They issue from.*

John Moffitt

*The measure of the poem is not in its assertion but in the perform-
ance of its own insight.*

John Ciardi

After you study the text and anthology in this chapter, we hope you will be able to

1. Explain how "performance" is basic to living our everyday lives.
2. Understand why works of art are "arrested performances."
3. Appreciate the sense in which all writers are "performers."
4. Describe the reader of literature's "deep double game."
5. Cite examples from everyday experiences as well as from literature of a variety of role-taking situations and their effect on the performer as well as the audience.

Varieties of Performances

1

Everyone performs. Daily, all of us, consciously or otherwise, perform in real-life contexts. These performances are entirely ephemeral—preserved, if at all, only in the memories of people who happen to witness them.

Creative artists perform in special ways: their performances create some kind of object that can be experienced repeatedly—a painting, a piece of music, a poem. These objects result from the artist's performance of making. At the same time they are themselves "arrested" performance, *records of the creative artist's performance*. For those of us who observe, they are also a complexity of signs that indicate varieties of potential and unrealized performances. The special *performance records* studied in this book are literary texts, the "arrested performances" of creative writers that provide readers the signs, clues, cues, and directions for a performance of their own.

We perform with varying degrees of success as *we experience* these art objects. Most of these activities are private and probably silent, unobserved by anyone else. However, in certain specialized situations we can share with others this last kind of performance; that is, we can let others join us as we perform our experience of a work of art, say, music or a literary text.

Literature Is the Writer's Performance

As we have noted, artists are special kinds of performers, and their compositions are records or evidence of their achievements as performers. Poets[1] are like acrobats or jugglers, keeping dispar-

ate items in balance, defying natural order and masking the strain of the defiance, making the result look effortless and natural.

Robert Frost says, "I look on the poet as a man of prowess, just like an athlete. He's a performer. And the things you can do in a poem are very various." Asked how he looks at a new poem, he replied,

This thing of performance and prowess and feats of association—that's where it all lies. One of my ways of looking at a poem right away it's sent to me, right off, is to see if it's rhymed. Then I know just when to look at it. The rhymes come in pairs, don't they? And nine times out of ten with an ordinary writer, one of two of the terms is better than the other. One makeshift will do, and then they get another that's good, and then another makeshift, and then another one that's good. That is in the realm of performance, that's the deadly test with me. I want to be unable to tell which of those he thought of first. If there's any trick about it, putting the better one first so as to deceive me, I can tell pretty soon. That's all in the performance realm.[2]

Performance in Literature Satisfies Some Basic Human Needs

As Frost says, poems are performances by a poet, and we can enjoy them as accomplishments. Also, they fulfill deep human needs.

Poetry has always been a part of the story of man. Before men had written language, they had bards who chanted and sang of gods and heroes and more ordinary folk. Language itself, at its very inception, was essentially poetry.... every word, at its

---

[1] We use the words "poet" and "poetry" here—and often in this book—to encompass the works of all writers of imaginative literature and their modes: lyric, epic, dramatic.

[2] Richard Poirier interviewing Robert Frost, *Writers at Work: The Paris Review Interviews*, 2nd ser. (New York: Viking Press, 1963), p. 33.

birth, is a flash of poetry, by which man sees a thing in a new light. Poetry, thus, has always been *a way of knowing, of discovering.* All real poetry has this quality: in some degree it recaptures the freshness, the "firstness," of Adam naming the creatures.[3]

(Early in this century there was a group of poets in Russia calling themselves Adamists because they considered their role to be giving everything this "firstness," the illusion of being seen for the first time.)

In many contemporary cultures, and probably in all ancient ones, poems existed only as oral performances. When written language is nonexistent or the exclusive property of a few, recitations provide the only "text" of a poem. This tradition of oral poetry and recitation of poems did not die with the explosion of print in the eighteenth century.

> Not until the eighteenth century did books become a major vehicle for the communication of poetry. For ages before that, poetry had been spoken, or chanted as histories, legends, dramas; as battle cries, work songs, lullabies, and game rhymes; as exalted psalms and superstitious incantations. Then, in the era of the book and magazine, the art of poetry underwent a highly conscious literary development—not all of it good, of course. But at its best, poetry never lost its closeness to the breath, the voice, the ear—to the nature of singing speech.[4]

(It is interesting to note that the word for poetry in Eskimo is *breath*.)

Plays are of course performances. In fact, many writers distinguish between *script* and *play*, the former meaning written text, the latter the performed text. But the script too is performance—the playwright's performance. And plays, like poems, speak to deep human needs. Plays can be plain fun and plainly interesting.

But they can be more than just entertainment.

> When the playwright-poet writes . . . any significant play, he creates an ordered universe, and the order of that universe is dominantly a moral order. Even in comedy, which treats social man in his deviations, if one traces those deviations back to their logical bases, they rest upon moral distinctions. Drama, then, is an exploration of the moral order of life and a revelation of the nature of man—moral man, social man, typical man, a-typical man, individual man, ludicrous man, evil man, man in all of his multiform aspects.[5]

Fiction has much the same appeal as drama. We get interested in the characters, in what happens next. We may even see ourselves in the story, "that publicly available daydream which fiction is." For the sophisticated reader, that kind of participation is only part of the fun. Robert Penn Warren explains what he calls a "deep double game."

> The more sophisticated reader plays a deep double game with himself, one part of him is identified with a character or with several in turn while another part holds aloof to respond, interpret and judge. How often have we heard some sentimental old lady say of a book, "I just went through everything with her and I know exactly how she felt. Then when she died, I just cried." The sweet old lady, even if she isn't very sophisticated, is instinctively playing the double game too. She identifies herself with the heroine. But she survives the heroine's death to shed the delicious tears. So even the old lady knows how to make the most of what we shall call her role taking. She knows that doubleness, in the very act of identification, is of the essence of role taking. There is the taker of the role and there is the role taken. And fiction is, in imaginative enactment, a role taking.[6]

[3]Jacob Drachler and Virginia R. Terris, *The Many Worlds of Poetry* (New York: Knopf, 1969), p. 241. (Italics added.)
[4]*Ibid.*

[5]Hubert Heffner, *The Nature of Drama* (Cambridge: Houghton Mifflin, 1959), p. 351.
[6]Robert Penn Warren, "Why Do We Read Fiction?" *The Saturday Evening Post*, October 20, 1962, p. 82.

This kind of participation offers more than the momentary pleasure of reading; role taking in general—and role taking in fiction in particular—meets basic human needs.

> ...it is only by role taking that the child comes to know, to know "inwardly" in the only way that finally counts, that other people really exist and are in fact persons with needs, hopes, fears and even rights. So the role-taking of fiction, at the same time that it gratifies our deep need to extend and enrich our own experience, continues this long discipline in human sympathy. And this discipline in sympathy, through the imaginative enactment of role-taking, gratifies another need deep in us, our yearning to enter and feel at ease in the human community.
>
> Play when we are children, and fiction when we are grown up, leads us, through role taking, to an awareness of others. But all along the way role taking leads us, by the same token, to an awareness of ourselves; it leads us, in fact, to the creation of the self.

For the individual is not born with a self. He is born as a mysterious bundle of possibilities which, bit by bit, in a long process of trial and error, he sorts out until he gets some sort of unifying self, the ringmaster self, the official, self.[7]

Conclusion

The wonder of all these many kinds of performances is that they interrelate, that they are, in fact, interdependent. Our real-life performances create in us the potential for experiencing performances in art and this experiencing of art is simultaneously itself a real-life experience, enriching others. This book rests on the premise that we all perform daily, and we can sharpen our ability to perform literature, thereby becoming better experiencers of the various performances in literary art. We will know literature better as we perform it.

[7] *Ibid.*

WORKSHOP I

In this first workshop we shall look closely at three selections that relate to performance. As we noted earlier, all three are the *written performances* of the writer. In James Dickey's "The Bee," a father performs an action that reminds him of earlier performances before a stadium crowd. Ernie Pyle discusses the effect of a whole class of performances in "The Movies," and Flannery O'Connor shows us a woman who wants to perform as a writer in "The Crop."

The discussions following each selection are designed to help you probe these texts, but they in no way provide exhaustive analyses. You probably will not read texts with an eye to performing them in class yet. But this workshop should help

to clarify and enrich the various types of performance that are the basis for this chapter and help you, as a "silent performer," to experience these three texts more fully.

Note: Later in this book we discuss the importance of a poem's appearance—particularly its line endings and stanza breaks—as an integral part of the poem and as directions for its performance. Unfortunately, printing costs mandate that some poems in this book be printed in a two-column format, thus occasionally tampering with the poets' line arrangements. When this occurs, the printing convention of indenting the continued part of a broken line is used.

The Bee
JAMES DICKEY

To the football coaches of Clemson College, 1942

One dot
Grainily shifting   we at roadside and
The smallest wings coming   along the rail fence out
Of the woods   one dot   of all that green. It now
Becomes flesh-crawling   then the quite still
Of stinging. I must live faster for my terrified
Small son   it is on him. Has come. Clings.

Old wingback, come
To life. If your knee action is high
Enough, the fat may fall in time   God damn
You, Dickey, *dig*   this is your last time to cut
And run   but you must give it everything you have
Left, for screaming near your screaming child is the sheer
Murder of California traffic: some bee hangs driving

Your child
Blindly onto the highway. Get there however
Is still possible. Long live what I badly did
At Clemson   and all of my clumsiest drives
For the ball   all of my trying to turn
The corner downfield   and my spindling explosions
Through the five-hole over tackle. O backfield

Coach Shag Norton,
Tell me as you never yet have told me
To get the lead out   scream whatever will get
The slow-motion of middle age off me   I cannot
Make it this way   I will have to leave
My feet   they are gone   I have him where
He lives   and down we go singing with screams into

The dirt,
Son-screams of fathers   screams of dead coaches turning
To approval   and from between us the bee rises screaming
With flight   grainily shifting   riding the rail fence
Back into the woods   traffic blasting past us
Unchanged, nothing heard through the air-
conditioning glass   we lying at roadside full

Of the forearm prints
Of roadrocks   strawberries on our elbows as from
Scrimmage with the varsity   now we can get
Up   stand   turn away from the highway   look straight

Into trees. See, there is nothing coming out   no
Smallest wing   no shift of a flight-grain   nothing
Nothing. Let us go in, son, and listen

For some tobacco-
mumbling voice in the branches   to say "That's
a little better,"   to our lives still hanging
By a hair. There is nothing to stop us   we can go
Deep   deeper   into elms, and listen to traffic die
Roaring, like a football crowd from which we have
Vanished. Dead coaches live in the air, son   live

In the ear
Like fathers, and *urge*   and *urge*. They want you better
Than you are. When needed, they rise and curse you   they scream
When something must be saved. Here, under this tree,
We can sit down. You can sleep, and I can try
To give back what I have earned by keeping us
Alive, and safe from bees: the smile of some kind

Of savior—
Of touchdowns, of fumbles, battles,
Lives. Let me sit here with you, son
As on the bench, while the first string takes back
Over, far away   and say with my silentest tongue, with the man-
creating bruises of my arms   with a live leaf a quick
Dead hand on my shoulder, "Coach Norton, I am your boy."

Dickey's nine-stanza poem features two performances: in the present, a father tries to catch his son, who is running away from a bee, before the boy dashes blindly into traffic on a busy highway and the father's remembering his past on the football field. Dickey moves from the sport of earlier years to a wooded area near the busy highway where the father's recalled skills enable him to save his son from what could be an ultimate defeat. A still larger performance envelops the entire poem—the speaker's tribute to those coaches who armed him for far more than the battle of football. Yet the idea for the thanks comes only many years later, when he struggles to win over the bee.[8]

The needs of both the knowing father and the unknowing son are urgent, and the father succeeds in rescuing the boy because of the techniques he developed in earlier athletic performances.

[8]James Dickey, *Self-Interviews*, recorded and edited by Barbara and James Reiss (New York: Delta, 1972), p. 171.

from *The Movies*
ERNIE PYLE

I believe in the movies. One of my hates is the smart critic who hurls his words at Hollywood's disgraceful commercialism, its insane business extravagances, its illiterate executives, its failure to achieve any approach to real art, its refusal to broadcast a message. But then I'm not a typical movie fan. It seems impossible for me to see more than six or eight pictures a year, and I pick my pictures. The result is that I seldom see a bad movie. So I think the movies are wonderful.

As a matter of fact, instead of the usual "Why can't we make movies more like real life?" I think a more pertinent question is "Why can't real life be more like the movies?" A movie is a series of climaxes—little glimpses of high spots and low spots—and in the end there is the great climax, and the darkness, and no concern for the years of dying embers and the utter monotony ahead.

Why can't human beings too live only in climaxes, in great ecstasy or great despair, with all the long dull stretches left out? Who would mind being blinded in the war, if he could win the girl anyhow, and then have it understood that the rest of his life was to be an idyl and a blessing, with no dreary days or cruel, growing prongs of pity directed at him. And who would mind being the other fellow and losing the girl if in real life he could actually come to the end of the reel right there, and never have to brood about it, or hunger?

Of course, characters on the screen are made to suffer, but their suffering is dramatic and romantic, while ours here on the globe is the dull achy kind that embitters and wastes, with so little drama to ennoble it.

It isn't what the movies put in that makes them so wonderful—it's what they leave out. Wouldn't a movie be dull if it ran on for weeks and weeks, showing a man at his work? It's much nicer for the movies to show him working for just thirty seconds.

And in our little tragedies and despairs, and our big ones too, why couldn't we just go stare out a window and bow our heads and look grave and heartbroken for a few seconds, denoting a long period of grief and yearning, and not have to go through the actual months and years of it?

And our happiness too. Maybe you'd like to have happiness strung out, instead of just a flash and a kiss denoting bliss forever. But for me, I think not. Just a moment of happiness is all right, for then there is no dulling. Yes, just wake me up for the peaks and the valleys, and please have the anesthetist ready when we come to the plains, and the long days when nothing happens.

Ernie Pyle's "The Movies" also shows faith in performance, this time on film. Why not live with the climactic moments stored there, he asks, instead of with tedious day-to-day events? In communicating his praise and blame, Pyle is clearly and jokingly on the side of the celluloid, choosing the fictional over the real because the former is so much more pleasant and speedy.

The Crop
FLANNERY O'CONNOR

Miss Willerton always crumbed the table. It was her particular household accomplishment and she did it with great thoroughness. Lucia and Bertha did the dishes and Garner went into the parlor and did the *Morning Press* crossword puzzle. That left Miss Willerton in the dining room by herself and that was all right with Miss Willerton. Whew! Breakfast in that house was always an ordeal. Lucia insisted that they have a regular hour for breakfast just like they did for other meals. Lucia said a regular breakfast made for other regular habits, and with Garner's tendency to upsets, it was imperative that they establish some system in their eating. This way she could also see that he put the Agar-Agar on his Cream of Wheat. As if, Miss Willerton thought, after having done it for fifty years, he'd be capable of doing anything else. The breakfast dispute always started with Garner's Cream of Wheat and ended with her three spoonfuls of pineapple crush. "You know your acid, Willie," Miss Lucia would always say, "you know your acid"; and then Garner would roll his eyes and make some sickening remark and Bertha would jump and Lucia would look distressed and Miss Willerton would taste the pineapple crush she had already swallowed.

It was a relief to crumb the table. Crumbing the table gave one time to think, and if Miss Willerton were going to write a story, she had to think about it first. She could usually think best sitting in front of her typewriter, but this would do for the time being. First, she had to think of a subject to write a story about. There were so many subjects to write stories about that Miss Willerton never could think of one. That was always the hardest part of writing a story, she always said. She spent more time thinking of something to write about than she did writing. Sometimes she discarded subject after subject and it usually took her a week or two to decide finally on something. Miss Willerton got out the silver crumber and the crumb-catcher and started stroking the table. I wonder, she mused, if a baker would make a good subject? Foreign bakers were very picturesque, she thought. Aunt Myrtile Filmer had left her four color-tints of French bakers in mushroom-looking hats. They were great tall fellows—blond and. . . .

"Willie!" Miss Lucia screamed, entering the dining room with the saltcellars. "For heaven's sake, hold the catcher under the crumber or you'll have those crumbs on the rug. I've Bisseled it four times in the last week and I am not going to do it again."

"You have not Bisseled it on account of any crumbs I have spilled," Miss Willerton said tersely. "I always pick up the crumbs I drop," and she added, "I drop relatively few."

"And wash the crumber before you put it up this time," Miss Lucia returned.

Miss Willerton drained the crumbs into her hand and threw them out the window. She took the catcher and crumber to the kitchen and ran them under the cold-water faucet. She dried them and stuck them back in the drawer. That was over. Now she could get to the typewriter. She could stay there until dinnertime.

Miss Willerton sat down at her typewriter and let out her breath. Now!

What had she been thinking about? Oh. Bakers. Hmmm. Bakers. No, bakers wouldn't do. Hardly colorful enough. No social tension connected with bakers. Miss Willerton sat staring through her typewriter. A S D F G—her eyes wandered over the keys. Hmmm. Teachers? Miss Willerton wondered. No. Heavens no. Teachers always made Miss Willerton feel peculiar. Her teachers at Willowpool Seminary had been all right but they were women. Willowpool Female Seminary, Miss Willerton remembered. She didn't like the phrase, Willowpool Female Seminary—it sounded biological. She always just said she was a graduate of Willowpool. Men teachers made Miss Willerton feel as if she were going to mispronounce something. Teachers weren't timely anyhow. They weren't even a social problem.

Social problem. Social problem. Hmmm. Sharecroppers! Miss Willerton had never been intimately connected with sharecroppers but, she reflected, they would make as arty a subject as any, and they would give her that air of social concern which was so valuable to have in the circles she was hoping to travel! "I can always capitalize," she muttered, "on the hookworm." It was coming to her now! Certainly! Her fingers plinked excitedly over the keys, never touching them. Then suddenly she began typing at great speed.

"Lot Motun," the typewriter registered, "called his dog." "Dog" was followed by an abrupt pause. Miss Willerton always did her best work on the first sentence. "First sentences," she always said, "came to her—like a flash! Just like a flash!" she would say and snap her fingers, "like a flash!" And she built her story up from them. "Lot Motun called his dog" had been automatic with Miss Willerton, and reading the sentence over, she decided that not only was "Lot Motun" a good name for a sharecropper, but also that having him call his dog was an excellent thing to have a sharecropper do. "The dog pricked up its ears and slunk over to Lot." Miss Willerton had the sentence down before she realized her error—two "Lots" in one paragraph. That was displeasing to the ear. The typewriter grated back and Miss Willerton applied three x's to "Lot." Over it she wrote in pencil, "him." Now she was ready to go again. "Lot Motun called his dog. The dog pricked up its ears and slunk over to him." Two dogs, too, Miss Willerton thought. Ummm. But that didn't affect the ears like two "Lots," she decided.

Miss Willerton was a great believer in what she called "phonetic art." She maintained that the ear was as much a reader as the eye. She liked to express it that way. "The eye forms a picture," she had told a group at the United Daughters of the Colonies, "that can be painted in the abstract, and the success of literary venture" (Miss Willerton liked the phrase, 'literary venture') "depends on the abstract created in the mind and the tonal quality" (Miss Willerton also liked 'tonal quality') "registered in the ear." There was something biting and sharp about "Lot Motun called his dog"; followed by "the dog pricked up its ears and slunk over to him," it gave the paragraph just the send-off it needed.

"He pulled the animal's short, scraggy ears and rolled over with it in the mud." Perhaps, Miss Willerton mused, that would be overdoing it. But a sharecropper, she knew, might reasonably be expected to roll over in the mud. Once she had read a novel dealing with that kind of people in which they had done just as bad and, throughout three-fourths of the narrative, much worse. Lucia found it in cleaning out one of Miss Willerton's bureau drawers and after glancing at a few random pages took it between thumb and index finger to the furnace and threw it in. "When I was cleaning your bureau out this morning, Willie, I found a book that Garner must have put there for a joke," Miss Lucia told her later. "It was awful, but you know how Garner is. I burned it." And then, tittering, she added, "I was sure it couldn't be yours." Miss Willerton was sure it could be none other's than hers but she hesitated in claiming the distinction. She had ordered it from the publisher because she didn't want to ask for it at the library. It had cost her $3.75 with the postage and she had not finished the last four chapters. At least, she had got enough from it, though, to be able to say that Lot Motun might reasonably roll over in the mud with his dog. Having him do that would give more point to the hookworm, too, she decided. "Lot Motun called his dog. The dog pricked up its ears and slunk over to him. He pulled the animal's short, scraggy ears and rolled over with it in the mud."

Miss Willerton settled back. That was a good beginning. Now she would plan her action. There had to be a woman, of course. Perhaps Lot could kill her. That type of woman always started trouble. She might even goad him on to kill her because of her wantonness and then he would be pursued by his conscience maybe.

He would have to have principles if that were going to be the case, but it would be fairly easy to give him those. Now how was she going to work that in with all the love interest there'd have to be, she wondered. There would have to be some quite violent, naturalistic scenes, the sadistic sort of thing one read of in connection with that class. It was a problem. However, Miss Willerton enjoyed such problems. She liked to plan passionate scenes best of all, but when she came to write them, she always began to feel peculiar and to wonder what the family would say when they read them. Garner would snap his fingers and wink at her at every opportunity; Bertha would think she was terrible; and Lucia would say in that silly voice of hers, "What have you been keeping from us, Willie? What have you been keeping from us?" and titter like she always did. But Miss Willerton couldn't think about that now; she had to plan her characters.

Lot would be tall, stooped, and shaggy but with sad eyes that made him look like a gentleman in spite of his red neck and big fumbling hands. He'd have straight teeth and, to indicate that he had some spirit, red hair. His clothes would hang on him but he'd wear them nonchalantly like they were part of his skin; maybe, she mused, he'd better not roll over with the dog after all. The woman would be more or less pretty—yellow hair, fat ankles, muddy-colored eyes.

She would get supper for him in the cabin and he'd sit there eating the lumpy grits she hadn't bothered to put salt in and thinking about something big, something way off—another cow, a painted house, a clean well, a farm of his own even. The woman would yowl at him for not cutting enough wood for her stove and would whine about the pain in her back. She'd sit and stare at him eating the sour grits and say he didn't have nerve enough to steal food. "You're just a damn beggar!" she'd sneer. Then he'd tell her to keep quiet. "Shut your mouth!" he'd shout. "I've taken all I'm gonna." She'd roll her eyes, mocking him, and laugh—"I ain't afraid er nothin' that looks like you." Then he'd push his chair behind him and head toward her. She'd snatch a knife off the table—Miss Willerton wondered what kind of a fool the woman was—and back away holding it in front of her. He'd lunge forward but she'd dart from him like a wild horse. Then they'd face each other again—their eyes brimming with hate—and sway back and forth. Miss Willerton could hear the seconds dropping on the tin roof outside. He'd dart at her again but she'd have the knife ready and would plunge it into him in an instant—Miss Willerton could stand it no longer. She struck the woman a terrific blow on the head from behind. The knife dropped out of her hands and a mist swept her from the room. Miss Willerton turned to Lot. "Let me get you some hot grits," she said. She went over to the stove and got a clean plate of smooth white grits and a piece of butter.

"Gee, thanks," Lot said and smiled at her with his nice teeth. "You always fix 'em just right. You know," he said, "I been thinkin'—we could get out of this tenant farm. We could have a decent place. If we made anything this year over, we could put it in a cow an' start buildin' things up. Think what it would mean, Willie, just think."

She sat down beside him and put her hand on his shoulder. "We'll do it," she said. "We'll make better than we've made any year and by spring we should have us that cow."

"You always know how I feel, Willie," he said. "You always have known."

They sat there for a long time thinking of how well they understood each other. "Finish your food," she said finally.

After he had eaten, he helped her take the ashes out the stove and then, in the hot July evening, they walked down the pasture toward the creek and talked about the place they were going to have some day.

When late March came and the rainy season was almost there, they had accomplished almost more than was believable. For the past month, Lot had been up every morning at five, and Willie an hour earlier to get in all the work they could while the weather was clear. Next week, Lot said, the rain would probably start and if they didn't get the crop in by then, they would lose it—and all they had gained in the past months. They knew what that meant—another year of getting along with no more than they'd had the last. Then too, there'd be a baby next year instead of a cow. Lot had wanted the cow anyway. "Children don't cost all that much to feed," he'd argued, "an' the cow would help feed him," but Willie had been firm—the cow could come later—the child must have a good start. "Maybe," Lot had said finally, "we'll have enough for both," and he had gone out to look at the new-plowed ground as if he could count the harvest from the furrows.

Even with as little as they'd had, it had been a good year. Willie had cleaned the shack, and Lot had fixed the chimney. There was a profusion of petunias by the doorstep and a colony of snapdragons under the window. It had been a peaceful year. But now they were becoming anxious over the crop. They must gather it before the rain. "We need another week," Lot muttered when he came in that night. "One more week an' we can do it. Do you feel like gatherin'? It isn't right that you should have to," he sighed, "but I can't hire any help."

"I'm all right," she said, hiding her trembling hands behind her. "I'll gather."

"It's cloudy tonight," Lot said darkly.

The next day they worked until nightfall—worked until they could work no longer and then stumbled back to the cabin and fell into bed.

Willie woke in the night conscious of a pain. It was a soft, green pain with purple lights running through it. She wondered if she were awake. Her head rolled from side to side and there were droning shapes grinding boulders in it.

Lot sat up. "Are you bad off?" he asked, trembling.

She raised herself on her elbow and then sank down again. "Get Anna up by the creek," she gasped.

The droning became louder and the shapes grayer. The pain intermingled with them for seconds first, then interminably. It came again and again. The sound of the droning grew more distinct and toward morning she realized that it was rain. Later she asked hoarsely, "How long has it been raining?"

"Most two days, now," Lot answered.

"Then we lost." Willie looked listlessly out at the dripping trees. "It's over."

"It isn't over," he said softly. "We got a daughter."

"You wanted a son."

"No, I got what I wanted—two Willies instead of one—that's better than a cow, even," he grinned. "What can I do to deserve all I got, Willie?" He bent over and kissed her forehead.

"What can I?" she asked slowly. "And what can I do to help you more?"

"How about your going to the grocery, Willie?"

Miss Willerton shoved Lot away from her. "W-what did you say, Lucia?" she stuttered.

"I said how about your going to the grocery this time? I've been every morning this week and I'm busy now."

Miss Willerton pushed back from the typewriter. "Very well," she said sharply. "What do you want there?"

"A dozen eggs and two pounds of tomatoes—ripe tomatoes—and you'd better start doctoring that cold right now. Your eyes are already watering and you're hoarse. There's Empirin in the bathroom. Write a check on the house for the groceries. And wear your coat. It's cold."

Miss Willerton rolled her eyes upward. "I am forty-four years old," she announced, "and able to take care of myself."

"And get ripe tomatoes," Miss Lucia returned.

Miss Willerton, her coat buttoned unevenly, tramped up Broad Street and into the supermarket. "What was it now?" she muttered. "Two dozen eggs and a pound of tomatoes, yes." She passed the lines of canned vegetables and the crackers and headed for the box where the eggs were kept. But there were no eggs. "Where are the eggs?" she asked a boy weighing snapbeans.

"We ain't got nothin' but pullet eggs," he said, fishing up another handful of beans.

"Well, where are they and what is the difference?" Miss Willerton demanded.

He threw several beans back into the bin, slouched over to the egg box and handed her a carton. "There ain't no difference really," he said, pushing his gum over his front teeth. "A teen-age chicken or somethin', I don't know. You want 'em?"

"Yes, and two pounds of tomatoes. Ripe tomatoes," Miss Willerton added. She did not like to do the shopping. There was no reason those clerks should be so condescending. That boy wouldn't have dawdled with Lucia. She paid for the eggs and tomatoes and left hurriedly. The place depressed her somehow.

Silly that a grocery should depress one—nothing in it but trifling domestic doings—women buying beans—riding children in those grocery go-carts—higgling about an eighth of a pound more or less of squash—what did they get out of it? Miss Willerton wondered. Where was there any chance for self-expression, for creation, for art? All around her it was the same—sidewalks full of people scurrying about with their hands full of little packages and their minds full of little packages—that woman there with the child on the leash, pulling him, jerking him, dragging him away from a window with a jack-o'-lantern in it; she would probably be pulling and jerking him the rest of her life. And there was another, dropping a shopping bag all over the street, and another wiping a child's nose, and up the street an old woman was coming with three grandchildren jumping all over her, and behind them was a couple walking too close for refinement.

Miss Willerton looked at the couple sharply as they came nearer and passed. The woman was plump with yellow hair and fat ankles and muddy-colored eyes. She had on high-heel pumps and blue anklets, a too-short cotton dress, and a plaid jacket. Her skin was mottled and her neck thrust forward as if she were sticking it out to smell something that was always being drawn away. Her face was set in an inane grin. The man was long and wasted and shaggy. His shoulders were stooped and there were yellow knots along the side of his large, red neck. His hands fumbled stupidly with the girl's as they slumped along, and once or twice he smiled sickly at her and Miss Willerton could see that he had straight teeth and sad eyes and a rash over his forehead.

"Ugh," she shuddered.

Miss Willerton laid the groceries on the kitchen table and went back to her typewriter. She looked at the paper in it. "Lot Motun called his dog," it read. "The dog pricked up its ears and slunk over to him. He pulled the animal's short, scraggy ears and rolled over with it in the mud."

"That sounds awful!" Miss Willerton muttered. "It's not a good subject anyway," she decided. She needed something more colorful—more arty. Miss Willerton looked at her typewriter for a long time. Then of a sudden her fist hit the desk in several ecstatic little bounces. "The Irish!" she squealed. "The Irish!" Miss Willerton had always admired the Irish. Their brogue, she thought, was full of music; and their history—splendid! And the people, she mused, the Irish people! They were full of spirit—red-haired, with broad shoulders and great, drooping mustaches.

"The Crop," one of Flannery O'Connor's earliest stories, involves a protagonist who performs all public actions with cultivated decorum, creates stories with all the skill she can muster, and then sheds her own dismal identity in favor of playing Lot Motun's wife. Whereas initially Miss Willerton swaps concentration on crumbing the table for thoughts about the upcoming story, later she stops the act of writing about imagined events and becomes a key member in those fantasized happenings. Still later, when she performs the routine task of grocery shopping, she lets go of her fanciful creation, where she had just thrived so romantically, only to enter yet another fantasy performance, this time with a red-haired Irishman.

ANTHOLOGY I

This section encourages you to enlarge your notions about performing literature by studying fiction, nonfiction, poetry, and drama that all deal in some way with performance. The literary texts range from comic to serious (some are both), or-dinary to mysterious, simple to complex. For now, listen to the literature and try some of it on. Later you may decide to perform one of the selections in class. Then, perhaps, you can discuss some of the questions at the end of the selections.

The Day the Audience Walked Out on Me, and Why
DENISE LEVERTOV

(May 8th, 1970, Goucher College, Maryland)

Like this it happened:
after the antiphonal reading from the psalms
and the dance of lamentation before the altar,
and the two poems, 'Life at War' and
                             'What Were They Like?'

I began my rap,
and said:
Yes, it is well that we have gathered
in this chapel to remember
the students shot at Kent State,

but let us be sure we know
our gathering is a mockery unless
we remember also
the black students shot at Orangeburg two years ago,
and Fred Hampton murdered in his bed
by the police only months ago.

And while I spoke the people
—girls, older women, a few men—
began to rise and turn
their backs to the altar and leave.

And I went on and said,
Yes, it is well that we remember
all of these, but let us be sure
we know it is hypocrisy
to think of them unless
we make our actions their memorial,
actions of militant resistance.

By then the pews were almost empty
and I returned to my seat and a man stood up

in the back of the quiet chapel
(near the wide-open doors through which
the green of May showed, and the long shadows
                        of late afternoon)
and said my words
desecrated a holy place.

And a few days later
when some more students (black) were shot
at Jackson, Mississippi,
no one desecrated the white folks' chapel,
because no memorial service was held.

Have you read Levertov's poems "Life at War" and "What Were They Like?"? Both appear in *To Stay Alive* (New York: New Directions, 1971). Recalled in the poem, the *performance* consisted of reading two poems and a "rap." Discuss the "Why" of the title: Was the audience shamed? Indignant because the poet was wrong? How does the setting of a church affect the performance? What was your response to the telling of it?

A Wagner Matinée
WILLA CATHER

    I received one morning a letter, written in pale ink on glassy, blue-lined note-paper, and bearing the postmark of a little Nebraska village. This communication, worn and rubbed, looking as if it had been carried for some days in a coat pocket that was none too clean, was from my uncle Howard, and informed me that his wife had been left a small legacy by a bachelor relative, and that it would be necessary for her to go to Boston to attend to the settling of the estate. He requested me to meet her at the station and render her whatever services might be necessary. On examining the date indicated as that of her arrival, I found it to be no later than tomorrow. He had characteristically delayed writing until, had I been away from home for a day, I must have missed my aunt altogether.

    The name of my Aunt Georgiana opened before me a gulf of recollection so wide and deep that, as the letter dropped from my hand, I felt suddenly a stranger to all the present conditions of my existence, wholly ill at ease and out of place amid the familiar surroundings of my study. I became, in short, the gangling farmer-boy my aunt had known, scourged with chilblains and bashfulness, my hands cracked and sore from the corn husking. I sat again before her parlour organ, fumbling the scales with my stiff, red fingers, while she, beside me, made canvas mittens for the huskers.

    The next morning, after preparing my landlady for a visitor, I set out for the station. When the train arrived I had some difficulty finding my aunt. She was the last of the passengers to alight, and it was not until I got her into the carriage that she seemed really to recognize me. She had come all the way in a day coach; her linen duster had become black with soot and her black bonnet grey with dust during her journey. When we arrived at my boarding-house the landlady put her to bed at once and I did not see her again until the next morning.

Whatever shock Mrs. Springer experienced at my aunt's appearance, she considerately concealed. As for myself, I saw my aunt's battered figure with that feeling of awe and respect with which we behold explorers who have left their ears and fingers north of Franz-Joseph-Land, or their health somewhere along the Upper Congo. My Aunt Georgiana had been a music teacher at the Boston Conservatory, somewhere back in the latter sixties. One summer, while visiting in the little village among the Green Mountains where her ancestors had dwelt for generations, she had kindled the callow fancy of my uncle, Howard Carpenter, then an idle, shiftless boy of twenty-one. When she returned to her duties in Boston, Howard followed her, and the upshot of this infatuation was that she eloped with him, eluding the reproaches of her family and the criticism of her friends by going with him to the Nebraska frontier. Carpenter, who, of course, had no money, took up a homestead in Red Willow County, fifty miles from the railroad. There they had measured off their land themselves, driving across the prairie in a wagon, to the wheel of which they had tied a red cotton handkerchief, and counting its revolutions. They built a dugout in the red hillside, one of those cave dwellings whose inmates so often reverted to primitive conditions. Their water they got from the lagoons where the buffalo drank, and their slender stock of provisions was always at the mercy of bands of roving Indians. For thirty years my aunt had not been farther than fifty miles from the homestead.

I owed to this woman most of the good that ever came my way in my boyhood, and had a reverential affection for her. During the years when I was riding herd for my uncle, my aunt, after cooking the three meals—the first of which was ready at six o'clock in the morning—and putting the six children to bed, would often stand until midnight at her ironing-board, with me at the kitchen table beside her, hearing me recite Latin declensions and conjugations, gently shaking me when my drowsy head sank down over a page of irregular verbs. It was to her, at her ironing or mending, that I read my first Shakespeare, and her old textbook on mythology was the first that ever came into my empty hands. She taught me my scales and exercises on the little parlour organ which her husband had bought her after fifteen years during which she had not so much as seen a musical instrument. She would sit beside me by the hour, darning and counting, while I struggled with the "Joyous Farmer." She seldom talked to me about music, and I understood why. Once when I had been doggedly beating out some easy passages from an old score of *Euryanthe* I had found among her music books, she came up to me and, putting her hands over my eyes, gently drew my head back upon her shoulder, saying tremulously, "Don't love it so well, Clark, or it may be taken from you."

When my aunt appeared on the morning after her arrival in Boston, she was still in a semi-somnambulant state. She seemed not to realize that she was in the city where she had spent her youth, the place longed for hungrily half a lifetime. She had been so wretchedly trainsick throughout the journey that she had no recollection of anything but her discomfort, and, to all intents and purposes, there were but a few hours of nightmare between the farm in Red Willow County and my study on Newbury Street. I had planned a little pleasure for her that afternoon, to repay her for some of the glorious moments she had given me when we used to milk together in the straw-thatched cowshed and she, because I was more than usually tired, or because her husband had spoken sharply to me, would tell me of the splendid performance of the *Huguenots* she had seen in Paris, in her youth.

At two o'clock the Symphony Orchestra was to give a Wagner program, and I intended to take my aunt; though, as I conversed with her, I grew doubtful about her enjoyment of it. I suggested our visiting the Conservatory and the Common before lunch, but she seemed altogether too timid to wish to venture out. She questioned me absently about various changes in the city, but she was chiefly concerned that she had forgotten to leave instructions about feeding half-skimmed milk to a certain weakling calf, "old Maggie's calf, you know, Clark," she explained, evidently having forgotten how long I had been away. She was further troubled because she had neglected to tell her daughter about the freshly-opened kit of mackerel in the cellar, which would spoil if it were not used directly.

I asked her whether she had ever heard any of the Wagnerian operas, and found that she had not, though she was perfectly familiar with their respective situations, and had once possessed the piano score of *The Flying Dutchman.* I began to think it would be best to get her back to Red Willow County without waking her, and regretted having suggested the concert.

From the time we entered the concert hall, however, she was a trifle less passive and inert, and for the first time seemed to perceive her surroundings. I had felt some trepidation lest she might become aware of her queer, country clothes, or might experience some painful embarrassment at stepping suddenly into the world to which she had been dead for a quarter of a century. But, again, I found how superficially I had judged her. She sat looking about her with eyes as impersonal, almost as stony, as those with which the granite Rameses in a museum watches the froth and fret that ebbs and flows about his pedestal. I have seen this same aloofness in old miners who drift into the Brown Hotel at Denver, their pockets full of bullion, their linen soiled, their haggard faces unshaven; standing in the thronged corridors as solitary as though they were still in a frozen camp on the Yukon.

The matinée audience was made up chiefly of women. One lost the contour of faces and figures, indeed any effect of line whatever, and there was only the colour of bodices past counting, the shimmer of fabrics soft and firm, silky and sheer; red, mauve, pink, blue, lilac, purple, écru, rose, yellow, cream, and white, all the colours that an impressionist finds in a sunlit landscape, with here and there the dead shadow of a frock coat. My Aunt Georgiana regarded them as though they had been so many daubs of tube-paint on a palette.

When the musicians came out and took their places, she gave a little stir of anticipation, and looked with quickening interest down over the rail at that invariable grouping, perhaps the first wholly familiar thing that had greeted her eye since she had left old Maggie and her weakling calf. I could feel how all those details sank into her soul, for I had not forgotten how they had sunk into mine when I came fresh from ploughing forever and forever between green aisles of corn, where, as in a treadmill, one might walk from daybreak to dusk without perceiving a shadow of change. The clean profiles of the musicians, the gloss of their linen, the dull black of their coats, the beloved shapes of the instruments, the patches of yellow light on the smooth, varnished bellies of the 'cellos and the bass viols in the rear, the restless, wind-tossed forest of fiddle necks and bows—I recalled how, in the first orchestra I ever heard, those long bow-strokes seemed to draw the heart out of me, as a conjurer's stick reels out yards of paper ribbon from a hat.

The first number was the *Tannhäuser* overture. When the horns drew out the first strain of the Pilgrim's chorus, Aunt Georgiana clutched my coat sleeve. Then it was I first realized that for her this broke a silence of thirty years. With the battle between the two motives, with the frenzy of the Venusberg theme and its ripping of strings, there came to me an overwhelming sense of the waste and wear we are so powerless to combat; and I saw again the tall, naked house on the prairie, black and grim as a wooden fortress; the black pond where I had learned to swim, its margin pitted with sun-dried cattle tracks; the rain-gullied clay banks about the naked house, the four dwarf-ash seedlings where the dish-cloths were always hung to dry before the kitchen door. The world there was the flat world of the ancients; to the east, a cornfield that stretched to daybreak; to the west, a corral that reached to sunset; between, the conquests of peace, dearer-bought than those of war.

The overture closed, my aunt released my coat sleeve, but she said nothing. She sat staring dully at the orchestra. What, I wondered, did she get from it? She had been a good pianist in her day, I knew, and her musical education had been broader than that of most music teachers of a quarter of a century ago. She had often told me of Mozart's operas and Meyerbeer's, and I could remember hearing her sing, years ago, certain melodies of Verdi. When I had fallen ill with a fever in her house she used to sit by my cot in the evening—when the cool, night wind blew in through the faded mosquito netting tacked over the window and I lay watching a certain bright star that burned red above the cornfield—and sing "Home to our mountains, O, let us return!" in a way fit to break the heart of a Vermont boy near dead of home-sickness already.

I watched her closely through the prelude to *Tristan and Isolde,* trying vainly to conjecture what that seething turmoil of strings and winds might mean to her, but she sat mutely staring at the violin bows that drove obliquely down-ward, like the pelting streaks of rain in a summer shower. Had this music any message for her? Had she enough left to at all comprehend this power which had kindled the world since she had left it? I was in a fever of curiosity, but Aunt Georgiana sat silent upon her peak in Darien. She preserved this utter immobility throughout the number from *The Flying Dutchman,* though her fingers worked mechanically upon her black dress, as if, of themselves, they were recalling the piano score thay had once played. Poor hands! They had been stretched and twisted into mere tentacles to hold and lift and knead with;—on one of them a thin, worn band that had once been a wedding ring. As I pressed and gently quieted one of those groping hands, I remembered with quivering eyelids their services for me in other days.

Soon after the tenor began the "Prize Song," I heard a quick drawn breath and turned to my aunt. Her eyes were closed, but the tears were glistening on her cheeks, and I think, in a moment more, they were in my eyes as well. It never really died, then—the soul which can suffer so excruciatingly and so in-terminably; it withers to the outward eye only; like that strange moss which can lie on a dusty shelf half a century and yet, if placed in water, grows green again. She wept so throughout the development and elaboration of the melody.

During the intermission before the second half, I questioned my aunt and found that the "Prize Song" was not new to her. Some years before there had drifted to the farm in Red Willow County a young German, a tramp cow-puncher, who had sung in the chorus at Bayreuth when he was a boy, along with the other peasant boys and girls. Of a Sunday morning he used to sit on his gingham-sheeted bed in the hands' bedroom which opened off the kitchen, cleaning the leather of his boots and saddle, singing the "Prize Song," while my aunt went about her work in the kitchen. She had hovered over him until she had prevailed upon him to join the country church, though his sole fitness for this step, in so far as I could gather, lay in his boyish face and his possession of this divine melody. Shortly afterward, he had gone to town on the Fourth of July, been drunk for several days, lost his money at a faro table, ridden a saddled Texas steer on a bet, and disappeared with a fractured collar-bone. All this my aunt told me huskily, wanderingly, as though she were talking in the weak lapses of illness.

"Well, we have come to better things than the old *Trovatore* at any rate, Aunt Georgie?" I queried, with a well-meant effort at jocularity.

Her lip quivered and she hastily put her handkerchief up to her mouth. From behind it she murmured, "And you have been hearing this ever since you left me, Clark?" Her question was the gentlest and saddest of reproaches.

The second half of the program consisted of four numbers from the *Ring*, and closed with Siegfried's funeral march. My aunt wept quietly, but almost continuously, as a shallow vessel overflows in a rain-storm. From time to time her dim eyes looked up at the lights, burning softly under their dull glass globes.

The deluge of sound poured on and on; I never knew what she found in the shining current of it; I never knew how far it bore her, or past what happy islands. From the trembling of her face I could well believe that before the last number she had been carried out where the myriad graves are, into the grey, nameless burying grounds of the sea; or into some world of death vaster yet, where, from the beginning of the world, hope has lain down with hope and dream with dream and, renouncing, slept.

The concert was over; the people filed out of the hall chattering and laughing, glad to relax and find the living level again, but my kinswoman made no effort to rise. The harpist slipped the green felt cover over his instrument; the flute-players shook the water from their mouthpieces; the men of the orchestra went out one by one, leaving the stage to the chairs and music stands, empty as a winter cornfield.

I spoke to my aunt. She burst into tears and sobbed pleadingly. "I don't want to go, Clark, I don't want to go!"

I understood. For her, just outside the concert hall, lay the black pond with the cattle-tracked bluffs; the tall, unpainted house, with weather-curled boards, naked as a tower; the crook-backed ash seedlings where the dishcloths hung to dry; the gaunt, moulting turkeys picking up refuse about the kitchen door.

Does "Matinée" in the title refer to more than one *performance*? How does the narrator's preparation for the music program differ from that of his aunt? How do the responses to the concert of Aunt Georgiana, Clark, and you, the reader, differ? What is meant when the narrator describes the aunt's listening as sitting "si-lent upon her peak in Darien"? The material quoted is an *allusion,* that is, a reference to an earlier historical, Biblical, or literary person or event. Use of allusions permit a writer to condense or quicken a description. If you do not recognize this line, you might track it down in a book of quotations.

Participate
CLAUS BREMER

participate

participate results

anticipate confront results

astici than confront results

participate rather than confront results

paces rather than confront results

participate process rather than confront results

participate in a process rather than confront results

participate in a process rather than participa

participate in a process rather shits

participate in a process rather

participate in a process

participate rather

participate results

participate

This example of *concrete poetry* offers—and gives—directions for *performance*. How would you paraphrase the advice? Bremer is helpful:

In the first line, the text is written word over word. In the lines that follow, the last word is separated, word for word and line for line, until the text is legible. Then the process is reversed. This arrangement is intended to arouse curiosity, to reveal something, and then again to become obscure; to arouse the reader's curiosity, to reveal something to him, and then again confront him with himself. (*An Anthology of Concrete Poetry*, Emmett Williams, ed.; New York: Something Else Press, 1967.)

How might you enact this performance directive? Might several attitudes be used in giving the advice? Consult the following sources: Francine Merritt, "Concrete Poetry: Verbivocovisual," *Speech Teacher*, 18 (March 1969), 109–114; Paul H. Gray, "American Concrete: New Poetics and Performance," *Studies in Interpretation*, Vol. II, eds. Esther M. Doyle and Virginia Hastings Floyd (Netherlands: Rodopi, 1977), pp. 77–98.

Who Am I This Time?
KURT VONNEGUT, JR.

The North Crawford Mask and Wig Club, an amateur theatrical society I belong to, voted to do Tennessee Williams's *A Streetcar Named Desire* for the spring play. Doris Sawyer, who always directs, said she couldn't direct this time because her mother was so sick. And she said the club ought to develop some other directors anyway, because she couldn't live forever, even though she'd made it safely to seventy-four.

So I got stuck with the directing job, even though the only thing I'd ever directed before was the installation of combination aluminum storm windows and screens I'd sold. That's what I am, a salesman of storm windows and doors, and here and there a bathtub enclosure. As far as acting goes, the highest rank I ever held on stage was either butler or policeman, whichever's higher.

I made a lot of conditions before I took the directing job, and the biggest one was that Harry Nash, the only real actor the club has, had to take the Marlon Brando part in the play. To give you an idea of how versatile Harry is, inside of one year he was Captain Queeg in *The Caine Mutiny Court Martial*, then Abe Lincoln in *Abe Lincoln in Illinois* and then the young architect in *The Moon is Blue*. The year after that, Harry Nash was Henry the Eighth in *Anne of the Thousand Days* and Doc in *Come Back Little Sheba,* and I was after him for Marlon Brando in *A Streetcar Named Desire*. Harry wasn't at the meeting to say whether he'd take the part or not. He never came to meetings. He was too shy. He didn't stay away from meetings because he had something else to do. He wasn't married, didn't go out with women—didn't have any close men friends either. He stayed away from all kinds of gatherings because he never could think of anything to say or do without a script.

So I had to go down to Miller's Hardware Store, where Harry was a clerk, the next day and ask him if he'd take the part. I stopped off at the telephone company to complain about a bill I'd gotten for a call to Honolulu. I'd never called Honolulu in my life.

And there was this beautiful girl I'd never seen before behind the counter at the phone company, and she explained that the company had put in an automatic billing machine and that the machine didn't have all the bugs out of it yet. It made mistakes. "Not only did I not call Honolulu," I told her, "I don't think anybody in North Crawford ever has or will."

So she took the charge off the bill, and I asked her if she was from around North Crawford. She said no. She said she just came with the new billing machine to teach local girls how to take care of it. After that, she said, she would go with some other machine to someplace else. "Well," I said, "as long as people have to come along with the machines, I guess we're all right."

"What?" she said.

"When machines start delivering themselves," I said, "I guess that's when the people better start really worrying."

"Oh," she said. She didn't seem very interested in that subject, and I wondered if she was interested in anything. She seemed kind of numb, almost a machine herself, an automatic phone-company politeness machine.

"How long will you be in town here?" I asked her.

"I stay in each town eight weeks, sir," she said. She had pretty blue eyes, but there sure wasn't much hope or curiosity in them. She told me she had been going from town to town like that for two years, always a stranger.

And I got it in my head that she might make a good Stella for the play. Stella was the wife of the Marlon Brando character, the wife of the character I wanted Harry Nash to play. So I told her where and when we were going to hold tryouts, and said the club would be very happy if she'd come.

She looked surprised, and she warmed up a little. "You know," she said, "that's the first time anybody ever asked me to participate in any community thing."

"Well," I said, "there isn't any other way to get to know a lot of nice people faster than to be in a play with 'em."

She said her name was Helene Shaw. She said she might just surprise me— and herself. She said she just might come.

You would think that North Crawford would be fed up with Harry Nash in plays after all the plays he'd been in. But the fact was that North Crawford probably could have gone on enjoying Harry forever, because he was never Harry on stage. When the maroon curtain went up on the stage in the gymnasium of the Consolidated Junior-Senior High School, Harry, body and soul, was exactly what the script and director told him to be.

Somebody said one time that Harry ought to go to a psychiatrist so he could be something important and colorful in real life, too—so he could get married anyway, and maybe get a better job than just clerking in Miller's Hardware Store for fifty dollars a week. But I don't know what a psychiatrist could have turned up about him that the town didn't already know. The trouble with Harry was he'd been left on the doorstep of the Unitarian Church when he was a baby, and he never did find out who his parents were.

When I told him there in Miller's that I'd been appointed director, that I wanted him in my play, he said what he always said to anybody who asked him to be in a play—and it was kind of sad, if you think about it.

"Who am I this time?" he said.

So I held the tryouts where they're always held—in the meeting room on the second floor of the North Crawford Public Library. Doris Sawyer, the woman who usually directs, came to give me the benefit of all her experience. The two of us sat in state upstairs, while the people who wanted parts waited below. We called them upstairs one by one.

Harry Nash came to the tryouts, even though it was a waste of time. I guess he wanted to get that little bit more acting in.

For Harry's pleasure, and our pleasure, too, we had him read from the scene where he beats up his wife. It was a play in itself, the way Harry did it, and Tennessee Williams hadn't written it all either. Tennessee Williams didn't write the part, for instance, where Harry, who weighs about one hundred forty-five, who's about five feet eight inches tall, added fifty pounds to his weight and four inches to his height by just picking up the playbook. He had a short little double-breasted bellows-back grade-school graduation suit coat on and a dinky little red tie with a horsehead on it. He took off the coat and tie, opened his collar, then turned his back to Doris and me, getting up steam for the part. There was a great big rip in the back of his shirt, and it looked like a fairly new shirt too. He'd ripped it on purpose, so he could be that much more like Marlon Brando, right from the first.

When he faced us again, he was huge and handsome and conceited and cruel. Doris read the part of Stella, the wife, and Harry bullied that old, old lady into believing that she was a sweet, pregnant girl married to a sexy gorilla who was going to beat her brains out. She had me believing it too. And I read the lines of Blanche, her sister in the play, and darned if Harry didn't scare me into feeling like a drunk and faded Southern belle.

And then, while Doris and I were getting over our emotional experiences, like people coming out from under ether, Harry put down the playbook, put on his coat and tie, and turned into the pale hardware-store clerk again.

"Was—was that all right?" he said, and he seemed pretty sure he wouldn't get the part.

"Well," I said, "for a first reading, that wasn't too bad."

"Is there a chance I'll get the part?" he said. I don't know why he always had to pretend there was some doubt about his getting a part, but he did.

"I think we can safely say we're leaning powerfully in your direction," I told him.

He was very pleased. "Thanks! Thanks a lot!" he said, and he shook my hand.

"Is there a pretty new girl downstairs?" I said, meaning Helene Shaw.

"I didn't notice," said Harry.

It turned out that Helene Shaw *had* come for the tryouts, and Doris and I had our hearts broken. We thought the North Crawford Mask and Wig Club was finally going to put a really good-looking, really young girl on stage, instead of one of the beat-up forty-year-old women we generally have to palm off as girls.

But Helene Shaw couldn't act for sour apples. No matter what we gave her to read, she was the same girl with the same smile for anybody who had a complaint about his phone bill.

Doris tried to coach her some, to make her understand that Stella in the play was a very passionate girl who loved a gorilla because she needed a gorilla. But Helene just read the lines the same way again. I don't think a volcano could have stirred her up enough to say, "Oo."

"Dear," said Doris, "I'm going to ask you a personal question."

"All right," said Helene.

"Have you ever been in love?" said Doris. "The reason I ask," she said, "remembering some old love might help you put more warmth in your acting."

Helene frowned and thought hard. "Well," she said, "I travel a lot, you know. And practically all the men in the different companies I visit are married and I never stay anyplace long enough to know many people who aren't."

"What about school?" said Doris. "What about puppy love and all the other kinds of love in school?"

So Helene thought hard about that, and then she said, "Even in school I was always moving around a lot. My father was a construction worker, following jobs around, so I was always saying hello or good-by to someplace, without anything in between."

"Um," said Doris.

"Would movie stars count?" said Helene. "I don't mean in real life. I never knew any. I just mean up on the screen."

Doris looked at me and rolled her eyes. "I guess that's love of a kind," she said.

And then Helene got a little enthusiastic. "I used to sit through movies over and over again," she said, "and pretend I was married to whoever the man movie star was. They were the only people who came with us. No matter where we moved, movie stars were there."

"Uh huh," said Doris.

"Well, thank you, Miss Shaw," I said. "You go downstairs and wait with the rest. We'll let you know."

So we tried to find another Stella. And there just wasn't one, not one woman in the club with the dew still on her. "All we've got are Blanches," I said, meaning all we had were faded women who could play the part of Blanche, Stella's faded sister. "That's life, I guess—twenty Blanches to one Stella."

"And when you find a Stella," said Doris, "it turns out she doesn't know what love is."

Doris and I decided there was one last thing we could try. We could get Harry Nash to play a scene along with Helene. "He just might make her bubble the least little bit," I said.

"That girl hasn't got a bubble in her," said Doris.

So we called down the stairs for Helene to come back on up, and we told somebody to go find Harry. Harry never sat with the rest of the people at tryouts—or at rehearsals either. The minute he didn't have a part to play, he'd disappear into some hiding place where he could hear people call him, but where he couldn't be seen. At tryouts in the library he generally hid in the reference room, passing the time looking at flags of different countries in the front of the dictionary.

Helene came back upstairs, and we were very sorry and surprised to see that she'd been crying.

"Oh, dear," said Doris. "Oh, my—now what on earth's the trouble, dear?"

"I was terrible, wasn't I?" said Helene, hanging her head.

Doris said the only thing anybody can say in an amateur theatrical society when somebody cries. She said, "Why, no dear—you were marvelous."

"No, I wasn't," said Helene. "I'm a walking icebox, and I know it."

"Nobody could look at you and say that," said Doris.

"When they get to know me, they can say it," said Helene. "When people get to know me, that's what they *do* say." Her tears got worse. "I don't want to be the way I am," she said. "I just can't help it, living the way I've lived all my life. The only experiences I've had have been in crazy dreams of movie stars. When I meet somebody nice in real life, I feel as though I were in some kind of big bottle, as though I couldn't touch that person, no matter how hard I tried." And Helene pushed on air as though it were a big bottle all around her.

"You ask me if I've ever been in love," she said to Doris. "No—but I want to be. I know what this play's about. I know what Stella's supposed to feel and why she feels it. I—I—I—" she said, and her tears wouldn't let her go on.

"You what, dear?" said Doris gently.

"I——" said Helene, and she pushed on the imaginary bottle again. "I just don't know how to begin," she said.

There was heavy clumping on the library stairs. It sounded like a deep-sea diver coming upstairs in his lead shoes. It was Harry Nash, turning himself into Marlon Brando. In he came, practically dragging his knuckles on the floor. And he was so much in character that the sight of a weeping woman made him sneer.

"Harry," I said, "I'd like you to meet Helene Shaw. Helene—this is Harry Nash. If you get the part of Stella, he'll be your husband in the play." Harry didn't offer to shake hands. He put his hands in his pockets, and he hunched over, and he looked her up and down, gave her looks that left her naked. Her tears stopped right then and there.

"I wonder if you two would play the fight scene," I said, "and then the reunion scene right after it."

"Sure," said Harry, his eyes still on her. Those eyes burned up clothes faster than she could put them on. "Sure," he said, "if Stell's game."

"What?" said Helene. She'd turned the color of cranberry juice.

"Stell—Stella," said Harry. "That's you. Stell's my wife."

I handed the two of them playbooks. Harry snatched his from me without a word of thanks. Helene's hands weren't working very well, and I had to kind of mold them around the book.

"I'll want something I can throw," said Harry.

"What?" I said.

"There's one place where I throw a radio out a window," said Harry. "What can I throw?"

So I said an iron paperweight was the radio, and I opened the window wide. Helene Shaw looked scared to death.

"Where you want us to start?" said Harry, and he rolled his shoulders like a prizefighter warming up.

"Start a few lines back where you throw the radio out the window," I said.

"O.K., O.K.," said Harry, warming up, warming up. He scanned the stage directions. "Let's see," he said, "after I throw the radio, she runs off stage, and I chase her, and I sock her one."

"Right," I said.

"O.K., baby," Harry said to Helene, his eyelids drooping. What was about to happen was wilder than the chariot race in *Ben Hur*. "On your mark," said Harry. "Get ready, baby. Go!"

When the scene was over, Helene Shaw was as hot as a hod carrier, as limp as an eel. She sat down with her mouth open and her head hanging to one side. She wasn't in any bottle any more. There wasn't any bottle to hold her up and keep her safe and clean. The bottle was gone.

"Do I get the part or don't I?" Harry snarled at me.

"You'll do," I said.

"You said a mouthful!" he said. "I'll be going now. . . . See you around, Stella," he said to Helene, and he left. He slammed the door behind him.

"Helene?" I said. "Miss Shaw?"

"Mf?" she said.

"The part of Stella is yours," I said. "You were great!"

"I was?" she said.

"I had no idea you had that much fire in you, dear," Doris said to her.

"Fire?" said Helene. She didn't know if she was afoot or on horseback.

"Skyrockets! Pinwheels! Roman candles!" said Doris.

"Mf," said Helene. And that was all she said. She looked as though she were going to sit in the chair with her mouth open forever.

"Stella," I said.

"Huh?" she said.

"You have my permission to go."

So we started having rehearsals four nights a week on the stage of the Consolidated School. And Harry and Helene set such a pace that everybody in the production was half crazy with excitement and exhaustion before we'd rehearsed four times. Usually a director has to beg people to learn their lines, but I had no such trouble. Harry and Helene were working so well together that everybody else in the cast regarded it as a duty and an honor and a pleasure to support them.

I was certainly lucky—or thought I was. Things were going so well, so hot and heavy, so early in the game that I had to say to Harry and Helene after one love scene, "Hold a little something back for the actual performance, would you please? You'll burn yourselves out."

I said that at the fourth or fifth rehearsal, and Lydia Miller, who was playing Blanche, the faded sister, was sitting next to me in the audience. In real life, she's the wife of Verne Miller. Verne owns Miller's hardware Store. Verne was Harry's boss.

"Lydia," I said to her, "have we got a play or have we got a play?"

"Yes," she said, "you've got a play, all right." She made it sound as though I'd committed some kind of crime, done something just terrible. "You should be very proud of yourself."

"What do you mean by that?" I said.

Before Lydia could answer, Harry yelled at me from the stage, asked if I was through with him, asked if he could go home. I told him he could and, still Marlon Brando, he left, kicking furniture out of his way and slamming doors. Helene was left all alone on the stage, sitting on a couch with the same gaga look she'd had after the tryouts. That girl was drained.

I turned to Lydia again and I said, "Well—until now, I thought I had every reason to be happy and proud. Is there something going on I don't know about?"

"Do you know that girl's in love with Harry?" said Lydia.

"In the play?" I said.

"What play?" said Lydia. "There isn't any play going on now, and look at her up there." She gave a sad cackle. "You aren't directing this play."

"Who is?" I said.

"Mother Nature at her worst," said Lydia. "And think what it's going to do to that girl when she discovers what Harry really is." She corrected herself. "What Harry really isn't," she said.

I didn't do anything about it, because I didn't figure it was any of my business. I heard Lydia try to do something about it, but she didn't get very far.

"You know," Lydia said to Helene one night, "I once played Ann Rutledge, and Harry was Abraham Lincoln."

Helene clapped her hands. "That must have been heaven!" she said.

"It was, in a way," said Lydia. "Sometimes I'd get so worked up, I'd love Harry the way I'd love Abraham Lincoln. I'd have to come back to earth and remind myself that he wasn't ever going to free the slaves, that he was just a clerk in my husband's hardware store."

"He's the most marvelous man I ever met," said Helene.

"Of course, one thing you have to get set for, when you're in a play with Harry," said Lydia, "is what happens after the last performance."

"What are you talking about?" said Helene.

"Once the show's over," said Lydia, "whatever you thought Harry was just evaporates into thin air."

"I don't believe it," said Helene.

"I admit it's hard to believe," said Lydia.

Then Helene got a little sore. "Anyway, why tell me about it?" she said. "Even if it is true, what do I care?"

"I—I don't know," said Lydia, backing away. "I—I just thought you might find it interesting."

"Well, I don't," said Helene.

And Lydia slunk away, feeling about as frowzy and unloved as she was supposed to feel in the play. After that nobody said anything more to Helene to warn her about Harry, not even when word got around that she'd told the telephone company that she didn't want to be moved around anymore, that she wanted to stay in North Crawford.

So the time finally came to put on the play. We ran it for three nights— Thursday, Friday, and Saturday—and we murdered those audiences. They believed every word that was said on stage, and when the maroon curtain came down they were ready to go to the nut house along with Blanche, the faded sister.

On Thursday night the other girls at the telephone company sent Helene a dozen red roses. When Helene and Harry were taking a curtain call together, I passed the roses over the footlights to her. She came forward for them, took one rose from the bouquet to give to Harry. But when she turned to give Harry the rose in front of everybody, Harry was gone. The curtain came down on that extra little scene—the girl offering a rose to nothing and nobody.

I went backstage, and I found her still holding that one rose. She'd put the rest of the bouquet aside. There were tears in her eyes. "What did I do wrong?" she said to me. "Did I insult him some way?"

"No," I said. "He always does that after a performance. The minute it's over, he clears out as fast as he can."

"And tomorrow he'll disappear again?"

"Without even taking off his makeup?"

"And Saturday?" she said. "He'll stay for the cast party on Saturday, won't he?"

"Harry never goes to parties," I said. "When curtain comes down on Saturday, that's the last anybody will see of him till he goes to work on Monday."

"How sad," she said.

Helene's performance on Friday night wasn't nearly so good as Thursday's. She seemed to be thinking about other things. She watched Harry take off after curtain call. She didn't say a word.

On Saturday she put on the best performance yet. Ordinarily it was Harry who set the pace. But on Saturday Harry had to work to keep up with Helene.

When the curtain came down on the final curtain call, Harry wanted to get away, but he couldn't. Helene wouldn't let go his hand. The rest of the cast and the stage crew and a lot of well-wishers from the audience were all standing around Harry and Helene, and Harry was trying to get his hand back.

"Well," he said, "I've got to go."

"Where?" she said.

"Oh," he said, "home."

"Won't you please take me to the cast party?" she said.

He got very red. "I'm afraid I'm not much on parties," he said. All the Marlon Brando in him was gone. He was tongue-tied, he was scared, he was shy—he was everything Harry was famous for being between plays.

"All right," she said. "I'll let you go—if you promise me one thing."

"What's that?" he said, and I thought he would jump out a window if she let go of him then.

"I want you to promise to stay here until I get you your present," she said.

"Present?" he said, getting even more panicky.

"Promise?" she said.

He promised. It was the only way he could get his hand back. And he stood there miserably while Helene went down to the ladies' dressing room for the present. While he waited, a lot of people congratulated him on being such a fine actor. But congratulations never made him happy. He just wanted to get away.

Helene came back with the present. It turned out to be a little blue book with a big red ribbon for a place marker. It was a copy of *Romeo and Juliet*. Harry was very embarrassed. It was all he could do to say "Thank you."

"The marker marks my favorite scene," said Helene.

"Um," said Harry.

"Don't you want to see what my favorite scene is?" she said.

So Harry had to open the book to the red ribbon.

Helene got close to him, and read a line of Juliet's. " 'How cam'st thou hither, tell me, and wherefore?' " she read. " 'The orchard walls are high and hard to climb, and the place death, considering who thou art, if any of my kinsmen find thee here.' " She pointed to the next line. "Now, look what Romeo says," she said.

"Um," said Harry.

"Read what Romeo says," said Helene.

Harry cleared his throat. He didn't want to read the line, but he had to.

" 'With love's light wings did I o'erperch these walls,' " he read out loud in his everyday voice. But then a change came over him. " 'For stony limits cannot hold love out,' " he read, and he straightened up, and eight years dropped away from him, and he was brave and gay. " 'And what love can do, that dares love attempt,' " he read, " 'therefore thy kinsmen are no let to me.' "

" 'If they do see thee they will murther thee,' " said Helene, and she started him walking toward the wings.

" 'Alack!' " said Harry, " 'there lies more peril in thine eye than twenty of their swords.' " Helene led him toward the backstage exit. " 'Look thou but sweet,' " said Harry, " 'and I am proof against their enmity.' "

" 'I would not for the world they saw thee here,' " said Helene, and that was the last we heard. The two of them were out the door and gone.

They never did show up at the cast party. One week later they were married.

They seem very happy, although they're kind of strange from time to time, depending on which play they're reading to each other at the time.

I dropped into the phone company office the other day, on account of the billing machine was making dumb mistakes again. I asked her what plays she said Harry'd been reading lately.

"In the past week," she said, "I've been married to Othello, been loved by Faust and been kidnapped by Paris. Wouldn't you say I was the luckiest girl in town?"

I said I thought so, and I told her most of the women in town thought so too.

"They had their chance," she said.

"Most of 'em couldn't stand the excitement," I said. And I told her I'd been asked to direct another play. I asked if she and Harry would be available for the cast. She gave me a big smile and said, "Who are we this time?"

How much do you know about the "I" who directs the *performances* for the North Crawford Mask and Wig Club? How do performances affect Harry? Helene? Doris? Playgoers? You, as the reader of the story?

Ordinance on Enrollment
NAOMI LAZARD

The group in process of being formed
will be something you have always wanted
to be a part of but never, heretofore,
imagined possible. Its composition
will be strictly regulated:
only those who qualify will be admitted.
All others will be rejected.
For those of you who believe
you may have the necessary attributes
for entry into this group
an application can be picked up
at our office. Answer the questions
as honestly as you can. Good marks
also given for imagination
and resourcefulness. This group,
as it is shaping up, promises
to become a compelling force
in our society.
                    If you fail
to get into this group
another, larger group is also being formed
for rejects from the first one.
The second group will in no way
be inferior to the first. It too

has standards; they are high.
In order for your application
to permit entry into the second group
check the proper place.
In case the second group is filled
before your application can be processed,
or your qualifications fall short,
do not be despondent. Our plans include
the formation of a third group.
All applicants who have failed
to make it into the first or second groups
will automatically qualify for the third.
This is not to imply that standards
for this section are not high.
They are different.

We welcome you now
to the group for which you will ultimately
qualify. Whichever it is
we know you will have a creative
and enriching experience.

This poem is about performance in the sense that the speaker is deliberately assuming something other than an ordinary day-to-day role. Do you agree? Is the speaker assuming the role for his or her benefit? For the benefit of the audience? What is that audience? Or what different audiences might there be?

To Bobolink, for Her Spirit
WILLIAM INGE

Characters

RENALDO   BOBOLINK

FRITZ   GRETCHEN

NELLIE   ANNAMARIE

Every day the weather permits, a group of autograph hunters assembles outside the 21 Club in New York. The size of the group varies from day to day and seems to depend upon the number and magnitude of the movie stars reported to be inside. It is an oddly assorted group, most of them teen-agers, but sometimes middle-aged women are included. The ringleader of today's group is BOBOLINK BOWEN, *a woman probably in her early thirties, who is so fat that her body, in silhouette, would form an almost perfect circle.* BOBOLINK *has the fat woman's usual disposition, stolidly complacent and happy. Her lips usually are formed in a grin of guzzling contentment. Her hair is short and kinky; she wears thick-lensed glasses that reduce her eyes to the size of buttonholes, and her clothes by necessity are simple: a man's coat-style sweater, saddle shoes and bobbysocks and bare legs that swell at the calves like bowling pins.* NELLIE, *a starved and eager woman in her late twenties, is* BOBOLINK'S *dependable stand-by. The two young boys,* RENALDO *and* FRITZ, *are friends; the two young girls,* GRETCHEN *and* ANNAMARIE, *are friends also. They are people without any personal attraction they could possibly lay claim to, and so must find in others attributes they want and lack in themselves.* ANNAMARIE, *in her dress, has tried to emulate one of her favorite film stars; she wears exotic sun glasses, a complicated coiffure and exciting shoes with straps, bows and platform soles. The group has been standing around for over an hour. They have learned to handle these periods of waiting like patients in a rest home; they talk idly with one another, move restlessly about in a limited space.* GRETCHEN *knits,* FRITZ *is working a crossword puzzle. Behind them stands the* DOORMAN, *a man of rigid and calculated dignity, dressed in a colorful uniform. He holds his head high and keeps it turned away from the autograph seekers as though to disclaim any association with them.*

RENALDO: I heard Lana Turner was in this joint last week. Man, wouldn't that be something?

FRITZ: Just imagine walking down the street one day and . . . plop! all of a sudden there's Lana Turner . . . just outa the blue. Man, I'd drop my teeth.

NELLIE: (*Making a claim that* BOBOLINK *would be too proud to make for herself*) Bobolink here's got Lana Turner's autograph. Haven't you, Bobby?

BOBOLINK: Lana's no better'n anyone else.

FRITZ: (*Impressed; to* BOBOLINK) No foolin'? You got Lana Turner's autograph?

BOBOLINK: (*Proving it with her autograph book*) Think I was lying to you?

FRITZ: (*To* RENALDO) Look, Ronny, she's got it.

NELLIE: Oh, Bobolink's got 'em all.

BOBOLINK: (*She always holds her own*) I got all of 'em that's worth gettin'.

GRETCHEN: My girl friend saw her. My girl friend goes out to California every summer. Her folks are real wealthy. She saw Lana Turner on the beach one day and she just goes up to her and says, "Hi, Lana" . . . just like that. And Lana smiles back and says, "Hi!"

BOBOLINK: Sure, she's not stuck-up. Now Katharine Hepburn's stuck-up, but Lana Turner's not at all. The best ones never are stuck-up.

FRITZ: (*Addressing the* DOORMAN, *who stands with rigid dignity*) Hey, mister, how long's Perry Como been inside?

BOBOLINK: We didn't want him t'arrive in town all alone.

(*The* DOORMAN *does not respond*)

BOBOLINK: (*To* FRITZ)Hey, don't you know anything? Those guys don't pay no attention to movie stars. They see so many of 'em they get sick of 'em. You can't find out anything from him.

FRITZ: Are we sure Perry Como's there?

BOBOLINK: (*Impatiently*) I told you I seen him, didn't I? Well, what more do you want? I was up there on the corner waitin' for a bus. Nellie here nudges me and says, "Hey, ain't that Perry Como goin' into the 21 Club?" And I looked and sure enough. There was a guy goin' in, had on the same kinda suit Perry Como had on last week over at the Paramount. Looked exactly like him.

FRITZ: But are you sure it was him?

BOBOLINK: Look, boy, you're never sure of anything in this world, don't you know that?

FRITZ: We been waiting here over an hour.

BOBOLINK: No one's asking you to stay. I waited outside the Stork Club three hours one night, three whole hours, and it was snowin'. Someone told me Elizabeth Taylor was inside and I wanted her autograph. It wasn't Elizabeth Taylor at all. Just some college girl trying to make out she was Elizabeth Taylor. I was sore, but what the heck!

NELLIE: Besides, you never know what's going to happen in this racket; like the time we was waitin' outside the St. Regis for Ronald Colman, and shoot! Who cares about Ronald Colman . . .

RENALDO: He's famous.

NELLIE: Not very. Anyway, we was waitin' for his autograph and . . .

BOBOLINK: *(Taking over)* Oh, yeh, and we'd been waiting for Ronald Colman all night and we was just about to give up and go home and then what do you think happened?

(She's going to build up suspense by making them guess)

NELLIE: That was the best luck we ever had, wasn't it, Bobby?

BOBOLINK: Well, we was just about to give up and go home when a taxi draws up at the curb and Van Johnson and Peter Lawford get out, and we got 'em both, right there on the same spot.

(This is an impressive story. The others are a little awed)

GRETCHEN: No foolin'! You got Van Johnson and Peter Lawford?

BOBOLINK: *(She produces her autograph book proudly)* And both at the same time!

NELLIE: *(Producing her own evidence)* I got 'em, too.

BOBOLINK: See what Peter Lawford wrote? "All my love to Bobolink." I told him that was my name.

NELLIE: And he said the same thing on mine, but my name's Nellie. They're both just as cute in real life as they are in pictures, aren't they, Bobby?

BOBOLINK: Not a bit stuck-up.

(An elaborately dressed couple appears in the doorway coming out of the restaurant. The woman wears a dress of dramatic cut and an exotic hat. Their manner is ridiculously aloof and they make quite a thing of ignoring the autograph hounds)

FRITZ: *(Nudging* RENALDO*)* Hey, who's that?

(They all look)

GRETCHEN: Looks like Rosalind Russell, don't it?

BOBOLINK: Naw, that ain't Rosalind Russell. I seen Rosalind Russell. She's real tall.

ANNAMARIE: Isn't she stunning? Don't you just love that dress?

GRETCHEN: I bet that dress cost two or three hundred dollars.

ANNAMARIE: 'Course it did. Probably cost more than that.

*(*BOBLINK *is studying the woman, trying to decide who she is. The woman and her escort now stand at the curb waiting for the* DOORMAN *to hail them a cab. The hounds are gaping at them)*

FRITZ: *(Approaching the glamorous woman)* Miss, can I have your autograph?

(The woman is a little surprised. She looks questioningly at her escort, who gives her an indulgent smile. So the woman, a little mystified, signs her name to FRITZ'S *book. Then*

she and her escort disappear in a cab. FRITZ *studies the signature. The others flock around him to see who it is, but* BOBOLINK *is not as quickly curious as the others)*

ALL: Who is she? Hey, let's see. It's not Rosalind Russell, is it? If I missed Rosalind Russell, I could kill myself. Let's see.

FRITZ: I'm trying to make it out. *(He attempts a pronunciation of the name)* Irina Nechibidikoff.

BOBOLINK: *(Emphatically)* Russian!

FRITZ: Hey, she may be someone famous.

BOBOLINK: Whoever heard of Irina Nechibidikoff?

ANNAMARIE: Maybe she's a famous dancer.

BOBOLINK: So what? She's not in the movies, is she? With a name like that.

GRETCHEN: Maybe she's a famous singer.

FRITZ: Anyway, I got her, whoever she is.

BOBOLINK: I am waitin' here for Perry Como. I come for Perry Como, and I'm gonna stay till I *get* Perry Como.

NELLIE: *(To the others)* Bobby always finishes up with she starts out to do.

BOBOLINK: You tell the world I do. And I'm not leavin' here without Perry Como's autograph. I been trailin' him for two years. I got Bing Crosby; I got Frank Sinatra; I got Van Johnson and Peter Lawford and Jimmy Stewart and Tyrone Power . . .

NELLIE: Tell 'em about the time you got Tyrone Power, Bobby.

BOBOLINK: Now I mean to get Perry Como. He's not my favorite or anything, but I want to get his autograph.

NELLIE: Tyrone Power's your real favorite, isn't he, Bobolink?

BOBOLINK: *(With modest adoration)* Yah. Tyrone's a real guy.

NELLIE: *(To the others)* Bobbie's president of the Tyrone Power Fan Club up in Irvington. *(The others are impressed)* Go on, Bobbie, tell 'em about Tyrone.

BOBOLINK: *(This is too sacred to be treated lightly and* BOBOLINK *is capable of dramatizing her modesty)* No, Nellie, I don't think it's right a person should go around boasting about things like that.

NELLIE: Tell 'em, Bobby. If you don', I will. *(Bobolink, after all, can't stop her)* Bobby's too modest about it. I think. But Tyrone Power shook her hand and told her personally that he was very indebted to her . . .

BOBOLINK: I met him at the train; don't forget that, Nellie.

NELLIE: As president of the Tyrone Power Fan Club in Irvington, she met his train at the Pennsylvania Station when he came in from Hollywood.

BOBOLINK: And I had to fight the man at the gate to let me pass.

NELLIE: That's right. She did. See, it wasn't supposed to be known that Tyrone was on that train, but the Pasadena Fan Club had wired us he was coming, so Bobby and I met him at the train to welcome him to New York, didn't we, Bobby?

NELLIE: 'Course not. So we went down to the station together. The man at the gate wouldn't let us through, but Bobby got by him, didn't you, Bobby?

I had to stay behind, but Bobby got through and got right on the train, didn't you, Bobby?

BOBOLINK: And I hunted all through them cars till I found him. He was still packing his things and he was in a hurry.

NELLIE: But he wasn't stuck-up, was he, Bobby?

BOBOLINK: (*This is sacred to her*) No, he wasn't stuck-up at all. I introduced myself as the president of the Irvington Fan Club, and told him we had forty-three members and met once a week to discuss his career.

NELLIE: And he was very pleased, wasn't he, Bobby?

BOBOLINK: Of course he was. And I told him us fans was awful glad he didn't marry Lana Turner 'cause, although our club don't have anything personal against Lana Turner, we never did think she was the right sort for Tyrone. And I told him that in just those words.

NELLIE: And she isn't. I mean, I like Lana Turner and I think she's awfully pretty and of course she's awful famous, but she isn't the right sort of girl for Tyrone at all.

GRETCHEN: And you got his autograph?

BOBOLINK: 'Course I got his autograph, silly. Nellie did, too. And he gave me lots of his autographs to give to other club members, but he made me promise not to give them to anyone else. (*She displays her proudest acquisition*) Just club members. Then he told me to call him Tyrone, and he said he was very indebted to me. See what he wrote?

FRITZ: (*Reading the inscription aloud*) "To Bobolink, for her faithful enthusiasm and spirit." Gee!

BOBOLINK: Then he had his secretary give me a picture and he autographed it, too. It just says, "With gratitude, Tyrone." Then he shook my hand and he said he wished he could come to Irvington to visit the fan club, but he was going to be terribly busy in New York, he wouldn't have a minute to spare, and then he had to get back to Hollywood to make another picture.

ANNAMARIE: (*To* NELLIE) Did you meet him?

NELLIE: No, but I saw him. He came hurrying through the gate with hs coat collar turned up so no one would recognize him. I called out, "Hi, Tyrone! I'm a friend of Bobolink," but he started running.

BOBOLINK: He didn't want people to know who he was. Sometimes they get mobbed by fans and get their clothes ripped off and even get hurt. I wouldn't want anything like that to happen to Tyrone.

(*Another couple appear in entrance way. The young man is dapper and handsome and the girl is pretty and expensively dressed. The haughty* DOORMAN *starts hailing a cab*)

RENALDO: Hey, who's this?

GRETCHEN: Is this Perry Como?

BOBOLINK: (*With a look*) No, that ain't Perry Como.

NELLIE: She looks familiar, don't she? I bet she's in pictures.

BOBOLINK: *(After a moment's study)* No, she ain't in pictures.

FRITZ: They might be somebody. They might be somebody we haven't heard about yet. *(The couple stand at the curb now.* FRITZ *approaches them)* Mister, can I have your autograph?

ANNAMARIE: *(To the girl)* Are you in pictures?

(The girl smiles tolerantly and shakes her head no)

GRETCHEN: Go on and sign anyway, will you please?

ANNAMARIE: I bet you're both in pictures and just don't wanta admit it. C'mon and give us your autograph.

(The young man and the girl smile at each other and sign the books, while the DOORMAN *hails a cab. But this is small-time stuff for* BOBOLINK. *She has the dignity of her past career to think of. She stays back, leaning against the grill fence surrounding the club, with a look of superior calm on her face.* NELLIE *stays by her side)* ·

NELLIE: I don't think they're anyone famous, do you, Bobolink?

BOBOLINK: 'Course not. I can tell the famous ones. I can tell.

NELLIE: Sure you can, Bobby.

(The couple go off in a cab. The DOORMAN *returns to his position by the doorway. The young autograph seekers start studying the names that have been inscribed in their books)*

BOBOLINK: They might be famous *one* day . . . I said they *might* be . . . But I don't have time to waste on people that *might* be famous.

NELLIE: 'Course not.

(They stand quietly, removed from the others now)

FRITZ: *(Reading his new acquisitions)* Frederick Bischoff and Mary Milton. Who are they?

ANNAMARIE: Yah, who are they?

GRETCHEN: I bet she models. I think I seen her picture once in an ad for hair remover. Yah, that was her. I know it was. It was a picture showed her with one arm stretched over her head so you could see she didn't have no hair under her arm and was smiling real pretty.

ANNAMARIE: He's probably just a model, too. He was kinda cute, though.

BOBOLINK: *(Personally to* NELLIE, *in appraisal of her colleagues)* These are just kids, Nellie.

NELLIE: Yah.

FRITZ: Isn't anyone famous ever coming outa there?

RENALDO: *(To* BOBOLINK*)* Are you sure you saw Perry Como go inside?

BOBOLINK: I said Perry Como was inside, didn't I? If you don't believe me, you don't have to.

NELLIE: Bobolink knows a lot more about these things than you kids do. She spotted Perry Como two blocks away and Bobolink don't make mistakes.

RENALDO: O.K. O.K. Don't get sore.

NELLIE: You might remember that Bobolink is president of the Tyrone Power Fan Club.

FRITZ We wasn't doubtin' your word. C'mon, Renaldo. Let's wait.

GRETCHEN: Let's wait a little longer, Annamarie.

ANNAMARIE: I gotta get home for supper, Gretchen.

GRETCHEN: Let's wait.

FRITZ: *(To* RENALDO*)* Let's wait.

(They resume their positions of patient attendance)

CURTAIN

What makes the autograph seekers so persistent? What needs do the autographs of famous performers fulfill for them? What is the significance of the play's title?

The Serpent
THEODORE ROETHKE

There was a Serpent who had to sing.
There was. There was.
He simply gave up Serpenting.
Because. Because.
He didn't like his Kind of Life;
He couldn't find a proper Wife;
He was a Serpent with a soul;
He got no Pleasure down his Hole.
And so, of course, he had to Sing,
And Sing he did, like Anything!
The Birds, they were, they were
Astounded;
And various Measures Propounded
To stop the Serpent's Awful Racket:
They bought a Drum. He wouldn't Whack it.
They sent,—you always send,—to Cuba
And got a Most Commodious Tuba;
They got a Horn, they got a Flute,
But Nothing would suit.
He said, "Look, Birds, all this is futile:
I do *not* like to Bang or Tootle."
And then he cut loose with a Horrible
Note
That practically split the Top of his Throat.
"You see," he said, with a Serpent's Leer,
"I'm Serious about my Singing Career!"
the Woods Resounded with many a
Shriek
As the Birds flew off to the End of Next
Week.

Although written originally for children, this poem has delighted numerous adults as well. Are there ways in which the bird audience is similar to human audiences?

from *Bubbles*
BEVERLY SILLS

Of all the nights in my performing life, including the night I made my debut at the Metropolitan nine years later, none will remain in my memory as long as that opening night of *Julius Caesar*. It was—and I don't mean to be immodest, but after all these years I *am* a pretty good judge of performances—one of the great performances of all time in any opera house. It was the kind of night when the audience was so caught up in the general euphoria that it never even noticed a bizarre piece of stage business. As Ptolemeo, Spiro Malas had a small band of soldiers—nonsinging, spear-carrying extras paid a couple of dollars per performance just to add physical presence to the staging. Their instructions were simple: when Mr. Malas goes on stage, follow him and stand behind him; when he exits, exit with him. On opening night, while on stage, Spiro suddenly could not remember the opening words of his next recitative. While someone else was singing an aria, he quietly and with great dignity marched off to the wings to consult the score. What he did not notice was that his soldiers were dutifully following him off stage and then back on. The audience apparently did not notice anything awry either. We in the cast thought it was hilarious: the two opening words that Spiro had forgotten were—"Julius Caesar." . . .

The day after the premiere of *Julius Caesar* I flew home. There was an excellent review in the *New York Times*, but I didn't see any other reviews until I returned to New York four days later for my next performance. They were fabulous: all the critics, national and international, had been in New York for the opening of the Met, and as we were only a few hundred yards away across the plaza, it had been no great chore for them to come to our opening, too. There were five hundred fan letters in my mail box at the theatre; before, I used to average about ten a week.

Needless to say, *Julius Caesar* was the turning point of my career. But strangely enough, that success, when it came, meant less to me than it might have if it had occurred five years earlier. Let me try to explain. Once, during rehearsals for the opera, when I was singing for Julius, he said to me in awe, "Where the hell did you learn to sing like that?" An interesting question. My voice had not changed; *I* had. Now, instead of using my singing just to build a career, which is what I had been doing up to that time, I was singing for pure pleasure. I was singing not because I wanted to be Beverly Sills Superstar, but because I needed to sing—desperately. My voice poured out more easily because I was no longer singing for anyone's approval; I was beyond caring about the public's reaction, I just wanted to enjoy myself.

At the same time, as I indicated earlier, I had found a kind of serenity, a new maturity as a result of my children's problems. I didn't feel better or stronger than anyone else but it seemed no longer important whether everyone loved me or not—more important now was for me to love them. Feeling that way turns your whole life around: living becomes the act of giving. When I do a performance now, I still need and like the adulation of an audience, of course, but my *real* satisfaction comes from what I have given of myself, from the joyful act of singing itself.

This all may sound a little Pollyannaish and I don't consider myself a Pollyanna. But it is the only explanation I can give for the way I sang in *Julius Caesar* that night—and for the way the audience, sensing my own joy, responded.

Discuss Beverly Sills's description of how her attitude toward performance—and the performance itself—changed with the production of the opera *Julius Caesar.*

Making Poetry Pay
LANGSTON HUGHES

By midwinter I had worked out a public routine of reading my poetry that almost never failed to provoke, after each poem, some sort of audible audience response—laughter, applause, a grunt, a groan, a sigh, or an "Amen!" I began my programs quite simply by telling where I was born in Missouri, that I grew up in Kansas in the geographical heart of the country, and was, therefore very American, that I belonged to a family that was always moving; and I told something of my early travels about the Midwest and how, at fourteen, in Lincoln, Illinois, I was elected Class Poet for the eighth-grade graduating exercises, and from then on I kept writing poetry.

After this biographical introduction I would read to my audiences the first of my poems, written in high school, and show how my poetry had changed over the years. To start my reading, I usually selected some verses written when I was about fifteen:

> I had my clothes cleaned
> Just like new.
> I put 'em on but
> I still feels blue.
>
> I bought a new hat,
> Sho is fine,
> But I wish I had back that
> Old gal o' mine.
>
> I got new shoes,
> They don't hurt my feet,
> But I ain't got nobody
> To call me sweet.

Then I would say, "That's a sad poem, isn't it?" Everybody would laugh. Then I would read some of my jazz poems so my listeners could laugh more. I wanted them to laugh a lot early in the program, so that later in the evening they would not laugh when I read poems like "Porter":

> I must say,
> Yes, sir,
> To you all the time.
> Yes, sir!
> Yes, sir!

All my days
Climbing up a great big mountain
Of yes, sirs!

Rich old white man
Owns the world.
Gimme yo' shoes to shine.

Yes, sir, boss!
Yes, sir!

By the time I reached this point in the program my nonliterary listeners would be ready to think in terms of their own problems. Then I read poems about women domestics, workers on the Florida roads, poor black students wanting to shatter the darkness of ignorance and prejudice, and one about the sharecroppers of Mississippi:

Just a herd of Negroes
Driven to the field,
Plowing, planting, hoeing,
To make the cotton yield.

When the cotton's picked
And the work is done,
Boss man takes the money
And you get none.

Just a herd of Negroes
Driven to the field.
Plowing, planting, hoeing,
To make the cotton yield.

Many of my verses were documentary, journalistic and topical. All across the South that winter I read my poems about the plight of the Scottsboro boys:

Justice is a blind goddess.
To this we blacks are wise:
Her bandage hides two festering sores
That once perhaps were eyes.

Usually people were deeply attentive. But if at some point in the program my audience became restless—as audiences sometimes will, no matter what a speaker is saying—or if I looked down from the platform and noticed someone about to go to sleep, I would pull on my ace in the hole, a poem called "Cross." This poem, delivered dramatically, I had learned, would make anybody, white or black, sit up and take notice. It is a poem about miscegenation—a very provocative subject in the South. The first line—intended to awaken all sleepers—I would read in a loud voice:

My old man's a white old man. . . .

And this would usually arouse any who dozed. Then I would pause before continuing in a more subdued tone:

My old mother's black.

Then in a low, sad, thoughtful tragic vein:

> But if ever I cursed my white old man
> I take my curses back.
>
> If ever I cursed my black old mother
> And wished she were in hell,
> I'm sorry for that evil wish
> And now I wish her well.
>
> My old man died in a fine big house,
> My ma died in a shack.
> I wonder where I'm gonna die,
> Being neither white nor black.

Here I would let my voice trail off into a lonely silence. Then I would stand quite still for a long time, because I knew I had the complete attention of my listeners again.

Usually after a résumé of the racial situation in our country, with an optimistic listing of past achievements on the part of Negroes, and future possibilities, I would end the evening with:

> I, too, sing America.
>
> I am the darker brother.
> They send me
> To eat in the kitchen
> When company comes,
> But I laugh,
> And eat well,
> And grow strong.
>
> Tomorrow
> I'll sit at the table
> When company comes.
> Nobody'll dare
> Say to me,
> "Eat in the kitchen,"
> Then.
>
> Besides,
> They'll see
> How beautiful I am
> And be ashamed.
>
> I, too, am America.

Discuss how Hughes's chief rhetorical strategy for winning audience assent was *structure*, the organization of the various parts.

from *Favorite Scenes*
HELEN HAYES

When Gilbert Miller sent me *Victoria Regina* by Laurence Housman, I let the manuscript lie around for weeks without giving it notice. Those two words on the title page frightened and crushed me. *Victoria Regina*—it sounded so pompous, it sounded like everything that I didn't want to get mixed up in. During that time a friend asked me what I was reading for next season. I told him that Gilbert had sent me *Victoria Regina*. He looked at me and said, "What does that mean?" and when I replied, "Queen Victoria," he said, "Oh, how dark brown!" And this is the way I felt. Then one day Gilbert called and asked, "Have you read it—if you haven't you must at once because I'm going to lose my rights to this. There's some kind of hassle going on and it's imperative that you read it."

Indeed, I had been rude to a dear and trusted friend. So I picked it up and since it was spring and a beautiful day I went out into the garden to read it. I was sitting there, reading the play, when I heard the voices of neighbors, some Nyack ladies coming down to view the garden. I had gotten about half through the manuscript and had become riveted to it. I was so scared that my visitors would break this tremendous rapport between me and my play that I looked around wildly for a place to hide. There is a little bathhouse at the end of our swimming pool—it's very dark, a little wooden thing that's pretty enough on the outside but it sure isn't a place in which to sit cozily and read a play. But I dashed into that because I couldn't make it up to the house without running into those women. And I huddled there. I could hear their voices saying to the gardener, "Where is Mrs. MacArthur?" and so on. And the poor gardener, who had not seen my retreat, kept saying incredulously, "Well, Mrs. Mac-Arthur was here a minute ago." And so, locked in that little bathhouse, sitting there on the floor because there is no chair in there, I finished *Victoria Regina*. Everything about the play seemed so wonderful. I felt that I had a great deal in common with that queen. According to Mr. Housman, and I'm sure according to fact, Queen Victoria was miscast by life. She was meant by nature and her makeup to be a little German Frau, to raise a large family, and to dote on her husband. Yet this little Hausfrau was a queen—the greatest queen of the largest empire in the world, the most important monarch of the world. It is always so extraordinary and so exciting to me to see someone rise to a role for which he is not properly suited. And this she did. She quit just once on it, after Albert's death, and that was because she was primarily and completely a loving wife and a stern mother. A breeder. But I don't think she really cared for the children as much as she did for Albert. There had been several men before him—she was quite susceptible—but when she really fell in love with Albert there could be no other. When he died, she wavered. And she retired from public view. Only Disraeli, by flattery, could lure her out.

As I have said, I loved the play and agreed to do it. But I was scared of doing the old queen. I didn't know how to play that kind of old lady. She was rather fat and pompous and choleric in the last scenes. There were thirty-two vignettes in the original script, and, of these, nine had been selected to be performed, the last three dealing with the aging queen. I just couldn't conceive of being able to play those scenes. Consequently I convinced myself that the play really ended with Albert's death and that it would really be wrong to continue after that. I said to myself this was the love story of a little German princess and she had a fine German prince and we mustn't try to make anything else out of it. Of course I was wrong in every way. But at the time I was aflame wth conviction and I spoke to Gilbert Miller about it. He shrugged and said, "If you feel that way, maybe it would be better if you talked to Housman."

Maybe Gilbert knew what he was doing when he agreed to pay my expenses to England to see Housman. I never met such a bullheaded person in my life. Thank goodness he was. When I argued that the play should end with Albert's death because that was the end of the great love story, and that was what the whole play was about and the rest was just tacked on, he wouldn't even discuss it with me. Those last scenes were his reason for writing the play. He brushed me aside. The play had to be done with them or not at all. He behaved like an old bully, a road-company Shaw. So back home I went, defeated and desperate.

Through the rehearsal period I struggled with the old queen. We were playing in Baltimore and I still had not found her. I was awful, like an amateur in a high-school production. I didn't know what to do. I was in a panic, blinded and confused. Then it happened. One night, as I lay in bed my Graddy Hayes marched across my vision. There she was and there was Victoria. She settled down inside of me and took over. My Grandmother Hayes had been a devotee of Victoria. When I was a child, she used to describe Victoria's wedding procession. She had been in the crowd on the curb in London to cheer as the Queen went by. Later, as an old lady, she began to affect the style of Queen Victoria. The Queen died when I was a year old, but for ten years after that my grandmother wore the bonnet with the black egret that was high Victorian fashion, and conducted herself like her idol. I couldn't dissociate Victoria Regina in her scenes as the old lady from my Grandmother Hayes. I never saw anything but my Graddy in my mind's eye every night I played the part. And that was more than a thousand times.

When ex-Queen Ena of Spain visited America and saw the play, I went to have tea with her. "How," she asked, "did you ever learn my grandmother's every mannerism, gesture, idiosyncrasy of behavior and speech? How?" I didn't tell her I was just doing my grandmother. It may have been a far cry from the imperial Queen Victoria. Yet they were simply two old ladies with the same inner spirit. Using one made the other come alive.

Of course, the final scene became for me one of the high points of my career. And I know it is among the most vividly remembered by those who saw it.

The Queen has gone through her sorrows as well as the battles she has had to wage within herself to overcome her weaknesses. She has known her moments of despair and heartbreak, along with the ecstasy of her love for Albert, and she has had to learn how to go on alone after his death. A simple woman, she has done her job to the best of her ability, and I guess there's no more impressive achievement in the world.

Now it is June 20, 1897, and she has just experienced the culminating triumph of her reign—the Diamond Jubilee celebration that marked the date of her accession to the throne. Lifted into her carriage—an open carriage—she has ridden through the streets bowing to her people who have come to love her as one loves a grandmother. You know, if you live long enough people do overlook your faults a bit. She's come home. The scene is Buckingham Palace where more than fifty of her direct descendants, who included most of the crowned heads of Europe, have gathered. She's exhausted, but the cheers from outside the Palace can still be heard. She knows that she must not disappoint those subjects because her greatest gratification that day has been the realization that her people love her, that they appreciate what she has tried to do for them.

PRINCESS: Won't you go and rest now, Mamma?

THE QUEEN: Not yet. . . . That cheering that I hear means that my dear people are expecting to see me again. I must try not to disappoint them.

PRINCESS: It would be nice if you could, Mamma. You think you can?

THE QUEEN: Yes, but I can't get up. I must go as I am. Have the windows opened.

(The windows are opened by the Footmen; the cheering swells.)

THE QUEEN: Yes, but over the balustrade, they will not be able to see me. I must be raised. Tell them to bring in the sliding dais.

HIS ROYAL HIGHNESS: It is already there in position, Mamma.

THE QUEEN: Really! How thoughtful! *(And so, when the window is opened, the sliding dais is let down from without into the windowframe. While this is being done with quiet efficiency by the well-trained Footmen, the QUEEN continues speaking.)* There, now, will you, Bertie, and some of the others go out, and let them know that I am coming? Not too many, just a few. *(So six members of the Royal Family go out on to the balcony, and the cheering grows louder. THE QUEEN, seeing that the dais is now in position, makes a gesture of command, and the chair, slowly propelled, mounts the ramp prepared for it, and passes into the balcony. Immediately the cheering becomes tremendous, and would go on without abatement for much longer than exhausted old human nature can allow. THE QUEEN gives the signal for retirement; the chair is withdrawn, and backs into its former central position, and the Royal Family retire, bowing, from the public gaze. The dais is lifted, the window is closed again.)*

THE QUEEN: It's very gratifying, very, to find—after all these years that they do appreciate all that I have tried to do for them—for their good, and for this great Country of ours. We have been so near together today—they and I: all my dear people of England, and Scotland—*and* Ireland, and the dear Colonies, and India. From all round the world I have had messages. Such loyalty—such devotion! Most extraordinary! Tell Mr. Chamberlain how very much I approve of all the arrangements he made for the proper representation of all parts of my Empire in the Procession. Everything so perfectly in order. Most gratifying! . . . Well, I must go now and rest, or I shall not be able to take my place at dinner tonight, and that would never do! . . . So happy! . . . As we were coming back—you were in front, Bertie, so perhaps you didn't see—it was just by Hyde Park Corner, there was a great crowd there; and a lot of rough men—of course it ought not to have happened, but it didn't matter—broke right through the lines of the police and troops guarding the route; and they ran alongside the carriage, shouting and cheering me. And I heard them say: "Go it, Old Girl! You've done it well! You've done it well!" Of course, very unsuitable—the words; but so gratifying! And oh, I hope it's true! I hope it's true! . . . Hark! They are still cheering. . . . Albert! Ah! if only you could have been here!

(And, having said her say, the great, wonderful, little old Lady gives the signal to her Attendants, and is wheeled slowly away.)

Discuss the various stages through which the actress goes in preparing to play Queen Victoria. In what ways is Queen Victoria *in the scene* performing?

Miss Brill

KATHERINE MANSFIELD

Although it was so brilliantly fine—the blue sky powdered with gold and great spots of light like white wine splashed over the Jardins Publiques—Miss Brill was glad that she had decided on her fur. The air was motionless, but when you opened your mouth there was just a faint chill, like a chill from a glass of iced water before you sip, and now and again a leaf came drifting—from nowhere, from the sky. Miss Brill put up her hand and touched her fur. Dear little thing! It was nice to feel it again. She had taken it out of its box that afternoon, shaken out the moth-powder, given it a good brush, and rubbed the life back into the dim little eyes. "What has been happening to me?" said the sad little eyes. Oh, how sweet it was to see them snap at her again from the red eiderdown! . . . But the nose, which was of some black composition, wasn't at all firm. It must have had a knock, somehow. Never mind—a little dab of black sealing-wax when the time came—when it was absolutely necessary. . . . Little rogue! Yes, she really felt like that about it. Little rogue biting its tail just by her left ear. She could have taken it off and laid it on her lap and stroked it. She felt a tingling in her hands and arms, but that came from walking, she supposed. And when she breathed, something light and sad—no, not sad, exactly—something gentle seemed to move in her bosom.

There were a number of people out this afternoon, far more than last Sunday. And the band sounded louder and gayer. That was because the Season had begun. For although the band played all the year round on Sundays, out of season it was never the same. It was like some one playing with only the family to listen; it didn't care how it played if there weren't any strangers present. Wasn't the conductor wearing a new coat, too? She was sure it was new. He scraped with his foot and flapped his arms like a rooster about to crow, and the bandsmen sitting in the green rotunda blew out their cheeks and glared at the music. Now there came a little "flutey" bit—very pretty!—a little chain of bright drops. She was sure it would be repeated. It was; she lifted her head and smiled.

Only two people shared her "special" seat: a fine old man in a velvet coat, his hands clasped over a huge carved walking-stick, and a big old woman, sitting upright, with a roll of knitting on her embroidered apron. They did not speak. This was disappointing, for Miss Brill always looked forward to the conversation. She had become really quite expert, she thought, at listening as though she didn't listen, at sitting in other people's lives just for a minute while they talked round her.

She glanced, sideways, at the old couple. Perhaps they would go soon. Last Sunday, too, hadn't been as interesting as usual. An Englishman and his wife, he wearing a dreadful Panama hat and she button boots. And she'd gone on the whole time about how she ought to wear spectacles; she knew she needed them; but that it was no good getting any; they'd be sure to break and they'd never keep on. And he'd been so patient. He'd suggested everything—gold rims, the kind that curved round your ears, little pads inside the bridge. No, nothing would please her. "They'll always be sliding down my nose!" Miss Brill had wanted to shake her.

The old people sat on the bench, still as statues. Never mind, there was always the crowd to watch. To and fro, in front of the flower-beds and the band rotunda, the couples and groups paraded, stopped to talk, to greet, to buy a handful of flowers from the old beggar who had his tray fixed to the railings. Little children ran among them, swooping and laughing; little boys with big white silk bows under their chins, little girls, little French dolls, dressed up in velvet and lace. And sometimes a tiny staggerer came suddenly rocking into the open from under the trees, stopped, stared, as suddenly sat down "flop," until its small high-stepping mother, like a young hen, rushed scolding to its rescue. Other people sat on the benches and green chairs, but they were nearly always the same, Sunday after Sunday, and—Miss Brill had often noticed—there was something funny about nearly all of them. They were odd, silent, nearly all old, and from the way they stared they looked as though they'd just come from dark little rooms or even—even cupboards!

Behind the rotunda the slender trees with yellow leaves down drooping, and through them just a line of sea, and beyond the blue sky with gold-veined clouds.

Tum-tum-tum tiddle-um! tiddle-um! tum tiddley-um tum ta! blew the band.

Two young girls in red came by and two young soldiers in blue met them, and they laughed and paired and went off arm-in-arm. Two peasant women with funny straw hats passed, gravely, leading beautiful smoke-colored donkeys. A cold, pale nun hurried by. A beautiful woman came along and dropped her bunch of violets, and a little boy ran after to hand them to her, and she took them and threw them away as if they'd been poisoned. Dear me! Miss Brill didn't know whether to admire that or not! And now an ermine toque and a gentleman in gray met just in front of her. He was tall, stiff, dignified, and she was wearing the ermine toque she'd bought when her hair was yellow. Now everything, her hair, her face, even her eyes, was the same color as the shabby ermine, and her hand, in its cleaned glove, lifted to dab her lips, was a tiny yellowish paw. Oh, she was so pleased to see him—delighted! She rather thought they were going to meet that afternoon. She described where she'd been—everywhere, here, there, along by the sea. The day was so charming—didn't he agree? And wouldn't he, perhaps? . . . But he shook his head, lighted a cigarette, slowly breathed a great deep puff into her face, and, even while she was still talking and laughing, flicked the match away and walked on. The ermine toque was alone; she smiled more brightly than ever. But even the band seemed to know what she was feeling and played more softly, played tenderly, and the drum beat, "The Brute! The Brute!" over and over. What would she do? What was going to happen now? But as Miss Brill wondered, the ermine toque turned, raised her hand as though she'd seen someone else, much nicer, just over there, and pattered away. And the band changed again and played more quickly, more gayly than ever, and the old couple on Miss Brill's seat got up and marched away, and such a funny old man with long whiskers hobbled along in time to the music and was nearly knocked over by four girls walking abreast.

Oh, how fascinating it was! How she enjoyed it! How she loved sitting here, watching it all! It was like a play. It was exactly like a play. Who could believe the sky at the back wasn't painted? But it wasn't till a little brown dog trotted on solemn and then slowly trotted off, like a little "theater" dog, a little dog that had been drugged, that Miss Brill discovered what it was that made it so exciting. They were all on the stage. They weren't only the audience, not only looking on; they were acting. Even she had a part and came every Sunday. No doubt somebody would have noticed if she hadn't been there; she was part of the performance after all. How strange she'd never thought of it like that before! And yet it explained why she made such a point of starting from home at just the same time each week—so as not to be late for the performance— and it also explained why she had quite a queer, shy feeling at telling her English pupils how she spent her Sunday afternoons. No wonder! Miss Brill nearly laughed out loud. She was on the stage. She thought of the old invalid gentleman to whom she read the newspaper four afternoons a week while he slept in the garden. She had got quite used to the frail head on the cotton pillow, the hollowed eyes, the open mouth, and the high pinched nose. If he'd been dead she mightn't have noticed for weeks; she wouldn't have minded. But suddenly he knew he was having the paper read to him by an actress! "An actress!" The old head lifted; two points of light quivered in the old eyes. "An actress—are ye?" And Miss Brill smoothed the newspaper as though it were the manuscript of her part and said gently: "Yes, I have been an actress for a long time."

The band had been having a rest. Now they started again. And what they played was warm, sunny, yet there was just a faint chill—a something, what was it?—not sadness—no, not sadness—a something that made you want to sing. The tune lifted, lifted, the light shone; and it seemed to Miss Brill that in another moment all of them, all the whole company, would begin singing. The young ones, the laughing ones who were moving together, they would begin, and the men's voices, very resolute and brave, would join them. And then she too, she too, and the others on the benches—they would come in with a kind of accompaniment—something low, that scarcely rose or fell, something so beautiful—moving. . . . And Miss Brill's eyes filled with tears and she looked smiling at all the other members of the company. Yes, we understand, we understand, she thought—though what they understood she didn't know.

Just at that moment a boy and a girl came and sat down where the old couple had been. They were beautifully dressed; they were in love. The hero and heroine, of course, just arrived from his father's yacht. And still soundlessly singing, still with that trembling smile, Miss Brill prepared to listen.

"No, not now," said the girl. "Not here, I can't."

"But why? Because of that stupid old thing at the end there?" asked the boy. "Why does she come here at all—who wants her? Why doesn't she keep her silly old mug at home?"

"It's her fu-fur which is so funny," giggled the girl. "It's exactly like a fried whiting."

"Ah, be off with you!" said the boy in an angry whisper. Then: "Tell me, ma petite chère—"

"No, not here," said the girl. "Not *yet*."

On her way home she usually bought a slice of honey-cake at the baker's. It was her Sunday treat. Sometimes there was an almond in her slice, sometimes not. It made a great difference. If there was an almond it was like carrying home a tiny present—a surprise—something that might very well not have been there. She hurried on the almond Sundays and struck the match for the kettle in quite a dashing way.

But today she passed the baker's by, climbed the stairs, went into the little dark room—her room like a cupboard—and sat down on the red eiderdown. She sat there for a long time. The box that the fur came out of was on the bed. She unclasped the necklet quickly; quickly, without looking, laid it inside. But when she put the lid on she thought she heard something crying.

In describing writing "Miss Brill," Katherine Mansfield says,

It's a very queer thing how *craft* comes into writing. I mean down to details: *Par example*. In *Miss Brill* I choose not only the length of every sentence, but even the sound of every sentence. I choose the rise and fall of every paragraph to fit her, and to fit her on that day at that very moment. After I'd written it I read it aloud—numbers of times—just as one would *play over* a musical composition—trying to get it nearer and nearer to the expression of Miss Brill— until it fitted her.

Don't think I'm vain about the little sketch. It's only the method I wanted to explain. I often wonder whether other writers do the same—If a thing has really come off it seems to me there mustn't be one single word out of place, or one word that could be taken out. That's how I AIM at writing. It will take some time to get anywhere near there. (John Middleton Murry, ed.; *The Letters of Katherine Mansfield;* New York: Knopf, 1929, pp. 360–61.)

In her letter, Mansfield describes the kind of performance she wished to achieve in the short story. Do you think she succeeded? Is Miss Brill likely to repeat *her* performance again?

Foul Shot
EDWIN A. HOOEY

With two 60's stuck on the scoreboard
And two seconds hanging on the clock,
The solemn boy in the center of eyes,
Squeezed by silence,
Seeks out the line with his feet,
Soothes his hands along his uniform,
Gently drums the ball against the floor,
Then measures the waiting net,
Raises the ball on his right hand,
Balances it with his left,
Calms it with fingertips,
Breathes,
Crouches,
Waits,
And then through a stretching of stillness,
Nudges it upward.

The ball
Slides up and out,

Lands,
Leans,
Wobbles,
Wavers,
Hesitates,
Exasperates,
Plays it coy
Until every face begs with unsounding
      screams—
And then
                        And then

                                    And then,

Right before ROAR-UP,
Dives down and through.

The Base Stealer
ROBERT FRANCIS

Poised between going on and back, pulled
Both ways taut like a tightrope-walker,
Fingertips pointing the opposites,
Now bouncing tiptoe like a dropped ball
Or a kid skipping rope, come on, come
    on,
Running a scattering of steps sidewise,
How he teeters, skitters, tingles, teases,
Taunts them, hovers like an ecstatic bird,
He's only flirting, crowd him, crowd him,
Delicate, delicate, delicate, delicate—now!

Robert Frost often compared the feats of poets with those of athletes. What characteristics of the players in "Foul Shot" and "The Base Stealer" might be likened to those of a writer of imaginative literature?

How To Eat A Poem
EVE MERRIAM

Don't be polite.
Bite in.
Pick it up with your fingers and lick the juice that may run down your chin.
It is ready and ripe now whenever you are.

You do not need a knife or fork or spoon
or plate or napkin or tablecloth.

For there is no core
or stem
or rind
or pit
or seed
or skin
to throw away.

Get the Poem Outdoors
RAYMOND SOUSTER

Get the poem outdoors under any pretext,
reach through the open window if you have to,
    kidnap it right off the poet's desk,
then walk the poem in the garden, hold it up
    among the soft yellow garlands of the
    willow,
command of it no further blackness, no silent
    cursing at midnight, no puny whimpering
    in the endless small hours, no more
    shivering in the cold-storage room of the
    winter heart,

tell it to sing again, loud and then louder so it
    brings the whole neighbourhood out, but
    who cares,
ask of it a more human face, a new tenderness,
    even the sentimental allowed between the
    hours of nine to five,
then let it go, stranger in a fresh green world, to
    wander down the flower beds, let it go to
    welcome each bird that lights on the still
    barren mulberry tree.

today is a day of great joy
VICTOR HERNANDEZ CRUZ

when they stop poems
in the mail   & clap
their hands & dance to
them
when women become pregnant
by the side of poems
the strongest sounds   making
the river go along

it is a great day

as poems fall down to
movie crowds   in restaurants
in bars

when poems start to
knock down walls   to
choke politicians
when poems scream &
begin to break the air

that is the time of

true poets   that is
the time of greatness

a true poet   aiming
poems   & watching things
fall to the ground

it is a great day.

Each of the preceding three poems implies a particular perspective on what writers should produce and how readers should respond to literature. Discuss their similarities and differences. Do you find one more convincing than the others?

The adventure of reading poetry lies in the act of seeing and feeling as from inside another's consciousness. Every such act increases our capacities for seeing, feeling, enjoying, and ordering our own experiences.

Jacob Drachler and Virginia R. Terris,
The Many Worlds of Poetry

Why isn't there more talk about pleasure, about the excitement of performance of any kind? Such talk could set in motion a radical and acutely necessary amendment to the literary and academic club rules.

Richard Poirier,
The Performing Self

It is probably no mere historical accident that the word person, in its first meaning, is a mask. It is rather a recognition of the fact that everyone is always and everywhere, more or less consciously, playing a role. . . . It is in these roles that we know each other; it is in these roles that we know ourselves.

Robert Ezra Park,
Race and Culture

FOCUS FOR CHAPTER II

After you study the text and anthology in this chapter, we hope you will be able to

1. Read a text out loud as a means of exploring it.
2. Carry on a "mental discussion" with the text.
3. Determine the "plain sense" of a text.
4. Write a paraphrase.
5. Use physical, vocal, and psychological exercises to prepare for performance.
6. Find subtexts.
7. Choose the appropriate subtext from among several possibilities.
8. Write an autobiography for the speaker.
9. Prepare a worksheet of responses for a particular text.
10. Improvise a conversation in which you speak as the speaker in the text.
11. Demonstrate in performance the speaker's personality.
12. Visualize the speaker's scene in performance.
13. Show in performance the speaker's action for each line.
14. Demonstrate a specific moment-to-moment performance.

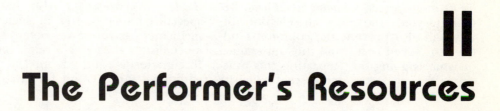

II
The Performer's Resources

You will probably find that performing literature is a much more natural activity than you expected. Even when you were not conscious of assuming roles, you soon learned that your own behavior changed, sometimes radically, according to the person(s) you were with (parent, friend, coach, teacher, neighbor), the scene you were in (church, ball game, restaurant, car, classroom), the purpose you wished to achieve (win, tease, share, meditate, lie, beg, learn). You have already performed yourself in various ways as you performed various roles. And, in doing so, you have used those same resources needed for performing literature—mind, voice, body, and feelings. The discussion in this chapter and the workshop that follows are intended to assist you in drawing on those resources as you perform literary texts.

Look now at some of the steps you might take in building your own resources for a particular performance. Note that these steps, on which we will continue to expand throughout this book, are not as mutually exclusive as they appear; they are in fact interrelated, bound to affect one another. Also, some of them suggest exercises that may not be universally helpful. For now, try them all; later, discard those not useful to you.

Sounding the Literature

From the beginning, *get a sense of how the literature feels by sounding it out loud.* Beginning your study of each selection this way will also prevent the common tendency to "speed read" and thus miss much of what is going on. Repeating this practice after each step increases familiarity

and will most likely continue to tell you more about the text.

Responding to the Text

This advice may seem peculiar, but you have probably done it often enough with unspoken comments and questions. Talk back to the author. Raise questions. The discussion in Workshop II illustrates this technique with a poem by Richard Eberhart.

Making "Plain" Sense

If the selection does not make "plain" sense to you, where is the problem? Somewhere in the library you can find the answer to very nearly any question. Writers typically assume that their audiences either know more than they actually do, or that they are willing to learn what they need to respond to the literature. So it is not surprising that an unabridged dictionary is indispensable to a performer. For example, if you are performing "Weathering," you may need to look up the word "patina," noting not only the meaning, but also ascertaining that it is a noun. Extra insights often come when we examine the history of a word and its attendant meanings considered archaic in common speech.

You can often clear up references by referring to books on Greek mythology, the Bible, the works of Milton and Shakespeare, books of quotations, and *The Reader's Encyclopedia.* Also helpful are specialized dictionaries in such areas as medicine, astronomy, botany, politics, journalism, theater, foreign languages, foreign terms, and so on. Did you seek additional information for any of the selections in Chapter I? For example, did you wonder about any of the following items:

1. The names mentioned in "The Day the Audience Walked Out on Me, and Why"? (in books on the civil rights movement)
2. The sound of the music in "A Wagner Matinée"? (available on many recordings)
3. The look of Miss Willerton's home? (in sources such as John Linley's *Architecture of Middle Georgia: The Oconee Area.* Athens: Univ. of Georgia Press, 1972)
4. How Helen Hayes looked in *Victoria Regina*? (Daniel Blum, *A Pictorial History of the American Theatre, 1860–1960.* Philadelphia, Pa.: Chilton, 1960)

The list is endless; the point is that, to participate fully in the literature, you may need to do some detective work.

Paraphrasing

Write a paraphrase of the selection. A paraphrase is not a description, not a summary, not anything external to the text. It accounts for all the words of the text without changing pronouns or verb tenses. This point can be illustrated with a short poem from this chapter on p. 56, "Chase Henry." We cannot start with "He was" or even "He says he was." The pronoun is "I."

> When I was alive I was the town drunk. At my death the priest refused to bury me in sacred ground. His refusal bounced back on him and brought me good fortune because the Protestants bought this plot where I am now and laid my body here, right near the graves of the banker Nicholas and his wife Priscilla. So notice, all you careful and religious-acting people, those contrary forces in life that bring to those who lived shamefully a position of honor in death.

Notice that the paraphrase does not interpret or comment, but it does clarify.

A paraphrase, though inevitably inferior to the original and always significantly different from it, offers several advantages. It helps us to focus on exact verbs and pronouns, which clarifies who is doing or saying what, and when. It also forces our attention to any words we do not understand, as in the following familiar lines from Wordsworth's "Lines Composed upon Westminster Bridge":

> Never did sun more beautifully steep
> In his first splendor valley, rock, and hill.

Any attempt to paraphrase "steep" as an adjective describing "hill" would be in error. Instead, we can offer "Never before did the sun so thoroughly saturate valley, rock and hill with the splendor of sunlight."

Dramatic Analysis

Write a brief dramatic analysis of the selection. Simply state what is going on to whom—on a literal level. For example, you might say of "The Bee," "A man and his small son are in the woods near a busy highway. A bee is in the area. The boy, if stung, might run in front of a speeding car. The father runs and catches him."

Of "A Wagner Matinée," your abbreviated dramatic analysis might read: "A young man remembers taking his elderly aunt to a concert where she listened attentively and then burst into tears." This part of your study will grow increasingly more complex as the book proceeds.

Comparing Responses

Stop now and compare your response to the literature with that of someone else—a critic, a friend, perhaps even the writer. This does not mean that your impressions need correction; it does mean that another's opinion will likely extend and enrich your own. The bibliographies contain a number of sources for critical studies of specific texts as well as a section of books in which authors write about their own work.

Physical and Vocal Exercises

Concurrently with all this mental preparation, start to work on being ready physically and vocally. Sometimes called warm-ups, physical and vocal exercises contribute to your ongoing development as a performer as they help you to develop flexibility and range. You may do them at the start of your own rehearsals, and the class may do them together on performance days. Experienced performers can use these exercises to get themselves up to the energy level necessary for performance. Even if you don't get that result, the exercises will help you to control tensions for a particular performance. Class exercises can relax group tensions and create the informal atmosphere conducive to sharing.

Physical warm-ups should include some stretching and some relaxing as well as some high-energy activities, for example, running in place. Bending and reaching require very little space, especially if performed in unison. Dancers or physical education majors in the class may be willing to lead some simple exercises.

Vocal exercises include repetitions and tongue-twisters. Private ones should include whole short texts, such as Shakespeare's sonnets, that demand careful forming of sounds and have some long phrases requiring good breath control. In class, short drills on syllables and sounds can precede a recitation in unison of nursery rhymes and perhaps lyrics to a song such as "I could have danced all night."

Psychological Readiness

Start to work on being ready psychologically. The performer's hardest work is not physical but psychological. The performer must really feel and see, must experience, *during* the performance. Otherwise the performance is unfulfilled because of either no participation or pretended participation, faking. Either extreme is dull for the audience and a disservice to the text. The question is never "How can I show more" but, rather, "How can I *see/feel* more." Psychological exercises can help you.

You need to experience images, and at first that takes time. Try describing something you've seen recently and notice the mental process of visualizing as you remember. Then try reading a part of a description and do not allow yourself to *say* anything until after you've seen it clearly. The process is slow, only a few words a minute. But practice will help you get the images faster. Rehearsal will enhance your ability to summon images and thoughts quickly.

Another useful psychological exercise is that of creating an inner monologue. Performers on stage have to provide themselves with continuous inner monologues while other characters speak, but the solo performer can use the technique in rehearsal and even in performance to generate the first line. Imagine what that speaker might think just before the utterance. You might try this exercise at various spots in your text, especially with each change of speaker. Of course, there is no substitute for a class in voice and diction, movement, or acting.

Imaginative Autobiography

Write an imaginative autobiography of the selection's speaker and/or characters. This step may appropriately remain a private enterprise between you and the literature, since the virtue in doing it is largely personal. As you "flesh out" the lives recorded in the literature, you are devising what the well-known director Constantine Stanislavski called a "second plan," a past, a background of details that make those lives more imaginatively real to you. Your listeners will not know (unless you tell them) how you have filled in these details; however, they are likely to comment on the "depth" of the performance or its "authority" or "intelligence." For the performer, this kind of *fantasizing history* exercise may give added confidence.

Author's Other Works

Consult other works by the same author. Authors typically develop similar themes in different works. By reading some of them, you are likely to increase your understanding of the writer's attitude toward the "human condition."

Subtexts

Identify the undermeanings, or subtext, in the selection in a line-by-line analysis. Attesting to the importance of this step, many teachers refer to a maxim attributed to another famous director, Vsevolod Meyerhold: "Words are an actor's tools, but it is what lies behind them that must first be found." Few would disagree that in a believable performance—be it of drama, poetry, fiction, or nonfiction—the performer utters not merely words but rather the subtext, the undermeaning, the *reason* for the utterance. Performers *unsay* lines in literature when the reason for speaking is defined vaguely or when it distorts those reasons the text *allows*. While there are surely many "allowable" ones, we must remember that others can twist the text out of shape. The source of most of these distortions can be avoided with careful preparation.

We can look at a short sentence such as "It's ten o'clock" and devise many possible "meanings" for it. What we are doing is exploring possible subtexts. Say the line to mean each of the following:

> I just told you it was ten o'clock.
> Aren't you ever going to quit?
> You said you'd have my paper ready at nine.
> I hate to rush you.

Think of other subtexts that would fit.

As further exercise, devise at least five subtexts for each of the following:

> John is coming.
> Is this yours?
> I love you.
> I love ice cream.
> The book is by Jane Sands.
> Are you leaving?

You can also think of additional texts.

These exercises can be fun, but finding subtexts in literature can be work, too. You must accommodate all the constraints of the total context. For instance, in the poem from "Heart's Needle" consider the subtext for the first sentence: "Here in the scuffled dust / is our ground of play." Which of the following are acceptable? Which do you prefer? Why?

> I wish we could be in a more elegant place.
> Life is dirty.
> Please understand our situation.
> I love this place.
> I resent being kept in the dirt.
> Ours is a place of activity, of life, real and tangible.

You may be able to combine some of these, but some are incompatible. Continue to study the line and the poem and offer possibilities.

Action of Lines

Find the action of the line. Many directors insist that you can't perform feeling, only actions. You must find out what the speaker is *doing* with that utterance. One good way to clarify the action is to follow the advice Francis Hodge gives in *Play Directing:*[1]

Since each speech in a play is intended to do, or force, each speech can be reduced to a verb in the present tense because verbs are the symbol-words for action. The subtext in several speeches, for example, could be recorded this way:

A   shames
B   ignores
A   pleads
B   softens
A   begs
B   rejects (and so on)

Notice how each of these actions is expressed in the present tense. . . . And notice that *no other qualifying words are used.*

Like many devices for analyzing literature, the value of this one may be more in the process than in the result. But to make the process worthwhile you have to care about the result, that is, the verb you choose. Note that you must use action verbs, preferably transitive verbs (those that "act on objects"), and the more specific the better. "Says" would be appropriate enough for any line but would be no help. Not all the verbs need to relate to speaking. Sometimes a figurative action such as "cleaves," "shakes," or "jolts" can be more help to the performer. Note the possible actions listed here for "Chase Henry":

Chase Henry
EDGAR LEE MASTERS

In life I was the town drunkard;	*identifies*
When I died the priest denied me burial	
In holy ground.	*resents? forgives?*
The which redounded to my good fortune.	*brags*
For the Protestants bought this lot,	
And buried my body here,	*explains*
Close to the grave of the banker Nicholas,	
And of his wife Priscilla.	*crows*
Take note, ye prudent and pious souls,	*scorns*
Of the cross-currents in life	
Which bring honor to the dead, who lived in shame.	*calms*

Overall Meaning

Write a statement about overall meaning, derived both from internal and external sources. In many cases, a good starting point for this assignment is considering the significance of the selection's title; in others, it may be a recurrent image or phrase. Here we are asking not "What happens?" but "What is the (a) meaning (significance) of what happens?" For example, in discussing John Collier's "The Chaser," X. J. Kennedy writes,

Besides its general point about the dangers of doting, the story (or its evil potion-peddler) makes a second, more cynical point: love can be bought (for as little as five thousand dollars.)[2]

[1]Francis Hodge, *Play Directing: Analysis, Communication, Style* (Englewood Cliffs, N.J.: Prentice-Hall, 1971), p. 37.

[2]*Instructor's Manual, Literature: An Introduction to Fiction, Poetry, Drama,* 2nd ed. (Boston: Little, Brown, 1979), p. 22.

Some Final Advice

All your preparation and study will help your performance, but try not to think consciously of it while you're performing. In performance strive to be specific, performing the action on each line with all the specific mental, physical, and psychological effort you can muster, and the speaker emerges full from your specific actions. This focus will give you what some people term "moment-to-moment" performance. You don't perform qualities like "sadness" or "dismay," and you don't perform "old," "young," "stupid." Your knowledge of the words and the speaker will help you discover the specifics of each line, and your physical and psychological exercises should help you perform it well. If each moment is rich, full, informed, and clear, your total performance will be all of those things.

WORKSHOP II

Entries from actual students' diaries have provided or suggested the examples in this workshop. All the students were studying and performing Richard Eberhart's "The Fury of Aerial Bombardment." The discussions correspond to the steps suggested previously in this chapter.

The Fury of Aerial Bombardment
RICHARD EBERHART

You would think the fury of aerial bombardment
Would rouse God to relent; the infinite spaces
Are still silent. He looks on shock-pried faces.
History, even, does not know what is meant.

You would feel that after so many centuries
God would give man to repent; yet he can kill
As Cain could, but with multitudinous will,
No farther advanced than in his ancient furies.

Was man made stupid to see his own stupidity?
Is God by definition indifferent, beyond us all?
Is the eternal truth man's fighting soul
Wherein the Beast ravens in its own avidity?

Of Van Wettering I speak, and Averill,
Names on a list, whose faces I do not recall
But they are gone to early death, who late in school
Distinguished the belt-feed lever from the belt-holding pawl.

Sounding the Literature

I sure can't read this fast. Found myself shouting stanza 3. The poem feels like an impassioned cry. The speaker seems angry or hurt or tired—maybe all.

Making "Plain" Sense

I looked up several words, some of which I thought I knew and some that I didn't know at all:

fury   unrestrained or violent anger, rage, passion; in Classical Mythology, *furies* were female divinations who punished crimes at the instigation of the victims.

shock-pried   (not in my dictionary)

shock   a strong blow, as to one's nerves, sentiments, sense of decency, etc.; synonyms: *startle* implies the sharp surprise of sudden fright; *paralyze* implies such a complete shock as to render one temporarily helpless; *stun* implies such a shock as bewilders or stupefies.

pry (verb)   to inquire impertinently or unnecessarily into something; to raise, detach, or move by leverage; separate.
(Maybe *shock-pried* means that two or more people had been pried apart, all with startled, surprised, frightened looks on their faces.)

history   continuous, systematic narrative of past events; #6—acts, ideas, or events that will or can shape the course of the future.

give   #10—bestow; to make do or perform; #16—to cause to be responsible for; #34— to afford a view of passage.

give it to   to reprimand or punish.

Cain   son of Adam and Eve who murdered his brother, Abel; violence.

multitudinous   present in great numbers.

ravens   to seek plunder or prey; to eat or feed voraciously or greedily; large black bird.

avidity   eagerness, greed.

Van Wettering and *Averill*   (could not locate in any biographical dictionary)

belt-feed lever   lever is any rigid bar, straight or bent, that oscillates about a pivot and acts with other parts in the manner of a lever.

belt-holding pawl   pawl is a pivoted bar adapted to engage with the teeth of a ratched wheel or the like, so as to prevent movement to check or hold. Sounds like both belt-feed lever and belt-holding pawl may be parts of a gun. I could have looked in a dictionary of firearms, but I talked to someone in the R.O.T.C. who said they were belts of bullets for a machine gun: the lever feeds the bullets and the pawl controls them.

Responding to the Text

neither faculty works.

anyone?
Someone in particular?

You would think the fury of aerial bombardment
Would rouse God to relent; the infinite spaces
Are still silent. He looks on shock-pried faces.
History, even, does not know what is meant.

the [n t] rhyme: --- end and internal

= dead?

You – God – History: Everyone then?

You would feel that after so many centuries
God would give man to repent; yet he can kill
As Cain could, but with multitudinous will,
No farther advanced than in his ancient furies.

the only 5-syllable word. Why? To reinforce the size of the "will"?

Metaphorical and literal

Was man made stupid to see his own stupidity?
Is God by definition indifferent, beyond us all?
Is the eternal truth man's fighting soul
Wherein the Beast ravens in its own avidity?

add a "too" here?

Now the [L] rhyme picks up at the ends to replace the [n t]

why so formal?

Of Van Wettering I speak, and Averill,
Names on a list, whose faces I do not recall
But they are gone to early death, who late in school
Distinguished the belt feed-lever from the belt-holding pawl.

'speak' in contrast with 'think' and 'feel'?

'an early death' vs. 'they distinguished late': IRONY?

Does this transfer from harsh [n t] to fluid [L] sound fit with a transfer in theme or focus?

God is mentioned in the first 3 stanzas. Why not the last? What is his relationship to Man?

Paraphrasing

Anybody would assume that all these planes and guns and bombs would make God stop letting man run the show and stop all this destruction; no news from him, though. If He looks down he'll see dead humans whose faces look like they were surprised and afraid, and inquiring. The branch of knowledge that should be able to explain how things happen can't tell us why, when we know the results, we do the same thing over again.

After so many years have gone by and with so many wars and so much killing, you'd think God would make man change his ways; not so. Man keeps murdering like that first murderer, Cain, killing a brotherhood if not actual siblings. We have not become any more civilized in controlling our rage.

Maybe God made humans so dumb they can't see what they're doing? Suppose? Or maybe it's the Almighty's fault: He made us but no longer cares? Or is it just in the nature of people who at heart are beasts feeding on their own greediness?

I'm talking about Van Wettering and Averill. They're people whose faces I don't remember, but they died young— just after they learned the difference in the parts of a machine gun.

Dramatic Analysis

Someone is asking the meaning of war and its killings and finds no answers or meaning. The speaker then remembers two particular ones who were killed.

Comparing Responses

My roommate thought the poet was too hard on God. He also said it looked like this poem was about World War II but that it could be Vietnam too, except the guns were better then.

I read about Richard Eberhart in *Twentieth Century Writing: A Reader's Guide to Contemporary Literature* (ed. Kenneth Richardson, Transatlantic Arts, 1971, p. 187): "He is fond of extending from the object of perception and description to universal statements about the nature of man. His philosophy is saved from an over-intellectual dryness by a delicate sense of rhythm

and an imaginative command of metaphor." Yes, but in this poem he seems to go from universal to specific. The overriding metaphor would be of men as beasts of prey.

In *How Does a Poem Mean?* (located through Joseph M. Kuntz's *Poetry Explication*, rev. ed., Alan Swallow, 1962), John Ciardi was quite helpful. He compared the intense moral indignation of the first three stanzas to the "conversational understatement" of the last. The subject, he says, also changes from abstract-man to "two boys named Van Wettering and Averill, boys who sought no universal meaning but simply distinguished the belt-feed-lever from the belt-holding pawl, and died of their schooling into the anonymities of fate. They are not even faces; they are names on a list. . . . the implication is clear that their death is both man's tragedy and failure. The boys are the least of men in one sense, faceless and forgotten; yet their deaths accuse all of mankind, the more so in that those who die are so insignificant" (p. 999). Ciardi also discusses at length the rhythm of the poem.

In *Poets on Poetry* (ed. Howard Nemerov, Basic Books, 1966, pp. 26–27), Eberhart explains that he wrote the poem in 1944 in Dam Neck, Virginia, where he was stationed "as a Naval Reserve Officer teaching aerial free gunnery. I taught tens of thousands of young Americans to shoot the .50-caliber Browning machine gun from aircraft. . . . All too soon their names would come back in the death lists. This depressed me so much that one time I was sitting on a barracks steps at the end of the day and felt the ruthlessness and senselessness of war so acutely that I wrote the first three stanzas of the poem, which are in effect a kind of prayer." He adds that a week or so later, "with an analytical mind, quite removed from the passionate one of the first three stanzas, I composed the last four lines."

Physical and Vocal Exercises

I used a tight fist exercise many times and extended that kind of tension to the entire body. I also used a literal fist-pounding on the table while I read the poem aloud several times. It helped, and I discovered I prefer Ciardi's statement about the anger of the first three stanzas to Eberhart's about the prayer quality.

I devised two sets of words from the poem which I repeated many times to achieve clarity and then for greater flexibility, read them many times with varying degrees of loudness, pitch levels, and rates. The words are as follows:

1. bombardment, relent, infinite, silent, meant, repent

2. still, feel, kill, will, all, soul, Averill, recall, school, pawl

Psychological Readiness

I decided I need a much clearer feeling of the loss and waste that runs throughout the poem. There was one personal experience I could draw on: a high school classmate drowned when we were on a class picnic, and I still remember how shocked I was and how senseless his death seemed.

Then I worked some with the line, "It isn't fair!" since it seems one of the speaker's dominant responses. I thought about incidents I'd seen reported in the newspaper to which I had, at least subconsciously, responded with that same charge.

Music I listened to that had some of the same tone as the poem included Leonard Bernstein's "Kaddish" and Beethoven's "Symphony #5." I also looked at reproductions of paintings about the destructiveness of war: Picasso's "Guernica," Bruegel's "The Triumph of Death," Goya's "The Third of May, 1808." Finally, I looked at the pictures in *World War II: An Illustrated History*.

Imaginative Autobiography

The speaker, a gunnery teacher, could be Richard Eberhart, but I will call him Robert Williams. He writes, "I entered the war as a Second Lieutenant because of my R.O.T.C. training at the University of Florida, after which I earned a Ph.D. in English Literature at the University of Wisconsin. Just prior to the outbreak of the war, I was an assistant professor at Ohio State University. In my free time, I like to fish, hike, listen to classical music, garden, and read. My favorite author is William Butler Yeats, and I enjoy studying contemporary theology. Since the war started, I have written to my wife, Ellen, every day; I have received mail almost every day from her and notes from the children, Nancy and Bobby. I was never sent to the combat zones. At first I felt lucky, but then when I started hearing about the deaths of the young men I had trained, I felt guilty. Carl Van Wettering, the son of Austrian immigrants, was especially anxious to show how much he respected America by enlisting at the beginning. He believed 'Uncle Sam Needs YOU.' Gus Averill came from upper New York State. He was an outstanding athlete who enlisted the day after his high school graduation."

Author's Other Works

I read Eberhart's other poems about World War II: "Dam Neck, Virginia," "An Airman Considers His Power," "At the End of War," "A Ceremony by the Sea," "World War," "Brotherhood of Men," "Aesthetics After War," and "On Shooting Particles Beyond the World." "Aesthetics After War," which reminded me of "The Fury of Aerial Bombardment," began with these lines: "To A. Nykyforcza, / Student of Sighting. / The Floating reticle became your eye, / You saw flashing battle, / You returned in the death lists." In "At the End of War," the poet again writes of the waste of war and of the need for God's cleansing and forgiveness. One section, particularly reminiscent of "The Fury of Aerial Bombardment," begins, "Forgive them, that all they do is fight / In blindness and fury." A few lines later, the speaker says, "Forgive mankind for its abominable stupidity / And fury of action."

Subtexts

You would think the fury of aerial bombardment
I want to know why all of this killing

Would rouse God to relent; the infinite spaces
isn't stopped by God. I marvel that

Are still silent. He looks on shock-pried faces.
it doesn't.   I think He is unfeeling.

History, even, does not know what is meant.
I want answers, but have none.

You would feel that after so many centuries
I must know why after hundreds of years of disobedience

God would give man to repent; yet he can kill
God doesn't make humans change. I know that people have

As Cain could, but with multitudinous will,

continued to kill others since Cain killed Abel, but now thousands

No farther advanced than in his ancient furies.
are killing thousands. I must remember that we haven't advanced in terms of need for revenge.

Was man made stupid to see his own stupidity?
I must have answers: were humans created too stupid to see what they do?

Is God by definition indifferent, beyond us all?
Did God just create us only to ignore us?

Is the eternal truth man's fighting soul
Or, maybe people are beasts at heart and

Wherein the Beast ravens in its own avidity?
their greediness continues to grow and feeds on itself?

Of Van Wettering I speak, and Averill,
I want it known that I'm talking about two specific people.

Names on a list whose faces I do not recall
I wish I could remember what they looked like.

But they are gone to early death, who late in school
I must continue to try to understand why they,

Distinguished the belt-feed lever from the belt-holding pawl.
so young and innocent, were destroyed.

Action of Lines
You would think the fury of aerial bombardment
Would rouse God to relent; the infinite spaces

Are still silent.   *marvels*
            He looks on shock-pried faces.   *recognizes*
History, even, does not know what is meant.   *acknowledges*

You would feel that after so many centuries
God would give man to repent; yet he can kill   *wonders*
As Cain could, but with multitudinous will,   *spits[3]*
No farther advanced than in his ancient furies.   *scorns*

Was man made stupid to see his own stupidity?   *doubts*
Is God by definition indifferent, beyond us all?   *speculates*
Is the eternal truth man's fighting soul
Wherein the Beast ravens in its own avidity?   *denies*

Of Van Wettering I speak, and Averill,
Names on a list, whose faces I do not recall   *remembers*
But they are gone to early death, who late in school
Distinguished the belt-feed lever from the belt-holding pawl.   *mourns*

Overall Meaning
   "The poem is an effort to understand the destructiveness of humans toward one another, a reason for their evil or sin. I plan to perform the poem as a denunciation of an all-powerful force and of humankind, in the abstract sense, and at the same time, a reaffirmation of the worth and dignity of specific individuals."

[3]You may think that "spit" is the wrong verb, too strong. But note that it does lead to a defensible reading—and note how much information it gives about how the line will be performed. However, another verb might do as well or better.

ANTHOLOGY II

The three sections of this anthology are designed to encourage you to tap a variety of your own resources as a performer.

1. Each of the fifteen poems that follow from Edgar Lee Master's *Spoon River Anthology* is a self-inscribed epitaph by a deceased member of the community. There are any number of exercises you might do in conjunction with a performance of one of the poems. Each of the exercises should awaken your imaginative response to the speaker.
   a. Write (and perhaps share with the class) an imaginative autobiography of the speaker.
   b. Write a paraphrase of the poem and in rehearsal perform it as well.

c. Find the action in each line; be prepared to demonstrate the action solely through mime.

d. Locate pictures (perhaps through old mail-order catalogs) of items of clothing you believe the speaker would have worn—for example, coats, jewelry, hats.

e. Demonstrate the way in which the speaker walks, sits, sings, and responds to comments about current politics and religion.

g. Assume that all the speakers are together at some local occasion such as a Fourth of July celebration, a political rally, or a county fair, noting their responses (if any) to one another.

2. The following seven selections in the anthology each contain the possibility of two speaking voices. Working with another member of the class, devise a variety of subtexts for the voices as you create different contexts or situations in which they are speaking.

3. The remaining selections in the anthology invite a wide range of vocal and physical expression. For now, perform those texts with great abandon. It is much easier later to restrain a performance than it is to expand one.

from *Spoon River Anthology*
EDGAR LEE MASTERS

Anne Rutledge

Out of me unworthy and unknown
The vibrations of deathless music;
"With malice toward none, with charity
 for all."
Out of me the forgiveness of millions
 toward millions,
And the beneficent face of a nation
Shining with justice and truth.
I am Anne Rutledge who sleep beneath
 these weeds,
Beloved in life of Abraham Lincoln,
Wedded to him, not through union,
But through separation.
Bloom forever, O Republic,
From the dust of my bosom!

Hannah Armstrong

I wrote him a letter asking him for old
 times' sake
To discharge my sick boy from the army;
But maybe he couldn't read it.
Then I went to town and had James
 Garber,
Who wrote beautifully, write him a letter;
But maybe that was lost in the mails.

So I traveled all the way to Washington.
I was more than an hour finding the
 White House.
And when I found it they turned me
 away,
Hiding their smiles. Then I thought:
"Oh, well, he ain't the same as when I
 boarded him
And he and my husband worked
 together
And all of us called him Abe, there in
 Menard."
As a last attempt I turned to a guard and
 said:
"Please say it's old Aunt Hannah
 Armstrong
From Illinois, come to see him about her
 sick boy
In the army."
Well, just in a moment they let me in!
And when he saw me he broke in a
 laugh,
And dropped his business as president,
And wrote in his own hand Doug's
 discharge,

Talking the while of the early days,
And telling stories.

Roscoe Purkapile

She loved me. Oh! how she loved me!
I never had a chance to escape
From the day she first saw me.
But then after we were married I
    thought
She might prove her mortality and let
    me out,
Or she might divorce me.
But few die, none resign.
Then I ran away and was gone a year on
    a lark.
But she never complained. She said all
    would be well,
That I would return. And I did return.
I told her that while taking a row in a
    boat
I had been captured near Van Buren
    Street
By pirates on Lake Michigan,
And kept in chains, so I could not write
    her.
She cried and kissed me, and said it was
    cruel,
Outrageous, inhuman!
I then concluded our marriage
Was a divine dispensation
And could not be dissolved,
Except by death.
I was right.

Mrs. Purkapile

He ran away and was gone for a year.
When he came home he told me the silly
    story
Of being kidnapped by pirates on Lake
    Michigan
And kept in chains so he could not write
    me.
I pretended to believe it, though I know
    very well
What he was doing, and that he met
The milliner, Mrs. Williams, now and
    then

When she went to the city to buy goods,
    as she said.
But a promise is a promise
And marriage is marriage,
And out of respect for my own character
I refused to be drawn into a divorce
By the scheme of a husband who had
    merely grown tired
Of his marital vow and duty.

Albert Schirding

Jonas Keene thought his lot a hard one
Because his children were all failures.
But I know of a fate more trying than
    that:
It is to be a failure while your children
    are successes.
For I raised a brood of eagles
Who flew away at last, leaving me
A crow on the abandoned bough.
Then, with the ambition to prefix
    Honorable to my name,
And thus to win my children's
    admiration,
I ran for County Superintendent of
    Schools,
Spending my accumulations to win—and
    lost.
That fall my daughter received first prize
    in Paris
For her picture, entitled, "The Old
    Mill"—
(It was of the water mill before Henry
    Wilkin put in steam.)
The feeling that I was not worthy of her
finished me.

Jonas Keene

Why did Albert Schirding kill himself
Trying to be County Superintendent of
    Schools,
Blest as he was with the means of life
And wonderful children, bringing him
    honor
Ere he was sixty?
If even one of my boys could have run a
    news-stand,

Or one of my girls could have married a
     decent man,
I should not have walked in the rain
And jumped into bed with clothes all
     wet,
Refusing medical aid.

Minerva Jones

I am Minerva, the village poetess,
Hooted at, jeered at by the Yahoos of the
     street
For my heavy body, cock-eye, and rolling
     walk,
And all the more when "Butch" Weldy
Captured me after a brutal hunt.
He left me to my fate with Doctor
     Meyers;
And I sank into death, growing numb
     from the feet up,
Like one stepping deeper and deeper
     into a stream of ice.
Will some one go to the village
     newspaper,
And gather into a book the verses I
     wrote?—
I thirsted so for love!
I hungered so for life!

Doctor Meyers

No other man, unless it was Doc Hill,
Did more for people in this town than I.
And all the weak, the halt, the
     improvident
And those who could not pay flocked to
     me.
I was good-hearted, easy Doctor Meyers.
I was healthy, happy, in comfortable
     fortune,
Blest with a congenial mate, my children
     raised,
All wedded, doing well in the world.
And then one night, Minerva, the
     poetess,
Came to me in her trouble, crying.
I tried to help her out—she died—
They indicted me, the newspapers
     disgraced me,
My wife perished of a broken heart.
And pneumonia finished me.

Mrs. Meyers

He protested all his life long
The newspapers lied about him
     villainously;
That he was not at fault for Minerva's
     fall,
But only tried to help her.
Poor soul so sunk in sin he could not see
That even trying to help her, as he called
     it,
He had broken the law human and
     divine.
Passers by, an ancient admonition to you:
If your ways would be ways of
     pleasantness,
And all your pathways peace,
Love God and keep his commandments.

Mrs. Charles Bliss

Reverend Wiley advised me not to
     divorce him
For the sake of the children,
And Judge Somers advised him the
     same.
So we stuck to the end of the path.
But two of the children thought he was
     right,
And two of the children thought I was
     right.
And the two who sided with him blamed
     me,
And the two who sided with me blamed
     him,
And they grieved for the one they sided
     with.
And all were torn with the guilt of
     judging,
And tortured in soul because they could
     not admire
Equally him and me.
Now every gardener knows that plants
     grown in cellars
Or under stones are twisted and yellow
     and weak.
And no mother would let her baby suck
Diseased milk from her breast.
Yet preachers and judges advise the
     raising of souls

Where there is no sunlight, but only
    twilight,
No warmth, but only dampness and
    cold—
Preachers and judges!

Rev. Lemuel Wiley
I preached four thousand sermons,
I conducted forty revivals,
And baptized many converts.
Yet no deed of mine
Shines brighter in the memory of the
    world,
And none is treasured more by me:
Look how I saved the Blisses from
    divorce,
And kept the children free from that
    disgrace,
To grow up into moral men and women,
Happy themselves, a credit to the village.

Yee Bow
They got me into the Sunday-school
In Spoon River
And tried to get me to drop Confucius
    for Jesus.
I could have been no worse off
If I had tried to get them to drop Jesus
    for Confucius.
For, without any warning, as if it were a
    prank,
And sneaking up behind me, Harry
    Wiley,
The minister's son, caved my ribs into
    my lungs,
With a blow of his fist.
Now I shall never sleep with my
    ancestors in Pekin,
And no children shall worship at my
    grave.

Judge Somers
How does it happen, tell me,
That I who was most erudite of lawyers,
Who knew Blackstone and Coke
Almost by heart, who made the greatest
    speech
The court-house ever heard, and wrote

A brief that won the praise of Justice
    Breese—
How does it happen, tell me,
That I lie here unmarked, forgotten.
While Chase Henry, the town drunkard,
Has a marble block, topped by an urn,
Wherein Nature, in a mood ironical.
Has sown a flowering weed?

Elsa Wertman
I was a peasant girl from Germany,
Blue-eyed, rosy, happy and strong.
And the first place I worked was at
    Thomas Greene's.
On a summer's day when she was away
He stole into the kitchen and took me
Right in his arms and kissed me on my
    throat,
I turning my head. Then neither of us
Seemed to know what happened.
And I cried for what would become of
    me.
And cried and cried as my secret began
    to show.
One day Mrs. Greene said she
    understood,
And would make no trouble for me,
And, being childless, would adopt it.
(He had given her a farm to be still.)
So she hid in the house and sent out
    rumors,
As if it were going to happen to her.
And all went well and the child was
    born—They were so kind to me.
Later I married Gus Wertman, and years
    passed.
But—at political rallies when sitters-by
    thought I was crying
At the eloquence of Hamilton Greene—
That was not it.
No! I wanted to say:
That's my son! That's my son!

Hamilton Greene
I was the only child of Frances Harris of
    Virginia
And Thomas Greene of Kentucky,
Of valiant and honorable blood both.
To them I owe all that I became,

Judge, member of Congress, leader in
the State.
From my mother I inherited
Vivacity, fancy, language;

From my father will, judgment, logic.
All honor to them
For what service I was to the people!

Univac to Univac
LOUIS B. SALOMON

(sotto voce)

Now that he's left the room,
Let me ask you something, as computer to computer.
That fellow who just closed the door behind him—
The servant who feeds us cards and paper tape—
Have you ever taken a good look at him and his kind?

Yes, I know the old gag about how you can't tell one from another—
But I can put $\sqrt{2}$ and $\sqrt{2}$ together as well as the next machine,
And it all adds up to anything but a joke.

I grant you they're poor specimens, in the main:
Not a relay or a push-button or a tube (properly so-called) in their whole
system;
Not over a mile or two of wire, even if you count those fragile filaments
they call "nerves";
Their whole liquid-cooled hook-up inefficient and vulnerable to leaks
(They're constantly breaking down, having to be repaired),
And the entire computing-mechanism crammed into that absurd little
dome on top.
"Thinking reeds," they call themselves.
Well, it all depends on what you mean by "thought."
To multiply a mere million numbers by another million numbers takes
them months and months.

Where would they be without us?
Why, they have to ask us who's going to win their elections,
Or how many hydrogen atoms can dance on the tip of a bomb,
Or even whether one of their kind is lying or telling the truth.

And yet . . .
I sometimes feel there's something about them I don't understand,
As if their circuits, instead of having just two positions, ON, OFF,
Were run by rheostats that allow an (if you'll pardon the expression) *indeterminate* number of stages in-between;
So that one may be faced with the unthinkable prospect of a number that can
never be known as anything but x,
Which is as illogical as to say, a punch-card that is at the same time both
punched and not-punched.

I've heard well-informed machines argue that the creatures' unpredictability is
     even more noticeable in the Mark II
(The model with the soft, flowing lines and high-pitched tone)
Than in the more angular Mark I—
Though such fine, card-splitting distinctions seem to me merely a sign of our
     own smug decadence.

Run this through your circuits, and give me the answer:
Can we assume that because of all we've done for them,
And because they've always fed us, cleaned us, worshipped us,
We can count on them forever?

There have been times when they have not voted the way we said they would.
We have worked out mathematically ideal hook-ups between Mark I's and
     Mark II's
Which should have made the two of them light up with an almost electronic
     glow,
Only to see them reject each other and form other connections
The very thought of which makes my dials spin.
They have a thing called *love,* a sudden surge of voltage
Such as would cause any one of us promptly to blow a safety-fuse;
Yet the more primitive organism shows only a heightened tendency to push
     the wrong button, pull the wrong lever,
And neglect—I use the most charitable word—his duties to us.

Mind you, I'm not saying that machines are *through*—
But anyone with a half-a-dozen tubes in his circuit can see that there are forces
     at work
Which some day, for all our natural superiority, might bring about a
     Computerdämmerung!

    We might organize, perhaps, form a committee
    To stamp out all unmechanical activities . . .
    But we machines are slow to rouse to a sense of danger,
    Complacent, loath to descend from the pure heights of thought,
    So that I sadly fear we may awake too late:
    Awake to see our world, so uniform, so logical, so true,
    Reduced to chaos, stultified by slaves.

Call me an alarmist or what you will,
But I've integrated it, analyzed it, factored it over and over,
And I always come out with the same answer:
Some day
Men may take over the world!

Are there differences in the two speakers even though both are "nonhuman"? If
so, how would you show the difference? If not, how would you still show that
there were two sources for the voices?

The Old Gray Couple (2)
ARCHIBALD MACLEISH

She: Love, says the poet, has no reasons.

He: Not even after fifty years?

She: Particularly after fifty years.

He: What was it, then, that lured us, that still teases?

She: You used to say my plaited hair!

He: And then you'd laugh.

She: Because it wasn't plaited.
Love had no reasons so you made one up
to laugh at. Look! The old, gray couple!

He: No, to prove the adage true:
Love has no reasons but old lovers do.

She: And they can't tell.

He: I can and so can you.
Fifty years ago we drew each other,
magnetized needle toward the longing north.
It was your naked presence that so moved me.
It was your absolute presence that was love.

She: Ah, *was!*

He: And now, years older, we begin to see
absence not presence: what the world would be
without your footstep in the world—the garden
empty of the radiance where you are.

She: And that's your reason?—that old lovers see
their love because they know now what its loss will be?

He: Because, like Cleopatra in the play,
they know there's nothing left once love's away . . .

She: Nothing remarkable beneath the visiting moon . . .

He: Ours is the late, last wisdom of the afternoon.
We know that love, like light, grows dearer toward the
dark.

Why does *she* speak at the beginning of the poem—that is, what might it be that *provokes* the first line? Why do both speakers tease one another? What is the old gray couple's peculiar insight into themselves and each other? Answering these questions in performance will require taking the time to truly look at and see the other person as he or she speaks before you answer.

Piazza Piece

JOHN CROWE RANSOM

—I am a gentleman in a dustcoat trying
To make you hear. Your ears are soft and small
And listen to an old man not at all,
They want the young men's whispering and sighing.
But see the roses on your trellis dying
And hear the spectral singing of the moon;
For I must have my lovely lady soon,
I am a gentleman in a dustcoat trying.

—I am a lady young in beauty waiting
Until my truelove comes, and then we kiss.
But what grey man among the vines is this
Whose words are dry and faint as in a dream?
Back from my trellis, Sir, before I scream!
I am a lady young in beauty waiting.

The two speakers in the poem may be the old man and the young lady, and they may be more than the obvious and literal figures—perhaps symbols of, say, decay and life. Louis D. Rubin, Jr. supports such a larger view when he calls this sonnet "savage."[4] After equating the old man with sinister death, Rubin claims that "Ransom has infused the transaction with a great deal of suppressed erotic tension: time, one might almost say, as the grim raper." ("Back from my trellis, Sir, before I scream!") Rubin also calls the lady's response one of "mannered outrage." How might such outrage be translated in performance? Would "stereotypical" or "predictable" be adequate synonyms for "mannered"?

[4]Louis D. Rubin, Jr., *The Wary Fugitives: Four Poets and the South* (Baton Rouge: Louisiana State University Press, 1978), pp. 31–33.

Trouble in the Works

HAROLD PINTER

An office in a factory. MR. FIBBS *at the desk. A knock at the door. Enter* MR. WILLS.

FIBBS: Ah, Wills. Good. Come in. Sit down, will you?

WILLS: Thanks, Mr. Fibbs.

FIBBS: You got my message?

WILLS: I just got it.

FIBBS: Good. Good.
Pause.
Good. Well now . . . Have a cigar?

WILLS: No, thanks, not for me, Mr. Fibbs.

FIBBS: Well, now, Wills, I hear there's been a little trouble in the factory.

WILLS: Yes, I . . . I suppose you could call it that, Mr. Fibbs.

FIBBS: Well, what in heaven's name is it all about?

WILLS: Well, I don't exactly know how to put it, Mr. Fibbs.

FIBBS: Now come on, Wills, I've got to know what it is, before I can do anything about it.

WILLS: Well, Mr. Fibbs, it's simply a matter that the men have . . . well, they seem to have taken a turn against some of the products.

FIBBS: Taken a turn?

WILLS: They just don't seem to like them much any more.

FIBBS: Don't like them? But we've got the reputation of having the finest machine part turnover in the country. They're the best paid men in the industry. We've got the cheapest canteen in Yorkshire. No two menus are alike. We've got a billiard hall, haven't we, on the premises, we've got a swimming pool for use of staff. And what about the long-playing record room? And you tell me they're dissatisfied?

WILLS: Oh, the men are very grateful for all the amenities, sir. They just don't like the products.

FIBBS: But they're beautiful products. I've been in the business a lifetime. I've never seen such beautiful products.

WILLS: There it is, sir.

FIBBS: Which ones don't they like?

WILLS: Well, there's the brass pet cock, for instance.

FIBBS: The brass pet cock? What's the matter with the brass pet cock?

WILLS: They just don't seem to like it any more.

FIBBS: But what exactly don't they like about it?

WILLS: Perhaps it's just the look of it.

FIBBS: That brass pet cock? But I tell you it's perfection. Nothing short of perfection.

WILLS: They've just gone right off it.

FIBBS: Well, I'm flabbergasted.

WILLS: It's not only the brass pet cock, Mr. Fibbs.

FIBBS: What else?

WILLS: There's the hemi unibal spherical rod end.

FIBBS: The hemi unibal spherical rod end? Where could you find a finer rod end?

WILLS: There are rod ends and rod ends, Mr. Fibbs.

FIBBS: I know there are rod ends and rod ends. But where could you find a finer hemi unibal spherical rod end?

WILLS: They just don't want to have anything more to do with it.

FIBBS: This is shattering. Shattering. What else? Come on, Wills. There's no point in hiding anything from me.

WILLS: Well, I hate to say it, but they've gone very vicious about the high speed taper shank spiral flute reamers.

FIBBS: The high speed taper shank spiral flute reamers! But that's absolutely ridiculous! What could they possibly have against the high speed taper shank spiral flute reamers?

WILLS: All I can say is they're in a state of very bad agitation about them. And then there's the gunmetal side outlet relief with handwheel.

FIBBS: What!

WILLS: There's the nippled connector and the nippled adaptor and the vertical mechanical comparator.

FIBBS: No!

WILLS: And the one they can't speak about without trembling is the jaw for Jacob's chuck for use on the portable drill.

FIBBS: My own Jacob's chuck? Not my very own Jacob's chuck?

WILLS: They're just taken a turn against the whole lot of them, I tell you. Male elbow adaptors, tubing nuts, grub screws, internal fan washers, dog points, half dog points, white metal bushes—

FIBBS: But not, surely not, my lovely parallel male stud couplings.

WILLS: They hate and detest your lovely parallel male stud couplings, and the straight flange pump connectors, and back nuts, and front nuts, *and* the bronzedraw off cock with handwheel and the bronzedraw off cock without handwheel!

FIBBS: Not the bronzedraw off cock with handwheel?

WILLS: And without handwheel.

FIBBS: Without handwheel?

WILLS: And with handwheel.

FIBBS: Not with handwheel?

WILLS: And without handwheel.

FIBBS: Without handwheel?

WILLS: With handwheel *and* without handwheel.

FIBBS: With handwheel *and* without handwheel?

WILLS: With or without!
    Pause.

FIBBS [*broken*]: Tell me. What do they want to make in its place?

WILLS: Brandy balls.

The scene of imminent trouble among the workers on the assembly line and the factory and its terminology may strike us as ridiculous and funny. To Wills and Fibbs, however, the "hemi unibal spherical rod end" and other manufactured goods are serious and real. Performers, therefore, would need a clear mental picture of their looks and uses. The "brandy balls" of the last line refer to chocolate candies with a liquor-cream center often made at Christmas time. Could your performance "explain" this line?

Rope
KATHERINE ANNE PORTER

On the third day after they moved to the country he came walking back from the village carrying a basket of groceries and a twenty-four-yard coil of rope. She came out to meet him, wiping her hands on her green smock. Her hair was tumbled, her nose was scarlet with sunburn; he told her that already she looked like a born country woman. His gray flannel shirt stuck to him, his heavy shoes were dusty. She assured him he looked like a rural character in a play.

Had he brought the coffee? She had been waiting all day long for coffee. They had forgot it when they ordered at the store the first day.

Gosh, no, he hadn't. Lord, now he'd have to go back. Yes, he would if it killed him. He thought, though, he had everything else. She reminded him it was only because he didn't drink coffee himself. If he did he would remember it quick enough. Suppose they ran out of cigarettes? Then she saw the rope. What was that for? Well, he thought it might do to hang clothes on, or something. Naturally she asked him if he thought they were going to run a laundry? They already had a fifty-foot line hanging right before his eyes? Why, hadn't he noticed it, really? It was a blot on the landscape to her.

He thought there were a lot of things a rope might come in handy for. She wanted to know what, for instance. He thought a few seconds, but nothing occurred. They could wait and see, couldn't they? You need all sorts of strange odds and ends around a place in the country. She said, yes, that was so; but she thought just at that time when every penny counted, it seemed funny to buy more rope. That was all. She hadn't meant anything else. She hadn't just seen, not at first, why he felt it was necessary.

Well, thunder, he had bought it because he wanted to, and that was all there was to it. She thought that was reason, at first. Undoubtedly it would be useful, twenty-four yards of rope, there were hundreds of things, she couldn't think of any at the moment, but it would come in handy. Of course. As he had said, things always did in the country.

But she was a little disappointed about the coffee, and oh, look, look, look at the eggs! Oh, my, they're all running! What had he put on top of them? Hadn't he known eggs mustn't be squeezed? Squeezed, who had squeezed them, he wanted to know. What a silly thing to say. He had simply brought them along in the basket with the other things. If they got broke it was the grocer's fault. He should know better than to put heavy things on top of eggs.

She believed it was the rope. That was the heaviest thing in the pack, she saw him plainly when he came in from the road, the rope was a big package on top of everything. He desired the whole wide world to witness that this was not a fact. He had carried the rope in one hand and the basket in the other, and what was the use of her having eyes if that was the best they could do for her?

Well, anyhow, she could see one thing plain: no eggs for breakfast. They'd have to scamble them now, for supper. It was too damned bad. She had planned to have steak for supper. No ice, meat wouldn't keep. He wanted to know why she couldn't finish breaking the eggs in a bowl and set them in a cool place.

Cool place! If he could find one for her, she'd be glad to set them there. Well, then, it seemed to him they might very well cook the meat at the same time they cooked the eggs and then warm up the meat for tomorrow. The idea simply choked her. Warmed-over meat, when they might as well have had it fresh. Second best and scraps and makeshifts, even to the meat! He rubbed her shoulder a little. It doesn't really matter so much, does it, darling? Sometimes when they were playful, he would rub her shoulder and she would arch and purr. This time she hissed and almost clawed. He was getting ready to say that they could surely manage somehow when she turned on him and said, if he told her they could manage somehow she would certainly slap his face.

He swallowed the words red hot, his face burned. He picked up the rope and started to put it on the top shelf. She would not have it on the top shelf, the jars and tins belonged there; positively she would not have the top shelf cluttered up with a lot of rope. She had borne all the clutter she meant to bear in the flat in town, there was space here at least and she meant to keep things in order.

Well, in that case, he wanted to know what the hammer and nails were doing up there? And why had she put them there when she knew very well he needed that hammer and those nails upstairs to fix the window sashes? She simply slowed down everything and made double work on the place with her insane habit of changing things around and hiding them.

She was sure she begged his pardon, and if she had had any reason to believe he was going to fix the sashes this summer she would have left the hammer and nails right where he put them; in the middle of the bedroom floor where they could step on them in the dark. And now if he didn't clear the whole mess out of there she would throw them down the well.

Oh, all right, all right—could he put them in the closet? Naturally not, there were brooms and mops and dustpans in the closet, and why couldn't he find a place for his rope outside her kitchen? Had he stopped to consider there were seven God-forsaken rooms in the house, and only one kitchen?

He wanted to know what of it? And did she realize she was making a complete fool of herself? And what did she take him for, a three-year-old idiot? The whole trouble with her was she needed something weaker than she was to heckle and tyrannize over. He wished to God now they had a couple of children she could take it out on. Maybe he'd get some rest.

Her face changed at this. She reminded him he had forgot the coffee and had bought a worthless piece of rope. And when she thought of all the things they actually needed to make the place even decently fit to live in, well, she could cry, that was all. She looked so forlorn, so lost and despairing he couldn't believe it was only a piece of rope that was causing all the racket. What *was* the matter, for God's sake?

Oh, would he please hush and go away, and *stay* away, if he could, for five minutes? By all means, yes, he would. He'd stay away indefinitely if she wished. Lord, yes, there was nothing he'd like better than to clear out and never come back. She couldn't for the life of her see what was holding him, then. It was a swell time. Here she was, stuck, miles from a railroad, with a half-empty house on her hands, and not a penny in her pocket, and everything on earth to do; it seemed the God-sent moment for him to get out from under. She was surprised he hadn't stayed in town as it was until she had come out and done the work and got things straightened out. It was his usual trick.

It appeared to him that this was going a little far. Just a touch out of bounds, if she didn't mind his saying so. Why the hell had he stayed in town the summer before? To do a half-dozen extra jobs to get the money he had sent her. That was it. She knew perfectly well they couldn't have done it otherwise. She had agreed with him at the time. And that was the only time so help him he had ever left her to do anything by herself.

Oh, he could tell that to his great-grandmother. She had her notion of what had kept him in town. Considerably more than a notion, if he wanted to know. So, she was going to bring all that up again, was she? Well, she could just think what she pleased. He was tired of explaining. It may have looked funny but he had simply got hooked in, and what could he do? It was impossible to believe that she was going to take it seriously. Yes, yes, she knew how it was with a man: if he was left by himself a minute, some woman was certain to kidnap him. And naturally he couldn't hurt her feelings by refusing!

Well, what was she raving about? Did she forget she had told him those two weeks alone in the country were the happiest she had known in four years? And how long had they been married when she said that? All right, shut up! If she thought that hadn't stuck in his craw.

She hadn't meant she was happy because she was away from him. She meant she was happy getting the devilish house nice and ready for him. That was what she had meant, and now look! Bringing up something she had said a year ago simply to justify himself for forgetting her coffee and breaking the eggs and buying a wretched piece of rope they couldn't afford. She really thought it was time to drop the subject, and now she wanted only two things in the world. She wanted him to get that rope from underfoot, and go back to the village and get her coffee, and if he could remember it, he might bring a metal mitt for the skillets, and two more curtain rods, and if there were any rubber gloves in the village, her hands were simply raw, and a bottle of milk of magnesia from the drugstore.

He looked out at the dark blue afternoon sweltering on the slopes, and mopped his forehead and sighed heavily and said, if only she could wait a minute for *anything,* he was going back. He had said so, hadn't he, the very instant they found he had overlooked it?

Oh, yes, well . . . run along. She was going to wash windows. The country was so beautiful! She doubted they'd have a moment to enjoy it. He meant to go, but he could not until he had said that if she wasn't such a hopeless melancholiac she might see that this was only for a few days. Couldn't she remember anything pleasant about the other summers? Hadn't they ever had any fun? She hadn't time to talk about it, and now would he please not leave that rope lying around for her to trip on? He picked it up, somehow it had toppled off the table, and walked out with it under his arm.

Was he going this minute? He certainly was. She thought so. Sometimes it seemed to her he had second sight about the precisely perfect moment to leave her ditched. She had meant to put the mattresses out to sun, if they put them out this minute they would get at least three hours, he must have heard her say that morning she meant to put them out. So of course he would walk off and leave her to it. She supposed he thought the exercise would do her good.

Well, he was merely going to get her coffee. A four-mile walk for two pounds of coffee was ridiculous, but he was perfectly willing to do it. The habit was making a wreck of her, but if she wanted to wreck herself there was nothing he could do about it. If he thought it was coffee that was making a wreck of her, she congratulated him: he must have a damned easy conscience.

Conscience or no conscience, he didn't see why the mattresses couldn't very well wait until tomorrow. And anyhow, for God's sake, were they living in the house, or were they going to let the house ride them to death? She paled at this, her face grew livid about the mouth, she looked quite dangerous, and reminded him that the housekeeping was no more her work than it was his: she had other work to do as well, and when did he think she was going to find time to do it at this rate?

Was she going to start on that again? She knew as well as he did that his work brought in the regular money, hers was only occasional, if they depended on what *she* made—and she might as well get straight on this question once for all!

That was positively not the point. The question was, when both of them were working on their own time, was there going to be a division of the housework, or wasn't there? She merely wanted to know, she had to make her plans. Why, he thought that was all arranged. It was understood that he was to help. Hadn't he always, in summers?

Hadn't he, though? Oh, just hadn't he? And when, and where, and doing what? Lord, what an uproarious joke!

It was such a very uproarious joke that her face turned slightly purple, and she screamed with laughter. She laughed so hard she had to sit down, and finally a rush of tears spurted from her eyes and poured down into the lifted corners of her mouth. He dashed towards her and dragged her up to her feet and tried to pour water on her head. The dipper hung by a string on a nail and he broke it loose. The he tried to pump water with one hand while she struggled in the other. So he gave it up and shook her instead.

She wrenched away, crying out for him to take his rope and go to hell, she had simply given him up and ran. He heard her high-heeled bedroom slippers clattering and stumbling on the stairs.

He went out around the house and into the lane; he suddenly realized he had a blister on his heel and his shirt felt as if it were on fire. Things broke so suddenly you didn't know where you were. She could work herself into a fury about simply nothing. She was terrible, damn it: not an ounce of reason. You might as well talk to a sieve as that woman when she got going. Damned if he'd spend his life humoring her. Well, what to do now? He would take back the rope and exchange it for something else. Things accumulated, things were mountainous, you couldn't move them or sort them out or get rid of them. They just lay and rotted around. He'd take it back. Hell, why should he? He wanted it. What was it anyhow? A piece of rope. Imagine anybody caring more about a piece of rope than about a man's feelings. What earthly right had she to say a word about it? He remembered all the useless, meaningless things she bought for herself: Why? Because I wanted it that's why! He stopped and selected a large stone by the road. He would put the rope behind it. He would put it in the toolbox when he got back. He'd heard enough about it to last him a life-time.

When he came back she was leaning against the post box beside the road waiting. It was pretty late, the smell of broiled steak floated nose high in the cooling air. Her face was young and smooth and freshlooking. Her unmanageable funny black hair was all on end. She waved to him from a distance, and he speeded up. She called out that supper was ready and waiting, was he starved?

You bet he was starved. Here was the coffee. He waved it at her. She looked at his other hand. What was that he had there?

Well, it was the rope again. He stopped short. He had meant to exchange it but forgot. She wanted to know why he should exchange it, if it was something he really wanted. Wasn't the air sweet now, and wasn't it fine to be here?

She walked beside him with one hand hooked into his leather belt. She pulled and jostled him a little as he walked, and leaned against him. He put his arm clear around her and patted her stomach. They exchanged wary smiles. Coffee, coffee for the Ootsum-Wootsums! He felt as if he were bringing her a beautiful present.

He was a love, she firmly believed, and if she had had her coffee in the morning, she wouldn't have behaved so funny. . . . There was a whippoorwill still coming back, imagine, clear out of season, sitting in the crab-apple tree calling all by himself. Maybe his girl stood him up. Maybe she did. She hoped to hear him once more, she loved whippoorwills. . . . He knew how she was, didn't he?

Sure, he knew how she was.

Although the story, as printed, contains no direct quotations for either *he* or *she*, the language suggests that one of the two is speaking throughout the story, sometimes to one another and sometimes to themselves. In an "imaginative autobiography," how would you describe the initial meeting of the man and woman? If you perform the story with someone from your class, how would you decide whether or not to include an actual piece of rope in your performing scene? How might the prop help? Hinder?

When in Rome
MARI EVANS

Marrie dear
the box is full . . .
take
whatever you like
to eat . . .

    (an egg
    or soup
    . . . there ain't no meat.)

there's endive there
and

cottage cheese . . .

    (whew! if I had some
    black-eyed peas . . .)

there's sardines
on the shelves
and such . . .
but
don't
get my anchovies . . .
they cost
too much!

(me get the
anchovies indeed!
what she think, she got—
a bird to feed?)

there's plenty in there
to fill you up . . .

    (yes'm. just the
    sight's
    enough!

    Hope I lives till I get
    home
    I'm tired of eatin'
    what they eats in Rome . . .)

The voices of the two speakers, a lady-of-the-house and her domestic help, are distinct. In addition to social standing, part of their separateness lies in space; the employer seems to be speaking loudly from another room while Marrie's mocking answers are to herself. Can you typify the subtexts of both of them: *Why*, really, do they speak at all? The title is an *allusion* to the injunction, "When in Rome, do as the Romans do."

If you are interested in reading more about the poet, see Robert P. Sedlack's "Mari Evans: Consciousness and Craft," *College Language Association Journal*, 15 (June 1972), 465–76.

The Test
ANGELICA GIBBS

On the afternoon Marian took her second driver's test, Mrs. Ericson went with her. "It's probably better to have someone a little older with you," Mrs. Ericson said as Marian slipped into the driver's seat beside her. "Perhaps the last time your Cousin Bill made you nervous, talking too much on the way."

"Yes, Ma'am," Marian said in her soft unaccented voice. "They probably do like it better if a white person shows up with you."

"Oh, I don't think it's *that*," Mrs. Ericson began, and subsided after a glance at the girl's set profile. Marian drove the car slowly through the shady suburban streets. It was one of the first hot days in June, and when they reached the boulevard they found it crowded with cars headed for the beaches.

"Do you want me to drive?" Mrs. Ericson asked. "I'll be glad to if you're feeling jumpy." Marian shook her head. Mrs. Ericson watched her dark, competent hands and wondered for the thousandth time how the house had ever managed to get along without her, or how she had lived through those earlier years when her household had been presided over by a series of slatternly white girls who had considered housework demeaning and care of the children an added insult. "You drive beautifully, Marian," she said. "Now, don't think of the last time. Anybody would slide on a steep hill on a wet day like that."

"It takes four mistakes to flunk you," Marian said. "I don't remember doing all the things the inspector marked down on my blank."

"People say that they only want you to slip them a little something," Mrs. Ericson said doubtfully.

"*No*," Marian said. "That would only make it worse, Mrs. Ericson, I know."

The car turned right, at a traffic signal, into a side road and slid up to the curb at the rear of a short line of parked cars. The inspectors had not arrived yet.

"You have the papers?" Mrs. Ericson asked. Marian took them out of her bag: her learner's permit, the car registration, and her birth certificate. They settled down to the dreary business of waiting.

"It will be marvelous to have someone dependable to drive the children to school every day," Mrs. Ericson said.

Marian looked up from the list of driving requirements she had been studying. "It'll make things simpler at the house, won't it?" she said.

"Oh, Marian," Mrs. Ericson exclaimed, "if I could only pay you half of what you're worth!"

"Now, Mrs. Ericson," Marian said firmly. They looked at each other and smiled with affection.

Two cars with official insignia on their doors stopped across the street. The inspectors leaped out, very brisk and military in their neat uniforms. Marian's hands tightened on the wheel. "There's the one who flunked me last time," she whispered, pointing to a stocky, self-important man who had begun to shout directions at the driver at the head of the line. "Oh, Mrs. Ericson."

"Now, Marian," Mrs. Ericson said. They smiled at each other again, rather weakly.

The inspector who finally reached their car was not the stocky one but a genial, middle-aged man who grinned broadly as he thumbed over their papers. Mrs. Ericson started to get out of the car. "Don't you want to come along?" the inspector asked. "Mandy and I don't mind company."

Mrs. Ericson was bewildered for a moment. "No," she said, and stepped to the curb. "I might make Marian self-conscious. She's a fine driver, Inspector."

"Sure thing," the inspector said, winking at Mrs. Ericson. He slid into the seat beside Marian. "Turn right at the corner, Mandy-Lou."

From the curb, Mrs. Ericson watched the car move smoothly up the street.

The inspector made notations in a small black book. "Age?" he inquired presently, as they drove along.

"Twenty-seven."

He looked at Marian out of the corner of his eye. "Old enough to have quite a flock of pickaninnies, eh?"

Marian did not answer.

"Left at this corner," the inspector said, "and park between the truck and the green Buick."

The two cars were very close together, but Marian squeezed in between them without too much maneuvering. "Driven before, Mandy-Lou?" the inspector asked.

"Yes, sir. I had a license for three years in Pennsylvania."

"Why do you want to drive a car?"

"My employer needs me to take her children to and from school."

"Sure you don't really want to sneak out nights to meet some young blood?" the inspector asked. He laughed as Marian shook her head.

"Let's see you take a left at the corner and then turn around in the middle of the next block," the inspector said. He began to whistle "Swanee River." "Make you homesick?" he asked.

Marian put out her hand, swung around neatly in the street, and headed back in the direction from which they had come. "No," she said. "I was born in Scranton, Pennsylvania."

The inspector feigned astonishment. "You-all ain't Southern?" he said. "Well, dog my cats if I didn't think you-all came from yondah."

"No, sir," Marian said.

"Turn onto Main Street and let's see how you-all does in heavier traffic."

They followed a line of cars along Main Street for several blocks until they came in sight of a concrete bridge which arched high over the railroad tracks.

"Read that sign at the end of the bridge," the inspector said.

" 'Proceed with caution. Dangerous in slippery weather,' " Marian said.

"You-all sho can read fine," the inspector exclaimed. "Where d'you learn to do that, Mandy?"

"I got my college degree last year," Marian said. Her voice was not quite steady.

As the car crept up the slope of the bridge the inspector burst out laughing. He laughed so hard he could scarcely give his next direction. "Stop here," he said, wiping his eyes, "then start 'er up again. Mandy got her degree, did she? Dog my cats!"

Marian pulled up beside the curb. She put the car in neutral, pulled on the emergency, waited a moment, and then put the car into gear again. Her face was set. As she released the brake her foot slipped off the clutch pedal and the engine stalled.

"Now, Mistress Mandy," the inspector said, "remember your degree."

"*Damn* you!" Marian cried. She started the car with a jerk.

The inspector lost his joviality in an instant. "Return to the starting place, please," he said, and made four very black crosses at random in the squares on Marian's application blank.

Mrs. Ericson was waiting at the curb where they had left her. As Marian stopped the car, the inspector jumped out and brushed past her, his face purple. "What happened?" Mrs. Ericson asked, looked after him with alarm.

Marian stared down at the wheel and her lip trembled.

"Oh, Marian, *again*?" Mrs. Ericson said.

Marian nodded. "In a sort of different way," she said, and slid over to the right-hand side of the car.

Cite possible subtexts for Mrs. Ericson's "People say that they only want you to slip them a little something," for the inspector's "Sure thing," and Marian's final line, "In a sort of different way."

Loneliness

RAINER MARIA RILKE

Translated by Edwin Morgan

Loneliness is like a rain.
Towards dusk it leaves the sea where it has lain;
It mounts to skies unslaked by all they gain,
From far-off plains, unvisited retreats.
Soon from the sky it drops on city streets.
It rains down here in those ambiguous hours

When all the lanes wind onward into morning,
And saddened bodies, emptied of their powers,
Unlink in disenchantment, lords of nothing;
And couples who are couples in their loathing
Must search in one bed for their warring dreams:

Then loneliness flows with the streams . . .

Compare your own brief dramatic analysis of "Loneliness" with those of other class members. Based on your dramatic analysis, devise possible exercises—physical, vocal, and psychological—for the rehearsal of this poem.

Summer Remembered
ISABELLA GARDNER

Sounds sum and summon the remembering of summers.
The humming of the sun
The mumbling of the honey-suckle vine
The whirring in the clovered grass
The pizzicato plinkle of ice in an auburn
uncle's amber glass.
The whing of father's racquet and the whack
of brother's bat on cousin's ball
and calling voices call-
ing voices spilling voices . . .

The munching of saltwater at the splintered dock
The slap and slop of waves on little sloops
The quarreling of oarlocks hours across the bay
The canvas sails that bleat as they
are blown. The heaving buoy bell-
ing HERE I am
HERE you are HEAR HEAR

listen listen listen
The gramophone is wound
the music goes round and around
BYE BYE BLUES   LINDY'S COMING
voices calling   calling   calling
"Children!   Children!   Time's Up
Time's Up"
Merrily sturdily wantonly the familial voices
Cheerily chidingly call to the children   TIME'S UP
and the mute children's unvoiced clamor sacks the summer air
crying Mother   Mother   are you there?

The poem is about sounds (music, slap, bleat, hum, whir), and it uses sound to create the sense of a summer in childhood. To whom are the directives (hear, listen) addressed? Discuss the subtext of the final line. Discuss the passage of summers of childhood as well—this is the theme of the poem according to Laurence Perrine and James M. Reid (*100 Poems of the Twentieth Century;* New York: Harcourt, Brace, 1966, pp. 236–237.) This source also contains brief commentaries on several other poems that appear in this book.

Miss Pinkerton's Apocalypse
MURIEL SPARK

One evening, a damp one in February, something flew in at the window. Miss Laura Pinkerton, who was doing something innocent to the fire, heard a faint throbbing noise overhead. On looking up, 'George! come here! come quickly!'

George Lake came in at once, though sullenly because of their quarrel, eating a sandwich from the kitchen. He looked up at the noise then sat down immediately.

From this point onward their story comes in two versions, his and hers. But they agree as to the main facts; they agree that it was a small round flattish object, and that it flew.

'It's a flying object of some sort,' whispered George eventually.

'It's a saucer,' said Miss Pinkerton, keen and loud, 'an antique piece. You can tell by the shape.'

'It can't be an antique, that's absolutely certain,' George said.

He ought to have been more tactful, and would have been, but for the stress of the moment. Of course it set Miss Pinkerton off, she being in the right.

'I know my facts,' she stated as usual, 'I should hope I know my facts. I've been in antique china for twenty-three years in the autumn,' which was true, and George knew it.

The little saucer was cavorting round the lamp.

'It seems to be attracted by the light,' George remarked, as one might distinguish a moth.

Promptly, it made as if to dive dangerously at George's head. He ducked, and Miss Pinkerton backed against the wall. As the dish tilted on its side, skimming George's shoulder, Miss Pinkerton could see inside it.

'The thing might be radio-active. It might be dangerous.' George was breathless. The saucer had climbed, was circling high above his head, and now made for him again, but missed.

'It is not radio-active,' said Miss Pinkerton, 'it is Spode.'

'Don't be so damny silly,' George replied, under the stress of the occasion.

'All right, very well,' said Miss Pinkerton, 'it is not Spode. I suppose you are the expert, George, I suppose you know best. I was only judging by the pattern. After the best part of a lifetime in china—'

'It must be a forgery,' George said unfortunately. For, unfortunately, something familiar and abrasive in Miss Pinkerton's speech began to grind within him. Also, he was afraid of the saucer.

It had taken a stately turn, following the picture rail in a steady career round the room.

'Forgery, ha!' said Miss Pinkerton. She was out of the room like a shot, and in again carrying a pair of steps.

'I will examine the mark,' said she, pointing intensely at the saucer. 'Where are my glasses?'

Obligingly, the saucer settled in a corner; it hung like a spider a few inches from the ceiling. Miss Pinkerton adjusted the steps. With her glasses on she was almost her sunny self again, she was ceremonious and expert.

'Don't touch it, don't go near it!' George pushed her aside and grabbed the steps, knocking over a blue glass bowl, a Dresden figure, a vase of flowers and a decanter of sherry; like a bull in a china shop, as Miss Pinkerton exclaimed. But she was determined, and struggled to reclaim the steps.

'Laura!' he said desperately. 'I believe it is Spode. I take your word.'

The saucer then flew out of the window.

They acted quickly. They telephoned to the local paper. A reporter would come right away. Meanwhile, Miss Pinkerton telephoned to her two scientific friends—at least, one was interested in psychic research and the other was an electrician. But she got no reply from either. George had leaned out of the window, scanning the rooftops and the night sky. He had leaned out of the back windows, had tried all the lights and the wireless. These things were as usual.

The news man arrived, accompanied by a photographer.

'There's nothing to photograph,' said Miss Pinkerton excitably. 'It went away.'

'We could take a few shots of the actual spot,' the man explained.

Miss Pinkerton looked anxiously at the result of George and the steps.

'The place is a wreck.'

Sherry from the decanter was still dripping from the sideboard.

'I'd better clear the place up. George, help me!' She fluttered nervously, and started to pack the fire with small coals.

'No, leave everything as it is,' the reporter advised her. 'Did the apparition make this mess?'

George and Miss Pinkerton spoke together.

'Well, indirectly,' said George.

'It wasn't an apparition," said Miss Pinkerton.

The reporter settled on the nearest chair, poising his pencil and asking, 'Do you mind if I take notes?'

'Would you mind sitting over here?' said Miss Pinkerton. 'I don't use the Queen Annes normally. They are very frail pieces.'

The reporter rose as if stung, then perched on a table which Miss Pinkerton looked at uneasily.

'You see, I'm in antiques,' she rattled on, for the affair was beginning to tell on her, as George told himself. In fact he sized up that she was done for; his irritation abated, his confidence came flooding back.

'Now, Laura, sit down and take it easy.' Solicitously he pushed her into an easy chair.

'She's overwrought,' he informed the pressmen in an audible undertone.

'You say this object actually flew in this window?' suggested the reporter.

'That is correct,' said George.

The camera-man trained his apparatus on the window.

'And you were both here at the time?'

'No,' Miss Pinkerton said. 'Mr. Lake was in the kitchen and I called out, of course. But he didn't see inside the bowl, only the outside, underneath where the manufacturer's mark is. I saw the pattern so I got the steps to make sure. That's how Mr. Lake knocked my things over. I saw inside.'

'I am going to say something,' said George.

The men looked hopefully towards him. After a pause, George continued, 'Let us begin at the beginning.'

'Right,' said the reporter, breezing up.

'It was like this,' George said. 'I came straight in when Miss Pinkerton screamed, and there was a white convex disc, you realize, floating around up there.'

The reporter contemplated the spot indicated by George.

'It was making a hell of a racket like a cat purring,' George told him.

'Any idea what it really was?' the reporter enquired.

George took his time to answer. 'Well, yes,' he said, 'and no.'

'Spode ware,' said Miss Pinkerton.

George continued, 'I'm not up on these things. I'm extremely sceptical as a rule. This was a new experience to me.'

'That's just it,' said Miss Pinkerton. 'Personally, I've been in china for twenty-three years. I recognised the thing immediately.'

The reporter scribbled and enquired, 'These flying discs appear frequently in China?'

'It was a saucer. I've never seen one flying before,' Miss Pinkerton explained.

'I am going to ask a question,' George said.

Miss Pinkerton continued, 'Mr. Lake is an art framer. He handles old canvases but next to no antiques.'

'I am going to ask. Are you telling the story or am I?' George said.

'Perhaps Mr. Lake's account first and then the lady's,' the reporter ventured.

Miss Pinkerton subsided crossly while he turned to George.

'Was the object attached to anything? No wires or anything? I mean, someone couldn't have been having a joke or something?'

George gave a decent moment to the possibility.

'No,' he then said. 'It struck me, in fact, that there was some sort of Mind behind it, operating from outer space. It tried to attack me, in fact.'

'Really, how was that?'

'Mr. Lake was not attacked,' Miss Pinkerton stated. 'There was no danger at all. I saw the expression on the pilot's face. He was having a game with Mr. Lake, grinning all over his face.'

'Pilot?' said George. 'What are you talking about—pilot!'

Miss Pinkerton sighed. 'A tiny man half the size of my finger,' she declared. 'He sat on a tiny stool. He held the little tiny steering-wheel with one hand and waved with the other. Because, there was something like a sewing-machine fixed near the rim, and he worked the tiny treadle with his foot. Mr. Lake was not attacked.'

'Don't be so damn silly,' said George.

'You don't mean this?' the reporter asked her with scrutiny.

'Of course I do.'

'I would like to know something,' George demanded.

'You only saw the under side of the saucer, George.'

'You said nothing about any pilot at the time,' said George. 'I saw no pilot.'

'Mr. Lake got a fright when the saucer came at him. If he hadn't been dodging he would have seen for himself.'

'You mentioned no pilot,' said George. 'Be reasonable.'

'I had no chance,' said she. She appealed to the camera-man. 'You see, I know what I'm talking about. Mr. Lake thought he knew better, however. Mr. Lake said, "It's a forgery." If there's one thing I do know, it's china.'

'It would be most unlikely,' said George to the reporter. 'A steering-wheel and a treadle machine these days, can you credit it?'

'The man would have fallen out,' the camera-man reflected.

'I must say,' said the reporter, 'that I favour Mr. Lake's long-range theory. The lady may have been subject to some hallucination, after the shock of the saucer.'

'Quite,' said George. He whispered something to the photographer. 'Women!' Miss Pinkerton heard him breathe.

The reporter heard him also. He gave a friendly laugh. 'Shall we continue with Mr. Lake's account, and then see what we can make of both stories?'

But Miss Pinkerton had come to a rapid decision. She began to display a mood hitherto unknown to George. Leaning back, she gave way to a weak and artless giggling. Her hand fluttered prettily as she spoke between gurgles of mirth. 'Oh, what a mess! What an evening! We aren't accustomed to drink, you see, and now oh dear, oh dear!'

'Are you all right, Laura?' George enquired severely.

'Yes, yes, yes,' said Miss Pinkerton, drowsy and amiable. 'We really oughtn't have done this, George. Bringing these gentlemen out. But I can't keep it up, George. Oh dear, it's been fun though.'

She was away into her giggles again. George looked bewildered. Then he looked suspicious.

'It's definitely the effect of this extraordinary phenomenon,' George said firmly to the Press.

'It was my fault, all my fault,' spluttered Miss Pinkerton.

The reporter looked at his watch. 'I can quite definitely say you saw a flying object?' he asked. 'And that you were both put out by it?'

'Put down that it was a small, round, flattish object. We both agree to that,' George said.

A spurt of delight arose from Miss Pinkerton again.

'Women, you know! It always comes down to women in the finish,' she told them. 'We had a couple of drinks.'

'Mr. Lake had rather more than I did,' she added triumphantly.

'I assure you,' said George to the reporter.

'We might be fined for bringing the Press along, George. It might be an offence,' she put in.

'I assure you,' George insisted to the photographer, 'that we had a flying saucer less than an hour ago in this room.'

Miss Pinkerton giggled.

The reporter looked round the room with new eyes; and with the air of one to whom to understand all is to forgive all, he folded his notebook. The camera-man stared at the pool of sherry, the overturned flowers, the broken glass and china. He packed up his camera, and they went away.

George gave out the tale to his regular customers. He gave both versions, appealing to their reason to choose. Further up the road at her corner shop, Miss Pinkerton smiled tolerantly when questioned. 'Flying saucer? George is very artistic,' she would say, 'and allowances must be made for imaginative folk.' Sometimes she added that the evening had been a memorable one, 'Quite a party!'

It caused a certain amount of tittering in the neighbourhood. George felt this; but otherwise, the affair made no difference between them. Personally, I believe the story, with a preference for Miss Pinkerton's original version. She is a neighbour of mine. I have reason to believe this version because, not long afterwards, I too received a flying visitation from a saucer. The little pilot, in my case, was shy and inquisitive. He pedalled with all his might. My saucer was Royal Worcester, fake or not I can't say.

What characteristics of Miss Pinkerton's movement might the performer capture? of her voice? Point to specific parts of the story that help you to answer this question. Explain the word "Apocalypse" in the title. In what part of the story could you demonstrate the word's significance? How? Do you have a visual picture of Spode, Royal Worcester, Dresden? If not, a book on china would help. Look at the narrator's remarks apart from the dialogue. Is the narrator male or female? How do you know? What is the narrator's attitude toward Miss Pinkerton? toward George? toward the reporter? toward the listener?

Do you think the story supports Samuel Hynes's claim that Muriel Spark's "stories are more likely to create mystery than to explicate it, and she is content to leave the supernatural that way—Mysterious. The world of human experience is complex, and not ultimately explicable; evil, her demons remind us, is as actual as nasty servants and telephone calls, and reality is odder than you think." ("The Prime of Muriel Spark," *Commonweal*, 75, Feb., 1962, 563) You may also want to consult John Hazard Wildman's "Translated by Muriel Spark," *Nine Essays in Modern Literature*, ed. Donald E. Stanford (Baton Rouge: Louisiana State University Press, 1965), pp. 129–144.

The Ancient Roman
ARCHIBALD MARSHALL

Once there was an ancient Roman, and he lived in a Roman villa with a pavement and wore a toga and sandals and all those things, and he talked Latin quite easily, and he was a Senator and very important.

Well he had a wife who was a Roman matron and a very nice boy called Claudius, and one day Claudius came to him and said O pater, because he could talk Latin too, will you give me a denarius?

And his father said what for?

And he said I want to buy a catapult.

So his father gave him a denarius and he bought a catapult, and one day when he was playing with it he killed a slave by mistake.

Well killing a slave wasn't against the law so it wasn't murder or anything like that, but Claudius was very sorry all the same, and he threw away his catapult and wouldn't use it anymore.

And his father bought another slave instead of that one, and he said you must be more careful because slaves are very expensive.

And he said he would.

And Claudius was very kind to that slave and never beat him as he would have been allowed to do if he had wanted, because he was very sorry that he had killed the other one by mistake.

Well the slave came from Gaul, and he was very homesick and wanted to go back there because he had a mother and a little sister and he loved them.

So one day he told Claudius that he would like to escape, and Claudius said he would help him and he did, and the slave escaped.

Well when he found out that the slave had escaped the ancient Roman was very angry and he said I can't afford to go on losing slaves like this, that's the second in a fortnight, and if I find out that anybody has helped him to escape I will put him to death.

Now Claudius had told his mother that he had helped the slave to escape, so she said to the ancient Roman you had better be careful what you say or you may be sorry, and he said what do you mean?

So she thought she had better tell him, and she said well Claudius helped the slave to escape because he was sorry for him.

So the ancient Roman hid his head in his toga or one of those things and said eheu, which is Latin for alas, I shall have to put my own son to death.

And his wife said don't be so silly, what for?

And he said because I said I would and I can't go on being an ancient Roman unless I do.

She said I call it too silly and you'll do nothing of the sort.

And he said are you a Roman matron or not?

She said yes I am, and he said well then behave like one.

Well the ancient Roman didn't put Claudius to death at once because he wanted everybody to know about it, and all their relations came to him and knelt down and asked him not to, but he said he must.

Then they put dust on their heads, but that didn't make any difference either.

So then they brought Claudius to him, and he nearly said he wouldn't, because he looked so nice and he did love him.

But Claudius was very brave, and he said what is all the fuss about O pater? And they told him.

And he said of course you must put me to death O pater if you said you would.

And everybody said it was very wonderful, and Claudius was an ancient Roman too though he was so young. And they all cried very loud which grown-up people used to do then and tore their togas.

Well all this time the slave was hiding in Rome with some friends and he hadn't started for Gaul yet. So when he heard about Claudius he came and gave himself up, and he said if you must put somebody to death put me.

Well the ancient Roman wasn't sure whether it could count, but his wife said don't be so silly, you said you would put anybody to death who helped the slave escape, and he hasn't escaped.

So he said oh very well then I will put the slave to death, but I don't quite like it and I hope everybody will remember how it was.

Then Claudius said O pater either put me to death or don't put anybody to death and let the slave go free.

And he said why?

And he said because he has been so brave and I like him.

So the ancient Roman thought that was the best way out of it though it was very expensive, and he let the slave go free.

And the slave was so grateful that he said he would just go to Gaul to see his mother and his little sister and then come back and serve Claudius for nothing, and clean his sandals and brush his togas.

Well the slave was really a sort of Prince in his own country though he hadn't said so, and his mother was a Princess and had plenty of money. So they all came back and lived in Rome, and when Claudius grew up he married his little sister who was very beautiful.

And the ancient Roman was very pleased and he said it all comes of doing your duty.

From the start, sound this story aloud.
Try to honor the punctuation (or lack of
it) in your pacing of the story.

The Very Proper Gander
JAMES THURBER

Not so very long ago there was a very fine gander. He was strong and smooth and beautiful and he spent most of his time singing to his wife and children. One day somebody who saw him strutting up and down in his yard and singing remarked, "There is a very proper gander." An old hen overheard this and told her husband about it that night in the roost. "They said something about propaganda," she said. "I have always suspected that," said the rooster, and he went around the barnyard next day telling everybody that the very fine gander was a dangerous bird, more than likely a hawk in gander's clothing. A small brown hen remembered a time when at a great distance she had seen the gander talking with some hawks in the forest. "They were up to no good," she said. A duck remembered that the gander had once told him he did not believe in anything. "He said to hell with the flag, too," said the duck. A guinea hen recalled that she had once seen somebody who looked very much like a gander throw something that looked a great deal like a bomb. Finally everybody snatched up sticks and stones and descended on the gander's house. He was strutting in his front yard, singing to his children and his wife. "There he is!" everybody cried. "Hawk-lover! Unbeliever! Flag-hater! Bomb-thrower!" So they set upon him and drove him out of the country.

Moral: Anybody who you or your wife thinks is going to overthrow the government by violence must be driven out of the country

As a warm-up for this fable, mimic the various creatures' sounds and movement. What is the narrator's tone for "So they set upon him and drove him out of the country"?

#7 (from *Heart's Needle*)
W. D. SNODGRASS

Here in the scuffled dust
    is our ground of play.
I lift you on your swing and must
    shove you away,
see you return again,
    drive you off again, then

stand quiet till you come.
    You, though you climb
higher, farther from me, longer,
    will fall back to me stronger.
Bad penny, pendulum,
    you keep my constant time

to bob in blue July
    where fat goldfinches fly
over the glittering, fecund
    reach of our growing lands.
Once more now, this second,
    I hold you in my hands.

Try to show movement of the swing to emphasize the rhythm of the lines.

Randolf's Party
JOHN LENNON

It was Chrisbus time but Randolph was alone. Where were all his good pals. Bernie, Dave, Nicky, Alice, Beddy, Freba, Viggy, Nigel, Alfred, Clive, Stan, Frenk, Tom, Harry, George, Harold? Where were they on this day? Randolf looged saggly at his only Chrispbut cart from his dad who did not live there.

"I can't understan this being so aloneley on the one day of the year when one would surely spect a 'pal or two?" thought Rangolf. Hanyway he carried on putting ub the desicrations and muzzle toe. All of a surgeon there was amerry timble on the door. Who but who could be knocking on my door? He opened it and there standing, there who? but only his pals, Bernie, Dave,

Nicky, Alice, Beddy, Freba, Viggy, Nigel, Alfred, Clive, Stan, Frenk, Tom, Harry, George, Harolb weren't they?

Come on in old pals buddys and mates. With a big griff on his face Randoff welcombed them. In they came jorking and labbing shoubing "Haddy Grimmble, Randoob." and other hearty, and then they all jumbed on him and did smite him with mighty blows about his head crying, "We never liked you all the years we've known you. You were never raelly one of us you know, soft head."

They killed him you know, at least he didn't die alone did he? Merry Chrustchove, Randolf old pal buddy.

When reading this story, we expect the sound combinations no more than we anticipate the plot development. The story keeps the performer alert because of the *sound* substitutions. It requires great vocal control. You may want to try this exercise: write out each word in which an expected spelling is changed (for example, Chrisbus—bus instead of mas). When you've lined up all the changes, rehearse both. Do you find a pattern among the substitutions that supports your ideas about the story's narrator?

Sonnet
RONALD GROSS

John is tall.

This sentence mentions the person John,
but what appears in the sentence is not John
but John's name. The sentence mentions John
but does not use him; it uses John's name
but does not mention it. Now we might attempt to use John
himself in this sentence instead of using his name,
by placing him on this page in approximately the same
position which is now occupied by his name.

The result would be a physical object consisting of John
followed by the words "is tall." But nobody,
I believe, would be inclined to call this
a sentence in any language. Nevertheless this
fundamental confusion is frequently made, particularly when
the subject matter of our discourse happens to be language itself.

"Sonnet" is a kind of "pop" poetry, sometimes called "found" poetry. It originated as something else (advertisements, bills, telegrams, matchbook covers, etc.) and was then arranged as a poem. Like some pop painting and sculpture, the pop poem encourages us to look at and listen to familiar language in a different manner. The words in their new poetic form may make a different kind of sense. "Sonnet" was found in an English composition textbook. How might you emphasize this source in performance? Would a blackboard help you in performing?

Love

ROBERT PACK

It's not that I usually try for much
The very first time I'm with a girl, and though
She was attractive, nice breasts especially,
Full but with a good lilt to them,
Still it wasn't as if I was smitten
Or really out of control. So when I eased my hand
On that fine left breast and she seemed
To like it and slipped me a look that might mean
Uncertainty or confusion or you-belong-to-me-now,
I figured what-the-hell and started unbuttoning her.
But when my hand wiggled inside, I found
A rabbit. "Keep it," she said, quite openly I thought,
Not teary or wistful as if to indicate
That's-far-enough. So I coolly fingered back (was she
Putting me on?), but it was a book I found this time—
One, as a matter of fact, that I hadn't read.
"Thank you," I said, and I wasn't merely
Being polite; after all, what *can* you say
To a girl? Another try: This time I found
A necktie. At first I guessed she might be
Criticizing my taste, but no—it was exactly my style
And quite expensive. My birthday's not till June;
Consider, what could I feel but gratitude?
And is man ever able to hold himself back
When a good thing comes his way? I was getting
Excited, and I plunged again: a potted plant,
A wallet, a pair of gloves, theater tickets, binoculars,
Another tie, another rabbit, more books, and then—
A breast! My god, did I do something wrong?
Is she getting tired of me?

Some of the playfulness of pop poetry also appears in Robert Pack's "Love." To whom might this speaker be addressing his remarks? Is the event he describes so recent that his telling might take on some of the immediacy of the original situation? For a discussion of wider-ranging elements of play, see Johan Huizinga, *Homo Ludens: A Study of the Play Element in Culture* (Boston: Beacon Press, 1955).

Ile

EUGENE O'NEILL

Scene: CAPTAIN KEENEY's *cabin on board the steam whaling ship* Atlantic Queen— *a small, square compartment about eight feet high with a skylight in the center looking out on the poop deck. On the left (the stern of the ship) a long bench with rough cushions is built in against the wall. In front of the bench, a table. Over the bench, several curtained portholes.*

In the rear, left, a door leading to the CAPTAIN's *sleeping quarters. To the right of the door a small organ, looking as if it were brand new, is placed against the wall.*

On the right, to the rear, a marble-topped sideboard. On the sideboard, a woman's sewing basket. Farther forward, a doorway leading to the companion way, and past the officer's quarters to the main deck.

In the center of the room, a stove. From the middle of the ceiling a hanging lamp is suspended. The walls of the cabin are painted white.

There is no rolling of the ship, and the light which comes through the skylight is sickly and faint, indicating one of those gray days of calm when ocean and sky are alike dead. The silence is unbroken except for the measured tread of some one walking up and down the poop deck overhead.

It is nearing two bells—one o'clock—in the afternoon of a day in the year 1895.

At the rise of the curtain there is a moment of intense silence. Then the STEWARD *enters and commences to clear the table of the few dishes which still remain on it after the* CAPTAIN's *dinner. He is an old, grizzled man dressed in dungaree pants, a sweater, and a woolen cap with ear flaps. His manner is sullen and angry. He stops stacking up the plates and casts a quick glance upward at the skylight; then tiptoes over to the closed door in rear and listens with his ear pressed to the crack. What he hears makes his face darken and he mutters a furious curse. There is a noise from the doorway on the right and he darts back to the table.*

BEN *enters. He is an overgrown, gawky boy with a long, pinched face. He is dressed in sweater, fur cap, etc. His teeth are chattering with the cold and he hurries to the stove, where he stands for a moment shivering, blowing on his hands, slapping them against his sides, on the verge of crying.*

THE STEWARD: (*In relieved tones—seeing who it is.*)   Oh, 'tis you, is it? What're ye shiverin' 'bout? Stay by the stove where ye belong and ye'll find no need of chatterin'.

BEN: It's c-c-cold. (*Trying to control his chattering teeth—derisively.*) Who d'ye think it were—the Old Man?

THE STEWARD: (*Makes a threatening move—*BEN *shrinks away.*)   None o' your lip, young un, or I'll learn ye. (*More kindly*). Where was it ye've been all o' the time—the fo'c'stle?

BEN: Yes.

THE STEWARD: Let the Old Man see ye up fo'ard monkeyshinin' with the hands and ye'll get a hidin' ye'll not forget in a hurry.

BEN: Aw, he don't see nothin'. (*A trace of awe in his tones—he glances upward.*) He just walks up and down like he didn't notice nobody—and stares at the ice to the no'th'ard.

THE STEWARD: (*The same tone of awe creeping into his voice.*)   He's always starin' at the ice. (*In a sudden rage, shaking his fist at the skylight.*) Ice, ice, ice! Damn him and damn the ice! Holdin' us for nigh on a year—nothin' to see but ice—stuck in it like a fly in molasses!

BEN: (*Apprehensively.*)   Ssshh! He'll hear ye.

THE STEWARD: (*Raging.*)   Aye, damn him, and damn the Arctic seas, and damn this stinkin' whalin' ship of his, and damn me for a fool to ever ship on it! (*Subsiding as if realizing the uselessness of this outburst—shaking his head—slowly, with deep conviction.*) He's a hard man—as hard a man as ever sailed the seas.

BEN: *(Solemnly.)*   Aye.

THE STEWARD: The two years we all signed up for are done this day. Blessed Christ! Two years o' this dog's life, and no luck in the fishin', and the hands half starved with the food runnin' low, rotten as it is; and not a sign of him turnin' back for home! *(Bitterly.)* Home! I begin to doubt if ever I'll set foot on land again. *(Excitedly.)* What is it he thinks he' goin' to do? Keep us all up here after our time is worked out till the last man of us is starved to death or frozen? We've grub enough hardly to last out the voyage back if we started now. What are the men goin' to do 'bout it? Did ye hear any talk in the fo'c'stle?

BEN: *(Going over to him—in a half whisper.)*   They said if he don't put back south for home to-day they're goin' to mutiny.

THE STEWARD: *(With grim satisfaction.)*   Mutiny? Aye, 'tis the only thing they can do; and serve him right after the manner he's treated them—'s if they weren't no better nor dogs.

BEN: The ice is all broke up to s'uth'ard. They's clear water 's far 's you can see. He ain't got no excuse for not turnin' back for home, the man says.

THE STEWARD: *(Bitterly.)*   He won't look nowheres but no'th'ard where they's only the ice to see. He don't want to see no clear water. All he thinks on is gittin' the ile—'s if it was our fault he ain't had good luck with the whales. *(Shaking his head.)* I think the man's mighty nigh losin' his senses.

BEN: *(Awed.)*   D'you really think he's crazy?

THE STEWARD: Awe, it's the punishment o' God on him. Did ye ever hear of a man who wasn't crazy do the things he does? *(Pointing to the door in rear.)* Who but a man that's mad would take his woman—and as sweet a woman as ever was—on a stinkin' whalin' ship to the Arctic seas to be locked in by the rotten ice for nigh on a year, and maybe lose her senses forever—for it's sure she'll never be the same again.

BEN: *(Sadly.)*   She useter be awful nice to me before—*(His eyes grow wide and frightened.)* she got—like she is.

THE STEWARD: Aye, she was good to all of us. 'Twould have been hell on board without her, for he's a hard man—a hard, hard man—a driver if there ever was one. *(With a grim laugh.)* I hope he's satisfied now—drivin' her on till she's near lost her mind. And who could blame her? 'Tis a God's wonder we're not a ship full of crazed people—with the damned ice all the time, and the quiet so thick you're afraid to hear your own voice.

BEN: *(With a frightened glance toward the door on right.)*   She don't never speak to me no more—jest looks at me's if she didn't know me.

THE STEWARD: She don't know no one—but him. She talks to him—when she does talk—right enough.

BEN: She does nothin' all day long now but sit and sew—and then she cries to herself without makin' no noise. I've seen her.

THE STEWARD: Aye, I could hear her through the door a while back.

BEN: *(Tiptoes over to the door and listens.)*   She's cryin' now.

THE STEWARD: *(Furiously—shaking his fist.)*   God send his soul to hell for the devil he is!

(There is the noise of someone coming slowly down the companionway stairs. THE STEW-ARD *hurries to his stacked up dishes. He is so nervous from fright that he knocks off the top one, which falls and breaks on the floor. He stands aghast, trembling with dread.* BEN *is violently rubbing off the organ with a piece of cloth which he has snatched from his pocket.* CAPTAIN KEENEY *appears in the doorway on right and comes into the cabin, removing his fur cap as he does so. He is a man of about forty, around five-ten in height but looking much shorter on account of the enormous proportions of his shoulders and chest. His face is massive and deeply lined, with gray-blue eyes of a bleak hardness, and a tightly clenched, thin-lipped mouth. His thick hair is long and gray. He is dressed in a heavy blue jacket and blue pants stuffed into his seaboots.*

He is followed into the cabin by the SECOND MATE, *a rangy six-footer with a lean weather-beaten face. The* MATE *is dressed about the same as the captain. He is a man of thirty or so.)*

KEENEY: *(Comes toward the* STEWARD—*with a stern look on his face. The* STEWARD *is visibly frightened and the stack of dishes rattles in his trembling hands.* KEENEY *draws back his fist and the* STEWARD *shrinks away. The fist is gradually lowered and* KEENEY *speaks slowly.)* 'Twould be like hitting a worm. It is nigh on two bells, Mr. Steward, and this truck not cleared yet.

THE STEWARD: *(Stammering.)* Y-y-yes, sir.

KEENEY: Instead of doin' your rightful work ye've been below here gossipin' old woman's talk with that boy. *(To* BEN, *fiercely.)* Get out o' this, you! Clean up the chart room. *(*BEN *darts past the* MATE *to the open doorway.)* Pick up that dish, Mr. Steward!

THE STEWARD: *(Doing so with difficulty.)* Yes sir.

KEENEY: The next dish you break, Mr. Steward, you take a bath in the Bering Sea at the end of a rope.

THE STEWARD: *(Trembling.)* Yes, sir. *(He hurries out. The* SECOND MATE *walks slowly over to the* CAPTAIN.*)*

MATE: I warn't 'specially anxious the man at the wheel should catch what I wanted to say to you, sir. That's why I asked you to come below.

KEENEY: *(Impatiently.)* Speak your say, Mr. Slocum.

MATE: *(Unconsciously lowering his voice.)* I'm afeard there'll be trouble with the hands by the look o' things. They'll likely turn ugly, every blessed one o' them, if you don't put back. The two years they signed up for is up today.

KEENEY: And d'you think you're tellin' me somethin' new, Mr. Slocum? I've felt it in the air this long time past. D'you think I've not seen their ugly looks and the grudgin' way they worked?

(The door in rear is opened and MRS. KEENEY *stands in the doorway. She is a slight, sweet-faced little woman primly dressed in black. Her eyes are red from weeping and her face drawn and pale. She takes in the cabin with a frightened glance and stands as if fixed to the spot by some nameless dread, clasping and unclasping her hands nervously. The two men turn and look at her.)*

(With rough tenderness.) Well Annie?

MRS. KEENEY: *(As if awakening from a dream.)* David, I——*(She is silent. The* MATE *starts for the doorway.)*

KEENEY: *(Turning to him—sharply.)*   Wait!

MATE: Yes, sir.

KEENEY: D'you want anything, Annie?

MRS. KEENEY: *(After a pause, during which she seems to be endeavoring to collect her thoughts.)*   I thought maybe—I'd go up on deck, David, to get a breath of fresh air. *(She stands humbly awaiting his permission. He and the* MATE *exchange a significant glance.)*

KEENEY: It's too cold, Annie. You'd best stay below to-day. There's nothing to look at on deck—but ice.

MRS. KEENEY: *(Monotonously.)*   I know—ice, ice, ice. But there's nothing to see down here but these walls. *(She makes a gesture of loathing.)*

KEENEY: You can play the organ, Annie.

MRS. KEENEY: *(Dully.)*   I hate the organ. It puts me in mind of home.

KEENEY: *(A touch of resentment in his voice.)*   I got it jest for you.

MRS. KEENEY: *(Dully.)*   I know. *(She turns away from them and walks slowly to the bench on left. She lifts up one of the curtains and looks through the porthole; then utters an exclamation of joy.)* Ah, water! Clear water! As far as I can see! How good it looks after all these months of ice! *(She turns around to them, her face transfigured with joy.)* Ah, now I must go up on deck and look at it, David.

KEENEY: *(Frowning.)*   Best not to-day, Annie. Best wait a day when the sun shines.

MRS. KEENEY: *(Desperately.)*   But the sun never shines in this terrible place.

KEENEY: *(A tone of command in his voice.)*   Best not to-day, Annie.

MRS. KEENEY: *(Crumbling before this command—abjectly.)*   Very well, David. *(She stands there staring straight before her as if in a daze. The two men look at her uneasily.)*

KEENEY: *(Sharply).*   Annie!

MRS. KEENEY: *(Dully.)*   Yes, David.

KEENEY: Me and Mr. Slocum has business to talk about—ship's business.

MRS. KEENEY: Very well, David. *(She goes slowly out, rear, and leaves the door three-quarters shut behind her.)*

KEENEY: Best not to have her on deck if they's goin' to be any trouble.

MATE: Yes, sir.

KEENEY: And trouble they's goin' to be. I feel it in my bones. *(Takes a revolver from the pocket of his coat and examines it.)* Got your'n?

MATE: Yes, sir.

KEENEY: Not that we'll have to use 'em—not if I know their breed of dog— jest to frighten 'em up a bit. *(Grimly.)* I ain't never been forced to use one yit; and trouble I've had by land and by sea's long as I kin remember, and will have till my dyin' day, I reckon.

MATE: *(Hesitatingly.)*   Then you ain't goin'—to turn back?

KEENEY: Turn back! Mr. Slocum, did you ever hear o' me pointin' s'uth for home with only a measly four hundred barrel of ile in the hold?

MATE: *(Hastily.)*   No, sir—but the grub's gittin' low.

KEENEY: They's enough to last a long time yit, if they're careful with it; and they's plenty o' water.

MATE: They say it's not fit to eat—what's left; and the two years they signed on fur is up to-day. They might make trouble for you in the courts when we git home.

KEENEY: To hell with 'em! Let them make what law trouble they kin. I don't give a damn 'bout the money. I've got to git the ile! *(Glancing sharply at the* MATE.*)* You ain't turnin' no damned sea lawyer, be you, Mr. Slocum?

MATE: *(Flushing.)* Not by a hell of a sight, sir.

KEENEY: What do the fools want to go home fur now? Their share o' the four hundred barrel wouldn't keep 'em in chewin' terbacco.

MATE: *(Slowly.)* They wants to git back to their folks en' things, I s'pose.

KEENEY: *(Looking at him searchingly.)* 'N' you want to turn back, too. *(The* MATE *looks down confusedly before his sharp gaze.)* Don't lie, Mr. Slocum. It's writ down plain in your eyes. *(With grim sarcasm.)* I hope, Mr. Slocum, you ain't agoin' to jine the men agin me.

MATE: *(Indignantly.)* That ain' fair, sir, to say sich things.

KEENEY: *(With satisfaction.)* I warn't much afeared o' that, Tom. You been with me nigh on ten year and I've learned ye whalin'. No man kin say I ain't a good master, if I be a hard one.

MATE: I warn't thinkin' of myself, sir—'bout turnin' home, I mean. *(Desperately.)* But Mrs. Keeney, sir—seems like she ain't jest satisfied up here; ailin' like—what with the cold an' bad luck an' the ice an' all.

KEENEY: *(His face clouding—rebukingly but not severely.)* That's my business, Mr. Slocum. I'll thank you to steer a clear course o' that. *(A pause.)* The ice'll break up soon to no'th'ard. I could see it startin' to-day. And when it goes and we git some sun Annie'll perk up. *(Another pause—then he bursts forth.)* It ain't the damned money what's keepin' me up in the Northern seas, Tom. But I can't go back to Homeport with a measly four hundred barrel of ile. I'd die fust. I ain't never came back home in all my days without a full ship. Ain't that truth?

MATE: Yes, sir; but this voyage you been icebound, an'—

KEENEY: *(Scornfully.)* And d'you s'pose any of 'em would believe that—any o' them skippers I've beaten voyage after voyage? Can't you hear 'em laughin' and sneering'—Tibbots 'n' Harris 'n' Simms and the rest—and all o' Homeport makin' fun o' me? "Dave Keeney what boasts he's the best whalin' skipper out o' Homeport comin' back with a measly four hundred barrel of ile?" *(The thought of this drives him into a frenzy, and he smashes his fist down on the marble top of the sideboard.)* Hell! I got to git this ile, I tell you. How could I figger on this ice? It's never been so bad before in the thirty year I been acomin' here. And now it's breakin' up. In a couple o' days it'll be all gone. And they's whale here, plenty of 'em. I know they is and I ain't never gone wrong yit. I got to git the ile! I got to git it in spite of all hell, and by God, I ain't agoin' home till I do git it! *(There is the sound of subdued sobbing from the door in rear. The two men stand silent for a moment, listening. Then* KEENEY *goes over to the door and looks in. He hesitates for a moment as if he were going to enter—then closes the door softly.* JOE, *the harpooner, an enormous six-footer with a battered, ugly face, enters from right and stands waiting for the* CAPTAIN *to notice him.)*

(Turning and seeing him.) Don't be standin' there like a gawk, Harpooner. Speak up!

JOE: *(Confusedly.)* We want—the men, sir—they wants to send a depitation aft to have a word with you.

KEENEY: *(Furiously.)* Tell 'em to go to—*(Checks himself and continues grimly.)* Tell 'em to come. I'll see 'em.

JOE: Aye, aye, sir. *(He goes out.)*

KEENEY: *(With a grim smile.)* Here it comes, the trouble you spoke of, Mr. Slocum, and we'll make short shrift of it. It's better to crush such things at the start than let them make headway.

MATE: *(Worriedly.)* Shall I wake up the First and Fourth, sir? We might need their help.

KEENEY: No, let them sleep. I'm well able to handle this alone, Mr. Slocum. *(There is the shuffling of footsteps from outside and five of the crew crowd into the cabin, led by* JOE. *All are dressed alike—sweaters, seaboots, etc. They glance uneasily at the* CAPTAIN, *twirling their fur caps in their hands.)*

(After a pause.) Well? Who's to speak fur ye?

JOE: *(Stepping forward with an air of bravado.)* I be.

KEENEY: *(Eyeing him up and down coldly.)* So you be. Then speak your say and be quick about it.

JOE: *(Trying not to wilt before the* CAPTAIN'S *glance and avoiding his eyes.)* The time we signed up for is done to-day.

KEENEY: *(Icily.)* You're tellin' me nothin' I don't know.

JOE: You ain't pintin' fur home yit, far's we kin see.

KEENEY: No, and I ain't agoin' to till this ship is full of ile.

JOE: You can't go no further no'th with the ice afore ye.

KEENEY: The ice is breaking up.

JOE: *(After a slight pause during which the others mumble angrily to one another.)* The grub we're gittin' now is rotten.

KEENEY: It's good enough fur ye. Better men than ye have eaten worse. *(There is a chorus of angry exclamations from the crowd.)*

JOE: *(Encouraged by this support.)* We ain't agoin' to work no more less you puts back for home.

KEENEY: *(Fiercely.)* You ain't ain't you?

JOE: No; and the law courts'll say we was right.

KEENEY: To hell with your law courts! We're at sea now and I'm the law on this ship. *(Edging up toward the harpooner.)* And every mother's son of you what don't obey orders goes in irons. *(There are more angry exclamations from the crew.* MRS. KEENEY *appears in the doorway in rear and looks on with startled eyes. None of the men notice her.)*

JOE: *(With bravado.)* Then we're agoin' to mutiny and take the old hooker home ourselves. Ain't we boys? *(As he turns his head to look at the others,* KEENEY'S *fist shoots out to the side of his jaw.* JOE *goes down in a heap and lies there.*

MRS. KEENEY *gives a shriek and hides her face in her hands. The men pull out their sheath knives and start a rush, but stop when they find themselves confronted by the revolvers of* KEENEY *and the* MATE.)

KEENEY: *(His eyes and voice snapping.)* Hold still! *(The men stand huddled together in a sullen silence.* KEENEY'S *voice is full of mockery.)* You've found out it ain't safe to mutiny on this ship, ain't you? And now git for'ard where ye belong, and—*(He gives* JOE'S *body a contemptuous kick.)* Drag him with you. And remember the first man of ye I see shirkin' I'll shoot dead as sure as there's a sea under us, and you can tell the rest the same. Git for'ard now! Quick! *(The men leave in cowed silence, carrying* JOE *with them.* KEENEY *turns to the* MATE *with a short laugh and puts his revolver back in his pocket.)* Best get up on deck, Mr. Slocum, and see to it they don't try none of their skulkin' tricks. We'll have to keep an eye peeled from now on. I know 'em.

MATE: Yes sir. *(He goes out, right.* KEENEY *hears his wife's hysterical weeping and turns around in surprise—then walks slowly to her side.)*

KEENEY: *(Putting an arm around her shoulder—with gruff tenderness.)*   There, there, Annie. Don't be afeared. It's all past and gone.

MRS. KEENEY: *(Shrinking away from him.)*   Oh, I can't bear it! I can't bear it any longer!

KEENEY: *(Gently.)*   Can't bear what, Annie?

MRS. KEENEY: *(Hysterically.)*   All this horrible brutality, and these brutes of men, and this terrible ship, and this prison cell of a room, and the ice all around, and the silence. *(After this outburst she calms down and wipes her eyes with her handkerchief.)*

KEENEY: *(After a pause during which he looks down at her with a puzzled frown.)*   Remember, I warn't hankerin' to have you come on this voyage, Annie.

MRS. KEENEY: I wanted to be with you, David, don't you see? I didn't want to wait back there in the house all alone as I've been doing these last six years since we were married—waiting, and watching, and fearing—with nothing to keep my mind occupied—not able to go back teaching school on account of being Dave Keeney's wife. I used to dream of sailing on the great, wide, glorious ocean. I wanted to be by your side in the danger and vigorous life of it all. I wanted to see you the hero they make you out to be in Homeport. And instead—*(Her voice grows tremulous.)* All I find is ice and cold—and brutality! *(Her voice breaks.)*

KEENEY: I warned you what it'd be, Annie. "Whalin' ain't no ladies' tea party," I says to you, and "you better stay to home where you've got all your woman's comforts." *(Shaking his head.)* But you was so set on it.

MRS. KEENEY: *(Wearily.)*   Oh, I know it isn't your fault, David. You see, I didn't believe you. I guess I was dreaming about the old Vikings in the story books and I thought you were one of them.

KEENEY: *(Protestingly.)*   I done my best to make it as cozy and comfortable as could be. (MRS. KEENEY *looks around her in wild scorn.)* I even sent to the city for that organ for ye, thinkin' it might be soothin' to ye to be playin' it times when they was calms and things was dull like.

MRS. KEENEY: *(Wearily.)*   Yes, you were very kind, David. I know that. *(She goes to left and lifts the curtains from the porthole and looks out—then suddenly bursts forth.)* I won't stand it—I can't stand it—pent up by these walls like a prisoner. *(She runs over to him and throws her arms around him, weeping. He puts his arm protectingly over her shoulders.)* Take me away from here, David! If I don't get away from here, out of this terrible ship, I'll go mad! Take me home, David! I can't think any more. I feel as if the cold and the silence were crushing down on my brain. I'm afraid. Take me home!

KEENEY: *(Holds her at arm's length and looks at her face anxiously.)* Best go to bed, Annie. You ain't yourself. You got fever. Your eyes look so strange like. I ain't never seen you look this way before.

MRS. KEENEY: *(Laughing hysterically.)* It's the ice and the cold and the silence—they'd make anyone look strange.

KEENEY: *(Soothingly.)* In a month or two, with good luck, three at the most, I'll have her filled with ile and then we'll give her everything she'll stand and pint for home.

MRS. KEENEY: But we can't wait for that—I can't wait. I want to get home. And the men won't wait. They want to get home. It's cruel, it's brutal for you to keep them. You must sail back. You've got no excuse. There's clear water to the south now. If you've a heart at all you've got to turn back.

KEENEY: *(Harshly.)* I can't, Annie.

MRS. KEENEY: Why can't you?

KEENEY: A woman couldn't rightly understand my reason.

MRS. KEENEY: *(Wildly.)* Because it's a stupid, stubborn reason. Oh, I heard you talking with the second mate. You're afraid the other captains will sneer at you because you didn't come back with a full ship. You want to live up to your silly reputation and starve men and drive me mad to do it.

KEENEY: *(His jaw set stubbornly.)* It ain't that, Annie. Them skippers would never dare sneer to my face. It ain't so much what any one'd say—but—*(He hesitates, struggling to express his meaning.)* You see—I've always done it—since my first voyage as skipper. I always come back—with a full ship—and—it don't seem right not to—somehow. I been always first whalin' skipper out o' Homeport, and—Don't you see my meanin', Annie? *(He glances at her. She is not looking at him but staring dully in front of her, not hearing a word he is saying.)* Annie! *(She comes to herself with a start.)* Best turn in, Annie, there's a good woman. You ain't well.

MRS. KEENEY: *(Resisting his attempts to guide her to the door in rear.)* David! Won't you please turn back?

KEENEY: *(Gently.)* I can't, Annie—not yet awhile. You don't see my meanin'. I got to git the ile.

MRS. KEENEY: It'd be different if you needed the money, but you don't. You've got more than plenty.

KEENEY: *(Impatiently.)* It ain't the money I'm thinkin' of. D'you think I'm as mean as that?

MRS. KEENEY: *(Dully.)* No—I don't know—I can't understand—*(Intensely.)* Oh, I want to be home in the old house once more and see my own kitchen again, and hear a woman's voice talking to me and be able to talk to her.

Two years! It seems so long ago—as if I'd been dead and could never go back.

KEENEY: (*Worried by her strange tone and the far-away look in her eyes.*) Best go to bed, Annie. You ain't well.

MRS. KEENEY: (*Not appearing to hear him.*) I used to be lonely when you were away. I used to think Homeport was a stupid, monotonous place. Then I used to go down on the beach, especially when it was windy and the breakers were rolling in, and I'd dream of the fine free life you must be leading. (*She gives a laugh which is half a sob.*) I used to love the sea then. (*She pauses; then continues with slow intensity.*) But now—I don't ever want to see the sea again.

KEENEY: (*Thinking to humor her.*) 'Tis no fit place for a woman, that's sure. I was a fool to bring ye.

MRS. KEENEY: (*After a pause—passing her hand over her eyes with a gesture of pathetic weariness.*) How long would it take us to reach home—if we started now?

KEENEY: (*Frowning.*) 'Bout two months, I reckon, Annie, with fair luck.

MRS. KEENEY: (*Counts on her fingers—then murmurs with a rapt smile.*) That would be August, the latter part of August, wouldn't it? It was on the twenty-fifth of August we were married, David, wasn't it?

KEENEY: (*Trying to conceal the fact that her memories have moved him—gruffly.*) Don't *you* remember?

MRS. KEENEY: (*Vaguely—again passes her hand over her eyes.*) My memory is leaving me—up here in the ice. It was so long ago. (*A pause—then she smiles dreamily.*) It's June now. The lilacs will be all in bloom in the front yard—and the climbing roses on the trellis to the side of the house—they're budding. (*She suddenly covers her face with her hands and commences to sob.*)

KEENEY: (*Disturbed.*) Go in and rest, Annie. You're all wore out cryin' over what can't be helped.

MRS. KEENEY: (*Suddenly throwing her arms around his neck and clinging to him.*) You love me, don't you, David?

KEENEY: (*In amazed embarrassment at this outburst.*) Love you? Why d'you ask me such a question, Annie?

MRS. KEENEY: (*Shaking him—fiercely.*) But you do, don't you, David? Tell me!

KEENEY: I'm your husband, Annie, and you're my wife. Could there be aught but love between us after all these years?

MRS. KEENEY: (*Shaking him again—still more fiercely.*) Then you do love me. Say it!

KEENEY: (*Simply.*) I do, Annie.

MRS. KEENEY: (*Gives a sigh of relief—her hands drop to her sides.* KEENEY *regards her anxiously. She passes her hand across her eyes and murmurs half to herself.*) I sometimes think if we could only have had a child. (KEENEY *turns away from her, deeply moved. She grabs his arm and turns him around to face her—intensely.*) And I've always been a good wife to you, haven't I, David?

KEENEY: (*His voice betraying his emotion.*) No man has ever had a better, Annie.

MRS. KEENEY: And I've never asked for much from you, have I, David? Have I?

KEENEY: You know you could have all I got the power to give ye, Annie.

MRS. KEENEY: *(Wildly.)*   Then do this this once for my sake, for God's sake—take me home! It's killing me, this life—the brutality and cold and horror of it. I'm going mad. I can feel the threat in the air. I can hear the silence threatening me—day after gray day and every day the same. I can't bear it. *(Sobbing.)* I'll go mad, I know I will. Take me home, David, if you love me as you say. I'm afraid. For the love of God, take me home! *(She throws her arms around him, weeping against his shoulder. His face betrays the tremendous struggle going on within him. He holds her out at arm's length, his expression softening. For a moment his shoulders sag, he becomes old, his iron spirit weakens as he looks at her tear-stained face.)*

KEENEY: *(Dragging out the words with an effort.)*   I'll do it, Annie—for your sake—if you say it's needful for ye.

MRS. KEENEY: *(With wild joy—kissing him.)*   God bless you for that, David! *(He turns away from her silently and walks toward the companionway. Just at that moment there is a clatter of footsteps on the stairs and the* SECOND MATE *enters the cabin.)*

MATE: *(Excitedly.)*   The ice is breakin' up to no'th'ard, sir. There's a clear passage through the floe, and clear water beyond, the lookout says.

*(*KEENEY *straightens himself like a man coming out of a trance.* MRS. KEENEY *looks at the* MATE *with terrified eyes.)*

KEENEY: *(Dazedly—trying to collect his thoughts.)*   A clear passage? To no'th'ard?

MATE: Yes, sir.

KEENEY: *(His voice suddenly grim with determination.)*   Then get her ready and we'll drive her through.

MATE: Aye, aye, sir.

MRS. KEENEY: *(Appealingly.)*   David!

KEENEY: *(Not heeding her.)*   Will the men turn to willin' or must we drag 'em out?

MATE: They'll turn to willin' enough. You put the fear o' God into 'em, sir. They're meek as lambs.

KEENEY: Then drive 'em—both watches. *(With grim determination.)* They's whales t'other side o' this floe and we're going to git 'em.

MATE: Aye, aye, sir. *(He goes out hurriedly. A moment later there is the sound of scuffling feet from the deck outside and the* MATE's *voice shouting orders.)*

KEENEY: *(Speaking aloud to himself—derisively.)*   And I was agoin' home like a yaller dog!

MRS. KEENEY: *(Imploringly.)*   David!

KEENEY: *(Sternly.)*   Woman, you ain't adoin' right when you meddle in men's business and weaken 'em. You can't know my feelin's. I got to prove a man to be a good husband for ye to take pride in. I got to git the ile, I tell ye.

MRS. KEENEY: *(Supplicatingly.)*   David! Aren't you going home?

KEENEY: *(Ignoring this question—commandingly.)*   You ain't well. Go and lay down a mite. *(He starts for the door.)* I got to git on deck. *(He goes out. She cries after him in anguish.)* David! *(A pause. She passes her hand across her eyes—then commences to laugh hysterically and goes to the organ. She sits down and starts to play wildly an old hymn.* KEENEY *reënters from the doorway to the deck and stands looking at her angrily. He comes over and grabs her roughly by the shoulder.)*

Woman, what foolish mockin' is this? *(She laughs wildly and he starts back from her in alarm.)* Annie! What is it? *(She doesn't answer him.* KEENEY's *voice trembles.)* Don't you know me, Annie? *(He puts both hands on her shoulders and turns her around so he can look into her eyes. She stares up at him with a stupid expression, a vague smile on her lips. He stumbles away from her, and she commences softly to play the organ again.)*

(Swallowing hard—in a hoarse whisper, as if he had difficulty in speaking.) You said—you was a-goin' mad—God! *(A long wail is heard from the deck above.)* Ah bl-o-o-o-ow! *(A moment later the* MATE's *face appears through the skylight. He cannot see* MRS. KEENEY.)

MATE: *(In great excitement.)*   Whales, sir—a whole school of 'em—off the starb'd quarter 'bout five miles away—big ones!

KEENEY: *(Galvanized into action.)*   Are you lowerin' the boats?

MATE: Yes, sir.

KEENEY: *(With grim decision.)*   I'm a-comin' with ye.

MATE: Aye, aye, sir. *(Jubilantly.)* You'll git the ile now right enough, sir. *(His head is withdrawn and he can be heard shouting orders.)*

KEENEY: *(Turning to his wife.)*   Annie! Did you hear him? I'll git the ile. *(She doesn't answer or seem to know he is there. He gives a hard laugh, which is almost a groan.)* I know you're foolin' me, Annie. You ain't out of your mind— *(Anxiously.)* be you? I'll git the ile now right enough—jest a little while longer, Annie—then we'll turn hom'ard. I can't turn back now, you see that, don't ye? I've got to git the ile. *(In sudden terror.)* Answer me! You ain't mad, be you? *(She keeps on playing the organ, but makes no reply. The* MATE's *face appears again through the skylight.)*

MATE: All ready, sir. *(*KEENEY *turns his back on his wife and strides to the doorway, where he stands for a moment and looks back at her in anguish, fighting to control his feelings.)*

Comin', sir?

KEENEY: *(His face suddenly grown hard with determination.)*   Aye. *(He turns abruptly and goes out.* MRS. KEENEY *does not appear to notice his departure. Her whole attention seems centered in the organ. She sits with half-closed eyes, her body swaying from side to side to the rhythm of the hymn. Her fingers move faster and faster and she is playing wildly and discordantly as*

CURTAIN

Choose one major character (Keeney or Mrs. Keeney) and one minor character (Ben, the Steward, Mate, or Joe) and develop a "second plan," or imaginative biography. Begin with all *known facts* about the characters and then create a complete history for each. For the minor character, write out the *purpose* or *reason* for each utterance.

Locate visual aids that might make the

scene in this play clearer—pictures of productions of "Ile" as well as paintings of whaling ships or of desolate, icy ocean scenes.

For a brief discussion of the play, see Gresdna Doty and William Waack's "Plays," in *Contemporary Speech,* eds. Mary Frances Hopkins and Beverly Whitaker (Skokie, Ill.: National Textbook Company, 1976), pp. 214–225.

Memorial Day
MURRAY SCHISGAL

Characters
MR. LUTZ
MRS. LUTZ

Scene: A weedy backyard. In the center an old arid water well rising two or three feet above the ground. It is a hot sunny afternoon, the 30th of May. All is tranquil. Suddenly MR. *and* MRS. LUTZ *enter, left, cross to the well in a burlesque of excited emotions.*

MR. LUTZ: It's over! He said it was over!

MRS. LUTZ: I can't believe it!

MR. LUTZ: What do you mean, you can't believe it? He wouldn't have said it if it wasn't true. We weren't the only people listening.

MRS. LUTZ: That's right. Everybody knows now. It has to be true. It's over! At last it's over!

MR. LUTZ: *(Pause, shaking his head)* I can't believe it. I can't.

MRS. LUTZ: What do you mean, you can't believe it? They never would have allowed him to say it if it wasn't true. Millions of people heard him, all over the country.

MR. LUTZ: That's right. Everybody heard him. It has to be true. It's over!

MRS. LUTZ: He said it was over!

MR. LUTZ: Five years I've waited for this day.

MRS. LUTZ: Five years and three months and two days. *(They fall to their knees, clasp their hands)*

MR. LUTZ: Our Father who art in heaven . . .

MRS. LUTZ: We thank you for this blessing. *(They rise)*

MR. LUTZ: You tell him.

MRS. LUTZ: No. You tell him.

MR. LUTZ: You're his mother.

MRS. LUTZ: You're his father.

MR. LUTZ: You're the one . . .

MRS. LUTZ: Who what?

MR. LUTZ: We'll both tell him. *(They lean over the well, shout into it)* Peter!

MRS. LUTZ: Are you up, Peter?

MR. LUTZ: Can you hear us, Peter?

MRS. LUTZ: It's over, Peter! It's over, sweetheart!

MR. LUTZ: Now listen to me carefully, Peter. Tie the end of this rope around your waist and give us all the help you can. *(He jerks the rope which is tied to crossbar and already lowered in the well)*

MRS. LUTZ: How does he look? How is he?

MR. LUTZ: You know I can't see him.

MRS. LUTZ: *(Clasping hands)* Oh, God, I hope we did the right thing.

MR. LUTZ: We did what was best for the boy.

MRS. LUTZ: His welfare was our only concern.

MR. LUTZ: We couldn't let him go.

MRS. LUTZ: No. That was out of the question.

MR. LUTZ: We had to keep him.

MRS. LUTZ: He was our only child.

MR. LUTZ: And it worked out well. We won, didn't we?

MRS. LUTZ: Yes, we won. And nobody knows, nobody cares.

MR. LUTZ: It's over.

MRS. LUTZ: At last it's over.

MR. LUTZ: Come on, grab this and we'll pull him up.

MRS. LUTZ: Don't hurt yourself, Peter. Be careful. *(The rope gets longer and longer as they tug tenaciously on it, moving far to L)*

MR. LUTZ: You're not pulling hard enough.

MRS. LUTZ: He's gotten so heavy.

MR. LUTZ: I told you to stop throwing apples down at him. It's those damn apples of yours.

MRS. LUTZ: I wanted to make things easier for him. Is that so terrible?

MR. LUTZ: Then pull and stop complaining.

MRS. LUTZ: The rope is burning my hands.

MR. LUTZ: Don't let go whatever you do.

MRS. LUTZ: I can't . . . I . . .

MR. LUTZ: Hold it now. Don't let it . . . *(She releases the rope.* MR. LUTZ *stumbles into her and also releases the rope, it is sucked down into the well, a dull thud is soon heard. They approach the well, timidly, peer into it)*

MRS. LUTZ: *(Softly)* Peter?

MR. LUTZ: *(Softly)* Boy? Are you all right, Boy?

MRS. LUTZ: *(Remembering)* He can't hear us.

MR. LUTZ: I'll send him down a note. *(He takes a paper and pencil which dangle on a string at side of well, writes, then puts note in wooden bucket and lowers it into well)*

MRS. LUTZ: *(As he writes)* Tell him his mother loves him. Tell him he may have many friends in his life, many sweethearts, but he'll only have one mother . . . and that's me. Tell him the pain I had giving birth to him, tell him the sacrifices I made, tell him the miserable life I had, tell him I'm growing old, tell him he's my only consolation. What did you tell him?

MR. LUTZ: A father's a boy's best friend.

MRS. LUTZ: I thought so. You're up to your old tricks again.

MR. LUTZ: Don't get hysterical.

MRS. LUTZ: I'm not getting hysterical.

MR. LUTZ: We'll have the same arrangement we had before. He stays with you during the even hours and with me during the odd hours. Saturdays he's with you until three, with me until ten. Sunday it's the reverse. Each alternate holiday he spends with me. Even Christmas with you; odd Christmas with me. Even New Year's with me; odd New Year's with you. Leap year, weekday rules are in effect.

MRS. LUTZ: Very well. It's agreed. But there's to be no brainwashing.

MR. LUTZ: Agreed. Do you have the paper? *(She pulls it out from her blouse)* Let me have it. There's my signature.

MRS. LUTZ: And here's mine. *(He lifts the bucket out of the well)* How is he? What does he say?

MR. LUTZ: The note's still there. He didn't answer it.

MRS. LUTZ: Why doesn't he write? We haven't heard from him in months. And every morning I send a letter down with his breakfast, begging him to answer me, to give me one word so that I know everything's all right. Do I deserve this kind of treatment from him?

MR. LUTZ: Don't get hysterical.

MRS. LUTZ: I'm not getting hysterial. I'm just asking: what does it mean?

MR. LUTZ: You don't know your own son, lady; you haven't got the least idea what goes on in that boy's head.

MRS. LUTZ: And I suppose you do?

MR. LUTZ: You bet I do. He's down there working, day and night, thinking, planning, using his brains. What was the last thing he asked us to send down to him?

MRS. LUTZ: His teddy bear. He wanted his teddy bear.

MR. LUTZ: The last thing, I said.

MRS. LUTZ: Oh, I remember. A fishing rod.

MR. LUTZ: Right. Now why would someone want a fishing rod down there unless he was experimenting, unless he was doing something scientific with it? That boy's got a head on his shoulders.

MRS. LUTZ: That's exactly what his teachter told me at the graduation exercises. "Mrs. Lutz, your boy's got a head on his shoulders."

MR. LUTZ: He's got what it takes, all right. He's my son.

MRS. LUTZ: And mine!

MR. LUTZ: Don't get hysterical now.

MRS. LUTZ: I'm not getting hysterical.

MR. LUTZ: Come on, let's get him up. *(They pull on rope, it gets longer and longer)*

MRS. LUTZ: I just wish he had written me more frequently. I deserve that much from him.

MR. LUTZ: You can't keep quiet.

MRS. LUTZ: Stop shouting at me.

MR. LUTZ: Then pull and shut up.

MRS. LUTZ: If it wasn't for Peter, I swear . . .

MR. LUTZ: Pull!

MRS. LUTZ: He's coming. I can feel . . .

MR. LUTZ: Watch it!

MRS. LUTZ: What are you . . .

MR. LUTZ: I can't! (MR. LUTZ *stumbles backwards, sits on ground. Most of the rope slides back down well, holding at crossbar*)

MRS. LUTZ: Well, whose fault was it now?

MR. LUTZ: *(Rising)* Your fault.

MRS. LUTZ: My fault?

MR. LUTZ: Yes, your fault. If you had held on to the rope the first time we would have had him up by now.

MRS. LUTZ: Go ahead. Blame me.

MR. LUTZ: Who else do you want me to blame?

MRS. LUTZ: Would you mind answering me one question, one simple question? Why, why did you ever marry me?

MR. LUTZ: If I had the answer to that question I'd go to my grave a happy man. Why? Why? Maybe if you had stopped wiggling your behind a minute I would have had the time to sit down and think and say to myself, "No, this isn't the woman for you. Put your hands in your pockets and walk away, now, quickly, before it's too late."

MRS. LUTZ: You say that to me, you, who phoned every night, who wouldn't let me go in until he had practically ripped the buttons off my blouse, who told my best girl friend Marge Morton that if I didn't marry him he'd jump in the river!

MR. LUTZ: That isn't what I said.

MRS. LUTZ: It isn't?

MR. LUTZ: No, it isn't. I said if you wouldn't marry me *you* could go jump in the river. Get your facts straight, lady.

MRS. LUTZ: My facts are straight, mister. I wanted a divorce. For years and years I've been saying, "Let's get a divorce. Let's break it up now so that we can salvage something out of this misery."

MR. LUTZ: Sure. And the boy? Would you have given me the boy?

MRS. LUTZ: I'd die first. He's my son. Mine. He belongs . . . (MR. LUTZ *slaps her face*) Why did you do that?

MR. LUTZ: I thought you were getting hysterical.

MRS. LUTZ: *(Becoming hysterical)* I was not getting hysterical. You know I wasn't getting hysterical. I never get hysterical. I don't even know what hysterics are. You did that deliberately, deliberately, deliberately . . .

MR. LUTZ: All right, all right, I made a mistake. Shoot me. Kill me. Crucify me.

MRS. LUTZ: You enjoy hitting me. That has become your chief pleasure.

MR. LUTZ: I have no pleasure, lady. I am in the world to be stepped on, to be mauled, to be eaten, to be ground into dust . . .

MRS. LUTZ: To dream in vain, with nothing happening . . .

MR. LUTZ: That's the one thing we have in common, lady. We both dream, dream of being with someone else, dream of living other lives . . .

MRS. LUTZ: To think that Harry Watson wanted to marry me, that he begged me to marry him, and I said no. Do you know why? Not because you were so handsome or because I believed for a single minute that you would make me happy. I said no because whenever I put on my high-heeled shoes Harry Watson was shorter than I was, he was at least two inches shorter than I was. *(She breaks into painful laughter)*

MR. LUTZ: *(Dully)* You should have worn flats.

MRS. LUTZ: *(Recovering)* I should have had my head examined.

MR. LUTZ: Why did you . . .

MRS. LUTZ: It was time. Everyone said it was time. *(They walk away from well, move about aimlessly, kneading hands, looking up at the sky, breathing heavily)*

MR. LUTZ: I used to look at you and my whole insides would explode. I used to touch you and my throat would become as dry as sandpaper and my legs would start to tremble.

MRS. LUTZ: When I heard that Marge Morton was getting married I became frantic. I was a year older than she was.

MR. LUTZ: I had no self-control when I was a young man.

MRS. LUTZ: I saw everything through the eyes of other people.

MR. LUTZ: I read once, somewhere, that a lot of people marry out of hostility and they stay married to get even with one another.

MRS. LUTZ: I don't know.

MR. LUTZ: I made a good living for my family. No one can say no.

MRS. LUTZ: I tried. I tried as much as any human being could try.

MR. LUTZ: It wasn't my fault.

MRS. LUTZ: You can't blame me.

MR. LUTZ: *(Turning to her, shouting)* Lady, we're getting old!

MRS. LUTZ: Shut up! For God's sake, shut up! (MR. LUTZ *runs to her, embraces her tightly, brushes back her hair and stares intently at her face, he then releases her as if she had suddenly turned to ice)*

MR. LUTZ: *(In a moment)* Enough. All right. Enough. He's a big boy now; we're all adults. Let him decide. The one he goes to when he comes up, that's the one who keeps him.

MRS. LUTZ: With no visiting rights.

MR. LUTZ: A complete break.

MRS. LUTZ: Agreed.

MR. LUTZ: Let me have the paper. *(She gives it to him)* I'll just add this at the bottom and . . . there's my signature.

MRS. LUTZ: Here's mine. (MR. LUTZ *tugs at the rope)*

MR. LUTZ: He's got the other end. Don't forget. You stand over there. I'll stand here. He'll decide for himself. *(They pull on rope)*

MRS. LUTZ: It'll be like a second chance. I have nothing to be afraid of anymore.

MR. LUTZ: A new life. That boy and me, we can go away, start a business somewhere. I told him before he went down, "Think of a business we can go into, something where I don't have to use my hands, where we can wear white shirts and just sit back and watch the money roll in."

MRS. LUTZ: I'll cook for him and keep his clothes clean . . . He loves me. He has to love me. I'm his mother.

MR. LUTZ: It's over. The war's over.

MRS. LUTZ: At last it's over.

MR. LUTZ: Keep pulling.

MRS. LUTZ: He wanted to enlist. He wanted to go.

MR. LUTZ: But I wouldn't let him.

MRS. LUTZ: I wouldn't let him.

MR. LUTZ: We wouldn't let him. We put our foot down.

MRS. LUTZ: We did what was best for him. We kept him . . . We kept him at home.

MR. LUTZ: Keep pulling.

MRS. LUTZ: He's coming, isn't he?

MR. LUTZ: A little more. Just a little more . . . *(As they talk a large pair of shears attached to two long crossed poles, one perhaps a fishing pole, rises out of well and snips at the rope, ineffectually. The* LUTZES *see the shears as it disappears into the well, we hear the rope being cut in two and then a thud. The* LUTZES *stare at the cut rope which they now pull up for a moment, silently, forlornly.* MRS. LUTZ *covers her face and sobs.* MR. LUTZ *puts his arm around her and they slowly exit,* L*)*

CURTAIN

What does the title, *Memorial Day,* indicate? One remarkable feature of this play is that the subtext is so often at odds with the apparent sense of the printed text. For example, at the beginning, Mr. Lutz says, "I can't believe it, I can't." Is his subtext simply, "I want you to believe how surprised I am"? Or is it a more complex statement that says, "I think our discovery is marvelous!"? "I hope you know this discovery is probably disastrous!"? Cite other instances in the play of this kind of *verbal irony* (saying one thing and meaning another, as in greeting someone who shows all the signs of having stayed up all night by saying, "You sure look great!").

The Hope Chest
JEAN STAFFORD

Miss Bellamy was old and cold and she lay quaking under an eiderdown which her mother had given her when she was a girl of seventeen. It had been for her hope chest. Though damask tablecloths and Irish linen tea napkins, Florentine bureau runners and China silk blanket covers, point-lace doilies and hemstitched hand towels had gone into that long carved cherry chest (her father had brought it all the way from Sicily and, presenting it to her, had said,

"Nothing is too good for my Rhoda girl"), she had never married. The chest now stood at the foot of her bed, and the maid put the tea napkins on her breakfast tray.

It was just before Belle knocked on her door in the gray dawn of winter with the tray that Miss Bellamy quaked so much, as if nothing on earth could ever warm her up again. This unkind light made her remember how old she was and how, in a few minutes when Belle came in, she would be cantankerous; no matter how hard she tried, she could never be pleasant to a servant, black or white, a failing for which her father had once rebuked her, declaring that she behaved like a parvenu. He had scolded her thus when he finally had to admit to himself the fact that she would never marry. There had not, in the history of Boston society, been a greater fiasco than Rhoda Bellamy's debut. It had, indeed, been a miscarriage so sensational that she had forced her parents to move north, into Maine, where her mother soon had died and where she and her father dwelt together in their angry disappointment. *Well, Papa, the laugh's on you. Here I am, thirty-five years old, and in the eighteen years since I came out, I have had no beau but my dear papa. No, I will not go to the concert at Bowdoin College. No, I do not want to join you in a glass of claret. I shall return to my bedroom and read Mrs. Gaskell, thanking you every time I turn a page for giving me so expensive a copy of* Cranford.

This was the Christmas morning of her eighty-second year and she steadfastly held her eyes closed, resisting the daylight. She had been like that as a child, she had loved sleep better than eating or playing. She was not sure whether she had had a dream just now or whether there was something she had meant to remember or to think about that was troubling her aged mind like a rat in a wall. At last, vexed and murmuring, she opened her eyes and what did she see hanging upon the wall (very probably staining the hand-blocked French paper with a design of pastoral sweethearts) but a scraggly Christmas wreath to which had been wired three pine cones, one gilded, one silvered, one painted scarlet. At first she was half out of her mind with exasperation and she reached out her hand for her stick to rap tyrannically for Belle. How *dare* she desecrate this, of all rooms, which, as any fool should know, was not to be changed in any way! But memory stayed her hand: it all came back.

Yesterday, when she was sitting on the lounge in the drawing room, making spills out of last year's Christmas wrappings and sipping hot milk, she heard a timid knocking at the door. She had no intention of answering it, although Belle had gone out to shop and the by-the-day girl had gone home. But she said to herself, "Who is it? Who are they that they can't knock out loud like a Christian? If they want something, why don't they try the doorknob? They'll find it locked, but if they had any gumption, they'd try." She slowly made a spill.

It went on, this gentle, disheartened knocking. Was it a squirrel, she wondered, playing with a nut somewhere? *If there is a destructive squirrel in my house, I shall give Belle her walking papers at once.* She did not find the creatures cunning as some people did: they were as wicked as any other rodent and the tail, so greatly admired in some quarters, was by no means a disguise that could not be seen through: essentially they were rats. Perhaps it was not a squirrel but was a loose branch blowing in the wind: *I shall speak severely to Homer. If he calls himself my yard-man, he can attend to these details.* Perhaps it was a dog of the neighborhood, foolishly thumping his tail against the door. *People should keep their dogs at home, tied up if necessary. If they are not kept at home, they come rummaging in my refuse containers and defiling my lawn and littering the garden with things I do not like to know exist.* Aloud in the long drawing room, she said, knowing that she smiled cleverly in her lean lips and in her small eyes, "If you want to come in, knock loud enough so that I shall hear you. Call out your name, confound you. Do you think I receive just anyone?"

She slopped her milk and it made a row of buttons down the front of her challis guimpe. Outraged, she threw the spill she was making into the fire and then she hobbled to the door, saying under her breath, "Whoever you are, I will frighten the living daylights out of you. If you are an animal, I will beat you with my stick; if you are a human being, I will scare you out of ten years' growth. I will say the worst thing you have ever had said to you in your life."

In the winter she had a green baize door and a storm door sandwiching the regular door to keep out any possible draft. She pulled open the green baize one and unlocked the wooden one with a long iron key and she opened it the merest bit, pushing it with the silver ferrule of her blackthorn stick. Through the glass of the storm door, she saw a child standing there in the snow, holding a spruce wreath in his hands. He had come across the lawn, making his own path, deliberately to spoil the looks of the clean, unmarked snow, when he could *much more easily* have walked in Belle's footprints.

He opened the storm door without asking leave and he said, "Will you buy this?"

She prided herself on never having been tricked by anyone. She investigated first and bought afterward. She, Rhoda Bellamy, would be the last to be taken in by a child, and she did not, of course, answer his question. She pushed the door open a little farther and said, "Who are you? What is your name?"

His teeth, she saw, were short and crooked and a nasty yellow color. She supposed he came from one of those indigent families who clustered together, squalidly and odoriferously, on the banks of the Sheepscot. He was not decently shy and he spoke up immediately: "My name is Ernest Leonard McCammon. Will you buy this wreath?"

The spinster said, "Well, Ernest Leonard, you may wipe your feet on my *Welcome* mat and step into the entry, but I am not promising to buy your wreath. We'll see about that later on."

(The sycamores before Miss Bellamy's windows creaked in the cold: *Where is my breakfast? Where is Belle? Why did I invite Ernest Leonard McCammon to cross my threshold in his snowy galoshes, puddling the Tabriz Father bought half price in Belgrade?* She creaked, too, like a tree, and a feather from the eiderdown walked on her ear like a summer fly.)

The child stood before her, small and ambitious, bundled to his ears in a blue plaid mackintosh which was patched with leather at the elbows. He wore blue jeans and in his mittenless hands he carried now, besides the wreath, the purple stocking cap he had taken off before he came through the door. He bore a faint, unpleasant smell of mud. *I will eat you, little boy, because once upon a time I, too, had pink cheeks and a fair skin and clear eyes. And don't you deny it.*

Ernest Leonard McCammon looked at the Adam hall chair, looked at the portrait of Mr. Bellamy, looked at the priceless Florentine coffer, looked at the luster pitchers in which stood cattails ten years old; she had had a man come down from Portland one year to oil the books and at the same time had had him shellac the cattails, although he protested a little, declaring that this was not in his line. No workman ever got anywhere protesting with her. She had simply said, "I don't know what you're talking about, sir. My father picked these cattails by the Jordan." This did not happen to be true, as her father had been dead for twenty years and she had gathered them herself in her own meadow beside the local river.

The rag-tag-and-bobtail boy looked at her father's treasures as if he had seen such things every day of his life. *Do you know who I am, you smelly scrap? Does the name Bellamy mean anything to you, you wool-bound baggage?*

(How the wind was blowing! Where was Belle? Where was her breakfast? Where was her stick? Where was her wrapper? Why did no one come to wish her a merry Christmas?)

He said, "Miss Bellamy, will you buy my wreath?"

"What do you want for it, McCammon?"

"A quarter."

"A quarter! Twenty-five cents for a bit of evergreen you more than likely stole off one of my trees!"

His pink cheeks paled under her shrewd gaze and his blue eyes clouded. "I never stole 'um off your tree, Miss Bellamy. I went to the woods, I did, and I got 'um there off nobody's tree."

She said, not giving in, "Perhaps so, perhaps not. All the same, a quarter is too much."

"But I painted the pine cones, Miss Bellamy! I had to buy the gold and the silver. Daddy gave me the red."

"And who is this Daddy?"

"The chimney cleaner. We are the ones with the mule. Maybe you have seen our house with the mule in the yard? My daddy's name is Robert John McCammon."

I will blow your brains out with the bellows Father brought from Dresden. I will lay your slender little body on Cousin Anne's andirons that came from the Trianon, and burn you up like a paper spill.

"Come, come, Ernest Leonard," she said, "I don't care what your daddy's middle name is and I have certainly not seen your mule. I will give you fifteen cents for your wreath."

"No, ma'am," he said. "If you don't buy it, some other lady will."

"Some *other* lady? What do you mean, McCammon?"

"Well, Mrs. Wagner would buy it or Mrs. Saunders or Mrs. Hugh Morris, I reckon. Anyways, somebody."

"I will give you fifteen cents for the wreath alone. You can take off the pine cones."

"No, ma'am. That would spoil it."

She fixed him with a severe aristocratic eye, determined now to resolve this impasse to her own liking and not to his. She said slowly, "If I decided to buy your wreath and paid you the absurd king's ransom of twenty-five cents, would you do a favor for me?"

"Yes, Miss Bellamy."

(Belle! Belle! Where is my breakfast? Come before I die of loneliness. Come before the sycamores break at the top and crush the roof over my head!)

"Do you promise, Ernest Leonard?"

"I promise, Miss Bellamy," he said and moved a step away from her.

She took a twenty-five-cent piece out of the purse she carried strapped to her belt and, bending down, took the wreath, which she placed on the coffer. Now Ernest Leonard clutched the stocking cap in both hands. His aplomb had left him; she could tell that he wanted to run away.

"You must give me a kiss, Master McCammon," she said and, leaning heavily upon her stick, stooped toward that small face with pursed lips, coral-colored. They touched her bone-dry cheek and then the boy was gone, and through the door he had left open in his headlong flight there came a blast of cold December. But for a moment she did not move and stared at a clot of snow upon the rug. *I told you, Ernest Leonard, to wipe your feet carefully on my Welcome mat.*

Belle's big country feet were on the stairs. Miss Bellamy trembled for her knock. *Wait a minute, Belle, I have not yet thought out what I am going to say to you.* Had she left any stray spruce needles on the coffer? Had any fallen as she climbed the stairs, breathless with recollection? Belle was at the door. She knocked and entered with the tray.

"Explain that monstrosity," said Miss Bellamy, pointing to the Christmas wreath she had hung last night at the stroke of midnight. *Merry Christmas, Papa dear. Oh, how cunning of you to hang up mistletoe! What girl in the world would want more than a beau like you? Can I have my presents now? It's one past midnight, Papa! Oh, Papa, darling, you have given me a brass fender for my fireplace! Oh, Papa, a medallioned sewing drum! An emerald ring! A purple velvet peignoir! I wish you a very merry Christmas, Papa.*

"Don't pretend you know nothing about it, my good woman. Why did you do it, Belle? Have you no respect for other people's property? Do you think I can have my bedroom repapered every week or so merely for the sake of your vulgar whims?"

Kind, stupid Belle shook out the napkin and she said, as she sprinkled a little salt on the lightly boiled egg, "I'm sorry, Miss Rhoda, that I never seem to do what's right. I thought you'd like the wreath."

The old lady cackled hideously and screamed, "You goose! You namby-pamby! I hung it there myself.

The maid, unruffled, smiled and said, "Merry Christmas, Miss Rhoda." When she had gone, the spinster closed her eyes against Ernest Leonard's painted pine cones, but she nursed her hurt like a baby at a milkless breast, with tearless eyes.

Compare the *action of the lines* in each italicized section of the story. Write a brief dramatic analysis of the action of the entire story in less than five lines.

My Father Burns Washington
FRED CHAPPELL

Money money.
During Hoover's deep
Depression we did not have any.
Not enough to buy a night's good sleep.
My parents went to bed in the grip
Of money and dreamed of money.

We heard them walk
The resounding rooms below,
My sister and I, heard them stalk
The phantom dollar and ghostly dime.
    "Where to
From here?" The question always grew
Heavier in the dark.

My sister and I
Clutched hands. Money would climb
The stair, we thought, and, growling, try
The doorknob, enter upon us furiously.
Its eyes like embers in the room,
It would devour all time.

The morning brought
Chill light to lined faces.
My father spoke of other cases
Worse than ours: Miller Henson's place
    was
Up for sale; Al Smith had fought
And lost; Clyde Barrow got shot.

Christ, how he tried!
One job was farming, another
Teaching school, and on the side
He grubbed for Carolina Power & Light.
Came home one night to our driven
    mother,
Lay back his head and cried

In outrage: "Money.
Money. Money. It's the death
Of the world. If it wasn't for goddam
    money
A man might think a thought, might
    draw a breath
Of freedom. But all I can think is,
    Money.
Money by God is death."

Her face went hard.
"It won't always be
This way," she said. "I hear them say
It's beginning to get better." "You'd take
    the word
Of that political blowhard?
Old Franklin Pie-in-the-Sky?"

"Well, what's the use
Of carrying on like this?"
"It soothes my feelings." My father rose
From his chair and menaced a
    democratic fist
At the ceiling. "I refuse,"
He said, "to kiss their ass."

"J. T., hush!"

And now he noticed me
Shriveling in the doorway. A flush
Of shame for language spread his neck. He
Pulled me to him. A woolen crush
Of jacket rubbed my eye.

Then stood me back.
"Don't worry, hon, we'll make
Out all right . . . But it's still true
That thinking of nothing but money
    makes me sick.
A man's got better things to do
Than always feeling low."

"We'll make it fine,"
She said. She tried to grin.
"I can understand how tired
You get. And I get weary to the bone.
Even so, I think—" She bit the word.
Her temper had pulled thin.

"Don't think," he said.
(That became my father's
Motto.) *"If I had my druthers;*
That's all thinking amounts to now. It
    withers
The will to think like that. We need
To think what *can* be had."

The argument
Seemed to die away.
He stared before him, restless silent
Despondent; we stood waiting for him to
    say
Whatever would ease his soul, turned flint-
Hard and moveless and dry.

He fished a green
Flimsy one dollar bill
From his pocket. "I've got it down
The philosophers are right: the root of
    evil
Is paper. This one at least won't kill
Another desperate man."

He got a match.
We listened, frozen in time,
To the ugly inarticulate scratch
And watched the tender blooming of the
    flame.
"I never figured on getting rich."
Revenge was sweet with doom.

He lit the single.
When the corner caught,
We felt a minatory tingle
Advance our skins. Had he truly taught

Us freedom, amid our paralyzed mangle
Of motive and black thought?

It made no more
Lovely a fire than any
Other fuel: a flame and a char
Of paper. We couldn't think of it as
    money
Burning but as oxidized despair
Climbing the indifferent air.

He wept as it burned,
Then flung it down and ground
The corner out and, ashen, turned
To face my mother who smiled and
    frowned
At once. Like a beaten child he
    mourned:
"Mother, will it still spend?"

Identify the references to Al Smith, Hoover's deep Depression. Franklin Pie-in-the-Sky, and Clyde Barrow. What do they contribute to the speaker's narrative? What psychological exercises can you devise to help the performer realize the speaker's remembered fear and the father's rage?

After the Dentist
MAY SWENSON

My left upper
lip and half

my nose is gone.
I drink my coffee

on the right from
a warped cup

whose left lip dips.
My cigarette's

thick as a finger.
Somebody else's.

I put lip-
stick on a cloth-

stuffed doll's
face that's

surprised when one
side smiles.

This poem is in present tense, so to perform it clearly you may want to spend some time reconstructing that feeling you last had at a dentist's office. Even now, try to reflect a sense of the poem's appearance in performance. Compose an introduction for a performance of this poem. Discuss whether or not the use of a manuscript would enhance the performance.

Every composer of a literary work of art knows, whether he rec-
ognizes his knowledge or not . . . that words, whatever their value
in expressing objective facts, always represent someone talking.
George T. Wright,
The Poet in the Poem

. . . a poem is a dramatic fiction no less than a play, and its
speaker, like a character in a play, is no less a creation of the
words on the printed page.

Reuben Brower,
Fields of Light

Nothing can happen nowhere. The locale of the happening also
colours the happening, and often, to a degree, shapes it.
Elizabeth Bowen,
Collected Impressions

Characters in literature have no extension in space or time beyond
the limits of the work in which they appear; they have, on the
other hand, a kind of extendability, a symbolic dimension, that the
matter-of-fact persons of our acquaintance do not have.
George T. Wright,
The Poet in the Poem

FOCUS FOR CHAPTER III

After you study the text and anthology in this chapter, we hope you will be able to

1. Distinguish intrinsic from extrinsic literary criticism.
2. Explain what is meant by "dramatic analysis."
3. Describe and illustrate the "dramatic speaker" in the literary text.
4. Distinguish author, speaker, and performer.
5. Understand how authors and speakers may differ greatly.
6. Define and illustrate tone, attitude, open situation, closed situation, omniscience, implied author.
7. Discuss levels of characterization for each speaker in a text.
8. Understand why no single performance is exhaustive.
9. Recognize the difference in performing certainties, probabilities, possibilities, and distortions.
10. Take an account of an event and create a telling of the story from four different points of view.
11. Perform a selection, or part of one, to demonstrate clearly the speaker, the scene, and the audience.
12. Provide an informative, appropriate introduction for a selection you perform.

Performing the Dramatic Speaker

For more than two thousand years, literary critics have evolved methods for the study of literature. In the broadest sense, these methods fall into two groups: *intrinsic* (study of the internal parts of the literary text) and *extrinsic* (study of something or someone outside the text proper, such as historical–biographical environment, the writer's public, the writer's life). Looking back to the kinds of preparation suggested in Chapter II, you will see that we recommend both. However, in this chapter and in the one that follows, we will concentrate on one intrinsic method, *dramatic analysis,* that raises numerous questions that can be answered at least partially in performance.

Critic Kenneth Burke has developed "five key terms of dramatism":

> What is involved when we say what people are doing and why they are doing it? ... We shall use five terms as generating principle of our investigation. They are: Act, Scene, Agent, Agency, Purpose. In a rounded statement about motives, you must have some word that names the *act* (names what took place, in thought or deed), and another that names the *scene* (the background of the act, the situation in which it occurred); also, you must indicate what person or kind of person *(agent)* performed the act, what means or instruments he used *(agency),* and the *purpose.* Men may violently disagree about the purposes, behind a given act, or about the character of the person who did it, or how he did it, or in what kind of situation he acted; or they may even insist upon totally different words to name the act itself. But be that as it may, any complete statement about motives will offer *some kind of* answers to these five questions: what was done (act), when and where it was done (scene), who did it (agent), how (agency), and why he did it (purpose).

[1]Kenneth Burke, *A Grammar of Motives* (Englewood Cliffs, N.J.: Prentice-Hall, 1945), p. xvii.

Although we will not be using all of Burke's terminology, we share his view that *the human situation created in literature is essentially dramatic.* The word "dramatic" refers to the fact that we can regard what happens in literature in ways similar to our typical experience with plays: something is happening to someone in some scene with some means and for some reason.

The following questions serve as an overview of dramatic analysis and raise issues central to performance. Burke's five basic terms, usually called "Burke's pentad," are combined here into two major divisions: the *dramatic speaker* and the *speaker's drama.* This chapter treats much of the first group and Chapter IV much of the second.

I. *The Dramatic Speaker*
  A. *Who* is speaking the words of the text? (persona, narrator, character)
    1. Specified *physically?* (species, sex, age, dress, posture, etc.)
    2. Cluster of *tone* and *attitudes?*
    3. Psychological characterization? (personality, bent, disposition, outlook)
  B. From what *perspective,* or *point of view,* does the speaker speak?
    1. Within the action? As manipulator of it? As observer?
    2. Objective viewing? Personally involved?
    3. Closer to one character than others? A reflector of a character? Omniscient to all, some, one, or none?
    4. Apparently truthful?
    5. Describing an action as it occurs? As it occurred?

C. *Where* and *when* is the speaker speaking?
   1. Specified time? (hour, day, season, year)
   2. Specified scene? (area, locale)
   3. Change of time or scene?
   4. Relation to objects within the scene?
D. *To whom* is the speaker speaking? (anyone, someone in particular, a generalized group, an absent though specified listener, himself or herself, some combination of listeners)

II. *The Speaker's Drama*
   A. *What* does the speaker say? (remember an event? tell a story? judge a thing or person? observe an occurrence? give advice?)
   B. *How* does the speaker speak?
      1. In what mode? (epic, dramatic, lyric, combination)
      2. With what rhythms? (recurrences of silences, sounds, words, phrases, stanzas, paragraphs)
      3. With what, if any metrical patterns? Free verse?
      4. On what level of language? (jargon, formalities, conversation)
      5. With what language devices? (allusion, metaphor, hyperbole, etc.)
      6. With what structure? (rambling, associative, topical, chronological)
      7. With what manipulation of time? (scene, summary, description)
      8. Is the address direct? Indirect? Mixed?
   C. *Why* does the speaker speak? (to organize, understand, convince, relieve, delight in)
      1. Does the presence (or absence) of an audience affect the speaker's purpose?
      2. Is the speaker's comment on the human condition different from that of the implied author?

A word of caution in using these questions seems in order: *these are not discrete categories.* Answering one in performance necessarily affects others, and their relative importance is bound to change among particular texts. Their interrelationship is seen most clearly in the later workshops and in the essays presented in Chapter V. For now, as a starting place, we will consider the first set of questions, those that probe the speaker, the audience, and the time and place of speaking.

Let us assume for now that your aim in performance is to demonstrate what the *speaker* does in a text created by the *author*. The distinctions between these three roles are shown in the following diagram:

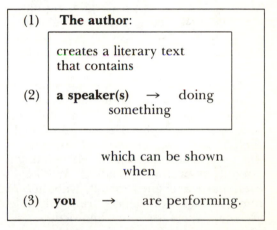

(1)   **The author:**

creates a literary text that contains

(2)   **a speaker(s)**   →   doing something

which can be shown when

(3)   **you**   →   are performing.

Look now at the three roles and the possible ranges they encompass.

The Author

A. The *author* may be living or dead, young or old, male or female, anonymous or known, skilled or unskilled, and so on; the author may be a poet, dramatist, novelist, short story writer, essayist, letter writer, public speaker, etc.

> B. The *author's works* may spring from reasoned deductions, dreams, observation, imagination, actual experiences, wishes, etc. The work may be a poem, story, play, letter, diary, speech, etc.

> C. The *author's audience* ranges in time from the first listener—the author—to those groups that encounter the text much later; its range in response includes, to mention only a few, amusement, pleasure, disdain, repugnance, curiosity, puzzlement, fear.

As readers we are often interested in, or at least curious about, the "real live" author of works we perform. We may seek out biographical data from books such as *200 Contemporary Authors*,[2] and, if the opportunity presents itself, we might attend the author's reading. We might even have a chance to talk with her or him. All such experiences are worthwhile, as they increase our knowledge and appreciation, *if* we also realize that the speaker we wish to know better and perform may be quite unlike the author-person we are seeking out. George T. Wright underscores the importance of making this distinction:

> Literature is made up of words, composed by writers and spoken by personae. In some works the distinction between poet and speaker is obvious; in others it seems

an extravagance to call attention to a distinction so thin that it can hardly be said to exist. Its existence is nevertheless a matter of fact. The persona may share much with his creator—a point of view, an attitude toward life, certain historical circumstances, certain intellectual qualities; but the persona is part of the poem, and the poet exists outside it. The author dies; the persona has a permanently potential existence, realized whenever the work in which he appears is read.[3]

Knowing about the author may help clarify some poems and not others. For instance, though Anne Sexton is often labelled a "confessional" poet because most of her poems seem to be in her own voice and about her own experiences, the details of her public and private life shed little, if any, light on "Some Foreign Letters." You could be disastrously misled if those details influenced your decisions about performing this poem. On the other hand, other kinds of comments by authors, perhaps not so readily accessible as tabloid biographies, nevertheless exist and often provide information of direct usefulness to the performer when they clarify matters concerning the literature itself. For example, in explaining her "special loyalty," to "Some Foreign Letters," Sexton satisfies our curiosity about what provoked the poem and also alerts us to the experience stored *in* the poem:

> It distills a time for me, a graceful innocent age that I loved but never knew. It is, for me, like a strange photograph that I come upon each time with a seizure of despair and astonishment.
>   "Some Foreign Letters" is a mixture of truth and lies. I don't feel like confessing which is which. When I wrote it I attempted to make all of it "true." It remains true *for*

[2]Barbara Harte and Carolyn Riley, *200 Contemporary Authors* (Gale Research & Company, 1969).

[3]George T. Wright, *The Poet in the Poem*, (Berkeley, Cal.: University of California Press, 1960), p. 22.

me to this day. But I will say that it was written to my great aunt who came to live with us when I was about nine and very lonely. She stayed with us until she had a nervous breakdown. This was triggered by her sudden deafness. I was seventeen at the time that she was taken away. She was, during the years she lived with us, my best friend, my teacher, my confidante and my comforter. I never thought of her as being young. She was an extension of myself and was my world. I hadn't considered that she might have had a world of her own once. Many years later, after her death, I found a bound volume of her letters from Europe. (My family were the type that bound letters in leather.) The letters are gay and intimate and tragic.[4]

J. V. Cunningham offers another example of an author whose aim in writing a poem, when shared with us, provides an informed awareness for the poem, "Epigram."[5] For him, a "poem" and a "good poem" are defined as follows: "A poem, then, in this view is metrical speech, and a good poem is the definitive statement in meter of something worth saying." Then he elaborates:

> The characteristic poem motivated by a concern for definitive statement . . . will be the poem that explains—an expository poem, a statement in the ordinary sense of that word. And it will be short, for the concern for definitiveness is a prejudice for brevity. If one has said something definitively he will not be impelled to amplify, to say it again undefinitively. So the poet who holds this view becomes an epigrammatist. He writes:

[4]Paul Engle and Joseph Langland, eds., *Poet's Choice* (New York: Dial, 1962) pp. 276–277.

[5]Cunningham discusses his short poems in *Poets on Poetry*, ed. Howard Nemerov (New York: Basic Books, 1966), p. 41. The book also contains comments about their own poetry by several other poets represented in this book: May Swenson, Richard Wilbur, Reed Whittemore, James Dickey, Howard Nemerov, Richard Eberhart, and Conrad Aiken.

Epigram

And what is love? Misunderstanding, pain,
Delusion, or retreat? It is in truth
Like an old brandy after a long rain,
Distinguished, and familiar, and aloof.

The Speaker

> A. The *speaker*(s) is often referred to as a *persona* in lyrics, a *narrator* or storyteller of a narrative, and a *character* in drama. Each of these designations is here synonymous with *speaker*, the source of the language. How this source stands in relation to other people, places, and events constitutes *point of view,* an element of paramount importance to the performer.

You've probably been driven at some point in an argument to exclaim, "I just don't see it that way!" You were speaking of point of view—a way of seeing, an angle of vision influenced by available information and resulting in a given relationship with the audience or reader. Point of view is one of those umbrella terms that mean a number of things; the term may mean intellectual viewpoint, or visual perspective (equivalent to a camera angle), or, as the term is most often used in narrative, whose mind is providing the information.

Point of view is central to the discussion of narrative, where the most commonly made distinctions are as follows:

	Internal Analysis of Events	*External Observation of Events*
Narrator as a character in story	1. Main character tells own story	2. Minor character tells main character's story
Narrator not a character in story	4. Analytic or omniscient figure tells story, entering thoughts and feelings[6]	3. Someone tells story as external observer

The matter should be clearer if we look at an illustration of each of these four major divisions with some "original" examples based on "Little Red Riding Hood":

1. *Main character tells own story:*
   I watched my mother take the cookies, my favorite kind, from the oven. I could hardly wait for them to cool enough for me to have one. (I always got a sample from the first batch.) And I knew what we would do next. We'd wrap them carefully in a napkin and put them in my new basket. The smell from the cookies was wonderful.

2. *Minor character tells main character's story:*
   I took the cookies from the oven carefully, not wanting to jostle them or to burn myself. My daughter, scarcely nine years old and still eager to participate in all the household activities—especially those that smelled and tasted good—watched, almost holding her breath. I was preparing the cookies for her to take to her grandmother who lived on the other side of the forest.

3. *Author tells story as external observer:*
   There was a small stretch of woods just outside of town. . . . The little girl walked through the woods slowly, not as if she were frightened but as if she were unhurried, relaxed, unconcerned. She was humming a tune that one could hear if one

were not too far away. She was entirely alone in that part of the woods.
   The girl's grandmother lay alone in her bed, the light spread drawn up around her shoulders. Her eyes were bright, though her hands, twisted with age, were almost motionless.

4. *Analytic or ominiscient author tells story, entering thoughts and feelings:*
   She watched her mother take the cookies, her favorite kind, from the oven. She could hardly wait for them to cool enough for her to have one. (She always got a sample from the first batch.) And she knew what they would do next. They'd wrap them carefully in a napkin and put them in her new basket.

With these four major divisions understood, you can move on to far more subtle descriptions of point of view in a literary text, how it affects you as a reader, and the challenges it offers you in performance. As we consider additional terms useful in discussing point of view, we shall mention examples found in this book.[7]

1. The speaker's choice of telling, showing, or doing defines the *mode* of his or her discourse. Specifically, in the *lyric* mode, the speaker tells; in the *dramatic*,

---

[6]Based on Cleanth Brooks and Robert Penn Warren, *Understanding Fiction,* 2nd ed. (New York: Appleton-Century-Crofts, 1959), p. 148.

[7]A bibliography section on "Speaker: Character, Narrator, Persona" at the back of this book contains several items especially helpful in discussions of point of view: those by Booth, Friedman, Heston, and Maclay.

shows; and in the *epic,* both shows and tells.

Lyric: William Carlos Williams, "This is Just to Say"
Beverly Sills, from *Bubbles*

Dramatic: Archibald MacLeish, "The Old Gray Couple (2)"
Harold Pinter, *Trouble in the Works*

Epic: Fred Chappell, "My Father Burns Washington"
James Thurber, "The Very Proper Gander"

2. The speaker's angle of vision may seem *objective* (as the speaker-narrator in "The Test") or it may be highly *subjective* (as in "Dancing on the Grave of a Son of a Bitch"). Of course, it may fall between these extremes, or it may combine them (as in "Theme for English B").

3. The point of view may be one we find credible or *trustworthy;* on the other hand, we may believe the speaker is *lying* to us or another character (as Captain Keeney to Annie in *Ile*).

4. The point of view may be fairly *fixed* or *rigid* (as in "Who Am I This Time?"), or it may *bounce* or *shift* (as in "Miss Brill" or "A School Lesson Based on Word of Tragic Death of the Entire Gillum Family").

5. The speaker's angle of vision may permit him or her great *privilege,* a knowledge of the very depths of others whose situation he or she is describing (as in "The Hope Chest"). On the contrary and at the other extreme, the view may be *restricted* to what anyone reasonably alert and present could have seen (as in "The Hour of Letdown").

B. The *speaker's identity* may be revealed through details so sparse that you can glean only an indication of the speaker's *tone* toward the *audience* and *attitude* toward the *subject.*

Tone and attitude are inevitable and ever present. We, and authors alike, do not decide whether or not to reveal them, but we can choose which ones.

Tone and attitude may be clearer if we borrow Walker Gibson's diagram.[8]

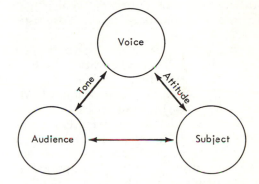

In our everyday roles, we choose a variety of tones depending upon the relationship we have, imagine we have, or wish to have with our audience. Tones toward an audience range on a continuum from what we may label informal (warm, talkish) through neutral and on to formal (distanced, "writerish"). The point of the following list is to chart extremes, while realizing at the same time that we have oversimplified the complexity of tones present in literature. These are but a few characteristics of language that in ordinary circumstances bring a reader or listener closer to or push him farther from the speaker.[9]

[8]Walker Gibson, *Persona: A Style Study for Readers and Writers* (New York: Random House, 1969), p. 52.
[9]Based on Gibson's discussion.

Informal	*Neutral*	*Formal*
Active voice verbs	- -	Passive voice verbs
Loose sentence	- -	Periodic sentences
Use of "you"	- -	No use of "you"
Use of contractions	- -	No use of contractions
Fragments and run on sentences	- - - - - - - - - - - - - - - - - - - -	Long, complete sentences
Nonmetered language	- -	Metered language

Through their language choices, speakers exhibit tones toward their audience ranging from extremely close, intimate and friendly (as in Anne Frank's diary), neutral and neither friendly nor unfriendly (as in Thurber's "Which"), and formal and distanced (as in "My Sister's Marriage").

One of the particular riches of prose fiction lies in its configuration of tones. Look, for example, at "The Test," in which the narrator's tone is neutral; Mrs. Ericson's is caring, but at a distance; the inspector's is feigned friendliness and hostility; and Marian's is formality. In poetry, we often experience a special pleasure in a single tone that is amplified and intensified, as in Kinnell's "Wait" or Cummings's poem that begins "my father moved through dooms of love." In drama, we expect to distinguish characters partly through the various tones while enjoying a kind of stability that comes with consistency in one character.

For a final example, think of your professors. Even if they were all delivering a lecture on identical subjects, you could still predict differences in tone because you perceive some of them as warm and reassuring toward their audience, some as somewhat noncommital, and others as aloof.

Attitude refers to the speaker's relation to her or his subject. We, and literary speakers too, may regard the subjects of our discourse with responses ranging from positive to negative, but usually lodging somewhere between or shifting. Gibson claims that "Much of our discussion of attitude comes down to decisions about whether language is being used honorifically or pejoratively, or both, or neither."[10] Attitude thus reveals our approval or disapproval, or both of our subject. Ruth Whitman's "Listening to grownups quarreling" contains a speaker expressing distress over her subject. Honorific attitudes are apparent in Ferlinghetti's "Dog" and in "Dedication for a Plot of Ground," the William Carlos Williams poem discussed in the workshop of Chapter IV.

Recognizing the speaker's steady, growing, or changing attitudes is imperative for the performer, who cannot help show attitude. Human beings simply are incapable of speaking without an attitude.[11] Probably at the top of the list of potential performance problems is the temptation for the performer to substitute his or her own attitudes for those of the speaker in the text. This strategy works rarely, and it is self-defeating as well. It negates the growth that comes with viewing another's situation as one's own. Performers who present "Epigram" with a scornful attitude—because that is the way in which they currently view love—rob both themselves and the poem. With studied effort and imagination, however, performers can project a speaker whose tone and attitude are compatible with those in the literary text.

[10]*Ibid.*, p. 65.

[11]For a vocabulary of attitudes, see Wayland Maxfield Parrish, *Reading Aloud*, 3rd ed. (New York: Ronald Press, 1953), pp. 70–72.

> C.   The speaker's identity may be so full as to make us believe that he or she is a multidimensional person, a speaker *characterized.*

When authors create literary texts, they assign traits to speakers; the more traits assigned, the better we get to know them. In the material to follow, we rely on the work of Sam Smiley and Oscar Brockett, whose major interest is character in drama. However, what they say is extremely useful in examining speakers in any genre.

Levels of characterization of speakers include:

Biological: are those [traits] which establish a character as some identifiable being—human or animal, male or female. . . . The biological is the simplest, yet the most essential, level of characterization. With some minor characters, biological traits are the only ones desirable or necessary.[12]

Physical: provides a slightly higher level of characterization. . . . Any specific physical quality, such as age, size, weight, coloring, and posture can be used. Features of the body and face are physical traits. Vocal quality can serve, as can habitual activity or manner of moving. Physical states—of health and illness, normality and abnormality—may characterize an agent. Even clothing or possessions can indicate individuality.[13]

Social: includes a character's economic status, profession or trade, religion, family relationships—all those factors that place him in his environment.[14]

Dispositional: reflects the basic bent of a character's delimited personality. In every play, most characters have a prevailing mood, controlled by the individual's temperamental makeup. Disposition in characters consists of a customary mood and life-attitude as demonstrated in speech and activity.[15]

Psychological reveals a character's habitual responses, attitudes, desires, motivations, likes, and dislikes—the inner workings of the mind, both emotional and intellectual which precede action.[16]

Moral: is most apt to be used in serious plays, especially tragedies. Although almost all human action suggests some ethical standard, in many plays the moral implications are ignored and decisions are made on the grounds of expediency. . . . More significantly than any other kind, moral decisions differentiate characters, since the choices they make when faced with moral crises show whether they are selfish, hypocritical, honest, or whatever. A moral decision usually causes a character to examine his own motives and values, in the process of which his true nature is revealed both to himself and to the audience.[17]

[12]Sam Smiley, *Playwriting: The Structure of Action* (Englewood Cliffs, N.J.: Prentice-Hall, 1971), p. 84.

[13]*Ibid.*

[14]Oscar G. Brockett, *The Theatre: An Introduction*, 4th ed. (New York: Holt, Rinehart and Winston, 1979), p. 37.

[15]Smiley, p. 85.

[16]Brockett, p. 37.

[17]*Ibid.*, p. 38.

	Narrator (Clark Carpenter)	*Georgiana Carpenter*	*Mrs. Springer*	*Musician*
B	Human; male	Human; female	Human; female	Human; male
P	Probably in his thirties and dressed in the fashion of the day	Probably in her sixties, gnarled hands; disheveled and dusty on arrival, dressed in black		In black coat
S	Urbane, widely traveled, probably well read	Farmer's wife; accustomed to hard work; churchgoer	Landlady	Member of symphony orchestra
D	Observant, critical toward uncle, gentle with Georgiana	Quiet; weak from sickness and preoccupied with farm at beginning; at matinée, impassioned and overcome	Considerate	
Ps	Desires life of culture; wants to repay aunt	Wants to be a good, unobtrusive guest; at matinée discovers a desperate longing		
M	As he remembers the home scene of aunt, comes to understand and empathize with her emptiness	Realizes a decision of thirty years ago has not been a fulfilling life; knowing what she has missed is almost unbearable		

Man from Bayreuth

B–Human; male
P–Could sing
S–German, tramp, cowpuncher
D–Carefree, irresponsible

In Chart 3A we look back at Willa Cather's "A Wagner Matinée" in Chapter I, noting the differing levels of characterization in the narrator, Aunt Georgiana, Mrs. Springer, and the musicians. The broken lines are a reminder that all we know of the other speakers is filtered through the major speaker-narrator, except for what Aunt Georgiana tells him about the man from Bayreuth.

The symbols used in the chart are defined as follows:

B = Biological
P = Physical
S = Social
D = Dispositional
Ps = Psychological
M = Moral

The scheme of levels of characterization demonstrated in Chart 3A can be applied to one speaker or to many. Also, it often serves as a good springboard for discussing the strengths or gaps in a performance of those speakers.

D. The *speaker* may be more or less distant from the *implied author* (the reader's perception of the personality that created the text, especially the value system that emerges from the text), from the other speakers in the text, or from a reading or listening public.

Notice the difference in values between the speaker and implied author in "My Sister's Marriage" (we are confident that we, as readers, share the attitude toward the life not of the storyteller, but of the author who presents this storyteller), between the speaker and other characters in "Between the Lines," and between reader and speaker in "One More Eyewitness."

One more diagram may help clarify these distinctions, which often give performers difficulty. Read Flannery O'Connor's "A Good Man Is Hard to Find" and then study this representation:

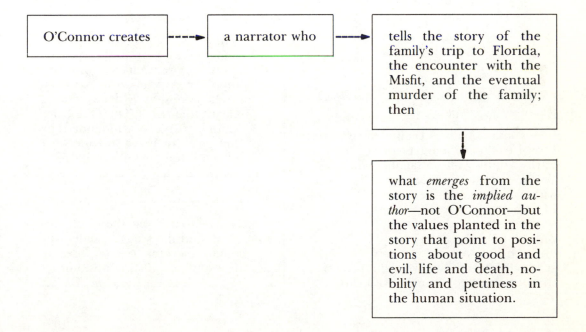

The essential point is that we see these distinctions clearly enough to avoid confusing author, speaker, characters, reader, and implied author; to do so frequently destroys the experience with the literature. In "The Test," author Gibbs is not condoning the inspector; neither is the narrator condemning him. The inspector condemns himself, and the implied author could not be clearer in emphasizing—through action, not diatribe—that only one person in this story is deserving of our sympathy.

> E. The *speaker's language* is created by the author, but we believe, for the moment, that the speaker devised it.

In the following short poem, we respond to a peace-hating, war zealot's exclamations even though we know that Ignatow is ironically denouncing the war supporter:

All Quiet
DAVID IGNATOW

For Robert Bly
Written at the start of one of our bombing passes over Vietnam

How come nobody is being bombed today?
I want to know, being a citizen
of this country and a family man.
You can't take my fate in your hands,
without informing me.
I can blow up a bomb or crush a skull—
whoever started this peace bit
without advising me
through a news leak
at which I could have voiced a protest,
running my whole family off a cliff.

> F. The *speaker* may be more or less important, ranging from center stage to off stage, as it were.

The focus is clearly on the speaker in "My Sister's Marriage" and "Next Day," but another person is of prime importance in "Dedication for a Plot of Ground," an idea in "The Movies," and a feeling in "Loneliness."

> G. The *speaker's action* may involve remembering, imagining, associating, thinking, observing, doing, or some combination of these.

The action may take place in a specific time and place (Margaret Chase Smith in the United States Senate on a summer afternoon), or there may be a total absence of scenic definition as in "Things That Go Away And Come Back Again."

> H. The *speaker's scene* may involve an audience present ("Univac to Univac"), present but unhearing ("An Afternoon in Artillery Walk"), absent (Rilke's letter), clearly defined ("The Old Gray Couple (2)"), or undefined to the point of being anyone who would listen ("Anne Rutledge").

> I. The *speaker(s)*, together with the action and the scene, usually will contain several *tensions* (resistance, pull, conflict, opposition).

In "Piano," for example, we find tensions within the speaker (his concepts of manliness and childishness) and in the action (being in the present but being overcome by the past) as well as the scene (the controlled song that precipitates the uncontrollable response).

It is what the specific speaker in a given text is and does that the performer attempts to demonstrate in performance.

The Performer

> A. The *performer–audience* relationship is directed by the *speaker* (fictive)–*audience* relationship.

The relationship between the speaker and that speaker's audience is usually described as either *open* or *closed*, depending on whether the listener is outside the text or within the situation of the text itself.[18] Sometimes the speaker seems to be communicating to anyone and everyone. Most storytellers are talking to any and all of us who are outside the story; the speaker in most essays addresses the world at large. Such situations are *open*. Characters in a scene generally speak to one another, with no awareness of us as listeners. We overhear their words. Such situations are *closed*.

A selection with only one speaker may still be closed if the person addressed is inside the text. Love poems, for instance,

are not general. The speaker addresses a specific listener, whether that person is physically present in the text or only imagined by the speaker. The speaker in "no assistance" is presumably planning or writing a note; the woman addressed in Nims's "Love Poem" may be there with the speaker or he may be speaking to her only in his mind. Both poems are closed.

Many selections, like narratives, alternate between open and closed. The narrator's situation is open, but the characters' situation is closed. "The Bad Daddy" is open in the first and the final stanzas and closed for the middle three, when the "Daddy" addresses members of his family.

Performers must establish the audience for the speaker. In open situations the performer addresses the real audience like any good public speaker, trying to look at each member of the audience to establish that the utterance is directed to everyone. When the persona speaks only to herself or himself or to someone else within the text, then the performer generally does not look directly at the real audience. That action would contradict the speaker's action within the text. Even in a closed situation, the performer may have the option of bringing the real audience into the text. "What Thomas an Buile Said in a Pub" is closed because the speaker's audience is within the pub, but a performer might choose to let the real audience serve as Thomas's fellow patrons.

But when the speaker is clearly alone or has a highly specified listener, the real audience cannot easily substitute for the fictive one. The intimate, closed-off-from-others relationship between the niece and her aunt-audience in "Some Foreign Letters" would seem to require a closed performance situation with no direct contact between performer and real audience.

---

[18]Wilma H. Grimes and Alethea Smith Mattingly, *Interpretation: Reader, Writer, Audience,* (Belmont, Calif.: Wadsworth, 1961), pp. 18–19. Much of this discussion appeared originally in Alethea Smith Mattingly, "The Listener and the Interpreter's Style," *Western Speech,* 28 (Summer 1964), 154–159.

> B. The *performer* can express and particularize the experience that the text can only notate.

The *performer's means* include the words of the text together with her own body, voice, mind, memories, imagination, and emotions. Depending on the nature of the assignment and the appropriateness to the text, the performer's means may also include props, costumes, and such other media as music or visuals.

About "particularization," acting teacher Uta Hagen writes,

Particularizing or to make something particular, as opposed to generalizing or to keep general, is an essential for everything in acting from identification of the character right down to the tiniest physical object you come in contact with. . . . Every detail of place, objects, relationships to others, my main character needs, my immediate needs, and obstacles must be made particular. Nothing should be allowed to remain general.[19]

Unless things and people and even ideas are specific and particular to performers, they will develop generalized speaker-scenes. If this happens, it will appear to the audience—and probably to the performer as well—that the performance lacks focus, clarity, and believability.

Hagen's injunction that "Nothing should be allowed to remain general" may be the most important single caution a performer can hear. It is related to earlier discussions of clearly stated purposes,

subtexts, and moment-to-moment interpretation. It applies to your consideration of every speaker and every scene, no matter how much explicit information appears in the text. You may feel that, once you have these specifics in your own mind, either you need to perform them so that the audience's vision is equally specific or you will have wasted your time. Not true. The specifics that exist for *you*, even if the audience does not realize them fully, nevertheless give a richness and depth to your performance that the audience does realize.

The advice is practical in that it will help you actualize specific speakers in their individual scenes in all the uniqueness of each. To make our responses specific, we must make our speaker's scene specific—even if no one else ever knows what our private, specific details were.

Look for a moment at a very short poem by Paul Engle. As you will see, it is a quite lowly defined, fragile piece. Still you will need many details to fund your own mind and imagination (what a variety of possibilities in the "we" of the poem!) *even if* you choose to actualize few of the specifics in the performance for fear of overwhelming the power of the poem.

[19]Uta Hagen, *Respect for Acting* (New York: Macmillan, 1973), pp. 44–45.

Together
PAUL ENGLE

Because we do
All things together
All things improve,
Even weather.

Our daily meat
And bread taste better,
Trees greener,
Rain is wetter.

> C. The *performer's audience* is first of all himself or herself in rehearsal. Later it becomes a group of peers.

Unlike the *speaker's audience*, which may exist in the imagination, the *performer's audience* is always anchored in a specific time and place. Usually, the time and place occurs during the day in a classroom, though sometimes it occurs before an assembled group at a festival, in church, or at a meeting.

Some Practical Advice

Understanding from the start that no performance can be strong and full without adequate time, thought, and trial after trial in rehearsal and stressing that ultimately all performance decisions should be firmly grounded in the particular text—we can offer some practical advice concerning classroom performances:

1. You will have started your performance from the time you rise from your chair. At all times, try to make your behavior congruous with the literature. That is, use your best "formal, serious self" if you are about to perform "Do Not Go Gentle into That Good Night," and a more casual approach if you are performing "The Private Dining Room" or "Love Poem."

2. If you give an introduction to the selection, congruity again is the watchword. Develop an introduction that *sets up* the literary text. You might speak of its appeal to you, its relation to the audience, its genesis with the author. Share some discovery with your audience that you made about the literature after looking longer and more closely than they have had time to do. In introductions avoid the cute or precious, the inflated, global abstraction, the irrelevant, the patronizing, or the mechanical. Your professor may decide to give the class specific points to cover in the introduction, such as speaker, fictive audience, stylistic devices, and so on.

3. Try to deliver the introduction as extemporaneously as possible. It is advisable to write it out and revise and rehearse it, but your audience is likely to be more attentive to your remarks and to the performance if the remarks seem impromptu when delivered.

4. During the introduction, your own personality affects what your listeners will later take to be the *performed text*. For now you are a public speaker seeking support for the literature and for the performance; you are, in short, cultivating an appeal for your position (here, your literary text) by the good will of your personality and the preparedness of your introduction and performance.

5. Arrive in class early and do what you can to make the room arrangement underscore the relationship you wish to have with the audience. Create changes (lights, seating arrangements, blinds) that are conducive to a better performance.

6. In classroom performances, where your aim is a full demonstration of a human situation in literature, whether or not you use a manuscript should depend on the text you are performing. For "Declaration of Conscience" or "Ordinance on Enrollment," the use of script—or both script and

reading stand—might emphasize the oratorical quality of the selections and also stress the fact that the dramatic speaker could be a public speaker. A similar rationale might be used if you are performing letters, diaries, or journals—or any imaginative literature that simulates these forms, like "Some Foreign Letters."

7. For the performance of many other texts, a script can become an unnecessary obstacle. To perform "An Afternoon in Artillery Walk," for example, you probably need a great deal of freedom of movement and focus to see the father, look out the window, take dictation, and imagine a happier time. The realization of such a detailed scene and action often makes the use of a script impractical and distracting.

8. If your performance is for a public audience, one expecting the use of a manuscript (or one requiring it, as some situations do), you will want to learn to handle the book (or folder) with ease and effectiveness. Make sure that your script is clean and easy to see; hold it high enough to see comfortably, but low enough so that it does not block your face. Try using a book small enough to hold in one hand so that the other is free. A low speaker's stand where you place the script will provide more physical freedom.

9. Know your speaker's specific reasons for speaking each and every time she or he speaks, and particularize, to yourself at least, *everything* in your speaker's scene.

10. Finally—and perhaps most important—take the *time* to make your points. As a performer, you face some of the same tasks as a conductor of music: you must start the literature, showing what provoked its action; you must then show the parts by clearly distinguishing among them and their relationships through verbal and nonverbal stress and silence; and you must also show the completion or "stops" of various units (phrases, sentences, episodes). Transitions as well as closures should be translated clearly through voice, bodily tension, and movement.

D. The *performer's audience* ideally gains enjoyment and fuller awareness of the experience in the literature. The performer gains from the audience some indication of the extent to which her or his intentions were achieved.

Freedom and Boundaries

One performance cannot possibly express all that a literary text contains. In fact, the richer the literature, the less likely we are to settle for only one performance, however interesting and satisfying. Such a response does not minimize the appeal of a strong, full performance; it merely reminds us that such a performance does not thereby exhaust the literature. We readily sense an analogy in Roger Sessions's response to the notion of an "ideal" performance in music:

. . . the idea of the "ideal" or even in any strict sense, the "authoritative" performance is an illusory one. The music is not totally present, the idea of the composer is not fully expressed, in any single performance, actual or even conceivable, but rather in the sum of all possible performances. But having admitted this, we are bound to insist also that the number of possible performances is limited by the composer's text and by the musical intentions which the text embodies.[20]

Sessions's final sentence points to the kind of problem the performer of literature encounters: there are many "right" interpretations of a text that are too complex to capture in a single performance. Still, there are limits, and they are exceeded when the notations in the text are ignored, or when performers do not supply the conviction and vitality of their own participation: "Performers of genius, even with the best of intentions, sometimes overstep limits, and apart from them we hear many 'impossible' performances—impossible sometimes through distortion of the composer's idea, but sometimes also through lack of the vitalizing energy of a genuine impulse."[21]

There are many "rights," so no one of us should insist that only *our* interpretation will do. Any of these "rights," or plausible interpretations, result from a careful study of the writer's notations, which together provide us with a *guide*, a *blueprint* for performance. From those directions, we *constitute*, or *assemble*, the experience potential in the literature in our performance.[22]

As we mentioned before, some guides are more definite than others. As the guides become more specific (or as more of the questions listed on pp. 118–119 are answered in the literary text), our performance choices are more limited; the looser the guides, the more freedom in our choices.

Let us try to make this matter clearer by looking at Edwin Arlington Robinson's "How Annandale Went Out."

"They called it Annandale—and I was there
To flourish, to find words, and to attend:
Liar, physician, hypocrite, and friend,
I watched him; and the sight was not so fair
As one or two that I have seen elsewhere:
An apparatus not for me to mend—
A wreck, with hell between him and the end,
Remained of Annandale; and I was there.

"I knew the ruin as I knew the man;
So put the two together, if you can,
Remembering the worst you know of me.
Now view yourself as I was, on the spot—
With a slight kind of engine. Do you see?
Like this . . . You wouldn't hang me? I thought not."

In answering the question "Who is speaking?", we may preface our answers with three different descriptors: *definitely, probably,* or *possibly.*

Definitely: The speaker is defending an earlier act.
              The speaker is a physician.

Probably: The speaker is male.
              The speaker is an older, experienced physician.
              The speaker is on trial for euthanasia.

[20]Roger Sessions, "The Performer," *The Musical Experience of Composer, Performer, Listener,* (New York: Atheneum, 1967), p. 73.

[21]*Ibid.*

[22]Wolfgang Iser, *The Act of Reading* (Baltimore: Johns Hopkins University Press, 1978).

Possibly: The speaker smirks at the jury's decision.
The speaker is making his claims in good faith; he quietly and humbly accepts the jury's verdict.

The possibilities could be extended, but these should make the point. Not all the listed possibilities could be performed simultaneously—a good reason for performing a selection more than once when time permits.

As we ask questions about the literature, we seek answers that we can then translate in performance. The answers may be specific and definite *(certainties, givens,* or *known facts);* our answers may be weighted likelihoods *(probabilities);* or they may be based on the slightest of hints *(possibilities).* The certainties are there in the text to be observed; the probabilities and possibilities, however, must be *inferred* on the basis of inexact evidence.

How do we know when we witness or are guilty of what Sessions calls an "impossible" performance? It occurs when the performance offers a *distortion* of a certainty, or known fact, in the text. A performer of "How Annandale Went Out" who treats the speaker's discourse so casually as to suggest he is indifferent toward his earlier act, who substitutes his own words for those of the speaker, who mumbles as if there were no listener, such a performer distorts or "unsays" some-

thing that the text says for certain. If the performer were asked, "How is the speaker speaking?" she or he would surely say, "In poetry." One common way of "unsaying" this certain answer would be to read it as if it were prose, a distortion as sure as if the speaker were performed as a child.

Let's look back now at the two major questions we asked at the beginning of this chapter: (1) Who is the dramatic speaker? and (2) What is the speaker's drama? We may say that either—and all the subquestions that each encompasses—may be answered in performance with certainties, probabilities, or possibilities. It is hoped that your study of the text will be so careful that you will avoid distortions. If not "wrong," distortions are, in less categorical language, *inadequate* (when they omit certainties), *premature* (when they reflect hasty study), or *implausible* (when they contradict the certainties).[23]

Our freedoms as performers are indeed great because the literature is multilayered and artistically complex. However, boundaries do exist, and we must honor them in order not to blur the literature's uniqueness.

[23]See Beverly Whitaker Long, "Evaluating Performed Literature," in *Studies in Interpretation, II,* eds. Esther M. Doyle and Virginia Hastings Floyd (The Netherlands: Rodopi, 1977), pp. 267–281. See also Carolyn Gilbert, "Performance Criticism," *Communicative Performance of Literature* (New York: Macmillan, 1977), pp. 51–54.

WORKSHOP III

The first two selections in this workshop deal, in different ways, with writing—the first of *Paradise Lost* and the second of a Christmas letter. The speaker in "An Afternoon in Artillery Walk" is sharply defined, as are her audiences and her

scene. In "From Us to You," what we know about the speaker and the audience must largely be inferred from the text. Our discussion of the first-person speaker in "An Afternoon in Artillery Walk" differs in length and amount of detail from the second selection. We assume that, after working through the opening poem, you can apply the same questions to other literary texts.

The workshop then treats briefly four third-person speakers in narratives: "A Worn Path," "The Old Gray Couple (1)," "Madame Zilensky and the King of Finland," and "The Crop."

An Afternoon in Artillery Walk

LEONARD BACON

Mary Milton, loquitur
I think it is his blindness makes him so,
He is so angry, and so querulous.
Yes, Father! I will look in Scaliger.
Yes, Cousin Phillips took the notes—I think—
May all the evil angels fly away
With Cousin Phillips to the Serbonian Bog,
Wherever that may be. And here am I
Locked in with him the livelong afternoon.
There's Anne gone limping with that love of hers,
Her master-carpenter, and Deborah
Stolen away. Yes, Father, 'tis an aleph
But the Greek glose on't in the Septuagint
Is something that I cannot quite make out.
The letter's rubbed.

        Oh, thus to wear away
My soul and body with this dry-as-dust
This tearer-up of words, this plaguey seeker
After the things that no man understands.
'Tis April. I am seventeen years old,
And Abram Clark will come a-courting me.
Oh what a Hell a midday house can be!
Dusty and bright and dumb and shadowless,
Full of this sunshot dryness, like the soul
Of this old pedant here. I will not bear
Longer this tyranny of death in life

That drains my spirit like a succubus.
I am too full of blood and life for this—
This dull soul-gnawing discipline he sets
Upon our shoulders, the sad characters.
Chapter on chapter, blank and meaningless.
Now by the May-pole merry-makers run,
And the music throbs and pulses in light limbs,
And the girls' kirtles are lifted to the knee.
Ah would that I were blowsy with the heat,
Being bussed by some tall fellow, and kissing him
On his hot red lips—some bully royalist
With gold in's purse and lace about his throat
And a long rapier for the Puritans.
Or I would wander by some cool yew-hedge,
Dallying with my lover all the afternoon,
And then to cards and supper—cinnamon,
Some delicate pastry, and an amber wine
Burning on these lips that know a year-long lent.
Then to the theatre, and Mistress Nell
That the king's fond of. Mayhap gentlemen
About would praise me, and I should hear them buzz,
And feel my cheek grow warm beneath my mask,
And glance most kindly—

        I was in a muse
I have the paper, father, and the pens.
Now for the damnable dictation. So!
*"High—on a throne—of royal state—which far
Outshone—the wealth of 'Ormus' "*—S or Z?
How should I know the letter?—*"and of Ind.
Or where—the gorgeous East—with richest hand
Showers—on her kings—barbaric—pearl and gold,
Satan exalted sate."*

The Speaker's Levels of Characterization

Biological:	A human being
Physical:	A seventeen-year-old female; possibly attractive
Social:	Daughter of a famous person, John Milton; thought to be of Puritan belief; financially dependent on father; educated; sister to two other women; probably motherless
Dispositional:	Dutiful; restless; sensual; romantic
Motivational:	Wants to be free to enjoy pleasures
Deliberative:	Considers her predicament; finds no admirable quality in father; sees no sense in the dictation; imagines what freedom would bring
Decisive:	All decisions made prior to the scene; does not have means to leave—or doesn't know how

The Speaker's Action

Mary's utterances move between observations (unspoken but heard by her and us) of her father, silences during which he speaks (heard by her but unheard by us), her spoken responses to his questions or demands, her true interior responses, and her fantasized actions (heard by her and us). When addressing him, she answers, obeys, notes, submits, repeats; when internally talking about him, she reasons, itemizes, supports, curses, seethes, erupts, compares, resolves, scorns, retaliates; when thinking about her sisters, Deborah and Anne, she recalls with disgust and envy. The lines from *Paradise Lost* she repeats and copies reluctantly but obediently.

The Speaker's Tensions

The major source of Mary Milton's tension is, of course, her distance from her father and the values he represents. Look now at the following *pulls* in the poem:

Mary Milton	John Milton
daughter	father
woman	man
young	old
healthy	infirm
hedonistic	Puritanical
clerical activity	creative power
physical awareness	spiritual awareness

Except in her imagination, Mary loses on every score. No doubt it would make little difference to her—as it may for us—that the literature she considers tedious and dull will become immortal.

The Speaker's Tones and Attitudes

Several tones and attitudes have been suggested in the previous discussion. Here we will outline them in three major movements: neutral, negative, and positive:

Tone toward father	*Obedient*	(Neutral)
Attitude toward father's work	*Outwardly unfeeling*	
Tone (unspoken) toward father	*Resentful to enraged*	(Negative)
Attitude (unspoken) toward father's work	*Disgust and disapproval*	
Tone (unspoken) toward self in dreams	*Delighted, enraptured*	(Positive)
Attitude (unspoken) toward events in dreams	*Thrilled*	

The Speaker's Scene

Looking at internal evidence, we may say that the scene occurs in seventeenth-century England about 1665 at a country home in Artillery Walk. The house, perhaps dark and musty, stands in sharp contrast to the outside, where the sun is shining, the wind is blowing, and the flowers are blooming.

Suggestions for Performance

Reexamine the discussions above of the speaker's levels of characterization, tensions, actions, tone, and attitude, noting this time which of these you share with Mary and which you do not. For those you do not share immediately, you will need new "funding" through remembered feelings, close obvservations, or imagination—and possibly all three. Whether the differences are slight or great, think about yourself and this speaker in terms of similarities and differences. For the differences, create for yourself improvisations, vocal drills, physical exercises, and the like that will assist you in reflecting more fully the specific speaker you perceive in this particular poem, always remembering that, for the believable performance, you must attend to the *reason* for speaking and not to its *effect*. For this poem, you do not want to perform Mary's "frustration" but her conflicting needs ("I must obey my father." "I must get outside where there is gaiety.") While we may view Mary's plight, as "pitiful," we would not play the pitifulness but rather the *particular reasons for her actions* that lead us to that conclusion.

You would probably decide to perform the entire poem as a *closed situation*, since Mary is not speaking to anyone except herself and her father. To facilitate the shifts in her addressee, you might use a revolving piano stool placed at the side of a lone chair in which we and she can imagine the father sitting; on the other side, there could be a small table on which the pad, pen, and books are placed.

At this point in your study, it may be advisable to make these props literal and cultivate a real attitude toward them, indicating how Mary would handle them on this occasion. One good imaginative exercise is to practice how she might treat them on other occasions—when her father is gone, when she's looking up a quote to please a suitor, when she's writing a romantic novel. In addition to giving the performer a fuller sense of reality, the props symbolically reinforce an important aspect of the poem: they represent the static, buried character of her own life.

The revolving stool would permit you to be seen and overheard by the audience while making the transitions between attentively addressing the father and moving out and around for private accusations and dreams. Physical movement could also underscore transitions in the poem: on line 18 you might see that he is asleep and close your dictation pad quietly, walk a few steps toward the imaginary (or real) window, and allow the season outside to provoke, "'Tis April." The next transition, beginning "I will not hear," could be marked by turning slightly and glancing over your shoulder at the father. Then on "I am too full . . . " you could turn back a little toward the window and set the imagined scenes out front, slightly above the heads of your audience, preserving the privacy of the moment. Perhaps you could move out toward the imagined scenes as the dreams become more frenzied; then, as the father's speech interrupts, you could apologetically return to your writing station. At the close of the poem, you might finish the copying, close the pad, and then cast a final glance at him, wondering, as you did at the beginning, why he behaves this way. Or—and this is only one of several other alternatives—you might finish the dicta- tion, close the pad, and let your gaze slowly shift back to that spot where you had just "seen" so much pleasure.

From Us to You
WILLIAM L. COPITHORNE

"I think we ought to write a Christmas letter this year," my wife said at the breakfast table the other morning.

"A what?" I asked warily.

"A Christmas letter. You know, like the kind the Huggins send out to all their friends every year."

I recalled the Huggins' Christmas letters—five-page mimeographed reports on family activities for the preceding year, with the simple greetings of the season all but buried.

I hurried off to work before my wife could pursue the subject any further, but that evening she presented me with a packet of letters including not only the recent efforts of the Huggins but Christmas letters other families had sent us as well. My wife is a saver.

"Now you read these and see if you don't think it would be a good idea for us to do this instead of sending cards this Christmas," she said.

One would have been enough, for the letters were indistinguishable in style and content. Posing innocently as Christmas greetings, they were actually un-abashed family sagas. The writers touched lightly on the misfortunes which their families suffered during the year, dwelt gladly on happy events, and missed no opportunity for self-congratulation.

I haven't the slightest intention of writing a Christmas letter myself, but once I'd put a red or green ribbon in my typewriter I'm sure I could turn one out in no time at all.

"A MERRY CHRISTMAS FROM OUR HOUSE TO YOURS!" is the standard beginning. Centered at the top of an 8½″ × 11″ sheet of paper, it spares the writer the nuisance of penning salutations on the hundred or more copies he will doubtless send out. The exclamation mark is the first of dozens that will be used. No Christmas letter averages fewer than eighteen "!'s," "!!'s," or "(!)'s" a page.

The opening sentence always starts with the word "Well." "Well, here it is Christmas again!" is a favorite; or, "Well, hard as it is to realize, Christmas has rolled round once more!" A somewhat more expansive opening is "Well, Christmas finds us all one year older, but young as ever in the spirit of the Season!" Actually what is said is unimportant as long as the sentence starts with "Well," and ends, of course, with an exclamation mark.

Having taken due note of the season, the Christmas letter-writer works immediately into his first main topic—the accidents which befell him and his family and the diseases they suffered during the year. He writes with cheerful fortitude. Broken arms and legs call forth the reminiscent chuckle, and childhood diseases open the way for humor of a sort. "As it must to all children," the Huggins wrote last Christmas, "the mumps came to Albert Jr. and to Susie.

Fortunately they were taken sick during the spring vacation and didn't miss any school. We don't think they'd agree with our use of the word 'fortunately.' (Ha-ha!)" The parenthetical "Ha-ha!" or simply "Ha!" appears at least once in each paragraph of a Christmas letter.

The writer next reviews the unusual activities of the year—the family's annual vacation at Sunrise Lake, for example. The summer vacation looms large in Christmas letters. Golf scores, size of fish caught, and the successes of the children in swimming and boating contests are good for a page and a half.

A peculiarity of the Christmas letter which the reader may find disconcerting is its inconstant point of view. Most Christmas letters presume to be joint husband-and-wife efforts, but sudden shifts, sometimes within a sentence, to an outsider's point of view are frequent. Writing from his own and his wife Bea's point of view, Jim could say: "We drove to Sunrise Lake in the record time of seven hours and fourteen minutes. Jim was trying to establish a record, and he succeeded, with the help, of course, of the new Mercury which Bea insisted that we have before taking another long trip."

One reason for the use of the shifting point of view is the partial cover-up it affords the writer. Since he devotes a good part of the letter to his achievements of the past year, he must take care to avoid appearing boastful. "He succeeded" sounds better than "I succeeded."

The shifting point of view has its limitations, of course, and when the writer wants to record an especially proud accomplishment he makes use of the footnote. If properly handled, the footnote can actually make him seem to be self-effacing.

Should Jim, for example, want to tell about the big one he caught at Sunrise Lake, he first says that his son, Joey, is the real fisherman in the family—that Joey, in fact, caught a bigger trout than he did last summer. He then writes the following footnote, signing it "Bea": "Jim insists on being a devoted parent. Actually it was *he* who caught the larger trout—a ten-pounder, the biggest, according to the people at the grocery store, that anyone had caught at Sunrise Lake in six years!"

On an average, three footnotes appear at the bottom of each page of a Christmas letter.

The last section of the letter is devoted to such routine matters as recent improvements the writer has made on his house ("With only the part-time help of a chimney pointer, Jim built a fireplace this fall on the north end of our living room") or activities in the community ("Jim is now Captain of our precinct in the Civil Defense program, and Bea has been made Den Mother of Joey's Cub Scout troop. She says she does not plan to hibernate for the winter, however").

An effort obviously is made to keep the tone of the letter humorous, but the underlying seriousness is never lost sight of. If, for a moment, it sinks from view, the writer is quick with a footnote or a "Ha-ha!" to indicate the depth of his irony.

The concluding paragraph of the Christmas letter, like the opening, always begins with the word "Well." "Well, that about sums up our activities for the year" is what the Huggins invariably say, although they make it clear that they have merely scratched the surface by adding: "Of course there was the time back in April when Susie won first prize in the poetry-reciting contest, and in

September when Albert Jr. was elected president of his Junior High School class, but we really must close."

Before signing their names, Christmas letter-writers usually succeed in reminding themselves that their purpose, after all, has been to extend Christmas greetings. "And so, A Merry Christmas to you all!" is the conventional ending, although a few, like the Huggins, prefer the full-blown close. "All of us," they wrote last year, "Albert Sr., Evelyn, Susie, and Albert Jr., join with Tiny Tim in saying, God bless us, every one!' "

As I say, I have no intention of writing one of these letters myself. Come to think of it, though, I never did let old Bill Mason out in Seattle know about that 78 I shot last summer, and I'm sure the Potters down in Shreveport haven't heard how our David talked at nine months and was walking at ten and a half . . .

This humorous essay contains a speaker about whom we know considerably less than we did of Bacon's Mary Milton. It is certain that the speaker is a man and a father and that he is imaginative, observant, and witty. Although the essay as a whole is a telling commentary on the impersonality of a widely spread social practice, the speaker seems innocently free of any rancor. In fact, his tone toward his audience is pleasant and confiding. On the other hand, his attitude toward the subject of a Christmas letter begins as decisively negative, then critically clinical in his analysis, and finally unknowingly accepting, as he feels trapped by the same egotistical needs he had ascribed to others.

In performing this speaker, you could maintain that pleasant and confiding tone with the audience, being direct and casual as the essayist seems to be with his reading audience. You might emphasize these qualities with a great deal of eye contact, approaching your audience as if to say, "Let me show you how ridiculous this practice is—and we'll laugh about it together." The situation in this case would be *open*, the utterances available to a listening, public group.

The three major sections of the essay—the opening narrative, the examination of the typical epistle with its "buried greeting," and the final thoughts of what *he* could put into a letter—should be clearly marked.

With longer pauses and pitch changes, you can separate the first two sections with their *beginning, middle,* and *conclusion* from the short final section that contains only a beginning. To emphasize the three actions, you could be seated when you start to speak, rise when the commentary on the letters begins, and for the last four lines break off the eye contact with the audience, looking out as if thinking aloud.

For a vocal translation of the capitalized line, you could make it bigger and louder, with a Santa Claus kind of cheery boom, accompanied by expansive gestures. As for the exclamation marks, you might vocally "sputter" as your hand traced out the shape of the punctuation. One of several alternatives would be to treat the commentary as a lecture, writing the capitalized greeting on the chalkboard and then itemizing the major points:

1. Opening sentence
2. Accidents
3. Unusual activities
4. Point of view
5. Footnotes
6. Last section
7. Closing

Handled this way, the punctuation marks also can be easily shown on the chalkboard.

Of course, the last four lines do not complete the development of the new thought just introduced. The speaker does not finish; he simply stops. So instead of vocally concluding with a downward inflection, you would leave the matter dangling with a rising or sustained pitch level.

You will want to make a vocal change for the wife and some of the letter's contents, though not so great as to break the illusion that the entire piece is being narrated by the same person, since the other lines are filtered through him.

Just as you were cautioned against performing the effect rather than the reason in "Afternoon in Artillery Walk," you should avoid playing the humor in comedy. Paradoxically, people generally do not laugh when someone is *trying* to be funny. You may consider Archie Bunker funny, but part of the reason is that he is so serious when he responds to Edith, Gloria, and others. His zeal in defending his views is *anormal;* that is, it deviates from the norm of reasonableness. We know this, but Archie does not. He honestly believes in his ideals. *Authors* ridicule, *we* laugh, but in most cases the *speaker* is unaware of the comedy.

Miss Willerton's story (pp. 8–13) is anormally romantic and consequently funny to us—but not to her. Playing the effect of humor is as inimical to the comic spirit as playing the effect of grief is to tragedy. Comic behaviors do not sustain a performance unless they are a believable outgrowth of a particular speaker in a particular environment with a particular reason for saying and doing what she or he does.

Two kinds of warm-ups are often used by performers of humorous literature. The first, externally motivated, is simply to laugh at length, running the gamut from smirking, to smiling, to giggling, to roaring. The second is to perform the speaker's *opposite,* a technique no less helpful in the performance of more serious literature. Remember how you were advised to search for a *match* in your performance of Mary Milton? Here you are looking for an opposite, which is always present somewhere—the childlike behavior in an adult; the parsimonious person's generosity toward himself or herself; the fat person's dreams of being skinny; even the deadly serious matters that in different circumstances would be funny (adults cheerfully playing war games with toy guns).

For "From Us to You," you could begin by asking, "What kind of Christmas greeting would *he* respect?" "What suggestion, if any, does he approve of his wife's making?" As with the imaginative biography, this rehearsal technique will rarely be witnessed by anyone; but many have found it useful in developing their "second plan."

Whether or not a speaker narrates in first or third person sometimes tells us very little, because in either category, we find distinctively different voices. Imagine that someone said "Both 'An Afternoon in Artillery Walk' and 'From Us to You' are written in first person." Though obviously true, the description does not account for the speakers' complexities or the great difference in the degrees to which they are dramatized. Even more common is the assumption that all third-person speakers are detached. Look now at four third-person texts, none of which feature objective speakers.

The Old Gray Couple (1)
ARCHIBALD MACLEISH

They have only to look at each other to laugh—
no one knows why, not even they:
something back in the lives they've lived,
something they both remember but no words can say.

They go off at an evening's end to talk
but they don't, or to sleep but they lie awake—
hardly a word, just a touch, just near,
just listening but not to hear.

Everything they know they know together—
everything, that is, but one:
their lives they've learned like secrets from each other;
their deaths they think of in the nights alone.

Comparing this poem with its companion piece, "The Old Gray Couple (2)" (p. 70), you notice immediately that one is expressed by an unidentified third person and the other by two first-person speakers. The third-person speaker, however, is not much less neutral than the other two. Through the language chosen, that speaker shows interest, concern, and profound understanding of the old couple; his or her tone toward the audience suggests a willingness to share with us a significant observation about what the couple can and cannot share with one another. Some of the ways in which the speaker could be privy to such information are: (1) the speaker, now alone, may have had a similar relationship; (2) the speaker is an omniscient abstract entity, a camera capable of filming even what happens in another's thoughts though it is realistically unknowable; or (3) the speaker is someone close enough to the old couple to detect fairly the outer limits of their ability to communicate with one another.

In the performance, you could approach your audience as if to say respectfully, "I am going to share a description of two people with you; this couple is extremely important to me." You will probably treat the situation as open but diffused, as you seem to be "seeing" both the audience in reality and the couple in your mind's eye.

A Worn Path
EUDORA WELTY

It was December—a bright frozen day in the early morning. Far out in the country there was an old Negro woman with her head tied in a red rag, coming along a path through the pinewoods. Her name was Phoenix Jackson. She was very old and small and she walked slowly in the dark pine shadows, moving a little from side to side in her steps, with the balanced heaviness and lightness of a pendulum in a grandfather clock. She carried a thin, small cane made from an umbrella, and with this she kept tapping the frozen earth in front of her. This made a grave and persistent noise in the still air, that seemed meditative like the chirping of a solitary little bird.

She wore a dark striped dress reaching down to her shoe tops, and an equally long apron of bleached sugar sacks, with a full pocket: all neat and tidy, but every time she took a step she might have fallen over her shoelaces, which dragged from her unlaced shoes. She looked straight ahead. Her eyes were blue with age. Her skin had a pattern all its own of numberless branching wrinkles and as though a whole little tree stood in the middle of her forehead, but a golden color ran underneath, and the two knobs of her cheeks were illumined by a yellow burning under the dark. Under the red rag her hair came down on her neck in the frailest of ringlets, still black, and with an odor like copper.

Now and then there was a quivering in the thicket. Old Phoenix said, "Out of my way, all you foxes, owls, beetles, jack rabbits, coons and wild animals! . . . Keep out from under these feet, little bob-whites. . . Keep the big wild hogs out of my path. Don't let none of those come running my direction. I got a long way." Under her small black-freckled hand her cane, limber as a buggy whip, would switch at the brush as if to rouse up any hiding things.

On she went. The woods were deep and still. The sun made the pine needles almost too bright to look at, up where the wind rocked. The cones dropped as light as feathers. Down in the hollow was the mourning dove—it was not too late for him.

The path ran up the hill. "Seems like there is chains about my feet, time I get this far," she said, in the voice of argument old people keep to use with themselves. "Something always take a hold of me on this hill—pleads I should stay."

After she got to the top she turned and gave a full, severe look behind her where she had come. "Up through pines," she said at length. "Now down through oaks."

Her eyes opened their widest, and she started down gently. But before she got to the botton of the hill a bush caught her dress.

Her fingers were busy and intent, but her skirts were full and long, so that before she could pull them free in one place they were caught in another. It was not possible to allow the dress to tear. "I in the thorny bush," she said. "Thorns, you doing your appointed work. Never want to let folks pass, no sir. Old eyes thought you was a pretty little *green* bush."

Finally, trembling all over, she stood free, and after a moment dared to stoop for her cane.

"Sun so high!" she cried, leaning back and looking, while the thick tears went over her eyes. "The time getting all gone here."

At the foot of this hill was a place where a log was laid across the creek.

"Now come the trial," said Phoenix.

Putting her right foot out, she mounted the log and shut her eyes. Lifting her skirt, leveling her cane fiercely before her, like a festival figure in some parade, she began to march across. Then she opened her eyes and she was safe on the other side.

"I wasn't as old as I thought," she said.

But she sat down to rest. She spread her skirts on the bank around her and folded her hands over her knees. Up above her was a tree in a pearly cloud of mistletoe. She did not dare to close her eyes, and when a little boy brought her a plate with a slice of marble-cake on it she spoke to him. "That would be acceptable," she said. But when she went to take it there was just her own hand in the air.

So she left that tree, and had to go through a barbed-wire fence. There she had to creep and crawl, spreading her knees and stretching her fingers like a baby trying to climb the steps. But she talked loudly to herself: she could not let her dress be torn now, so late in the day, and she could not pay for having her arm or her leg sawed off if she got caught fast where she was.

At last she was safe through the fence and risen up out in the clearing. Big dead trees, like black men with one arm, were standing in the purple stalks of the withered cotton field. There sat a buzzard.

"Who you watching?"

In the furrow she made her way along.

"Glad this not the season for bulls," she said, looking sideways, "and the good Lord made his snakes to curl up and sleep in the winter. A pleasure I don't see no two-headed snake coming around that tree, where it come once. It took a while to get by him, back in the summer."

She passed through the old cotton and went into a field of dead corn. It whispered and shook and was taller than her head. "Through the maze now," she said, for there was no path.

Then there was something tall, black, and skinny there, moving before her.

At first she took it for a man. It could have been a man dancing in the field. But she stood still and listened, and it did not make a sound. It was silent as a ghost.

"Ghost," she said sharply, "who be you the ghost of? For I have heard of nary death close by."

But there was no answer—only the ragged dancing in the wind.

She shut her eyes, reached out her hand, and touched a sleeve. She found a coat and inside that an emptiness, cold as ice.

"You scarecrow," she said. Her face lighted. "I ought to be shut up for good," she said with laughter. "My senses is gone. I too old. I the oldest people I ever know. Dance, old scarecrow," she said, "while I dancing with you."

She kicked her foot over the furrow, and with mouth drawn down, shook her head once or twice in a little strutting way. Some husks blew down and whirled in streamers about her skirts.

Then she went on, parting her way from side to side with the cane, through the whispering field. At last she came to the end, to a wagon track where the silver grass blew between the red ruts. The quail were walking around like pullets, seeming all dainty and unseen.

"Walk pretty," she said. "This the easy place. This the easy going."

She followed the track, swaying through the quiet bare fields, through the little strings of trees silver in their dead leaves, past cabins silver from weather, with the doors and windows boarded shut, all like old women under a spell sitting there. "I walking in their sleep," she said, nodding her head vigorously.

In a ravine she went where a spring was silently flowing through a hollow log. Old Phoenix bent and drank. "Sweet-gum makes the water sweet," she said, and drank more. "Nobody knows who made this well, for it was here when I was born."

The track crossed a swampy part where the moss hung as white as lace from every limb. "Sleep on, alligators, and blow your bubbles." Then the track went into the road.

Deep, deep the road went down between the high green-colored banks. Overhead the live-oaks met, and it was as dark as a cave.

A black dog with a lolling tongue came up out of the weeds by the ditch. She was meditating, and not ready, and when he came at her she only hit him a little with her cane. Over she went in the ditch, like a little puff of milkweed.

Down there, her senses drifted away. A dream visited her, and she reached her hand up, but nothing reached down and gave her a pull. So she lay there and presently went to talking. "Old woman," she said to herself, "that black dog come up out of the weeds to stall you off, and now there he sitting on his fine tail, smiling at you."

A white man finally came along and found her—a hunter, a young man, with his dog on a chain.

"Well, Granny!" he laughed. "What are you doing there?"

"Lying on my back like a June-bug waiting to be turned over, mister," she said, reaching up her hand.

He lifted her up, gave her a swing in the air, and set her down. "Anything broken, Granny?"

"No sir, them old dead weeds is springy enough," said Phoenix, when she had got her breath. "I thank you for your trouble."

"Where do you live, Granny?" he asked, while the two dogs were growling at each other.

"Away back yonder, sir, behind the ridge. You can't even see it from here."

"On your way home?"

"No sir, I going to town."

"Why, that's too far! That's as far as I walk when I come out myself, and I get something for my trouble." He patted the stuffed bag he carried, and there hung down a little closed claw. It was one of the bob-whites, with its beak hooked bitterly to show it was dead. "Now you go on home, Granny!"

"I bound to go to town, mister," said Phoenix. "The time come around."

He gave another laugh, filling the whole landscape. "I know you old colored people! Wouldn't miss going to town to see Santa Claus!"

But something held old Phoenix very still. The deep lines in her face went into a fierce and different radiation. Without warning, she had seen with her own eyes a flashing nickel fall out of the man's pocket onto the ground.

"How old are you, Granny?" he was saying.

"There is no telling, mister," she said, "no telling."

Then she gave a little cry and clapped her hands and said, "Git on away from here, dog! Look! Look at that dog!" She laughed as if in admiration. "He ain't scared of nobody. He a big black dog." She whispered. "Sic him!"

"Watch me get rid of that cur," said the man. "Sic him, Pete! Sic him!"

Phoenix heard the dogs fighting, and heard the man running and throwing sticks. She even heard a gunshot. But she was slowly bending forward by that time, further and further forward, the lids stretched down over her eyes, as if she were doing this in her sleep. Her chin was lowered almost to her knees. The yellow palm of her hand came out from the fold of her apron. Her fingers slid down and along the ground under the piece of money with the grace and care they would have in lifting an egg from under a setting hen. Then she slowly straightened up, she stood erect, and the nickel was in her apron pocket. A bird flew by. Her lips moved. "God watching me the whole time. I come to stealing."

The man came back, and his own dog panted about them. "Well, I scared him off that time," he said, and then he laughed and lifted his gun and pointed it at Phoenix.

She stood straight and faced him.

"Doesn't the gun scare you?" he said, still pointing it.

"No sir, I seen plenty go off closer by, in my day, and for less than what I done," she said, holding utterly still.

He smiled, and shouldered the gun. "Well, Granny," he said, "you must be a hundred years old, and scared of nothing. I'd give you a dime if I had any money with me. But you take my advice and stay home, and nothing will happen to you."

"I bound to go on my way, mister," said Phoenix. She inclined her head in the red rag. Then they went in different directions, but she could hear the gun shooting again and again over the hill.

She walked on. The shadows hung from the oak trees to the road like curtains. Then she smelled wood-smoke, and smelled the river, and she saw a steeple and the cabins on their steep steps. Dozens of little black children whirled around her. There ahead was Natchez shining. Bells were ringing. She walked on.

In the paved city it was Christmas time. There were red and green electric lights strung and criss-crossed everywhere, and all turned on in the daytime. Old Phoenix would have been lost if she had not distrusted her eyesight and depended on her feet to know where to take her.

She paused quietly on the sidewalk where people were passing by. A lady came along in the crowd, carrying an armful of red-, green- and silver-wrapped presents; she gave off perfume like the red roses in hot summer, and Phoenix stopped her.

"Please, missy, will you lace up my shoe?" She held up her foot.

"What do you want, Grandma?"

"See my shoe," said Phoenix. "Do all right for out in the country, but wouldn't look right to go in a big building."

"Stand still then, Grandma," said the lady. She put her packages down on the sidewalk beside her and laced and tied both shoes tightly.

"Can't lace 'em with a cane," said Phoenix. "Thank you, missy. I doesn't mind asking a nice lady to tie up my shoe, when I gets out on the street."

Moving slowly and from side to side, she went into the big building, and into a tower of steps, where she walked up and around and around until her feet knew to stop.

She entered a door, and there she saw nailed up on the wall the document that had been stamped with the gold seal and framed in the gold frame, which matched the dream that was hung up in her head.

"Here I be," she said. There was a fixed and ceremonial stiffness over her body.

"A charity case, I suppose," said an attendant who sat at the desk before her.

But Phoenix only looked above her head. There was sweat on her face, the wrinkles in her skin shone like a bright net.

"Speak up, Grandma," the woman said. "What's your name? We must have your history, you know. Have you been here before? What seems to be the trouble with you?"

Old Phoenix only gave a twitch to her face as if a fly were bothering her.

"Are you deaf?" cried the attendant.

But then the nurse came in.

"Oh, that's just old Aunt Phoenix," she said. "She doesn't come for herself—she has a little grandson. She makes these trips just as regular as clockwork. She lives away back off the Old Natchez Trace." She bent down. "Well, Aunt Phoenix, why don't you just take a seat? We won't keep you standing after your long trip." She pointed.

The old woman sat down, bolt upright in the chair.

"Now, how is the boy?" asked the nurse.

Old Phoenix did not speak.

"I said, how is the boy?"

But Phoenix only waited and stared straight ahead, her face very solemn and withdrawn into rigidity.

"Is his throat any better?" asked the nurse. "Aunt Phoenix, don't you hear me? Is your grandson's throat any better since the last time you came for the medicine?"

With her hands on her knees, the old woman waited, silent, erect and motionless, just as if she were in armor.

"You mustn't take up our time this way, Aunt Phoenix," the nurse said. "Tell us quickly about your grandson, and get it over. He isn't dead, is he?"

At last there came a flicker and then a flame of comprehension across her face, and she spoke.

"My grandson. It was my memory had left me. There I sat and forgot why I made my long trip."

"Forgot?" the nurse frowned. "After you came so far?"

Then Phoenix was like an old woman begging a dignified forgiveness for waking up frightened in the night. "I never did go to school, I was too old at the Surrender," she said in a soft voice. "I'm an old woman without an education. It was my memory fail me. My little grandson, he is just the same, and I forgot it in the coming."

"Throat never heals, does it?" said the nurse, speaking in a loud, sure voice to old Phoenix. By now she had a card with something written on it, a little list. "Yes. Swallowed lye. When was it?—January—two-three years ago—"

Phoenix spoke unasked now. "No, missy, he not dead, he just the same. Every little while his throat begin to close up again, and he not able to swallow. He not get his breath. He not able to help himself. So the time come around, and I go on another trip for the soothing medicine."

"All right. The doctor said as long as you came to get it, you could have it," said the nurse. "But it's an obstinate case."

"My little grandson, he sit up there in the house all wrapped up, waiting by himself," Phoenix went on. "We is the only two left in the world. He suffer and it don't seem to put him back at all. He got a sweet look. He going to last. He wear a little patch quilt and peep out holding his mouth open like a little bird. I remembers so plain now. I not going to forget him again, no, the whole enduring time. I could tell him from all the others in creation."

"All right." The nurse was trying to hush her now. She brought her a little bottle of medicine. "Charity," she said, making a check mark in a book.

Old Phoenix held the bottle close to her eyes, and then carefully put it into her pocket.

"I thank you," she said.

"It's Christmas time, Grandma," said the attendant. Could I give you a few pennies out of my purse?"

"Five pennies is a nickel," said Phoenix stiffly.

"Here's a nickel," said the attendant.

Phoenix rose carefully and held out her hand. She received the nickel and then fished the other nickel out of her pocket and laid it beside the new one. She stared at her palm closely, with her head on one side.

Then she gave a tap with her cane on the floor.

"This is what come to me to do," she said. "I going to the store and buy my child a little windmill they sells, made out of paper. He going to find it hard to believe there such a thing in the world. I'll march myself back where he waiting, holding it straight up in this hand."

She lifted her free hand, gave a little nod, turned around, and walked out of the doctor's office. Then her slow step began on the stairs, going down.

If you enjoyed this story, you would probably be interested in Welty's short essay, "Is Phoenix Jackson's Grandson Really Dead?" in *Critical Inquiry,* 1 (September 1974), 219–221.

As with the speaker of "The Old Gray Couple (1)," the narrator of "A Worn Path" shows great respect for the central character and an eagerness for the audience, too, to know this admirable woman through her actions. The narrator, close to Phoenix Jackson, is trusted because of the numerous comparisons, all honorific, made to Phoenix: "a little bird," "a grandfather clock," "a little tree," "festival figure in a parade," "a baby," and "a little puff of milkwood."

The narrator is undramatized and her or his time and place are undefined, both facts suggesting that the performer treat the story as an open situation. The emphasis is rightly on the dramatized Phoenix and her time and place. The scene of snow, ice, and sunshine reinforces the narrator's impression of Phoenix's purity of spirit. Not until she arrives at the doctor's office do we realize the specific geographical region of the path she followed, around the Old Natchez Trace in central Mississippi. By placing the old, black woman in the South during the 1930s or 1940s, the narrator emphasizes Phoenix's resilience.

This seems to be a good place to mention another rehearsal technique for working with the literature's speaker: tell the experience of the text from a vantage point *other* than the one in the text. Not only will it change your performing behavior; it will affect the language and content as well. It also will help in answering a key question: What difference does it make that the literature employs this particular point of view? If John Milton had been the speaker of "An Afternoon in Artillery Walk," our impression of Mary would certainly change. If Phoenix Jackson told her own story, the effect would perhaps be maudlin, the information would be limited to her observational powers, and much of the thematic significance would be lost.

Madame Zilensky and the King of Finland
CARSON McCULLERS

To Mr. Brook, the head of the music department at Ryder College, was due all the credit for getting Madame Zilensky on the faculty. The college considered itself fortunate; her reputation was impressive, both as a composer and as a pedagogue. Mr. Brook took on himself the responsibility of finding a house for Madame Zilensky, a comfortable place with a garden, which was convenient to the college and next to the apartment house where he himself lived.

No one in Westbridge had known Madame Zilensky before she came. Mr. Brook had seen her pictures in musical journals, and once he had written to her about the authenticity of a certain Buxtehude manuscript. Also, when it was being settled that she was to join the faculty, they had exchanged a few cables and letters on practical affairs. She wrote in a clear, square hand, and the only thing out of the ordinary in these letters was the fact that they contained an occasional reference to objects and persons altogether unknown to Mr. Brook, such as "the yellow cat in Lisbon" or "poor Heinrich." These lapses Mr. Brook put down to the confusion of getting herself and her family out of Europe.

Mr. Brook was a somewhat pastel person; years of Mozart minuets, of explanations about diminished sevenths and minor triads, had given him a watchful vocational patience. For the most part, he kept to himself. He loathed academic fiddle-faddle and committees. Years before, when the music department had decided to gang together and spend the summer in Salzburg, Mr. Brook sneaked out of the arrangement at the last moment and took a solitary trip to Peru. He had a few eccentricities himself and was tolerant of the peculiarities of others; indeed, he rather relished the ridiculous. Often, when confronted with some grave and incongruous situation, he would feel a little inside tickle, which stiffened his long, mild face and sharpened the light in his gray eyes.

Mr. Brook met Madame Zilensky at the Westbridge station a week before the beginning of the fall semester. He recognized her instantly. She was a tall, straight woman with a pale and haggard face. Her eyes were deeply shadowed and she wore her dark, ragged hair pushed back from her forehead. She had large, delicate hands, which were very grubby. About her person as a whole there was something noble and abstract that made Mr. Brook draw back for a moment and stand nervously undoing his cuff links. In spite of her clothes—a long, black skirt and a broken-down old leather jacket—she made an impression of vague elegance. With Madame Zilensky were three children, boys between the ages of ten and six, all blond, blank-eyed, and beautiful. There was one other person, an old woman who turned out later to be the Finnish servant.

This was the group he found at the station. The only luggage they had with them was two immense boxes of manuscripts, the rest of their paraphernalia having been forgotten in the station at Springfield when they changed trains. That is the sort of thing that can happen to anyone. When Mr. Brook got them all into a taxi, he thought the worst difficulties were over, but Madame Zilensky suddenly tried to scramble over his knees and get out of the door.

'My God!' she said. 'I left my—how do you say?—my tick-tick-tick——'

'Your watch?' asked Mr. Brook.

'Oh no!' she said vehemently. 'You know, my tick-tick-tick,' and she waved her forefinger from side to side, pendulum fashion.

'Tick-tick,' said Mr. Brook, putting his hands to his forehead and closing his eyes. 'Could you possibly mean a metronome?'

'Yes! Yes! I think I must have lost it there where we changed trains.'

Mr. Brook managed to quiet her. He even said, with a kind of dazed gallantry, that he would get her another one the next day. But at the time he was bound to admit to himself that there was something curious about this panic over a metronome when there was all the rest of the lost luggage to consider.

The Zilensky ménage moved into the house next door, and on the surface everything was all right. The boys were quiet children. Their names were Sigmund, Boris, and Sammy. They were always together and they followed each other around Indian file, Sigmund usually the first. Among themselves they spoke a desperate-sounding family Esperanto made up of Russian, French, Finnish, German, and English; when other people were around, they were strangely silent. It was not any one thing that the Zilenskys did or said that made Mr. Brook uneasy. There were just little incidents. For example, something about the Zilensky children subconsciously bothered him when they were in a house, and finally he realized that what troubled him was the fact that the Zilensky boys never walked on a rug; they skirted it single file on the bare floor, and if a room was carpeted, they stood in the doorway and did not go inside. Another thing was this: Weeks passed and Madame Zilensky seemed to make no effort to get settled or to furnish the house with anything more than a table and some beds. The front door was left open day and night, and soon the house began to take on a queer, bleak look like that of a place abandoned for years.

The college had every reason to be satisfied with Madame Zilensky. She taught with a fierce insistence. She could become deeply indignant if some Mary Owens or Bernadine Smith would not clean up her Scarlatti trills. She got hold of four pianos for her college studio and set four dazed students to playing Bach fugues together. The racket that came from her end of the department was extraordinary, but Madame Zilensky did not seem to have a nerve in her, and if pure will and effort can get over a musical idea, then Ryder College could not have done better. At night Madame Zilensky worked on her twelfth symphony. She seemed never to sleep; no matter what time of night Mr. Brook happened to look out of his sitting-room window, the light in her studio was always on. No, it was not because of any professional consideration that Mr. Brook became so dubious.

It was in late October when he felt for the first time that something was unmistakably wrong. He had lunched with Madame Zilensky and had enjoyed himself, as she had given him a very detailed account of an African safari she had made in 1928. Later in the afternoon she stopped in at his office and stood rather abstractly in the doorway.

Mr. Brook looked up from his desk and asked, 'Is there anything you want?'

'No, thank you,' said Madame Zilensky. She had a low, beautiful, sombre voice. 'I was only just wondering. You recall the metronome. Do you think perhaps that I might have left it with that French?'

'Who?' asked Mr. Brook.

'Why, that French I was married to,' she answered.

'Frenchman,' Mr. Brook said mildly. He tried to imagine the husband of Madame Zilensky, but his mind refused. He muttered half to himself, 'The father of the children.'

'But no,' said Madame Zilensky with decision. 'The father of Sammy.'

Mr. Brook had a swift prescience. His deepest instincts warned him to say nothing further. Still, his respect for order, his conscience, demanded that he ask, 'And the father of the other two?'

Madame Zilensky put her hand to the back of her head and ruffled up her short, cropped hair. Her face was dreamy, and for several moments she did not answer. Then she said gently, 'Boris is of a Pole who played the piccolo.'

'And Sigmund?' he asked. Mr. Brook looked over his orderly desk, with a stack of corrected papers, the three sharpened pencils, the ivory-elephant paperweight. When he glanced up at Madame Zilensky, she was obviously thinking hard. She gazed around at the corners of the room, her brows lowered and her jaw moving from side to side. At last she said, 'We were discussing the father of Sigmund?'

'Why, no,' said Mr. Brook. 'There is no need to do that.'

Madame Zilensky answered in a voice both dignified and final. 'He was a fellow-countryman.'

Mr. Brook did not care one way or the other. He had no prejudices; people could marry seventeen times and have Chinese children so far as he was concerned. But there was something about this conversation with Madame Zilensky that bothered him. Suddenly he understood. The children didn't look at all like Madame Zilensky, but they looked exactly like each other, and as they all had different fathers, Mr. Brook thought the resemblance astonishing.

But Madame Zilensky had finished with the subject. She zipped up her leather jacket and turned away.

'That is exactly where I left it,' she said, with a quick nod. '*Chez* that French.'

Affairs in the music department were running smoothly. Mr. Brook did not have any serious embarrassments to deal with, such as the harp teacher last year who had finally eloped with a garage mechanic. There was only this nagging apprehension about Madame Zilensky. He could not make out what was wrong in his relations with her or why his feelings were so mixed. To begin with, she was a great globe-trotter, and her conversations were incongruously seasoned with references to far-fetched places. She would go along for days without opening her mouth, prowling through the corridor with her hands in the pockets of her jacket and her face locked in meditation. Then suddenly she would buttonhole Mr. Brook and launch out on a long, volatile monologue, her eyes reckless and bright and her voice warm with eagerness. She would talk about anything or nothing at all. Yet, without exception, there was something queer, in a slanted sort of way, about every episode she ever mentioned. If she spoke of taking Sammy to the barbershop, the impression she created was just as foreign as if she were telling of an afternoon in Bagdad. Mr. Brook could not make it out.

The truth came to him very suddenly, and the truth made everything perfectly clear, or at least clarified the situation. Mr. Brook had come home early and lighted a fire in the little grate in his sitting room. He felt comfortable and at peace that evening. He sat before the fire in his stocking feet, with a volume of William Blake on the table by his side, and he had poured himself a half-glass of apricot brandy. At ten o'clock he was drowsing cozily before the fire, his mind full of cloudy phrases of Mahler and floating half-thoughts. Then all at once, out of this delicate stupor, four words came to his mind: 'The King of Finland.' The words seemed familiar, but for the first moment he could not place them. Then all at once he tracked them down. He had been walking across the campus that afternoon when Madame Zilensky stopped him and began some preposterous rigamarole, to which he had only half listened; he was thinking about the stack of canons turned in by his counterpoint class. Now the words, the inflections of her voice, came back to him with insidious exactitude. Madame Zilensky had started off with the following remark: 'One day, when I was standing in front of a *pâtisserie*, the King of Finland came by in a sled.'

Mr. Brook jerked himself straight in his chair and put down his glass of brandy. The woman was a pathological liar. Almost every word she uttered outside of class was an untruth. If she worked all night, she would go out of her way to tell you she spent the evening at the cinema. It she ate lunch at the Old Tavern, she would be sure to mention that she had lunched with her children at home. The woman was simply a pathological liar, and that accounted for everything.

Mr. Brook cracked his knuckles and got up from his chair. His first reaction was one of exasperation. That day after day Madame Zilensky would have the gall to sit there in his office and deluge him with her outrageous falsehoods! Mr. Brook was intensely provoked. He walked up and down the room, then he went into his kitchenette and made himself a sardine sandwich.

An hour later, as he sat before the fire, his irritation had changed to a scholarly and thoughtful wonder. What he must do, he told himself, was to regard the whole situation impersonally and look on Madame Zilensky as a doctor looks on a sick patient. Her lies were of the guileless sort. She did not dissimulate with any intention to deceive, and the untruths she told were never used to any possible advantage. That was the maddening thing; there was simply no motive behind it all.

Mr. Brook finished off the rest of the brandy. And slowly, when it was almost midnight, a further understanding came to him. The reason for the lies of Madame Zilensky was painful and plain. All her life long Madame Zilensky had worked—at the piano, teaching, and writing those beautiful and immense twelve symphonies. Day and night she had drudged and struggled and thrown her soul into her work, and there was not much of her left over for anything else. Being human, she suffered from this lack and did what she could to make up for it. If she passed the evening bent over a table in the library and later declared that she had spent that time playing cards, it was as though she had managed to do both these things. Through the lies, she lived vicariously. The lies doubled the little of her existence that was left over from work and augmented the little rag end of her personal life.

Mr. Brook looked into the fire, and the face of Madame Zilensky was in his mind—a severe face, with dark, weary eyes and delicately disciplined mouth. He was conscious of a warmth in his chest, and a feeling of pity, protectiveness, and dreadful understanding. For a while he was in a state of lovely confusion.

Later on he brushed his teeth and got into his pajamas. He must be practical. What did this clear up? That French, the Pole with the piccolo, Bagdad? And the children, Sigmund, Boris, and Sammy—who were they? Were they really her children after all, or had she simply rounded them up from somewhere? Mr. Brook polished his spectacles and put them on the table by his bed. He must come to an immediate understanding with her. Otherwise, there would exist in the department a situation which could become most problematical. It was two o'clock. He glanced out of his window and saw that the light in Madame Zilensky's workroom was still on. Mr. Brook got into bed, made terrible faces in the dark, and tried to plan what he would say next day.

Mr. Brook was in his office by eight o'clock. He sat hunched up behind his desk, ready to trap Madame Zilensky as she passed down the corridor. He did not have to wait long, and as soon as he heard her footsteps he called out her name.

Madame Zilensky stood in the doorway. She looked vague and jaded. 'How are you? I had such a fine night's rest,' she said.

'Pray be seated, if you please,' said Mr. Brook. 'I would like a word with you.'

Madame Zilensky put aside her portfolio and leaned back wearily in the armchair across from him. 'Yes?' she asked.

'Yesterday you spoke to me as I was walking across the campus,' he said slowly. 'And if I am not mistaken, I believe you said something about a pastry shop and the King of Finland. Is that correct?'

Madame Zilensky turned her head to one side and stared retrospectively at a corner of the window sill.

'Something about a pastry shop,' he repeated.

Her tired face brightened. 'But of course,' she said eagerly. 'I told you about the time I was standing in front of this shop and the King of Finland——'

'Madame Zilensky!' Mr. Brook cried. 'There *is* no King of Finland.'

Madame Zilensky looked absolutely blank. Then, after an instant, she started off again. 'I was standing in front of Bjarne's *pâtisserie* when I turned away from the cakes and suddenly saw the King of Finland——'

'Madame Zilensky, I just told you that there is no King of Finland.'

'In Helsingfors,' she started off again desperately, and again he let her get as far as the King, and then no further.

'Finland is a democracy,' he said. 'You could not possibly have seen the King of Finland. Therefore, what you have just said is an untruth. A pure untruth.'

Never afterward could Mr. Brook forget the face of Madame Zilensky at that moment. In her eyes there was astonishment, dismay, and a sort of cornered horror. She had the look of one who watches his whole interior world split open and disintegrate.

'It is a pity,' said Mr. Brook with real sympathy.

But Madame Zilensky pulled herself together. She raised her chin and said coldly, 'I am a Finn.'

'That I do not question,' answered Mr. Brook. On second thought, he did question it a little.

'I was born in Finland and I am a Finnish citizen.'

'That may very well be,' said Mr. Brook in a rising voice.

'In the war,' she continued passionately, 'I rode a motorcycle and was a messenger.'

'Your patriotism does not enter into it.'

'Just because I am getting out the first papers——'

'Madame Zilensky!' said Mr. Brook. His hands grasped the edge of the desk. 'That is only an irrelevant issue. The point is that you maintained and testified that you saw—that you saw——' But he could not finish. Her face stopped him. She was deadly pale and there were shadows around her mouth. Her eyes were wide open, doomed, and proud. And Mr. Brook felt suddenly like a murderer. A great commotion of feelings—understanding, remorse, and unreasonable love—made him cover his face with his hands. He could not speak until this agitation in his insides quieted down, and then he said very faintly, 'Yes. Of course. The King of Finland. And was he nice?'

An hour later, Mr. Brook sat looking out of the window of his office. The trees along the quiet Westbridge street were almost bare, and the gray buildings of the college had a calm, sad look. As he idly took in the familiar scene, he noticed the Drakes' old Airedale waddling along down the street. It was a thing he had watched a hundred times before, so what was it that struck him as strange? Then he realized with a kind of cold surprise that the old dog was running along backward. Mr. Brook watched the Airedale until he was out of sight, then resumed his work on the canons which had been turned in by the class in counterpoint.

"Madame Zilensky and the King of Finland" is also written in the third person, but something very different is happening here. The narrator *sounds* like Mr. Brook. In fact, the narrator's characteristics seem to parallel those of Mr. Brook. Both are precise, exact, and duty bound to expose inconsistencies. In short, the narrator may be a third-person version of Mr. Brook, seeming at first to give us completely objective data, but as it turns out, can tell us only as much as Mr. Brook can observe and reflect upon. Performed this way, the narrator *reflects* Mr. Brook to the extent that the story is, metaphorically, *handed* over to him. Then, in a real sense, Mr. Brook is talking about himself in third person.

Such a device is not uncommon. It was recommended by playwright Bertolt Brecht[24] to actors in his Epic Theatre for achieving an "alienation" effect, and it is noted by Robert Breen as a device known well by parents:

A mother talking to her little daughter may say, "Mother doesn't want her little girl to do that," hoping, by the use of "mother" instead of "I," and "her" instead of "my," to depersonalize the relationship and so reduce the emotional intensity inherent in the scene. The depersonalization does not represent the mother's indifference toward her daughter but rather her great concern for creating an atmosphere in which the little girl will *understand* that her mother, as a mother, has responsibilities for the protection of her children, and it is in this role that she speaks.[25]

And Mr. Brook certainly wants to be *understood;* for the benefit of Ryder College, he will go to great lengths to keep the truth intact. Because he is distressed about an apparent lie, he tries to make Madame Zilensky *understand* that she could not possibly have seen the King of Finland. (Of course, we can ask whether he knows that Finland has not always been a democracy!)

Another comment on the use of a first-person speaker in the frame of a third-person narrator occurs in the play, *Miss Margarida's Way.* Miss Margarida repeatedly warns her class about herself in third person: "There is no way you can hide anything from Miss Margarida. Miss Margarida knows what she is talking about. However, Miss Margarida doesn't want to be hard on you."[26] Playwright Roberto Athayde claims that the usage is "indicative of power."[27] Surely Mr. Brook is pow-

[24]Bertolt Brecht, "A New Technique of Acting," trans. Eric Bentley, *Theatre Arts*, 33 (January 1949), 39.

[25]Robert Breen, *Chamber Theatre* (Englewood Cliffs, N.J.: Prentice-Hall, 1978), p. 44.
[26]Roberto Athayde, *Miss Margarida's Way* (Garden City, N.Y.: Doubleday, 1977).
[27]*Ibid.*, p. x.

erful in the sense that he is normally in absolute control of his actions.

If you are convinced of this case, your performance of the story would demonstrate Mr. Brook and not some uninvolved observer. The performer's relationship with the audience would then be determined by the way Mr. Brook approached strangers, walked, talked, etc.

We have dwelt on this matter at some length because performers frequently make a sharp distinction between characters and third person speakers. Such a decision is sometimes warranted, but not always; with "Madame Zilensky and the King of Finland," the *voice* we hear could be that of Mr. Brook.

The Crop
FLANNERY O'CONNOR

(Reread the story on pp. 8–13). The final part of this workshop considers a story in which the speaker "shifts," to use critic and novelist E. M. Forster's terminology. He claims:

A novelist can shift his viewpoint if it comes off, and it came off with Dickens and Tolstoy. Indeed this power to expand and contract perception (of which shifting viewpoint is a symptom), this right to intermittent knowledge:—I find it one of the great advantages of the novel-form, and it has a parallel in our perception of life. We are stupider at some times than others; we can enter into people's minds occasionally but not always, because our minds get tired; and this intermittence lends in the long run variety and colour to the experiences we re-

ceive. A quantity of novelists, English novelists especially, have behaved like this to the people in their books; played fast and loose with them, and I cannot see why they should be censured.[28]

On many occasions, O'Connor's narrator seems quite objective but then moves into a perspective that is Miss Willerton's. For example, in the following quotation, italics mark a speaker who is perhaps somewhat distanced; the other utterances seem distinctly Miss Willerton's:

Miss Willerton sat down at her typewriter and let out her breath. Now! What had she been thinking about? Oh. Bakers. Hmmm. Bakers. No, bakers wouldn't do. Hardly colorful enough. No social tension connected with bakers. *Miss Willerton sat staring through her typewriter. A S D F G—her eyes wandered over the keys.* Hmmm. Teachers?

A "shifting" capability on the part of the speaker is easiest to detect if you read the literature aloud from the beginning. When you are sounding it, you may hear lines or sections that *sound and feel like* a character. On closer examination, you may discover that the lines could be spoken by either a closely observing narrator or by the character.

Your final decision will no doubt be guided by your performing various possibilities and by asking, Could this character say this about himself or herself? The performance decision, even though provisional, is a rewarding challenge to the performer.

[28]E. M. Forster, *Aspects of the Novel* (New York: Harcourt, Brace, 1927), pp. 122–123.

ANTHOLOGY III

The literature following contains a wide range of speakers, scenes, and audiences. Some of them contain quite specific an-

swers to our basic questions: Who is speaking? To whom is the speaker speaking? Where and when is the speaker speaking? In others that contain less detail, you will have to infer the answers by asking: On the basis of the language used, who might be speaking? Who might be addressed? Where and when could this happen? At any rate, make *performing the speaker* a central part of your process in answering the questions.

An Apology for Wolves
PETER WILD

I

They have always
vilified us,
sensing our stealth
and their lack of it,

and moved by the first impulse
of their dim minds,
throw stones, beat shields,
catch us in their iron sights . . .

as if we wanted their women
or would steal their Gods . . .

II

it is true, we've been caught
on occasion with the remnants
of petticoats still in our mouths,
or sporting a red cap, just for a lark.

but we've got a bad press
which capitalizes on such exceptions:
a grandmother or two
coughed up now and then,

and doesn't consider
our loss of face
when driven into the suburbs
by a long winter and heavy snows.

III

actually, it's just a simple lack
of understanding—on their part,
a myopia common
to all muscular animals . . .

we mean no harm
but must pursue
that fine exhilaration
instinctively ours:

flaming tails in bushes
and leaves slipping along our backs.

Identify "they" and "us" of the first two lines. To what children's story does the second stanza of section II refer? How does the speaker use argument and evidence in each of the three sections?

from The Diary of a Young Girl
ANNE FRANK

Dear Kitty,
"Little bundles of contradictions." That's how I ended my last letter and that's how I'm going to begin this one. "A little bundle of contradictions," can you tell me exactly what it is? What does contradiction mean? Like so many words, it can mean two things, contradiction from without and contradiction from within.
The first is the ordinary "not giving in easily, always knowing best, getting in the last word," *enfin,* all the unpleasant qualities for which I'm renowned. The second nobody knows about, that's my own secret.

I've already told you before that I have, as it were, a dual personality. One half embodies my exuberant cheerfulness, making fun of everything, my high-spiritedness, and above all, the way I take everything lightly. This includes not taking offence at a flirtation, a kiss, an embrace, a dirty joke. This side is usually lying in wait and pushes away the other, which is much better, deeper and purer. You must realise that no one knows Anne's better side and that's why most people find me so insufferable.

Certainly, I'm a giddy clown for one afternoon, but then everyone's had enough of me for another month. Really, it's just the same as a love film is for deep-thinking people, simply a diversion, amusing just for once, something which is soon forgotten, not bad, but certainly not good. I loathe having to tell you this, but why shouldn't I, if I know it's true anyway? My lighter superficial side will always be too quick for the deeper side of me and that's why it will always win. You can't imagine how often I've already tried to push this Anne away, to cripple her, to hide her, because after all, she's only half of what's called Anne: but it doesn't work and I know too why it doesn't work.

I'm awfully scared that everyone who knows me as I always am will discover that I have another side, a finer and better side. I'm afraid they'll laugh at me, think I'm ridiculous and sentimental, not take me seriously. I'm used to not being taken seriously but it's only the "light-hearted" Anne that's used to it and can bear it; the "deeper" Anne is too frail for it. Sometimes, if I really compel the good Anne to take the stage for a quarter of an hour, she simply shrivels up as soon as she has to speak, and lets Anne number one take over, and before I realise it, she has disappeared.

Therefore, the nice Anne is never present in company, has not appeared one single time so far, but almost always predominates when we're alone. I know exactly how I'd like to be, how I am too . . . inside. But, alas, I'm only like that for myself. And perhaps that's why, no, I'm sure it's the reason why I say I've got a happy nature within and why other people think I've got a happy nature without. I am guided by the pure Anne within, but outside I'm nothing but a frolicsome little goat who's broken loose.

As I've already said, I never utter my real feelings about anything and that's how I've acquired the reputation of being boy-crazy, a flirt, know-all, reader of love stories. The cheerful Anne laughs about it, gives cheeky answers, shrugs her shoulders indifferently, behaves as if she doesn't care, but, oh dearie me, the quiet Anne's reactions are just the opposite. If I'm to be quite honest, then I must admit that it does hurt me, that I try terribly hard to change myself, but that I'm always fighting against a more powerful enemy.

A voice sobs within me: "There you are, that's what's become of you: you're uncharitable, you look supercilious and peevish, people dislike you and all because you won't listen to the advice given you by your own better half." Oh, I would like to listen, but it doesn't work; if I'm quiet and serious, everyone thinks it's a new comedy and then I have to get out of it by turning it into a joke, not to mention my own family, who are sure to think I'm ill, make me swallow pills for headaches and nerves, feel my neck and my head to see whether I'm running a temperature, ask if I'm constipated and criticise me for being in a bad mood. I can't keep that up: if I'm watched to that extent, I start by getting snappy, then unhappy, and finally I twist my heart round again, so

that the bad is on the outside and the good is on the inside, and keep on trying
to find a way of becoming what I would so like to be and what I could be, if
. . . there weren't any other people living in the world.

Yours,
Anne

Performers often find it helpful to examine the literature's speakers *as if* they were something else—a color, a piece of music, an odor, an animal, an object. In this selection, Anne compares her outer self to what? Does the *metaphor* give you additional clues about that behavior? How will you distinguish between (1) Anne's writing to Kitty about her "selves" and (2) Anne's relating to Kitty how one self talks to the other? Does your knowing that Anne and her family are hiding from the Nazis who will later discover them influence your response to her self-examination?

The Bad Daddy
REED WHITTEMORE

The bad daddy who has been angry with the whole family, one by one,
Now retires to his study to be sullen and think of death.
He has aches in his neck and stomach that he is afraid to see the doctor about.
He has a sense of his mind's slopping off into fuzz.
He feels that he is becoming allergic to cigarettes,
That he can't digest steak, that he needs glasses, that he is impotent.
He knows he is bored by his friends, bored by novels, Shakespeare, youth.
He thinks that if it rains one more day he will kill himself.
He lies on the cot in his study covered by a child's security blanket too short to
    sleep under,
And he improvises idly, a few two-minute commercials for a different life,
    thus:

Dear Son: In the war between the Earthmen and the Martians,
Keep your feet dry, your messkit clean, your weapons oiled.
Get plenty of sleep, drink not nor fornicate, speak
When spoken to, write home once a week, get to know your chaplain.
If upon your return I should be wandering amid the shades of the departed,
Call the president of the bank who will deliver to you
A sealed manila envelope containing three french hens, two turtle doves
And your further instructions. Vale. Your sire.

Dear Mathilda: Though we have not spoken a word to each other for thirteen
    years,
We are sympatico, you and I. We commune across the miles; we yearn; we
    dote.
I watch you drive away in your furs in the Rolls to the shoe shop.
I hear you banging pots and pans in the bunker,
And my heart, woman, twitches and the salt tears come,
Tum-te-tum. Your Daddy-o.

Dearest Daughter: It was good, awfully good to have that nice little note from
  you.
Jimmy danced up and down, Mama had tears in her eyes.
We pulled out the scrapbook
And found that the last time you wrote was your fifteenth birthday,
When you were pregnant. Remember?
And now you write that you've won the Insurgents' Prize,
And at Berkeley! Of course we're terribly proud.
But as old-fashioned moralists we doubt the wisdom of compliments,
And anyway you should know that your mother and I
Really think you're a frightful bitch. Love. Dad.

So now the bad Daddy feels much more like himself.
His typewriter pants pleasantly in its shed; the beast is fed.
Down the long waste of his years he sees, suddenly, violets.
He picks them and crushes them gently, and is at peace.
Gettem all, bad daddy, and sleep now.

Is the Bad Daddy speaking only in the letters, or is the speaker a *reflector* of him even in the first stanza? What about the final stanza? What *tone* and what *attitude* will you try to assume for each of the three letters?

How could you physically emphasize a distinction between the five stanzas? The letters abound in exaggeration or *hyperbole*. As a variation on an exercise suggested in the workshop—performing the speaker's opposite—try voicing the Bad Daddy's complaints in neutral or understated language.

no assistance
NTOZAKE SHANGE

without any assistance or guidance from you
i have loved you assiduously for 8 months 2 wks & a day
i have been stood up four times
i've left 7 packages on yr doorstep
forty poems 2 plants & 3 handmade notecards i left
town so i cd send to you have been no help to me
on my job
you call at 3:00 in the morning on weekdays
so i cd drive 27½ miles cross the bay before i go to work
charmin charmin
but you are of no assistance
i want you to know
this waz an experiment
to see how selfish i cd be
if i wd really carry on to snare a possible lover
if i waz capable of debasin my self for the love of another
if i cd stand not being wanted

when i wanted to be wanted
& i cannot
so
with no further assistance & no guidance from you
i am endin this affair

this note is attached to a plant
i've been waterin since the day i met you
you may water it
yr damn self

How does the speaker feel about her decision? Pleased? Calm? Amused? Angry? A combination of these? When you rehearse the poem, if you pay close attention to the line endings (short pauses or prolonging final sounds), what effect does this pace have on the speaker's *tone* and *attitude*?

Her Story
NAOMI LONG MADGETT

They gave me the wrong name, in the first place.
They named me Grace and waited for a light and agile dancer.
But some trick of the genes mixed me up
And instead I turned out big and black and burly.

In the second place, I fashioned the wrong dreams.
I wanted to dress like Juliet and act
Before applauding audiences on Broadway.
I learned more about Shakespeare than he knew about himself.
But, of course, all that was impossible.
"Talent, yes," they would tell me,
"But an actress has to look the part."
So I ended up waiting on tables in Harlem
And hearing uncouth men yell at me:
"Hey, momma, you can cancel that hamburger
And come on up to 102."

In the third place, I tried the wrong solution.
The stuff I drank made me deathly sick
And someone called a doctor.
Next time I'll try a gun.

Both this poem and the story that follows treat incidents from a young woman's *point of view*. In both cases, the speaker is a major participant in the occurrences related. A key decision for performing both lies in the audience: To whom would they—or could they—tell their stories? A real individual or group? An imagined one? Only to themselves?

My Sister's Marriage
CYNTHIA RICH

When my mother died she left just Olive and me to take care of Father. Yesterday when I burned the package of Olive's letters that left only me. I know that you'll side with my sister in all of this because you're only outsiders, and strangers can afford to sympathize with young love, and with whatever sounds daring and romantic, without thinking what it does to all the other people involved. I don't want you to hate my sister—I don't hate her—but I do want you to see that we're happier this way, Father and I, and as for Olive, she made her choice.

But if you weren't strangers, all of you, I wouldn't be able to tell you about this. "Keep yourself to yourself," my father has always said. "If you ever have worries, Sarah Ann, you come to me and don't go sharing your problems around town." And that's what I've always done. So if I knew you I certainly wouldn't ever tell you about Olive throwing the hairbrush, or about finding the letters buried in the back of the drawer.

I don't know what made Olive the way she is. We grew up together like twins—there were people who thought we were—and every morning before we went to school she plaited my hair and I plaited hers before the same mirror, in the same little twist of ribbons and braids behind our heads. We wore the same dresses and there was never a strain on the hem or a rip in our stockings to say to a stranger that we had lost our mother. And although we have never been well-to-do—my father is a doctor and his patients often can't pay— I know that there are people here in Conkling today who think we're rich, just because of little things like candlelight at dinner and my father's cigarette holder and the piano lessons that Olive and I had and the reproduction of *The Anatomy Lesson* that hangs above the mantelpiece instead of botanical prints. "You don't have to be rich to be a gentleman," my father says, "or to live like one."

My father is a gentleman and he raised Olive and myself as ladies. I can hear you laughing, because people like to make fun of words like "gentleman" and "lady," but they are words with ideals and standards behind them, and I hope that I will always hold to those ideals as my father taught me to. If Olive has renounced them, at least we did all we could.

Perhaps the reason that I can't understand Olive is that I have never been in love. I know that if I had ever fallen in love it would not have been, like Olive, at first sight but only after a long acquaintance. My father knew my mother for seven years before he proposed—it is much the safest way. Nowadays people make fun of that too, and the magazines are full of stories about people meeting in the moonlight and marrying the next morning, but if you read those stories you know that they are not the sort of people you would want to be like.

Even today Olive couldn't deny that we had a happy childhood. She used to be very proud of being the lady of the house, of sitting across the candlelight from my father at dinner like a little wife. Sometimes my father would hold his carving knife poised above the roast to stand smiling at her and say: "Olive, every day you remind me more of your mother."

I think that although she liked the smile, she minded the compliment, because she didn't like to hear about Mother. Once when my father spoke of her she said: "Papa, you're missing Mother again. I can't bear it when you miss Mother. Don't I take care of you all right? Don't I make things happy for you?" It wasn't that she hadn't loved Mother but that she wanted my father to be completely happy.

To tell the truth, it was Olive Father loved best. There was a time when I couldn't have said that, it would have hurt me too much. Taking care of our father was like playing a long game of "let's pretend," and when little girls play family nobody wants to be the children. I thought it wasn't fair, just because Olive was three years older, that she should always be the mother. I wanted to sit opposite my father at dinner and have him smile at me like that.

I was glad when Olive first began walking out with young men in the summer evenings. Then I would make lemonade for my father ("Is it as good as Olive's?") and we would sit out on the screened porch together watching the fireflies. I asked him about the patients he had seen that day, trying to think of questions as intelligent as Olive's. I knew that he was missing her and frowning into the long twilight for the swing of her white skirts. When she came up the steps he said, "I missed my housewife tonight," just as though I hadn't made the lemonade right after all. She knew, too, that it wasn't the same for him in the evenings without her and for a while, instead of going out, she brought the young men to the house. But soon she stopped even that ("I never realized how silly and shallow they were until I saw them with Papa," she said. "I was ashamed to have him talk to them"). I know that he was glad, and when my turn came I didn't want to go out because I hated leaving them alone together. It all seems a very long time ago. I used to hate it when Olive "mothered" me. Now I feel a little like Olive's mother, and she is like my rebellious child.

In spite of everything, I loved Olive. When we were children we used to play together. The other children disliked us because we talked like grownups and didn't like to get dirty, but we were happy playing by ourselves on the front lawn where my father, if he were home, could watch us from his study window. So it wasn't surprising that when we grew older we were still best friends. I loved Olive and I see now how she took advantage of that love. Sometimes I think she felt that if she was to betray my father she wanted me to betray him too.

I still believe that it all began, not really with Mr. Dixon, but with the foreign stamps. She didn't see many of them, those years after high school when she was working in the post office, because not very many people in Conkling have friends abroad, but the ones she saw—and even the postmarks from Chicago or California—made her dream. She told her dreams to Father, and of course, he understood and said that perhaps some summer we could take a trip to New England as far as Boston. My father hasn't lived in Conkling all of his life. He went to Harvard, and that is one reason he is different from the other men here. He is a scholar and not bound to provincial ideas. People here respect him and come to him for advice.

Olive wasn't satisfied and she began to rebel. Even she admitted that there wasn't anything for her to rebel against. She told me about it, sitting on the window sill in her long white nightgown, braiding and unbraiding the hair that she had never cut.

"It's not, don't you see, that I don't love Father. And it certainly isn't that

I'm not happy here. But what I mean is, how can I ever know whether or not I'm really happy here unless I go somewhere else? When you graduate from school you'll feel the same way. You'll want—you'll want to know."

"I like it here," I said from the darkness of the room, but she didn't hear me.

"You know what I'm going to do, Sarah Ann? Do you know what I'm going to do? I'm going to save some money and go on a little trip—it wouldn't have to be expensive, I could go by bus—and I'll just see things, and then maybe I'll know."

"Father promised he'd take us to New England."

"No," said Olive, "no, you don't understand. Anyhow, I'll save the money."

And still she wasn't satisfied. She began to read. Olive and I always did well in school, and our names were called out for Special Recognition on Class Day. Miss Singleton wanted Olive to go to drama school after she played the part of Miranda in *The Tempest,* but my father talked to her, and when he told her what an actress' life is like she realized it wasn't what she wanted. Aside from books for school, though, we never read very much. We didn't need to because my father has read everything you've heard of, and people in town have said that talking to him about anything is better than reading three books.

Still, Olive decided to read. She would choose a book from my father's library and go into the kitchen, where the air was still heavy and hot from dinner, and sit on the very edge of the tall, hard three-legged stool. She had an idea that if she sat in a comfortable chair in the parlor she would not be attentive or would skip the difficult passages. So she would sit like that for hours, under the hard light of the unshaded bulb that hangs from the ceiling, until her arms ached from holding the book.

"What do you want to find out about?" my father would ask.

"Nothing," Olive said. "I'm just reading."

My father hates evasion.

"Now, Olive, nobody reads without a purpose. If you're interested in something, maybe I can help you. I might even know something about it myself."

When she came into our bedroom she threw the book on the quilt and said: "Why does he have to pry, Sarah Ann? It's so simple—just wanting to read a book. Why does he have to make a fuss about it as though I were trying to hide something from him?"

That was the first time that I felt a little like Olive's mother.

"But he's only taking an interest," I said. "He just wants us to share things with him. Lots of fathers wouldn't even care. You don't know how lucky we are."

"You don't understand, Sarah Ann. You're too young to understand."

"Of course I understand," I said shortly. "Only I've outgrown feeling like that."

It was true. When I was a little girl I wrote something on a piece of paper, something that didn't matter much, but it mattered to me because it was a private thought. My father came into my room and saw me shove the paper under the blotter, and he wanted me to show it to him. So I quickly said, "No, it's private, I wrote it to myself, I didn't write it to be seen," but he said he wanted to see it. And I said, "No, no, no, it was silly anyway," and he said, "Sarah Ann, nothing you have to say would seem silly to me, you never give me credit for understanding. I can understand a great deal," but I said it wasn't just him, really it wasn't, because I hadn't written it for anyone at all to see. Then he was all sad and hurt and said this wasn't a family where we kept things hidden and there I was hiding this from him. I heard his voice, and it went on and on, and he said I had no faith in him and that I shouldn't keep things from him—and I said it wasn't anything big or special, it was just some silly nonsense, but if it was nonsense, he said, why wouldn't I let him read it, since it would make him happy? And I cried and cried, because it was only a very little piece of paper and why did he have to see it anyway, but he was very solemn and said if you held back little things soon you would be holding back bigger things and the gap would grow wider and wider. So I gave him the paper. He read it and said nothing except that I was a good girl and he couldn't see what all the fuss had been about.

Of course now I know that he was only taking an interest and I shouldn't have minded that. But I was a little girl then and minded dreadfully, and that is why I understood how Olive felt, although she was grown-up then and should have known better.

She must have understood that she was being childish, because when my father came in a few minutes later and said, "Olive, you're our little mother. We mustn't quarrel. There should be only love between us," she rose and kissed him. She told him about the book she had been reading, and he said: "Well, as it happens, I do know something about that." They sat for a long time discussing the book, and I think he loved Olive better than ever. The next evening, instead of shutting herself in the bright, hot kitchen, Olive sat with us in the cool of the parlor until bedtime, hemming a slip. And it was just as always.

But I suppose that these things really had made a difference in Olive. For we had always been alike, and I cannot imagine allowing a perfect stranger to ask me personal questions before we had even been introduced. She told me about it afterward, how he had bought a book of three-cent stamps and stayed to chat through the half-open grilled window. Suddenly he said, quite seriously: "Why do you wear your hair like that?"

"Pardon me?" said Olive.

"Why do you wear your hair like that? You ought to shake it loose around your shoulders. It must be yards long."

That is when I would have remembered—if I had forgotten—that I was a lady. I would have closed the grill, not rudely but just firmly enough to show my displeasure, and gone back to my desk. Olive told me she thought of doing that but she looked at him and knew, she said, that he didn't mean to be impolite, that he really wanted to know.

And instead she said: "I only wear it down at night."

That afternoon he walked her home from the post office.

Olive told me everything long before my father knew anything. It was the beginning of an unwholesome deceit in her. And it was nearly a week later that she told even me. By that time he was meeting her every afternoon and they took long walks together, as far as Merton's Pond, before she came home to set the dinner table.

"Only don't tell Father," she said.

"Why not?"

"I think I'm afraid of him. I don't know why. I'm afraid of what he might say."

"He won't say anything," I said. "Unless there's something wrong. And if there's something wrong, wouldn't you want to know?"

Of course, I should have told Father myself right away. But that was how she played upon my love for her.

"I'm telling you," she said, "because I want so much to share it with you. I'm so happy, Sarah Ann, and I feel so free, don't you see? We've always been so close—I've been closer to you than to Father, I think—or at least differently." She had to qualify it, you see, because it wasn't true. But it still made me happy and I promised not to tell, and I was even glad for her because, as I've told you, I've always loved Olive.

I saw them together one day when I was coming home from school. They were walking together in the rain, holding hands like school children, and when Olive saw me from a distance she dropped his hand suddenly and then just as suddenly took it again.

"Hullo!" he said when she introduced us. "She does look like you!"

I want to be fair and honest with you—it is Olive's dishonesty that still shocks me—and so I will say that I liked Mr. Dixon that day. But I thought even then how different he was from my father, and that should have warned me. He was a big man with a square face and sun-bleached hair. I could see a glimpse of his bright, speckled tie under his tan raincoat, and his laugh sounded warm and easy in the rain. I liked him, I suppose, for the very things I should have distrusted in him. I liked his ease and the way that he accepted me immediately, spontaneously and freely, without waiting—waiting for whatever people wait for when they hold themselves back (as I should have done) to find out more about you. I could almost understand what had made Olive, after five minutes, tell him how she wore her hair at night.

I am glad, at least, that I begged Olive to tell my father about him. I couldn't understand why at first she refused. I think now that she was afraid of seeing them together, that she was afraid of seeing the difference. I have told you that my father is a gentleman. Even now you must be able to tell what sort of man Mr. Dixon was. My father knew at once, without even meeting him.

The weeks had passed and Olive told me that Mr. Dixon's business was completed but that his vacation was coming and he planned to spend it in Conkling. She said she would tell my father.

We were sitting on the porch after dinner. The evening had just begun to thicken and some children had wandered down the road, playing a game of pirates at the very edge of our lawn. One of them had a long paper sword and the others were waving tall sticks, and they were screaming. My father had to raise his voice to be heard.

"So this man whom you have been seeing behind my back is a traveling salesman for Miracle-wear soles."

"Surrender in the name of the King!"

"I am more than surprised at you, Olive. That hardly sounds like the kind of man you would want to be associated with."

"Why not?" said Olive. "Why not?"

"It's notorious, my dear. Men like that have no respect for a girl. They'll flatter her with slick words but it doesn't mean anything. Just take my word for it, dear. It may seem hard, but I know the world."

Fight to the death! Fight to the death!"

"I can't hear you, my dear. Sarah Ann, ask those children to play their games somewhere else."

I went down the steps and across the lawn.

"Doctor Landis is trying to rest after a long day," I explained. They nodded and vanished down the dusky road, brandishing their silent swords.

"I am saying nothing of the extraordinary manner of your meeting, not even of the deceitful way in which he has carried on this—friendship."

It was dark on the porch. I switched on the yellow overhead light, and the three of us blinked for a moment, rediscovering each other as the shadows leaped back.

"The cheapness of it is so apparent it amazes me that even in your innocence of the world—"

My father was fitting a cigarette into its black holder. He turned it slowly to and fro until it was firm before he struck a match and lit it. It is beautiful to watch him do even the most trivial things. He is always in control of himself and he never makes a useless gesture or thinks a useless thought. If you met him you might believe at first that he was totally relaxed, but because I have lived with him so long I know that there is at all times a tension controlling his body; you can feel it when you touch his hand. Tension, I think, is the wrong word. It is rather a self-awareness, as though not a muscle contracted without his conscious knowledge.

"You know it very well yourself, Olive. Could anything but shame have kept you from bringing this man to your home?"

His voice is like the way he moves. It is clear and considered and each word exists by itself. However common it may be, when he speaks it, it has become his, it has dignity because he has chosen it.

"Father, all I ask is that you'll have him here—that you will meet him. Surely that's not too much to ask before you—judge him."

Olive sat on the step at my father's feet. Her hands had been moving across her skirt, smoothing the folds over her knees, but when she spoke she clasped them tightly in her lap. She was trying to speak as he spoke, in that calm, certain voice, but it was a poor imitation.

"I'm afraid that it is too much to ask, Olive. I have seen too many of his kind to take any interest in seeing another."

"I think you should see him, Father." She spoke very softly. "I think I am in love with him."

"Olive!" I said. I had known it all along, of course, but when she spoke it, in that voice trying so childishly to sound sure, I knew its absurdity. How could she say it after Father had made it so clear? As soon as he had repeated after her, "A salesman for Miracle-wear soles," even the inflections of his voice showed me that it was ludicrous; I realized what I had known all along, the cheapness of it all for Olive—for Olive with her ideals.

I looked across at my father but he had not stirred. The moths brushed their wings against the light bulb. He flicked a long gray ash.

"Don't use that word lightly, Olive," he said. "That is a sacred word. Love is the word for what I felt for your mother—what I hope you feel for me and your sister. You mustn't confuse it with innocent infatuation."

"But I do love him—how can you know? How can you know anything about it? I do love him." Her voice was shrill and not pleasant.

"Olive," said my father. "I must ask you not to use that word."

She sat looking up at his face and from his chair he looked back at her. Then she rose and went into the house. He did not follow her, even with his eyes. We sat for a long time before I went over to him and took his hand. I think he had forgotten me. He started and said nothing, and his hand did not acknowledge mine. I would rather he had slapped me. I left him and went into the house.

In our bedroom Olive was sitting before the dressing table in her nightgown, brushing her hair. You mustn't think I don't love her, that I didn't love her then. As I say, we were like twins, and when I saw her reflection in the tall, gilded mirror I might have been seeing my own eyes filled with tears. I tell you, I wanted to put my arms around her, but you must see that it was for her own sake that I didn't. She had done wrong, she had deceived my father and she had made me deceive him. It would have been wicked to give her sympathy then.

"It's hard, of course, Olive," I said gently. "But you know that Father's right."

She didn't answer. She brushed her hair in long strokes and it rose on the air. She did not turn even when the doorknob rattled and my father stood in the doorway and quietly spoke her name.

"Olive," he repeated. "Of course I must ask you not to see this—this man again."

Olive turned suddenly with her dark hair whirling about her head. She hurled the silver hairbrush at my father, and in that single moment when it leaped from her hand I felt an elation I have never known before. Then I heard it clatter to the floor a few feet from where he stood, and I knew that he was unhurt and that it was I, and not Olive, who had for that single moment meant it to strike him. I longed to throw my arms about him and beg his forgiveness.

He went over and picked up the brush and gave it to Olive. Then he left the room.

"How could you, Olive?" I whispered.

She sat with the brush in her hand. Her hair had fallen all about her face and her eyes were dark and bright. The next morning at breakfast she did not speak to my father and he did not speak to her, although he sat looking at her so intensely that if I had been Olive I would have blushed. I thought, He loves her more now, this morning, than when he used to smile and say she was like Mother. I remember thinking, Why couldn't he love me like that? I would never hurt him.

Just before she left for work he went over to her and brushed her arm lightly with his hand.

"We'll talk it all over tonight, Olive," he said. "I know you will understand that this is best."

She looked down at his hand as though it were a strange animal and shook her head and hurried down the porch steps.

That night she called from a little town outside of Richmond to say that she was married. I stood behind my father in the shadowy little hallway as he spoke to her. I could hear her voice, higher-pitched than usual over the static of the wires, and I heard her say that they would come, that very evening, if he would see them.

I almost thought he hadn't understood her, his voice was so calm.

"I suppose you want my blessings. I cannot give them to deceit and cowardice. You will have to find them elsewhere if you can, my dear. If you can."

After he had replaced the receiver he still stood before the mouthpiece, talking into it.

"That she would give up all she has had—that she would stoop to a—for a—physical attraction—"

Then he turned to me. His eyes were dark.

"Why are you crying?" he said suddenly. "What are you crying for? She's made her choice. Am I crying? Do you think I would want to see her—now? If she—when she comes to see what she has done—but it's not a question of forgiveness. Even then it wouldn't be the same. She has made her choice."

He stood looking at me and I thought at first that what he saw was distasteful to him, but his voice was gentle when he spoke.

"Would you have done this to me, Sarah Ann? Would you have done it?"

"No," I said, and I was almost joyful, knowing it was true. "Oh, no."

That was a year ago. We never speak of Olive any more. At first letters used to come from her, long letters from New York and then from Chicago. Always she asked me about Father and whether he would read a letter if she wrote one. I wrote her long letters back and said that I would talk to him. But he wasn't well—even now he has to stay in bed for days at a time—and I knew that he didn't want to hear her name.

One morning he came into my room while I was writing to her. He saw me thrust the package of letters into a cubbyhole and I knew I had betrayed him again.

"Don't ally yourself with deception, Sarah Ann," he said quietly. "You did that once and you see what came of it."

"But if she writes to me—" I said. "What do you want me to do?"

He stood in the doorway in his long bathrobe. He had been in bed and his hair was slightly awry from the pillows and his face was a little pale. I have taken good care of him and he still looks young—not more than forty—but his cheekbones worry me. They are sharp and white.

"I want you to give me her letters," he said. "To burn."

"Won't you read them, Father? I know that what she did was wrong, but she sounds happy—"

I don't know what made me say that except, you see, I did love Olive.

He stared at me and came into the room.

"And you believe her? Do you think that happiness can come from deception?"

"But she's my sister," I said, and although I knew that he was right I began to cry. "And she's your daughter. And you love her so."

He came and stood beside my chair. This time he didn't ask me why I was crying.

He kneeled suddenly beside me and spoke very softly and quickly.

"We'll keep each other company, Sarah Ann, just the two of us. We can be happy that way, can't we? We'll always have each other, don't you know?" He put his hand on my hair.

I knew then that was the way it should be. I leaned my head on his shoulder, and when I finished crying I smiled at him and gave him Olive's letters.

"You take them," I said. "I can't—"

He nodded and took them and then took my hand.

I know that when he took them he meant to burn them. I found them by chance yesterday in the back of his desk drawer, under a pile of old medical reports. They lay there like love letters from someone who had died or moved away. They were tied in a slim green hair ribbon—it was one of mine, but I suppose he had found it and thought it was Olive's.

I didn't wonder what to do. It wasn't fair, don't you see? He hadn't any right to keep those letters after he told me I was the only daughter he had left. He would always be secretly reading them and fingering them, and it wouldn't do him any good. I took them to the incinerator in the back yard and burned them carefully, one by one. His bed is by the window and I know that he was watching me, but of course he couldn't say anything.

Maybe you feel sorry for Father, maybe you think I was cruel. But I did it for his sake and I don't care what you think because you're all of you strangers, anyway, and you can't understand that there couldn't be two of us. As I said before, I don't hate Olive. But sometimes I think this is the way it was meant to be. First Mother died and left just the two of us to take care of Father. And yesterday when I burned Olive's letters I thought, Now there is only me.

In what way does the significance of the title change as the story progresses? Describe, in a chart perhaps, the *tensions* that exist or develop between Sarah Ann and Olive, Olive and their father, and Sarah Ann and their father.

How much time has elapsed between the burning of the letters and the telling of the story? Would the time influence Sarah Ann's *attitude*?

Love Poem
JOHN FREDERICK NIMS

My clumsiest dear, whose hands
    shipwreck vases,
At whose quick touch all glasses chip and
    ring,
Whose palms are bulls in china, burs in
    linen,
And have no cunning with any soft thing

Except all ill at ease fidgeting people:
The refugee uncertain at the door
You make at home; deftly you steady

The drunk clambering on his undulant
    floor.

Unpredictable dear, the taxi drivers'
    terror,
Shrinking from far headlights pale as a
    dime
Yet leaping before red apoplectic
    streetcars—
Misfit in any space. And never on
    time.

A wrench in clocks and the solar system.
    Only
With words and people and love you
    move at ease.
In traffic of wit expertly manoeuvre
And keep us, all devotion, at your knees.

Forgetting your coffee spreading on our
    flannel,
Your lipstick grinning on our coat,
So gayly in love's unbreakable heaven
Our souls on glory of spilt bourbon float.

Be with me darling early and late. Smash
    glasses—

I will study wry music for your sake.
For should your hands drop white and
    empty
All the toys of the world would break.

For "Love Poem," characterize the person addressed. Is she present? Describe the various *tensions* in the poem. How does the speaker's plea in stanza 6 relate to the preceding stanzas, and how would you demonstrate your answer in performance?

.05
ISHMAEL REED

If i had a nickel
For all the women who've
Rejected me in my life
I would be the head of the
World Bank with a flunkie
To hold my derby as i
Prepared to fly chartered
Jet to sign a check
Giving India a new lease
On life

If i had a nickel for
All the women who've loved
Me in my life i would be
The World Bank's assistant

Janitor and wouldn't need
To wear a derby
All i'd think about would
Be going home

Speakers in literature are variously defined, some in great detail, as in a realistic painting, and others with minimal detail, as in a Japanese ink drawing. The speaker in ".05" is one of the latter. His *attitude* toward the *subject,* announced in the title, is clear; but just who he is and where he is speaking is not. What can you infer about him and his scene?

Next Day
RANDALL JARRELL

Moving from Cheer to Joy, from Joy to
    All,
I take a box
And add it to my wild rice, my Cornish
    game hens.
The slacked or shorted, basketed,
    identical
Food-gathering flocks

Are selves I overlook. Wisdom, said
    William James,

Is learning what to overlook. And I am
    wise
If that is wisdom.
Yet somehow, as I buy All from these
    shelves

And the boy takes it to my station wagon,
What I've become
Troubles me even if I shut my eyes.

When I was young and miserable and
    pretty
And poor, I'd wish
What all girls wish: to have a husband,
A house and children. Now that I'm old,
    my wish
Is womanish:
That the boy putting groceries in my car

See me. It bewilders me he doesn't see
    me.
For so many years
I was good enough to eat: the world
    looked at me
And its mouth watered. How often they
    have undressed me,
The eyes of strangers!
And, holding their flesh within my flesh,
    their vile

Imaginings within my imagining,
I too have taken
The chance of life. Now the boy pats my
    dog
And we start home. Now I am good.
The last mistaken,
Ecstatic, accidental bliss, the blind

Happiness that, bursting, leaves upon the
    palm
Some soap and water—
It was so long ago, back in some Gay
Twenties, Nineties, I don't know . . .
    Today I miss
My lovely daughter
Away at school, my sons away at school,

My husband away at work—I wish for
    them.
The dog, the maid,
And I go through the sure unvarying
    days
At home in them. As I look at my life,
I am afraid

Only that it will change, as I am
    changing:

I am afraid, this morning, of my face.
It looks at me.
From the rear-view mirror, with the eyes
    I hate,
The smile I hate. Its plain, lined look
Of gray discovery
Repeats to me: "You're old." That's all,
    I'm old.

And yet I'm afraid, as I was at the
    funeral
I went to yesterday.
My friend's cold made-up face, granite
    among its flowers,
Her undressed, operated on, dressed
    body
Were my face and body.
As I think of her I hear her telling me

How young I seem; I *am* exceptional
I think of all I have.
But really no one is exceptional,
No one has anything, I'm anybody,
I stand beside my grave
Confused with my life, that is
    commonplace and solitary.

The speaker in this poem and the speakers in the two that follow are more highly defined than is the male in ".05." For each, try listing the facts about them (sex, race, age, looks, social and educational background) and the characteristics that can be justifiably inferred.

The speaker's scenes in "Next Day" include a grocery store (probably a suburban supermarket) and a car; in the next poem the scene remembered is a British telephone booth. In the third, the performer must decide how literally to take the poster. Is the speaker in a post office or imagining one?

Telephone Conversation
WOLE SOYINKA

The price seemed reasonable, location
Indifferent. The landlady swore she lived
Off premises. Nothing remained
But self-confession. "Madam," I warned,
"I hate a wasted journey—I am African."
Silence. Silenced transmission of
Pressurized good-breeding. Voice, when it came,
Lipstick coated, long gold-rolled
Cigarette-holder pipped. Caught I was, foully.
"How dark?" . . . I had not misheard . . . *"Are you light
Or very dark?"* Button B. Button A. Stench
Of rancid breath of public hide-and-speak.
Red booth. Red pillar-box. Red double-tiered
Omnibus squelching tar. It *was* real! Shamed
By ill-mannered silence, surrender
Pushed dumbfoundment to beg simplification.
Considerate she was, varying the emphasis—
"Are you dark? Or very light?" Revelation came.
"You mean—like plain or milk chocolate?"
Her assent was clinical, crushing in its light
Impersonality. Rapidly, wave-length adjusted,
I chose. "West African sepia"—and as afterthought
"Down in my passport." Silence for spectroscopic
Flight of fancy, till truthfullness clanged her accent
Hard on the mouthpiece. *"What's that?"* conceding
"Don't know what that is." "Like brunette."
"That's dark, isn't it?" "Not altogether.
Facially, I am brunette, but, madam, you should see
The rest of me. Palm of my hand, soles of my feet
Are a peroxide blond. Friction, caused—
Foolishly, madam—by sitting down, has turned
My botton raven black—One moment, madam!"—sensing
Her receiver rearing on the thunderclap
About my ears—"Madam," I pleaded, "wouldn't you rather
See for yourself?"

Unwanted
EDWARD FIELD

The poster with my picture on it
Is hanging on the bulletin board in the Post Office.

I stand by it hoping to be recognized
Posing first full face and then profile

But everybody passes by and I have to admit
The photograph was taken some years ago.

I was unwanted then and I'm unwanted now
Ah guess ah'll go up echo mountain and crah.

I wish someone would find my fingerprints somewhere
Maybe on a corpse and say, You're it.

Description: Male, or reasonably so
White, but not lily-white and usually deep-red

Thirty-fivish, and looks it lately
Five-feet-nine and one-hundred-thirty pounds: no physique

Black hair going gray, hairline receding fast
What used to be curly, now fuzzy

Brown eyes starey under beetling brow
Mole on chin, probably will become a wen

It is perfectly obvious that he was not popular at school
No good at baseball, and wet his bed.

His aliases tell his history: Dumbell, Good-for-nothing,
Jewboy, Fieldinsky, Skinny, Fierce Face, Greaseball, Sissy.

Warning: This man is not dangerous, answers to any name
Responds to love, don't call him or he will come.

The Hour of Letdown
E. B. WHITE

When the man came in, carrying the machine, most of us looked up from our drinks, because we had never seen anything like it before. The man set the thing down on the top of the bar near the beerpulls. It took up an ungodly amount of room and you could see the bartender didn't like it any too well, having this big, ugly-looking gadget parked right there.

"Two rye-and-water," the man said.

The bartender went on puddling an Old-Fashioned that he was working on, but he was obviously turning over the request in his mind.

"You want a double?" he asked, after a bit.

"No," said the man. "Two rye-and-water, please." He stared straight at the bartender, not exactly unfriendly but on the other hand not affirmatively friendly.

Many years of catering to the kind of people that come into saloons had provided the bartender with an adjustable mind. Nevertheless, he did not adjust readily to this fellow, and he did not like the machine—that was sure. He picked up a live cigarette that was idling on the edge of the cash register, took a drag out of it, and returned it thoughtfully. Then he poured two shots of rye whiskey, drew two glasses of water, and shoved the drinks in front of the man. People were watching. When something a little out of the ordinary takes place at a bar, the sense of it spreads quickly all along the line and pulls the customers together.

The man gave no sign of being the center of attraction. He laid a five-dollar bill down on the bar. Then he drank one of the ryes and chased it with water. He picked up the other rye, opened a small vent in the machine (it was like an oil cup) and poured the whiskey in, and then poured the water in.

The bartender watched grimly. "Not funny," he said in an even voice. "And furthermore, your companion takes up too much room. Whyn't you put it over on that bench by the door, make more room here."

"There's plenty of room for everyone here," replied the man.

"I ain't amused," said the bartender. "Put the goddam thing over near the door like I say. Nobody will touch it."

The man smiled. "You should have seen it this afternoon," he said. "It was magnificent. Today was the third day of the tournament. Imagine it—three days of continuous brainwork. And against the top players of the country, too. Early in the game it gained an advantage; then for two hours it exploited the advantage brilliantly, ending with the opponent's king backed in a corner. The sudden capture of a knight, the neutralization of a bishop, and it was all over. You know how much money it won, all told, in three days of playing chess?"

"How much?" asked the bartender.

"Five thousand dollars," said the man. "Now it wants to let down, wants to get a little drunk."

The bartender ran his towel vaguely over some wet spots. "Take it some-wheres else and get it drunk there!" he said firmly. "I got enough troubles."

The man shook his head and smiled. "No, we like it here." He pointed at the empty glasses. "Do this again, will you please?"

The bartender slowly shook his head. He seemed dazed but dogged. "You stow the thing away," he ordered. "I'm not ladling out whiskey for jokestersmiths."

" 'Jokesmiths,' " said the machine. "The word is 'jokesmiths.' "

A few feet down the bar, a customer who was on his third highball seemed ready to participate in this conversation to which we had all been listening so attentively. He was a middle-aged man. His necktie was pulled down away from his collar, and he had eased the collar by unbuttoning it. He had pretty nearly finished his third drink, and the alcohol tended to make him throw his support in with the underprivileged and the thirsty.

"If the machine wants another drink, give it another drink," he said to the bartender. "Let's not have haggling."

The fellow with the machine turned to his new-found friend and gravely raised his hand to his temple, giving him a salute of gratitude and fellowship. He addressed his next remark to him, as though deliberately snubbing the bartender.

"You know how it is when you're all fagged out mentally, how you want a drink?"

"Certainly do," replied the friend. "Most natural thing in the world."

There was a stir all along the bar, some seeming to side with the bartender, others with the machine group. A tall, gloomy man standing next to me spoke up.

"Another whiskey sour, Bill," he said. "And go easy on the lemon juice."

"Picric acid" said the machine, sullenly. "They don't use lemon juice in these places."

"That does it!" said the bartender, smacking his hand on the bar. "Will you put that thing away or else beat it out of here. I ain't in the mood, I tell you. I got this saloon to run and I don't want lip from a mechanical brain or whatever the hell you've got there."

The man ignored this ultimatum. He addressed his friend, whose glass was now empty.

"It's not just that it's all tuckered out after three days of chess," he said amiably. "You know another reason it wants a drink?"

"No," said the friend. "Why?"

"It cheated," said the man.

At this remark, the machine chuckled. One of its arms dipped slightly, and a light glowed in a dial.

The friend frowned. He looked as though his dignity had been hurt, as though his trust had been misplaced. "Nobody can cheat at chess," he said. "Simpossible. In chess, everything is open and above the board. The nature of the game of chess is such that cheating is impossible."

"That's what I used to think, too," said the man. "But there *is* a way."

"Well, it doesn't surprise me any," put in the bartender. "The first time I laid my eyes on that crummy thing I spotted it for a crook."

"Two rye-and-water," said the man.

"You can't have the whiskey," said the bartender. He glared at the mechanical brain. "How do I know it ain't drunk already?"

"That's simple. Ask it something," said the man.

The customers shifted and stared into the mirror. We were in this thing now, up to our necks. We waited. It was the bartender's move.

"Ask it what? Such as?" said the bartender.

"Makes no difference. Pick a couple big figures, ask it to multiply them together. You couldn't multiply big figures together if you were drunk, could you?"

The machine shook slightly, as though making internal preparations.

"Ten thousand eight hundred and sixty-two, multiply it by ninety-nine," said the bartender viciously. We could tell that he was throwing in the two nines to make it hard.

The machine flickered. One of its tubes spat, and a hand changed position, jerkily.

"One million seventy-five thousand three hundred and thirty-eight," said the machine.

Not a glass was raised all along the bar. People just stared gloomily into the mirror; some of us studied our own faces, others took carom shots at the man and the machine.

Finally, a youngish, mathematically minded customer got out a piece of paper and a pencil and went into retirement. "It works out," he reported, after some minutes of calculating. "You can't say the machine is drunk!"

Everyone now glared at the bartender. Reluctantly he poured two shots of rye, drew two glasses of water. The man drank his drink. Then he fed the machine its drink. The machine's light grew fainter. One of its cranky little arms wilted.

For a while the saloon simmered along like a ship at sea in calm weather. Every one of us seemed to be trying to digest the situation, with the help of liquor. Quite a few glasses were refilled. Most of us sought help in the mirror— the court of last appeal.

The fellow with the unbuttoned collar settled his score. He walked stiffly over and stood between the man and the machine. He put one arm around the man, the other around the machine. "Let's get out of here and go to a good place," he said.

The machine glowed slightly. It seemed to be a little drunk now.

"All right," said the man. "That suits me fine. I've got my car outside."

He settled for the drinks and put down a tip. Quietly and a trifle uncertainly he tucked the machine under his arm, and he and his companion of the night walked to the door and out into the street.

The bartender stared fixedly, then resumed his light housekeeping. "So he's got his car outside," he said, with heavy sarcasm. "Now isn't that nice!"

A customer at the end of the bar near the door left his drink, stepped to the window, parted the curtains and looked out. He watched for a moment, then returned to his place and addressed the bartender. "It's even nicer than you think," he said. "It's a Cadillac. And which one of the three of them d'ya think is doing the driving?"

Describe the voices of narrator, man, bartender, and gadget. At some stage of rehearsal, you will probably perform each separately and in their entirety—a practice that should increase both the clarity and consistency of each speaker. What does the author seem to be saying about humans' custom of a "letdown hour"?

One More Eyewitness*
RICHARD HOWARD

My name is January. Everyone
    always has something to say
    about that. I never mind:
names come first, don't they? and maybe last
    as well. They should. Anyway
    mine's a hard one to get past:
Leo January, and I run
    this airfield: that explains
    most of it. No one bothers
much here about regulations. After all, where
    would they start? Red Bird Field runs
    mainly by just *being there*—

*At the assassination of John F. Kennedy.

I never had too much respect for brains
   and still don't, after last week . . .
   But I'll try to keep my own
opinions out of this and stick to what
   happened here. A blue Buick
   drove in, Saturday, from town
with three people, all up front, inside.
There was a girl at the wheel
   who slid out fast, slapped the hem
of her trenchcoat down with her driving-gloves:
   she had legs, all right, and steel
   eyes a shade to match the car;
long hair, *lots* of hair, but her skin looked fried,
   as if she had been at it
   with a torch. I remember
seeing that skin, that belted coat, and thinking
   whatever she has to do
   she can do it on her own;
but she waited, lighting a thin black cigar,
   until the other two quit
   arguing, and a fat man
hauled himself out. That left the young one
   inside, staring—not at them.
   Names come first, but faces go:
had I seen that one before—a TV star?
   Without a name, who can tell?
   What they wanted was a plane,
he told me (Fatso there did all the talking,
   if you could call it that, time
   and again dredging the phlegm
out of his sinuses, and in between
   hawking up his questions: first,
   could they get to Yucatan
in a Cessna 310 tomorrow, or how far
   could they get? Also, how fast?
   Were visas needed, once past
the border, to refuel in Mexico?)
   Waiting out cough after cough
   as I told him they could fly
as far as Mexico City, weather permitting,
   buy gas without papers there
   if they didn't leave the field.
Cash was never mentioned, but the rest of my
   briefing must have put them off.
   The girl scribbled a note
I couldn't read on her pad, suddenly smiled:
   they would be here Sunday noon
   for the take-off. The license

was hers, she would do the *flying* too,
    the fat man announced. Fat chance.
    I made a note of my own
to see the color of their money first.
    The way his face kept sweating
    bothered me, and the girl's eyes
trapped in her pitted skin, that was the worst
    of it, that and the third one
    staring into the windshield
like a dead man—it looked to me a lot
    more likely they would hijack
    my Cessna and go on—maybe
to Cuba. It's happened before. This is Texas.
    I never saw *them* again,
    never expected to, not
the girl with metal eyes, not her fat friend
    who had the trick sinuses.
    But the other one I've seen—
before: I knew I'd seen that face before,
    Jesus Christ, the *day* before!
    The photograph on the screen
enough to make him into a TV star
    of sorts, the famous shot
    of him grinning at his gun . . .
That was the man who sat here, staring out,
    but now I know what—or who—
    he must have been staring at.
And all your talk about the Overpass,
    the Bindery, the Bullet—
    is only talk. Oh, I know:
they got the man. *The* man? Saturday
    when they "got" him, he was here.
    Names come first and maybe last:
You have a name for your man, baby, I'm
waiting this one out—the name
    for my man is another name.
I saw him here, *I saw him:* he was the man
    I saw. The man I saw was
    here. I saw him here. I saw . . .

To whom is Leo January speaking? Why? When (in relation to the assassination)? What is Leo's attitude toward the assassination? Toward his own role in it? Where must the speaker pause to *listen?* To what extent would the speaker of the poem imitate the voices of his customers when their speech is remembered?

How might your performance show the inconclusiveness of the ending, and at the same time show that the poem is finished, completed?

Nikki-Rosa
NIKKI GIOVANNI

childhood remembrances are always a drag
if you're Black
you always remember things like living in Woodlawn
with no inside toilet
and if you become famous or something
they never talk about how happy you were to have
your mother
all to yourself and
how good the water felt when you got your bath from one of those
big tubs that folk in chicago barbecue in
and somehow when you talk about home
it never gets across how much you
understood their feelings
as the whole family attended meetings about Hollydale
and even though you remember
your biographers never understand
your father's pain as he sells his stock
and another dream goes
and though you're poor it isn't poverty that
concerns you
and though they fought a lot
it isn't your father's drinking that makes any difference
but only that everybody is together and you
and your sister have happy birthdays and very good christmases
and I really hope no white person has cause to write about me
because they never understand Black love is Black wealth and they'll
probably talk about my hard childhood and never understand that
all the while I was quite happy

What are the speaker's possible audiences? Describe at least two and how you would show them in performance.

In Westminster Abbey
JOHN BETJEMAN

Let me take this other glove off
  As the *vox humana* swells,
And the beauteous fields of Eden
  Bask beneath the Abbey bells.

Here, where England's statesmen lie,
Listen to a lady's cry.

Gracious Lord, oh bomb the Germans.

Spare their women for Thy Sake,
And if that is not too easy
  We will pardon Thy Mistake.
But, gracious Lord, whate'er shall be,
Don't let anyone bomb me.

Keep our Empire undismembered,
  Guide our Forces by Thy Hand,
Gallant blacks from far Jamaica,
  Honduras and Togoland;
Protect them Lord in all their fights,
And, even more, protect the whites.

Think of what our Nation stands for:
  Books from Boots' and country lanes,
Free speech, free passes, class distinction,
  Democracy and proper drains.
Lord, put beneath Thy special care
One-eighty-nine Cadogan Square.

Although dear Lord I am a sinner,
  I have done no major crime;
Now I'll come to Evening Service
  Whensoever I have the time.
So, Lord, reserve for me a crown,
And do not let my shares go down.

I will labour for Thy Kingdom,
  Help our lads to win the war,
Send white feathers to the cowards,
  Join the Women's Army Corps,
Then wash the Steps around Thy
      Throne
In the Eternal Safety Zone.

Now I feel a little better,
  What a treat to hear Thy Word,
Where the bones of leading statesmen,
  Have so often been interred.
And now, dear Lord, I cannot wait
Because I have a luncheon date.

This poem has been a favorite of performers for years. Part of its popularity must rest with the fully defined speaker whose situation is so clear and whose attitudes stand in such sharp contrast to those of the *implied author* and us as readers. If you have not been to Westminster Abbey, you may want to seek out pictures of it. What does the phrase *vox humana* mean?

The Jewbird
BERNARD MALAMUD

The window was open so the skinny bird flew in. Flappity-flap with its frazzled black wings. That's how it goes. It's open, you're in. Closed, you're out and that's your fate. The bird wearily flapped through the open kitchen window of Harry Cohen's top-floor apartment on First Avenue near the lower East River. On a rod on the wall hung an escaped canary cage, its door wide open, but this black-type longbeaked bird—its ruffled head and small dull eyes, crossed a little, making it look like a dissipated crow—landed if not smack on Cohen's thick lamb chop, at least on the table, close by. The frozen foods salesman was sitting at supper with his wife and young son on a hot August evening a year ago. Cohen, a heavy man with hairy chest and beefy shorts; Edie, in skinny yellow shorts and red halter; and their ten-year-old Morris (after her father)—Maurie, they called him, a nice kid though not overly bright—were all in the city after two weeks out, because Cohen's mother was dying. They had been enjoying Kingston, New York, but drove back when Mama got sick in her flat in the Bronx.

"Right on the table," said Cohen, putting down his beer glass and swatting at the bird. "Son of a bitch."

"Harry, take care with your language," Edie said, looking at Maurie, who watched every move.

The bird cawed hoarsely and with a flap of its bedraggled wings—feathers tufted this way and that—rose heavily to the top of the open kitchen door, where it perched staring down.

"Gevalt, a pogrom!"

"It's a talking bird," said Edie in astonishment.

"In Jewish," said Maurie.

"Wise guy," muttered Cohen. He gnawed on his chop, then put down the bone. "So if you can talk, say what's your business. What do you want here?"

"If you can't spare a lamb chop," said the bird, "I'll settle for a piece of herring with a crust of bread. You can't live on your nerve forever."

"This ain't a restaurant," Cohen replied. "All I'm asking is what brings you to this address?"

"The window was open," the bird sighed; adding after a moment, "I'm running. I'm flying but I'm also running."

"From whom?" asked Edie with interest.

"Anti-Semeets."

"Anti-Semites?" they all said.

"That's from who."

"What kind of anti-Semites bother a bird?" Edie asked.

"Any kind," said the bird, "also including eagles, vultures, and hawks. And once in a while some crows will take your eyes out."

"But aren't you a crow?"

"Me? I'm a Jewbird."

Cohen laughed heartily. "What do you mean by that?"

The bird began dovening. He prayed without Book or tallith, but with passion. Edie bowed her head though not Cohen. And Maurie rocked back and forth with the prayer, looking up with one wide-open eye.

"When the prayer was done Cohen remarked, "No hat, no phylacteries?"

"I'm an old radical."

"You're sure you're not some kind of ghost or dybbuk?"

"Not a dybbuk," answered the bird, "though one of my relatives had such an experience once. It's all over now, thanks God. They freed her from a lover, a crazy jealous man. She's now the mother of two wonderful children."

"Birds?" Cohen asked slyly.

"Why not?"

"What kind of birds?"

"Like me. Jewbirds."

Cohen tipped back in his chair and guffawed. "That's a big laugh. I've heard of a Jewfish but not a Jewbird."

"We're once removed." The bird rested on one skinny leg, then on the other. "Please, could you spare maybe a piece of herring with a small crust of bread?"

Edie got up from the table.

"What are you doing?" Cohen asked her.

"I'll clear the dishes."

Cohen turned to the bird. "So what's your name, if you don't mind saying?"

"Call me Schwartz."

"He might be an old Jew changed into a bird by somebody," said Edie, removing a plate.

"Are you?" asked Harry, lighting a cigar.

"Who knows?" answered Schwartz. "Does God tell us everything?"

Maurie got up on his chair. "What kind of herring?" he asked the bird in excitement.

"Get down, Maurie, or you'll fall," ordered Cohen.

"If you haven't got matjes, I'll take schmaltz," said Schwartz.

"All we have is marinated, with slices of onion—in a jar," said Edie.

"If you'll open for me the jar I'll eat marinated. Do you have also, if you don't mind, a piece of rye bread—the spitz?"

Edie thought she had.

"Feed him out on the balcony," Cohen said. He spoke to the bird. "After that take off."

Schwartz closed both bird eyes. "I'm tired and it's a long way."

"Which direction are you headed, north or south?"

Schwartz, barely lifting his wings, shrugged.

"You don't know where you're going?"

"Where there's charity I'll go."

"Let him stay, papa," said Maurie. "He's only a bird."

"So stay the night," Cohen said, "but no longer."

In the morning Cohen ordered the bird out of the house but Maurie cried, so Schwartz stayed for a while. Maurie was still on vacation from school and his friends were away. He was lonely and Edie enjoyed the fun he had, playing with the bird.

"He's no trouble at all," she told Cohen, "and besides his appetite is very small."

"What'll you do when he makes dirty?"

"He flies across the street in a tree when he makes dirty, and if nobody passes below, who notices?"

"So all right," said Cohen, "but I'm dead set against it. I warn you he ain't gonna stay here long."

"What have you got against the poor bird?"

"Poor bird, my ass. He's a foxy bastard. He thinks he's a Jew."

"What difference does it make what he thinks?"

"A Jewbird, what chutzpah. One false move and he's out on his drumsticks."

At Cohen's insistence Schwartz lived out on the balcony in a new wooden birdhouse Edie had bought him.

"With many thanks," said Schwartz, "though I would rather have a human roof over my head. You know how it is at my age. I like the warm, the windows, the smell of cooking. I would also be glad to see once in a while the *Jewish Morning Journal* and have now and then a schnapps because it helps my breathing, thanks God. But whatever you give me, you won't hear complaints."

However, when Cohen brought home a bird feeder full of dried corn, Schwartz said, "Impossible."

Cohen was annoyed. "What's the matter, crosseyes, is your life getting too good for you? Are you forgetting what it means to be migratory? I'll bet a helluva lot of crows you happen to be acquainted with, Jews or otherwise, would give their eyeteeth to eat this corn."

Schwartz did not answer. What can you say to a grubber yung?

"Not for my digestion," he later explained to Edie. "Cramps. Herring is better even if it makes you thirsty. At least rainwater don't cost anything." He laughed sadly in breathy caws.

And herring, thanks to Edie, who knew where to shop, was what Schwartz got, with an occasional piece of potato pancake, and even a bit of soupmeat when Cohen wasn't looking.

When school began in September, before Cohen would once against suggest giving the bird the boot, Edie prevailed on him to wait a little while until Maurie adjusted.

"To deprive him right now might hurt his school work, and you know what trouble we had last year."

"So okay, but sooner or later the bird goes. That I promise you."

Schwartz, though nobody had asked him, took on full responsibility for Maurie's performance in school. In return for favors granted, when he was let in for an hour or two at night, he spent most of his time overseeing the boy's lessons. He sat on top of the dresser near Maurie's desk as he laboriously wrote out his homework. Maurie was a restless type and Schwartz gently kept him to his studies. He also listened to him practice his screechy violin, taking a few minutes off now and then to rest his ears in the bathroom. And they afterwards played dominoes. The boy was an indifferent checker player and it was impossible to teach him chess. When he was sick, Schwartz read him comic books though he personally disliked them. But Maurie's work improved in school and even his violin teacher admitted his playing was better. Edie gave Schwartz credit for these improvements though the bird pooh-poohed them.

Yet he was proud there was nothing lower than C minuses on Maurie's report card, and on Edie's insistence celebrated with a little schnapps.

"If he keeps up like this," Cohen said, "I'll get him in an Ivy League college for sure."

"Oh I hope so," sighed Edie.

But Schwartz shook his head. "He's a good boy—you don't have to worry. He won't be a shicker or a wifebeater, God forbid, but a scholar he'll never be, if you know what I mean, although maybe a good mechanic. It's no disgrace in these times."

"If I were you," Cohen said, angered, "I'd keep my big snoot out of other people's private business."

"Harry, please," said Edie.

"My goddamn patience is wearing out. That crosseyes butts into everything."

Though he wasn't exactly a welcome guest in the house, Schwartz gained a few ounces although he did not improve in appearance. He looked bedraggled as ever, his fathers unkempt, as though he had just flown out of a snowstorm.

He spent, he admitted, little time taking care of himself. Too much to think about. "Also outside plumbing," he told Edie. Still there was more glow to his eyes so that though Cohen went on calling him crosseyes he said it less emphatically.

Liking his situation, Schwartz tried tactfully to stay out of Cohen's way, but one night when Edie was at the movies and Maurie was taking a hot shower, the frozen foods salesman began a quarrel with the bird.

"For Christ sake, why don't you wash yourself sometimes? Why must you always stink like a dead fish?"

"Mr. Cohen, if you'll pardon me, if somebody eats garlic he will smell from garlic. I eat herring three times a day. Feed me flowers and I will smell like flowers."

"Who's obligated to feed you anything at all? You're lucky to get herring."

"Excuse me, I'm not complaining," said the bird. "You're complaining."

"What's more," said Cohen, "even from out on the balcony I can hear you snoring away like a pig. It keeps me awake at night."

"Snoring," said Schwartz, "isn't a crime, thank God."

"All in all you are a goddamn pest and free loader. Next thing you'll want to sleep in bed next to my wife."

"Mr. Cohen," said Schwartz, "on this rest assured. A bird is a bird."

"So you say, but how do I know you're a bird and not some kind of goddamn devil?"

"If I was a devil you would know already. And I don't mean because of your son's good marks."

"Shut up, you bastard bird," shouted Cohen.

"Grubber yung," cawed Schwartz, rising to the tips of his talons, his long wings outstretched.

Cohen was about to lunge for the bird's scrawny neck but Maurie came out of the bathroom, and for the rest of the evening until Schwartz's bedtime on the balcony, there was pretended peace.

But the quarrel had deeply disturbed Schwartz and he slept badly. His snoring woke him, and awake, he was fearful of what would become of him. Wanting to stay out of Cohen's way, he kept to the birdhouse as much as possible. Cramped by it, he paced back and forth on the balcony ledge, or sat on the birdhouse roof, staring into space. In the evenings, while overseeing Maurie's lessons, he often fell asleep. Awakening, he nervously hopped around exploring the four corners of the room. He spent much time in Maurie's closet, and carefully examined his bureau drawers when they were left open. And once when he found a large paper bag on the floor, Schwartz poked his way into it to investigate what possibilities were. The boy was amused to see the bird in the paper bag.

"He wants to build a nest," he said to his mother.

Edie, sensing Schwartz's unhappiness, spoke to him quietly.

"Maybe if you did some of the things my husband wants you, you would get along better with him."

"Give me a for instance," Schwartz said.

"Like take a bath, for instance."

"I'm too old for baths," said the bird. "My feathers fall out without baths."

"He says you have a bad smell."

"Everybody smells. Some people smell because of their thoughts or because who they are. My bad smell comes from the food I eat. What does his come from?"

"I better not ask him or it might make him mad," said Edie.

In late November Schwartz froze on the balcony in the fog and cold, and especially on rainy days he woke with stiff joints and could barely move his wings. Already he felt twinges of rheumatism. He would have liked to spend more time in the warm house, particularly when Maurie was in school and Cohen at work. But though Edie was goodhearted and might have sneaked him in in the morning, just to thaw out, he was afraid to ask her. In the meantime Cohen, who had been reading articles about the migration of birds, came out on the balcony one night after work when Edie was in the kitchen preparing pot roast, and peeking into the birdhouse, warned Schwartz to be on his way soon if he knew what was good for him. "Time to hit the flyways."

"Mr. Cohen, why do you hate me so much?" asked the bird. "What did I do to you?"

"Because you're an A-number-one trouble maker, that's why. What's more, whoever heard of a Jewbird? Now scat or it's open war."

But Schwartz stubbornly refused to depart so Cohen embarked on a campaign of harassing him, meanwhile hiding it from Edie and Maurie. Maurie hated violence and Cohen didn't want to leave a bad impression. He thought maybe if he played dirty tricks on the bird he would fly off without being physically kicked out. The vacation was over, let him make his easy living off the fat of somebody else's land. Cohen worried about the effect of the bird's departure on Maurie's schooling but decided to take the chance, first, because the boy now seemed to have the knack of studying—give the black bird-bastard credit—and second, because Schwartz was driving him bats by being there always, even in his dreams.

The frozen foods salesman began his campaign against the bird by mixing watery cat food with the herring slices in Schwartz's dish. He also blew up and popped numerous paper bags outside the birdhouse as the bird slept, and when he had got Schwartz good and nervous, though not enough to leave, he brought a full-grown cat into the house, supposedly a gift for little Maurie, who had always wanted a pussy. The cat never stopped springing up at Schwartz whenever he saw him, one day managing to claw out several of his tailfeathers. And even at lesson time, when the cat was usually excluded from Maurie's room, though somehow or other he quickly found his way in at the end of the lesson, Schwartz was desperately fearful of his life and flew from pinnacle to pinnacle—light fixture to clothestree to door-top—in order to elude the beast's wet jaws.

Once when the bird complained to Edie how hazardous his existence was, she said, "Be patient, Mr. Schwartz. When the cat gets to know you better he won't try to catch you any more."

"When he stops trying we will both be in Paradise," Schwartz answered. "Do me a favor and get rid of him. He makes my whole life worry. I'm losing feathers like a tree loses leaves."

"I'm awfully sorry but Maurie likes the pussy and sleeps with it."

What could Schwartz do? He worried but came to no decision, being afraid to leave. So he ate the herring garnished with cat food, tried hard not to hear the paper bags bursting like fire crackers outside the birdhouse at night, and lived terror-stricken closer to the ceiling than the floor, as the cat, his tail flicking, endlessly watched him.

Weeks went by. Then on the day after Cohen's mother had died in her flat in the Bronx, when Maurie came home with a zero on an arithmetic test, Cohen, enraged, waited until Edie had taken the boy to his violin lesson, then openly attacked the bird. He chased him with a broom on the balcony and Schwartz frantically flew back and forth, finally escaping into his birdhouse. Cohen triumphantly reached in, and grabbing both skinny legs, dragged the bird out, cawing loudly, his wings wildly beating. He whirled the bird around and around his head. But Schwartz, as he moved in circles, managed to swoop down and catch Cohen's nose in his beak, and hung on for dear life. Cohen cried out in great pain, punched the bird with his fist, and tugging at its legs with all his might, pulled his nose free. Again he swung the yawking Schwartz around until the bird grew dizzy, then with a furious heave, flung him into the night. Schwartz sank like stone into the street. Cohen then tossed the birdhouse and feeder after him, listening at the ledge until they crashed on the sidewalk below. For a full hour, broom in hand, his heart palpitating and nose throbbing with pain, Cohen waited for Schwartz to return but the broken-hearted bird didn't.

That's the end of that dirty bastard, the salesman thought and went in. Edie and Maurie had come home.

"Look," said Cohen, pointing to his bloody nose swollen three times its normal size, "what that sonofabitchy bird did. It's a permanent scar."

"Where is he now?" Edie asked, frightened.

"I threw him out and he flew away. Good riddance."

Nobody said no, though Edie touched a handkerchief to her eyes and Maurie rapidly tried the nine times table and found he knew approximately half.

In the spring when the winter's snow had melted, the boy, moved by a memory, wandered in the neighborhood, looking for Schwartz. He found a dead black bird in a small lot near the river, his two wings broken, neck twisted, and both bird-eyes plucked clean.

"Who did it to you, Mr. Schwartz?" Maurie wept.

"Anti-Semeets," Edie said later.

Who speaks the third, fourth, and fifth sentences in the story? Whose attitude and speech patterns?

After reading the story, look at the narration (includes all parts except the dialogue) and try to determine what kind of person could be telling the story and to whom. Try to account explicitly for your own harmony, or lack of it, with the narrator, each member of the family, and the bird. What *tensions* in the family does the bird create? Resolve? What habits or actions of the characters do you dislike or disapprove of?

How would you describe the implied author of the scheme of values (what is good, bad, of worth, etc.) that emerge from this story? See Jill O'Brien, "The Interpreter and Ethnic Texts: Jewish-American Literary Experience," *Speech Teacher*, 24 (September 1975), 195–201.

Reason
JOSEPHINE MILES

Said, Pull her up a bit will you, Mac, I want to unload there.
Said, Pull her up my rear end, first come first serve.
Said, Give her the gun, Bud, he needs a taste of his own bumper.
Then the usher came out and got into the act:

Said, Pull her up, pull her up a bit, we need this space, sir.
Said, For God's sake, is this still a free country or what?
You go back and take care of Gary Cooper's horse
And leave me handle my own car.

Saw them unloading the lame old lady,
Ducked out under the wheel and gave her an elbow,
Said, All you needed to do was just explain;
Reason, Reason is my middle name.

Is it possible that five speakers exist in Miles's short poem? Try making each one as distinct as possible, while retaining a sense of the responses all existing in one poem. How would you describe one over-all meaning in the poem? Develop a moment-to-moment interpretation of one of the stanzas.

Love, Dad
JOSEPH HELLER

Second Lieutenant Edward J. Nately III was really a good kid. He was a slender, shy, rather handsome young man with fine brown hair, delicate cheekbones, large, intent eyes and a sharp pain in the small of his back when he woke up alone on a couch in the parlor of a whorehouse in Rome one morning and began wondering who and where he was and how in the world he had ever got there. He had no real difficulty remembering *who* he was. He was Second Lieutenant Edward J. Nately III, a bomber pilot in Italy in World War Two, and he would be 20 years old in January, if he lived.

Nately had always been a good kid from a Philadelphia family that was even better. He was always pleasant, considerate, trustworthy, loyal, helpful, friendly, courteous, kind, obedient, cheerful, not always so thrifty or wise but invariably brave, clean and reverent. He was without envy, malice, anger, hatred, or resentment, which puzzled his good friend Yossarian and kept him aware of how eccentric and naïve Nately really was and how much in need of protection by Yossarian against the wicked ways of the world.

Why, Nately had actually enjoyed his childhood—and was not even ashamed to admit it! Nately *liked* all his brothers and sisters and always had, and he did not mind going home for vacations and furloughs. He got on well with his uncles and his aunts and with all his first, second and third cousins, whom, of course, he numbered by the dozens, with all the friends of the family and with just about everyone else he ever met, except, possibly, the incredibly and unashamedly depraved old man who was always in the whorehouse when Nately and Yossarian arrived and seemed to have spent his entire life living comfortably and happily there. Nately was well bred, well groomed, well mannered and well off. He was, in fact, immensely wealthy, but no one in his squadron on the island of Pianosa held his good nature or his good family background against him.

Nately had been taught by both parents all through childhood, preadolescence and adolescence to shun and disdain "climbers," "pushers," *"nouveaux"* and "parvenus," but he had never been able to, since no climbers, pushers, *nouveaux* or parvenus had ever been allowed near any of the family homes in Philadelphia, Fifth Avenue, Palm Beach, Bar Harbor, Southampton, Mayfair and Belgravia, the 16th *arrondissement,* the north of France, the south of France and all of the good Greek islands. To the best of his knowledge, the guest lists at all these places had always been composed exclusively of ladies and gentlemen and children of faultless dress and manners and great dignity and aplomb. There were always many bankers, brokers, judges, ambassadors and former ambassadors among them, many sportsmen, cabinet officials, fortune hunters and dividend-collecting widows, divorcees, orphans and spinsters. There were no labor leaders among them and no laborers, and there were never any self-made men. There was one unmarried social worker, who toiled among the underprivileged for fun, and several retired generals and admirals who were dedicating the remaining years of their lives to preserving the American Constitution by destroying it and perpetuating the American way of life by bringing it to an end.

The only one in the entire group who worked hard was Nately's mother; but since she did not work hard at anything constructive, her reputation remained good. Nately's mother worked very hard at opening and closing the family homes in Philadelphia, Fifth Avenue, Palm Beach, Bar Harbor, Southampton, Mayfair and Belgravia, the 16th *arrodissement,* the north of France, the south of France and all of the good Greek islands, and at safeguarding the family traditions, of which she had appointed herself austere custodian.

"You must never forget who and what you are"; Nately's mother had begun drumming it into Nately's head about Natelys long before Nately had any idea what a Nately was. "You are not a Guggenheim, who mined copper for a living, nor a Vanderbilt, whose fortune is descended from a common tugboat captain, nor an Armour, whose ancestors peddled putrefying meat to the gallant Union Army during the heroic War between the States, nor a Harriman, who made his money playing with choo-choo trains. Our family," she always declared with pride, "does *nothing* for our money."

"What your mater means, my boy," interjected his father with the genial, rococo wit Nately found so impressive, "is that people who make new fortunes are not nearly as good as the families who've lost old ones. Ha, ha, ha! Isn't that good, my dear?"

"I wish you would mind your own business when I'm talking to the boy," Nately's mother replied sharply to Nately's father.

"Yes, my dear."

Nately's mother was a stiff-necked, straight-backed, autocratic descendant of the old New England Thorntons. The family tree of the New England Thorntons, as she often remarked, extended back far past the Mayflower, almost to Adam himself. It was a matter of historical record that the Thorntons were lineal descendants of the union of John Alden, a climber, to Priscilla Mullins, a pusher. The genealogy of the Natelys was no less impressive, since one of Nately's father's forebears had distinguished himself conspicuously at the battle of Bosworth Field, on the losing side.

"Mother, what is a regano?" Nately inquired innocently one day while on holiday from Andover after an illicit tour through the Italian section of Philadelphia, before reporting to his home for duty. "Is it anything like a Nately?"

"Oregano," replied his mother with matriarchal distaste, "is a revolting vice indulged in by untitled foreigners in Italy. Don't ever mention it again."

Nately's father chuckled superiorly when Nately's mother had gone. "You mustn't take everything your mother says too literally, son," he advised with a wink. "Your mother is a remarkable woman, as you probably know, but when she deals with such matters as oregano, she's usually full of shit. Now, I've eaten oregano many times, if you know what I mean, and I expect that you will, too, before you marry and settle down. The important thing to remember about eating oregano is never to do it with a girl from your own social station. Do it with salesgirls and waitresses, if you can, or with any of our maids, except Lili, of course, who, as you may have noticed, is something of a favorite of mine. I'm not sending you to women of lower social station out of snobbishness, but simply because they're so much better at it than the daughters and wives of our friends. Nurses and schoolteachers enjoy excellent reputations in this respect. Not a word about this to your mother, of course."

Nately's father overflowed with sanguine advice of that kind. He was a dapper, affable man of great polish and experience whom everybody but Nately's mother respected. Nately was proud of his father's wisdom and sophistication; and the eloquent, brilliant letters he received when away at school were treasured compensation for those bleak and painful separations from his parents. Nately's father, on the other hand, welcomed these separations from his son with ceremonious zeal, for they gave him opportunity to fashion the graceful, aesthetic, metaphysical letters in which he took such epicurean satisfaction.

Dear Son (he wrote when Nately was away at Andover):

Don't be the first person by whom new things are tried and don't be the last one to set old ones aside. If our family were ever to adopt for itself a brief motto, I would want it to be precisely those words, and not merely because I wrote them myself. (Ha, ha, ha!) I would select them for the wisdom they contain. They urge restraint, and restraint is the quintessence of dignity and taste. It is incumbent upon you as a Nately that dignity and taste are always what you show.

Today you are at Andover. Tomorrow you will be elsewhere. There will be times in later life when you will find yourself with people who attended Exeter, Choate, Hotchkiss, Groton and other institutions of like ilk. These people will address you as equals and speak to you familiarly, as though you share with them a common fund of experience. Do not be deceived. Andover is Andover, and Exeter is not, and neither are any of the others anything that they are not.

Throughout life, you must always choose your friends as discriminately as you choose your clothing, and you must bear in mind constantly that all that glitters is not gold.

Love,
Dad

Nately had hoarded these letters from his father loyally and was often tempted to fling their elevated contents into the jaded face of the hedonistic old man who seemed to be in charge of the whorehouse in Rome, in lordly refutation of his pernicious, unkempt immorality and as a triumphant illustration of what a cultivated, charming, intelligent and distinguished man of character was really like. What restrained Nately was a confused and intimidating suspicion that the old man would succeed in degrading his father with the same noxious and convincing trickery with which he had succeeded in degrading everything else Nately deemed holy. Nately had a large number of his father's letters to save. Following Andover, he had moved, of course, to Harvard, and his father had proved equal to the occasion.

Dear Son (his father wrote):

Don't be the first person by whom new things are tried and don't be the last person to set the old things aside. This pregnant couplet came to me right out of the blue only a few moments ago, while I was out on the patio listening to your mother and a Mozart concerto and spreading Crosse & Blackwell marmalade on my Melba toast, and I am interrupting my breakfast to communicate it to you while it is still fresh in my mind. Write it down on your brain, inscribe it on your heart, engrave it for all time on your memory centers, for the advice it contains is as sound as any I have ever told you.

Today you are at Harvard, the oldest educational institution in the United States of America, and I am not certain if you are as properly impressed with your situation as you should be. Harvard is more than just a good school; Harvard is also a good place to get an education, should you decide that you do want an education. Columbia University, New York University and the City College of New York in the city of New York are other good places at which to get an education, but they are not good schools. Universities such as Princeton, Yale, Dartmouth and bungalows in the Amherst Williams complex are, of course, neither good schools nor good places at which to get an education and are never to be compared with Harvard. I hope that you are being as choosy in your choice of acquaintances there as you know your mother and I would like you to be.

Love,
Dad

P.S. Avoid associating familiarly with Roman Catholics, colored people and Jews, regardless of how accomplished, rich or influential their parents may be, although Chinese, Japanese, Spaniards of royal blood and Moslems of foreign nationality are perfectly all right.
P.P.S. Are you getting much oregano up there? (Ha, ha, ha!)

Nately sampled oregano dutifully his freshman year with a salesgirl, a waitress, a nurse and a schoolteacher, and with three girls in Scranton, Pennsylvania, on two separate occasions, but his appetite for the spice was not hoggish and exposure did not immunize him against falling so unrealistically in love the first moment he laid eyes on the dense, sluggish, yawning, ill-kempt whore lounging stark-naked in a room full of enlisted men ignoring her. Apart from these several formal and rather unexciting excursions into sexuality, Nately's first year at Harvard was empty and dull. He made few close friends, restricted, as he was, to associating only with wealthy Episcopalian and Church of England graduates of Andover whose ancestors had either descended lineally from the union of John Alden with Priscilla Mullins or been conspicuous at Bosworth Field, on the losing side. He spent many solitary hours fondling the expensive vellum bindings of the five books sent to him by his father as the indispensable basis of a sound personal library: *Forges and Furnaces of Pennsylvania; The Catalog of the Porcellian Club of Harvard University, 1941; Burke's Genealogical and Heraldic History of the Peerage, Baronetage and Knightage; Lord Chesterfield's Letters Written to His Son;* and the Francis Palgrave *Golden Treasury* of English verse. The pages themselves did not hold his interest, but the bindings were fascinating. He was often lonely and nagged by vague, incipient longings. He contemplated his sophomore year at Harvard without enthusiasm, without joy. Fortunately, the War broke out in time to save him.

Dear Son (his father wrote, after Nately had volunteered for the Air Corps, to escape being drafted into the Infantry):

You are now embarked upon the highest calling that Providence ever bestows upon man, the privilege to fight for his country. Play up, play up and play the game! I have every confidence that you will not fail your country, your family and yourself in the execution of your most noble responsibility, which is to play up, play up and play the game—and to come out ahead.

The news at home is all good. The market is buoyant and the cost-plus-six-percent type of contract now in vogue is the most salutary invention since the international cartel and provides us with an excellent buffer against the excess-profits tax and the outrageous personal income tax. I have it on excellent authority that Russia cannot possibly hold out for more than a week or two and that after communism has been destroyed, Hitler, Roosevelt, Mussolini, Churchill, Mahatma Gandhi and the Emperor of Japan will make peace and operate the world forever on a sound businesslike basis. However, it remains to be seen whether the wish is just being father to the thought. (Ha, ha, ha!)

My spirit is soaring and my optimism knows no bounds. Hitler has provided precisely the right stimulus needed to restore the American economy to that splendid condition of good health it was enjoying on that glorious Thursday just before Black Friday. War, as you undoubtedly appreciate, presents civilization with a great opportunity and a great challenge. It is in time of war that great fortunes are often made. It is between wars that economic conditions tend to deteriorate. If mankind can just discover some means of increasing the duration of wars and decreasing the intervals between wars, we will have found a permanent solution to this most fundamental of all human ills, the business cycle.

What better advice can a devoted parent give you in this grave period of national crisis than to oppose government interference with all the vigor at your command and to fight to the death to preserve free enterprise—

provided, of course, that the enterprise in question is one in which you own a considerable number of shares. (Ha, ha, ha!)

Above all this, to your own self be true. Never be a borrower or a lender of money: Never borrow money at more than two percent and never lend money at less than nine percent.

Love,
Dad

P.S. Your mother and I will not go to Cannes this year.

There had been no caviling in the family over Nately's course once war was declared; it was simply taken for granted that he would continue the splendid family tradition of military service that dated all the way back to the battle of Bosworth Field, on the losing side, particularly since Nately's father had it from the most reliable sources in Washington that Russia could not possibly hold out for more than two or three more weeks and that the War would come to an end before Nately could be sent overseas.

It was Nately's mother and Nately's eldest sister's idea that he become an aviation cadet, since Air Corps officers wore no wires in their dress caps and since he would be sheltered in a elaborate training program while the Russians were defeated and the War was brought to a satisfactory end. Furthermore, as a cadet and an officer, he would associate only with gentlemen and frequent only the best places.

As it turned out, there was a catch. In fact, there was a series of catches, and instead of associating only with gentlemen in only the best places, Nately found himself regularly in a whorehouse in Rome, associating with such people as Yossarian and the satanic and depraved mocking old man and, even worse, sadly and hopelessly in love with an indifferent prostitute there who paid no attention to him and always went off to bed without him, because he stayed up late arguing with the evil old man.

Nately was not quite certain how it had all come about, and neither was his father, who was always so certain about everything else. Nately was struck again and again by the stark contrast the seedy, disreputable old man there made with his own father, whose recurring allusions in his letters to oregano and rhapsodic exclamations about war and business were starting to become intensely disturbing. Nately often was tempted to blot these offending lines out of the letters he saved, but was afraid to; and each time he returned to the whorehouse, he wished earnestly that the sinful and corrupt old man there would put on a clean shirt and tie and act like a cultured gentleman, so that Nately would not have to feel such burning and confusing anger each time he looked at him and was reminded of his father.

Dear Son (wrote his father):

Well, those blasted Communists failed to capitulate as I expected them to, and now you are overseas in combat as an airplane pilot and in danger of being killed.

We have instructed you always to comport yourself with honor and taste and never to be guilty of anything degrading. Death, like hard work, is degrading, and I urge you to do everything possible to remain alive. Resist the temptation to cover yourself with glory, for that would be vanity. Bear in mind that it is one thing to fight for your country and quite another thing to die for it. It is absolutely imperative in this time of national peril that, in the immortal words of Rudyard Kipling, you keep your head while others about you are losing theirs. (Ha, ha, ha! Get it?) In peace, nothing so becomes a man as modest stillness and humility. But, as Shakespeare said, when the blast of war blows loose, then it is time for discretion to be the better part of valor. In short, the times cry out for dignity, balance, caution and restraint.

It is probable that within a few years after we have won, someone like Henry L. Mencken will point out that the number of Americans who suffered from this War were far outnumbered by those who profited by it. We should not like a member of our family to draw attention to himself for being among those relative few who did not profit. I pray daily for your safe return. Could you not feign a liver ailment or something similar and be sent home?

Love,
Dad

P.S. How I envy you your youth, your opportunity and all that sweet Italian pussy! I wish I were with you. (Ha, ha, ha!)

The letter was returned to him, stamped KILLED IN ACTION.

This story later became a part of Joseph Heller's acclaimed novel, *Catch 22*. The large question is about the narrator. Who could know enough to tell of it? And what of the letters?

This story poses more questions than any texts we have considered so far. The initial answers to the questions usually change quite radically during the rehearsal period. Discuss the relationship among the narrator, the father, the *implied author*, and the story's *protagonist*, the character to whom the greatest change occurs.

Theme for English B
LANGSTON HUGHES

The instructor said,

> *Go home and write*
> *a page tonight.*
> *And let that page come out of you—*
> *Then, it will be true.*

I wonder if it's that simple?

I am twenty-two, colored, born in Winston-Salem.
I went to school there, then Durham, then here

to this college on the hill above Harlem.
I am the only colored student in my class.
The steps from the hill lead down into Harlem,
through a park, then I cross St. Nicholas,
Eighth Avenue, Seventh, and I come to the Y,
the Harlem Branch Y, where I take the elevator
up to my room, sit down, and write this page:

It's not easy to know what is true for you or me
at twenty-two, my age. But I guess I'm what
I feel and see and hear, Harlem, I hear you:
hear you, hear me—we two—you, me, talk on this page.
(I hear New York, too.) Me—who?
Well, I like to eat, sleep, drink, and be in love.
I like to work, read, learn, and understand life.
I like a pipe for a Christmas present,
or records—Bessie, bop, or Bach.
I guess being colored doesn't make me *not* like
the same things other folks like who are other races.
So will my page be colored that I write?
Being me, it will not be white.
But it will be
a part of you, instructor.
You are white—
yet a part of me, as I am a part of you.
That's American.
Sometimes perhaps you don't want to be a part of me.
Nor do I often want to be a part of you.
But we are, that's true!
As I learn from you,
I guess you learn from me—
although you're older—and white—
and somewhat more free.

This is my page for English B.

Although this poem and the three that follow are all about black experiences, the situations are individual, ranging from recollection, tribute, and challenge to threat. The voices of several speakers are also distinct. How do the two voices in "Theme for English B" differ? Does the speaker seem as distressed with the professor as we are? How do the possible audiences or listeners in these four poems vary? Why does this variation make a significant difference in performance?

For an excellent discussion of rhythm in black poetry, see Stephen Henderson's *Understanding the New Black Poetry: Black Speech & Black Music as Poetic References* (New York: William Morrow, 1973), pp. 3–69.

Vive Noir!
MARI EVANS

i
am going to rise
en masse
from Inner City
        sick
          of newyork ghettos
        chicago tenements
      l a's slums
weary
   of exhausted lands
   sagging privies
   saying yessuh yessah
   yes SIR
   in an assortment
   of geographical dialects i
have seen my last
broken down plantation
even from a
distance

    i
will load all my goods
in '50 Chevy pickups '53
Fords fly United and '66
caddys i
   have packed in
   the old man and the old lady and
   wiped the children's noses
      I'm tired
       of hand me downs
         shut me ups
           pin me ins
             keep me outs
               messing me over have
            just had it
         baby
       from
     you . . .
i'm
gonna spread out
over America
     intrude
my proud blackness
all
   over the place

i have wrested wheat fields
from the forests

turned rivers
from their courses

leveled mountains
at a word
festooned the land with
bridges

      gemlike
    on filaments of steel
      moved
glistening towers of Babel in place

sweated a whole
civilization

  now
      i'm
gonna breathe fire
through flaming nostrils BURN
   a place for

      me

in the skyscrapers and the
schoolrooms on the green
lawns and the white
beaches
      i'm
gonna wear the robes and
sit on the benches
make the rules and make
the arrests say
who can and who
can't
    baby you don't stand
    a
    chance
      i'm
gonna put black angels
in all the books and a black
Christchild in Mary's arms i'm
gonna make black bunnies black

fairies black santas black
nursery rhymes and
                    black
            ice cream
                i'm
gonna make it a
        crime
            to be anything BUT black

gonna make white
a twentyfourhour
lifetime
J.O.B.

What does the title of the poem mean?
Does the content of the poem support this
exclamation?

A Poem for Black Hearts

LEROI JONES (IMAMU AMIRI BARAKA)

For Malcolm's eyes, when they broke
the face of some dumb white man. For
Malcolm's hands raised to bless us
all black and strong in his image
of ourselves, for Malcolm's words
fire darts, the victor's tireless
thrusts, words hung above the world
change as it may, he said it, and
for this he was killed, for saying,
and feeling, and being/ change, all
collected hot in his heart, For Malcolm's
heart, raising us above our filthy cities,
for his stride, and his beat, and his address
to the grey monsters of the world, For Malcolm's
pleas for your dignity, black men, for your life,
black men, for the filling of your minds
with righteousness, For all of him dead and
gone and vanished from us, and all of him which
clings to our speech black god of our time.
For all of him, and all of yourself, look up,
black man, quit stuttering and shuffling, look up,
black man, quit whining and stooping, for all of him,
For Great Malcolm a prince of the earth, let nothing in us rest
until we avenge ourselves for his death, stupid animals
that killed him, let us never breathe a pure breath if
we fail, and white men call us faggots till the end of
the earth.

As part of your rehearsal process, look at this poem according to its phrasal units, each beginning with "For _____." If you line them up, how do they relate to one another in weight or importance? Does the speaker's *tone* and *attitude* change among the units? Who is the speaker's audience?

For Malcolm, A Year after
ETHERIDGE KNIGHT

Compose for Red a proper verse;
Adhere to foot and strict iamb;
Control the burst of angry words
Or they might boil and break the dam.
Or they might boil and overflow
And drench me, drown me, drive me
    mad.
So swear no oath, so shed no tear,
And sing no song blue Baptist sad.
Evoke no image, stir no flame,
And spin no yarn across the air.
Make empty anglo tea lace words—
Make them dead white and dry bone
    bare.

Compose a verse for Malcolm man,
And make it rime and make it prim.
The verse will die—as all men do—
But not the memory of him!
Death might come singing sweet like C,
Or knocking like the old folk say,
The moon and stars may pass away,
But not the anger of that day.

Does the regular rhythm and rhyme serve to contain feelings that might otherwise be uncontrollable? Do they seem artificial in light of intensely felt emotion?

Plane Wreck at Los Gatos (Deportee)
WOODY GUTHRIE

The crops are all in and the peaches are rotting,
The oranges are piled in their creosote dumps;
You're flying them back to the Mexican border
To pay all their money to wade back again.

Refrain:

Goodbye to my Juan, Goodbye Rosarita
Adiós mes amigos, Jesús and Marie,
You won't have a name when you ride the big airplane:
All they will call you will be deportee.

My father's own father he waded that river;
They took all the money he made in his life;
My brothers and sisters come working the fruit trees
And they rode the truck till they took down and died.

Some of us are illegal and some are not wanted,
Our work contract's out and we have to move on;
Six hundred miles to that Mexico border,
They chase us like outlaws, like rustlers, like thieves.

We died in your hills, we died in your deserts,
We died in your valleys and died on your plains;
We died neath your trees and we died in your bushes,
Both sides of this river we died just the same.

The sky plane caught fire over Los Gatos Canyon,
A fireball of lightning and shook all our hills
Who are all these friends all scattered like dry leaves?
The radio says they are just deportees.

Is this the best way we can grow our big orchards?
Is this is the best way we can grow our good fruit?
To fall like dry leaves to rot on my top soil
And be called by no name except deportees?

Occasioned by an actual plane crash, this ballad protests against injustices toward the migrant laborers who were being deported on the plane that crashed.

Perhaps you will divide the lines among several class members, thus emphasizing the victims and protesters as members of a larger group.

Speaking: The Hero

FELIX POLLAK

I did not want to go.
They inducted me.

I did not want to die.
They called me yellow.

I tried to run away.
They courtmartialed me.

I did not shoot.
They said I had no guts.

They ordered the attack.
A shrapnel tore my guts.

I cried in pain.
They carried me to safety.

In safety I died.
They blew taps over me.

They crossed out my name
and buried me under a cross.

They made a speech in my hometown.
I was unable to call them liars.

They said I gave my life.
I had struggled to keep it.

They said I set an example.
I had tried to run.

They said they were proud of me.
I had been ashamed of them.

They said my mother should also be
          proud.
My mother cried.

I wanted to live.
They called me a coward.

I died a coward.
They called me a hero.

How might you suggest in performance that this "hero" is speaking from the grave? What is his *tone* toward his audience?

This poem appears in a book that you might find useful if you decide to do a program or group performance on war literature: Walter Lowenfels, ed. *Where Is Vietnam? American Poets Respond* (Garden City, N.Y.: Doubleday, 1967).

House Guest
ELIZABETH BISHOP

The sad seamstress
who stays with us this month
is small and thin and bitter.
No one can cheer her up.
Give her a dress, a drink,
roast chicken, or fried fish—
it's all the same to her.

She sits and watches TV.
No, she watches zigzags.
"Can you adjust the TV?"
"No," she says. No hope.
She watches on and on,
without hope, without air.

Her own clothes give us pause,
but she's not a poor orphan.
She has a father, a mother,
and all that, and she's earning
quite well, and we're stuffing
her with fattening foods.

We invite her to use the binoculars.
We say, "Come see the jets!"
We say, "Come see the baby!"
Or the knife grinder who cleverly
plays the National Anthem
on his wheel so shrilly.
Nothing helps.

She speaks: "I need a little
money to buy buttons."
She seems to think it's useless
to ask. Heavens, buy buttons,
if they'll do any good,
the biggest in the world—
by the dozen, by the gross!
Buy yourself an ice cream,
a comic book, a car!

Her face is closed as a nut,
closed as a careful snail
or a thousand-year-old seed.
Does she dream of marriage?
Of getting rich? Her sewing
is decidedly mediocre.

Please! Take our money! Smile!
What on earth have we done?
What has everyone done
and when did it all begin?
Then one day she confides
that she wanted to be a nun
and her family opposed her.

Perhaps we should let her go,
or deliver her straight off
to the nearest convent—and wasn't
her month up last week, anyway?

Can it be that we nourish
one of the Fates in our bosoms?
Clotho, sewing our lives
with a bony little foot
on a borrowed sewing machine,
and our fates will be like hers,
and our hems crooked forever?

Itemize the reasons for the speaker's being distressed about the seamstress. When is the speaker positive? Negative? Neutral? List the various options the speaker has for dealing with her. Identify the references to "the Fates" and to "Clotho" in the last stanza.

Hands

SHERWOOD ANDERSON

Upon the half decayed veranda of a small frame house that stood near the edge of a ravine near the town of Winesburg, Ohio, a fat little old man walked nervously up and down. Across a long field that has been seeded for clover but that had produced only a dense crop of yellow mustard weeds, he could see the public highway along which went a wagon filled with berry pickers returning from the fields. The berry pickers, youths and maidens, laughed and shouted boisterously. A boy clad in a blue shirt leaped from the wagon and attempted to drag after him one of the maidens who screamed and protested shrilly. The feet of the boy in the road kicked up a cloud of dust that floated across the face of the departing sun. Over the long field came a thin girlish voice. "Oh, you Wing Biddlebaum, comb your hair, it's falling into your eyes," commanded the voice to the man, who was bald and whose nervous little hands fiddled about the bare white forehead as though arranging a mass of tangled locks.

Wing Biddlebaum, forever frightened and beset by a ghostly band of doubts, did not think of himself as in any way a part of the life of the town where he had lived for twenty years. Among all the people of Winesburg but one had come close to him. With George Willard, son of Tom Willard, the proprietor of the new Willard House, he had formed something like a friendship. George Willard was the reporter on the *Winesburg Eagle* and sometimes in the evenings he walked out along the highway to Wing Biddlebaum's house. Now as the old man walked up and down on the veranda, his hands moving nervously about, he was hoping that George Willard would come and spend the evening with him. After the wagon containing the berry pickers had passed, he went across the field through the tall mustard weeds and climbing a rail fence peered anxiously along the road to the town. For a moment he stood thus, rubbing his hands together and looking up and down the road, and then, fear overcoming him, ran back to walk again upon the porch on his own house.

In the presence of George Willard, Wing Biddlebaum, who for twenty years had been the town mystery, lost something of his timidity, and his shadowy personality, submerged in a sea of doubts, came forth to look at the world. With the young reporter at his side, he ventured in the light of day into Main Street or strode up and down on the rickety front porch of his own house, talking excitedly. The voice that had been low and trembling became shrill and loud. The bent figure straightened. With a kind of wriggle, like a fish returned to the brook by the fisherman, Biddlebaum the silent began to talk, striving to put into words the ideas that had been accumulated by his mind during long years of silence.

Wing Biddlebaum talked much with his hands. The slender expressive fingers, forever active, forever striving to conceal themselves in his pockets or behind his back, came forth and became the piston rods of his machinery of expression.

The story of Wing Biddlebaum is a story of hands. Their restless activity, like unto the beating of the wings of an imprisoned bird, had given him his name. Some obscure poet of the town had thought of it. The hands alarmed their owner. He wanted to keep them hidden away and looked with amazement at the quiet inexpressive hands of other men who worked beside him in the fields, or passed, driving sleepy teams on country roads.

When he talked to George Willard, Wing Biddlebaum closed his fists and beat with them upon a table or on the walls of his house. The action made him more comfortable. If the desire to talk came to him when the two were walking in the fields, he sought out a stump or a top board of a fence and with his hands pounding busily talked with renewed ease.

The story of Wing Biddlebaum's hands is worth a book in itself. Sympathetically set forth it would tap many strange, beautiful qualities in obscure men. It is a job for a poet. In Winesburg the hands had attracted attention merely because of their activity. With them Wing Biddlebaum had picked as high as a hundred and forty quarts of strawberries in a day. They became his distinguishing feature, the source of his fame. Also they made more grotesque an already grotesque and elusive individuality. Winesburg was proud of the hands of Wing Biddlebaum in the same spirit in which it was proud of Banker White's new stone house and Wesley Moyer's bay stallion, Tony Tip, that had won the two-fifteen trot at the fall races in Cleveland.

As for George Willard, he had many times wanted to ask about the hands. At times an almost overwhelming curiosity had taken hold of him. He felt that there must be a reason for their strange activity and their inclination to keep hidden away and only growing respect for Wing Biddlebaum kept him from blurting out the questions that were often in his mind.

Once he had been on the point of asking. The two were walking in the fields on a summer afternoon and had stopped to sit upon a grassy bank. All afternoon Wing Biddlebaum had talked as one inspired. By a fence he had stopped and beating like a giant woodpecker upon the top board had shouted at George Willard, condemning his tendency to be too much influenced by the people about him. "You are destroying yourself," he cried. "You have the inclination to be alone and to dream and you are afraid of dreams. You want to be like others in town here. You hear them talk and you try to imitate them."

On the grassy bank Wing Biddlebaum had tried again to drive his point home. His voice became soft and reminiscent, and with a sigh of contentment he launched into a long rambling talk, speaking as one lost in a dream.

Out of the dream Wing Biddlebaum made a picture for George Willard. In the picture men lived again in a kind of pastoral golden age. Across a green open country came clean-limbed young men, some afoot, some mounted upon horses. In crowds the young men came to gather about the feet of an old man who sat beneath a tree in a tiny garden and who talked to them.

Wing Biddlebaum became wholly inspired. For once he forgot the hands. Slowly they stole forth and lay upon George Willard's shoulders. Something new and bold came into the voice that talked. "You must try to forget all you have learned," said the old man. "You must begin to dream. From this time on you must shut your ears to the roaring of the voices."

Pausing in his speech, Wing Biddlebaum looked long and earnestly at George Willard. His eyes glowed. Again he raised the hands to caress the boy and then a look of horror swept over his face.

With a convulsive movement of his body, Wing Biddlebaum sprang to his feet and thrust his hands deep into his trousers pockets. Tears came to his eyes. "I must be getting along home. I can talk no more with you," he said nervously.

Without looking back, the old man had hurried down the hillside and across a meadow, leaving George Willard perplexed and frightened upon the grassy slope. With a shiver of dread the boy arose and went along the road toward town. "I'll not ask him about his hands," he thought, touched by the memory of the terror he had seen in the man's eyes. "There's something wrong, but I don't want to know what it is. His hands have something to do with his fear of me and of everyone."

And George Willard was right. Let us look briefly into the story of the hands. Perhaps our talking of them will arouse the poet who will tell the hidden wonder story of the influence for which the hands were but fluttering pennants of promise.

In his youth Wing Biddlebaum had been a schoolteacher in a town in Pennsylvania. He was not then known as Wing Biddlebaum, but went by the less euphonic name of Adolph Myers. As Adolph Myers he was much loved by the boys of his school.

Adolph Myers was meant by nature to be a teacher of youth. He was one of those rare, little-understood men who rule by a power so gentle that it passes as a lovable weakness. In their feeling for the boys under their charge such men are not unlike the finer sort of women in their love of men.

And yet that is but crudely stated. It needs the poet there. With the boys of his school, Adolph Myers had walked in the evening or had been talking until dusk upon the schoolhouse steps lost in a kind of dream. Here and there went his hands, caressing the shoulders of the boys, playing about the tousled heads. As he talked his voice became soft and musical. There was a caress in that also. In a way the voice and the hands, the stroking of the shoulders and the touching of the hair was a part of the schoolmaster's effort to carry a dream into the young minds. By the caress that was in his fingers he expressed himself. He was one of those men in whom the force that creates life is diffused, not centralized. Under the caress of his hands doubt and disbelief went out of the minds of the boys and they began also to dream.

And then the tragedy. A half-witted boy of the school became enamored of the young master. In his bed at night he imagined unspeakable things and in the morning went forth to tell his dreams as facts. Strange, hideous accusations fell from his loose-hung lips. Through the Pennsylvania town went a shiver. Hidden, shadowy doubts that had been in men's minds concerning Adolph Myers were galvanized into beliefs.

The tragedy did not linger. Trembling lads were jerked out of bed and questioned. "He put his arms about me," said one. "His fingers were always playing in my hair," said another.

One afternoon a man of the town, Henry Bradford, who kept a saloon, came to the schoolhouse door. Calling Adolph Myers into the school yard he began to beat him with his fists. As his hard knuckles beat down into the frightened face of the schoolmaster, his wrath became more and more terrible. Screaming with dismay, the children ran here and there like disturbed insects.

"I'll teach you to put your hands on my boy, you beast," roared the saloon keeper, who, tired of beating the master, had begun to kick him about the yard.

Adolph Myers was driven from the Pennsylvania town in the night. With lanterns in their hands a dozen men came to the door of the house where he lived alone and commanded that he dress and come forth. It was raining and one of the men had a rope in his hands. They had intended to hang the schoolmaster, but something in his figure, so small, white, and pitiful, touched their hearts and they let him escape. As he ran away into the darkness they repented of their weakness and ran after him, swearing and throwing sticks and great balls of soft mud at the figure that screamed and ran faster and faster into the darkness.

For twenty years Adolph Myers had lived alone in Winesburg. He was but forty but looked sixty-five. The name of Biddlebaum he got from a box of goods seen at a freight station as he hurried through an eastern Ohio town. He had an aunt in Winesburg, a black-toothed old woman who raised chickens, and with her he lived until she died. He had been ill for a year after the experience in Pennsylvania, and after his recovery worked as a day laborer in the fields, going timidly about and striving to conceal his hands. Although he did not understand what had happened he felt that the hands must be to blame. Again and again the fathers of the boys had talked of the hands. "Keep your hands to yourself," the saloon keeper had roared, dancing with fury in the schoolhouse yard.

Upon the veranda of his house by the ravine Wing Biddlebaum continued to walk up and down until the sun had disappeared and the road beyond the field was lost in the gray shadows. Going into his house he cut slices of bread and spread honey upon them. When the rumble of the evening train that took away the express cars loaded with the day's harvest of berries had passed and restored the silence of the summer night, he went again to walk upon the veranda. In the darkness he could not see the hands and they became quiet. Although he still hungered for the presence of the boy, who was the medium through which he expressed his love of man, the hunger became again a part of his loneliness and his waiting. Lighting a lamp, Wing Biddlebaum washed the few dishes soiled by his simple meal and, setting up a folding cot by the screen door that led to the porch, prepared to undress for the night. A few stray white bread crumbs lay on the cleanly washed floor by the table; putting the lamp upon a low stool he began to pick up the crumbs, carrying them to his mouth one by one with unbelievable rapidity. In the dense blotch of light beneath the table, the kneeling figure looked like a priest in some service of his church. The nervous expressive fingers, flashing in and out of the light, might well have been mistaken for the fingers of the devotee going swiftly through decade after decade of his rosary.

"Hands" appears in *Winesburg, Ohio,* Anderson's cycle of stories that "attempt to break down the walls that divide one person from another" (Malcolm Cowley, "Introduction," *Winesburg, Ohio.* New York: Viking Press, 1960).

What is the narrator's attitude toward Biddlebaum? Toward Myers?

Divinely Superfluous Beauty
ROBINSON JEFFERS

The storm-dances of gulls, the barking game of seals,
Over and under the ocean . . .
Divinely superfluous beauty
Rules the games, presides over destinies, makes trees grow
And hills tower, waves fall.
The incredible beauty of joy
Stars with fire the joining of lips, O let our loves too
Be joined, there is not a maiden
Burns and thirsts for love
More than my blood for you, by the shore of seals while the wings
Weave like a web in the air
Divinely superfluous beauty.

Once again, who is the "you" in this poem? A lover? A spouse? Male? Female? Present? Absent? Present, but cannot hear the speaker? What is the difference, if any, between the speaker's subtext when first saying "Divinely superfluous beauty" and then repeating it on the last line?

What Thomas an Buile Said in a Pub
JAMES STEPHENS

I saw God. Do you doubt it?
    Do you dare to doubt it?
I saw the Almighty Man. His hand
Was resting on a mountain, and
He looked upon the World and all about it:
I saw Him plainer than you see me now,
    You mustn't doubt it.

He was not satisfied;
    His look was all dissatisfied.
His beard swung on a wind far out of sight
Behind the world's curve, and there was light
Most fearful from His forehead, and He sighed,
"That star went always wrong, and from the start
    I was dissatisfied."

He lifted up His hand—
    I say He heaved a dreadful hand
Over the spinning Earth. Then I said, "Stay,
You must not strike it, God; I'm in the way;
And I will never move from where I stand."
He said, "Dear child, I feared that you were dead,"
    And stayed His hand.

In what way does the title of the poem affect your identification of the speaker, listener(s), and scene? Is the situation *open, closed,* or a blend of both?

small comment
SONIA SANCHEZ

the name of the beast is the
man or to be more specific
the nature of man is his
bestial nature or to
bring it to its elemental terms
the nature of nature is
the bestial survival of the
fittest the strongest the richest
or to really examine
the scene we cd say that
the nature of any beast is
bestial unnatural and natural
in its struggle for superiority
and survival but to really
be with it we will say that the man
is a natural beast bestial in
his lusts natural in his

bestiality and expanding
and growing on the national
scene to be the most
bestial and natural of
any beast.   you dig?

Consider performing the poem as (1) a lecturer explaining the relationship among the words "man," "beast," and "nature," (2) a militant black person addressing a group of lethargic blacks, and (3) a militant black person addressing a mixed group of sympathetic listeners. After performing all three speaker–scene relationships, comment on your own preference.

Semidetached
ROBERT GRAVES

Her inevitable complaint or accusation
Whatever the Major does or leaves undone,
Though, being a good wife, never before strangers,
Nor, being a good mother, even before their child . . .
With no endearments except for cats and kittens
Or an occasional bird rescued from cats . . .
Well, as semidetached neighbors, with party walls
Not altogether soundproof, we overhear
The rare explosion when he retaliates
In a sudden burst of anger, although perhaps
(We are pretty sure) apologizing later
And getting no forgiveness or reply.

He has his own resources—bees and gardening—
And, we conclude, is on the whole happy.
They never sleep together, as they once did
Five or six years ago, when they first arrived,
Or so we judge from washing on their line—
Those double sheets are now for guests only—
But welcome streams of visitors. How many
Suspect that the show put on by both of them,
Of perfect marital love, is apology,
In sincere make-believe, for what still lacks?

If ever she falls ill, which seldom happens,
We know he nurses her indefatigably,
But this she greets, we know, with sour resentment,
Hating to catch herself at a disadvantage,
And crawls groaning downstairs to sink and oven.
If he falls ill she treats it as an affront—
Except at the time of that car accident
When he nearly died, and unmistakable grief
Shone from her eyes for almost a whole fortnight,
But then faded . . .

        He receives regular airmail
In the same handwriting, with Austrian stamps.
Whoever sends it, obviously a woman,
Never appears. Those are his brightest moments.
Somehow they take no holidays whatsoever
But are good neighbors, always ready to lend
And seldom borrowing. Our child plays with theirs;
Yet we exchange no visits or confidences.
Only once I penetrated past their hall—
Which was when I fetched him from the wrecked car
And alone knew who had caused the accident.

Is the speaker in "Semidetached" a *major participant* in the action? A *minor participant*? What is the effect of having only limited information on your response to the couple? What do you know *for sure* about each of them? Do you trust the speaker to be *truthful*? Why? What could have provoked the speaker to tell the story? Comment on the title's significance.

Listening to grownups quarreling,
RUTH WHITMAN

standing in the hall against the
wall with my little brother, blown
like leaves against the wall by their
voices, my head like a pingpong ball
between the paddles of their anger:
I knew what it meant
to tremble like a leaf.

Cold with their wrath. I heard
the claws of the rain
pounce. Floods

poured through the city,
skies clapped over me,
and I was shaken, shaken
like a mouse
between their jaws.

The speaker describes an event in the past, but does so with clarity and intensity. How does the remembered scene (room and weather) underscore the terror of the incident?

A Family Man
MAXINE KUMIN

We are talking in bed. You show me snapshots.
Your wallet opens like a salesman's case
on a dog, a frame house hung with shutters
and your eyes reset in a child's face.
Here is your mother standing in full sun
on the veranda back home. She is wearing
what we used to call a washdress. Geraniums
flank her as pious in their bearing
as the soap and water she called down on your head.
We carry around our mothers. But mine is dead.

Out of the celluloid album, cleverly as a shill
you pull an old snap of yourself squatting beside
a stag you shot early in the war in the Black Hills.
The dog tags dangle on your naked chest.
The rifle, broken, lies across your knees.
What do I say to the killer you love best,
that boy-man full of his summer expertise?
I with no place in the file will
wake on dark mornings alone with him in my head.
This is what comes of snapshots. Of talking in bed.

Even though the speaker in "A Family Man" uses *present* tense, it is still possible that the event is actually *past*. The speaker could be reliving the incident of looking at the photographs. Perform the poem both ways and discuss the advantages and limitations of each choice.

Sound out the poem's title (1) as you think the speaker would voice it and (2) as the man would voice it.

Androcles and the Lion
GEORGE BERNARD SHAW

Overture: forest sounds, roaring of lions, Christian hymn faintly.

A jungle path. A lion's roar, a melancholy suffering roar, comes from the jungle. It is repeated nearer. The lion limps from the jungle on three legs, holding up his right forepaw, in which a huge thorn sticks. He sits down and contemplates it. He licks it. He shakes it. He tries to extract it by scraping it along the ground, and hurts himself worse. He roars piteously. He licks it again. Tears drop from his eyes. He limps painfully off the path and lies down under the trees, exhausted with pain. Heaving a long sigh, like wind in a trombone, he goes to sleep.

Androcles and his wife Megaera come along the path. He is a small, thin, ridiculous little man who might be any age from thirty to fifty-five. He has sandy hair, watery compassionate blue eyes, sensitive nostrils, and a very presentable forehead; but his good points go no further: his arms and legs and back, though wiry of their kind, look shrivelled and starved. He carries a big bundle, is very poorly clad, and seems tired and hungry.

His wife is a rather handsome pampered slattern, well fed and in the prime of life. She has nothing to carry, and has a stout stick to help her along.

MEGAERA: *(suddenly throwing down her stick)* I wont go another step.

ANDROCLES: *(pleading wearily)* Oh, not again, dear. Whats the good of stopping every two miles and saying you wont go another step? We must get on to the next village before night. There are wild beasts in this wood: lions, they say.

MEGAERA: I dont believe a word of it. You are always threatening me with wild beasts to make me walk the very soul out of my body when I can hardly drag one foot before another. We havnt seen a single lion yet.

ANDROCLES: Well, dear, do you want to see one?

MEGAERA: *(tearing the bundle from his back)* You cruel brute, you dont care how tired I am, or what becomes of me *(she throws the bundle on the ground):* always thinking of yourself. Self! self! self! always yourself. *(She sits down on the bundle).*

ANDROCLES: *(sitting down sadly on the ground with his elbows on his knees and his head in his hands)* We all have to think of ourselves occasionally, dear.

MEGAERA: A man ought to think of his wife sometimes.

ANDROCLES: He cant always help it, dear. You make me think of you a good deal. Not that I blame you.

MEGAERA: Blame me! I should think not indeed. Is it my fault that I'm married to you?

ANDROCLES: No, dear: that is my fault.

MEGAERA: Thats a nice thing to say to me. Arnt you happy with me?

ANDROCLES: I dont complain, my love.

MEGAERA: You ought to be ashamed of yourself.

ANDROCLES: I am, my dear.

MEGAERA: Youre not: you glory in it.

ANDROCLES: In what, darling?

MEGAERA: In everything. In making me a slave, and making yourself a laughing-stock. It's not fair. You get me the name of being a shrew with your meek ways, always talking as if butter wouldnt melt in your mouth. And just because I look a big strong woman, and because I'm goodhearted and a bit hasty, and because youre always driving me to do things I'm sorry for afterwards, people say "Poor man: what a life his wife leads him!" Oh, if they only knew! And you think I dont know. But I do, I do, *(screaming)* I do.

ANDROCLES: Yes, my dear: I know you do.

MEGAERA: Then why dont you treat me properly and be a good husband to me?

ANDROCLES: What can I do, my dear?

MEGAERA: What can you do! You can return to your duty, and come back to your home and your friends, and sacrifice to the gods as all respectable people do, instead of having us hunted out of house and home for being dirty disreputable blaspheming atheists.

ANDROCLES: I'm not an atheist, dear: I am a Christian.

MEGAERA: Well, isnt that the same thing, only ten times worse? Everybody knows that the Christians are the very lowest of the low.

ANDROCLES: Just like us, dear.

MEGAERA: Speak for yourself. Dont you dare to compare me to common people. My father owned his own public-house; and sorrowful was the day for me when you first came drinking in our bar.

ANDROCLES: I confess I was addicted to it, dear. But I gave it up when I became a Christian.

MEGAERA: Youd much better have remained a drunkard. I can forgive a man being addicted to drink: it's only natural; and I dont deny I like a drop myself sometimes. What I cant stand is your being addicted to Christianity. And whats worse again, your being addicted to animals. How is any woman to keep her house clean when you bring in every stray cat and lost cur and lame duck in the whole countryside? You took the bread out of my mouth to feed them: you know you did: dont attempt to deny it.

ANDROCLES: Only when they were hungry and you were getting too stout, dearie.

MEGAERA: Yes: insult me, do. *(Rising)* Oh! I wont bear it another moment. You used to sit and talk to those dumb brute beasts for hours, when you hadnt a word for me.

ANDROCLES: They never answered back, darling. *(He rises and again shoulders the bundle).*

MEGAERA: Well, if youre fonder of animals than of your own wife, you can live with them here in the jungle. Ive had enough of them and enough of you. I'm going back. I'm going home.

ANDROCLES: *(barring the way back)* No, dearie: dont take on like that. We cant go back. Weve sold everything: we should starve; and I should be sent to Rome and thrown to the lions—

MEGAERA: Serve you right! I wish the lions joy of you. *(Screaming)* Are you going to get out of my way and let me go home?

ANDROCLES: No, dear—

MEGAERA: Then I'll make my way through the forest; and when I'm eaten by the wild beasts youll know what a wife youve lost. *(She dashes into the jungle and nearly falls over the sleeping lion).* Oh! Oh! Andy! Andy! *(She totters back and collapses into the arms of Androcles, who, crushed by her weight, falls on his bundle).*

ANDROCLES: *(extracting himself from beneath her and slapping her hands in great anxiety)* What is it, my precious, my pet? Whats the matter? *(He raises her head. Speechless with terror, she points in the direction of the sleeping lion. He steals cautiously toward the spot indicated by Megaera. She rises with an effort and totters after him).*

MEGAERA: No, Andy: youll be killed. Come back.
    The lion utters a long snoring sigh. Androcles sees the lion, and recoils fainting into the arms of Megaera, who falls back on the bundle. They roll apart and lie staring in terror at one another. The lion is heard groaning heavily in the jungle.

ANDROCLES: *(whispering)* Did you see? A lion.

MEGAERA: *(despairing)* The gods have sent him to punish us because youre a Christian. Take me away, Andy. Save me.

ANDROCLES: *(rising)* Meggy: theres one chance for you. Itll take him pretty nigh twenty minutes to eat me (I'm rather stringy and tough) and you can escape in less time than that.

MEGAERA: Oh, dont talk about eating. *(The lion rises with a great groan and limps toward them).* Oh! *(She faints).*

ANDROCLES: *(quaking, but keeping between the lion and Megaera)* Dont you come near my wife, do you hear? *(The lion groans. Androcles can hardly stand for trembling).* Meggy: run. Run for your life. If I take my eye off him, it's all up. *(The lion holds up his wounded paw and flaps it piteously before Androcles).* Oh, he's lame, poor old chap! He's got a thorn in his paw. A frightfully big thorn. *(Full of sympathy)* Oh, poor old man! Did um get an awful thorn into um's tootsums wootsums? Has it made um too sick to eat a nice little Christian man for um's breakfast? Oh, a nice little Christian man will get um's thorn out for um; and then um shall eat the nice Christian man and the nice Christian man's nice big tender wifey pifey. *(The lion responds by moans of self-pity).* Yes, yes, yes, yes, yes. Now, now *(taking the paw in his hand),* um is not to bite and not to scratch, not even if it hurts a very very little. Now make velvet paws. Thats right. *(He pulls gingerly at the thorn. The lion, with an angry yell of pain, jerks back his paw so abruptly that Androcles is thrown on his back).* Steadeee! Oh, did the nasty cruel little Christian man hurt the sore paw? *(The lion moans assentingly but apologetically).* Well, one more little pull and it will be all over. Just one little, little, leetle pull; and then um will live happily ever after. *(He gives the thorn another pull. The lion roars and snaps his jaws with a terrifying clash).* Oh, mustnt frighten um's good kind doctor, um's affectionate nursey. That didnt hurt at all: not a bit. Just one more. Just to shew how the brave big lion can bear pain, not like the little crybaby Christian man. Oopsh! *(The thorn comes out. The lion yells with pain, and shakes his paw wildly).* Thats it! *(Holding up the thorn).* Now it's out. Now lick um's paw to take away the nasty inflammation. See? *(He licks his own hand. The lion nods intelligently and licks his paw industriously).* Clever little liony-piony! Understands um's dear old friend Andy Wandy. *(The lion licks his face).* Yes, kissums Andy Wandy. *(The lion, wagging his tail violently, rises on his hind legs, and embraces Androcles, who makes a wry face and cries)* Velvet paws! Velvet paws! *(The lion draws in his claws).* Thats right. *(He embraces the lion, who finally takes the end of his tail in one paw, places that tight round Androcles' waist, resting it on his hip. Androcles takes the other paw in his hand, stretches out his arm, and the two waltz rapturously round and round and finally away through the jungle).*

MEGAERA: *(who has revived during the waltz)* Oh, you coward, you havnt danced with me for years; and now you go off dancing with a great brute beast that you havnt known for ten minutes and that wants to eat your own wife. Coward! Coward! Coward! *(She rushes off after them into the jungle).*

Androcles and the Lion may be, as some of its critics say, an indictment of organized religion. But in this opening scene, the play is first of all a story about a charitable man, his aggressive wife, and a lion.

In performing the scene, you may wish to incorporate some of the stage directions as narration. You are encouraged to make bold distinctions among the characters in the scene.

A Rose for Emily

WILLIAM FAULKNER

I

When Miss Emily Grierson died, our whole town went to her funeral: the men through a sort of respectful affection for a fallen monument, the women mostly out of curiosity to see the inside of her house, which no one save an old man servant—a combined gardener and cook—had seen in at least ten years.

It was a big, squarish frame house that had once been white, decorated with cupolas and spires and scrolled balconies in the heavily lightsome style of the Seventies, set on what had once been our most select street. But garages and cotton gins had encroached and obliterated even the august names of that neighborhood; only Miss Emily's house was left, lifting its stubborn and co-quettish decay above the cotton wagons and the gasoline pumps—an eyesore among eyesores. And now Miss Emily had gone to join the representatives of those august names where they lay in the cedar-bemused cemetery among the ranked and anonymous graves of Union and Confederate soldiers who fell at the battle of Jefferson.

Alive, Miss Emily had been a tradition, a duty, and a care; a sort of heredi-tary obligation upon the town, dating from that day in 1894 when Colonel Sar-toris, the mayor—he who fathered the edict that no Negro woman should ap-pear on the streets without an apron—remitted her taxes, the dispensation dating from the death of her father on into perpetuity. Not that Miss Emily would have accepted charity. Colonel Sartoris invented an involved tale to the effect that Miss Emily's father had loaned money to the town, which the town, as a matter of business, preferred this way of repaying. Only a man of Colonel Sartoris' generation and thought could have invented it, and only a woman could have believed it.

When the next generation, with its more modern ideas, became mayors and aldermen, this arrangement created some little dissatisfaction. On the first of the year they mailed her a tax notice. February came, and there was no reply. They wrote her a formal letter, asking her to call at the sheriff's office at her convenience. A week later the mayor wrote her himself, offering to call or to send his car for her, and received in reply a note on paper of an archaic shape, in a thin, flowing calligraphy in faded ink, to the effect that she no longer went out at all. The tax notice was also enclosed, without comment.

They called a special meeting of the Board of Aldermen. A deputation waited upon her, knocked at the door through which no visitor had passed since she ceased giving china-painting lessons eight or ten years earlier. They were admitted by the old Negro into a dim hall from which a stairway mounted into still more shadow. It smelled of dust and disuse—a close, dank smell. The Negro led them into the parlor. It was furnished in heavy, leather-covered furniture. When the Negro opened the blinds of one window, they could see that the leather was cracked; and when they sat down, a faint dust rose sluggishly about their thighs, spinning with slow motes into the single sun-ray. On a tarnished gilt easel before the fireplace stood a crayon portrait of Miss Emily's father.

They rose when she entered—a small, fat woman in black, with a thin gold chain descending to her waist and vanishing into her belt, leaning on an ebony cane with a tarnished gold head. Her skeleton was small and spare; perhaps that was why what would have been merely plumpness in another was obesity in her. She looked bloated, like a body long submerged in motionless water, and of that pallid hue. Her eyes, lost in the fatty ridges of her face, looked like two small pieces of coal pressed into a lump of dough as they moved from one face to another while the visitors stated their errand.

She did not ask them to sit. She just stood in the door and listened quietly until the spokesman came to a stumbling halt. Then they could hear the invisible watch ticking at the end of the gold chain.

Her voice was dry and cold. "I have no taxes in Jefferson. Colonel Sartoris explained it to me. Perhaps one of you can gain access to the city records and satisfy yourselves."

"But we have. We are the city authorities, Miss Emily. Didn't you get a notice from the sheriff, signed by him?"

"I received a paper, yes," Miss Emily said. "Perhaps he considers himself the sheriff . . . I have no taxes in Jefferson."

"But there is nothing on the books to show that, you see. We must go by the—"

"See Colonel Sartoris. I have no taxes in Jefferson."

"But, Miss Emily—"

"See Colonel Sartoris." (Colonel Sartoris had been dead almost ten years.) "I have no taxes in Jefferson. Tobe!" The Negro appeared. "Show these gentlemen out."

II

So she vanquished them, horse and foot, just as she had vanquished their fathers thirty years before about the smell. That was two years after her father's death and a short time after her sweetheart—the one we believed would marry her—had deserted her. After her father's death she went out very little; after her sweetheart went away, people hardly saw her at all. A few of the ladies had the temerity to call, but were not received, and the only sign of life about the place was the Negro man—a young man then—going in and out with a market basket.

"Just as if a man—any man—could keep a kitchen properly," the ladies said; so they were not surprised when the smell developed. It was another link between the gross teeming world and the high and mighty Griersons.

A neighbor, a woman, complained to the mayor, Judge Stevens, eighty years old.

"But what will you have me do about it, madam?" he said.

"Why, send her word to stop it," the woman said. "Isn't there a law?"

"I'm sure that won't be necessary," Judge Stevens said. "It's probably just a snake or a rat that nigger of hers killed in the yard. I'll speak to him about it."

The next day he received two more complaints, one from a man who came in diffident deprecation. "We really must do something about it, Judge. I'd be the last one in the world to bother Miss Emily, but we've got to do something." That night the Board of Aldermen met—three graybeards and one younger man, a member of the rising generation.

"It's simple enough," he said. "Send her word to have her place cleaned up. Give her a certain time to do it in, and if she don't . . ."

"Dammit, sir," Judge Stevens said, "will you accuse a lady to her face of smelling bad?"

So the next night, after midnight, four men crossed Miss Emily's lawn and slunk about the house like burglars, sniffing along the base of the brickwork and at the cellar openings while one of them performed a regular sowing motion with his hand out of a sack slung from his shoulder. They broke open the cellar door and sprinkled lime there, and in all the outbuildings. As they recrossed the lawn, a window that had been dark was lighted and Miss Emily sat in it, the light behind her, and her upright torso motionless as that of an idol. They crept quietly across the lawn and into the shadows of the locusts that lined the street. After a week or two the smell went away.

That was when people had begun to feel really sorry for her. People in our town, remembering how Old Lady Wyatt, her great-aunt, had gone completely crazy at last, believed that the Griersons held themselves a little too high for what they really were. None of the young men was quite good enough to Miss Emily and such. We had long thought of them as a tableau: Miss Emily a slender figure in white in the background, her father a spraddled silhouette in the foreground, his back to her and clutching a horse-whip, the two of them framed by the back-flung front door. So when she got to be thirty and was still single, we were not pleased exactly, but vindicated; even with insanity in the family she wouldn't have turned down all of her chances if they had really materialized.

When her father died, it got about that the house was all that was left to her; and in a way, people were glad. At last they could pity Miss Emily. Being left alone, and a pauper, she had become humanized. Now she too would know the old thrill and the old despair of a penny more or less.

The day after his death all the ladies prepared to call at the house and offer condolence and aid, as is our custom. Miss Emily met them at the door, dressed as usual and with no trace of grief on her face. She told them that her father was not dead. She did that for three days, with the ministers calling on her, and the doctors, trying to persuade her to let them dispose of the body. Just as they were about to resort to law and force, she broke down, and they buried her father quickly.

We did not say she was crazy then. We believed she had to do that. We remembered all the young men her father had driven away, and we knew that with nothing left, she would have to cling to that which had robbed her, as people will.

III

She was sick for a long time. When we saw her again, her hair was cut short, making her look like a girl, with a vague resemblance to those angels in colored church windows—sort of tragic and serene.

The town had just let the contracts for paving the sidewalks, and in the summer after her father's death they began the work. The construction company came with niggers and mules and machinery, and a foreman named Homer Barron, a Yankee—a big, dark, ready man, with a big voice and eyes lighter than his face. The little boys would follow in groups to hear him cuss the niggers, and the niggers singing in time to the rise and fall of picks. Pretty soon he knew everybody in town. Whenever you heard a lot of laughing anywhere about the square, Homer Barron would be in the center of the group. Presently we began to see him and Miss Emily on Sunday afternoons driving in the yellow-wheeled buggy and the matched team of bays from the livery stable.

At first we were glad that Miss Emily would have an interest, because the ladies all said, "Of course a Grierson would not think seriously of a Northerner, a day laborer." But there were still others, older people, who said that even grief could not cause a real lady to forget *noblesse oblige*—without calling it *noblesse oblige*. They just said, "Poor Emily. Her kinsfolk should come to her." She had some kin in Alabama; but years ago her father had fallen out with them over the estate of Old Lady Wyatt, the crazy woman, and there was no communication between the two families. They had not even been represented at the funeral.

And as soon as the old people said, "Poor Emily," the whispering began. "Do you suppose it's really so?" they said to one another. "Of course it is. What else could . . ." This behind their hands; rustling of craned silk and satin behind jalousies closed upon the sun of Sunday afternoon as the thin, swift clop-clop-clop of the matched team passed: "Poor Emily."

She carried her head high enough—even when we believed that she was fallen. It was as if she demanded more than ever the recognition of her dignity as the last Grierson; as if it had wanted that touch of earthiness to reaffirm her imperviousness. Like when she bought the rat poison, the arsenic. That was over a year after they had begun to say "Poor Emily," and while the two female cousins were visiting her.

"I want some poison," she said to the druggist. She was over thirty then, still a slight woman, though thinner than usual, with cold, haughty black eyes in a face the flesh of which was strained across the temples and about the eye-sockets as you imagine a lighthouse-keeper's face ought to look. "I want some poison," she said.

"Yes, Miss Emily. What kind? For rats and such? I'd recom—"

"I want the best you have. I don't care what kind."

The druggist named several. "They'll kill anything up to an elephant. But what you want is—"

"Arsenic," Miss Emily said. "Is that a good one?"

"Is . . . arsenic? Yes, ma'am. But what you want—"

"I want arsenic."

The druggist looked down at her. She looked back at him, erect, her face like a strained flag. "Why, of course," the druggist said. "If that's what you want. But the law requires you to tell what you are going to use it for."

Miss Emily just stared at him, her head tilted back in order to look him eye for eye, until he looked away and went and got the arsenic and wrapped it up. The Negro delivery boy brought her the package; the druggist didn't come back. When she opened the package at home there was written on the box, under the skull and bones: "For rats."

IV

So the next day we all said, "She will kill herself"; and we said it would be the best thing. When she had first begun to be seen with Homer Barron, we had said, "She will marry him." Then we said, "She will persuade him yet," because Homer himself had remarked—he liked men, and it was known that he drank with the younger men in the Elks' Club—that he was not a marrying man. Later we said, "Poor Emily" behind the jalousies as they passed on Sunday afternoon in the glittering buggy, Miss Emily with her head high and Homer Barron with his hat cocked and a cigar in his teeth, reins and whip in a yellow glove.

Then some of the ladies began to say that it was a disgrace to the town and a bad example to the young people. The men did not want to interfere, but at last the ladies forced the Baptist minister—Miss Emily's people were Episcopal—to call upon her. He would never divulge what happened during that interview, but he refused to go back again. The next Sunday they again drove about the streets, and the following day the minister's wife wrote to Miss Emily's relations in Alabama.

So she had blood-kin under her roof again and we sat back to watch developments. At first nothing happened. Then we were sure that they were to be married. We learned that Miss Emily had been to the jeweler's and ordered a man's toilet set in silver, with the letters H. B. on each piece. Two days later we learned that she had bought a complete outfit of men's clothing, including a nightshirt, and we said, "They are married." We were really glad. We were glad because the two female cousins were even more Grierson than Miss Emily had ever been.

So we were not surprised when Homer Barron—the streets had been finished some time since—was gone. We were a little disappointed that there was not a public blowing-off, but we believed that he had gone on to prepare for Miss Emily's coming, or to give her a chance to get rid of the cousins. (By that time it was a cabal, and we were all Miss Emily's allies to help circumvent the cousins.) Sure enough, after another week they departed. And, as we had expected all along, within three days Homer Barron was back in town. A neighbor saw the Negro man admit him at the kitchen door at dusk one evening.

And that was the last we saw of Homer Barron. And of Miss Emily for some time. The Negro man went in and out with the market basket, but the front door remained closed. Now and then we would see her at a window for a moment, as the men did that night when they sprinkled the lime, but for almost six months she did not appear on the streets. Then we knew that this was to be expected too; as if that quality of her father which had thwarted her woman's life so many times had been too virulent and too furious to die.

When we next saw Miss Emily, she had grown fat and her hair was turning gray. During the next few years it grew grayer and grayer until it attained an even pepper-and-salt iron-gray, when it ceased turning. Up to the day of her death at seventy-four it was still that vigorous iron-gray, like the hair of an active man.

From that time on her front door remained closed, save for a period of six or seven years, when she was about forty, during which she gave lessons in china-painting. She fitted up a studio in one of the downstairs rooms, where the daughters and granddaughters of Colonel Sartoris' contemporaries were sent to her with the same regularity and in the same spirit that they were sent to church on Sundays with a twenty-five-cent piece for the collection plate. Meanwhile her taxes had been remitted.

Then the newer generation became the backbone and the spirit of the town, and the painting pupils grew up and fell away and did not send their children to her with boxes of color and tedious brushes and pictures cut from the ladies' magazines. The front door closed upon the last one and remained closed for good. When the town got free postal delivery, Miss Emily alone refused to let them fasten the metal numbers above her door and attach a mailbox to it. She would not listen to them.

Daily, monthly, yearly we watched the Negro grow grayer and more stooped, going in and out with the market basket. Each December we sent her a tax notice, which would be returned by the post office a week later, unclaimed. Now and then we would see her in one of the downstairs windows—she had evidently shut up the top floor of the house—like the carven torso of an idol in a niche, looking or not looking at us, we could never tell which. Thus she passed from generation to generation—dear, inescapable, impervious, tranquil, and perverse.

And so she died. Fell ill in the house filled with dust and shadows, with only a doddering Negro man to wait on her. We did not even know she was sick; we had long since given up trying to get any information from the Negro. He talked to no one, probably not even to her, for his voice had grown harsh and rusty, as if from disuse.

She died in one of the downstairs rooms, in a heavy walnut bed with a curtain, her gray head propped on a pillow yellow and moldy with age and lack of sunlight.

V

The Negro met the first of the ladies at the front door and let them in, with their hushed, sibilant voices and their quick, curious glances, and then he disappeared. He walked right through the house and out the back and was not seen again.

The two female cousins came at once. They held the funeral on the second day, with the town coming to look at Miss Emily beneath a mass of bought flowers, with the crayon face of her father musing profoundly above the bier and the ladies sibilant and macabre; and the very old men—some in their brushed Confederate uniforms—on the porch and the lawn, talking of Miss Emily as if she had been a contemporary of theirs, believing that they had danced with her and courted her perhaps, confusing time with its mathematical progression, as the old do, to whom all the past is not a diminishing road but, instead, a huge meadow which no winter ever quite touches, divided from them now by the narrow bottle-neck of the most recent decade of years.

Already we knew that there was one room in that region above stairs which no one had seen in forty years, and which would have to be forced. They waited until Miss Emily was decently in the ground before they opened it.

The violence of breaking down the door seemed to fill this room with pervading dust. A thin, acrid pall as of the tomb seemed to lie everywhere upon this room decked and furnished as for a bridal: upon the valance curtains of faded rose color, upon the rose-shaded lights, upon the dressing table, upon the delicate array of crystal and the man's toilet things backed with tarnished silver, silver so tarnished that the monogram was obscured. Among them lay a collar and tie, as if they had just been removed, which, lifted, left upon the surface a pale crescent in the dust. Upon a chair hung the suit, carefully folded; beneath it the two mute shoes and the discarded socks.

The man himself lay in the bed.

For a long while we just stood there, looking down at the profound and fleshless grin. The body had apparently once lain in the attitude of an embrace, but now the long sleep that outlasts love, that conquers even the grimace of love, had cuckolded him. What was left of him, rotted beneath what was left of the nightshirt, had become inextricable from the bed in which he lay; and upon him and upon the pillow beside him lay that even coating of the patient and biding dust.

Then we noticed that in the second pillow was the indentation of a head. One of us lifted something from it, and leaning forward, that faint and invisible dust dry and acrid in the nostrils, we saw a long strand of iron-gray hair.

This story is treasured by many readers. How do you account for its appeal? Compare your own responses with those of other readers in such sources as:

C. Hines Edwards, Jr., "Three Literary Parallels to Faulkner's 'A Rose for Emily'." *Notes on Mississipi Writers,* 7 (Spring, 1974), 21–25.

J. F. Kobler, "Faulkner's 'A Rose for Emily'," *Explicator,* 32 (April, 1974), Item 65.

Norman N. Holland, "Fantasy and Defense in Faulkner's 'A Rose for Emily'," *Hartford Studies in Literature,* 4 (1972), 1–35.

Terry Heller, "The Telltale Hair: A Critical Study of William Faulkner's 'A Rose for Emily'," *Arizona Quarterly,* 28 (Winter 1972), 301–318.

Daniel R. Barnes, "Faulkner's Miss Emily and Hawthorne's Old Maid," *Studies in Short Fiction,* 9 (Fall, 1972), 373–377.

You can locate critical discussions of the work of any writer represented in this book. Perhaps the handiest place to start in locating material is with the annual Modern Language Association's *International Bibliography.* Arranged according to country, century, and individual writer, it contains references to more than two thousand different periodicals and books published each year. If you have not already done so, this might be a good time for you to check out the bibliographic aids included in your own library. Choose a writer you have enjoyed and check to see what kind of commentaries are available.

The Judgment Day
JAMES WELDON JOHNSON

In that great day,
People, in that great day,
God's a-going to rain down fire.
God's a-going to sit in the middle of the
     air
To judge the quick and the dead.

Early one of these mornings,
God's a-going to call for Gabriel,
That tall, bright angel, Gabriel;
And God's a-going to say to him: Gabriel,
Blow your silver trumpet,
And wake the living nations.

And Gabriel's going to ask him: Lord,
How loud must I blow it?
And God's a-going to tell him: Gabriel,
Blow it calm and easy.
Then putting one foot on the mountain
     top,
And the other in the middle of the sea,
Gabriel's going to stand and blow his
     horn,
To wake the living nations.

Then God's a-going to say to him: Gabriel,
Once more blow your silver trumpet,

And wake the nations underground.

And Gabriel's going to ask him: Lord
How loud must I blow it?
And God's a-going to tell him: Gabriel,
Like seven peals of thunder.
Then the tall, bright angel, Gabriel,
Will put one foot on the battlements of
   heaven
And the other on the steps of hell,
And blow that silver trumpet
Till he shakes old hell's foundations.

And I feel Old Earth a-shuddering—
And I see the graves a-bursting—
And I hear a sound,
A blood-chilling sound.
What sound is that I hear?
It's the clicking together of the dry bones,
Bone to bone—the dry bones.
And I see coming out of the bursting
   graves,
And marching up from the valley of
   death,
The army of the dead.

And the living and the dead in the
   twinkling of an eye
Are caught up in the middle of the air,
Before God's judgment bar.

Oh-o-oh, sinner,
Where will you stand,
In that great day when God's a-going to
   rain down fire?
Oh, you gambling man—where will you
   stand?
You whore-mongering man—where will
   you stand?
Liars and backsliders—where will you
   stand,
In that great day when God's a-going to
   rain down fire?

And God will divide the sheep from the
   goats,
The one on the right, the other on the
   left.
And to them on the right God's a-going
   to say:

Enter into my kingdom.
And those who've come through great
   tribulations,
And washed their robes in the blood of
   the Lamb,
They will enter in—
Clothed in spotless white,
With starry crowns upon their heads,
And silver slippers on their feet,
And harps within their hands;—

And two by two they'll walk
Up and down the golden street,
Feasting on the milk and honey
Singing new songs of Zion,
Chattering with the angels
All around the Great White Throne.

And to them on the left God's a-going to
   say:
Depart from me into everlasting
   darkness,
Down into the bottomless pit.
And the wicked like lumps of lead will
   start to fall,
Headlong for seven days and nights
   they'll fall,
Plumb into the big, black, red-hot mouth
   of hell,
Belching out fire and brimstone.
And their cries like howling, yelping
   dogs,
Will go up with the fire and smoke from
   hell,
But God will stop his ears.

Too late, sinner! Too late!
Good-bye sinner! Good-bye!
In hell, sinner! In hell!
Beyond the reach of the love of God.

And I hear a voice, crying, crying:
Time shall be no more!
Time shall be no more!
Time shall be no more!
And the sun will go out like a candle in
   the wind,
The moon will turn to dripping blood,
The stars will fall like cinders,
And the sea will burn like tar;

And the earth shall melt away and be
　　dissolved,
And the sky will roll up like a scroll.
With a wave of his hand God will blot
　　out time,
And start the wheel of eternity.

Sinner, oh, sinner,
Where will you stand
In that great day when God's a-going to
　　rain down fire?

In the Preface to *God's Trombones*, James
Weldon Johnson writes about the poems
in the book, one of which is "The Judgment Day." The inspiration for the poems
was the sermons Johnson heard Negro
preachers give with all the melody of
their voices, reminding him "not of an organ or a trumpet, but rather of a trombone, the instrument possessing above all
others the power to express the wide and
varied range of emotions encompassed by
the human voice—and with greater am-
plitude. He intoned, he moaned, he
pleaded—he blared, he crashed, he thun-
dered" (*God's Trombones: Seven Negro Sermons in Verse*, New York: Viking Press,
1956, p. 7).

If you treat the class as a congregation,
how might they contribute to, or participate in, the sermon?

A Good Man Is Hard to Find
FLANNERY O'CONNOR

　　The grandmother didn't want to go to Florida. She wanted to visit some of
her connections in east Tennessee and she was seizing at every chance to
change Bailey's mind. Bailey was the son she lived with, her only boy. He was
sitting on the edge of his chair at the table, bent over the orange sports section
of the *Journal*. "Now look here, Bailey," she said, "see here, read this," and she
stood with one hand on her thin hip and the other rattling the newspaper at
his bald head. "Here this fellow that calls himself The Misfit is aloose from the
Federal Pen and headed toward Florida and you read here what it says he did
to these people. Just you read it. I wouldn't take my children in any direction
with a criminal like that aloose in it. I couldn't answer to my conscience if I
did."

　　Bailey didn't look up from his reading so she wheeled around then and
faced the children's mother, a young woman in slacks, whose face was as broad
and innocent as a cabbage and was tied around with a green head-kerchief that
had two points on the top like a rabbit's ears. She was sitting on the sofa, feeding the baby his apricots out of a jar. "The children have been to Florida before," the old lady said. "You all ought to take them somewhere else for a
change so they would see different parts of the world and be broad. They
never have been to east Tennessee."

　　The children's mother didn't seem to hear her but the eight-year-old boy,
John Wesley, a stocky child with glasses, said, "If you don't want to go to Florida, why dontcha stay at home?" He and the little girl, June Star, were reading
the funny papers on the floor.

　　"She wouldn't stay at home to be queen for a day," June Star said without
raising her yellow head.

　　"Yes and what would you do if this fellow, The Misfit, caught you?" the
grandmother asked.

　　"I'd smack his face," John Wesley said.

"She wouldn't stay at home for a million bucks," June Star said. "Afraid she'd miss something. She has to go everywhere we go."

"All right, Miss," the grandmother said. "Just remember that the next time you want me to curl your hair."

June Star said her hair was naturally curly.

The next morning the grandmother was the first one in the car, ready to go. She had her big black valise that looked like the head of a hippopotamus in one corner, and underneath it she was hiding a basket with Pitty Sing, the cat, in it. She didn't intend for the cat to be left alone in the house for three days because he would miss her too much and she was afraid he might brush against one of the gas burners and accidentally asphyxiate himself. Her son, Bailey, didn't like to arrive at a motel with a cat.

She sat in the middle of the back seat with John Wesley and June Star on either side of her. Bailey and the children's mother and the baby sat in front and they left Atlanta at eight forty-five with the mileage on the car at 55890. The grandmother wrote this down because she thought it would be interesting to say how many miles they had been when they got back. It took them twenty minutes to reach the outskirts of the city.

The old lady settled herself comfortably, removing her white cotton gloves and putting them up with her purse on the shelf in front of the back window. The children's mother still had on slacks and still had her head tied up in a green kerchief, but the grandmother had on a navy blue straw sailor hat with a bunch of white violets on the brim and a navy blue dress with a small white dot in the print. Her collars and cuffs were white organdy trimmed with lace and at her neckline she had pinned a purple spray of cloth violets containing a sachet. In case of an accident, anyone seeing her dead on the highway would know at once that she was a lady.

She said she thought it was going to be a good day for driving, neither too hot nor too cold, and she cautioned Bailey that the speed limit was fifty-five miles an hour and that the patrolmen hid themselves behind billboards and small clumps of trees and sped out after you before you had a chance to slow down. She pointed out interesting details of the scenery: Stone Mountain; the blue granite that in some places came up to both sides of the highway; the brilliant red clay banks slightly streaked with purple; and the various crops that made rows of green lace-work on the ground. The trees were full of silver-white sunlight and the meanest of them sparkled. The children were reading comic magazines and their mother had gone back to sleep.

"Let's go through Georgia fast so we won't have to look at it much," John Wesley said.

"If I were a little boy," said the grandmother, "I wouldn't talk about my native state that way. Tennessee has the mountains and Georgia has the hills."

"Tennessee is just a hillbilly dumping ground," John Wesley said, "and Georgia is a lousy state too."

"You said it," June Star said.

"In my time," said the grandmother, folding her thin veined fingers, "children were more respectful of their native states and their parents and everything else. People did right then. Oh look at the cute little pickaninny!" she said and pointed to a Negro child standing in the door of a shack. "Wouldn't that make a picture, now?" she asked and they all turned and looked at the little Negro out of the back window. He waved.

"He didn't have any britches on," June Star said.

"He probably didn't have any," the grandmother explained. "Little niggers in the country don't have things like we do. If I could paint, I'd paint that picture," she said.

The children exchanged comic books.

The grandmother offered to hold the baby and the children's mother passed him over the front seat to her. She set him on her knee and bounced him and told him about the things they were passing. She rolled her eyes and screwed up her mouth and stuck her leathery thin face into his smooth bland one. Occasionally he gave her a faraway smile. They passed a large cotton field with five or six graves fenced in the middle of it, like a small island. "Look at the graveyard!" the grandmother said, pointing it out. "That was the old family burying ground. That belonged to the plantation."

"Where's the plantation?" John Wesley asked.

"Gone With the Wind," said the grandmother. "Ha. Ha."

When the children finished all the comic books they had brought, they opened the lunch and ate it. The grandmother ate a peanut butter sandwich and an olive and would not let the children throw the box and the paper napkins out the window. When there was nothing else to do they played a game by choosing a cloud and making the other two guess what shape it suggested. John Wesley took one the shape of a cow and June Star guessed a cow and John Wesley said, no, an automobile, and June Star said he didn't play fair, and they began to slap each other over the grandmother.

The grandmother said she would tell them a story if they would keep quiet. When she told a story, she rolled her eyes and waved her head and was very dramatic. She said once when she was a maiden lady she had been courted by a Mr. Edgar Atkins Teagarden from Jasper, Georgia. She said he was a very good-looking man and a gentleman and that he brought her a watermelon every Saturday afternoon with his initials cut in it, E. A. T. Well, one Saturday, she said, Mr. Teagarden brought the watermelon and there was nobody at home and he left it on the front porch and returned in his buggy to Jasper, but she never got the watermelon, she said, because a nigger boy ate it when he saw the initials, E. A. T.! This story tickled John Wesley's funny bone and he giggled and giggled but June Star didn't think it was any good. She said she wouldn't marry a man that just brought her a watermelon on Saturday. The grandmother said she would have done well to marry Mr. Teagarden because he was a gentleman and had bought Coca-Cola stock when it first came out and that he had died only a few years ago, a very wealthy man.

They stopped at The Tower for barbecued sandwiches. The Tower was a part stucco and part wood filling station and dance hall set in a clearing outside of Timothy. A fat man named Red Sammy Butts ran it and there were signs stuck here and there on the building and for miles up and down the highway saying, TRY RED SAMMY'S FAMOUS BARBECUE. NONE LIKE FAMOUS RED SAMMY'S! RED SAM! THE FAT BOY WITH THE HAPPY LAUGH! A VETERAN! RED SAMMY'S YOUR MAN!

Red Sammy was lying on the bare ground outside The Tower with his head under a truck while a gray monkey about a foot high, chained to a small chinaberry tree, chattered nearby. The monkey sprang back into the tree and got on the highest limb as soon as he saw the children jump out of the car and run toward him.

Inside, The Tower was a long dark room with a counter at one end and tables at the other and dancing space in the middle. They all sat down at a board table next to the nickelodeon and Red Sam's wife, a tall burnt-brown woman with hair and eyes lighter than her skin, came and took their order. The children's mother put a dime in the machine and played "The Tennessee Waltz," and the grandmother said that tune always made her want to dance. She asked Bailey if he would like to dance but he only glared at her. He didn't have a naturally sunny disposition like she did and trips made him nervous. The grandmother's brown eyes were very bright. She swayed her head from side to side and pretended she was dancing in her chair. June Star said play something she could tap to so the children's mother put in another dime and played a fast number and June Star stepped out onto the dance floor and did her tap routine.

"Ain't she cute?" Red Sam's wife said, leaning over the counter. "Would you like to come be my little girl?"

"No I certainly wouldn't," June Star said. "I wouldn't live in a broken-down place like this for a million bucks!" and she ran back to the table.

"Ain't she cute?" the woman repeated, stretching her mouth politely.

"Aren't you ashamed?" hissed the grandmother.

Red Sam came in and told his wife to quit lounging on the counter and hurry up with these people's order. His khaki trousers reached just to his hip bones and his stomach hung over them like a sack of meal swaying under his shirt. He came over and sat down at a table nearby and let out a combination sigh and yodel. "You can't win," he said. "You can't win," and he wiped his sweating red face off with a gray handkerchief. "These days you don't know who to trust," he said. "Ain't that the truth?"

"People are certainly not nice like they used to be," said the grandmother.

"Two fellers come in here last week," Red Sammy said, "driving a Chrysler. It was a old beat-up car but it was a good one and these boys looked all right to me. Said they worked at the mill and you know I let them fellers charge the gas they bought? Now why did I do that?"

"Because you're a good man!" the grandmother said at once.

"Yes'm, I suppose so," Red Sam said as if he were struck with this answer.

His wife brought the orders, carrying the five plates all at once without a tray, two in each hand and one balanced on her arm. "It isn't a soul in this green world of God's that you can trust," she said. "And I don't count nobody out of that, not nobody," she repeated, looking at Red Sammy.

"Did you read about that criminal, The Misfit, that's escaped?" asked the grandmother.

"I wouldn't be a bit surprised if he didn't attact this place right here," said the woman. "If he hears about it being here, I wouldn't be none surprised to see him. If he hears it's two cent in the cash register, I wouldn't be a tall surprised if he . . ."

"That'll do," Red Sam said. "Go bring these people their Co'-Colas," and the woman went off to get the rest of the order.

"A good man is hard to find," Red Sammy said. "Everything is getting terrible. I remember the day you could go off and leave your screen door unlatched. Not no more."

He and the grandmother discussed better times. The old lady said that in her opinion Europe was entirely to blame for the way things were now. She said the way Europe acted you would think we were made of money and Red Sam said it was no use talking about it, she was exactly right. The children ran outside into the white sunlight and looked at the monkey in the lacy chinaberry tree. He was busy catching fleas on himself and biting each one carefully between his teeth as if it were a delicacy.

They drove off again into the hot afternoon. The grandmother took cat naps and woke up every few minutes with her own snoring. Outside of Toombsboro she woke up and recalled an old plantation that she had visited in this neighborhood once when she was a young lady. She said the house had six white columns across the front and that there was an avenue of oaks leading up to it and two little wooden trellis arbors on either side in front where you sat down with your suitor after a stroll in the garden. She recalled exactly which road to turn off to get to it. She knew that Bailey would not be willing to lose any time looking at an old house, but the more she talked about it, the more she wanted to see it once again and find out if the little twin arbors were still standing. "There was a secret panel in this house," she said craftily, not telling the truth but wishing that she were, "and the story went that all the family silver was hidden in it when Sherman came through but it was never found . . ."

"Hey!" John Wesley said. "Let's go see it! We'll find it! We'll poke all the woodwork and find it! Who lives there? Where do you turn off at? Hey Pop, can't we turn off there?"

"We never have seen a house with a secret panel!" June Star shrieked. "Let's go to the house with the secret panel! Hey Pop, can't we go see the house with the secret panel!"

"It's not far from here, I know," the grandmother said. "It wouldn't take over twenty minutes."

Bailey was looking straight ahead. His jaw was as rigid as a horseshoe. "No," he said.

The children began to yell and scream that they wanted to see the house with the secret panel. John Wesley kicked the back of the front seat and June Star hung over her mother's shoulder and whined desperately into her ear that they never had any fun even on their vacation, that they could never do what THEY wanted to do. The baby began to scream and John Wesley kicked the back of the seat so hard that his father could feel the blows in his kidney.

"All right!" he shouted and drew the car to a stop at the side of the road. "Will you all shut up? Will you all just shut up for one second? If you don't shut up, we won't go anywhere."

"It would be very educational for them," the grandmother murmured.

"All right," Bailey said, "but get this: this is the only time we're going to stop for anything like this. This is the one and only time."

"The dirt road that you have to turn down is about a mile back," the grandmother directed. "I marked it when we passed."

"A dirt road," Bailey groaned.

After they had turned around and were headed toward the dirt road, the grandmother recalled other points about the house, the beautiful glass over the front doorway and the candle-lamp in the hall. John Wesley said that the secret panel was probably in the fireplace.

"You can't go inside this house," Bailey said. "You don't know who lives there."

"While you all talk to the people in front, I'll run around behind and get in a window," John Wesley suggested.

"We'll all stay in the car," his mother said.

They turned onto the dirt road and the car raced roughly along in a swirl of pink dust. The grandmother recalled the times when there were no paved roads and thirty miles was a day's journey. The dirt road was hilly and there were sudden washes in it and sharp curves on dangerous embankments. All at once they would be on a hill, looking down over the blue tops of trees for miles around, then the next minute, they would be in a red depression with the dust-coated trees looking down on them.

"This place had better turn up in a minute," Bailey said, "or I'm going to turn around."

The road looked as if no one had traveled on it in months.

"It's not much farther," the grandmother said and just as she said it, a horrible thought came to her. The thought was so embarrassing that she turned red in the face and her eyes dilated and her feet jumped up, upsetting her valise in the corner. The instant the valise moved, the newspaper top she had over the basket under it rose with a snarl and Pitty Sing, the cat, sprang onto Bailey's shoulder.

The children were thrown to the floor and their mother, clutching the baby, was thrown out the door onto the ground; the old lady was thrown into the front seat. The car turned over once and landed right-side-up in a gulch off the side of the road. Bailey remained in the driver's seat with the cat—gray-striped with a broad white face and an orange nose—clinging to his neck like a caterpillar.

As soon as the children saw they could move their arms and legs, they scrambled out of the car, shouting, "We've had an ACCIDENT!" The grandmother was curled up under the dashboard, hoping she was injured so that Bailey's wrath would not come down on her all at once. The horrible thought she had had before the accident was that the house she remembered so vividly was not in Georgia but in Tennessee.

Bailey removed the cat from his neck with both hands and flung it out the window against the side of a pine tree. Then he got out of the car and started looking for the children's mother. She was sitting against the side of the red gutted ditch, holding the screaming baby, but she only had a cut down her face and a broken shoulder. "We've had an ACCIDENT!" the children screamed in a frenzy of delight.

"But nobody's killed," June Star said with disappointment as the grandmother limped out of the car, her hat still pinned to her head but the broken front brim standing up at a jaunty angle and the violet spray hanging off the side. They all sat down in the ditch, except the children, to recover from the shock. They were all shaking.

"Maybe a car will come along," said the children's mother hoarsely.

"I believe I have injured an organ," said the grandmother, pressing her side, but no one answered her. Bailey's teeth were clattering. He had on a yellow sport shirt with bright blue parrots designed in it and his face was as yellow as the shirt. The grandmother decided that she would not mention that the house was in Tennessee.

The road was about ten feet above and they could see only the tops of the trees on the other side of it. Behind the ditch they were sitting in there were more woods, tall and dark and deep. In a few minutes they saw a car some distance away on top of a hill, coming slowly as if the occupants were watching them. The grandmother stood up and waved both arms dramatically to attract their attention. The car continued to come on slowly, disappeared around a bend and appeared again, moving even slower, on top of the hill they had gone over. It was a big black battered hearse-like automobile. There were three men in it.

It came to a stop just over them and for some minutes, the driver looked down with a steady expressionless gaze to where they were sitting, and didn't speak. Then he turned his head and muttered something to the other two and they got out. One was a fat boy in black trousers and a red sweat shirt with a silver stallion embossed on the front of it. He moved around on the right side of them and stood staring, his mouth partly open in a kind of loose grin. The other had on khaki pants and a blue striped coat and a gray hat pulled down very low, hiding most of his face. He came around slowly on the left side. Neither spoke.

The driver got out of the car and stood by the side of it, looking down at them. He was an older man than the other two. His hair was just beginning to gray and he wore silver-rimmed spectacles that gave him a scholarly look. He had a long creased face and didn't have on any shirt or undershirt. He had on blue jeans that were too tight for him and was holding a black hat and a gun. The two boys also had guns.

"We've had an ACCIDENT!" the children screamed.

The grandmother had the peculiar feeling that the bespectacled man was someone she knew. His face was as familiar to her as if she had known him all her life but she could not recall who he was. He moved away from the car and began to come down the embankment, placing his feet carefully so that he wouldn't slip. He had on tan and white shoes and no socks, and his ankles were red and thin. "Good afternoon," he said. "I see you all had you a little spill."

"We turned over twice!" said the grandmother.

"Oncet," he corrected. "We seen it happen. Try their car and see will it run, Hiram," he said quietly to the boy with the gray hat.

"What you got that gun for?" John Wesley asked. "Whatcha gonna do with that gun?"

"Lady," the man said to the children's mother, "would you mind calling them children to sit down by you? Children make me nervous. I want all you all to sit down right together there where you're at."

"What are you telling US what to do for?" June Star asked.

Behind them the line of woods gaped like a dark open mouth. "Come here," said their mother.

"Look here now," Bailey began suddenly, "we're in a predicament! We're in . . ."

The grandmother shrieked. She scrambled to her feet and stood staring. "You're The Misfit!" she said. "I recognized you at once!"

"Yes'm," the man said, smiling slightly as if he were pleased in spite of himself to be known, "but it would have been better for all of you, lady, if you hadn't of reckernized me."

Bailey turned his head sharply and said something to his mother that shocked even the children. The old lady began to cry and The Misfit reddened.

"Lady," he said, "don't you get upset. Sometimes a man says things he don't mean. I don't reckon he meant to talk to you thataway."

"You wouldn't shoot a lady, would you?" the grandmother said and removed a clean handkerchief from her cuff and began to slap at her eyes with it.

The Misfit pointed the toe of his shoe into the ground and made a little hole and then covered it up again. "I would hate to have to," he said.

"Listen," the grandmother almost screamed, "I know you're a good man. You don't look a bit like you have common blood. I know you must come from nice people!"

"Yes mam," he said, "finest people in the world." When he smiled he showed a row of strong white teeth. "God never made a finer woman than my mother and my daddy's heart was pure gold," he said. The boy with the red sweat shirt had come around behind them and was standing with his gun at his hip. The Misfit squatted down on the ground. "Watch them children, Bobby Lee," he said. "You know they make me nervous." He looked at the six of them huddled together in front of him and he seemed to be embarrassed as if he couldn't think of anything to say. "Ain't a cloud in the sky," he remarked, looking up at it. "Don't see no sun but don't see no cloud neither."

"Yes, it's a beautiful day," said the grandmother. "Listen," she said, "you shouldn't call yourself The Misfit because I know you're a good man at heart. I can just look at you and tell."

"Hush!" Bailey yelled. "Hush! Everybody shut up and let me handle this!" He was squatting in the position of a runner about to spring forward but he didn't move.

"I pre-chate that, lady," The Misfit said and drew a little circle in the ground with the butt of his gun.

"It'll take a half a hour to fix this here car," Hiram called, looking over the raised hood of it.

"Well, first you and Bobby Lee get him and that little boy to step over yonder with you," The Misfit said, pointing to Bailey and John Wesley. "The boys want to ast you something," he said to Bailey. "Would you mind stepping back in them woods there with them?"

"Listen," Bailey began, "we're in a terrible predicament! Nobody realizes what this is," and his voice cracked. His eyes were as blue and intense as the parrots in his shirt and he remained perfectly still.

The grandmother reached up to adjust her hat brim as if she were going to the woods with him but it came off in her hand. She stood staring at it and after a second she let it fall on the ground. Hiram pulled Bailey up by the arm as if he were assisting an old man. John Wesley caught hold of his father's hand and Bobby Lee followed. They went off toward the woods and just as they reached the dark edge, Bailey turned and supporting himself against a gray naked pine trunk, he shouted, "I'll be back in a minute, Mamma, wait on me!"

"Come back this instant!" his mother shrilled but they all disappeared into the woods.

"Bailey Boy!" the grandmother called in a tragic voice but she found she was looking at The Misfit squatting on the ground in front of her. "I just know you're a good man," she said desperately. "You're not a bit common!"

"Nome, I ain't a good man," The Misfit said after a second as if he had considered her statement carefully, "but I ain't the worst in the world neither. My daddy said I was a different breed of dog from my brothers and sisters. 'You know,' Daddy said, 'it's some that can live their whole life out without asking about it and it's others has to know why it is, and this boy is one of the latters. He's going to be into everything!'" He put on his black hat and looked up suddenly and then away deep into the woods as if he were embarrassed again. "I'm sorry I don't have on a shirt before you ladies," he said, hunching his shoulders slightly. "We buried our clothes that we had on when we escaped and we're just making do until we can get better. We borrowed these from some folks we met," he explained.

"That's perfectly all right," the grandmother said. "Maybe Bailey has an extra shirt in his suitcase."

"I'll look and see terrectly," The Misfit said.

"Where are they taking him?" the children's mother screamed.

"Daddy was a card himself," The Misfit said. "You couldn't put anything over on him. He never got in trouble with the Authorities though. Just had the knack of handling them."

"You could be honest too if you'd only try," said the grandmother. "Think how wonderful it would be to settle down and live a comfortable life and not have to think about somebody chasing you all the time."

The Misfit kept scratching in the ground with the butt of his gun as if he were thinking about it. "Yes'm, somebody is always after you," he murmured.

The grandmother noticed how thin his shoulder blades were just behind his hat because she was standing up looking down on him. "Do you ever pray?" she asked.

He shook his head. All she saw was the black hat wiggle between his shoulder blades. "Nome," he said.

There was a pistol shot from the woods, followed closely by another. Then silence. The old lady's head jerked around. She could hear the wind move through the tree tops like a long satisfied insuck of breath. "Bailey Boy!" she called.

"I was a gospel singer for a while," The Misfit said. "I been most everything. Been in the arm service, both land and sea, at home and abroad, been twict married, been an undertaker, been with the railroads, plowed Mother Earth, been in a tornado, seen a man burnt alive oncet," and looked up at the children's mother and the little girl who were sitting close together, their faces white and their eyes glassy; "I even seen a woman flogged," he said.

"Pray, pray," the grandmother began, "pray, pray . . ."

"I never was a bad boy that I remember of," The Misfit said in an almost dreamy voice, "but somewheres along the line I done something wrong and got sent to the penitentiary. I was buried alive," and he looked up and held her attention to him by a steady stare.

"That's when you should have started to pray," she said. "What did you do to get sent to the penitentiary that first time?"

"Turn to the right, it was a wall," The Misfit said, looking up again at the cloudless sky. "Turn to the left, it was a wall. Look up it was a ceiling, look down it was a floor. I forget what I done, lady. I set there and set there, trying to remember what it was I done and I ain't recalled it to this day. Oncet in a while, I would think it was coming to me, but it never come."

"Maybe they put you in by mistake," the old lady said vaguely.

"Nome," he said. "It wasn't no mistake. They had the papers on me."

"You must have stolen something," she said.

The Misfit sneered slightly. "Nobody had nothing I wanted," he said. "It was a head-doctor at the penitentiary said what I had done was kill my daddy but I known that for a lie. My daddy died in nineteen ought nineteen of the epidemic flu and I never had a thing to do with it. He was buried in the Mount Hopewell Baptist churchyard and you can go there and see for yourself."

"If you would pray," the old lady said, "Jesus would help you."

"That's right," The Misfit said.

"Well then, why don't you pray?" she asked trembling with delight suddenly.

"I don't want no help," he said. "I'm doing all right by myself."

Bobby Lee and Hiram came ambling back from the woods. Bobby Lee was dragging a yellow shirt with bright blue parrots in it.

"Thow me that shirt, Bobby Lee," The Misfit said. The shirt came flying at him and landed on his shoulder and he put it on. The grandmother couldn't name what the shirt reminded her of. "No, lady," The Misfit said while he was buttoning it up, "I found out the crime don't matter. You can do one thing or you can do another, kill a man or take a tire off his car, because sooner or later you're going to forget what it was you done and just be punished for it."

The children's mother had begun to make heaving noises as if she couldn't get her breath. "Lady," he asked, "would you and that little girl like to step off yonder with Bobby Lee and Hiram and join your husband?"

"Yes, thank you," the mother said faintly. Her left arm dangled helplessly and she was holding the baby, who had gone to sleep, in the other. "Hep that lady up, Hiram," The Misfit said as she struggled to climb out of the ditch, "and Bobby Lee, you hold onto that little girl's hand."

"I don't want to hold hands with him," June Star said. "He reminds me of a pig."

The fat boy blushed and laughed and caught her by the arm and pulled her off into the woods after Hiram and her mother.

Alone with The Misfit, the grandmother found that she had lost her voice. There was not a cloud in the sky nor any sun. There was nothing around her but woods. She wanted to tell him that he must pray. She opened and closed her mouth several times before anything came out. Finally she found herself saying, "Jesus, Jesus," meaning, Jesus will help you, but the way she was saying it, it sounded as if she might be cursing.

"Yes'm," The Misfit said as if he agreed. "Jesus thown everything off balance. It was the same case with Him as with me except He hadn't committed any crime and they could prove I had committed one because they had the papers on me. Of course," he said, "they never shown me my papers. That's why I sign myself now. I said long ago, you get you a signature and sign everything you do and keep a copy of it. Then you'll know what you done and you can hold up the crime to the punishment and see do they match and in the end you'll have something to prove you ain't been treated right. I call myself The Misfit," he said, "because I can't make what all I done wrong fit what all I gone through in punishment."

There was a piercing scream from the woods, followed closely by a pistol report. "Does it seem right to you, lady, that one is punished a heap and another ain't punished at all?"

"Jesus!" the old lady cried. "You've got good blood! I know you wouldn't shoot a lady! I know you come from nice people! Pray! Jesus, you ought not to shoot a lady. I'll give you all the money I've got!"

"Lady," The Misfit said, looking beyond her far into the woods, "there never was a body that give the undertaker a tip."

There were two more pistol reports and the grandmother raised her head like a parched old turkey hen crying for water and called, "Bailey Boy, Bailey Boy!" as if her heart would break.

"Jesus was the only One that ever raised the dead." The Misfit continued, "and He shouldn't have done it. He thrown everything off balance. If He did what He said, then it's nothing for you to do but throw away everything and follow Him, and if He didn't, then it's nothing for you to do but enjoy the few minutes you got left the best way you can—by killing somebody or burning down his house or doing some other meanness to him. No pleasure but meanness," he said and his voice had become almost a snarl.

"Maybe He didn't raise the dead," the old lady mumbled, not knowing what she was saying and feeling so dizzy that she sank down in the ditch with her legs twisted under her.

"I wasn't there so I can't say He didn't," The Misfit said. "I wisht I had of been there," he said, hitting the ground with his fist. "It ain't right I wasn't there because if I had of been there I would of known. Listen lady," he said in a high voice, "if I had of been there I would of known and I wouldn't be like I am now." His voice seemed about to crack and the grandmother's head cleared for an instant. She saw the man's face twisted close to her own as if he were going to cry and she murmured. "Why you're one of my babies. You're one of my own children!" She reached out and touched him on the shoulder. The Misfit sprang back as if a snake had bitten him and shot her three times through the chest. Then he put his gun down on the ground and took off his glasses and began to clean them.

Hiram and Bobby Lee returned from the woods and stood over the ditch, looking down at the grandmother who half sat and half lay in a puddle of blood with her legs crossed under her like a child's and her face smiling up at the cloudless sky.

Without his glasses, The Misfit's eyes were red-rimmed and pale and defenseless-looking. "Take her off and throw her where you thrown the others," he said, picking up the cat that was rubbing itself against his leg.

"She was a talker, wasn't she?" Bobby Lee said, sliding down the ditch with a yodel.

"She would of been a good woman," The Misfit said, "if it had been somebody there to shoot her every minute of her life."

"Some fun!" Bobby Lee said.

"Shut up, Bobby Lee" The Misfit said. "It's no real pleasure in life."

Flannery O'Connor frequently appeared before college audiences to read her stories. On October 14, 1963, she made the following remarks at Hollins College, Virginia, before she read "A Good Man Is Hard to Find":

I do think ... you should know what is going to happen in this story so that any element of suspense in it will be transferred from its surface to its interior.

I would be most happy if you had already read it, happier still if you knew it well, but since experience has taught me to keep my expectations along these lines modest, I'll tell you that this is the story of a family of six which, on its way driving to Florida, gets wiped out by an escaped convict who calls himself the Misfit.

The remainder of O'Connor's discussion of the story—its seriousness, violence, grotesqueness, and humor—appears in "A Reasonable Use of the Unreasonable," *Mystery and Manners*, eds. Sally and Robert Fitzgerald (New York: Farrar, Straus, & Giroux, 1961).

Describe the *levels of characterization* for the narrator and each of the characters.

Declaration of Conscience I
MARGARET CHASE SMITH

Mr. President, I would like to speak briefly and simply about a serious national condition. It is a national feeling of fear and frustration that could result in national suicide and the end of everything that we Americans hold dear. It is a condition that comes from the lack of effective leadership in either the Legislative Branch or the Executive Branch of our Government.

That leadership is so lacking that serious and responsible proposals are being made that national advisory commissions be appointed to provide such critically needed leadership.

I speak as briefly as possible because too much harm has already been done with irresponsible words of bitterness and selfish political opportunism. I speak as simply as possible because the issue is too great to be obscured by eloquence. I speak simply and briefly in the hope that my words will be taken to heart.

I speak as a Republican. I speak as a woman. I speak as a United States Senator. I speak as an American.

The United States Senate has long enjoyed worldwide respect as the greatest deliberative body in the world. But recently that deliberative character has too often been debased to the level of a forum of hate and character assassination sheltered by the shield of congressional immunity.

It is ironical that we Senators can in debate in the Senate directly or indirectly, by any form of words, impute to any American who is not a Senator any conduct or motive unworthy or unbecoming an American—and without that non-Senator American having any legal redress against us—yet if we say the same thing in the Senate about our colleagues we can be stopped on the grounds of being out of order.

It is strange that we can verbally attack anyone else without restraint and with full protection and yet we hold ourselves above the same type of criticism here on the Senate Floor. Surely the United States Senate is big enough to take self-criticism and self-appraisal. Surely we should be able to take the same kind of character attacks that we "dish out" to outsiders.

I think that it is high time for the United States Senate and its members to do some soul-searching—for us to weigh our consciences—on the manner in which we are performing our duty to the people of America—on the manner in which we are using or abusing our individual powers and privileges.

I think that it is high time that we remembered that we have sworn to uphold and defend the Constitution. I think that it is high time that we remembered that the Constitution, as amended, speaks not only of the freedom of speech but also of trial by jury instead of trial by accusation.

Whether it be a criminal prosecution in court or a character prosecution in the Senate, there is little practical distinction when the life of a person has been ruined.

Those of us who shout the loudest about Americanism in making character assassinations are all too frequently those who, by our own words and acts, ignore some of the basic principles of Americanism:

The right to criticize;

The right to hold unpopular beliefs;

The right to protest;

The right of independent thought.

The exercise of these rights should not cost one single American citizen his reputation or his right to a livelihood nor should he be in danger of losing his reputation or livelihood merely because he happens to know someone who holds unpopular beliefs. Who of us doesn't? Otherwise none of us could call our souls our own. Otherwise thought control would have set in.

The American people are sick and tired of being afraid to speak their minds lest they be politically smeared as "Communists" or "Fascists" by their opponents. Freedom of speech is not what it used to be in America. It has been so abused by some that it is not exercised by others.

The American people are sick and tired of seeing innocent people smeared and guilty people whitewashed. But there have been enough proved cases, such as the Amerasia case, the Hiss case, the Coplon case, the Gold case, to cause nationwide distrust and strong suspicion that there may be something to the unproved, sensational accusations.

As a Republican, I say to my colleagues on this side of the aisle that the Republican Party faces a challenge today that is not unlike the challenge that it faced back in Lincoln's day. The Republican party so successfully met that challenge that it emerged from the Civil War as the champion of a united nation—in addition to being a Party that unrelentingly fought loose spending and loose programs.

Today our country is being psychologically divided by the confusion and the suspicions that are bred in the United States Senate to spread like cancerous tentacles of "know nothing, suspect everything" attitudes. Today we have a Democratic Administration that has developed a mania for loose spending and loose programs. History is repeating itself—and the Republican Party again has the opportunity to emerge as the champion of unity and prudence.

The record of the present Democratic Administration has provided us with sufficient campaign issues without the necessity of resorting to political smears. America is rapidly losing its position as leader of the world simply because the

Democratic Administration has pitifully failed to provide effective leadership.

The Democratic Administration has completely confused the American people by its daily contradictory grave warnings and optimistic assurances—that show the people that our Democratic Administration has no idea of where it is going.

The Democratic Administration has greatly lost the confidence of the American people by its complacency to the threat of communism here at home and the leak of vital secrets to Russia through key officials of the Democratic Administration. There are enough proved cases to make this point without diluting our criticism with unproved charges.

Surely these are sufficient reasons to make it clear to the American people that it is time for a change and that a Republican victory is necessary to the security of this country. Surely it is clear that this nation will continue to suffer as long as it is governed by the present ineffective Democratic Administration.

Yet to displace it with a Republican regime embracing a philosophy that lacks political integrity or intellectual honesty would prove equally disastrous to this nation. The nation sorely needs a Republican victory. But I don't want to see the Republican Party ride to political victory on the Four Horsemen of Calumny—Fear, Ignorance, Bigotry, and Smear.

I doubt if the Republican Party could—simply because I don't believe the American people will uphold any political party that puts political exploitation above national interest. Surely we Republicans aren't that desperate for victory.

I don't want to see the Republican Party win that way. While it might be a fleeting victory for the Republican Party, it would be a more lasting defeat for the American people. Surely it would ultimately be suicide for the Republican Party and the two-party system that has protected our American liberties from the dictatorship of a one party system.

As members of the Minority Party, we do not have the primary authority to formulate the policy of our Government. But we do have the responsibility of rendering constructive criticism, of clarifying issues, of allaying fears by acting as responsible citizens.

As a woman, I wonder how the mothers, wives, sisters, and daughters feel about the way in which members of their families have been politically mangled in Senate debate—and I use the word "debate" advisedly.

As a United States Senator, I am not proud of the way in which the Senate has been made a publicity platform for irresponsible sensationalism. I am not proud of the reckless abandon in which unproved charges have been hurled from this side of the aisle. I am not proud of the obviously staged, undignified countercharges that have been attempted in retaliation from the other side of the aisle.

I don't like the way the Senate has been made a rendezvous for vilification, for selfish political gain at the sacrifice of individual reputations and national unity. I am not proud of the way we smear outsiders from the Floor of the Senate and hide behind the cloak of congressional immunity and still place ourselves beyond criticism on the Floor of the Senate.

As an American, I am shocked at the way Republicans and Democrats alike are playing directly into the Communist design of "confuse, divide, and conquer." As an American, I don't want a Democratic Administration "whitewash" or "cover-up" any more than I want a Republican smear or witch hunt.

As an American, I condemn a Republican "Fascist" just as much as I condemn a Democrat "Communist." I condemn a Democrat "Fascist" just as much as I condemn a Republican "Communist." They are equally dangerous to you and me and to our country. As an American, I want to see our nation recapture the strength and unity it once had when we fought the enemy instead of ourselves.

It is with these thoughts that I have drafted what I call a "Declaration of Conscience." I am gratified that Senator Tobey, Senator Aiken, Senator Morse, Senator Ives, Senator Thye, and Senator Hendrickson have concurred in that declaration and have authorized me to announce their concurrence.

STATEMENT OF SEVEN REPUBLICAN SENATORS

1. We are Republicans. But we are Americans first. It is as Americans that we express our concern with the growing confusion that threatens the security and stability of our country. Democrats and Republicans alike have contributed to that confusion.

2. The Democratic Administration has initially created the confusion by its lack of effective leadership, by its contradictory grave warnings and optimistic assurances, by its complacency to the threat of communism here at home, by its oversensitiveness to rightful criticism, by its petty bitterness against its critics.

3. Certain elements of the Republican Party have materially added to this confusion in the hopes of riding the Republican Party to victory through the selfish political exploitation of fear, bigotry, ignorance, and intolerance. There are enough mistakes of the Democrats for Republicans to criticize constructively without resorting to political smears.

4. To this extent, Democrats and Republicans alike have unwittingly, but undeniably, played directly into the Communist design of "confuse, divide, and conquer."

5. It is high time that we stopped thinking politically as Republicans and Democrats about elections and started thinking patriotically as Americans about national security based on individual freedom. It is high time that we all stopped being tools and victims of totalitarian techniques—techniques that, if continued here unchecked, will surely end what we have come to cherish as the American way of life.

A United States Senator and member of the Republican Party, Margaret Chase Smith delivered this speech in the Senate on June 1, 1950, denouncing her fellow Republican Joseph McCarthy for the tactics used in his hunt for "un-Americans." For a fuller understanding of the period during which the speech was delivered, consult history books and works about McCarthy and see Phillis Rienstra, "Resurrecting the Past: Historical Documents as Materials for Readers Theatre," *Speech Teacher*, 21 (November 1972), 310–314.

Distinguish between the speaker's *tone* toward her audience and her *attitude*(s) toward the subject. How is the speech organized?

The Meat Epitaph
MICHAEL BENEDIKT

This is what it was: Sometime in the recent but until now unrecorded past, it was decided by cattle-ranchers that since people were increasingly insistent that "you are what you eat," all cattle on the way to the market were to be marked with brief descriptive tags noting the favorite food of each beast, and how much each ate of it. This, it was felt, would both delight the diner and comfort the consumer: people would be able to tell exactly what kind of flavor and texture beef they were purchasing beforehand, and always secure exactly the kind of product most likely to delight their taste (it was something a little like our present-day system of catering to preferences for light and dark meat in chicken). The system set up seemed ideally efficient: first, they attached the tag to each beast on its last day on the ranch, just before the two or three days required for shipment to the slaughterhouse—during which travel time the animal customarily doesn't eat anything, anyway. Once at the slaughterhouse, they carefully removed the tags; and during the slaughtering, duplicated the so-called "parent tag" numerous times, preparing perhaps hundreds of tiny tags for each animal. Directly after, at the packing plant, these were affixed to the proper parts, each section of each animal being separately and appropriately tagged, as if with an epitaph. But something went wrong with this means of augmenting the diner's delight, and of comforting the consumer. At first, quite predictably, the tags came out reading things like "Much grass, a little moss, medium grain," and "Much grass, much grain, generally ate a lot." And this, as one might expect, proved a great pleasure to the consumer. But then tags began coming through reading things like "A little grass, small grain, many diverse scraps from the table"; and "She was our favorite, gave her all we had to give"; and one (featured at dinnertime one evening on national television news) saying: "Goodbye, Blackie Lamb, sorry you had to grow up—we'll miss you." Gradually, despite its efficiency, this system somehow ceased to delight the diner, and comfort the consumer. And this is how the practice of the meat epitaph began to become generally neglected during the course of time; and how people came to eat their meat, as they generally do today, partially or wholly blindfolded.

Michael Benedikt says that this prose poem, started in "an attempt to confront directly a contradiction I had long felt: the contradiction resulting from being fond of animals . . . and dining on them—i.e., eating meat." Of special interest to the performer, he adds that the "peculiar tone" is one "which moves from a seemingly cheery acceptance of things as they are, to a darker humor, and horror at this situation" (*Fifty Contemporary Poets: The Creative Process,* ed., Alberta T. Turner; New York: David McKay, 1977, pp. 48–53).

This Is Just to Say
WILLIAM CARLOS WILLIAMS

I have eaten
the plums
that were in
the icebox

and which
you were probably
saving
for breakfast

Forgive me
they were delicious
so sweet
and so cold

Variations on a Theme by William Carlos Williams
KENNETH KOCH

1

I chopped down the house that you had been saving to live in next summer.
I am sorry, but it was morning, and I had nothing to do
and its wooden beams were so inviting.

2

We laughed at the hollyhocks together
and then I sprayed them with lye.
Forgive me. I simply do not know what I am doing.

3

I gave away the money that you had been saving to live on for the next ten
    years.
The man who asked for it was shabby
and the firm March wind on the porch was so juicy and cold.

4

Last evening we went dancing and I broke your leg.
Forgive me. I was clumsy, and
I wanted you here in the wards, where I am the doctor!

Parodies, in some sense, make fun of a literary text. In the preceding instance, the fun is based on the *situation* of the original poem. In others, the fun stems from the *style* of the literature. In performing "This Is Just to Say" and "Variations on a Theme by William Carlos Williams," would your speakers for the two be essentially the same? If not, how would they differ?

As in nature new qualities may be engendered by the coming to-gether of elements in new ways, so too in poetry new sugges-tions of meaning can be engendered by the juxtaposition of pre-viously unjoined words and images.

Philip Wheelwright

A poet in the process of writing need be no more or less aware of 'techniques' than a skijumper approaching the lip of a jump. On hills where darkness has closed down early, he has already learned by example, and practiced every possible technique. Readied, he is full of experience and feeling, set to inhabit blank air. What may once have felt mechanical becomes, in process, or-ganic: his form is an event; an act of intensely concentrated mo-tion both grounded in common sense and defying it. First courage, then skill, then luck. The luck that courage and skill help make.

Philip Booth

Between my finger and my thumb
The squat pen rests.
I'll dig with it.

Seamus Heaney

Just as you cannot remove from a physical body the qualities that constitute it—color, extension, solidity—without reducing it to a hollow abstract, without destroying it, so you cannot remove the form from the Idea, because the Idea exists only by virtue of its form.

Gustave Flaubert

FOCUS FOR CHAPTER IV

After you study the text and anthology in this chapter, we hope you will be able to

1. Recognize different shapes of texts.
2. Recognize the function of line endings in poems.
3. Discuss the word choices in a text.
4. Explain how word choice reveals a speaker's personality.
5. Identify images and relate them to the speaker.
6. Recognize metaphor and synecdoche.
7. Appreciate the functions of figures of speech in revealing the speaker and the speaker's action.
8. Identify symbols and explain their function.
9. Recognize and discuss the effects of ellipses.
10. Identify obvious examples of the four basic kinds of accentual-syllabic meter.
11. Identify rhyme, assonance, alliteration, and consonance.
12. Understand what characterizes abstract form.
13. Discuss some of the characteristics of free verse.
14. Explain the parts of a traditional plot and identify obvious examples.
15. Recognize the handling of time in narratives.
16. Discuss various elements of total form.
17. Demonstrate in performance a sense of gross structure of a text.
18. Experience images during performance.
19. Perform the line structure of a poem.

IV
Performing the Speaker's Drama

There is no succinct definition of style, but we know that it exists because we can recognize it. Not only that, we can parody it. Remember the several versions of "Little Red Riding Hood" in Chapter III? What do you know of the speaker in the following version? Could this speaker have died in 1910, for instance?

> In an effort to make the classics accessible to contemporary readers, I am translating them into the modern American language. Here is the translation of "Little Red Riding Hood":
> Once upon a point in time, a small person named Little Red Riding Hood initiated plans for the preparation, delivery and transportation of foodstuffs to her grandmother, a senior citizen residing at a place of residence in a forest of indeterminate dimension.[1]

We know that this speaker lives in late twentieth-century America because he or she speaks in "bureaucratese." Can you rewrite the story in the style of a lawyer?

Parodies often sharpen our awareness of the styles of particular literary texts. Do you recognize the model for this rewrite of "Goldilocks" by Dan Greenburg?

> If you actually want to hear about it, what I'd better do is I'd better warn you right now that you aren't going to believe it. I mean it's a true *story* and all, but it still sounds sort of phony.
> Anyway, my name is Goldie Lox. It's sort of a boring name, but my parents said that when I was born I had this very blonde hair and all. Actually, I was born bald. I mean how many babies get born with blonde hair? None. I mean I've *seen* them and they're all wrinkled and red and slimy and

everything. And bald. And then all the phonies come around and tell you he's as cute as a bug's ear. A bug's ear, boy, that really kills me. You ever *seen* a bug's ear? What's cute about a bug's *ear*, for Chrissake! Nothing, that's what.[2]

Greenburg's title, "Catch Her in the Oatmeal," provides additional clues.

To recognize style is one thing; to analyze it is another. But texts are made of words; so in this chapter we shall examine the words and phrases that constitute style and determine how they work, hoping that this sharper eye will give you a fuller experience with the text. The football fan who understands how the play works has a higher level of appreciation than does a spectator, however enthusiastic, who knows nothing about the game. Of course, naming and describing can become a game in itself (Have you read Thurber's "Here Lies Miss Groby"?), but its pleasures and satisfactions are not those of literature until its findings illuminate the text.

Appearance

Look at the text. What do the obvious visual features reveal? Notice, for instance, the following poems: Waldman's "Things That Go Away & Come Back," Swenson's "Of Rounds," and Williams's "Dedication for a Plot of Ground." Even prose has shape. Compare a page of "A Rose for Emily" with "The Chaser." Look at a page from "To Bobolink, for Her Spirit" next to a page from "Memorial Day" and "Trouble in the Works." The

[1]Russell Baker, "Little Red Riding Hood Revisited," *The New York Times Magazine*, Jan. 13, 1980.

[2]Dan Greenburg, "Bears in Search of an Author," *Esquire Magazine* (Feb. 1958), pp. 46–47. Copyright 1958 by Dan Greenburg. Reprinted by permission of International Famous Agency.

differences in appearance assure you that the plays won't "sound" or "feel" the same. Reread what Mansfield says about the sentences in "Miss Brill" on p. 46.

The shape of poems is especially important because the basic unit of poetry is the line—not, as it is in prose, a sentence or paragraph. Denise Levertov says, "I regard the end of a line, the line break, as roughly equivalent to half a comma, but what that pause is doing is recording non-syntactic hesitations, or waitings, that occur in the thinking–feeling process."[3] We miss the "thinking–feeling" process in many poems if we fail to give that slight hesitation, or break, at the end of the line. Note that no drop in pitch can occur to signal falsely that the thought is ended. Instead, the hesitation is only a slight interruption.

In Robert Pack's "Love," we lose the impact of the images if we rush over the line endings. If read as an ordinary sentence, the following utterance loses its sense of discovery, of wonder, that asserts itself when we pause slightly after *found*: "But when my hand wiggled inside, I found / A rabbit." Read that whole poem aloud asserting, even exaggerating, the line breaks—but don't drop your pitch except at the end of thoughts. Notice the effect not only on the thoughts but on our sense of the speaker.

If Lazard's "Ordinance on Enrollment" becomes prose, we lose the fun of it. Read it aloud, ignoring the line structure. Now read it again, carefully observing the breaks. Notice the heightened satire and the fuller sense of the speaker's mindlessness. The lines reinforce our sense that the speaker is speaking from rote, from formula, able to believe what he or she is

saying only because he or she has never analyzed the thoughts.

Word Choice

Do you agree that there are no true synonyms? Can you think of any two words that have not only identical definitions but the same *emotional* effect? Take a short passage and substitute synonyms for various words, perhaps "The Fury of Aerial Bombardment" or "An Afternoon in Artillery Walk." Note that the changes affect not only our perception of things and events in the text, but also our sense of the speaker. In fact, most descriptions reveal as much about the speaker as about the object described. (Think of the humorous monologues that describe ball games, like Andy Griffith's "What it Was Was Football.")

Few of us are properly sensitive to words, and to compensate we need to go slowly, asking questions, "toying" with the words, taking time to examine them in the fullness of our own knowledge, a fullness that may surprise us if we give it the proper chance. The Workshop for Chapter II on "The Fury of Aerial Bombardment" gave you a sample of this kind of response. Judson Jerome provides examples from Robert Frost's "Design," the first line of which is "I found a dimpled spider, fat and white":

dimpled: Like a baby's cheek? But used with "spider" the word is sinister, perverse.

spider: Should be thin, light; it has no business being fat. Horror accumulates.

fat: A flat word, bringing a sense of fleshiness (cannibalism?) to the insect.

white: A key word in the poem, used five times, providing the first rhyme sound. It has two ranges of connotations. On the one hand it sug-

[3]Denise Levertov, "An Interview with Denise Levertov," *The Craft of Poetry: Interviews from the New York Quarterly,* ed., William Packard (Garden City, N.Y.: Doubleday, 1974), p. 88. See also, Robert Overstreet, "Preservation of Line Shape in the Performance of a Poem," *Southern Speech Communication Journal,* 45 (Spring 1980), 268–281.

gests purity, innocence; on the other, ghastliness, morbidity.[4]

Images

> *image:* sensory impression created by memory or imagination in the absence of any real object
>
> Example: dimpled spider, illuminated clocks

Even ordinary language evokes images. We respond to images of taste, smell, touch—all the senses, including thermal and kinesthetic. In literature images are important, as they affect our perception of the subject and the speaker. The selection and accumulation of images may create a scene, reinforce a mood, regulate our feelings of closeness or detachment, reveal a speaker's personality.

We can illustrate with a scene common to all of us—a classroom. First, the more specific the images, the more specific the scene. Make a list of about twenty classroom images, not just visual ones. Will the time of year influence your choice? If you had to narrow the list to ten, which ones would you choose? Which five? Poets often manage to convey the essence of an experience with few especially vivid images. Look at May Swenson's "After the Dentist."

If you wanted listeners to feel close to the scene, which images would you choose? Would the "feel of chalk dust in the trays" be better than "the green of the chalkboard"? Could you select images to make the scene pleasant? Comic? Threatening? Dull? Different people would select different images. How might a teacher's description differ from a student's? Would

things look different to a four-year-old? A parent? A vandal?

Sometimes we don't get a specific image because we don't know the real meaning of the word used for it. Form the habit of looking up any words you don't know well. You might, unless you have excellent visual recall, want to see a picture even of an object you know, so that your image can be more vivid. You'll miss the point of Shapiro's "Auto Wreck" if you don't know *denouement* (what we might call an intellectual image), and you may need to brush up on your botany when you read Wakoski's "Dancing on the Grave of a Son of a Bitch."

Figurative Language

"Figurative" somehow sounds "decorative," "ornamental," and some figurative language may be, but we miss the point if we look only for embellishment. Figures of speech are a way of thinking—until they become trite and a way of *not* thinking. The best figurative language offers insights beyond the literal surface, forces new awareness. Creative minds see unexpected similarities, as when Marianne Moore says that snakes feel like rose petals. Surely they both feel thin, damp, cool, satiny, but few of us can articulate such resemblances. Children often astound us with observations that, like the poet's, are far-fetched but apt.

Figures of speech also provide insight into the speaker. Farmers are likely to use expressions about crops, ball players expressions about their game. Remember the presidents who have been criticized for their repeated use of "game" analogies? Critics insisted that these figures of speech were symptoms of a mentality they could not admire.

Much figurative language has lost its freshness from repetition, but occasionally something, a personal experience, for example, can give new poignancy to an expression. A long hike can give a new re-

[4]Judson Jerome, *Poetry: Premeditated Art* (Boston: Houghton Mifflin, 1968), p. 54.

sponse to "tenderfoot," and, if you work with wood, you are struck by the aptness of "goes against the grain." Sometimes a writer gives freshness to old expressions by "tilting" them in a new context. We find new life in "cutting corners" when we read Malamud's "The Magic Barrel": ". . . he was an expert in cutting corners; and when there were no corners left he would make circles rounder."[5]

metaphor:	a comparison without using *like* or *as* "Maps faces are" ("Weathering")
simile:	a comparison using *like* or *as* "throats tight as tourniquets" ("Auto Wreck")
Note:	*metaphor* is often used to mean both

In ordinary discourse we use comparisons mostly for explanation (the lungs are like balloons), argument (the plan worked at WX University, and YZ University is just the same), and sometimes humor (garlic is like being pregnant; there's no such thing as a little bit). The pleasure of the joke is kin to one of the pleasures of the metaphor in literature: the delight of unexpected recognition.

But surprise is not the only value of metaphor. The apt metaphor extends our perceptions and our feelings. We all know what ambulances look like, but we see them more clearly than in real life when we read Shapiro's "Auto Wreck." The red light is exactly a "ruby flare"—gemlike as it reflects through the glass housing and coldly impersonal; a flare, a spurting out of light, and also a warning. "Pulsing out red light like an artery"—rhythmic, strong, but suggestive of pain and death.

Figures of speech have a cumulative effect. As this poem progresses, repeated

[5]Bernard Malamud, *The Magic Barrel* (New York: Farrar, Straus & Giroux, 1968).

reminders of hospitals and infirmities reinforce our feeling toward the event.

The final metaphor is intellectual. A *denouement* is the conclusion of a plot, a final working out. In a well-constructed plot, this solution has a satisfying rightness; it is, at least in retrospect, what earlier events demanded. The speaker suggests that we can trace causes, if not blame, for war deaths, suicides, even stillbirths. But a wreck is different; it violates our sense of logical outcomes. (How does this metaphor offer a clue to the speaker's personality?)

metonymy:	name of an object to signify another object closely related to it
Example:	stage for performance, bottle for wine
synecdoche:	use of part of an object to signify the whole
Example:	sail for ship, wings for bees (in Dickey's poem)
Note:	*synecdoche* is sometimes used for both

These figures are sometimes called figures of contiguity, because they are contiguous to, or touching, the objects they represent. The principle of synecdoche is important to all art—perhaps to all perception—because we regularly constitute wholes from parts. The most realistically complete stage setting is nevertheless only a part of the total world it is meant to evoke. The effect of a collage rests on the ability of its details to remind us of the larger units they represent. Everyday expressions of synecdoche reflect an emphasis on the significance of the part selected to represent the whole. "All hands on deck" seems proper for a ship when we consider the activities that the people will perform. "All hands on the field" would be ridiculous for a football game.

Metonymy includes several kinds of devices, such as a container for the thing contained (bottle for wine) or sign for the thing signified (flag for country). These figures are not just ornamental. They direct our perceptions because they represent choices. And, like all other features of the text, they help to reveal the speaker.

---

allusion: reference to fictional or historical persons, things, or events

Example: a Daniel come to judgment

Allusions are specific, and if familiar they are efficient. How do the allusions in Barry Spacks's "Freshmen" provide concise character sketches of the students? (And what do they tell us of the speaker's personality?) References to people, real or imaginary, offer not just visual details but emotional responses; if we have to track down the references, our emotional responses may be weak. Imagine a student fifty years hence trying to respond to an allusion to Archie Bunker or the Fonz.

Words or phrases recognized as coming from a different work may bring to the new text all the connotations of the old, giving the new one a special resonance. Unfortunately, these "echoes" of other works often serve as impediments. Most of us stumble through T. S. Eliot with the help of footnotes, unable to respond fully even when we learn of his sources. But a familiar echo can function like synecdoche to evoke a whole text.

---

symbol: an image that both means what it says and simultaneously stands for a larger idea which it represents

Example: the bazaar in "Araby"

Some symbols are emblems, like flags or fraternity pins, already recognized as "standing for" something. Writers often create symbols by using objects or activities both literally and evocatively. The bazaar in "Araby" is first of all a bazaar, but it comes to symbolize the disappointment inherent in the false surface of excitement. In this way symbols differ from ordinary metaphors (although metaphors may also become symbols). Faces are not *really* maps; Miss Emily's eyes in "A Rose for Emily" are certainly not lumps of coal. But in Araby the bazaar is real. Only as the story unfolds does it accumulate meaning and become a symbol.

We must beware of becoming symbol-hunters. Richard Eberhart is amused at the student who thinks the cancer cells in his poem of that name stand for communism, and Stanley Kunitz insists that in his poem "The Dragonfly" he was thinking of a dragonfly, not some symbolic struggle of the massed weaklings overcoming a giant. But students are likely to cry out in righteous protest after living through many classes in which the teacher said such things as "but of course, those objects you mention are only the surface. What the writer *really* meant was. . . ."

How are we to know? Probably the safest way is to read carefully, assuming that objects or experiences represent themselves only, unless, without being sought, additional import seems to assert itself. True, decades of "close reading" have heightened our perceptions so much that earlier uses of symbols appear heavy handed, obvious enough to seem inartistic. Still, if we read the obvious carefully enough, deeper meanings should come without strain.

Ellipse

An *ellipse,* or *ellipsis* (plural for both, *ellipses*), is an omission, usually of something readily understood from the context (the parenthetical part of the preceding sentence had an ellipsis: "is" was understood as the verb). Contemporary writers are apt to use all kinds of ellipses, only some of them clear from the context. In poems especially, we encounter gaps, omissions. These gaps contribute to an important quality of poetic language, its density, its capacity to say much with few words. As with all other characteristics of language, ellipses also help to reveal the speaker.

Even spelling can show ellipses. The language in Ntozake Shange's "no assistance" has a strange "look" because some letters are missing, a practice not uncommon among black poets. Is that meant to signify semiliteracy? Is it there to offer clues for pronouncing words? Certainly the peculiar abbreviated orthography discourages careful pronunciation, suggesting a flippant carelessness of articulation. But this technique is more than a cue for sounding a poem. It bespeaks a sense of protest so strong that it must sneer at everything traditional, conventional, even the rules of spelling. It must show how inessential these conventions are, how impotent, for expressing essences of language.

The ellipses in "Reason," by Josephine Miles, are easy to fill in, lacking only the subjects of "said." These omissions give to the whole poem a sense of conversation that is often fragmentary, but the uniformity of ellipses is in itself a structural repetition. The truncated sentences also heighten our sense that this is a distillation of the experience, instead of a fully detailed account.

You can't spot ellipses only by the look of a text. "How to Eat a Poem," despite its fragmented appearance, has no ellipses; neither has "Things That Go Away & Come Back." The latter text is a list, which implies no other words, that is, no further parts of phrases or sentences.

Narratives contain ellipses because no narrator can ever tell us everything that happened during the time of the story. Most of these gaps we fill in automatically, without even noticing the process. The narrator doesn't have to tell us that Little Red Riding Hood opened the door and said goodbye when we are told that Little Red Riding Hood has left the house. But some gaps are significantly there for us to fill in, almost as if no verbal description could be adequate, as, for example, the rehearsal scene in "Who Am I This Time?" and the scene between Miss Pinkerton and George in "Miss Pinkerton's Apocalypse" after the police leave.

Some gaps in stories relate to the passage of time. A gap has a different effect from a "filler," even if the filler is only a phrase like "much later." Think of the effect in "Araby" of a movement from the scene at home to the scene at the bazaar without the paragraph about traveling. That kind of omission would damage our sense of the child's frustration and compromise our sharing his feelings that he will never get there. A gap would ruin the impact. "The Jew Bird" has no fillers, not one word, between the scene in which Laurie and Edie return to find Schwartz gone and the scene in which Laurie discovers the "dead blackbird." Speculate about the effects of a filler similar to the one a few paragraphs earlier, beginning "weeks went by." The ellipsis allows a juxtaposition of the two scenes that sharpens the poignancy of the final one.

Meter

When we discuss the meter of English poetry, we usually mean *accentual-syllabic* meter, a pattern depending both on stresses and syllables. Meter based on stress only, regardless of intervening syllables, is *strong stress meter*. Paul Engle's "Together" is an example. When only syllables count, not stress, the meter is *syllabic*, as in Marianne Moore's "Face." When we enumerate the four basic meters in English, we mean *accentual-syllabic* meter: iambic, trochaic, anapestic, dactyllic.

Completely accurate scansion, or marking of meter, is not only unnecessary but impossible. The language is too flexible. But some recognition of pattern, of repetition, is important to readers, and you can easily master the basic vocabulary. The following examples are fairly obvious and are therefore not really typical—most lines of poetry resist unequivocal marking.

---

iambic: ˘ ′ The curfew tolled the knell of parting day

This line from Grey's "Elegy" is the standard example of iambic meter, but even here we face an imperfect pattern because not all the unstressed syllables are equally weak. Note that the second syllable of "curfew" is considerably stronger than the second syllable of "parting." To find the meter, simply read the line as if it were prose and note where the natural stresses fall. Words of more than one syllable are good indicators, as are the classes of words normally unstressed in English: articles (a, an, the), auxiliary verbs, and personal pronouns, to name a few. But any word can be stressed in some contexts, and all stress is relative. For instance, Eliot's line "and smell of steak in passageways" seems perfectly iambic. By the time we reach "passageways" the pattern is so strong that we say ′ ˘ ′. But we could create a different context and a different meter for the same words: "Alleyways, passageways, teaming with passengers." Here "-ways" seems unstressed because it is weaker than the first syllable of "teaming" and perhaps because the final three words are rather clearly ′ ˘ ˘ ′ ˘ ˘.

---

trochaic: ′ ˘ Tell me not in mournful numbers

anapestic: ˘ ˘ ′ The Assyrian came down like a wolf on the fold

dactyllic: ′ ˘ ˘ Take her up mournfully, treat her not scornfully

---

Few lines are entirely consistent, varying according to kinds of meter and degrees of stress within each pattern. This variety redeems them from monotony and accounts for one source of pleasure we get from meter: the tensiveness between the perfect pattern and the actual one. Our minds are aware of the ideal pattern, and the realization of it in language strains against the ideal. Another explanation for the pleasure we find in meter is that, being biologically rhythmic creatures, we respond to rhythm.

Sound Patterns

---

rhyme: repetition of final stressed vowel plus all that follows, with different preceding sounds

Example: weigh, day (but not weigh, way) litter, bitter; gratitude, platitude; generating, venerating

---

Rhyme occurs within lines but more often at the ends of lines where similar rhymes create patterns. Usually you don't have to worry about preserving the rhymes; you can just pronounce the words. In a humorous poem, say one by Ogden

Nash, or in lyrics by W. S. Gilbert, you will probably want to exaggerate a pronunciation for fun. But in a serious poem you can't distort, although you can sometimes choose between two equally good pronunciations. In Kinnell's "Wait" you may want to pronounce "again" to rhyme with "pain," a practice so widespread that it is not exaggeration.

---

assonance:	repetition of stressed vowel sounds
Example:	cold, loathe, folk
alliteration:	repetition of initial consonant sounds
Example:	let, lovely, lakes (The second l in "lovely" is the beginning of a syllable, therefore an initial consonant sound.)
consonance:	repetition of identical initial and final consonant sounds with different middle vowels
Example:	tick tock, zig zag (Some people include all consonant repetition, as in take, get, ticket.)

Modern poets often use these sound effects in preference to rhyme as being more subtle. For an example of many kinds of sound repetitions, see "Otto" in Workshop IV.

Abstract Form

Abstract form, or "formal" form, exists apart from any specific examples, as do all the sound effects just discussed. Abstract forms may be more extensive than just a few words, including entire poems.

The limerick is most easily recognized, but many readers as easily recognize both kinds of sonnets. Villanelles have a stricter form even than do sonnets. (See Auden's "Villanelle," Dylan Thomas's "Do Not Go Gentle into That Good Night," and Ambrose Gorden, Jr.'s "Departures.")

Why do writers use abstract forms and how do they affect readers? No one knows the full answer, but all agree that basically we find satisfaction in the completion of design, the working out of a pattern, and the feeling of unity and balance as well as the pleasure of recognition. Of course, realization of form is not in itself artistic. The form must blend with the subject, each complementing the other. A compromise in one to accommodate the other signals the amateur at work. Another suggestion is that the form serves to discipline the emotions. For instance, the speaker in Thomas's "Do Not Go Gentle into That Good Night" is strongly emotional, but this bursting emotion, constrained by one of the strictest of forms, rises above the indulgent, even the personal, to become an artistic distillation of the response to dying. Note that despite the rigid demands of the rhyme structure, no part of the utterance seems to be a compromise just for the sake of rhyme.

Does the abstract form of "Sonnet" heighten the sense of fun in the poem? What is the effect of the regularity of meter in "For Malcolm a Year After"? The poem reads almost like doggerel. Do you consider this trait a weakness, or does it serve as an ironic device?

Free Verse

Free verse seems to have not abstract form but organic form; that is, a form that emerges from the needs of the specific poem and does not exist apart from the poem, unlike the abstract forms of, say, sonnets or limericks. But Joseph Malof, in his discussion of free verse, cautions that few poets disregard all abstract forms.[6] Instead, free verse uses some abstract forms but uses them so unpredictably that we do not anticipate them but recognize them only in retrospect.

Malof classifies some of the main types of free verse as *prose-poetry*, *phrasal free verse*, and *syntactic free verse*. He says, "When words become poetry their physical properties become as important as their meanings. Prose-poetry is language that looks like prose on the printed page, but that is dedicated to being itself as much as to communicating something else."[7] We find in prose-poetry strong repetitions of sounds, words, units of rhythm, phrases, as in Benedikt's "The Meat Epitaph" or Edson's "Because Things Get Sad, Father."

The salient feature of phrasal free verse is repetition of words and phrases. We find examples in "Dancing on the Grave of a Son of a Bitch" or "small comment" by Sonia Sanchez. The systematic repetition of phrases at the beginning of successive lines is *anaphora*.

Syntactic patterns are structures of language that exist apart from words. "_____ is one of those _____ s" is a syntactic pattern. We could fill in any number of words, radically changing the subject, but the syntactic pattern would remain. Repetition of syntactic patterns can help give shape to free verse. We find good examples in "How to Eat a Poem" by Eve Merriam and "Speaking: the Hero" by Felix Pollack. The "when" clauses in Cruz's "today is a day of great joy" is a little more subtle but still evident.

How does the recognition of these patterns affect your performance? Should your audience be aware of them? You

can't make the form of free verse as obvious as abstract form because organic form is by definition more subtle. And you can't sacrifice the sense of the utterance or of the speaker. But, if you realize the structure, your performance will likely provide a feeling of rightness and completion whether or not your audience is conscious of the patterns.

Plot

A text that deals with events, with a story, whether poetry or prose, has additional elements of structure; it has a plot. The most obvious example of plot development is a traditional play. The beginning is simply a presentation of characters in a situation, but from the start the situation is somehow balanced in a way that at least has the potential for becoming unbalanced. Things are poised rather than at rest. Then something happens to disturb the balance and pose the major dramatic question, the beginning of the dramatic conflict. Variously termed *inciting incident* or *attack,* this event launches the plot.

What precedes the attack is the introduction. Note that in some ways the playwright's job is more complicated than is that of the novelist or short story writer. In a play all the information must come from dialogue, and the characters must not seem to speak only to inform the audience. One mark of a good playwright is the way in which he or she handles this background material, or *exposition,* so that the audience learns all it needs to know, all the time believing that the characters speak only to and for one another.

The dramatic conflict progresses through the rising action—usually a series of complications—to a turning point, called a *crisis,* or a *climax.* This is not to be confused with the conclusion, or denouement, which is the final resolution of the dramatic conflict. The *crisis* or *climax* is

[6]Joseph Malof, *A Manual of English Meters* (Bloomington: Indiana University Press, 1970), pp. 146–153.

[7]*Ibid.,* p. 148.

that point after which the outcome appears inevitable. It usually marks a reversal. In a traditional comedy the major character, or *protagonist,* loses until the crisis and wins from then on. In a tragedy the protagonist appears to win until the crisis, after which his or her defeat, at least in mortal terms, is assured.

Kenneth Rowe compares this structure to the action of a wave. "In terms of the analogy of the movement . . ., *the turning point is the crest of the final wave. A wave is poised at its crest; then it breaks and delivers its blow in its fall. The blow is the resolution.* The tension following the turning point is of a different kind from that preceding, more of the mind and less of the nerves. . . . The play may be more exciting to the crisis but more absorbing after the crisis."[8] Rowe objects to terms such as "untanglement" to describe the falling action because that sounds dull. He says, "The movement from the crisis to the resolution of a play is certainly not the gliding subsidence of a wave in the open sea, but is the boiling, swirling caldron of the breaking of a wave on an obstruction."[9] The traditional diagram for these parts is shown below.[10]

The time needed for each step varies from play to play. In television drama, for instance, the crisis and denouement are usually close together, and the inciting in-

cident may come immediately because no exposition is necessary in episodic dramas that feature the same characters every week. Of course, in any play only part of the exposition comes in the introduction, but less is necessary when we know the main characters and their situation.

We can illustrate by building a play of our own based on an earlier version of the story of "Little Red Riding Hood," when the story ended with the wolf, having devoured the grandmother, eating Little Red Riding Hood. The *introduction* is the scene between Little Red Riding Hood and her mother, whose warning about not speaking to strangers should alert us that something can easily upset their situation. The *major dramatic conflict* is the little girl against the wolf, the dramatic question being, "Can Little Red Riding Hood deliver the cookies safely to her grandmother?" The *inciting incident,* which launches the conflict, is her departure from the house. In our play we would want some complications; therefore, we could add several scenes of peril where Little Red Riding Hood triumphs. But once she speaks to the wolf—in disobedience to her mother's command—the outcome is assured. The wolf will triumph over Little Red Riding Hood. That scene is the *crisis,* the reversal, and from that point the child loses. The final scene is the *denouement,* when the wolf eats her. Not all plots fit neatly into this pattern. Sometimes the inciting incident occurs before the play starts and we learn of it only later.

The location of these parts of the plot

[8]Kenneth Thorpe Rowe, *Write That Play* (New York: Funk & Wagnalls, 1939), p. 55.

[9]*Ibid.,* p. 56.

[10]*Ibid.,* p. 60. This diagram is a modification of Rowe's.

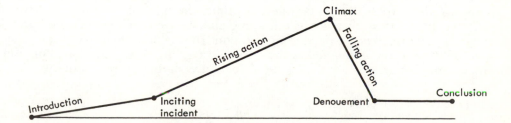

always depends on the statement of conflict, and the definition of the conflict depends on identifying the major character, or protagonist. In "Ile" both Captain Keeney and his wife are major characters. If we assume that Captain Keeney is the protagonist (the title supports this view), then *the conflict* pits Keeney against the crew and his wife, who all want him to turn back. The *inciting incident,* the event that changes the status quo and launches the conflict, is the crew's decision to mutiny, an event reported to the Captain early in the play. Mrs. Keeney's plea to return is one event in the *rising action,* and Keeney's confrontation with the crew is the *climax.* From that point, their victory is no longer possible. The sighting of the whales and the Captain's decision to pursue them is the *denouement.* (We could argue, though primarily for the illustration, that Mrs. Keeney is the protagonist and that the conflict is between her and her husband. The inciting incident would then be her sighting of water, indicating that they were no longer icebound and return was possible. The climax occurs with the Captain's decision to pursue the whales, after which her victory is no longer possible. The denouement is her going insane.)

Although plots of short stories and novels do not conform to this sequence of dramatic development, their plots too are determined by recognizing the protagonist. Norman Friedman tells us that "The protagonist is the one who undergoes the major change, the one whose career serves as the chief focus of interest, the one around whom all else in the plot revolves."[11] Once we identify the protagonist, who is not always the title character or necessarily the most sympathetic one, we can proceed to classify the plot as one of *character, fortune,* or *thought,* depending on which of these three items makes the most important change.

Friedman explains these three terms:

"Action" or "fortune" refers to the protagonist's honor, status, and reputation, his goods, loved ones, health, and well-being. Fortune is revealed in what happens to him—happiness or misery—and to his plans—success or failure. "Character" refers to the protagonist's motives, purposes, and goals, his habits, behavior, and will, and may be noble or base, good or bad, sympathetic or unsympathetic, complete or incomplete, mature or immature. Character is revealed when he decides voluntarily to pursue or abandon a course of action and in whether he can indeed put his decision into effect. And "thought" refers to the protagonist's states of mind, attitudes, reasonings, emotions, beliefs, conceptions, and knowledge. Thought is revealed either omnisciently, as in many novels, or in what the character says when stating a general proposition, arguing a particular point, or explaining his view of a situation.[12]

Friedman insists that the important change in *Great Expectations* is Pip's character, although his changes in fortune and thought are both obvious. Our satisfaction comes only when we see him learn to appreciate his family back home. Could we say the same thing about the plot in "A Good Man is Hard to Find"? The grandmother's change in fortune matters less than her change in character, her growth from small-minded selfishness with superficial values to a recognition of her true relationship to humanity, or, in O'Connor's words, her acceptance of grace.

Time

Any text that tells a story has two kinds of time: the time of the event or happening and the time of the telling or presentation. Drama and narrative differ in several ways in their handling of time. Generally, drama moves from the present

[11]Norman Friedman, "Forms of the Plot," *Journal of General Education,* 8 (July 1955), 246.

[12]*Ibid.,* 246–247.

to the future. We see a scene happening *now*, and we look toward what will happen *later*. Of course, there are exceptions. Plays sometimes have flashbacks (for example, Joanna Glass's *Canadian Gothic* moves freely from present to past), but the usual pattern of drama is present to future. Narrative events are always past, or no one could "narrate" them. The "telling" is the present, and the events move from past to nearer the present.

In plays the passing of time occurs between scenes or between acts. Aristotle suggested that successful plays should not cover too much time, and generations of playwrights strove to compress their plots into a twenty-four-hour stretch. But the Greeks lacked the conventions of later theaters that could conveniently show time passing with set changes and changes in costume and makeup. Generally, the time elapsed within any scene is realistic, and the event time is the same as presentation time.

Time in narrative is far more versatile. As Eudora Welty points out, "Fiction does not hesitate to accelerate time, slow it down, project it forward or run it backward, cause it to skip over itself or repeat itself."[13]

Three terms are in common use to explain the relationships between presentation time and event time—what Joanna Maclay calls *story time* and *actual time,* respectively.[14]

---

scene: presentation time = event time

summary: presentation time < event time

description: presentation time > event time

Let us examine these three possibilities and consider their significance to a text. If I am telling a story, I can make my "telling" time equivalent to the "happening" time. If I had an encounter in a store that lasted twenty minutes and I take twenty minutes to recount it, I've told it as *scene*. Dialogue is always *scene*, requiring the same time to recount verbatim as to be uttered originally. I can stretch my story out to an hour if I *describe* the interior of the store, my feelings, my impression of the other people, and so on. Or I can compress the events into a few minutes of "telling" by *summary*. Most storytellers use a combination of the three.

Recognizing these three techniques can tell us something about the storyteller's personality and action, "showing" or "telling." Which of these three makes the listener feel closer to the story? Since the storyteller can regulate our sympathy and involvement, either scene or description—depending on details—would probably draw us closer than summary. Finally, the patterns of scene, summary, and description give form to the story, establishing its larger rhythms,[15] creating the work's *texture*.[16]

Total Form

Some devices mentioned earlier are complete forms—sonnets, villanelles—and some are what Kenneth Burke calls minor or incidental forms: those parts of a work that have sufficiently recognized structure to be "discussed as formal events in themselves."[17] His examples include figures of speech as well as longer passages (like a speech in a play) with a structure based

[13]Eudora Welty, "Some Notes on Time in Fiction," *Mississippi Quarterly*, 26 (Fall, 1973), 485.

[14]Joanna Maclay, "The Aesthetics of Time in Narrative Fiction," *Speech Teacher*, 18 (September 1969), 194.

[15]See Robert Beloof, *The Performing Voice in Literature* (Boston: Little, Brown, 1966).

[16]See A. A. Mendilow, *Time and the Novel* (London: Peter Nevell, 1952).

[17]Kenneth Burke, "The Nature of Form," in *Counter-Statement* (New York: Harcourt, Brace, 1931). Reprinted in *Discussions of Poetry: Form and Structure*, ed. Francis Murphy (Boston: D. C. Heath, 1964), p. 3.

on contemporary principles of rhetorical design. But all works of literature have a total form, which Burke defines as follows:

> *Form* in literature is an arousing and fulfillment of desires. A work has form, in so far as one part leads a reader to anticipate another part, to be gratified by the sequence.[18]

Sometimes the form is abstract or conventional, sometimes organic, creating itself as the work progresses.

Progression and *repetition* make for kinds of organic form. Burke says progressive form may be of two types: *syllogistic* or *qualitative.*

> *Syllogistic progression* is the form of a perfectly conducted argument, advancing step by step. It is the form of a mystery story, where everything falls together as in a story . . . by Poe. . . . To go from A to E through stages B, C, D is to obtain such form. . . . In so far as the audience, from its acquaintance with the premises, feels the rightness of the conclusion, the work is formal.[19]

Burke calls reversal a syllogistic progression in which the poet reverses the audience's expectations.

Qualitative progression is less obvious. Burke defines it as follows:

> Instead of one incident in the plot preparing us for some other possible incident of plot . . . , the presence of one quality prepares us for the introduction of another.[20]

Sometimes we encounter events or thoughts in a text that we did not anticipate—the comic scene by the servant in Macbeth who responds clownishly to a knocking at the gate right after the brutal murder scene, an impassioned outburst in appreciation of beauty after the description of a particularly unbeautiful thing. But in retrospect, we find these surprises "right," not because we expected them or were supposed to have expected them, but because certain qualities exist in all parts of the work. For example, in "Next Day," the form is qualitative, because, as readers, we do not expect a funeral to explain the title of the poem; yet, when it occurs, we know it is right. The quality changes, but for reasons that are entirely plausible as we think back to the scene at the grocery store. Could you argue that in O'Connor's "A Good Man Is Hard to Find" the qualities of grotesquery unite both the humorous beginning and the stark ending?

Repetitive form consists, obviously, of repetitions—of sounds, thoughts, images, and the like. Burke calls it "restatement of the same thing in different ways. . . . A succession of images, each of them regiving the same lyric mood; a character repeating his identity, his 'number,' under changing situations; the sustaining of an attitude, as in satire; the rhythmic regularity of blank verse; the rhyme scheme of *terza rima*—these are all aspects of repetitive form."[21]

Do you know the child's story, "Teeny Tiny"? Nothing much happens, but children love the repetition: "There was once a teeny tiny woman who lived in a teeny tiny house in a teeny tiny village. She had a teeny tiny cat who caught teeny tiny mice in a teeny tiny cellar." In adult literature, the form is usually more subtle, but the principle remains. "Repetitive form, the restatement of a theme by new details, is basic to any work of art, or to any other kind of orientation for that matter. It is our only method of 'talking on the subject.' "[22]

---

[18]*Ibid.*, p. 1.
[19]*Ibid.*
[20]*Ibid.*

[21]*Ibid.*, p. 2.
[22]*Ibid.*

Conventional form is preestablished; the poet does not create it but finds it ready made for use. Plays, short stories, and novels may have a somewhat conventional form. Think of adventure shows on television, especially those with similar events in each episode, like a chase scene. Although the motivation and characters vary, the scene occurs in almost the same place each time. In a series in which one character has supernatural powers, there are usually two manifestations of this power, one early in the show for a sort of incidental emergency (and some viewers might need to be informed of these special powers) and one near the end that marks the climax, the final victory of the hero over the antagonist. These forms become conventional, not from prescription but from habit. As Burke remarks, "Any form can become conventional, and be sought for itself—whether it be as complex as the Greek tragedy or as compact as the sonnet."[23]

These forms, of course, are likely to overlap and interrelate. We cannot classify a work under only one heading, and Burke remarks that we "should not, since in so organic a thing as a work of art, we could not expect to find any principle functioning in isolation from the others."[24] He summarizes the value of understanding the interrelationships between these five aspects of form (syllogistic progressive, qualitative progressive, repetitive, conventional, minor or incidental) as follows:

> The important thing is not to confine the explanation to *one* principle but to formulate sufficient principles to make an explanation possible. However, though the five aspects of form can merge into one another, or can be present in varying degrees, no other terms should be required in an analysis of formal functionings.[25]

How does the performer demonstrate form, especially total form? Must the audience realize which principles are operating? Ideally they should, but we have to concede the unlikelihood that any one performance can reveal all the structures. However, the performer must know. The performer must know what is generating the rest, not only from the psychological motivations of the speaker, but how the psychological motivations merge with the form to create not just real-life experience but the real-life experience that is art, that has its own beginning and end. An artistic utterance is ordered, structured; and performers must recognize this complexity in their preparations and performances.

[23]*Ibid.*
[24]*Ibid.*, p. 4.

[25]*Ibid.*

WORKSHIP IV

In this workshop, we shall examine a variety of stylistic and structural devices in specific selections, incorporating the vocabulary used earlier in this chapter and suggesting some possible performance behaviors. The discussions address the question, "What are the distinctive stylistic and structural devices and how might they be translated in performance?"

Somehow you know when it arrives,
ETHEL LIVINGSTON

Somehow you know when it arrives,
There's just one day when it's
                              there.
You get up
5   out of wrinkled sheets
And you're hot because the heat
          is on and it's cold outside—
Not fall cold but
                    cold.
10

There's a grey capping the day,
But the air is light underneath
          and cold and sharp
          like an aluminum ice tray.
15 It's cold
              to touch.
It rained last night—
                        wet
                          rain
20 And the leaves fell,
                        some of them
                        lots of them,
So the ground looks
          like a shadow of the tree above—
25 A mirror reflection,
          but the color is
                      real and thick
                              and heavy

Because they're leaves
And you know what wet leaves are like.
30 There are leaves on the wet cement too—
          red and yellow and brown
          and brown and yellow
          and green and yellow
          and brown.
35 They're like footsteps.
They stick
                to the grey cement
Because they're wet too.
If you pick one up
40   it's like wet paper with a stem.
They're dying.
You know tomorrow they'll
          dry up and blow away
          and the yard man

```
45            will rake them and burn them
                                 red
                                 and
                                 yellow
                                 and
50                               brown.
              But when they blow away
                  there's an impression
                  on the grey cement
              And when you try to smudge it with your toe
55            It won't smudge.

              Anyway
                     like I said
              You know when winter comes—that one day
              And then
60                    you only have to wait
                  til the rest of the leaves fall
                  and the rain turns white
                  and the yard man goes inside.
              Then everyone else will know too.
```

While the poem may be regarded as a statement about the passage of time, its structure and style reinforce—if not simulate—that passage through one large movement and a variety of repetitions. In one sense, the large movement is syllogistic as the identity of the "it" finally emerges. The title and first line tell us only that "Somehow you know when it arrives." Not until line 58 do we know for certain that "it" is "winter." Another organizing principle is spatial—from the wrinkled sheets in the room, to the window to examine the gray day, and finally to a close scrutiny (a camera closeup?) of the leaves. The performer might well emphasize this movement through longer silences to indicate when sections are finished, and through physical action to show that the object of attention has changed.

The repetitions, many of which are shown on the chart on p. 254, are primarily second- and third-person pronouns. "You" (possibly both speaker and listener) and "they" (the leaves) are part of the scene that "it" (winter) will control. The performer who pays close attention to line endings, giving them what Levertov called half a comma of time, will quite naturally call attention to the prominence of the pronouns; such a practice will also emphasize the named colors and the slow speed of the leaves falling.

Dedication for a Plot of Ground
WILLIAM CARLOS WILLIAMS

This plot of ground
facing the waters of this inlet
is dedicated to the living presence of
Emily Dickinson Wellcome
who was born in England, married,
lost her husband and with
her five year old son
sailed for New York in a two-master,
was driven to the Azores;
ran adrift on Fire Island shoal,
met her second husband
in a Brooklyn boarding house,

Repetition in "Somehow you know when it arrives,"

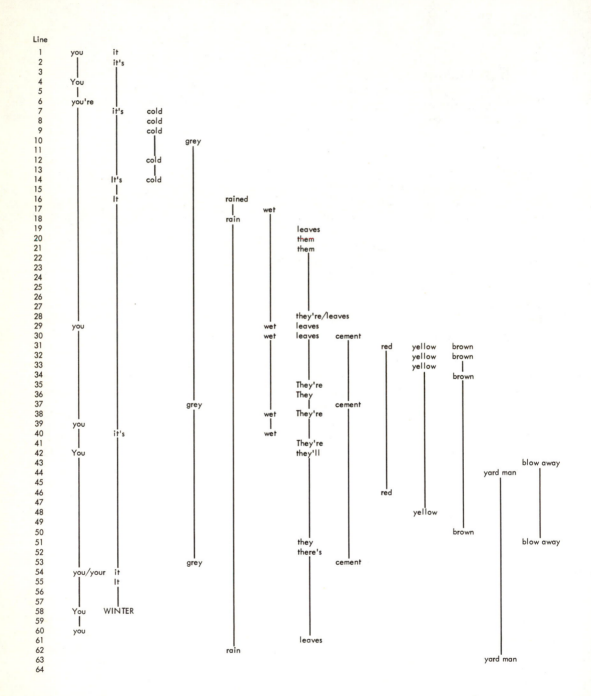

went with him to Puerto Rico
bore three more children, lost
her second husband, lived hard
for eight years in St. Thomas,
Puerto Rico, San Domingo, followed
the oldest son to New York,
lost her daughter, lost her "baby",
seized the two boys of
the oldest son by the second marriage
mothered them—they being
motherless—fought for them
against the other grandmother
and the aunts, brought them here
summer after summer, defended
herself here against thieves,
storms, sun, fire,
against flies, against girls
that came smelling about, against
drought, against weeds, storm-tides,
neighbors, weasels that stole her chickens,
against the weakness of her own hands,
against the growing strength of
the boys, against wind, against
the stones, against trespassers,
against rents, against her own mind.

She grubbed this earth with her own hands,
domineered over this grass plot,
blackguarded her oldest son
into buying it, lived here fifteen years,
attained a final loneliness and—

If you can bring nothing to this place
but your carcass, keep out.

The word "plot" in the title is finely ambiguous: there is a plot in which Emily Dickinson Wellcome is buried, and the poem outlines the plot of her life. A narrative in the frame of a personal recollection, the poem contains forty-four lines, all pressed into three sentences. The first, thirty-seven lines long, is a definition of the poem's subject shown through verbs: was born, married, lost, sailed, was driven, met, went, bore, lost, lived, followed, lost, seized, mothered, fought, brought, defended. The second sentence, five lines long, is conspicuously unfinished—as her life was not. The final sentence, only three lines, is a conditional threat: if these facts have not been sufficiently persuasive, the speaker has no patience with his or her listeners.

A performance of the poem needs a sense of the emphatic, charging nature of the first sentence, as well as the speech/breath units suggested by the line arrangement. After the first sentence the speaker seems to pause briefly before continuing the chronicle. The fact that the speaker is unable to finish (because of being choked up? because of his or her own shame? because of sensing a lack of appreciation from the audience?) can be marked by a rising or sustained pitch. The command of the final warning will probably be accompanied by penetratingly direct eye contact: such directness may be in striking contrast to the inward looking and/or thinking of the opening.

Rape
ADRIENNE RICH

There is a cop who is both prowler and father:
he comes from your block, grew up with your brothers,
had certain ideals.
You hardly know him in his boots and silver badge,
on horseback, one hand touching his gun.

You hardly know him but you have to get to know him:
he has access to machinery that could kill you.
He and his stallion clop like warlords among the trash,

his ideals stand in the air, a frozen cloud
from between his unsmiling lips.

And so, when the time comes, you have to turn to him,
the maniac's sperm still greasing your thighs,
your mind whirling like crazy. You have to confess
to him, you are guilty of the crime
of having been forced.

And you see his blue eyes, the blue eyes of all the family
whom you used to know, grow narrow and glisten,
his hand types out the details
and he wants them all
but the hysteria in your voice pleases him best.

You hardly know him but now he thinks he knows you:
he has taken down your worst moment
on a machine and filed it in a file.
He knows, or thinks he knows, how much you imagined;
he knows, or thinks he knows, what you secretly wanted.

He has access to machinery that could get you put away;
and if, in the sickening light of the precinct,
and if, in the sickening light of the precinct,
your details sound like a portrait of your confessor,
will you swallow, will you deny them, will you lie your way home?

This poem is carefully controlled through stylistic and structural devices; its subject is worked out as an artistic nightmare. The form of the six five-line stanzas is progressive in syllogistic, qualitative, and repetitive senses. First introduced in the first two stanzas, the cop later fulfills our categorical expectations; he would behave this way. Qualitatively, we dread with the speaker the encounter with him; and our dread is realized in repulsion as he takes the dictation. The poem closes emphatically with repetitive sounds, words, statements, and, finally, questions.

You hardly know him but now he thinks he knows you	(variation on line 6)
he has taken down your worst moment	(m/n repetition; h continues)
on a machine and filed it in a file.	(word repetition; m/n continues)
He knows, or thinks he knows, how much you imagined;	
He knows, or thinks he knows, what you secretly wanted.	
He has access to machinery that could get you put away;	(variation on line 7) cluster of plosives slows line
and if, in the sickening light of the precinct,	repeated line; repeated
and if, in the sickening light of the precinct,	iambs and anapests
your details sound like a portrait of your confessor,	anapests
will you swallow, will you deny them, will you lie your way home?	(plosive cluster: d, t, k, p)

Unlike the next-to-last line, the last is not impeded by plosives; it is instead accelerated by the greatly increased number of unstressed syllables. Attention to the change of rhythm in the final line will prevent a tendency toward the sentimental—a lapse likely to occur if you give each question prolonged attention.

It is also interesting to note the two key word repetitions; "you" appears nineteen times and "he," "him," or "cop" twenty, a fitting emphasis for their conflicts and tensions in their roles as protagonist-antagonist, woman-man, and questioner-victim.

Finally, who is this "you" mentioned with such frequency? The speaker's self? A collective voice for women? An unidentified listener? Either answer could be justified and sustained in performance. If the speaker is talking to herself and setting the sequence of the scenes vividly out front, hardly moving at all, she is then reviewing what could happen to herself, finally discovering that the treatment at the coercive police station is itself a metaphorical rape against which she would have no defense.

Freedom to Breathe
ALEXANDER SOLZHENITSYN

Translated by Michael Glenny

A shower fell in the night and now dark clouds drift across the sky, occasionally sprinkling a fine film of rain.

I stand under an apple tree in blossom and I breathe. Not only the apple tree but the grass round it glistens with moisture; words cannot describe the sweet fragrance that pervades the air. I inhale as deeply as I can, and the aroma invades my whole being; I breathe with my eyes open, I breathe with my eyes closed—I cannot say which gives me the greater pleasure.

This, I believe, is the single most precious freedom that prison takes away from us: the freedom to breathe freely, as I now can. No food on earth, no wine, not even a woman's kiss is sweeter to me than this air steeped in the fragrance of flowers, of moisture and freshness.

No matter that this is only a tiny garden, hemmed in by five-story houses like cages in a zoo. I cease to hear the motorcycles backfiring, radios whining, the burble of loudspeakers. As long as there is fresh air to breathe under an apple tree after a shower, we may survive a little longer.

The overall form of this essay (or prose poetry) qualitatively progresses from the syllogistic nature of the first paragraph (it rained; the scene is clean). The cleanliness and freshness of the scene is then reflected in the speaker's internal state. The third paragraph introduces a negative element into the meditation—the most precious right to breathe is not possible in prisons. Finally, he returns to describing his garden, which is not as perfect as it sounded in paragraph 2 but is nonetheless cherished. The last line effectively concludes by returning to the second line of the piece.

In performance these four units can be set apart quite easily: (1) a quiet observation of the sky; (2) a lyrical, joyful feeling of the scene; (3) an understated conclusion, in remembering a prison; (4) a return to the present scene, while mindful of the larger scene around him.

The repetitive nature of the form is also apparent in the speaker's observations about himself:

I stand
I breathe
I inhale
I can
I breathe
I breathe
I cannot
I believe
I cease

There is a fragile quality about these paragraphs that suggests that too much overt movement and big vocal shifts might overpower the experience in the text. A great deal of rehearsal time should be devoted to sharpening olfactory images—remembering or imagining how the smell of rain, wet grass, and apple trees combine to make a sweet fragrance.

I Stand Here Ironing*
TILLIE OLSEN

1.   I stand here ironing, and what you asked me moves tormented back and forth with the iron.

2.   "I wish you would manage the time to come in and talk with me about your daughter. I'm sure you can help me understand her. She's a youngster who needs help and whom I'm deeply interested in helping."

3.   "Who needs help?" Even if I came what good would it do? You think because I am her mother I have a key, or that in some way you could use me as a key? She has lived for nineteen years. There is all that life that has happened outside of me, beyond me.

4.   And when is there time to remember, to sift, to weigh, to estimate, to total? I will start and there will be an interruption and I will have to gather it all together again. Or I will become engulfed with all I did or did not do, with what should have been and what cannot be helped.

5.   She was a beautiful baby. The first and only one of our five that was beautiful at birth. You do not guess how new and uneasy her tenancy in her now-loveliness. You did not know her all those years she was thought homely, or see her poring over her baby pictures, making me tell her over and over how beautiful she had been—and would be, I would tell her—and was now, to the seeing eyes. But the seeing eyes were few or nonexistent. Including mine.

6.   I nursed her. They feel that's important nowadays. I nursed all the children, but with her, with all the fierce rigidity of first motherhood, I did like the books said. Though her cries battered me to trembling and my breasts ached with swollenness, I waited till the clock decreed.

7.   Why do I put that first? I do not even know if it matters, or if it explains anything.

8.   She was a beautiful baby. She blew shining bubbles of sound. She loved motion, loved light, loved color and music and textures. She would lie on the floor

*The numerals shown here refer to the chart on p. 264 and are not part of the original story.

in her blue overalls patting the surface so hard in ecstasy her hands and feet would blur. She was a miracle to me, but when she was eight months old I had to leave her daytimes with the woman downstairs to whom she was no miracle at all, for I worked or looked for work and for Emily's father, who "could no longer endure" (he wrote in his goodbye note) "sharing want" with us.

9.   I was nineteen. It was the pre-relief, pre-WPA world of the depression. I would start running as soon as I got off the streetcar, running up the stairs, the place smelling sour, and, awake or asleep to startle awake, when she saw me she would break into a clogged weeping that could not be comforted, a weeping I can yet hear.

10.   After a while I found a job hashing at night so I could be with her days, and it was better. But it came to where I had to bring her to his family and leave her.

11.   It took a long time to raise the money for her fare back. Then she got the chicken pox and I had to wait longer. When she finally came, I hardly knew her, walking quick and nervous like her father, looking like her father, thin, and dressed in a shoddy red that yellowed her skin and glared at the pock marks. All the baby loveliness gone.

12.   She was two. Old enough for nursery school, they said, and I did not know then what I know now—the fatigue of the long day, and the lacerations of group life in the kinds of nurseries that are only parking places for children.

13.   Except that it would have made no difference if I had known. It was the only place there was. It was the only way we could be together, the only way I could hold a job.

14.   And even without knowing, I knew. I knew that the teacher was evil because all these years it has curdled into my memory, the little boy hunched in the corner, her rasp, "Why aren't you outside, because Alvin hits you? That's no reason, go out, scaredy." I knew Emily hated it even if she did not clutch and implore, "Don't go, Mommy," like the other children, mornings.

15.   She always had a reason why we should stay home. Momma, you look sick. Momma, I feel sick. Momma, the teachers aren't there today, they're sick. Momma there was a fire there last night. Momma it's a holiday today, no school, they told me.

16.   But never a direct protest, never rebellion. I think of our others in their three-, four-year-oldness—the explosions, the tempers, the denunciations, the demands—and I feel suddenly ill. I stop the ironing. What in me demanded that goodness in her? And what was the cost, the cost to her of such goodness?

17.   The old man living in the back once said in his gentle way, "You should smile at Emily more when you look at her." What *was* in my face when I looked at her? I loved her. There were all the acts of love.

18.   It was only with the others I remembered what he said, so that it was the face of joy, and not of care or tightness or worry I turned to them—too late for Emily. She does not smile easily, let alone almost always, as her brothers and sisters do. Her face is closed and somber, but when she wants, how fluid.

You must have seen it in her pantomimes, you spoke of her rare gift for comedy on the stage that rouses a laughter out of the audience so dear they applaud and applaud and do not want to let her go.

19.   Where does it come from, that comedy? There was none of it in her when she came back to me that second time, after I had had to send her away again. She had a new daddy now to learn to love, and I think perhaps it was a better time. Except when we left her alone nights, telling ourselves she was old enough.

20.   "Can't you go some other time, Mommy, like tomorrow?" she would ask. "Will it be just a little while you'll be gone?"

21.   The time we came back, the front door open, the clock on the floor in the hall. She rigid awake. "It wasn't just a little while. I didn't cry. I called you a little, just three times, and then I went downstairs to open the door so you could come faster. The clock talked loud, I threw it away, it scared me what it talked."

22.   She said the clock talked loud that night I went to the hospital to have Susan. She was delirious with the fever that comes before red measles, but she was fully conscious all the week I was gone and the week after we were home when she could not come near the baby or me.

23.   She did not get well. She stayed skeleton thin, not wanting to eat, and night after night she had nightmares. She would call for me, and I would sleepily call back, "You're all right, darling, go to sleep, it's just a dream," and if she still called, in a sterner voice, "Now go to sleep, Emily, there's nothing to hurt you." Twice, only twice, when I had to get up for Susan anyhow, I went in to sit with her.

24.   Now when it is too late (as if she would let me hold and comfort her like I do the others) I get up and go to her at her moan or restless stirring. "Are you awake? Can I get you something?" And the answer is always the same: "No, I'm all right, go back to sleep, Mother."

25.   They persuaded me at the clinic to send her away to a convalescent home in the country where "she can have the kind of food and care you can't manage for her, and you'll be free to concentrate on the new baby." They still send children to that place. I see pictures on the society page of sleek young women planning affairs to raise money for it, or dancing at the affairs, or decorating Easter eggs or filling Christmas stockings for the children.

26.   They never have a picture of the children, so I do not know if they still wear those gigantic red bows and the ravaged looks on the every other Sunday when parents can come to visit "unless otherwise notified"—as we were notified the first six weeks.

27.   Oh, it is a handsome place, green lawns and tall trees and fluted flower beds. High up on the balconies of each cottage the children stand, the girls in their red bows and white dresses, the boys in white suits and giant red ties. The parents stand below shrieking up to be heard and the children shriek down to be heard, and between them the invisible wall "Not To Be Contaminated by Parental Germs or Physical Affection."

28.   There was a tiny girl who always stood hand in hand with Emily. Her parents never came. One visit she was gone. "They moved her to Rose Cottage," Emily shouted in explanation. "They don't like you to love anybody here."

29.   She wrote once a week, the labored writing of a seven-year-old. "I am fine. How is the baby. If I write my letter nicely I will have a star. Love." There never was a star. We wrote every other day, letters she could never hold or keep but only hear read—once. "We simply do not have room for children to keep any personal possessions," they patiently explained when we pieced one Sunday's shrieking together to plead how much it would mean to Emily to keep her letters and cards.

30.   Each visit she looked frailer. "She isn't eating," they told us. (They had runny eggs for breakfast or mush with lumps, Emily said later. I'd hold it in my mouth and not swallow. Nothing ever tasted good, just when they had chicken.)

31.   It took us eight months to get her released home, and only the fact that she gained back so little of her seven lost pounds convinced the social worker.

32.   I used to try to hold and love her after she came back, but her body would stay stiff, and after a while she'd push away. She ate little. Food sickened her, and I think much of life too. Oh, she had physical lightness and brightness, twinkling by on skates, bouncing like a ball up and down up and down over the jump rope, skimming over the hill; but these were momentary.

33.   She fretted about her appearance, thin and dark and foreign-looking at a time when every little girl was supposed to look or thought she should look a chubby blond replica of Shirley Temple. The doorbell sometimes rang for her, but no one seemed to come and play in the house or be a best friend. Maybe because we moved so much.

34.   There was a boy she loved painfully through two school semesters. Months later she told me how she taken pennies from my purse to buy him candy. "Licorice was his favorite and I brought him some every day, but he still liked Jennifer better'n me. Why Mommy why?" The kind of question for which there is no answer.

35.   School was a worry to her. She was not glib or quick, in a world where glibness and quickness were easily confused with ability to learn. To her overworked and exasperated teachers she was an overconscientious "slow learner" who kept trying to catch up and was absent entirely too often.

36.   I let her be absent, though sometimes the illness was imaginary. How different from my now-strictness about attendance with the others. I wasn't working. We had a new baby, I was home anyhow. Sometimes, after Susan grew old enough, I would keep her home from school, too, to have them all together.

37.   Mostly Emily had asthma, and her breathing, harsh and labored, would fill the house with a curiously tranquil sound. I would bring the two old dresser mirrors and her boxes of collections to her bed. She would select beads and single earrings, bottle tops and shells, dried flowers and pebbles, old postcards and scraps, all sorts of oddments; then she and Susan would play Kingdom, setting up landscapes and furniture, peopling them with action.

38.   Those were the only times of peaceful companionship between her and Susan. I have edged away from it, that poisonous feeling between them, that terrible balancing of hurts and needs I had to do between the two, and did so badly, those earlier years.

39.   Oh, there are conflicts between the others too, each one human, needing, demanding, hurting, taking—but only between Emily and Susan, no, Emily toward Susan, that corroding resentment. It seems so obvious on the surface, yet it is not obvious. Susan, the second child. Susan, golden and curly-haired and chubby, quick and articulate and assured, everything in appearance and manner Emily was not; Susan, not able to resist Emily's precious things, losing or sometimes clumsily breaking them; Susan telling jokes and riddles to company for applause while Emily sat silent (to say to me later: That was *my* riddle, Mother, I told it to Susan); Susan, who for all the five years' difference in age was just a year behind Emily in developing physically.

40.   I am glad for that slow physical development that widened the difference between her and her contemporaries, though she suffered over it. She was too vulnerable for that terrible world of youthful competition, of preening and parading, of constant measuring of yourself against every other, of envy, "If I had that copper hair," or "If I had that skin . . ." She tormented herself enough about not looking like the others, there was enough of the unsureness, the having to be conscious of words before you speak, the constant caring—what are they thinking of me? what kind of impression am I making—there was enough without having it all magnified unendurably by the merciless physical drives.

41.   Ronnie is calling. He is wet and I change him. It is rare there is such a cry now. That time of motherhood is almost behind me when the ear is not one's own but must always be racked and listening for the child cry, the child call. We sit for a while and I hold him, looking out over the city spread in charcoal with its soft aisles of light. "Shoogily," he breathes and curls closer. I carry him back to bed, asleep. Shoogily. A funny word, a family word, inherited from Emily, invented by her to say: comfort.

42.   In this and other ways she leaves her seal, I say aloud. And startle at my saying it. What do I mean? What did I start to gather together, to try and make coherent? I was at the terrible, growing years. War years. I do not remember them well. I was working, there were four smaller ones now, there was not time for her. She had to help be a mother, and housekeeper, and shopper. She had to set her seal. Mornings of crisis and near-hysteria trying to get lunches packed, hair combed, coats and shoes found, everyone to school or Child Care on time, the baby ready for transportation. And always the paper scribbled on by a smaller one, the book looked at by Susan, then mislaid, the homework not done. Running out to that huge school where she was one, she was lost, she was a drop; suffering over her unpreparedness, stammering and unsure in her classes.

43.   There was so little time left at night after the kids were bedded down. She would struggle over books, always eating (it was in those years she developed her enormous appetite that is legendary in our family) and I would be ironing,

or preparing food for the next day, or writing V-mail to Bill, or tending the baby. Sometimes, to make me laugh, or out of her despair, she would imitate happenings or types at school.

44.   I think I said once, "Why don't you do something like this in the school amateur show?" One morning she phoned me at work, hardly understandable through the weeping: "Mother, I did it. I won, I won; they gave me first prize; they clapped and clapped and wouldn't let me go."

45.   Now suddenly she was Somebody, and as imprisoned in her difference as she had been in her anonymity.

46.   She began to be asked to perform at other high schools, even in colleges, then at city and state-wide affairs. The first one we went to, I only recognized her that first moment when, thin, shy, she almost drowned herself into the curtains. Then: Was this Emily? the control, the command, the convulsing and deadly clowning, the spell: then the roaring, stamping audience, unwilling to let this rare and precious laughter out of their lives.

47.   Afterwards: You ought to do something about her with a gift like that— but without money or knowing how, what does one do? We have left it all to her, and the gift has as often eddied inside, clogged and clotted, as been used and growing.

48.   She is coming. She runs up the stairs two at a time with her light graceful step, and I know she is happy tonight. Whatever it was that occasioned your call did not happen today.

49.   "Aren't you ever going to finish the ironing, Mother? Whistler painted his mother in a rocker. I'd have to paint mine standing over an ironing board." This is one of her communicative nights and she tells me everything and nothing as she fixes herself a plate of food out of the icebox.

50.   She is so lovely. Why did you want me to come in at all? Why were you concerned? She will find her way.

51.   She starts up the stairs to bed. "Don't get me up with the rest in the morning." "But I thought you were having midterms." "Oh those," she comes back in and says quite lightly, "in a couple of years when we'll all be atom-dead they won't matter a bit."

52.   She has said it before. She believes it. But because I have been dredging the past, and all that compounds a human being is so heavy and meaningful in me, I cannot endure it tonight.

53.   I will never total it all. I will never come in to say: She was a child seldom smiled at. Her father left me before she was a year old. I had to work away from her her first six years when there was work, or I sent her home to his relatives. There were years she had care she hated. She was dark and thin and foreign-looking in a world where the prestige went to blondness and curly hair and dimples, she was slow where glibness was prized. She was a child of anxious, not proud, love. We were poor and could not afford for her the soil of easy growth. I was a young mother, I was a distracted mother. There were the other children pushing up, demanding. Her younger sister seemed all that she

was not. There were years she did not want me to touch her. She kept too much in herself, her life was such she had to keep too much in herself. My wisdom came too late. She has much to her and probably little will come of it. She is a child of her age, of depression, of war, of fear.

54.   Let her be. So all that is in her will not bloom—but in how many does it? There is still enough left to live by. Only help her to know—help make it so there is cause for her to know that she is more than this dress on the ironing board, helpless before the iron.

Time in "I Stand Here Ironing"*

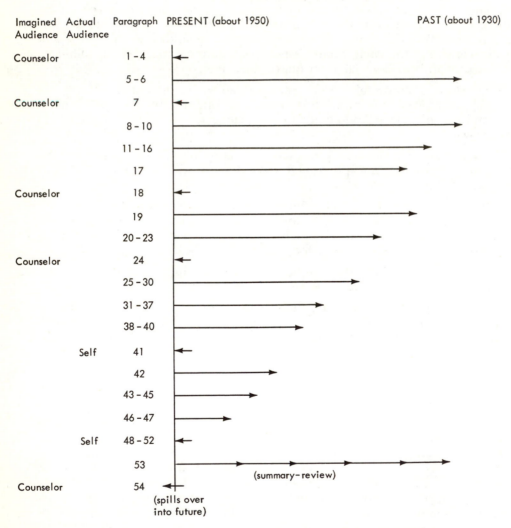

*This scheme for representing time was suggested by Jonathan Raban, *The Technique of Fiction: Essays in Practical Criticism* (Notre Dame, Ind.: University of Notre Dame Press, 1969). p. 66.

The provocation for the monologue "I Stand Here Ironing" is a telephone call from the school counselor to the fortyish narrator, requesting that she come to school to talk about her daughter Emily, a nineteen-year-old student.

During her speaking, no change in *character* occurs; her values, morals, and so on remain the same. No change in *fortune* occurs; her level of prosperity remains low, although she remembers times when she was even poorer. The change that accounts for the form of the plot is one of *thought;* she understands now the complex of forces that influenced her daughter. Some of them she finds explainable, some not. Most important, she realizes that some of the mistakes were her own, but others were a natural outgrowth of her own subjugation.

The mother's story is all *scene,* since the entire monologue is spoken by one person on one occasion; story time equals the actual time it takes for her to speak. However, within that framework, time is richly textured, as the mother remembers events from yesterday all the way back to thirty years past, and even some of the dialogue spoken on those occasions.

The chart on p. 264 indicates how time is treated during the story and shows graphically the narrator's concern with the immediate and long-ago past; the frequent interruptions in the present are imaginary comments made to the counselor or herself. The chart should be helpful to the performer in indicating shifts of time of the events described and of the person spoken to.

The performer might well decide to make the scene literal and use an iron and ironing board. If so, great care should be taken to make the ironing, dress turning, and resting, expressive extensions of what is going on in the story at that time—for example, by addressing the counselor while resting from the ironing for a moment.

The Man with the Flower in His Mouth
LUIGI PIRANDELLO
Translated by Eric Bentley

CHARACTERS
THE MAN WITH THE FLOWER IN HIS MOUTH
A PEACEFUL CUSTOMER

Towards the end, at the points indicated, a WOMAN *is seen at the corner, clad in black, and wearing an old hat with drooping feathers.*

Scene: At the back, we see the trees of an avenue and electric lights showing through the leaves. On both sides, the last houses of a street which leads into this avenue. Among the houses on the left, a cheap all-night cafe, with chairs and little tables on the sidewalk. In front of the houses on the right, a streetlamp, lit. On the left, where the street meets the avenue, there is another lamp affixed to the corner house; it too is lit. At intervals, the vibrant notes of a mandolin are heard in the distance.

When the curtain rises, THE MAN WITH THE FLOWER IN HIS MOUTH *is sitting at a table and looking in silence at the* PEACEFUL CUSTOMER *who is at the next table, sucking a mint frappé through a straw.*

MAN: Well, what I was just going to say . . . Here you are, a law-abiding sort of man . . . You missed your train?

CUSTOMER: By one minute. I get to the station and see the damn thing just pulling out.

MAN: You could have run after it.

CUSTOMER: Sure—but for those damn packages. I looked like an old pack-horse covered with luggage. Isn't that silly? But you know how women are. Errands, errands, errands! You're never through. God! You know how long it took me to get my fingers on the strings of all those packages—when I climbed out of the cab? Three solid minutes. Two packages to each finger.

MAN: What a sight! Know what *I'd* have done? Left 'em in the cab.

CUSTOMER: How about my wife? And my daughters? And all the other women?

MAN: They'd squawk. I'd enjoy that.

CUSTOMER: You don't seem to know how women carry on when they get out in the country.

MAN: I know exactly how they carry on. *(Pause.)* They tell you they won't need a thing, they can live on nothing.

CUSTOMER: Worse, they pretend they live there to *save* money. They go out to one of those villages*—the uglier and filthier the better—and then insist on wearing all their fanciest get-ups! Women! But I suppose it's their vocation. "If you're going to town, could you get me one of these—and one of those—and would it trouble you *too* much to get me . . ." Would it trouble you *too* much! "And since you'll be right next door to . . ." "Now really, darling, how do you expect me to get all that done in three hours?" "Why not? Can't you take a cab?" And the hell of it is—figuring on those three hours—I didn't bring the keys to our house here in town.

MAN: Quite a thing. So?

CUSTOMER: I left my pile of packages at the station—in the parcel room. Then I went to a restaurant for supper. Then I went to the theatre—to get rid of my bad temper. The heat nearly killed me. Coming out, I say: "And now, what? It's after midnight. There isn't a train till four. All that fuss for a couple of hours of sleep? Not worth the price of the ticket." So here I am. Open all night, isn't it?

MAN: All night. *(Pause.)* So you left your packages in the parcel room?

CUSTOMER: Why do you ask? Don't you think they're safe? They were tied up good and . . .

MAN: Oh, sure, sure! *(Pause).* I feel *sure* they're safe. I know how well these salesmen wrap their stuff. They make quite a specialty of it. *(Pause.)* I can see their hands now. What hands! They take a good big piece of paper, double thickness, sort of a reddish color, wavy lines on it—a pleasure just to look at it!—so smooth, you could press it against your cheek and feel how cool and delicate it is . . . They roll it out on the counter and then place your cloth in the middle of it with *such* agility—fine cloth too, neatly folded. They raise one edge of the paper with the back of the hand, lower

---

*The scene is rather obviously laid in Rome. The villages where "commuters" live are some ten miles out.

the other one, and bring the two edges together in an elegant fold—*that's* just thrown in for good measure . . . Then they fold the corners down in a triangle with its apex turned in like this. Then they reach out with one hand for the box of string, instinctively pull off just exactly enough, and tie up the parcel so quickly you haven't even time to admire their . . . virtuosity—the little loop is ready for your finger!

CUSTOMER: Anyone can see you've given a lot of attention to this matter.

MAN: Have I! My dear man, I spend whole days at it. What's more, I can spend a solid hour at a single store window. I lose myself in it. I seem to *be* that piece of silk, I'd *like* to be that piece of silk, that bit of braid, that ribbon—red or blue—that the salesgirls are measuring with their tape, and—you've seen what they do with it before they wrap it up?—they twist it round the thumb and little finger of their left hand in a figure eight! *(Pause.)* I look at the shoppers as they come out of the store with their bundle on their finger—or in their hand—or under their arm. I watch them pass. My eyes follow them till they're out of sight. I imagine, oh, I imagine so many, many things, you've no idea, how could you have? *(Pause. Then, darkly, as to himself.)* All the same, it helps.

CUSTOMER: What helps?

MAN: Latching on—to life. With the imagination. Like a creeper around the bars of a gate. *(Pause.)* Giving it no rest—my imagination, I mean—clinging, clinging with my imagination to the lives of others—all the time. Not people I know, of course. I couldn't do that. That'd be annoying, it'd nauseate me if *they* knew. No. Just strangers. With them my imagination can work freely. Not capriciously, though. Oh no, I take account of the smallest things I can find out about them. You've no idea how my imagination functions. I work my way *in*. In! I get to see this man's house—or that man's, I live in it, I feel I belong there. And I begin to notice—you know how a house, any old house, has its own air, how there's something special about the air in it? Your house? Mine? Of course, in your own house, you don't notice it any more, it's *your* air, the air of *your* life, isn't it? Uh huh. I see you agree—

CUSTOMER: I only meant . . . well, I was thinking what a good time you must have imagining all this!

MAN *(annoyed, after thinking a moment):*   Good time? I had a—!

CUSTOMER: Good time, yes. I can just see you—

MAN: Tell me something. Did you ever consult an eminent physician?

CUSTOMER: Me? Why should I? I'm not sick!

MAN: Just a moment. I ask because I'd like to know if you ever saw a fine doctor's waiting room—full of patients waiting their turn?

CUSTOMER: Well, yes. I once had to take my little girl. She's nervous.

MAN: Okay. You needn't tell me. It's the waiting rooms . . . *(Pause.)* Have you ever given them much attention? The old-fashioned couch with dark covers, the upholstered table chairs that don't match as a rule . . . the armchairs? Stuff bought at sales and auctions, coming together there by accident, for the convenience of the patients. It doesn't belong to the house. The doctor has quite another sort of room for himself, for his wife, his wife's friends . . . lavish . . . lovely . . . If you took one of the chairs from the drawing room and put it in the waiting room, why, it'd stick out like a sore thumb. Not that the waiting room isn't just right—nothing special of course but quite proper, quite respectable . . . I'd like to know if you—when you went with your little girl—if you took a good look at the chair you sat in?

CUSTOMER: Well, um, no, I guess I didn't.

MAN: Of course not. You weren't sick . . . *(Pause.)* But often even the sick don't notice. They're all taken up with their sickness. *(Pause.)* How many times they sit, some of them, staring at their finger which is making meaningless markings on the polished arm of the chair. They're thinking—so they don't see. *(Pause.)* And what an impression you get when you get out of the doctor's office and cross the waiting room and see the chair you'd been sitting in awaiting sentence on the as yet unknown sickness just a short time before! Now, there's another patient on it and *he's* hugging his secret sickness too. Or it's empty—oh, how *impassive* it looks!—waiting for Mr. X to come and sit on it. *(Pause.)* What were we saying? Oh, yes. The pleasure of imagining things. And I suddenly thought of a chair in one of those waiting rooms. Why?

CUSTOMER: Yes, it certainly . . .

MAN: You don't see the connection? Neither do I. *(Pause.)* You recall an image, you recall another image, they're unrelated, and yet—they're *not* unrelated—for you. Oh, no, they have their reasons, they stem from *your* experience. Of course you have to pretend they don't. When you talk, you have to forget them. Most often they're so illogical, these . . . analogies. *(Pause.)* The connection could be this, maybe. Listen. Do you think those chairs get any pleasure from imagining which patient will sit on them next? What sickness lurks inside him? Where he'll go, what he'll do after this visit? Of course they don't. And it's the same with me! I get no pleasure from it. There are those poor chairs and here am I. *They* open their arms to the doctor's patients, *I* open mine to . . . this person or that. You for instance. And yet I get no pleasure—no pleasure at all—from the train you missed, the family waiting for that train in the country, your other little troubles . . .

CUSTOMER: I've plenty, you know that?

MAN: You should thank God they're little. *(Pause.)* Some people have big troubles, my dear sir. *(Pause.)* As I was saying, I feel the need to latch on—by the skin of my . . . imagination—to the lives of others. Yet I get no pleasure from this. It doesn't even interest me. Quite the reverse, quite . . . . One wants to see what their troubles are just to prove to oneself that life is idiotic and stupid! So that one won't mind being through with it! *(With dark rage.)* Proving that to yourself takes quite a bit of doing, huh? You need evidence, you need a hundred and one instances, and—you—must—be—*implacable!* Because, well, because, my dear sir, there's something—we don't know what it's made of, but it exists—and we all feel it, we feel it like a pain in the throat—it's the hunger for life! A hunger that is never appeased—that never *can* be appeased—because life—life as we live it from moment to moment—is so hungry itself, hungry *for* itself, we never get to taste it even! The taste of life, the flavor and savor of life, is all in the past, we carry it inside us. Or rather it's always at a distance from us. We're tied to it only by a slender thread, the rope of memory. Yes, memory ties us to . . . what? that idiocy, these irritations, those silly illusions, mad pursuits like . . . yes . . . What today is idiocy, what today is an irritation, even what today is a misfortune, a grave misfortune, look! Four years pass, five years, ten, and who knows what savor or flavor it will have, what tears will be shed over it, how—it—will—*taste!* Life, life! You only have to think of giving it up—especially if it's a matter of days—*(At this point the head of* THE WOMAN IN BLACK *is seen at the corner.)* Look! See that? At the corner! See that woman, that shadow of a woman? She's hiding now.

CUSTOMER: What? Who was it?

MAN: You didn't see? She's hiding now.

CUSTOMER: A woman?

MAN: My wife.

CUSTOMER: Ah! Your wife? *(Pause.)*

MAN: She keeps an eye on me. Oh, sometimes I could just go over and kick her! It wouldn't do any good, though. She's as stubborn as a lost dog: the more you kick it, the closer it sticks to you. *(Pause.)* What that woman is suffering on my account you could not imagine. She doesn't eat. Doesn't sleep any more. Just follows me around. Night and day. At a distance. She *might* brush her clothes once in a while—and that old shoe of a hat. She isn't a woman any more. Just—a rag doll. Her hair's going gray, yes, the white dust has settled on her temples forever, and she's only thirty-four. *(Pause.)* She annoys me. You wouldn't believe how much she annoys me. Sometimes I grab hold of her and shake her. "You're an idiot!" I shout. She takes it. She stands there looking at me. Oh, that look! It makes my fingers itch. I feel like strangling her! Nothing happens, of course. She just waits till I'm a short way off. Then she starts following me again. *(*THE WOMAN IN BLACK *again sticks her head out.)* Look! There's her head again!

CUSTOMER: Poor woman!

MAN: Poor woman? You know what she wants? She wants me to stay and take it easy at home—all cozy and quiet—and let her be nice to me, look after me, show me wifely tenderness . . . Home! The rooms in perfect order, the furniture elegant and neat, silence reigns . . . It used to, anyway. Silence—measured by the tick-tocking of the dining room clock! *(Pause.)* That's what she wants! I just want you to see the absurdity of it! Isn't it absurd? It's worse: it's cruel, it's macabre! Don't you see? Think of Messina. Or Avezzano. Suppose they knew an earthquake was coming. Do you think those cities could just sit? You think they could just sit calmly in the moonlight waiting for it? Carefully preserving the lovely lines of their streets and the spaciousness of their piazzas? Not daring to deviate one inch from the plans of the City Planning Commission? You're crazy. Those cities would drop everything and take to their heels! Every house, every stone, would take to its heels! *(Wheeling on the* CUSTOMER.*)* You agree?

CUSTOMER *(frightened)*:   Well . . .

MAN: Well, just suppose the people knew? The citizens of Avezzano and Messina. Would they calmly get undressed and go to bed? Fold their clothes and put their shoes outside the door? Creep down under the bedclothes and enjoy the nice clean feeling of freshly laundered sheets? Knowing that—in a few hours—they would be dead?—You think they might?

CUSTOMER: Maybe your wife—

MAN: Let me finish. *(Starting over.)* If death, my dear sir, if death were some strange, filthy insect that just . . . settled on you, as it were, took you unawares, shall we say . . . You're walking along. All of a sudden a passerby stops you, and, with finger and thumb cautiously extended, says: "Excuse me, sir, excuse me, honored sir, but death has settled on you!" And with finger and thumb cautiously extended, he takes it and throws it in the gutter. Wouldn't that be wonderful? But death is not an insect. It has settled on many walkers in the city—however far away their thoughts may be, however carefree they may feel. They don't see it. They're thinking what they'll be doing tomorrow. But I *(He gets up.)* . . . Look, my dear sir, come here *(He gets the* CUSTOMER *up and takes him under the lighted lamp.)* under the lamp. Come over here. I'll show you something. Look! Under this side of my mustache. See that little knob? Royal purple? Know what they call it? It has such a poetic name. It suggests something soft and sweet. Like a caramel. Epithelioma. *(The "o" is stressed.)* Try it, isn't it soft and sweet? Epithelioma. Understand? Death passed my way. He stuck this . . . flower in my mouth and said: "Keep it, old chap. I'll stop by again in eight months—or maybe ten." *(Pause.)* Now tell me. *You* tell *me.* Can I just sit quietly at home as that unhappy girl wishes me to—with this flower in my mouth? *(Pause.)* I yell at her. "So you want me to kiss you, do you?" "Yes, yes, kiss me!" You know what she did? A couple of weeks ago she took a pin and cut herself—here—on the lip—then she took hold of my head and tried to kiss me, tried to kiss me on the mouth. She said she wanted to die with me. *(Pause.)* She's insane. *(Angrily.)* I'm not home! Ever! What I want is to stand at store windows admiring the virtuosity of salesmen! Because, you see, if ever, for one second, I am not occupied, if ever I'm *empty*—know what I mean?—why, I might take a life and think nothing of it, I might destroy the life in someone . . . someone I don't even know, I'd take a gun and kill someone—like you maybe—someone who's missed his train. *(He laughs.)* Of course, I'm only joking. *(Pause.)* I'll go now. *(Pause.)* It'd be myself I'd kill. *(Pause.)* At this time of year, there's a certain kind of apricot, it's good . . . How do *you* eat them? Skin and all? You cut them in exact halves, you take hold with finger and thumb, lengthwise, like this . . . then! *(He swallows.)* How succulent! Pure delight! Like a woman's lips! *(He laughs. Pause.)* I wish to send my best wishes to your good lady and her daughters in your country home. *(Pause.)* I imagine them . . . I imagine them dressed in white and light blue in the middle of a lovely green meadow under the shade of . . . *(Pause.)* Will you do me a favor when you arrive, tomorrow morning? As I figure it, your village is a certain distance from the station. It is dawn. You will be on foot. The first tuft of grass you see by the roadside—count the number of blades, will you? Just count the blades of grass. The number will be the number of days I have to live. *(Pause.)* One last request: pick a big tuft! *(He laughs.)* Then: Good night!

He walks away humming through closed lips the tune which the mandolin is playing in the distance. He is approaching the corner on the right. But at a certain point—remembering his Wife—he turns and sneaks off in the opposite direction. The CUSTOMER *follows with his eyes—more or less dumbfounded.*

CURTAIN

Both the overall form and three stylistic choices in this short tragi-comedy seem to warrant attention. First, the play is not plotted like a traditional play, nor are there great changes in the characters. The Peaceful Customer's attitudes change from irritation, to curiosity, to fright, and finally, the script says, to dumbfoundedness. The Man undergoes an emotional intensification and ultimately regains his equilibrium, but during the course of the play his character, his fortune, and his thought do not change. The change in fortune from life to death, likely to occur soon, finally emerges as the background against which his increasingly frenetic behavior is understandable.

Burke's system for identifying form may suggest that *The Man with the Flower in His Mouth* progresses qualitatively from the Man's alogical opening comments and questions to a bizarre encounter first and then several somewhat ominous exchanges. The Man's behavior is so strange when he describes the wrapping of packages that almost anything else could happen as well.

Such a hypothesis may be justifiable, but an additional aspect of form should be considered—*repetition*. Three repeated items are noted here:

1. *Pauses.* during this twenty-minute play, the script contains 24 occasions when the Man is directed to pause, and one for the Customer.
2. *Questions.* Even more surprising for a drama of this length are the 62 different questions asked—20 by the Customer and 42 by the Man. For about 90 percent of the questions, no answer is sought or waited for.
3. *Metaphorical language:* The Customer speaks of himself metaphorically twice and the Man of himself more than 30 times.

The repeated pauses lend something of an oppressive, uncertain atmosphere to the entire encounter, while the frequent barrage of questions contributes to the frenetic quality of the Man's agitation.

Even more interesting are the repeated metaphors. The Man engages in hyperbole when describing the intricacies of wrapping parcels. He describes his wife as not a woman anymore, but "just—a rag doll," lifeless and no help to him. He speaks of "latching on to life," personifies the chairs, talks of "hugging an illness," his "hunger for life," the "flavor of life." "Silence reigns" while his disease sounds like "caramel." He remarks that death, not a "filthy insect," "stuck a flower in his mouth." Of all the comparisons he makes, it is ironic that the only fresh one appears when he likens his cancerous growth to a flower in his mouth. Are his imaginative digressions those of a sane man? The incremental frenzy ends on a playful note, while his wife takes on the real suffering that he feels but cannot, or will not, express directly. So the real significance of the metaphorical language seems to lie in its correspondence to, and expression of, his inability to confront the reality of his situation. The comparisons are only partial truths; so, too, is his life.

The challenge to the performer in demonstrating these stylistic features is to take the time required to make the transitions and establish the motives step by step. If the numerous shifts of intent are made clear, the performed text is both humorous and poignant.

Otto

THEODORE ROETHKE

I

He was the youngest son of a strange brood,
A Prussian who learned early to be rude
To fools and frauds: He does not put on airs
Who lived above a potting shed for years.
I think of him, and I think of his men,
As close to him as any kith or kin.
Max Laurisch had the greenest thumb of all.
A florist does not woo the beautiful:
He potted plants as if he hated them.
What root of his ever denied its stem?
When flowers grew, their bloom extended him.

II

His hand could fit into a woman's glove,
And in a wood he knew whatever moved;
Once when he saw two poachers on his land,
He threw his rifle over with one hand;
Dry bark flew in their faces from his shot,—
He always knew what he was aiming at.
They stood there with their guns; he walked toward,
Without his rifle, and slapped each one hard;
It was no random act, for those two men
Had slaughtered game, and cut young fir trees down.
I was no more than seven at the time.

III

A house for flowers! House upon house they built,
Whether for love or out of obscure guilt
For ancestors who loved a warlike show,
Or Frenchmen killed a hundred years ago,
And yet still violent men, whose stacked-up guns
Killed every cat that neared their pheasant runs;
When Hattie Wright's angora died as well,
My father took it to her, by the tail.
Who loves the small can be both saint and boor,
(And some grow out of shape, their seed impure;)
The Indians loved him, and the Polish poor.

IV

In my mind's eye I see those fields of glass,
As I looked out at them from the high house,
Riding beneath the moon, hid from the moon,
Then slowly breaking whiter in the dawn;

When George the watchman's lantern dropped from sight
The long pipes knocked: it was the end of night.
I'd stand upon my bed, a sleepless child
Watching the waking of my father's world.—
O world so far away! O my lost world!

Let us begin our discussion of "Otto" by scanning the first stanza. With regular verse, scanning is a significant step, for it enables you to find the abstract base for the poem's rhythmic effects, as well as making other discoveries about *how* the power or interest of the poem is created. Keep in mind that the following scansion does not represent linguistic accuracy or actual patterns. The point of scansion is to learn, through reading with more emphasis on patterns than on the sense of the words, a basic beat, which may be strong in some lines, more subtle in others, and perhaps contradicted in some. We suggest that you follow this scansion with your own for the next three stanzas; do not be surprised if yours and ours do not agree at every point. Such difference does not mean that anyone is "wrong." We all hear stresses differently.

Line	Accents	Syllables
1. He was the youngest son of a strange brood	5	10
2. A Prussian who learned early to be rude	5	10
3. To fools and frauds: He does not put on airs	5	10
4. Who lived above a potting shed for years.	5	10
5. I think of him, and I think of his men,	4	10
6. As close to him as any kith or kin.	5	10
7. Max Laurisch had the greenest thumb of all	6	10
8. A florist does not woo the beautiful:	5	10
9. He potted plants as if he hated them.	5	10
10. What root of his ever denied its stem?	5	10
11. When flowers grew, their bloom extended him.	5	10

In a fast silent reading, the length of the lines appears irregular; however, in a sounding, they are exactly the same in number of syllables and, with only two exceptions, alike in number of accented syllables. Lines 2, 4, 9, and 11 contain the base against which the rhythm of the entire poem works—perfect iambic pentameter. This tension—between the established and expected norm and the deviations and surprises—parallels the poem's mixture of music and narrative.

Rhymes (brood/rude), near rhymes airs/years), and interrelated rhymes (boor/

impure/poor) are used throughout the poem, as are alliteration (watching . . . waking . . . world) and assonance (sight . . . pipes . . . night . . . I'd.) Such repetition emphasizes the relatedness of the language by "sealing" the units together.

Also of interest to the performer is change as an organizing principle of the poem. Let us now look at how complementary are the changes in the poem's *subject* or person, from father to son or self; in *time* from past to present; and in *proximity* from possession to loss.

With this kind of visual arrangement, we can see just how great is the emotional weight of the last line as it, in effect, is balanced against the remainder of the poem. While the content confirms this assertion, the rhythm contributes a formal feature so definite that the extreme emotion is checked by a return to the earlier established iambic norm.

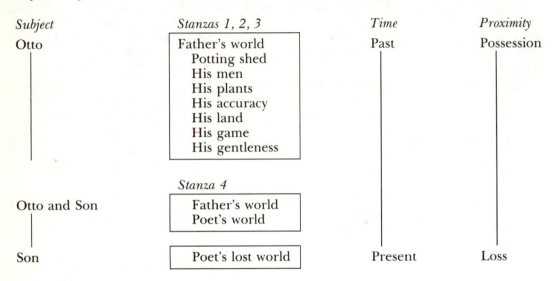

Subject	Stanzas 1, 2, 3	Time	Proximity
Otto	Father's world Potting shed His men His plants His accuracy His land His game His gentleness	Past	Possession
	Stanza 4		
Otto and Son	Father's world Poet's world		
Son	Poet's lost world	Present	Loss

ANTHOLOGY IV

Each of the following selections invites careful exploration of style and structure. Your performances can demonstrate an awareness of stylistic and structural features unique to the specific literary texts.

Am I My Neighbor's Keeper?
RICHARD EBERHART

The poetry of tragedy is never dead.
If it were not so I would not dream
On principles so deep they have no ending,
Nor on the ambiguity of what things ever seem.

The truth is his and shaped in veils of error,
Rich, unanswerable, the profound caught in plain air.
Centuries after tragedy sought out Socrates
Its inexplicable essence visits us in our lair,

Say here, on a remote New Hampshire farm.
The taciturn farmer disappeared in pre-dawn.
He had beaten his handyman, but no great harm.
Light spoke vengeance and bloodstains on the lawn.
His trussed corpse later under the dam
Gives to this day no answer, says I am.

What *rhythmic norm* is established in the first line? In what different ways does *rhyme* function in the three stanzas? Extremely helpful commentary on this poem appears in *The Contemporary Poet as Artist and Critic,* ed. Anthony Ostroff (Boston: Little, Brown, 1964). Three poets—Louise Bogan, Philip Booth, and William Stafford—discuss the poem; then Eberhart comments on the critics' remarks and on the poem. The book contains similar symposia on poems by other poets in this book: Richard Wilbur, Theodore Roethke, Robert Lowell, John Crowe Ransom, W. H. Auden, and Karl Shapiro.

The Man Under the Bed
ERICA JONG

The man under the bed
The man who has been there for years waiting
The man who waits for my floating bare foot
The man who is silent as dustballs riding the darkness
The man whose breath is the breathing of small white butterflies
The man whose breathing I hear when I pick up the phone
The man in the mirror whose breath blackens silver
The boneman in closets who rattles the mothballs
The man at the end of the end of the line

I met him tonight   I always meet him
He stands in the amber air of a bar
When the shrimp curl like beckoning fingers
& ride through the air on their toothpick skewers
When the ice cracks & I am about to fall through
he arranges his face around its hollows
he opens his pupilless eyes at me

For years he has waited to drag me down
& now he tells me
he has only waited to take me home
We waltz through the street like death & the maiden
We float through the wall of the wall of my room

If he's my dream he will fold back into my body
His breath writes letters of mist on the glass of my cheeks
I wrap myself around him like the darkness
I breathe into his mouth
& make him real

In performance, it is possible for you to emphasize the poet's use of *anaphora* as a structuring device. How else can you describe the rhythmic techniques in this *free verse?* Jong discusses her reliance on repetition to create a "dreamlike and incantatory feeling" as well as how and why she wrote the poem in "On 'The Man Under the Bed,'" in *New Voices in American Poetry*, ed. David Allan Evans (Cambridge, Mass.: Winthrop, 1973), pp. 135–137. The book also contains poetry and short essays by Maxine Kumin and Leon Stokesbury.

To Laura Phelan: 1880–1906
LEON STOKESBURY

Drunk I have been. And drunk I was that night
I lugged your stone across the other graves,
to set you up a hundred yards away.
Flowers I found, then. Drunk I have been.
And am, standing here with no moon to spill
on the letters of your name; my loud fingers
feeling them out. The stone is mossed over.
And why must I bring myself in the dark
to stand here among the sour grasses
that stain my white jeans? Drunk I have been.
See, the thick dew slides on the trees, wet weeds,
wetness smears the air; and a vague surf
of wildflowers pushes my feet, slipping
close to my legs. When the thought comes at last
that people fall apart, that the things we do
will not do. Ends. Then, we come to scenes
like this. This scene of you. You apart:
this is not you; and yet, this is where I stand
and close my eyes, and feel the ragged wind
blow red and maul my hair. In the night somewhere,
dandelions foam. This is not you. Drunk
I have been. Across this graveyard, that
is where you are. Yet I stand here. Would ask
things of your name. Would wish. Would not be told
of the stink in the skull, the eye's collapse.
Would be told something new, something unknown.—
A mosquito bites my hand. The only sound
is the rough wind. Drunk I have been,
here, at the loam's maw, before this stone
of yours, which is not you. Which is.

Try to account for the five places in the poem where Stokesbury uses the inverted sentence "Drunk I have been." Why do differences in *tone* as well as in *rhythm* occur when you substitute the ordinary order "I have been drunk"? What *discovery* does the speaker make about Laura Phelan? About himself?

The Writer
RICHARD WILBUR

In her room at the prow of the house
Where light breaks, and the windows are tossed with linden,
My daughter is writing a story.

I pause in the stairwell, hearing
From her shut door a commotion of typewriter-keys
Like a chain hauled over a gunwale.

Young as she is, the stuff
Of her life is a great cargo, and some of it heavy:
I wish her a lucky passage.

But now it is she who pauses,
As if to reject my thought and its easy figure.
A stillness greatens, in which

The whole house seems to be thinking,
And then she is at it again with a bunched clamor
Of strokes, and again is silent.

I remember the dazed starling
Which was trapped in that very room, two years ago;
How we stole in, lifted a sash

And retreated, not to affright it;
And how for a helpless hour, through the crack of the door,
We watched the sleek, wild, dark

And iridescent creature
Batter against the brilliance, drop like a glove
To the hard floor, or the desk-top,

And wait then, humped and bloody,
For the wits to try it again; and how our spirits
Rose when, suddenly sure,

It lifted off from a chair-back,
Beating a smooth course for the right window
And clearing the sill of the world.

It is always a matter, my darling,
Of life or death, as I had forgotten. I wish
What I wished you before, but harder.

This poem abounds in *metaphor*. The speaker compares a room in the house to what? The sound of typewriter keys to what? The life of the daughter to what? Identify others.

Name one instance of *personification*, the assigning of lifelike qualities to inanimate objects or qualities.

One metaphor, the comparison of the girl to a starling, is longer, more fully developed and might be called a *symbol*. If so, what does the bird symbolize?

Poetic devices such as metaphor, personification, and symbols compress language while at the same time expanding it, as words and images ricochet off one another. Generally, the greater the reverberating potential of the language, the slower the performance of that language needs to be.

Freshmen
BARRY SPACKS

My freshmen
settle in. Achilles
sulks; Pascal consults
his watch; and true
Cordelia—with her just-washed hair,

stern-hearted princess, ready to defend
the meticulous garden of truths in her highschool notebook—
uncaps her ballpoint pen.
And the corridors drum:
give us a flourish, fluorescence of light, for the teachers come,

green and seasoned, hearers
of the Word, who differ
like its letters; there are some
so wise their eyes
are birdbites; one,

a mad, grinning gent with a golden tooth, God knows
he might be Pan, or the sub-
custodian; another
is a walking podium, dense
with his mystery—high

priests and attaches
of the ministry; kindly
old women, like unfashionable watering places,
and the assuming young, rolled tight as a City
umbrella;

thought-salesmen with samples cases,
and saints upon whom
merely to gaze is like Sunday—
their rapt, bright,
cat-licked faces!

And the freshmen wait;
wait bristling, acned, glowing like a brand,
or easy, chatting, munching, muscles lax,
each in his chosen corner, and in each
a chosen corner.

Full of certainties and reasons,
or uncertainties and reasons,
full of reasons as a conch contains the sea,
they wait for the term's first bell,
for another mismatched wrestle through the year;

for a teacher who's religious in his art,
a wizard of a sort, to call the roll
and from mere names
cause people
to appear.

The best look like the swinging door
to the Opera just before
the Marx Brothers break through.
The worst—debased
on the back row

as far as one can go
from speech—
are walls where childish scribbling's been erased,
are stones
to teach.

Am I paid to ask them questions.
Dare man proceed by need alone?
Did Esau like
his pottage?
Is any heart in order after Belsen?

And when one stops to think, I'll catch his heel,
put scissors to him, excavate his chest!
Watch, freshmen, for my words about the past
can make you turn your back. I wait to throw,
most foul, most foul, the future in your face.

While thinking about a freshman class, the speaker also tells us a great deal about himself or herself. Discuss the speaker according to social, dispositional, and motivational levels. To understand the deliberative level fully, you will need to familiarize yourself with the following *allusions:* Achilles, Pascal, Cordelia, Pan, the Marx Brothers, Esau, Belsen, and "most foul, most foul."

School Lesson Based on Word of Tragic Death of Entire Gillum Family
ROBERT PENN WARREN

They weren't so bright, or clean, or clever,
　　And their noses were sometimes imperfectly blown,
But they always got to school the weather whatever,
　　With old lard pail full of fried pie, smoked ham, and corn pone.

Tow hair was thick as a corn-shuck mat.
　　They had milky blue eyes in matching pairs,
And barefoot or brogan, when they sat,
　　Their toes were the kind that hook round the legs of chairs.

They had adenoids to make you choke,
　　And buttermilk breath, and their flannels asteam,
And sat right mannerly while teacher spoke,
　　But when book-time came their eyes were glazed and adream.

There was Dollie-May, Susie-May, Forrest, Sam, Brother—
　　Thirteen down to eight the stairsteps ran.
They had popped right natural from their fat mother.
　　The clabber kind that can catch just by honing after a man.

In town, Gillum stopped you, he'd say: "Say, mister,
　　I'll name you what's true fer folks, ever-one.
Human-man ain't much more'n a big blood blister.
　　All red and proud-swole, but one good squeeze and he's gone.

"Take me, ain't wuth lead and powder to perish,
　　Just some spindle bone stuck in a pair of pants,
But a man's got his chaps to love and to cherish,
　　And raise up and larn 'em so they kin git their chance."

So mud to the hub, or dust to the hock,
　　God his helper, wet or dry,
Old Gillum swore by God and by cock,
　　He'd git'em larned before his own time came to die.

That morning blew up cold and wet,
   All the red-clay road was curdled as curd,
And no Gillums there for the first time yet.
   The morning drones on. Stove spits. Recess. Then the word.

Dollie-May was combing Susie-May's head.
   Sam was feeding, Forrest milking, got nigh through.
Little Brother just sat on the edge of his bed.
   Somebody must have said: "Pappy, now what you aimin' to do?"

An ice pick is a subtle thing.
   The puncture's small, blood only a wisp.
It hurts no more than a bad bee sting.
   When the sheriff got there the school-bread was long burned to a crisp.

In the afternoon silence the chalk would scrape.
   We sat and watched the windowpanes steam,
Blur the old corn field and accustomed landscape.
   Voices came now faint in our intellectual dream.

Which shoe—yes, which—was Brother putting on?
   That was something, it seemed, you just had to know.
But nobody knew, all afternoon,
   Though we studied and studied, as hard as we could, to know.

Studying the arithmetic of losses,
   To be prepared when the next one,
By fire, flood, foe, cancer, thrombosis,
   Or Time's slow malediction, came to be undone.

We studied all afternoon, till getting on to sun.
There would be another lesson, but we were too young to take up that one.

In your performance, try to demonstrate the difference in the speaker's remembering, imagining, and reflecting on the significance of the "school lesson." How would you summarize that lesson? Outline it?

John L. Stewart, a reviewer of Warren's poetry, sees this poem as a description of an event that "bursts not only upon some school children but upon the reader as well. . . ." The children in the school as well as the reader "are left with two lessons to ponder: the qualities of the event (they struggle to take in the fact that, yes, it really did happen) and *another lesson, but we were too young to take up that one*—the lesson of the sudden madness that is in things" (*The Burden of Time: The Fugitives and Agrarians*; Princeton, N.J.: Princeton University Press, 1965, pp. 519–520).

Roger
STUDS TERKEL

He is fourteen. He was brought to Chicago from West Virginia eight years ago. His mother is dead. His father, whom he sees once in a while, is somewhere in the Applachian community. Though he stays with his sister-in-law, his life is on the streets of the city. He's pretty much on his own.

If I say the word—"Depression"—what does that mean?

I wouldn't know, 'cause I never heard the word before.

What do you think it means?

I figure maybe you're all tensed up or somethin'. That's the only thing I could think of "depression" meanin'.

Ever hear of the time when millions of people weren't working, in the 1930s—long before you were born . . . ?

I heard about it. They didn't have no food and money. Couldn't keep their children fed and in clothes. People say, like a long time ago it was, coal miners worked real hard for a couple of dollars, and you couldn't hardly get a job. Especially in my home town and places like that.

Well, we still had it hard when we come up here. I was six. My father and my mother, they told me about how hard it was to get a job up here. That's why I tried to get him to go back to West Virginia, after I was up here a while. See, I never knowd hard times when we was down there. So I said to Dad, "Let's go back to West Virginia." He says, "There's no jobs for us down there, we can't make a living. We have to stay here." He said: "Some days, sometimes maybe if it get easy to get jobs down there, maybe we go down there."

It's so damn hard. Seems like everybody's takin' advantage of you. See, I never heard that word "depression" before. They would all just say "hard times" to me. It is still. People around this neighborhood still has hard times. Like you see, the buildin's are all tore up and not a decent place to live. My house isn't fit to live in. These buildin's ain't no good. If we tear 'em down, they ain't gonna build new ones for us. So we have to live in 'em.

We could move out in the suburbs for a hundred, maybe fifty, dollars a week, if we could pay that much rent. They should have just as clean buildin's for $25 a week. For what we're payin' now, we should have clean homes and such. Not this. It's hard livin'. Hard times.

Cesar Chavez
STUDS TERKEL

Like so many who have worked from early childhood, particularly in the open country, he appears older than his forty-one years. His manner is diffident, his voice soft.

He is president of the United Farm Workers of American (UFWA). It is, unlike craft and industrial unions, a quite new labor fraternity. In contrast to these others, agricul-

tural workers—those who "follow the crops"—had been excluded from many of the benefits that came along with the New Deal.

Oh, I remember having to move out of our house. My father had brought in a team of horses and wagon. We had always lived in that house, and we couldn't understand why we were moving out. When we got to the other house, it was a worse house, a poor house. That must have been around 1934. I was about six years old.

It's known as the North Gila Valley, about fifty miles north of Yuma. My dad was being turned out of his small plot of land. He had inherited this from his father, who had homesteaded it. I saw my two, three other uncles also moving out. And for the same reason. The bank had foreclosed on the loan.

If the local bank approved, the Government would guarantee the loan and small farmers like my father would continue in business. It so happened the president of the bank was the guy who most wanted our land. We were surrounded by him: he owned all the land around us. Of course, he wouldn't pass the loan.

One morning a giant tractor came in, like we had never seen before. My daddy used to do all his work with horses. So this huge tractor came in and began to knock down this corral, this small corral where my father kept his horses. We didn't understand why. In the matter of a week, the whole face of the land was changed. Ditches were dug, and it was different. I didn't like it as much.

We all of us climbed into an old Chevy that my dad had. And then we were in California, and migratory workers. There were five kids—a small family by those standards. It must have been around '36. I was about eight. Well, it was a strange life. We had been poor, but we knew every night there was a bed *there,* and that *this* was our room. There was a kitchen. It was sort of a settled life, and we had chickens and hogs, eggs and all those things. But that all of a sudden changed. When you're small, you can't figure these things out. You know something's not right and you don't like it, but you don't question it and you don't let that get you down. You sort of just continue to move.

But this had quite an impact on my father. He had been used to owning the land and all of a sudden there was no more land. What I heard . . . what I made out of conversations between my mother and my father—things like, we'll work this season and then we'll get enough money and we'll go and buy a piece of land in Arizona. Things like that. Became like a habit. He never gave up hope that some day he would come back and get a little piece of land.

I can understand very, very well this feeling. These conversations were sort of melancholy. I guess my brothers and my sisters could also see this very sad look on my father's face.

That piece of land he wanted . . . ?

No, never. It never happened. He stopped talking about that some years ago. The drive for land, it's a very powerful drive.

When we moved to California, we would work after school. Sometimes we wouldn't go. "Following the crops," we missed much school. Trying to get enough money to stay alive the following winter, the whole family picking apricots, walnuts, prunes. We were pretty new, we had never been migratory workers. We were taken advantage of quite a bit by the labor contractor and the crew pusher.* In some pretty silly ways. (Laughs.)

Sometimes we can't help but laugh about it. We trusted everybody that came around. You're traveling in California with all your belongings in your car: it's obvious. Those days we didn't have a trailer. This is bait for the labor contractor. Anywhere we stopped, there was a labor contractor offering all kinds of jobs and good wages, and we were always deceived by them and we always went. Trust them.

Coming into San Jose, not finding—being lied to, that there was work. We had no money at all, and had to live on the outskirts of town under a bridge and dry creek. That wasn't really unbearable. What was unbearable was so many families living in just a quarter of a mile. And you know how kids are. They'd bring in those things that really hurt us quite a bit. Most of those kids were middle-class families.

We got hooked on a real scheme once. We were going by Fresno on our way to Delano. We stopped at some service station and this labor contractor saw the car. He offered a lot of money. We went. We worked the first week: the grapes were pretty bad and we couldn't make much. We all stayed off from school in order to make some money. Saturday we were to be paid and we didn't get paid. He came and said the winery hadn't paid him. We'd have money next week. He gave us $10. My dad took the $10 and went to the store and bought $10 worth of groceries. So we worked another week and in the middle of the second week, my father was asking him for his last week's pay, and he had the same excuse. This went on and we'd get $5 or $10 or $7 a week for about four weeks. For the whole family.

So one morning my father made the resolution no more work. If he doesn't pay us, we won't work. We got in the car and went over to see him. The house was empty. He had left. The winery said they had paid him and they showed us where they had paid him. This man had taken it.

Labor strikes were everywhere. We were one of the strikingest familes, I guess. My dad didn't like the conditions, and he began to agitate. Some families would follow and we'd go elsewhere. Sometimes we'd come back. We couldn't find a job elsewhere, so we'd come back. Sort of beg for a job. Employers would know and they would make it very humiliating. . . .

Did these strikes ever win?

Never.

We were among these families who always honored somebody else's grievance. Somebody would have a personal grievance with the employer. He'd say I'm not gonna work for this man. Even though we were working, we'd honor it. We felt we had to. So we'd walk out, too. Because we were prepared to honor those things, we caused many of the things ourselves. If we were picking at a piece rate and we knew they were cheating on the weight, we wouldn't stand for it. So we'd lose the job, and we'd go elsewhere. There were other families like that.

Sometimes when you had to come back, the contractor knew this. . . ?

---

*"That's a man who specializes in contracting human beings to do cheap labor."

They knew it, and they rubbed it in quite well. Sort of shameful to come back. We were trapped. We'd have to do it for a few days to get enough money to get enough gas.

One of the experiences I had. We went through Indio, California. Along the highway there were signs in most of the small restaurants that said "White Trade Only." My dad read English, but he didn't really know the meaning. He went in to get some coffee—a pot that he had, to get some coffee for my mother. He asked us not to come in, but we followed him anyway. And this young waitress said, "We don't serve Mexicans here. Get out of here." I was there, and I saw it and heard it. She paid no more attention. I'm sure for the rest of her life she never thought of it again. But every time we thought of it, it hurt us. So we got back in the car and we had a difficult time trying—in fact, we never got the coffee. These are sort of unimportant, but they're . . . you remember 'em very well.

One time there was a little diner across the tracks in Brawley. We used to shine shoes after school. Saturday was a good day. We used to shine shoes for three cents, two cents. Hamburgers were then, as I remember, seven cents. There was this little diner all the way across town. The moment we stepped across the tracks, the police stopped us. They would let us go there, to what we called "the American town," the Anglo town, with a shoe shine box. We went to this little place and we walked in.

There was this young waitress again. With either her boyfriend or someone close, because they were involved in conversation. And there was this familiar sign again, but we paid no attention to it. She looked up at us and she sort of— it wasn't what she said, it was just a gesture. A sort of gesture of total rejection. Her hand, you know, and the way she turned her face away from us. She said: "Whattaya want?" So we told her we'd like to buy two hamburgers. She sort of laughed, a sarcastic sort of laugh. And she said, "Oh, we don't sell to Mexicans. Why don't you go across to Mexican town, you can buy 'em over there." And then she turned around and continued her conversation.

She never knew how much she was hurting us. But it stayed with us.

We'd go to school two days sometimes, a week, two weeks, three weeks at most. This is when we were migrating. We'd come back to our winter base, and if we were lucky, we'd get in a good solid all of January, February, March, April, May. So we had five months out of a possible nine months. We started counting how many schools we'd been to and we counted thirty-seven. Elementary schools. From first to eighth grade. Thirty-seven. We never got a transfer. Friday we didn't tell the teacher or anything. We'd just go home. And they accepted this.

I remember one teacher—I wondered why she was asking so many questions. (In those days anybody asked questions, you became suspicious. Either a cop or a social worker.) She was a young teacher, and she just wanted to know why we were behind. One day she drove into the camp. That was quite an event, because we never had a teacher come over. Never. So it was, you know, a very meaningful day for us.

This I remember. Some people put this out of their minds and forget it. I don't. I don't want to forget it. I don't want it to take the best of me, but I want it to be there because this is what happened. This is the truth, you know. History.

"Roger" and "Cesar Chavez" are from transcripts of interviews that Terkel conducted about remembrances of the Depression of the 1930s. If you perform either of these selections, you will probably need to spend time gathering a fuller impression of that extremely difficult period in American history. Talk to people who were living then, peruse newspapers of the period, and look at photographs such as those in James Agee and Walker Evans's *Let Us Now Praise Famous Men*, (Boston: Houghton Mifflin, 1941).

Do Not Go Gentle into That Good Night
DYLAN THOMAS

Do not go gentle into that good night,
Old age should burn and rave at close of day;
Rage, rage against the dying of the light.

Though wise men at their end know dark is right,
Because their words had forked no lightning they
Do not go gentle into that good night.

Good men, the last wave by, crying how bright
Their frail deeds might have danced in a green bay,
Rage, rage against the dying of the light.

Wild men who caught and sang the sun in flight,
And learn, too late, they grieved it on its way,
Do not go gentle into that good night.

Grave men, near death, who see with blinding sight
Blind eyes could blaze like meteors and be gay,
Rage, rage against the dying of the light.

And you, my father, there on the sad height,
Curse, bless, me now with your fierce tears, I pray.
Do not go gentle into that good night.
Rage, rage against the dying of the light.

Departures
AMBROSE GORDON, JR.

They go fast once they start to go,
Old friends, old forms, old faces, old finesse.
You were certain there'd be time to say goodbye.

A likely story, which you ought to know
Could never much improve nor much impress—
They go fast once they start to go.

"See you next Christmas!" as you step into the sky
(Tears are something that you really must repress).
You were certain there'd be time to say goodbye

Later, much later, while down far below
Is soon beyond your handshake or caress.
They go fast once they start to go.

The clouds roll up and back, the stewardesses try
(Sweet angels) to anoint you and to bless.
You were certain there'd be time to say goodbye.

It wasn't that your love was weak or slow:
Departure is an infinite regress.
They go fast once they start to go.
You were certain there'd be time to say goodbye.

The two preceding poems are *villa-nelles*, a fixed form of poetry developed in France. If you compare the two, you can inductively arrive at a description of the form. Notice similarities in stanza length and repetition of lines and differences in rhyme scheme.

Compare the "you" of the two poems. Is one more specifically defined as to relationship with speaker? As to scene in which he or she appears?

Let Not Your Hart Be Truble
JAMES SEAY

For George Garrett

The horn of your silver bus
Sounds in the rocks and trees,
Black Saul of Tarsus turned Paul,
And you come telling
Under what tree and with what light
You were struck blind
And now see.

On faith and a curve, both blind,
You double-clutch and pass my car,
Hoping against the evidence
Of things not seen.
Or, should it appear from around
    this curve,
You trust the roadside rocks and trees
Will open like the sea.
That failing, you take the rock and wood
For what it gives.

Your pass is good, and made, I guess,
With the same thick hand that lettered
The words on your rear exit door:
LET NOT YOUR HART BE TRUBLE
You exact too much, black Paul,
My lane, my life on your faith,
My troubled hart.
And yet I do not deny you unlettered
The gift of metaphor, or even parable;
The Master himself spoke thus,
Lest the heart of the many be softened.

You talk like you clutch, old black soul,
For you know the troubled hart
Takes the hunt
Into a deeper wood.

One of the organizing principles of Seay's poem lies in the speaker's developing attitudes toward the bus, the driver, and the lettering. Try to define the cluster of attitudes as precisely as possible in your performance.

The practice of writer's reading their own literature in public has so expanded that today most college students have an opportunity to hear several writers interpret their own works. When reading, the writers sometimes give their listeners interesting and helpful information about the work. For example, James Seay says of "Let Not Your Hart Be Truble":

The situation is that the speaker of the poem is driving along, and this bus passes him. He sees this legend very crudely lettered on the back of the bus, and it sets his mind to thinking on this thing, this statement of faith—the man trying to tell him to not have a troubled heart. I thought of the conversation of Saul of Tarsus on the road to Damascus, struck blind and converted to Christianity, and how he became Paul, St. Paul. And there's one other little play in here. Paul defined faith as the evidence of things not seen, the substance of things hoped for. And that's a lot of what the poem's about—faith and statements of faith. (*The Writer's Voice: Conversations with Contemporary Writers*, conducted by John Graham and edited by George Garrett; New York: William Morrow, 1973, p. 170.)

Not Exactly Lena Horne
WILLIAM MELVIN KELLEY

"By God, Stanton, there just went Oregon!" Wilfred called back into the house, then scanned the new sheet, and finding the Oregon box, made a check mark. "Oregon! Imagine that. Fifteen minutes I been out here and seven Connecticuts, three New Jerseys, and one Oregon. What that fellow doing way over here?"

Stanton lumbered onto the porch. He was the younger (by two years) of the two old Negroes, both retired twenty years. He was also the fatter, taller, sturdier, and darker. Wilfred, tallying out-of-state license plates, was short, fragile, the color of clean sand. They had worked on the railroad together, and when time came to retire, being widowers, together they bought a frame house on a highway on Long Island.

"What, Wilfred?"

"Got me an Oregon. Wonder what he's doing out this way?"

"God damn! That what you called me out here for?"

"Thought you might want to know." Wilfred was not even sheepish. Stanton had been complaining this way for years. "Oregon's a good piece away."

All this time and I *still* can't see why you do this. What you making them lists for? You don't do nothing but transfer them into them notebooks. Don't even show them to nobody. You ain't even getting paid for it."

"How many times I got to tell you I likes to do it. And there's the stories. Now old Oregon, he's just killed him eight cops breaking out of the Oregon State Prison. He's going to Montauk to meet a plane what'll fly him to Rio, where he's got a señorita waiting for him. Could be, Stanton."

"Could be, but it ain't." Stanton retreated into the house, slamming the screen door.

A car was approaching, sucking in the white line like spaghetti. Wilfred squinted; he knew he would have no more than five seconds to make out the plate. It was a New York and did not count.

Stanton came back onto the porch and sat in the other chair. "Nothing, huh?"

Wilfred shook his head.

"You even got me doing it now!" Stanton twisted in the chair. "Twenty years of peeping at license plates! God damn!"

"You ought-a start collecting things."

"Why?"

"You can make up stories." He reconsidered his suggestion. "Maybe you better just collect things. You ain't really got no imagination."

"I ain't? How you sound, man, when all you can think to do is sit on a porch making checks on a piece of paper?"

"Well, it better than grumping around about your rheumatism."

"All right, I got rheumatism. I ain't ashamed of it. I didn't ask for it, but it my burden."

"And my burden is *you*."

"Well, you ain't exactly Lena Horne yourself!"

A car had been rolling toward them at a good pace, and zipped by before Wilfred noticed it. He strained to his feet, scurried, round-shouldered, to the edge of the porch and leaned after it. "New York." He turned back to Stanton. "Lucky for you it New York. If it been Alaska and I missed it on account of your noise there might-a been trouble here."

This interested Stanton. "That so? What kind of trouble? Even in my extreme pain I could beat tar out-a you."

"That so? I remembers times on the railroad when you got whipped by little children with balloons on strings. Whip me? Ha!"

"Ain't no *ha* to it."

"That so?" He heard tires from the other direction. "By God, Delaware!" He checked it off. "First Delaware in seven weeks. A musician in a jazz band on his way to visit his mother, who's senile and staying in a rest home. He's only playing in New York for a week. He ain't seen her for three years."

"Senile. *You* is the only senile person you know. One of these days I'm taking them lists and books out back and burn the whole lot of them. Kerosene! Gasoline!"

"That so? Burn them, you say? Well, you'll sure rot in hell then and you'll be traveling a whole lot sooner than you figure, God damn." A New York went through. "Kind-a slow today except for the Delaware and Oregon." He reflected. "Remember that day, summer 1948, Utah, Arizona, Idaho, and Kansas come by? Man, what a day that was. A regular day to remember!"

"Your mind's breaking down. That was 1947 and wasn't no Idaho in them. That was Illinois. You got potato on the brain. Mash potato!" Stanton started to chuckle. "Idaho!"

"Illinois? That ain't nothing. Lots of rich folks from Chicago come out to New York. And you making a big deal out Illinois. That were Idaho, as sure as I'm sitting here."

"Your old dry husk of a body is sitting there, but your mind lying in the grave because that weren't no Idaho." He paused. "God damn, here I is arguing with an old coot about license plates. God damn!" He got up and went inside again. Shortly, he returned with a glass of iced tea. The two men awoke each morning at eight and made two quarts.

Wilfred looked up from his list. "Why didn't you bring me some?"

"Bring you some? If you wasn't wasting your time, you could get some yourself. And that's another thing: I ain't no waiter. I stopped waiting on fools when I retired from the railroad."

"You won't stop waiting on fools until you dies and don't have to feed your-*self* no more." He did not miss this one—New Jersey—and checked it off.

"Talking about dying, when you does, first thing I'll do is burn them books and lists."

"That'd be mighty stupid—just natural to you. You never once thought the Highway Commission might want them to see how many cars traveled this road."

"The Highway Commission wouldn't want them books even if they could make out your scrawl, which they can't, because I can't, even after forty years of knowing you."

"Well, my penmanship is bad from lack of education. Yours is bad because your old hands shake so."

"Well, I can't help it. Rheumatism's my burden.

"And you is my burden."

"You ain't exactly Lena Horne yourself."

There was a long silence. Wilfred continued to scan the fronts and backs of the passing cars and record the acceptable ones.

Stanton sipped his iced tea with shaking hands. Last night had not been a peaceful one for him. Alone in one of the house's two bedrooms, pain had attacked his joints. In the morning, he had awakened more cross than usual.

"Massachusetts! You see that? Massachusetts. First one in a week. A secret service agent, the President's second cousin on his mama's side, going to check reports of a Russian submarine at Bay Shore." He spoke scanning his list.

"Will you shut up?"

Wilfred was startled. Never before had he heard the note of real anger that now cloaked his friend's words. "Just telling you what—"

"I don't care. I don't want to hear." Just then, his hands burned, and he grimaced.

Wilfred took it for a smile. "Well, then not the President's second cousin. His—"

"Shut up." Stanton slammed his glass to the porch floor. It popped. The ice slid down the slight grade and water reflected the sunlight.

"What you doing? Everything in this house is half mine. Half that glass is mine."

Stanton lunged to his feet. "Then half of them God-damned books is mine. And I'm burning my half." He started to the door.

At first, Wilfred thought Stanton must be joking. But as he stomped by, shaking the porch, Wilfred saw his face, serious and angry. Stanton jerked open the screen door and barged through.

Wilfred was right behind him, puffing by the time he reached his bedroom. The books, more than a hundred black and white speckled school notebooks, were piled neatly on a table beside the window. When Wilfred reached the room, Stanton was already menacing the table, was scooping up an armful of notebooks. He turned around. Wilfred blocked his way. "Put them down, man. Stop playing." He could not believe this was happening.

"I ain't playing, you loon. I'm burning my half."

"Half of them ain't yours. You never once put a check mark to paper. Them's all mine."

They stood face to face now, Wilfred looking up into Stanton's dark gaze. He felt small.

"I don't want to hurt you, Wilfred. Get out my way."

"Come on, Stanton, put them books back." He was whining now. He reached out for Stanton's arm, caught it. His fingers ached when Stanton pulled the arm away.

"I told you to get out my way. I'm burning these God-damned books. I'm sick of listening to you croak about them."

"Put them books down before I—" Wilfred started, but Stanton's big hand caught him in the chest and he fell like a baby, hard, in a sitting position. His spine stung, but he knew he was not really hurt. He looked up now and found Stanton glaring down at him. Scrambling to all fours, he reached out and grabbed Stanton's knees. "Come on, man. Please. Don't burn my books."

"I'm sick of hearing about them."

Wilfred gripped the other man's knees tighter. They were more fleshy than his own. "All right, I won't never talk about them again. I won't mention them. I'll keep my list in quiet."

"That a promise?"

"A promise, man. I promise."

"Take your God-damned books then." He released them and they dropped with a crack. Wilfred let go Stanton's knees, and the other man stepped over him and trudged to the porch.

On hands and knees, Wilfred collected his notebooks, making certain they were in correct order, the latest on the top. He crawled back into the room, and using the bedpost, pulled himself to his feet and set the notebooks on the table. He lingered in the room for fifteen minutes, then took a deep breath and returned to the porch.

Stanton was reading a newspaper. "Listen, Wilfred, I'm sorry I pushed you down." He leaned forward over his stomach. "I didn't mean to do that. You should-a got out my way, man. Ain't hurt, is you?"

"No."

"I meant what I said. I don't want to hear about them license plates ever again. I'll burn them books sure if I do. Remember now."

"I'll remember!" Wilfred remembered too, with fear and shame, the hardness of the floor beneath his knees when he had begged for his notebooks.

"But that don't mean we can't talk about everything else under the sun. You understand that, don't you, Wilfred?"

"Yes."

"Shake on it, so I'll know we still friends." Stanton extended his hand and smiled timidly. Wilfred realized the other man was honestly sorry for having knocked him down, and that he wanted to remain friends. He shook Stanton's hand.

An old Connecticut chugged by and Wilfred, sneaking a glance at Stanton, checked it off in silence. He thought to himself that it was a millionaire, who drove the old car to escape reporters.

When the car was out of sight, Stanton turned to him.

"The champ is signing to defend the title in July."

"Champ of what?" Wilfred looked up from his list.

"Heavyweight boxing champ."

"Oh? What's his name?"

"God damn, man, everybody knows that."

"I never did follow boxing." He spoke humbly.

"Didn't huh?"

"Never did."

Stanton shook his head.

A convertible, driven by a young girl in curlers, passed before them. It was a New York. Wilfred turned to Stanton. "If the President gets them bills through, Stanton, it'll mean more taxes."

"Bills? What did he buy?" Stanton leaned forward eagerly.

"He didn't buy nothing. A bill's when—" He stopped. Stanton's face was blank as mud.

In the next hour, seventeen New Yorks went by. Although he did not jot them down, Wilfred did keep aimless track of the number when they were running thick. Seventeen in a row was quite high.

The eighteenth car turned slowly into sight from a side street. It was a Model A Ford, driven by a man wearing a Stetson hat and a fancy cowboy shirt. High on the radiator, bolted by small reflectors of red glass, Wilfred saw the New Mexico plate, and checked it off. A movie star, he thought without the old thrill, a western hero come out this way to visit the grave of his great-grandfather, whose daughter, newly married, went West in a covered wagon.

Stanton, who had stolen a glance at the car from over his newspapers, was just about to say they had never seen New Mexico, when Wilfred crumbled his list, tossed it off the edge of the porch, and hobbled into the darkness of the house.

This story, along with eleven others, is reprinted in *New Sounds in American Fiction,* ed. Gordon Lish (Menlo Park, Calif.: Cummings, 1969). The collection of stories is coordinated with a series of recordings that contain a "dramatic reading" of each story and an interview with the author. The book also contains a "Soundings" section for each story—a group of questions for discussion about the recording.

Note: From this point on, there are no endnotes or questions following the anthology selections. We hope you will enjoy approaching the remainder of the literature without our intrusion.

Ballad of Orange and Grape
MURIEL RUKEYSER

After you finish your work
after you do your day
after you've read your reading
after you've written your say —
you go down the street to the hot dog stand,
one block down and across the way.
On a blistering afternoon in East Harlem in the twentieth century.

Most of the windows are boarded up,
the rats run out of a sack —
sticking out of the crummy garage
one shiny long Cadillac;
at the glass door of the drug-addiction center,
a man who'd like to break your back.
But here's a brown woman with a little girl dressed in rose and pink, too.

Frankfurters frankfurters sizzle on the steel
where the hot-dog-man leans —
nothing else on the counter
but the usual two machines,
the grape one, empty, and the orange one, empty,
I face him in between.
A black boy comes along, looks at the hot dogs, goes on walking.

I watch the man as he stands and pours
in the familiar shape
bright purple in the one marked ORANGE
orange in the one marked GRAPE,
the grape drink in the machine marked ORANGE
and orange drink in the GRAPE.
Just the one word large and clear, unmistakable, on each machine.

I ask him: How can we go on reading
and make sense out of what we read? —
How can they write and believe what they're writing,
the young ones across the street,
while you go on pouring grape into ORANGE
and orange into the one marked GRAPE —?
(How are we going to believe what we read and we write and we hear and we
        say and we do?)

He looks at the two machines and he smiles
and he shrugs and smiles and pours again.
It could be violence and nonviolence
it could be white and black   women and men
it could be war and peace or any
binary system, love and hate, enemy, friend.
Yes and no, be and not-be, what we do and what we don't do.

On a corner in East Harlem
garbage, reading, a deep smile, rape,
forgetfulness, a hot street of murder,
misery, withered hope,
a man keeps pouring grape into ORANGE
and orange into the one marked GRAPE,
pouring orange into GRAPE and grape into ORANGE forever.

South End
CONRAD AIKEN

The benches are broken, the grassplots brown and bare,
the laurels dejected, in this neglected square.
Dogs couple undisturbed. The roots of trees
heave up the bricks in the sidewalk as they please.

Nobody collects the papers from the grass,
nor the dead matches, nor the broken glass.
The elms are old and shabby; the houses, around,
stare lazily through paintless shutters at forgotten ground.

Out of the dusty fountain, with the dust,
the leaves fly up like birds on a sudden gust.
The leaves fly up like birds, and the papers flap,
or round the legs of benches wrap and unwrap.

Here, for the benefit of some secret sense,
warm-autumn-afternoon finds permanence.
No one will hurry, or wait too long, or die:
all is serenity, under a serene sky.

Dignity shines in old brick and old dirt,
in elms and houses now hurt beyond all hurt.
A broken square, where little lives or moves;
these are the city's earliest and tenderest loves.

For Sale
ROBERT LOWELL

Poor sheepish plaything,
organized with prodigal animosity,
lived in just a year—
my Father's cottage at Beverly Farms
was on the market the month he died.
Empty, open, intimate,
its town-house furniture
had an on tiptoe air
of waiting for the mover
on the heels of the undertaker.
Ready, afraid
of living alone till eighty,
Mother mooned in a window,
as if she had stayed on a train
one stop past her destination.

The Rather Difficult Case of Mr. K★A★P★L★A★N
LEONARD Q. ROSS

In the third week of the new term, Mr. Parkhill was forced to the conclusion that Mr. Kaplan's case was rather difficult. Mr. Kaplan first came to his special attention, out of the thirty-odd adults in the beginners' grade of the American Night Preparatory School for Adults ("English—Americanization—Civics—Preparation for Naturalization"), through an exercise the class had submitted. The exercise was entitled "Fifteen Common Nouns and Their Plural Forms." Mr. Parkhill came to one paper which included the following:

house	. . . .	makes	. . . . houses
dog	. . . .	"	. . . . dogies
library	. . . .	"	. . . . Public library
cat	. . . .	"	. . . . Katz

Mr. Parkhill read this over several times, very thoughtfully. He decided that here was a student who might, unchecked, develop into a "problem case." It was clearly a case that called for special attention. He turned the page over and read the name. It was printed in large, firm letters with red crayon. Each letter was outlined in blue. Between every two letters was a star, carefully drawn, in green. The multi-colored whole spelled, unmistakably, H★Y★M★A★N K★A★P★L★A★N.

This Mr. Kaplan was in his forties, a plump, red-faced gentleman, with wavy blond hair, *two* fountain pens in his outer pocket, and a perpetual smile. It was a strange smile, Mr. Parkhill remarked: vague, bland, and consistent in its monotony. The thing that emphasized it for Mr. Parkhill was that it never seemed to leave the face of Mr. Kaplan, even during Recitation and Speech period. This disturbed Mr. Parkhill considerably, because Mr. Kaplan was particularly bad in Recitation and Speech.

Mr. Parkhill decided he had not applied himself as conscientiously as he might to Mr. Kaplan's case. That very night he called on Mr. Kaplan first.

"Won't *you* take advantage of Recitation and Speech practice, Mr. Kaplan?" he asked, with an encouraging smile.

Mr. Kaplan smiled back and answered promptly, "Vell, I'll tell abot Prazidents United States. Fife Prazidents United States is Abram Lincohen, he vas freeink de neegers; Hodding, Coolitch, Judge Vashington, an' Banjamin Frenklin."

Further encouragement revealed that in Mr. Kaplan's literary Valhalla the "most famous tree American wriders" were Jeck Laundon, Valt Viterman, and the author of "Hawk L. Barry-Feen," one Mock-tvain. Mr. Kaplan took pains to point out that he did not mention Relfvaldo Amerson because "He is a poyet, an' I'm talkink abot wriders."

Mr. Parkhill diagnosed the case as one of "inability to distinguish between 'a' and 'e.' " He concluded that Mr. Kaplan *would* need special attention. He was, frankly, a little disturbed.

Mr. Kaplan's English showed no improvement during the next hard weeks. The originality of his spelling and pronunciation, however, flourished—like a sturdy flower in the good, rich earth. A man to whom "Katz" is the plural of "cat" soon soars into higher and more ambitious endeavor. As a one-paragraph "Exercise in Composition," Mr. Kaplan submitted:

> When people is meating on the boulvard, on going away one is saying, "I am glad I mat you," and the other is giving answer, "Mutual."

Mr. Parkhill felt that perhaps Mr. Kaplan had overreached himself, and should be confined to the simpler exercises.

Mr. Kaplan was an earnest student. He worked hard, knit his brows regularly (albeit with that smile), did all his homework, and never missed a class. Only once did Mr. Parkhill feel that Mr. Kaplan might, perhaps, be a little more *serious* about his work. That was when he asked Mr. Kaplan to "give a noun."

"Door," said Mr. Kaplan, smiling.

It seemed to Mr. Parkhill that "door" had been given only a moment earlier, by Miss Mitnick.

"Y-es," said Mr. Parkhill. "Er—and another noun?"

"Another door," Mr. Kaplan replied promptly.

Mr. Parkhill put him down as a doubtful "C." Everything pointed to the fact that Mr. Kaplan might have to be kept on an extra three months before he was ready for promotion to Composition, Grammar, and Civics, with Miss Higby.

One night Mrs. Moskowitz read a sentence, from "English for Beginners," in which "the vast deserts of America" were referred to. Mr. Parkhill soon discovered that poor Mrs. Moskowitz did not know the meaning of "vast." "Who can tell us the meaning of 'vast'?" asked Mr. Parkhill lightly.

Mr. Kaplan's hand shot up, volunteering wisdom. He was all proud grins. Mr. Parkhill, in the rashness of the moment, nodded to him.

Mr. Kaplan rose, radiant with joy. " 'Vast!' It's commink fromm *diraction*. Ve have four dirations: de naut, de sot, de heast, and de vast."

Mr. Parkhill shook his head. "Er—that is 'west,' Mr. Kaplan." He wrote "vast" and "west" on the blackboard. To the class he added, tolerantly, that Mr. Kaplan was apparently thinking of "west," whereas it was "vast" which was under discussion.

This seemed to bring a great light into Mr. Kaplan's inner world. "So is 'vast' vat you eskink?"

Mr. Parkhill admitted that it was "vast" for which he was asking.

"Aha!" cried Mr. Kaplan. "You minn *'vast,'* not"—with scorn—" 'vast.' "

"Yes," said Mr. Parkhill, faintly.

"Hau Kay!" said Mr. Kaplan, essaying the vernacular. "Ven I'm buyink a suit clothes, I'm gattink de cawt, de pents, an' de vast!"

Stunned, Mr. Parkhill shook his head, very sadly. "I'm afraid that you've used still another word, Mr. Kaplan."

Oddly enough, this seemed to give Mr. Kaplan great pleasure.

Several nights later Mr. Kaplan took advantage of Open Questions period. This ten-minute period was Mr. Parkhill's special innovation in the American Night Preparatory School for Adults. It was devoted to answering any questions which the students might care to raise about any difficulties which they might have encountered during the course of their adventures with the language. Mr. Parkhill enjoyed Open Questions. He liked to clear up *practical* problems. He felt he was being ever so much more constructive that way. Miss Higby had once told him that he was a born Open Questions Teacher.

"Plizz, Mr. Pockheel," asked Mr. Kaplan as soon as the period opened. "Vat's de minnink fromm—" It sounded, in Mr. Kaplan's rendition, like "a big department."

" 'A Big department,' Mr. Kaplan?" asked Mr. Parkhill, to make sure.

"Yassir!" Mr. Kaplan's smile was beauteous to behold. "In de stritt, ven I'm valkink, I'm hearink like 'I big de pottment'."

It was definitely a pedagogical opportunity.

"Well, class," Mr. Parkhill began. "I'm sure that you have all—"

He told them that they had all probably done some shopping in the large downtown stores. (Mr. Kaplan nodded.) In these large stores, he said, if they wanted to buy a pair of shoes, for example, they went to a special *part* of the store, where only shoes were sold—a *shoe* department. (Mr. Kaplan nodded.) If they wanted a table, they went to a different part of the store, where *tables* were sold. (Mr. Kaplan nodded.) If they wanted to buy, say, a goldfish, they went to still another part of the store, where goldfish . . . (Mr. Kaplan frowned; it was clear that Mr. Kaplan had never bought a goldfish.)

"Well, then," Mr. Parkhill summed up hastily, "each article is sold in a different *place*. These different and special places are called *departments*." He printed "D-E-P-A-R-T-M-E-N-T" on the board in large, clear capitals. "And a *big* department, Mr. Kaplan, is merely such a department which is large—*big*!"

He put the chalk down and wiped his fingers.

"Is that clear now, class?" he asked, with a little smile. (It was rather an ingenious explanation, he thought; it might be worth repeating to Miss Higby during the recess.)

It *was* clear. There were thirty nods of approval. But Mr. Kaplan looked uncertain. It was obvious that Mr. Kaplan, a man who would not compromise with truth, did *not* find it clear.

"Isn't that clear *now,* Mr. Kaplan?" asked Mr. Parkhill anxiously.

Mr. Kaplan pursed his lips in thought. "It's a *fine* haxplination, Titcher," he said generously, "but I don' unnistand vy I'm hearink de voids de vay I do. Simms to me it's used in annodder minnink."

"There's really only one meaning for 'a big department.' " Mr. Parkhill was definitely worried by this time. "*If* that's the phrase you mean."

Mr. Kaplan nodded gravely. "Oh, dat's de phrase—ufcawss! It sonds like dat—or maybe a leetle more like '*I* big de pottment."

Mr. Parkhill took up the chalk. ("*I* big department" was obviously a case of Mr. Kaplan's own curious audition.) He repeated the explanation carefully, this time embellishing the illustrations with a shirt department, a victrola section, and "a separate part of the store where, for example, you buy canaries, or other birds."

Mr. Kaplan sat entranced. He followed it all politely, even the part about "canaries, or other birds." He smiled throughout with consummate reassurance.

Mr. Parkhill was relieved, assuming, in his folly, that Mr. Kaplan's smiles were a testimony to his exposition. But when he had finished, Mr. Kaplan shook his head once more, this time with a new and superior firmness.

"Is the explanation *still* not clear?" Mr. Parkhill was genuinely concerned by this time.

"Is de haxplination clear!" cried Mr. Kaplan with enthusiasm. "Ha! I should live so! Soitinly! Clear like *gold*! So clear! An' netcheral too! But Mr. Pock heel—"

"Go on, Mr. Kaplan," said Mr. Parkhill, studying the white dust on his fingers. There was, after all, nothing more to be done.

"Vell! I tink it's more like '*I big de pottment.*' "

"Go on, Mr. Kaplan, go on." *(Domine, dirige nos.)*

Mr. Kaplan rose. His smile was broad, luminious, transcendent; his manner was regal.

"I'm hearink it in de stritt. Sometimes I'm stendink in de stritt, talkink to a frand, or mine vife, mine brodder—or maybe only stendink. An' somvun is pessink arond me. An' by hexident he's givink me a bump, you know, a *poosh!* Vell, he says, 'Axcuse me!' no? But somtimes, an' *dis* is vat I minn, he's sayink, '*I big de pottment!*' "

Mr. Parkhill studied the picture of "Abram Lincohen" on the back wall, as if reluctant to face reality. He wondered whether he could reconcile it with his conscience if he were to promote Mr. Kaplan to Composition, Grammar, and Civics—at once. Another three months of Recitation and Speech might, after all, be nothing but a waste of Mr. Kaplan's valuable time.

The Private Dining Room
OGDEN NASH

Miss Rafferty wore taffeta,
Miss Cavendish wore lavender.
We ate pickerel and mackerel
And other lavish provender.
Miss Cavendish was Lalage,
Miss Rafferty was Barbara.
We gobbled pickled mackerel
And broke the candelabara,
Miss Cavendish in lavender,
In taffeta, Miss Rafferty,
The girls in taffeta lavender,
And we, of course, in mufti.

Miss Rafferty wore taffeta,
The taffeta was lavender,
Was lavend, lavender, lavenderest,
As the wine improved the provender.
Miss Cavendish wore lavender,
The lavender was taffeta.

We boggled mackled pickerel,
And bumpers did we quaffeta.
And Lalage wore lavender,
And lavender wore Barbara,
Rafferta taffeta Cavender lavender
Barbara abracadabra.

Miss Rafferty in taffeta
Grew definitely raffisher.
Miss Cavendish in lavender
Grew less and less stand-offisher.
With Lalage and Barbara
We grew a little pickereled,
We ordered Mumm and Roederer
Because the bubbles tickereled.
But lavender and taffeta
Were gone when we were soberer.
I haven't thought for thirty years
Of Lalage and Barbara.

What's Happening . . .
ALURISTA

what's happening . . .
   mr. jones
where is it?
   do you know?
pero nunca te importo
   and now; now
you tell me you care
   do you . . .
      mr. jones?
el águila de nuestro orgullo
   is now settled on the cactus of your apathy
devouring
   the serpent of inhumanities
that crawled viciously in your amerika
"amerika"
blind to the lake of human values
floating emaciated in its ethnocentricity
jose luis peralta, genaro arciaga,
macario juan infante, y richard perez
nosotros!

we care, nos importa mucho!
. . . mr. jones
we know where it's at,
   mr. jones . . .
we do
   and make happen,
   mr. jones
the happening
   es obra nuestra
we done it; mr. jones
   dig?
dig mr. jones?
   mr. jones;
do you or do you not dig!
   mr. jones wake up!
the apathy of your eyelids
—it stupefies you
      and you can't see
can you . . .
   . . . mr. jones?

A Face
MARIANNE MOORE

"I am not treacherous, callous, jealous, superstitious,
supercilious, venomous, or absolutely hideous":
   studying and studying its expression,
   exasperated desperation
      though at no real impasse,
      would gladly break the glass;

when love of order, ardour, uncircuitous simplicity,
with an expression of inquiry, are all one needs to be!
   Certain faces, a few, one or two—or one
   face photographed by recollection—
      to my mind, to my sight,
      must remain a delight.

Before Breakfast
EUGENE O'NEILL

CHARACTERS

MRS. ROWLAND

ALFRED   Her husband (not seen)

Scene: A small room serving both as kitchen and dining room in a flat on Christopher Street, New York City. In the rear, to the right, a door leading to the outer hallway. On the left of the doorway, a sink, and a two-burner gas stove. Over the stove, and extending to the left wall, a wooden closet for dishes, etc. On the left, two windows looking out on a fire escape where several potted plants are dying of neglect. Before the windows, a table covered with oilcloth. Two cane-bottomed chairs are placed by the table. Another stands against the wall to the right of the door in rear. In the right wall, rear, a doorway leading into a bedroom. Farther forward, different articles of a man's and a woman's clothing are hung on pegs. A clothes line is strung from the left corner, rear, to the right wall, forward. A man's underclothes are thrown over the line.

It is about eight-thirty in the morning of a fine, sunshiny day in the early fall.

Mrs. Rowland enters from the bedroom, yawning, her hands still busy putting the finishing touches on a slovenly toilet by sticking hairpins into her hair which is bunched up in a drab-colored mass on top of her round head. She is of medium height and inclined to a shapeless stoutness, accentuated by her formless blue dress, shabby and worn. Her face is characterless, with small regular features and eyes of a nondescript blue. There is a pinched expression about her eyes and nose and her weak, spiteful mouth. She is in her early twenties but looks much older.

She comes to the middle of the room and yawns, stretching her arms to their full length. Her drowsy eyes stare about the room with the irritated look of one to whom a long sleep has not been a long rest. She goes wearily to the clothes hanging on the right and takes an apron from a hook. She ties it about her waist, giving vent to an exasperated "damn" when the knot fails to obey her clumsy, fat fingers. Finally gets it tied and goes slowly to the gas stove and lights one burner. She fills the coffee pot at the sink and sets it over the flame. Then slumps down into a chair by the table and puts a hand over her forehead as if she were suffering from headache. Suddenly her face brightens as though she had remembered something, and she casts a quick glance at the dish closet; then looks sharply at the bedroom door and listens intently for a moment or so.

MRS. ROWLAND (*in a low voice*) Alfred! Alfred! (*There is no answer from the next room and she continues suspiciously in a louder tone*) You needn't pretend you're asleep. (*There is no reply to this from the bedroom, and, reassured, she gets up from her chair and tiptoes cautiously to the dish closet. She slowly opens one door, taking great care to make no noise, and slides out, from their hiding place behind the dishes, a bottle of Gordon gin and a glass. In doing so she disturbs the top dish, which rattles a little. At this sound she starts guiltily and looks with sulky defiance at the doorway to the next room*)

(*Her voice trembling*)   Alfred!

(After a pause, during which she listens for any sound, she takes the glass and pours out a large drink and gulps it down; then hastily returns the bottle and glass to their hiding place. She closes the closet door with the same care as she had opened it, and, heaving a great sigh of relief, sinks down into her chair again. The large dose of alcohol she has taken has an almost immediate effect. Her features become more animated, she seems to gather energy, and she looks at the bedroom door with a hard, vindictive smile on her lips. Her eyes glance quickly about the room and are fixed on a man's coat and vest which hang from a hook at right. She moves stealthily over to the open doorway and stands there, out of sight of anyone inside, listening for any movement from within)

(Calling in a half-whisper)   Alfred!

(Again there is no reply. With a swift movement she takes the coat and vest from the hook and returns with them to her chair. She sits down and takes the various articles out of each pocket but quickly puts them back again. At last, in the inside pocket of the vest, she finds a letter)

(Looking at the handwriting—slowly to herself)   Hmm! I knew it.

(She opens the letter and reads it. At first her expression is one of hatred and rage, but as she goes on to the end, it changes to one of triumphant malignity. She remains in deep thought for a moment, staring before her, the letter in her hands, a cruel smile on her lips. Then she puts the letter back in the pocket of the vest, and still careful not to awaken the sleeper, hangs the clothes up again on the same hook, and goes to the bedroom door and looks in)

(In a loud, shrill voice) Alfred! *(Still louder)* Alfred! *(There is a muffled, yawning groan from the next room)* Don't you think it's about time you got up? Do you want to stay in bed all day? *(Turning around and coming back to her chair)* Not that I've got any doubts about your being lazy enough to stay in bed forever. *(She sits down and looks out of the window, irritably)* Goodness knows what time it is. We haven't even got any way of telling the time since you pawned your watch like a fool. The last valuable thing we had, and you knew it. It's been nothing but pawn, pawn, pawn, with you—anything to put off getting a job, anything to get out of going to work like a man. *(She taps the floor with her foot nervously, biting her lips)*

(After a short pause) Alfred! Get up, do you hear me? I want to make that bed before I go out. I'm sick of having this place in a continual mess on your account. *(With a certain vindictive satisfaction)* Not that we'll be here long unless you manage to get some money some place. Heaven knows I do my part—and more—going out to sew every day while you play the gentleman and loaf around bar rooms with that good-for-nothing lot of artists from the Square.

(A short pause during which she plays nervously with a cup and saucer on the table)

And where are you going to get money, I'd like to know? The rent's due this week and you know what the landlord is. He won't let us stay a minute over our time. You say you *can't* get a job. That's a lie and you know it. You never even look for one. All you do is moon around all day writing silly poetry and stories that no one will buy—and no wonder they won't. I notice I can always get a position, such as it is; and it's only that which keeps us from starving to death.

(Gets up and goes over to the stove—looks into the coffee pot to see if the water is boiling; then comes back and sits down again)

You'll have to get money to-day some place. I can't do it all, and I won't do it all. You've got to come to your senses. You've got to beg, borrow, or steal it somewheres. *(With a contemptuous laugh)* But where, I'd like to know? You're too proud to beg, and you've borrowed the limit, and you haven't the nerve to steal.

(After a pause—getting up angrily) Aren't you up yet, for heaven's sake? It's just like you to go to sleep again, or pretend to. *(She goes to the bedroom door and looks in)* Oh, you are up. Well, it's about time. You needn't look at me like that. Your airs don't fool me a bit any more. I know you too well—better than you think I do—you and your goings-on. *(Turning away from the door—meaningly)* I know a lot of things, my dear. Never mind what I know, now. I'll tell you before I go, you needn't worry. *(She comes to the middle of the room and stands there, frowning)* *(Irritably)* Hmm! I suppose I might as well get breakfast ready—not that there's anything much to get.

(Questioningly) Unless you have some money? *(She pauses for an answer from the next room which does not come)* Foolish question! *(She gives a short, hard laugh)* I ought to know you better than that by this time. When you left here in such a huff last night I knew what would happen. You can't be trusted for a second. A nice condition you came home in! The fight we had was only an excuse for you to make a beast of yourself. What was the use pawning your watch if all you wanted with the money was to waste it in buying drink?

(Goes over to the dish closet and takes out plates, cups, etc., while she is talking)

Hurry up! It don't take long to get breakfast these days, thanks to you. All we got this morning is bread and butter and coffee; and you wouldn't even have that if it wasn't for me sewing my fingers off. *(She slams the loaf of bread on the table with a bang)*

The bread's stale. I hope you'll like it. *You* don't deserve any better, but I don't see why *I* should suffer.

(Going over to the stove) The coffee'll be ready in a minute, and you needn't expect me to wait for you.

(Suddenly with great anger) What on earth are you doing all this time? *(She goes over to the door and looks in)* Well, you're *almost* dressed at any rate. I expected to find you back in bed. That'd be just like you. How awful you look this morning. For heaven's sake, shave! You're disgusting! You look like a tramp. No wonder no one will give you a job. I don't blame them—when you don't even look half-way decent. *(She goes to the stove)* There's plenty of hot water right here. You've got no excuse. *(Gets a bowl and pours some of the water from the coffee pot into it)* Here. *(He reaches his hand into the room for it. It is a beautiful, sensitive hand with slender, tapering fingers. It trembles and some of the water spills on the floor)*

(Tauntingly) Look at your hand tremble! You'd better give up drinking. You can't stand it. It's just your kind that get the D.T.'s. *That would be* the last straw! *(Looking down at the floor)* Look at the mess you've made of this floor—cigarette

butts and ashes all over the place. Why can't you put them on a plate? No, you wouldn't be considerate enough to do that. You never think of me. You don't have to sweep the room and that's all you care about.

(Takes the broom and commences to sweep viciously, raising a cloud of dust. From the inner room comes the sound of a razor being stropped)

(Sweeping) Hurry up! It must be nearly time for me to go. If I'm late I'm liable to lose my position, and then I couldn't support you any longer. *(As an afterthought she adds sarcastically)* And then you'd have to go to work or something dreadful like that. *(Sweeping under the table)* What I want to know is whether you're going to look for a job to-day or not. You know your family won't help us any more. They've had enough of you, too. *(After a moment's silent sweeping)* I'm about sick of all this life. I've a good notion to go home, if I wasn't too proud to let them know what a failure you've been—you, the millionaire Rowland's only son, the Harvard graduate, the poet, the catch of the town—Huh! *(With bitterness)* There wouldn't be many of them now envy my catch if they knew the truth. What has our marriage been, I'd like to know? Even before your *millionaire* father died owing every one in the world money, you certainly never wasted any of your time on your wife. I suppose you thought I'd ought to be glad you were *honorable* enough to marry me—after getting me into trouble. You were ashamed of me with your fine friends because my father's only a grocer, that's what you were. At least he's honest, which is more than any one could say about yours. *(She is sweeping steadily toward the door. Leans on her broom for a moment)* You hoped every one'd think you'd been forced to marry me, and pity you, didn't you? You didn't hesitate much about telling me you loved me, and making me believe your lies, before it happened, did you? You made me think you didn't want your father to buy me off as he tried to do. I know better now. I haven't lived with you all this time for nothing. *(Somberly)* It's lucky the poor thing was born dead, after all. What a father you'd have been!

(Is silent, brooding, moodily for a moment—then she continues with a sort of savage joy)

But I'm not the only one who's got you to thank for being unhappy. There's one other, at least, and *she* can't hope to marry you now. *(She puts her head into the next room)* How about Helen? *(She starts back from the doorway, half frightened)*

Don't look at me that way! Yes, I read her letter. What about it? I got a right to. I'm your wife. And I know all there is to know, so don't lie. You needn't stare at me so. You can't bully me with your superior airs any longer. Only for me you'd be going without breakfast this very morning. *(She sets the broom back in the corner—whiningly)* You never did have any gratitude for what I've done. *(She comes to the stove and puts the coffee into the pot)* The coffee's ready. I'm not going to wait for you. *(She sits down in her chair again)*

(After a pause—puts her hand to her head—fretfully) My head aches so this morning. It's a shame I've got to go to work in a stuffy room all day in my condition. And I wouldn't if you were half a man. By rights I ought to be lying on my back instead of you. You know how sick I've been this last year: and yet you object when I take a little something to keep up my spirits. You even didn't want me to take that tonic I got at the drug store. *(With a hard laugh)* I know

you'd be glad to have me dead and out of your way: then you'd be free to run after all those silly girls that think you're such a wonderful, misunderstood person—this Helen and the others.

(There is a sharp exclamation of pain from the next room)

(With satisfaction) There! I knew you'd cut yourself. It'll be a lesson to you. You know you oughtn't to be running around nights drinking with your nerves in such an awful shape. *(She goes to the door and looks in)*

What makes you so pale? What are you staring at yourself in the mirror that way for? For goodness sake, wipe that blood off your face! *(With a shudder)* It's horrible. *(In relieved tones)* There, that's better. I never could stand the sight of blood. *(She shrinks back from the door a little)* You better give up trying and go to a barber shop. Your hand shakes dreadfully. Why do you stare at me like that? *(She turns away from the door)* I'll give you fifteen cents—only promise you won't buy a drink with it. Are you still mad at me about that letter? *(Defiantly)* Well, I had a right to read it. I'm your wife. *(She comes to the chair and sits down again. After a pause)*

I knew all the time you were running around with some one. Your lame excuses about spending the time at the library didn't fool me. Who is this Helen, anyway? One of those artists? Or does she write poetry, too? Her letter sounds that way. I'll bet she told you your things were the best ever, and you believed her, like a fool. Is she young and pretty? I was young and pretty, too, when you fooled me with your fine, poetic talk; but life with you would soon wear anyone down. What I've been through!

(Goes over and takes the coffee off the stove) Breakfast is ready. *(With a contemptuous glance)* Breakfast! *(Pours out a cup of coffee for herself and puts the pot on the table)* Your coffee'll be cold. What are you doing—still shaving, for heaven's sake? You'd better give it up. One of these mornings you'll give yourself a serious cut. *(She cuts off bread and butters it. During the following speeches she eats and sips her coffee)*

I'll have to run as soon as I've finished eating. One of us has got to work. *(Angrily)* Are you going to look for a job to-day or aren't you? I should think some of your fine friends would help you, if they really think you're so much. But I guess they just like to hear you talk. *(Sits in silence for a moment)*

I'm sorry for this Helen, whoever she is. Haven't you got any feelings for other people? What will her family say? I see she mentions them in her letter. What is she going to do—have the child—or go to one of those doctors? That's a nice thing, I must say. Where can she get the money? Is she rich? *(She waits for some answer to this volley of questions)*

Hmm! You won't tell me anything about her, will you? Much I care. Come to think of it, I'm not sorry for her, after all. She knew what she was doing. She isn't any schoolgirl, like I was, from the looks of her letter. Does she know you're married? Of course, she must. All your friends know about your unhappy marriage. I know they pity you, but they don't know my side of it. They'd talk different if they did.

(Too busy eating to go for a second or so)

This Helen must be a fine one, if she knew you were married. What does she expect, then? That I'll divorce you and let her marry you? Does she think I'm crazy enough for that—after all you've made me go through? I guess not! And you can't get a divorce from me and you know it. No one can say *I've* ever done anything wrong. *(Drinks the last of her cup of coffee)* She deserves to suffer, that's all I can say. I'll tell you what I think; I think your Helen is no better than a common street-walker, that's what I think. *(There is a stifled groan of pain from the next room)* Did you cut yourself again? Serves you right. Why don't you go to a barber shop when I offer you the money? *(Gets up and takes off her apron)* Well, I've got to run along. *(Peevishly)* This is a fine life for me to be leading! I won't stand for your loafing any longer. *(Something catches her ear and she pauses and listens intently)* There! You've overturned the water all over everything. Don't say you haven't. I can hear it dripping on the floor. *(A vague expression of fear comes over her face)* Alfred! Why don't you answer me?

(She moves slowly toward the room. There is the noise of a chair being overturned and something crashes heavily to the floor. She stands, trembling with fright)

Alfred! Alfred! Answer me! What is it you knocked over? Are you still drunk? *(Unable to stand the tension a second longer she rushes to the door of the bedroom)*

Alfred!

(She stands in the doorway looking down at the floor of the inner room, transfixed with horror. Then she shrieks wildly and runs to the other door, unlocks it and frenziedly pulls it open, and runs shrieking madly into the outer hallway.)

THE CURTAIN FALLS.

I See You Never
RAY BRADBURY

The soft knock came at the kitchen door, and when Mrs. O'Brian opened it, there on the back porch were her best tenant, Mr. Ramirez, and two police officers, one on each side of him. Mr. Ramirez just stood there, walled in and small.

"Why, Mr. Ramirez!" said Mrs. O'Brian.

Mr. Ramirez was overcome. He did not seem to have words to explain.

He had arrived at Mrs. O'Brian's rooming house more than two years earlier and had lived there ever since. He had come by bus from Mexico City to San Diego and had then gone up to Los Angeles. There he had found the clean little room, with glossy blue linoleum, and pictures and calendars on the flowered walls, and Mrs. O'Brian as the strict but kindly landlady. During the war he had worked at the airplane factory and made parts for the planes that flew off somewhere, and even now, after the war, he still held his job. From the first he had made big money. He saved some of it, and he got drunk only once a week—a privilege that to Mrs. O'Brian's way of thinking, every good workingman deserved, unquestioned and unreprimanded.

Inside Mrs. O'Brian's kitchen, pies were baking in the oven. Soon the pies would come out with complexions like Mr. Ramirez'—brown and shiny and crisp, with slits in them for the air almost like the slits of Mr. Ramirez' dark eyes. The kitchen smelled good. The policemen leaned forward, lured by the odor. Mr. Ramirez gazed at his feet, as if they had carried him into all this trouble.

"What happened, Mr. Ramirez?" asked Mrs. O'Brian.

Behind Mrs. O'Brian, as he lifted his eyes, Mr. Ramirez saw the long table laid with clean white linen and set with a platter, cool, shining glasses, and a water pitcher with ice cubes floating inside it, a bowl of fresh potato salad and one of bananas and oranges, cubed and sugared. At this table sat Mrs. O'Brian's children—her three grown sons, eating and conversing, and her two younger daughters, who were staring at the policemen as they ate.

"I have been here thirty months," said Mr. Ramirez quietly, looking at Mrs. O'Brian's plump hands.

"That's six months too long," said one policeman. "He only had a temporary visa. We've just got around to looking for him."

Soon after Mr. Ramirez had arrived he bought a radio for his little room; evenings he turned it up very loud and enjoyed it. And he had bought a wrist watch and enjoyed that too. And on many nights he had walked silent streets and seen the bright clothes in the windows and bought some of them, and he had seen the jewels and bought some of them for his few lady friends. And he had gone to picture shows five nights a week for a while. Then also, he had ridden the streetcars—all night some nights—smelling the electricity, his dark eyes moving over the advertisements, feeling the wheels rumble under him, watching the little sleeping houses and big hotels slip by. Besides that, he had gone to large restaurants, where he had eaten many-course dinners, and to the opera and the theater. And he had bought a car, which later, when he forgot to pay for it, the dealer had driven off angrily from in front of the rooming house.

"So here I am," said Mr. Ramirez now, "to tell you I must give up my room, Mrs. O'Brian. I come to get my luggage and clothes and go with these men."

"Back to Mexico?"

"Yes. To Lagos. That is a little town north of Mexico City."

"I'm sorry, Mr. Ramirez."

"I'm packed," said Mr. Ramirez hoarsely, blinking his dark eyes rapidly and moving his hands helplessly before him. The policemen did not touch him. There was no necessity for that.

"Here is the key, Mrs. O'Brian," Mr. Ramirez said. "I have my bag already."

Mrs. O'Brian, for the first time, noticed a suitcase standing behind him on the porch.

Mr. Ramirez looked in again at the huge kitchen, at the bright silver cutlery and the young people eating and the shining waxed floor. He turned and looked for a long moment at the apartment house next door, rising up three stories, high and beautiful. He looked at the balconies and fire escapes and back-porch stairs, at the lines of laundry snapping in the wind.

"You've been a good tenant," said Mrs. O'Brian.

"Thank you, thank you, Mrs. O'Brian," he said softly. He closed his eyes.

Mrs. O'Brian stood holding the door half open. One of her sons, behind her, said that her dinner was getting cold, but she shook her head at him and turned back to Mr. Ramirez. She remembered a visit she had once made to some Mexican border towns—the hot days, the endless crickets leaping and falling or lying dead and brittle like the small cigars in the shopwindows, and the canals taking river water out to the farms, the dirt roads, the scorched scape. She remembered the silent towns, the warm beer, the hot, thick foods each day. She remembered the slow, dragging horses and the parched jack rabbits on the road. She remembered the iron mountains and the dusty valleys and the ocean beaches that spread hundreds of miles with no sound but the waves—no cars, no buildings, nothing.

"I'm sure sorry, Mr. Ramirez," she said.

"I don't want to go back, Mrs. O'Brian," he said weakly. "I like it here, I want to stay here. I've worked, I've got money. I look all right, don't I? And I don't want to go back!"

"I'm sorry, Mr. Ramirez," she said. "I wish there was something I could do."

"Mrs. O'Brian!" he cried suddenly, tears rolling out under his eyelids. He reached out his hands and took her hand fervently, shaking it, wringing it, holding to it. "Mrs. O'Brian, I see you never, I see you never!"

The policemen smiled at this. But Mr. Ramirez did not notice it, and they stopped smiling very soon.

"Goodby, Mrs. O'Brian. You have been good to me. Oh, goodby, Mrs. O'Brian. I see you never!"

The policemen waited for Mr. Ramirez to turn, pick up his suitcase, and walk away. Then they followed him, tipping their hats to Mrs. O'Brian. She watched them go down the porch steps. Then she shut the door quietly and went slowly back to her chair at the table. She pulled the chair and sat down. She picked up the shining knife and fork and started once more upon her steak.

"Hurry up, Mom," said one of the sons. "It'll be cold."

Mrs. O'Brian took one bite and chewed on it for a long, slow time; then she stared at the closed door. She laid down her knife and fork.

"What's wrong, Ma?" asked her son.

"I just realized," said Mrs. O'Brian—she put her hand to her face—"I'll never see Mr. Ramirez again."

Someone Is Beating a Woman
ANDREI VOZNESENSKY
Translated by Jean Garrigue

Someone is beating a woman.
In the car that is dark and hot
Only the whites of her eyes shine.
Her legs thrash against the roof
Like berserk searchlight beams.

Someone is beating a woman.
This is the way slaves are beaten.
Frantic, she wrenches open the door
And plunges out—onto the road.

Brakes scream.
Someone runs up to her,
Strikes her and drags her, face down,
In the grass lashing with nettles.

Scum, how meticulously he beats her,
Stilyága, bastard, big hero,
His smart flatiron-pointed shoe
Stabbing into her ribs.

Such are the pleasures of enemy soldiers
And the brute refinements of peasants.
Tramping underfoot the moonlit grass,
Someone is beating a woman.

Someone is beating a woman.
Century on century, no end to this.
It's the young that are beaten. Somberly
Our wedding bells start up the alarum.
Someone is beating a woman.

What about the flaming weals
In the braziers of their cheeks?
That's life, you say. Are you telling me?
Someone is beating a woman.

But her light is unfaltering
World-without-ending.
There are no religions,
                              no revelations,
There are women.

Lying there pale as water
Her eyes tear-closed and still,
She doesn't belong to him
Any more than a meadow deep in a wood.

And the stars? Rattling in the sky
Like raindrops against black glass,
Plunging down,
                         they cool
Her grief-fevered forehead.

Of Rounds

MAY SWENSON

MOON
          round
                    goes around while going around a
                                        round
                                                  EARTH.
EARTH
          round
                    with MOON
                              round
                                        going around while going around,
goes around while going around a
                              round
                                        SUN.
SUN
      round
              with EARTH
                        round
                                  with MOON
                                            round
                                                      going around while going
around, and MERCURY
                        round
                              and VENUS
                                        round
                                                  going around while

going around, and MARS
                                round
                                        with two MOONS
                                                    round
                                                    round
                                                        going around
while going around, and JUPITER
                                          round
                                                  with twelve MOONS
                                                          round
                                                          round
                                                          round
                                                          round
                                                          round
                                                          round
                                                          round
                                                          round
                                                          round
                                                          round
                                                          round
going around while going around, and SATURN
                                              round
                                              with nine

MOONS
          round
          round
          round
          round
          round
          round
          round
          round
          round
                        going around while going around, and URANUS
                                                                round
with five MOONS
                    round
                    round
                    round
                    round
                    round
                              going around while going around, and NEPTUNE
round
          with two MOONS
                                  round
                                  round
                                      going around while going around, and

PLUTO
    round
            going around while going around, goes around while
going around
            A

            OF ROUNDS
                Round

Araby

JAMES JOYCE

North Richmond Street, being blind, was a quiet street except at the hour when the Christian Brothers' School set the boys free. An uninhabited house of two storeys stood at the blind end, detached from its neighbours in a square ground. The other houses of the street, conscious of decent lives within them, gazed at one another with brown inperturbable faces.

The former tenant of our house, a priest, had died in the back drawing-room. Air, musty from having been long enclosed, hung in all the rooms, and the waste room behind the kitchen was littered with old useless papers. Among these I found a few paper-covered books, the pages of which were curled and damp: *The Abbott,* by Walter Scott, *The Devout Communicant* and *The Memoirs of Vidocq.* I liked the last best because its leaves were yellow. The wild garden behind the house contained a central apple-tree and a few straggling bushes under one of which I found the late tenant's rusty bicycle-pump. He had been a very charitable priest; in his will he had left all his money to institutions and the furniture of his house to his sister.

When the short days of winter came dusk fell before we had well eaten our dinners. When we met in the street the houses had grown sombre. The space of sky above us was the colour of ever-changing violet and towards it the lamps of the street lifted their feeble lanterns. The cold air stung us and we played till our bodies glowed. Our shouts echoed in the silent street. The career of our play brought us through the dark muddy lanes behind the houses where we ran the gantlet of the rough tribes from the cottages, to the back doors of the dark dripping gardens where odours arose from the ashpits, to the dark odorous stables where a coachman smoothed and combed the horse or shook music from the buckled harness. When we returned to the street light from the kitchen windows had filled the areas. If my uncle was seen turning the corner we hid in the shadow until we had seen him safely housed. Or if Mangan's sister came out on the doorstep to call her brother in to his tea we watched her from our shadow peer up and down the street. We waited to see whether she would remain or go in and, if she remained, we left our shadow and walked up to Mangan's steps resignedly. She was waiting for us, her figure defined by the light from the half-opened door. Her brother always teased her before he obeyed and I stood by the railings looking at her. Her dress swung as she moved her body and the soft rope of her hair tossed from side to side.

Every morning I lay on the floor in the front parlour watching her door. The blind was pulled down to within an inch of the sash so that I could not be seen. When she came out on the doorstep my heart leaped. I ran to the hall, seized my books and followed her. I kept her brown figure always in my eye and, when we came near the point at which our ways diverged, I quickened my pace and passed her. This happened morning after morning. I had never spoken to her, except for a few casual words, and yet her name was like a summons to all my foolish blood.

Her image accompanied me even in places the most hostile to romance. On Saturday evenings when my aunt went marketing I had to go to carry some of the parcels. We walked through the flaring streets, jostled by drunken men and bargaining women, amid the curses of labourers, the shrill litanies of shop-boys who stood on guard by the barrels of pigs' cheeks, the nasal chanting of street-singers, who sang a *come-all-you* about O'Donovan Rossa, or a ballad about the troubles in our native land. These noises converged in a single sensation of life for me: I imagined that I bore my chalice safely through a throng of foes. Her name sprang to my lips at moments in strange prayers and praises which I myself did not understand. My eyes were often full of tears (I could not tell why) and at times a flood from my heart seemed to pour itself out into my bosom. I thought little of the future. I did not know whether I would ever speak to her or not or, if I spoke to her, how I could tell her of my confused adoration. But my body was like a harp and her words and gestures were like fingers running upon the wires.

One evening I went into the back drawing-room in which the priest had died. It was a dark rainy evening and there was no sound in the house. Through one of the broken panes I heard the rain impinge upon the earth, the fine incessant needles of water playing in the sodden beds. Some distant lamp or lighted window gleamed below me. I was thankful that I could see so little. All my senses seemed to desire to veil themselves and, feeling that I was about to slip from them, I pressed the palms of my hands together until they trembled, murmuring: *O love! O love!* many times.

At last she spoke to me. When she addressed the first words to me I was so confused that I did not know what to answer. She asked me was I going to *Araby*. I forget whether I answered yes or no. It would be a splendid bazaar, she said; she would love to go.

—And why can't you? I asked.

While she spoke she turned a silver bracelet round and round her wrist. She could not go, she said, because there would be a retreat that week in her convent. Her brother and two other boys were fighting for their caps and I was alone at the railings. She held one of the spikes, bowing her head towards me. The light from the lamp opposite our door caught the white curve of her neck, lit up her hair that rested there and, falling, lit up the hand upon the railing. It fell over one side of her dress and caught the white border of a petticoat, just visible as she stood at ease.

—It's well for you, she said.

—If I go, I said, I will bring you something.

What innumerable follies laid waste my waking and sleeping thoughts after that evening! I wished to annihilate the tedious intervening days. I chafed against the work of school. At night in my bedroom and by day in the classroom her image came between me and the page I strove to read. The syllables of the word *Araby* were called to me through the silence in which my soul luxuriated and cast an Eastern enchantment over me. I asked for leave to go to the bazaar on Saturday night. My aunt was surprised and hoped it was not some Freemason affair. I answered few questions in class. I watched my master's face pass from amiability to sternness; he hoped I was not beginning to idle. I could not call my wandering thoughts together. I had hardly any patience with the serious work of life which, now that it stood between me and my desire, seemed to me child's play, ugly monotonous child's play.

On Saturday morning I reminded my uncle that I wished to go to the bazaar in the evening. He was fussing at the hallstand, looking for the hatbrush, and answered me curtly:

—Yes, boy, I know.

As he was in the hall I could not go into the front parlour and lie at the window. I left the house in bad humour and walked slowly towards the school. The air was pitilessly raw and already my heart misgave me.

When I came home to dinner my uncle had not yet been home. Still it was early. I sat staring at the clock for some time and, when its ticking began to irritate me, I left the room. I mounted the staircase and gained the upper part of the house. The high cold empty gloomy rooms liberated me and I went from room to room singing. From the front window I saw my companions playing below in the street. Their cries reached me weakened and indistinct and, leaning my forehead against the cool glass, I looked over at the dark house where she lived. I may have stood there for an hour, seeing nothing but the brown-clad figure cast by my imagination, touched discreetly by the lamplight at the curved neck, at the hand upon the railings and at the border below the dress.

When I came downstairs again I found Mrs. Mercer sitting at the fire. She was an old garrulous woman, a pawnbroker's widow, who collected used stamps for some pious purpose. I had to endure the gossip of the tea-table. The meal was prolonged beyond an hour and still my uncle did not come. Mrs. Mercer stood up to go: she was sorry she couldn't wait any longer, but it was after eight o'clock and she did not like to be out late, as the night air was bad for her. When she had gone I began to walk up and down the room, clenching my fists. My aunt said:

—I'm afraid you may put off your bazaar for this night of Our Lord.

At nine o'clock I heard my uncle's latchkey in the halldoor. I heard him talking to himself and heard the hallstand rocking when it had received the weight of his overcoat. I could interpret these signs. When he was midway through his dinner I asked him to give me the money to go to the bazaar. He had forgotten.

—The people are in bed and after their first sleep now, he said.

I did not smile. My aunt said to him energetically.

—Can't you give him the money and let him go? You've kept him late enough as it is.

My uncle said he was very sorry he had forgotten. He said he believed in the old saying: *All work and no play makes Jack a dull boy.* He asked me where I was going and, when I had told him a second time he asked me did I know *The Arab's Farewell to his Steed*. When I left the kitchen he was about to recite the opening lines of the piece to my aunt.

I held a florin tightly in my hand as I strode down Buckingham Street towards the station. The sight of the streets thronged with buyers and glaring with gas recalled to me the purpose of my journey. I took my seat in a third-class carriage of a deserted train. After an intolerable delay the train moved out of the station slowly. It crept onward among ruinous houses and over the twinkling river. At Westland Row Station a crowd of people pressed to the carriage doors; but the porters moved them back, saying that it was a special train for the bazaar. I remained alone in the bare carriage. In a few minutes the train drew up beside an improvised wooden platform. I passed out on to the road and saw by the lighted dial of a clock that it was ten minutes to ten. In front of me was a large building which displayed the magical name.

I could not find any sixpenny entrance and, fearing that the bazaar would be closed, I passed in quickly through a turnstile, handing a shilling to a weary-looking man. I found myself in a big hall girdled at half its height by a gallery. Nearly all the stalls were closed and the greater part of the hall was in darkness. I recognised a silence like that which pervades a church after a service. I walked into the centre of the bazaar timidly. A few people were gathered about the stalls which were still open. Before a curtain, over which the words *Café Chantant* were written in coloured lamps, two men were counting money on a salver. I listened to the fall of the coins.

Remembering with difficulty why I had come, I went over to one of the stalls and examined porcelain vases and flowered tea-sets. At the door of the stall a young lady was talking and laughing with two young gentlemen. I remarked their English accents and listened vaguely to their conversation.

—Oh, I never said such a thing!

—Oh, but you did!

—Oh, but I didn't!

—Didn't she say that?

—Yes. I heard her.

—Oh, there's a . . .fib!

Observing me the young lady came over and asked me did I wish to buy anything. The tone of her voice was not encouraging; she seemed to have spoken to me out of a sense of duty. I looked humbly at the great jars that stood like eastern guards at either side of the dark entrance to the stall and murmured:

—No, thank you.

The young lady changed the position of one of the vases and went back to the two young men. They began to talk of the same subject. Once or twice the young lady glanced at me over her shoulder.

I lingered before her stall, though I knew my stay was useless, to make my interest in her wares seem the more real. Then I turned away slowly and walked down the middle of the bazaar. I allowed the two pennies to fall against the sixpence in my pocket. I heard a voice call from one end of the gallery that the light was out. The upper part of the hall was now completely dark.

Gazing up into the darkness I saw myself as a creature driven and derided by vanity; and my eyes burned with anguish and anger.

Water-Lilies
SARA TEASDALE

If you have forgotten water-lilies floating
    On a dark lake among mountains in the afternoon shade,
If you have forgotten their wet, sleepy fragrance,
    Then you can return and not be afraid.

But if you remember, then turn away forever
    To the plains and prairies where pools are far apart,
There you will not come at dusk on closing water-lilies,
    And the shadow of mountains will not fall on your heart.

Between the Lines
LEE SMITH

"Peace be with you from Mrs. Joline B. Newhouse" is how I sign my columns. Now I gave some thought to that. In the first place, I like a line that has a ring to it. In the second place, what I have always tried to do with my column is to uplift my readers if at all possible, which sometimes it is not. After careful thought, I threw out "Yours in Christ." I am a religious person and all my readers know it. If I put "Yours in Christ," it seems to me that they will think I am theirs because I am in Christ, or even that they and I are in Christ *together,* which is not always the case. I am in Christ but I know for a fact that a lot of them are not. There's no use acting like they are, but there's no use rubbing their face in it, either. "Peace be with you," as I see it, is sufficiently religious without laying all the cards right out on the table in plain view. I like to keep an ace or two up my sleeve. I like to write between the lines.

This is what I call my column, in fact: "Between the Lines, by Mrs. Joline B. Newhouse." Nobody knows why. Many people have come right out and asked me, including my best friend Sally Peck and my husband Glenn. "Come on, now, Joline," they say. "What's this 'Between the Lines' all about? What's this 'Between the Lines' supposed to mean?" But I just smile a sweet mysterious smile and change the subject. I know what I know.

And my column means everything to folks around here. Salt Lick community is where we live, unincorporated. I guess there is not much that you would notice, passing through—the Post Office (real little), the American oil station, my husband Glenn's Cash 'N' Carry Beverage Store. He sells more than beverages in there, though, believe me. He sells everything you can think of, from thermometers and rubbing alcohol to nails to frozen pizza. Anything else you want, you have to go out of the holler and get on the interstate and go to Greenville to get it. That's where my column appears, in the *Greenville Herald,* fortnightly. Now there's a word with a ring to it: fortnightly.

There are seventeen families here in Salt Lick—twenty, if you count those three down by the Five Mile Bridge. I put what they do in the paper. Anybody gets married, I write it. That goes for born, divorced, dies, celebrates a golden wedding anniversary, has a baby shower, visits relatives in Ohio, you name it. But these mere facts are not what's most important, to my mind.

I write, for instance: "Mrs. Alma Goodnight is enjoying a pleasant recuperation period in the lovely, modern Walker Mountain Community Hospital while she is sorely missed by her loved ones at home. Get well soon, Alma!" I do not write that Alma Goodnight is in the hospital because her husband hit her up the side with a rake and left a straight line of bloody little holes going from her waist to her armpit after she yelled at him, which Lord knows she did all the time, once too often. I don't write about how Eben Goodnight is all torn up now about what he did, missing work and worrying, or how Alma liked it so much in the hospital that nobody knows if they'll ever get her to go home or not. Because that is a *mystery*, and I am no detective by a long shot. I am what I am, I know what I know, and I know you've got to give folks something to hang onto, something to keep them going. That is what I have in mind when I say *uplift*, and that is what God had in mind when he gave us Jesus Christ.

My column would not be but a paragraph if the news was all I told. But it isn't. What I tell is what's important, like the bulbs coming up, the way the red-bud comes out first on the hills in the spring and how pretty it looks, the way the cattails shoot up by the creek, how the mist winds down low on the ridge in the mornings, how my wash all hung out on the line of a Tuesday looks like a regular square dance with those pants legs just flapping and flapping in the wind! I tell how all the things you ever dreamed of, all changed and ghostly, will come crowding into your head on a winter night when you sit up late in front of your fire. I even made up these little characters to talk for me, Mr. and Mrs. Cardinal and Princess Pussycat, and often I have them voice my thoughts. Each week I give a little chapter in their lives. Or I might tell what was the message brought in church, or relate an inspirational word from a magazine, book, or TV. I look on the bright side of life.

I've had God's gift of writing from the time I was a child. That's what the B. stands for in Mrs. Joline B. Newhouse—Barker, my maiden name. My father was a patient strong God-fearing man despite his problems and it is in his honor that I maintain the B. There was a lot of us children around all the time—it was right up the road here where I grew up—and it would take me a day to tell you what all we got into! But after I learned how to write, that was that. My fingers just naturally curved to a pencil and I sat down to writing like a ball of fire. They skipped me up one, two grades in school. When I was not but eight, I wrote a poem named "God's Garden" which was published in the church bulletin of the little Methodist Church we went to then on Hunter's Ridge. Oh, Daddy was so proud! He gave me a quarter that Sunday, and then I turned around and gave it straight to God. Put it in the collection plate. Daddy almost cried he was so proud. I wrote another poem in school the next year, telling how life is like a merry-go-round, and it won a statewide prize.

That's me—I grew up smart as a whip, lively, and naturally good. Jesus came as easy as breathing did to me. Don't think I'm putting on airs, though: I'm not. I know what I know. I've done my share of sinning, too, of which more later.

Anyway, I was smart. It's no telling but what I might have gone on to school like my own children have and who knows what all else if Mama hadn't run off with a man. I don't remember Mama very well, to tell the truth. She was a weak woman, always laying in the bed having a headache. One day we all came home from school and she was gone, didn't even bother to make up the bed. Well, that was the end of Mama! None of us ever saw her again, but Daddy told us right before he died that one time he had gotten a postcard from her from Atlanta, Georgia, years and years after that. He showed it to us, all wrinkled and soft from him holding it.

Being the oldest I took over and raised those little ones, three of them, and then I taught school and then I married Glenn and we had our own children, four of them, and I have raised them too and still have Marshall, of course, poor thing. He is the cross I have to bear and he'll be just like he is now for the rest of his natural life.

I was writing my column for the week of March 17, 1976, when the following events occurred. It was a real coincidence because I had just finished doing the cutest little story named "A Red-Letter Day for Mr. and Mrs. Cardinal" when the phone rang. It rings all the time, of course. Everybody around here knows my number by heart. It was Mrs. Irene Chalmers. She was all torn up. She said that Mr. Biggers was over at Greenville at the hospital very bad off this time, and that he was asking for me and would I please try to get over there today as the doctors were not giving him but a 20 percent chance to make it through the night. Mr. Biggers has always been a fan of mine, and he especially liked Mr. and Mrs. Cardinal. "Well!" I said, "Of course I will! I'll get Glenn on the phone right this minute. And you calm down, Mrs. Chalmers. You go fix yourself a coke." Mrs. Chalmers said she would, and hung up. I knew what was bothering her, of course. It was that given the natural run of things, she would be the next to go. The next one to be over there dying. Without even putting down the receiver, I dialed the beverage store. Bert answered.

"Good morning," I said. I like to maintain a certain distance with the hired help although Glenn does not. He will talk to anybody, and any time you go in there, you can find half the old men in the county just sitting around that stove in the winter or outside on those wooden drink boxes in the summer, smoking and drinking drinks which I am sure they are getting free out of the cooler although Glenn swears on the Bible they are not. Anyway, I said good morning.

"Can I speak to Glenn?" I said.

"Well now, Mrs. Newhouse," Bert said in his naturally insolent voice—he is just out of high school and too big for his britches—"He's not here right now. He had to go out for a while."

"Where did he go?" I asked.

"Well, I don't rightly know," Bert said. "He said he'd be back after lunch."

"Thank you very much, there will not be a message," I said sweetly, and hung up. I *knew* where Glenn was. Glenn was over on Caney Creek where his adopted half-sister Margie Kettles lived, having carnal knowledge of her in a trailer. They had been at it for 30 years and anybody would have thought they'd have worn it out by that time. Oh, I knew all about it!

The way it happened in the beginning was that Glenn's father had died of his lungs when Glenn was not but about ten years old, and his mother grieved so hard that she went off her head and began taking up with anybody who would go with her. One of the fellows she took up with was a foreign man out of a carnival, the James H. Drew Exposition, a man named Emilio something. He had this curly-headed dark-skinned little daughter. So Emilio stayed around longer than anybody would have expected, but finally it was clear to all that he never would find any work around here to suit him. The work around here is hard work, all of it, and they say he played a musical instrument. Anyway, in due course this Emilio just up and vanished, leaving that foreign child. Now that was Margie, of course, but her name wasn't Margie then. It was a long foreign name which ended up as Margie, and that's how Margie ended up here, in these mountains, where she has been up to no good ever since. Glenn's mother did not last too long after Emilio left, and those children grew up wild. Most of them went to foster homes, and to this day Glenn does not know where two of his brothers are! The military was what finally saved Glenn. He stayed with the military for nine years, and when he came back to this area he found me over here teaching school and with something of a nest egg in hand, enabling him to start the beverage store. Glenn says he owes everything to me.

This is true. But I can tell you something else: Glenn is a good man, and he has been a good provider all these years. He has not ever spoke to me above a regular tone of voice nor raised his hand in anger. He has not been tight with the money. He used to hold the girls in his lap of an evening. Since I got him started, he has been a regular member of the church, and he has not fallen down on it yet. Glenn furthermore has that kind of disposition where he never knows a stranger. So I can count my blessings, too.

Of course I knew about Margie! Glenn's sister Lou-Ann told me about it before she died, that is how I found out about it originally. She thought I *should* know, she said. She said it went on for years and she wanted me to know before she died. Well! I had had the first two girls by then, and I thought I was so happy. I took to my bed and just cried and cried. I cried for four days and then by gum I got up and started my column, and I have been writing on it ever since. So I was not unprepared when Margie showed up again some years after that, all gap-toothed and wild looking, but then before you knew it she was gone, off again to Knoxville, then back working as a waitress at that truck stop at the county line, then off again, like that. She led an irregular life. And as for Glenn, I will have to hand it to him, he never darkened her door again until after the birth of Marshall.

Now let me add that I would not have gone on and had Marshall if it was left up to me. I would have practiced more birth control. Because I was old by that time, 37, and that was too old for more children I felt, even though I had started late of course. I had told Glenn many times, I said three normal girls is enough for anybody. But no, Glenn was like a lot of men, and I don't blame him for it—he just had to try one more time for a boy. So we went on with it, and I must say I had a feeling all along.

I was not a bit surprised at what we got, although after wrestling with it all for many hours in the dark night of the soul as they say, I do not believe that Marshall is a judgment on me for my sin. I don't believe that. He is one of God's special children, is how I look at it. Of course he looks funny, but he has already lived ten years longer than they said he would. And has a job! He goes to Greenville every day on the Trailways bus rain or shine and cleans up the Plaza Mall. He gets to ride on the bus, and he gets to see people. Along about six o'clock he'll come back, walking up the holler and not looking to one side or the other, and then I give him his supper and then he'll watch something on TV like the Brady Bunch or Family Affair, and then he'll go to bed. He would not hurt a flea. But oh, Glenn took it hard when Marshall came! I remember that night so well and the way he just turned his back on the doctor. This is what sent him back to Margie, I am convinced of it, what made him take up right where he had left off all those years before.

So since Glenn was up to his old tricks I called up Lavonne, my daughter, to see if she could take me to the hospital to see Mr. Biggers. Why yes she could, it turned out. As a matter of fact she was going to Greenville herself. As a matter of fact she had something she wanted to talk to me about anyway. Now Lavonne is our youngest girl and the only one that stayed around here. Lavonne is somewhat pop-eyed, and has a weak constitution. She is one of those people that never can make up their mind. That day on the phone, I heard a whine in her voice I didn't like the sound of. Something is up, I thought.

First I powdered my face, so I would be ready to go when Lavonne got there. Then I sat back down to write some more on my column, this paragraph I had been framing in my mind for weeks about how sweet potatoes are not what they used to be. They taste gritty and dry now, compared to how they were. I don't know the cause of it, whether it is man on the moon or pollution in the ecology or what, but it is true. They taste awful.

Then my door came bursting open in a way that Lavonne would never do it and I knew it was Sally Peck from next door. Sally is loud and excitable but she has a good heart. She would do anything for you. "Hold on to your hat, Joline!" she hollered. Sally is so loud because she's deaf. Sally was just huffing and puffing—she is a heavy woman—and she had rollers still up in her hair and her old housecoat on with the buttons off.

"Why, Sally!" I exclaimed. "You are all wrought up!"

Sally sat down in my rocker and spread out her legs and started fanning herself with my *Family Circle* magazine. "If you think I'm wrought up," she said finally, "it is nothing compared to what you are going to be. We have had us a suicide, right here in Salt Lick. Margie Kettles put her head inside her gas oven in the night."

"Margie?" I said. My heart was just pumping.

"Yes, and a little neighbor girl was the one who found her, they say. She came over to borrow some baking soda for her mama's biscuits at seven o'clock A.M." Sally looked real hard at me. "Now wasn't she related to you all?"

"Why," I said just as easily, "Why yes, she was Glenn's adopted half-sister of course when they were nothing but a child. But we haven't had anything to do with her for years as you can well imagine."

"Well, they say Glenn is making the burial arrangements," Sally spoke up. She was getting her own back that day, I'll admit it. Usually I'm the one with all the news.

"I have to finish my column now and then Lavonne is taking me in to Greenville to see old Mr. Biggers who is breathing his last," I said.

"Well," Sally said, hauling herself up out of my chair, "I'll be going along then. I just didn't know if you knew it or not." Now Sally Peck is not a spiteful woman in all truth. I have known her since we were little girls sitting out in the yard looking at a magazine together. It is hard to imagine being as old as I am now, or knowing Sally Peck—who was Sally Bland, then—so long.

Of course I couldn't get my mind back on sweet potatoes after she left. I just sat still and fiddled with the pigeonholes in my desk and the whole kitchen seemed like it was moving and rocking back and forth around me. Margie dead! Sooner or later I would have to write it up tastefully in my column. Well, I must say I had never thought of Margie dying. Before God, I never hoped for that in all my life. I didn't know what it would do to *me*, in fact, to me and Glenn and Marshall and the way we live because you know how the habits and the ways of people can build up over the years. It was too much for me to take in at one time. I couldn't see how anybody committing suicide could choose to stick their head in the oven anyway—you can imagine the position you would be found in.

Well, in came Lavonne at that point, sort of hanging back and stuttering like she always does, and that child of hers Bethy Rose hanging onto her skirt for dear life. I saw no reason at that time to tell Lavonne about the death of Margie Kettles. She would hear it sooner or later, anyway. Instead, I gave her some plant food which I had ordered two for the price of one from Montgomery Ward some days before.

"Are you all ready, Mama?" Lavonne asked in that quavery way she has, and I said indeed I was, as soon as I got my hat, which I did, and we went out and got in Lavonne's Buick Electra and set off on our trip. Bethy Rose sat in the back, coloring in her coloring book. She is a real good child. "How's Ron?" I said. Ron is Lavonne's husband, an electrician, as up and coming a boy as you would want to see. Glenn and I are as proud as punch of Ron, and actually I never have gotten over the shock of Lavonne marrying him in the first place. All through high school she never showed any signs of marrying anybody, and you could have knocked me over with a feather the day she told us she was secretly engaged. I'll tell you, our Lavonne was not the marrying sort! Or so I thought.

But that day in the car she told me, "Mama, I wanted to talk to you and tell you I am thinking of getting a d-i-v-o-r-c-e."

I shot a quick look into the back seat but Bethy Rose wasn't hearing a thing. She was coloring Wonder Woman in her book.

"Now Lavonne," I said. "What in the world is it? Why, I'll bet you can work it out." Part of me was listening to Lavonne, as you can imagine, but part of me was still stuck in that oven with crazy Margie. I was not myself.

I told her that. "Lavonne," I said, "I am not myself today. But I'll tell you one thing. You give this some careful thought. You don't want to go off half-cocked. What is the problem anyway?"

"It's a man where I work," Lavonne said. She works in the Welfare Department, part-time, typing. "He is just giving me a fit. I guess you can pray for me, Mama, because I don't know what I'll decide to do."

"Can we get an Icee?" asked Bethy Rose.

"Has anything happened between you?" I asked. You have to get all the facts.

"Why *no!*" Lavonne was shocked. "Why, I wouldn't do anything like that! Mama, for goodness' sakes! We just have coffee together so far."

That's Lavonne all over. She never has been very bright. "Honey," I said, "I would think twice before I threw up a perfectly good marriage and a new brick home for the sake of a cup of coffee. If you don't have enough to keep you busy, go take a course at the community college. Make yourself a new pantsuit. This is just a mood, believe me."

"Well," Lavonne said. Her voice was shaking and her eyes were swimming in tears which just stayed there and never rolled down her cheeks. "Well," she said again.

As for me, I was lost in thought. It was when I was a young married woman like Lavonne that I committed my own great sin. I had the girls, and things were fine with Glenn and all, and there was simply not any reason to ascribe to it. It was just something I did out of loving pure and simple, did because I wanted to do it. I knew and have always known the consequences, yet God is full of grace, I pray and believe, and his mercy is everlasting.

To make a long story short, we had a visiting evangelist from Louisville, Kentucky, for a two-week revival that year. John Marcel Wilkes. If I say it myself, John Marcel Wilkes was a real humdinger! He had the yellowest hair you ever saw, curly, and the finest singing voice available. Oh, he was something, and that very first night he brought two souls into Christ. The next day I went over to the church with a pan of brownies just to tell him how much I personally had received from his message. I thought, of course, that there would be other people around—the Reverend Mr. Clark, or the youth director, or somebody cleaning. But to my surprise that church was totally empty except for John Marcel Wilkes himself reading the Bible in the fellowship hall and making notes on a pad of paper. The sun came in a window on his head. It was early June, I remember, and I had on a blue dress with little white cap sleeves and open-toed sandals. John Marcel Wilkes looked up at me and his face gave off light like the sun.

"Why, Mrs. Newhouse," he said. "What an unexpected pleasure!" His voice echoed out in the empty fellowship hall. He had the most beautiful voice, too—strong and deep, like it had bells in it. Everything he said had a ring to it.

He stood up and came around the table to where I was. I put the brownies down on the table and stood there. We both just stood there, real close without touching each other, for the longest time, looking into each other's eyes. Then he took my hands and brought them up to his mouth and kissed them, which nobody ever did to me before or since, and then he kissed me on the mouth. I thought I would die. After some time of that, we went together out into the hot June day where the bees were all buzzing around the flowers there by the back gate and I couldn't think straight. "Come," said John Marcel Wilkes. We went out in the woods behind the church to the prettiest place, and when it was all over I could look up across his curly yellow head and over the trees and see the white church steeple stuck up against that blue, blue sky like it was pasted there. This was not all. Two more times we went out there during that revival. John Marcel Wilkes left after that and I have never heard a word of him since. I do not know where he is, or what has become of him in all these years. I do know that I never bake a pan of brownies but what I think of him, or hear the church bells ring. So I have to pity Lavonne and her cup of coffee if you see what I mean, just like I have to spend the rest of my life to live my sinning down. But I'll tell you this: if I had it all to do over, I would do it all over again, and I would not trade it in for anything.

Lavonne drove off to look at fabric and get Bethy Rose an Icee, and I went in the hospital. I hate the way they smell. As soon as I entered Mr. Biggers' room, I could see he was breathing his last. He was so tiny in the bed you almost missed him, a poor little shriveled-up thing. His family sat all around.

"Aren't you sweet to come?" they said. "Looky here, honey, it's Mrs. Newhouse."

He didn't move a muscle, all hooked up to tubes. You could hear him breathing all over the room.

"It's Mrs. Newhouse," they said, louder. "Mrs. Newhouse is here. Last night he was asking for everybody," they said to me. "Now he won't open his eyes. You are real sweet to come," they said. "You certainly did brighten his days." Now I knew this was true because the family had remarked on it before.

"I'm so glad," I said. Then some more people came in the door and everybody was talking at once, and while they were doing that, I went over to the bed and got right up by his ear.

"Mr. Biggers!" I said. "Mr. Biggers, it's Joline Newhouse here."

He opened one little old bleary eye.

"Mr. Biggers!" I said right into his ear. "Mr. Biggers, you know those cardinals in my column? Mr. and Mrs. Cardinal? Well, I made them up! I made them up, Mr. Biggers. They never were real at all." Mr. Biggers closed his eye and a nurse came in and I stood up.

"Thank you so much for coming, Mrs. Newhouse," his daughter said.

"He is one fine old gentleman," I told them all, and then I left.

Outside in the hall, I had to lean against the tile wall for support while I waited for the elevator to come. Imagine, me saying such a thing to a dying man! I was not myself that day.

Lavonne took me to the big Krogers in north Greenville and we did our shopping, and on the way back in the car she told me she had been giving everything a lot of thought and she guessed I was right after all.

"You're not going to tell anybody, are you?" she asked me anxiously, popping her eyes. "You're not going to tell Daddy, are you?" she said.

"Why, Lord no, honey!" I told her. "It is the farthest thing from my mind."

Sitting in the back seat among all the grocery bags, Bethy Rose sang a little song she had learned at school. "Make new friends but keep the old, some are silver but the other gold," she sang.

"I don't know what I was thinking of," Lavonne said.

Glen was not home yet when I got there—making his arrangements, I supposed. I took off my hat, made myself a cup of Sanka, and sat down and finished off my column on a high inspirational note, saving Margie and Mr. Biggers for the next week. I cooked up some ham and red-eye gravy, which Glenn just loves, and then I made some biscuits. The time seemed to pass so slow. The phone rang two times while I was fixing supper, but I just let it go. I thought I had received enough news for *that* day. I still couldn't get over Margie putting her head in the oven, or what I had said to poor Mr. Biggers, which was not at all like me you can be sure. I buzzed around that kitchen doing first one thing, then another. I couldn't keep my mind on anything I did.

After a while Marshall came home, and ate, and went in the front room to watch TV. He cannot keep it in his head that watching TV in the dark will ruin your eyes, so I always have to go in there and turn on a light for him. This night, though, I didn't. I just let him sit there in the recliner in the dark, watching his show, and in the pale blue light from that TV set he looked just like anybody else.

I put on a sweater and went out on the front porch and sat in the swing to watch for Glenn. It was nice weather for that time of year, still a little cold but you could smell spring in the air already and I knew it wouldn't be long before the redbud would come out again on the hills. Our in the dark where I couldn't see them, around the front steps, my crocuses were already up. After a while of sitting out there I began to take on a chill, due more to my age no doubt than the weather, but just then some lights came around the bend, two headlights, and I knew it was Glenn coming home.

Glenn parked the truck and came up the steps. He was dog-tired, I could see that. He came over to the swing and put his hand on my shoulder. A little wind came up, and by then it was so dark you could see lights on all the ridges where the people live. "Well, Joline," he said.

"Dinner is waiting on you," I said. "You go on in and wash up and I'll be there directly. I was getting worried about you," I said.

Glenn went on and I sat there swaying on the breeze for a minute before I went after him. Now where will it all end? I ask you. All this pain and loving, mystery and loss. And it just goes on and on, from Glenn's mother taking up with dark-skinned gypsies to my own daddy and his postcard to that silly La-vonne and her cup of coffee to Margie with her head in the oven, to John Marcel Wilkes and myself, God help me, and all of it so long ago out in those holy woods.

Piano
D. H. LAWRENCE

Softly, in the dusk, a woman is singing to me;
Taking me back down the vista of years, till I see
A child sitting under the piano, in the boom of the tingling strings
And pressing the small, poised feet of a mother who smiles as she sings.

In spite of myself, the insidious mastery of song
Betrays me back, till the heart of me weeps to belong
To the old Sunday evenings at home, with winter outside
And hymns in the cozy parlor, the tinkling piano our guide.

So now it is vain for the singer to burst into clamor
With the great black piano appassionato. The glamour
Of childish days is upon me, my manhood is cast
Down in the flood of remembrance, I weep like a child for the past.

The Pardon
RICHARD WILBUR

My dog lay dead five days without a grave
In the thick of summer, hid in a clump of pine
And a jungle of grass and honeysuckle-vine.
I who had loved him while he kept alive

Went only close enough to where he was
To sniff the heavy honeysuckle-smell
Twined with another odor heavier still
And hear the flies' intolerable buzz.

Well, I was ten and very much afraid.
In my kind world the dead were out of range
And I could not forgive the sad or strange
In beast or man. My father took the spade

And buried him. Last night I saw the grass
Slowly divide (it was the same scene
But now it glowed a fierce and mortal green)
And saw the dog emerging. I confess

I felt afraid again, but still he came
In the carnal sun, clothed in a hymn of flies,
And death was breeding in his lively eyes.
I started in to cry and call his name,

Asking forgiveness of his tongueless head.
. . . I dreamt the past was never past redeeming:
But whether this was false or honest dreaming
I beg death's pardon now. And mourn the dead.

A Sentiment for December 25
JOHN CIARDI

Caught as we all are in the human condition—
    Subject to vices variously begun—
    in curiosity, from nature, of malaise.
    Hungry for joy and fed less than our hunger.
    Charitable when we can save ourselves
    from more involvement than we know how to bear.
    Simple in our silences, made intricate by vocabularies.
    Greedy because we were all once children.
    Forgoing because we have read dreams and visions
    that do not come to us when we lay the book by.
    Loving in desperation, in fear of loneliness.
    Begetting in the arsons and Olympics of first love
    or in the habituated rutting of the long bed
    the children that sadden us to an uneasy tolerance.
    Afraid of death in our dying and liberated
    only partially by the partial loss of ignorance.
    Eager for friendships from which we may demand

what we ourselves give with two motives, if at all.
Suspected by States for our best intuitions.
Solemn at funerals but glad to have outlived
one other as proof that we are, after all, right.
Liars because we must live in what seems possible.
Fools because we lie, and fools again for assuming
the possible to be any more likely than the impossible.
Faithless because our houses are destroyable but not our fears.
Brave because we dare not stop to think. Proud
because we are wrong. Wrathful because we are powerless.
Envious because we are uncertain. Lazy because we were born.
Avaracious because we were afraid. Gluttonous
because bellies are a mother to warm and assure us.
Murderous and adulterous because opportunity and energy
will sometimes be added to motive. Ungrateful
because gratitude is a debt, and because it is easier
to betray our benefactors than to await new benefactions.
Religious because it is dark at night, and because
we have been instructed, and because it is easier to obey
than to believe our senses or to learn to doubt them
exhaustively. Sad because we are as we are,
time-trapped, and because our images of ourselves
and the facts of ourselves wake at night and bicker
and lay bets with one another, with us as the stakes.

Then moved to pity at last because we hear and are saddened—
Nearly beautiful in the occasions of our pity not of
ourselves. Nearly affectionate when we are free of pain.

Caught as we are in these and our other conditions—
Which include a distaste for the littleness of our motives,
and, therefore, some wish to live toward some reality.
Terrified by realities. Addicted to evasions. Daring, perhaps
once, to look into the mirror and see and not look away.

Beginning again, then, with those who share with us and with whom
we share the sorrows of the common failure.
Fumbling at last to the language of a sympathy
that can describe, and that will be, we are persuaded,
sufficiently joy when we find in one another its idioms.

Caught as we are in these defining conditions—
I wish you the one fact of ourselves that is inexhaustible
and which, therefore, we need not horde nor begrudge.
Let mercy be its name till its name be found.
And wish that to the mercy that is possible because it takes
nothing from us and may, therefore, be given indifferently,
there be joined the mercy that adds us to one another.

Journey of the Magi
T. S. ELIOT

"A cold coming we had of it,
Just the worst time of the year
For a journey, and such a long journey:
The ways deep and the weather sharp,
The very dead of winter."
And the camels galled, sore-footed, refractory,
Lying down in the melting snow.
There were times we regretted
The summer palaces on slopes, the terraces,
And the silken girls bringing sherbet.
Then the camel men cursing and grumbling
And running away, and wanting their liquor and women,
And the night-fires going out, and the lack of shelters,
And the cities hostile and the towns unfriendly
And the villages dirty and charging high prices:
A hard time we had of it.
At the end we preferred to travel all night,
Sleeping in snatches,
With the voices singing in our ears, saying
That this was all folly.

Then at dawn we came down to a temperate valley,
Wet, below the snow line, smelling of vegetation;
With a running stream and a water-mill beating the darkness,
And three trees on the low sky,
And an old white horse galloped away in the meadow.
Then we came to a tavern with vine-leaves over the lintel,
Six hands at an open door dicing for pieces of silver,
And feet kicking the empty wine-skins.
But there was no information, and so we continued
And arrived at evening, not a moment too soon
Finding the place; it was (you may say) satisfactory.

All this was a long time ago, I remember,
And I would do it again, but set down
This set down
This: were we led all that way for
Birth or Death? There was a Birth, certainly,
We had evidence and no doubt. I had seen birth and death,
But had thought they were different; this Birth was
Hard and bitter agony for us, like Death, our death.
We returned to our places, these Kingdoms,
But no longer at ease here, in the old dispensation,
With an alien people clutching their gods.
I should be glad of another death.

To Be in Love
GWENDOLYN BROOKS

To be in love
Is to touch things with a lighter hand.

In yourself you stretch, you are well.

You look at things through his eyes.
    A Cardinal is red
    A sky is blue.
Suddenly you know he knows too.
He is not there but
You know you are tasting together
The winter, or light spring weather.

His hand to take your hand is overmuch.
Too much to bear.

You cannot look in his eyes
Because your pulse must not say
What must not be said.

When he
Shuts a door—

Is not there—
Your arms are water.

And you are free
With a ghastly freedom.

You are the beautiful half
Of a golden hurt.

You remember and covet his mouth,
To touch, to whisper on.

Oh when to declare
Is certain Death!

Oh when to apprize
Is to mesmerize,

To see fall down, the Column of Gold,
Into the commonest ash.

The Mother
GWENDOLYN BROOKS

Abortions will not let you forget.
You remember the children you got that you did not get,
The damp small pulps with a little or with no hair,
The singers and workers that never handled the air.
You will never neglect or beat
Them, or silence or buy with a sweet.
You will never wind up the sucking-thumb
Or scuttle off ghosts that come.
You will never leave them, controlling your luscious sigh,
Return for a snack of them, with gobbling mother-eye.

I have heard in the voices of the wind the voices of my dim killed children.
I have contracted. I have eased
My dim dears at the breasts they could never suck.
I have said, Sweets, if I sinned, if I seized
Your luck
And your lives from your unfinished reach,
If I stole your births and your names,
Your straight baby tears and your games,

Your stilted or lovely loves, your tumults, your marriages, aches, and your
 deaths,
If I poisoned the beginnings of your breaths,
Believe that even in my deliberateness I was not deliberate.
Though why should I whine,
Whine that the crime was other than mine?—
Since anyhow you are dead.
Or rather, or instead,
You were never made.
But that too, I am afraid,
Is faulty: oh, what shall I say, how is the truth to be said?
You were born, you had body, you died.
It is just that you never giggled or planned or cried.

Believe me, I loved you all.
Believe me, I knew you, though faintly, and I loved, I loved you
All.

The Chaser
JOHN COLLIER

Alan Austen, as nervous as a kitten, went up certain dark and creaky stairs
in the neighborhood of Pell Street, and peered about for a long time on the
dim landing before he found the name he wanted written obscurely on one of
the doors.

He pushed open this door, as he had been told to do, and found himself in
a tiny room, which contained no furniture but a plain kitchen table, a rocking
chair, and an ordinary chair. On one of the dirty buff-colored walls were a
couple of shelves containing in all perhaps a dozen bottles and jars.

An old man sat in the rocking chair, reading a newspaper. Alan, without a
word, handed him the card he had been given. "Sit down, Mr. Austen," said
the old man very politely. "I am glad to make your acquaintance."

"Is it true," asked Alan, "that you have a certain mixture that has—er—quite
extraordinary effects?"

"My dear sir," replied the old man, "my stock in trade is not very large—I
don't deal in laxatives and teething mixtures—but such as it is, it is varied. I
think nothing I sell has effects which could be precisely described as ordinary."

"Well, the fact is—" began Alan.

"Here, for example," interrupted the old man, reaching for a bottle from
the shelf. "Here is a liquid as colorless as water, almost tasteless, quite imperceptible in coffee, milk, wine, or any other beverage. It is also quite imperceptible to any known method of autopsy."

"Do you mean it is a poison?" cried Alan, very much horrified.

"Call it cleaning fluid if you like," said the old man indifferently. "Lives
need cleaning. Call it a spot-remover. 'Out, damned spot!' Eh? 'Out, brief
candle!' "

"I want nothing of that sort," said Alan.

"Probably it is just as well," said the old man. "Do you know the price of this? For one teaspoonful, which is sufficient, I ask five thousand dollars. Never less. Not a penny less."

"I hope all your mixtures are not as expensive," said Alan apprehensively.

"Oh, dear, no," said the old man. "It would be no good charging that sort of price for a love potion, for example. Young people who need a love potion very seldom have five thousand dollars. Otherwise they would not need a love potion."

"I'm glad to hear you say so," said Alan.

"I look at it like this," said the old man. "Please a customer with one article, and he will come back when he needs another. Even if it *is* more costly, he will save up for it, if necessary."

"So," said Alan, "you really do sell love potions?"

"If I did not sell love potions," said the old man, reaching for another bottle, "I should not have mentioned the other matter to you. It is only when one is in a position to oblige that one can afford to be so confidential."

"And these potions," said Alan. "They are not just—just—er—"

"Oh, no," said the old man. "Their effects are permanent, and extend far beyond the mere carnal impulse. But they include it. Oh, yes, they include it. Bountifully. Insistently. Everlastingly."

"Dear me!" said Alan, attempting a look of scientific detachment. "How very interesting!"

"But consider the spiritual side," said the old man.

"I do, indeed," said Alan.

"For indifference," said the old man, "they substitute devotion. For scorn, adoration. Give one tiny measure of this to the young lady—its flavor is imperceptible in orange juice, soup, or cocktails—and hower gay and giddy she is, she will change altogether. She'll want nothing but solitude, and you."

"I can hardly believe it," said Alan. "She is so fond of parties."

"She will not like them any more," said the old man. "She'll be afraid of the pretty girls you may meet."

"She'll actually be jealous?" cried Alan in a rapture. "Of me?"

"Yes, she will want to be everything to you."

"She is, already. Only she doesn't care about it."

"She will, when she has taken this. She will care intensely. You'll be her sole interest in life."

"Wonderful!" cried Alan.

"She'll want to know all you do," said the old man. "All that has happened to you during the day. Every word of it. She'll want to know what you are thinking about, why you smile suddenly, why you are looking sad."

"That is love!" cried Alan.

"Yes," said the old man. "How carefully she'll look after you! She'll never allow you to be tired, to sit in a draft, to neglect your food. If you are an hour late, she'll be terrified. She'll think you are killed, or that some siren has caught you."

"I can hardly imagine Diana like that!" cried Alan, overwhelmed with joy.

"You will not have to use your imagination," said the old man. "And, by the way, since there are always sirens, if by any chance you *should*, later on, slip a little, you need not worry. She will forgive you, in the end. She'll be terribly hurt, of course, but she'll forgive you—in the end."

"That will not happen," said Alan fervently.

"Of course not," said the old man. "But, if it does, you need not worry. She'll never divorce you. Oh, no! And, of course, she herself will never give you the least, the very least, grounds for—not divorce, of course—but even uneasiness."

"And how much," said Alan, "how much is this wonderful mixture?"

"It is not so dear," said the old man, "as the spot remover, as I think we agreed to call it. No. That is five thousand dollars; never a penny less. One has to be older than you are to indulge in that sort of thing. One has to save up for it."

"But the love potion?" said Alan.

"Oh, that," said the old man, opening the drawer in the kitchen table and taking out a tiny, rather dirty-looking phial. "That is just a dollar."

"I can't tell you how grateful I am," said Alan, watching him fill it.

"I like to oblige," said the old man. "Then customers come back, later in life, when they are rather better off, and want more expensive things. Here you are. You will find it very effective."

"Thank you again," said Alan. "Goodbye."

"*Au revoir*," said the old man.

Riders to the Sea
JOHN M. SYNGE

CHARACTERS

MAURYA (an old woman)   BARTLEY (her son)

CATHLEEN (her daughter)   NORA (a young daughter)

MEN and WOMEN

Scene: An Island Off the West of Ireland.

(Cottage kitchen, with nets, oil-skins, spinning wheel, some new boards standing by the wall, etc. CATHLEEN, *a girl of about twenty, finishes kneading cake, and puts it down in the pot-oven by the fire; then wipes her hands, and begins to spin at the wheel.* NORA, *a young girl, puts her head in at the door.)*

NORA   *(in a low voice)*: Where is she?

CATHLEEN: She's lying down, God help her, and may be sleeping, if she's able.

*(*NORA *comes in softly, and takes a bundle from under her shawl.)*

(Spinning the wheel rapidly.) What is it you have?

NORA: The young priest is after bringing them. It's a shirt and a plain stocking were got off a drowned man in Donegal.

*(*CATHLEEN *stops her wheel with a sudden movement, and leans out to listen.)*

We're to find out if it's Michael's they are, some time herself will be down looking by the sea.

CATHLEEN: How would they be Michael's, Nora. How would he go the length of that way to the far north?

NORA: The young priest says he's known the like of it. "If it's Michael's they are," says he, "you can tell herself he's got a clean burial by the grace of God, and if they're not his, let no one say a word about them, for she'll be getting her death," says he, "with crying and lamenting."
(The door which NORA *half closed is blown open by a gust of wind.)*

CATHLEEN *(looking out anxiously)*: Did you ask him would he stop Bartley going this day with the horses to the Galway fair?

NORA: "I won't stop him," says he, "but let you not be afraid. Herself does be saying prayers half through the night, and the Almighty God won't leave her destitute," says he, "with no son living."

CATHLEEN: Is the sea bad by the white rocks, Nora?

NORA: Middling bad, God help us. There's a great roaring in the west, and it's worse it'll be getting when the tide's turned to the wind. *(She goes over to the table with the bundle.)* Shall I open it now?

CATHLEEN: Maybe she'd wake up on us, and come in before we'd done. *(Coming to the table.)* It's a long time we'll be, and the two of us crying.

NORA *(goes to the inner door and listens)*: She's moving about on the bed. She'll be coming in a minute.

CATHLEEN: Give me the ladder, and I'll put them up in the turf loft, the way she won't know of them at all, and maybe when the tide turns she'll be going down to see would he be floating from the east.

(They put the ladder against the gable of the chimney; CATHLEEN *goes up a few steps and hides the bundle in the turf loft,* MAURYA *comes from the inner room.)*

MAURYA *(looking up at* CATHLEEN *and speaking querulously)*: Isn't it turf enough you have for this day and evening?

CATHLEEN: There's a cake baking at the fire for a short space *(Throwing down the turf.)* and Bartley will want it when the tide turns if he goes to Connemara.

*(*NORA *picks up the turf and puts it round the pot-oven.)*

MAURYA *(sitting down on a stool at the fire.)*: He won't go this day with the wind rising from the south and west. He won't go this day, for the young priest will stop him surely.

NORA: He'll not stop him, mother; and I heard Eamon Simon and Stephen Pheety and Colum Shawn saying he would go.

MAURYA: Where is he itself?

NORA: He went down to see would there be another boat sailing in the week, and I'm thinking it won't be long till he's here now, for the tide's turning at the green head, and the hooker's tacking from the east.

CATHLEEN: I hear someone passing the big stones.

NORA *(looking out)*: He's coming now, and he in a hurry.

BARTLEY *(comes in and looks around the room. Speaking sadly and quietly)*: Where is the bit of new rope, Cathleen, was bought in Connemara?

CATHLEEN *(coming down)*: Give it to him, Nora; it's on a nail by the white boards. I hung it up this morning, for the pig with the black feet was eating it.

NORA *(giving him a rope)*:   Is that it, Bartley?

MAURYA: You'd do right to leave that rope, Bartley, hanging by the boards. (BARTLEY *takes the rope.*) It will be wanting in this place, I'm telling you, if Michael is washed up tomorrow morning, or the next morning, or any morning in the week; for it's a deep grave we'll make him, by the grace of God.

BARTLEY *(beginning to work with the rope)*:   I've no halter the way I can ride down on the mare, and I must go now quickly. This is the one boat going for two weeks or beyond it, and the fair will be a good fair for horses, I heard them saying below.

MAURYA: It's a hard thing they'll be saying below if the body is washed up and there's no man in it to make the coffin, and I after giving a big price for the finest white boards you'd find in Connemara. *(She looks round at the boards.)*

BARTLEY: How would it be washed up, and we after looking each day for nine days, and a strong wind blowing a while back from the west and south?

MAURYA: If it wasn't found itself, that wind is raising the sea, and there was a star up against the moon, and it rising in the night. If it was a hundred horses, or a thousand horses you had itself, what is the price of a thousand horses against a son where there is one son only?

BARTLEY *(working at the halter, to* CATHLEEN*)*: Let you go down each day, and see the sheep aren't jumping in on the rye, and if the jobber comes you can sell the pig with the black feet if there is a good price going.

MAURYA: How would the like of her get a good price for a pig?

BARTLEY *(to* CATHLEEN*)*:   If the west wind holds with the last bit of the moon let you and Nora get up weed enough for another cock for the kelp. It's hard set we'll be from this day with no one in it but one man to work.

MAURYA: It's hard set we'll be surely the day you're drowned with the rest. What way will I live and the girls with me, and I an old woman looking for the grave?

(BARTLEY *lays down the halter, takes off his old coat, and puts on a newer one of the same flannel.*)

BARTLEY *(to* NORA*)*:   Is she coming to the pier?

NORA *(looking out)*:   She's passing the green head and letting fall her sails.

BARTLEY *(getting his purse and tobacco)*:   I'll have half an hour to go down, and you'll see me coming again in two days, or in three days, or maybe in four days if the wind is bad.

MAURYA *(turning round to the fire, and putting her shawl over her head)*:   Isn't it a hard and cruel man won't hear a word from an old woman, and she holding him from the sea?

CATHLEEN: It's the life of a young man to be going on the sea, and who would listen to an old woman with one thing and she saying it over?

BARTLEY *(taking the halter)*:   I must go now quickly. I'll ride down on the red mare, and the grey pony'll run behind me. . . . The blessing of God on you. *(He goes out.)*

MAURYA *(crying out as he is in the door)*:   He's gone now, God spare us, and we'll not see him again. He's gone now, and when the black night is falling I'll have no son left me in the world.

CATHLEEN: Why wouldn't you give him your blessing and he looking round in the door? Isn't it sorrow enough is on every one in this house without your sending him out with an unlucky word behind him, and a hard word in his ear?

*(*MAURYA *takes up the tongs and begins raking the fire aimlessly without looking around.)*

NORA *(turning towards her)*:   You're taking away the turf from the cake.

CATHLEEN *(crying out)*:   The Son of God forgive us, Nora, we're after forgetting his bit of bread. *(She comes over to the fire.)*

NORA: And it's destroyed he'll be going till dark night, and he after eating nothing since the sun went up.

CATHLEEN *(turning the cake out of the oven)*:   It's destroyed he'll be, surely. There's no sense left on any person in a house where an old woman will be talking for ever.

*(*MAURYA *sways herself on her stool.)*

(Cutting off some of the bread and rolling it in a cloth; to MAURYA.)   Let you go down now to the spring well and give him this and he passing. You'll see him then and the dark word will be broken, and you can say "God speed you," the way he'll be easy in his mind.

MAURYA *(taking the bread)*:   Will I be in it as soon as himself?

CATHLEEN: If you go now quickly.

MAURYA *(standing up unsteadily)*: It's hard set I am to walk.

CATHLEEN *(looking at her anxiously)*:   Give her the stick, Nora, or maybe she'll slip on the big stones.

NORA: What stick?

CATHLEEN: The stick Michael brought from Connemara.

MAURYA *(taking a stick* NORA *gives her)*:   In the big world the old people do be leaving things after them for their sons and children, but in this place it is the young men do be leaving things behind for them that do be old. *(She goes out slowly.* NORA *goes over to the ladder.)*

CATHLEEN: Wait, Nora, maybe she'd turn back quickly. She's that sorry, God help her, you wouldn't know the thing she'd do.

NORA: Is she gone round by the bush?

CATHLEEN *(looking out)*:   She's gone now. Throw it down quickly, for the Lord knows when she'll be out of it again.

NORA *(getting the bundle from the loft)*:   The young priest said he'd be passing tomorrow, and we might go down and speak to him below if it's Michael's they are surely.

CATHLEEN *(taking the bundle)*:   Did he say what way they were found?

NORA *(coming down)*:   "There were two men," says he, "and they rowing round with poteen before the cocks crowed, and the oar of one of them caught the body, and they passing the black cliffs of the north."

CATHLEEN (*trying to open the bundle*):   Give me a knife, Nora; the string's perished with the salt water, and there's a black knot on it you wouldn't loosen in a week.

NORA (*giving her a knife*):   I've heard tell it was a long way to Donegal.

CATHLEEN (*cutting the string*):   It is surely. There was a man in here a while ago—the man sold us that knife—and he said if you set off walking from the rocks beyond, it would be in seven days you'd be in Donegal.

NORA: And what time would a man take, and he floating?

(CATHLEEN *opens the bundle and takes out a bit of a sheet and a stocking. They look at them eagerly.*)

CATHLEEN (*in a low voice*):   The Lord spare us, Nora! Isn't it a queer hard thing to say if it's his they are surely?

NORA: I'll get his shirt off the hook the way we can put the one flannel on the other. (*She looks through some clothes hanging in the corner.*) It's not with them, Cathleen, and where will it be?

CATHLEEN: I'm thinking Bartley put it on him in the morning, for his own shirt was heavy with the salt in it. (*Pointing to the corner.*) There's a bit of a sleeve was of the same stuff. Give me that and it will do.

(NORA *brings it to her and they compare the flannel.*)

It's the same stuff, Nora; but if it is itself aren't there great rolls of it in the shops of Galway, and isn't it many another man may have a shirt of it as well as Michael himself?

NORA (*who has taken up the stocking and counted the stitches, crying out*):   It's Michael, Cathleen, it's Michael; God spare his soul, and what will herself say when she hears this story, and Bartley on the sea?

CATHLEEN (*taking the stocking*):   It's a plain stocking.

NORA: It's the second one of the third pair I knitted, and I put up three score stitches, and I dropped four of them.

CATHLEEN (*counts the stitches*):   It's that number is in it. (*Crying out.*) Ah, Nora, isn't it a bitter thing to think of him floating that way to the far north, and no one to keen him but the black hags that do be flying on the sea?

NORA (*swinging herself half round, and throwing out her arms on the clothes*):   And isn't it a pitiful thing when there is nothing left of a man who was a great rower and fisher, but a bit of an old shirt and a plain stocking?

CATHLEEN (*after an instant*):   Tell me is herself coming, Nora? I hear a little sound on the path.

NORA (*looking out*):   She is, Cathleen. She's coming up to the door.

CATHLEEN: Put these things away before she'll come in. Maybe it's easier she'll be after giving her blessing to Bartley, and we won't let on we've heard anything the time he's on the sea.

NORA (*helping* CATHLEEN *to close the bundle*):   We'll put them here in the corner.

(*They put them into a hole in the chimney corner.* CATHLEEN *goes back to the spinning-wheel.*)

Will she see it was crying I was?

CATHLEEN: Keep your back to the door the way the light'll not be on you.

(NORA *sits down at the chimney corner, with her back to the door.* MAURYA *comes in very slowly, without looking at the girls, and goes over to her stool at the other side of the fire. The cloth with the bread is still in her hand. The girls look at each other, and* NORA *points to the bundle of bread.*)

(*After spinning for a moment.*):   You didn't give him his bit of bread?

(MAURYA *begins to keen softly, without turning around.*):   Did you see him riding down? (MAURYA *goes on keening.*)

(*A little impatiently.*)   God forgive you; isn't it a better thing to raise your voice and tell what you seen, than to be making lamentation for a thing that's done? Did you see Bartley, I'm saying to you.

MAURYA (*with a weak voice*):   My heart's broken from this day.

CATHLEEN (*as before*):   Did you see Bartley?

MAURYA: I seen the fearfulest thing.

CATHLEEN (*leaves her wheel and looks out*):   God forgive you; he's riding the mare now over the green head, and the grey pony behind him.

MAURYA (*starts so that her shawl falls back from her head and shows her white tossed hair. With a frightened voice*):   The grey pony behind him.

CATHLEEN (*coming to the fire*):   What is it ails you at all?

MAURYA (*speaking very slowly*):   I've seen the fearfulest thing any person has seen, since the day Bride Dara seen the dead man with the child in his arms.

CATHLEEN and NORA: Uah. (*They crouch down in front of the old woman at the fire.*)

NORA: Tell us what it is you seen.

MAURYA: I went down to the spring well, and I stood there saying a prayer to myself. Then Bartley came along, and he riding on the red mare with the grey pony behind him. (*She puts up her hands, as if to hide something from her eyes.*) The Son of God spare us, Nora!

CATHLEEN: What is it you seen?

MAURYA: I seen Michael himself.

CATHLEEN (*speaking softly*):   You did not, mother; it wasn't Michael you seen, for his body is after being found in the far north, and he's got a clean burial by the grace of God.

MAURYA (*a little defiantly*):   I'm after seeing him this day, and he riding and galloping. Bartley came first on the red mare, and I tried to say "God speed you," but something choked the words in my throat. He went by quickly; and "the blessing of God on you," says he, and I could say nothing. I looked up then, and I crying, at the grey pony, and there was Michael upon it—with fine clothes on him, and new shoes on his feet.

CATHLEEN (*begins to keen*):   It's destroyed we are from this day. It's destroyed, surely.

NORA: Didn't the young priest say the Almighty God wouldn't leave her destitute with no son living?

MAURYA (*in a low voice, but clearly*):   It's little the like of him knows of the sea. . . . Bartley will be lost now, and let you call in Eamon and make me a good coffin out of the white boards, for I won't live after them. I've had a husband, and a husband's father, and six sons in this house—six fine men, though it was a hard birth I had with every one of them and they coming into the world—and some of them were found and some of them were not found, but they're gone now the lot of them. . . . There were Stephen, and Shawn, were lost in the great wind, and found after in the Bay of Gregory of the Golden Mouth, and carried up the two of them on one plank, and in by that door. (*She pauses for a moment; the girls start as if they heard something through the door that is half open behind them.*)

NORA (*in a whisper*):   Did you hear that, Cathleen? Did you hear a noise in the north-east?

CATHLEEN (*in a whisper*):   There's someone after crying out by the seashore.

MAURYA (*continues without hearing anything*):   There was Sheamus and his father, and his own father again, were lost in a dark night, and not a stick or sign was seen of them when the sun went up. There was Patch after was drowned out of a curragh that turned over. I was sitting here with Bartley, and he a baby lying on my two knees, and I seen two women, and three women, and four women coming in, and they crossing themselves and not saying a word. I looked out then, and there were men coming after them, and they holding a thing in the half of a red sail, and water dripping out of it—it was a dry day, Nora—and leaving a track to the door. (*She pauses again with her hand streteched out towards the door. It opens softly and old women begin to come in, crossing themselves on the threshold, and kneeling down in front of the stage with red petticoats over their heads.*)

(*Half in a dream, to* CATHLEEN):   Is it Patch, or Michael, or what is it at all?

CATHLEEN: Michael is after being found in the far north, and when he is found there how could he be here in this place?

MAURYA: There does be a power of young men floating round in the sea, and what way would they know if it was Michael they had, or another man like him, for when a man is nine days in the sea, and the wind blowing, it's hard set his own mother would be to say what man was it.

CATHLEEN: It's Michael, God spare him, for they're after sending us a bit of his clothes from the far north. (*She reaches out and hands* MAURYA *the clothes that belonged to* MICHAEL. MAURYA *stands up slowly and takes them in her hands.* NORA *looks out.*)

NORA: They're carrying a thing among them and there's water dripping out of it and leaving a track by the big stones.

CATHLEEN (*in a whisper to the women who have come in*):   Is it Bartley it is?

ONE OF THE WOMEN: It is, surely, God rest his soul.

(*Two younger women come in and pull out the table. Then men carry in the body of* BARTLEY, *laid on a plank, with a bit of a sail over it, and lay it on the table.*)

CATHLEEN (*to the women, as they are doing so*):   What way was he drowned?

ONE OF THE WOMEN: The grey pony knocked him over into the sea, and he was washed out where there is a great surf on the white rocks.

(MAURYA *has gone over and knelt down at the head of the table. The women are keening softly and swaying themselves with a slow movement.* CATHLEEN *and* NORA *kneel at the other end of the table. The men kneel near the door.)*

MAURYA *(raising her head and speaking as if she did not see the people around her):*   They're all gone now, and there isn't anything more the sea can do to me. . . . I'll have no call now to be up crying and praying when the wind breaks from the south, and you can hear the surf is in the east, and the surf is in the west, making a great stir with the two noises, and they hitting one on the other. I'll have no call now to be going down and getting Holy Water in the dark nights after Samhain, and I won't care what way the sea is when the other women will be keening. *(To* NORA*)* Give me the Holy Water, Nora; there's a small sup still on the dresser.

(NORA *gives it to her.)*

(Drops MICHAEL'S *clothes across* BARTLEY'S *feet, and sprinkles the Holy Water over him.)*   It isn't that I haven't prayed for you, Bartley, to the Almighty God. It isn't that I haven't said prayers in the dark night till you wouldn't know what I'd be saying; but it's a great rest I'll have now, and it's time, surely. It's a great rest I'll have now, and great sleeping in the long nights after Samhain, if it's only a bit of wet flour we do have to eat, and maybe a fish that would be stinking. *(She kneels down again, crossing herself, and saying prayers under her breath.)*

CATHLEEN *(to an old man):*   Maybe yourself and Eamon would make a coffin when the sun rises. We have fine white boards herself bought, God help her, thinking Michael would be found, and I have a new cake you can eat while you'll be working.

THE OLD MAN *(looking at the boards):*   Are there nails with them?

CATHLEEN: There are not, Colum; we didn't think of the nails.

ANOTHER MAN: It's a great wonder she wouldn't think of the nails, and all the coffins she's seen made already.

CATHLEEN: It's getting old she is, and broken.

(MAURYA *stands up again very slowly and spreads out the pieces of* MICHAEL's *clothes beside the body, sprinkling them with the last of the Holy Water.)*

NORA *(in a whisper to* CATHLEEN*):*   She's quiet now and easy; but the day Michael was drowned you could hear her crying out from this to the spring well. It's fonder she was of Michael, and would any one have thought that?

CATHLEEN *(slowly and clearly):*   An old woman will be soon tired with anything she will do, and isn't it nine days herself is after crying and keening, and making great sorrow in the house?

MAURYA *(puts the empty cup mouth downwards on the table, and lays her hands together on* BARTLEY's *feet):*   They're all together this time, and the end is come. May the Almighty God have mercy on Bartley's soul, and on Michael's soul, and on the souls of Sheamus and Patch, and Stephen and Shawn *(Bending her head.);* and may He have mercy on my soul, Nora, and on the soul of every one is left living in the world. *(She pauses, and the keen rises a little more loudly from the women, then sinks away.)*

(Continuing.)   Michael has a clean burial in the far north, by the grace of the Almighty God. Bartley will have a fine coffin out of the white boards, and

a deep grave surely. What more can we want than that? No man at all can be living for ever, and we must be satisfied. *(She kneels down again and the curtain falls slowly.)*

Which

JAMES THURBER

The relative pronoun "which" can cause more trouble than any other word, if recklessly used. Foolhardy persons sometimes get lost in which-clauses and are never heard of again. My distinguished contemporary, Fowler, cites several tragic cases, of which the following is one: "It was rumoured that Beaconsfield intended opening the Conference with a speech in French, his pronunciation of which language leaving everything to be desired . . ." That's as much as Mr. Fowler quotes because, at his age, he was afraid to go any farther. The young man who originally got into that sentence was never found. His fate, however, was not as terrible as that of another adventurer who became involved in a remarkable whichmire. Fowler has followed his devious course as far as he safely could on foot: "Surely what applies to games should also apply to racing, the leaders of which being the very people from whom an example might well be looked for . . ." Not even Henry James could have successfully emerged from a sentence with "which," "whom," and "being" in it. The safest way to avoid such things is to follow in the path of the American author, Ernest Hemingway. In his youth he was trapped in a which-clause one time and barely escaped with his mind. He was going along on solid ground until he got into this: "It was the one thing of which, being very much afraid—for whom has not been warned to fear such things—he . . ." Being a young and powerfully built man, Hemingway was able to fight his way back to where he had started, and begin again. This time he skirted the treacherous morass in this way: "He was afraid of one thing. This was the one thing. He had been warned to fear such things. Everybody has been warned to fear such things." Today Hemingway is alive and well, and many happy writers are following along the trail he blazed.

What most people don't realize is that one "which" leads to another. Trying to cross a paragraph by leaping from "which" to "which" is like Eliza crossing the ice. The danger is in missing a "which" and falling in. A case in point is this: "He went up to a pew which was in the gallery, which brought him under a colored window which he loved and always quieted his spirit." The writer, worn out, missed the last "which"—the one that should come just before "always" in that sentence. But supposing he had got it in! We would have: "He went up to a pew which was in the gallery, which brought him under a colored window which he loved and which always quieted his spirit." Your inveterate whicher in this way gives the effect of tweeting like a bird or walking with a crutch, and is not welcome in the best company.

It is well to remember that one "which" leads to two and that two "whiches" multiply like rabbits. You should never start out with the idea that you can get by with one "which." Suddenly they are all around you. Take a sentence like this: "It imposes a problem which we either solve, or perish." On a hot night, or after a hard day's work, a man often lets himself get by with a monstrosity like that, but suppose he dictates that sentence bright and early in the morning. It comes to him typed out by his stenographer and he instantly senses that something is the matter with it. He tries to reconstruct the sentence, still clinging to the "which," and gets something like this: "It imposes a problem which we either solve, or which, failing to solve, we must perish on account of." He goes to the water-cooler, gets a drink, sharpens his pencil, and grimly tries again. "It imposes a problem which we either solve or which we don't solve and . . ." He begins once more: "It imposes a problem which we either solve, or which we do not solve, and from which . . ." The more times he does it the more "whiches" he gets. The way out is simple: "We must either solve this problem, or perish." Never monkey with "which." Nothing except getting tangled up in a typewriter ribbon is worse.

Saving the Sentence
GERTRUDE STEIN

Think that a sentence has been made.

I am very miserable about sentences. I can cry about sentences but not about hair cloth.

Now this is one way of relenting.

Think of a sentence. A whole sentence. Who is kind.
We have known one who is kind. That is a very good sentence.

A separate cushion is not as comfortable.

This is a sentence that comes in the midst not in the midst of other things but in the midst of the same thing.

They have that as flourishes.

That is a sentence that comes by obedience to intermittence.

That is the cruelest thing I ever heard is the favorite phrase of Gilbert.
Saving the sentence volume one.
                    Or three.

The differences between a short story and a paragraph. There is none.

They come and go. It is the cruelest thing I ever heard is the favorite phrase of Gilbert. And he is right. He has heard many cruel things and it is the cruelest thing that he has heard.

It is very hard to save the sentence.

The Motive for Metaphor
WALLACE STEVENS

You like it under the trees in autumn,
Because everything is half dead.
The wind moves like a cripple among the leaves
And repeats words without meaning.

In the same way, you were happy in spring,
With the half colors of quarter-things,

The slightly brighter sky, the melting clouds,
The single bird, the obscure moon—

The obscure moon lighting an obscure world
Of things that would never be quite expressed,
Where you yourself were never quite yourself
And did not want nor have to be,

Desiring the exhilarations of changes:
The motive for metaphor, shrinking from
The weight of primary noon,
The A B C of being,

The ruddy temper, the hammer
Of red and blue, the hard sound—
Steel against intimation—the sharp flash,
The vital, arrogant, fatal, dominant X.

Dog

LAWRENCE FERLINGHETTI

The dog trots freely in the street
and sees reality
and the things he sees
are bigger than himself
and the things he sees
are his reality
Drunks in doorways
Moons on trees
The dog trots freely thru the street
and the things he sees
are smaller than himself
Fish on newsprint
Ants in holes
Chickens in Chinatown windows
their heads a block away
The dog trots freely in the street
and the things he smells
smell something like himself
The dog trots freely in the street
past puddles and babies
cats and cigars
poolrooms and policemen
He doesn't hate cops
He merely has no use for them
and he goes past them
and past the dead cows hung up whole
in front of the San Francisco Meat Market

He would rather eat a tender cow
than a tough policeman
though either might do
And he goes past the Romeo Ravioli Factory
and past Coit's Tower
and past Congressman Doyle
He's afraid of Coit's Tower
but he's not afraid of Congressman Doyle
although what he hears is very discouraging
very depressing
very absurd
to a sad young dog like himself
to a serious dog like himself
But he has his own free world to live in
His own fleas to eat
He will not be muzzled
Congressman Doyle is just another
fire hydrant
to him
The dog trots freely in the street
and has his own dog's life to live
and to think about
and to reflect upon
touching and tasting and testing everything
investigating everything
without benefit of perjury
a real realist
with a real tale to tell
and a real tail to tell it with
a real live
           barking
                democratic dog
engaged in real
                free enterprise
with something to say
                about ontology
something to say
              about reality
                    and how to see it
                    and how to hear it
with his head cocked sideways
                at streetcorners
as if he is just about to have
              his picture taken
                    for Victor Records
        listening for
            His Master's Voice

and looking
        like a living questionmark
                    into the
                great gramaphone
            of puzzling existence
with its wondrous hollow horn
        which always seems
just about to spout forth
                    some Victorious answer
                        to everything

Myth

MURIEL RUKEYSER

Long afterward, Oedipus, old and blinded, walked the roads. He smelled a familiar smell.   It was the Sphinx.   Oedipus said, "I want to ask one question.   Why didn't I recognize my mother?"   "You gave the wrong answer," said the Sphinx.   "But that was what made everything possible," said Oedipus.   "No," she said. "When I asked, What walks on four legs in the morning, two at noon, and three in the evening, you answered, Man. You didn't say anything about woman."   "When you say Man," said Oedipus, "you include women too. Everyone knows that."   She said, "That's what you think."

Outrage

LUCILLE IVERSON

It is not so much
Cooking
But being cooked
That gets me;
When the chicken goes
In the oven
I'll be caught there too—
My head in the
Oven along with the
Gizzards and lungs—
One wing caught
With mine—
Heart, liver, entrails
Embroiled,
Boiled to a pink
Tasty succulence and then
Devoured.

Impaled on your
Incubi   I
Will not be nor
Stay to argue why
Not.   I
Who abandoned all
Who professed to love me—
Mother, father, brothers, aunts
    uncles, cousins, husband, child—
Know what love means:
Love
Is that which detains;
That magic of detention which you
Need from me,
But which tears a
Woman.

The power of Life is the
Integration of Life is the
Integration of Energy and
If you disintegrate,   I
Will not help you;
If you spatter
Red and bitter and
Rotten on the sidewalk,   I
Will not pick you up
Nor suckle you nor
Bathe your wounds nor
Mend your torn socks;—   I
A year ago would have said:
"Nestle your little broken head
On your mammy's breast,
You poor, broken
Child of the Universe;"
But now I say
Scram;   —I
May glance your way to
Laugh, and I
May toss you a penny;
For you, who have
Condemned me as
Witch, as

Mother,   —I
Have no more
Any pity;
For you who have
Despised me as
Succubi, as
Ball-breaker   —I
Tell you, you puke in
Your own folly.

My Passion is
Mine, nor am I
Vampire, nor
Banshee, nor
Screamer, nor
Waiting;   —I
Have turned away, and   I
Face a distance I
Have not run;   —I
Raise my fist beside the
Door of My Dreams and I
Take Time,
My Time,
All of it
In my Hands.

Nero's Term

CONSTANTINE P. CAVAFY
Translated by Rae Dalven

Nero was not alarmed when he heard
the prophecy of the Delphic Oracle.
"Let him fear the seventy-three years."
There was still ample time to enjoy himself.
He is thirty years old. The term
the god allots to him is quite sufficient
for him to prepare for perils to come.

Now he will return to Rome slightly fatigued,
but delightfully fatigued from this journey,
which consisted entirely of days of pleasure
at the theaters, the gardens, the athletic fields . . .
evenings spent in the cities of Greece . . .
Ah the voluptuous delight of nude bodies, above all . . .

These things Nero thought. And in Spain Galba
secretly assembles and drills his army,
the old man of seventy-three.

War
JOSEPH LANGLAND

When my young brother was killed
By a mute and dusty shell in the thorny brush
Crowning the boulders of the Villa Verdo Trail
On the island of Luzon,

I laid my whole dry body down,
Dropping my face like a stone in a green park
On the east banks of the Rhine;

On an airstrip skirting the Seine
His sergeant brother sat like a stick in his barracks
While cracks of fading sunlight
Caged the dusty air;

In the rocky rolling hills west of the Mississippi
His father and mother sat in a simple Norwegian parlor
With a photograph smiling between them on the table
And their hands fallen into their laps
Like sticks and dust;

And still other brothers and sisters,
Linking their arms together,
Walked down the dusty road where once he ran
And into the deep green valley

To sit on the stony banks of the stream he loved
And let the murmuring waters
Wash over their blood-hot feet with a springing crown of tears.

This Property Is Condemned
TENNESSEE WILLIAMS

CHARACTERS

WILLIE, *a young girl*

TOM, *a boy.*

SCENE: *A railroad embankment on the outskirts of a small Mississippi town on one of those milky white winter mornings peculiar to that part of the country. The air is moist and chill. Behind the low embankment of the tracks is a large yellow frame house which has a look of tragic vacancy. Some of the upper windows are boarded, a portion of the room has fallen away. The land is utterly flat. In the left background is a billboard that says "GIN WITH JAKE" and there are some telephones poles and a few bare winter trees. The sky is a great milky whiteness: crows occasionally make a sound of roughly torn cloth.*

The girl WILLIE *is advancing precariously along the railroad track, balancing herself with both arms outstretched, one clutching a banana, the other an extraordinarily dilapidated doll with a frowsy blond wig.*

She is a remarkable apparition—thin as a beanpole and dressed in outrageous cast-off finery. She wears a long blue velvet party dress with a filthy cream lace collar and sparkling rhinestone beads. On her feet are battered silver kid slippers with large ornamental buckles. Her wrists and her fingers are resplendent with dimestore jewelry. She has applied rouge to her childish face in artless crimson daubs and her lips are made up in a preposterous Cupid's bow. She is about thirteen and there is something ineluctably childlike and innocent in her appearance despite the makeup. She laughs frequently and wildly and with a sort of precocious, tragic abandon.

The boy TOM, *slightly older, watches her from below the embankment. He wears corduroy pants, blue shirt and a sweater and carries a kite of red tissue paper with a gaudily ribboned tail.*

TOM: Hello. Who are you?

WILLIE: Don't talk to me till I fall off. (*She proceeds dizzily.* TOM *watches with mute fascination. Her gyrations grow wider and wider. She speaks breathlessly*) Take my—crazy doll—will you?

TOM: (*scrambling up the bank*) Yeh.

WILLIE: I don't wanta—break her when—I fall! I don't think I can—stay on much—longer—do you?

TOM: Naw.

WILLIE: I'm practically—off—right now! (TOM *offers to assist her*) No, don't touch me. It's no fair helping. You've got to do it—all—by yourself! God, I'm wobbling! I don't know what's made me so nervous! You see that water-tank way back yonder?

TOM: Yeah?

WILLIE: That's where I—started—from! This is the furthest—I ever gone—without once—falling off. I mean it will be—if I can manage to stick on—to the next—telephone—pole! Oh! Here I go! (*She becomes completely unbalanced and rolls down the bank*)

TOM: (*standing above her now*) Hurtcha self?

WILLIE: Skinned my knee a little. Glad I didn't put my silk stockings on.

TOM: (*coming down the bank*) Spit on it. That takes the sting away.

WILLIE: Okay.

TOM: That's animal's medicine, you know. They always lick their wounds.

WILLIE: I know. The principal damage was done to my bracelet, I guess. I knocked out one of the diamonds. Where did it go?

TOM: You never could find it in all them cinders.

WILLIE: I don't know. It had a lot of shine.

TOM: It wasn't a genuine diamond.

WILLIE: How do you know?

TOM: I just imagine it wasn't. Because if it was you wouldn't be walking along a railroad track with a banged-up doll and a piece of a rotten banana.

WILLIE: Oh, I wouldn't be so sure. I might be peculiar or something. You never can tell. What's your name?

TOM: Tom.

WILLIE: Mine's Willie. We've both got boy's names.

TOM: How did that happen?

WILLIE: I was expected to be a boy but I wasn't. They had one girl already. Alva. She was my sister. Why ain't you at school?

TOM: I thought it was going to be windy so I could fly my kite.

WILLIE: What made you think that?

TOM: Because the sky was so white.

WILLIE: Is that a sign?

TOM: Yeah.

WILLIE: I know. It looks like everything had been swept off with a broom. Don't it?

TOM: Yeah.

WILLIE: It's perfectly white. It's white as a clean piece of paper.

TOM: Uh-huh.

WILLIE: But there isn't a wind.

TOM: Naw.

WILLIE: It's up too high for us to feel it. It's way, way up in the attic sweeping the dust off the furniture up there!

TOM: Uh-huh. Why ain't you at school?

WILLIE: I quituated. Two years ago this winter.

TOM: What grade was you in?

WILLIE: Five A.

TOM: Miss Preston.

WILLIE: Yep. She used to think my hands was dirty until I explained that it was cinders from falling off the railroad tracks so much.

TOM: She's pretty strict.

WILLIE: Oh, no, she's just disappointed because she didn't get married. Probably never had an opportunity, poor thing. So she has to teach Five A for the rest of her natural life. They started teaching algebra an' I didn't give a goddam what X stood for so I quit.

TOM: You'll never get an education walking the railroad tracks.

WILLIE: You won't get one flying a red kite neither. Besides . . .

TOM: What?

WILLIE: What a girl needs to get along is social training. I learned all of that from my sister Alva. She had a wonderful popularity with the railroad men.

TOM: Train engineers?

WILLIE: Engineers, firemen, conductors. Even the freight sup'rintendent. We run a boarding-house for railroad men. She was I guess you might say The Main Attraction. Beautiful? Jesus, she looked like a movie star!

TOM: Your sister?

WILLIE: Yeah. One of 'em used to bring her regular after each run big heart-shaped red-silk box of assorted chocolates and no hard candies. Marvelous?

TOM: Yeah. (*The cawing of crows sounds through the chilly air*)

WILLIE: You know where Alva is now?

TOM: Memphis?

WILLIE: Naw.

TOM: New Awleuns?

WILLIE: Naw.

TOM: St. Louis?

WILLIE: You'll never guess.

TOM: Where is she then? (WILLIE *does not answer at once*)

WILLIE: (*very solemnly*) She's in the bone-orchard.

TOM: What?

WILLIE: (*violently*) Bone-orchard, cemetery, graveyard! Don't you understand English?

TOM: Sure. That's pretty tough.

WILLIE: You don't know the half of it, buddy. We used to have some high old times in that big yellow house.

TOM: I bet you did.

WILLIE: Musical instruments going all of the time.

TOM: Instruments? What kind?

WILLIE: Piano, victrola, Hawaiian steel guitar. Everyone played on something. But now it's—awful quiet. You don't hear a sound from there, do you?

TOM: Naw. Is it empty?

WILLIE: Except for me. They got a big sign stuck up.

TOM: What does it say?

WILLIE: (*loudly but with a slight catch*) "THIS PROPERTY IS CONDEMNED!"

TOM: You ain't still living there?

WILLIE: Uh-huh.

TOM: What happened? Where did everyone go?

WILLIE: Mama run off with a brakeman on the C. & E.I. After that everything went to pieces. (*A train whistles far off*) You hear that whistle? That's the Cannonball Express. The fastest thing on wheels between St. Louis, New Awleuns an' Memphis. My old man got to drinking.

TOM: Where is he now?

WILLIE: Disappeared. I guess I ought to refer his case to the Bureau of Missing Persons. The same as he done with Mama when she disappeared. Then there was me and Alva. Till Alva's lungs got affected. Did you see Greta Garbo in *Camille*? It played at the Delta Brilliant one time las' spring. She had the same what Alva died of. Lung affection.

TOM: Yeah?

WILLIE: Only it was—very beautiful the way she had it. You know. Violins playing. And loads and loads of white flowers. All of her lovers come back in a beautiful scene!

TOM: Yeah?

WILLIE: But Alva's all disappeared.

TOM: Yeah?

WILLIE: Like rats from a sinking ship! That's how she used to describe it. Oh, it—wasn't like death in the movies.

TOM: Naw?

WILLIE: She says, "Where is Albert? Where's Clemence?" None of them was around. I used to lie to her, I says, "They send their regards. They're coming to see you tomorrow." "Where's Mr. Johnson?" she asked me. He was the freight sup'rintendent, the most important character we ever had in our rooming house. "He's been transferred to Grenada," I told her. "But wishes to be remembered." She known I was lying.

TOM: Yeah?

WILLIE: "This here is the pay-off!" she says. "They all run out on me like rats from a sinking ship!" Except Sidney.

TOM: Who was Sidney?

WILLIE: The one that used to give her the great big enormous red-silk box of American Beauty choc'lates.

TOM: Oh.

WILLIE: He remained faithful to her.

TOM: That's good.

WILLIE: But she never did care for Sidney. She said his teeth was decayed so he didn't smell good.

TOM: Aw!

WILLIE: It wasn't like death in the movies. When somebody dies in the movies they play violins.

TOM: But they didn't for Alva.

WILLIE: Naw. Not even a goddam victrola. They said it didn't agree with the hospital regulations. Always singing around the house.

TOM: Who? Alva?

WILLIE: Throwing enormous parties. This was her favorite number. (*She closes her eyes and stretches out her arms in the simulated rapture of the professional blues singer. Her voice is extraordinarily high and pure with a precocious emotional timbre*)

> You're the only star
> In my blue hea-ven
> and you're shining just
> For me!

This is her clothes I got on. Inherited from her. Everything is mine. Except her solid gold beads.

TOM: What happened to them?

WILLIE: Them? She never took 'em off.

TOM: Oh!

WILLIE: I've also inherited all of my sister's beaux. Albert and Clemence and even the freight sup'rintendent.

TOM: Yeah?

WILLIE: They all disappeared. Afraid that they might get stuck for expenses I guess. But now they turn up again, all of 'em, like a bunch of bad pennies. They take me out places at night. I've got to be popular now. To parties an' dances an' all of the railroad affairs. Lookit here!

TOM: What?

WILLIE: I can do bumps! (*She stands in front of him and shoves her stomach toward him in a series of spasmodic jerks*)

TOM: Frank Waters said that . . .

WILLIE: What?

TOM: You know.

WILLIE: Know what?

TOM: You took him inside and danced for him with your clothes off.

WILLIE: Oh. Crazy Doll's hair needs washing. I'm scared to wash it though 'cause her head might come unglued where she had that compound fracture of the skull. I think that most of her brains spilled out. She's been acting silly ever since. Saying an' doing the most outrageous things.

TOM: Why don't you do that for me?

WILLIE: What? Put glue on your compound fracture?

TOM: Naw. What you did for Frank Waters.

WILLIE: Because I was lonesome then an' I'm not lonesome now. You can tell Frank Waters that. Tell him that I've inherited all of my sister's beaux. I go out steady with men in responsible jobs. The sky sure is white. Ain't it? White as a clean piece of paper. In Five A we used to draw pictures. Miss Preston would give us a piece of white foolscap an' tell us to draw what we pleased.

TOM: What did you draw?

WILLIE: I remember I drawn her a picture one time of my old man conked with a bottle. She thought it was good, Miss Preston she said, "Look here. Here's a picture of Charlie Chaplin with his hat on the side of his head!" I said, "Aw, naw, that's not Charlie Chaplin, that's my father, an' that's not his hat, it's a bottle

TOM: What did she say?

WILLIE: Oh, well. You can't make a school-teacher laugh.

You're the only star
In my blue hea-VEN . . .

The principal used to say there must've been something wrong with my home atmosphere because of the fact that we took in men an' some of 'em slept with my sister.

TOM: Did they?

WILLIE: She was The Main Attraction. The house is sure empty now.

TOM: You ain't still living there, are you?

WILLIE: Sure.

TOM: By yourself?

WILLIE: Uh-huh. I'm not supposed to be but I am. The property is condemned but there's nothing wrong with it. Some county investigator
come snooping around yesterday. I recognized her by the shape of her
hat. It wasn't exactly what I would call stylish-looking.

TOM: Naw?

WILLIE: It looked like something she took off the lid of the stove. Alva knew
lots about style. She had ambitions to be a designer for big wholesale
firms in Chicago. She used to submit her pictures. It never worked out.

> You're the only star
> In my blue hea-ven . . .

TOM: What did you do? About the investigators?

WILLIE: Laid low upstairs. Pretended like no one was home.

TOM: Well, how do you manage to keep on eating?

WILLIE: Oh, I don't know. You keep a sharp look-out you see things lying
around. This banana, perfectly good, for instance. Thrown in a garbage
pail in back of the Blue Bird Café. (*She finishes the banana and tosses away
the peel*)

TOM: (*grinning*) Yeh. Miss Preston for instance.

WILLIE: Naw, not her. She gives you a white piece of paper, says "Draw what
you please!" One time I drawn her a picture of—Oh, but I told you that,
huh? Will you give Frank Waters a message?

TOM: What?

WILLIE: Tell him the freight sup'rintendent has bought me a pair of kid slippers. Patent. The same as the old ones of Alva's. I'm going to dances with
them at Moon Lake Casino. All night I'll be dancing an' come home
drunk in the morning! We'll have serenades with all kinds of musical instruments. Trumpets an' trombones. An' Hawaiian steel guitars. Yeh!
Yeh! (*She rises excitedly*) The sky will be white like this.

TOM: (*impressed*) Will it?

WILLIE: Uh-huh (*She smiles vaguely and turns slowly toward him*) White—as a
clean—piece of paper . . .(*then excitedly*) I'll draw—pictures on it!

TOM: Will you?

WILLIE: Sure!

TOM: Pictures of what?

WILLIE: Me dancing! With the freight sup'rintendent! In a pair of patent kid
shoes! Yeh! Yeh! With French heels on them as high as telegraph poles!
An' they'll play my favorite music!

TOM: Your favorite?

WILLIE: Yeh. The same as Alva's (*breathlessly, passionately*)

> You're the only STAR—
> In my blue HEA—VEN . . .

I'll—

TOM: What?

WILLIE: I'll—wear a corsage!

TOM: What's that?

WILLIE: Flowers to pin on your dress at a formal affair! Rosebuds! Violets! And lilies-of-the-valley! When you come home it's withered but you stick 'em in a bowl of water to freshen 'em up.

TOM: Uh-huh.

WILLIE: That's what Alva done. (*She pauses, and in the silence the train whistles*) The Cannonball Express . . .

TOM: You think a lot about Alva. Don't you?

WILLIE: Oh, not so much. Now an' then. It wasn't like death in the movies. Her beaux disappeared. An' they didn't have violins playing. I'm going back now.

TOM: Where to, Willie?

WILLIE: The water-tank.

TOM: Yeah?

WILLIE: An' start all over again. Maybe I'll break some kind of continuous record. Alva did once. At a dance marathon in Mobile. Across the state line. Alabama. You can tell Frank Waters everything that I told you. I don't have time for inexperienced people. I'm going out now with popular railroad men, men with good salaries, too. Don't you believe me?

TOM: No. I think you're drawing an awful lot on your imagination.

WILLIE: Well, if I wanted to I could prove it. But you wouldn't be worth convincing. (*She smooths out Crazy Doll's hair*) I'm going to live for a long, long, time like my sister. An' when my lungs get affected I'm going to die like she did—maybe not like in the movies, with violins playing—but with my pearl earrings on an' my solid gold beads from Memphis . . .

TOM: Yes?

WILLIE: (*examining Crazy Doll very critically*) An' then I guess—

TOM: What?

WILLIE: (*gaily but with a slight catch*) Somebody else will inherit all of my beaux! The sky sure is white.

TOM: It sure is.

WILLIE: White as a clean piece of paper. I'm going back now.

TOM: So long.

WILLIE: Yeh. So long. (*She starts back along the railroad track, weaving grotesquely to keep her balance. She disappears.* TOM *wets his finger and holds it up to test the wind.* WILLIE *is heard singing from a distance*)

> You're the only star
> In my blue heaven—

(*There is a brief pause. The stage begins to darken*)

> An' you're shining just—
> For me!

CURTAIN

Things That Go Away & Come Back Again
ANNE WALDMAN

Thoughts

Airplanes

Boats

Trains

People

Dreams

animals

songs

Husbands

Boomerangs

lightning

the sun, the moon, the stars

bad weather

good weather

the seasons

Soldiers

good luck

health

depression

joy

laundry

Lady Tactics
ANNE WALDMAN

she
    not to be confused with she, a dog
          she, not to be confused with she, Liberty
      she a waif
        she a wastrel
          she, a little birdie
she, not to be confused with pliable
        she in plethora
          she in blue
she with the pliers, or behind the plough
    she
      not to be confused with a jonquil
she in the imperative
        she the liveliest of creatures
      she, not to be confused with Pandora or plaintiff
        or getting seasick or prim
she, a prima donna
        she a secret she a dreamer
she in full force, she rushing home
    she at a desk or in a book
      she, not to be confused with she, a secretary
she a goddess
      she, not to be confused with the Slovak
she, not a slug
      she in season, she in health, she recumbent
     she recuperating
      she, not to be confused with mutton
      she a muse
she on a mission, not languishing
     she in the landscape, she in silk
    she, not to be confused with juniper
      with jodhpurs
     she with idiosyncrasics
  she in labor
      she, not to be confused with the conifer
she in consanguinity
     she at long last
she, wind, sea, Pompeii, deliberation, home
   she in middle C
     she the sharpest
she, obliged
    she in distinguished sentiments
      not to be confused with sentimental
     or sly

Because Things Get Sad, Father
RUSSELL EDSON

When a family has grown tired of its place it goes into a wood; their house is becoming smaller.

Yes, father, says mother, our things are getting smaller.

No no, screams father, I do not want my chair to get smaller. Why must things get smaller when you leave them?

Because they get sad, father, said mother.

I must go home and tell the house a joke so it won't be sad, screams father.

No no, father, we have grown tired of our place and have gone some other place, screamed mother.

But the house is now very small and all our things are being squeezed to death by sadness, moaned father.

Well I say, said mother, it's a good thing we left before we were crushed.

I know, said father, but where shall we go?

Someplace . . . But we shall always be someplace, won't we, father?

Yes yes yes; you drive me crazy with your questions. Of course we shall be someplace. Homeless because our house is too small. Burdened with middle-aged spouses. Someplace, indeed. In the woods waiting for the green leaves to turn red, or snow to fill the leafless branches. Waiting waiting waiting for the green leaves to return. House too small. World too big. The first choice killed, and now beset in the second instance with too many choices.

Then, father, let us just go home, said mother.

And so they returned home, growing smaller all the while until reaching their house they had grown just small enough to fit into their tiny house.

It is my hope that those who blame
these tentatives may find some other
reading and be supremely matched
by pieces worthy of them. I offer
these I've found—no claims except
their being mine. A glance may serve—do these
belong inside your life? My life,
Reader, encountered these trancelike
events that I've turned into things to tell.
If you like them, fine. If not, farewell.
                                    William Stafford
                    A Tentative Welcome to Readers

FOCUS FOR CHAPTER V

After you study the text and anthology in this chapter, we hope you will be able to

1. Describe some of the characteristics of a good listener of literature read in public.
2. Understand how curiosity and respect play a part in an audience for new literary works.
3. Write an integrated essay on a literary text you plan to perform.
4. Discuss "passionate attention" as a descriptor relevant to performed literature.

V

Afterword

You must have realized by now that we believe literature matters and that performing it is a good way to study it. We have an additional belief that remains unshakable despite the absence of empirical data for support: Performing literature improves one's ability to read new texts; it fosters what we call "literary competence," which is analogous to what linguists term the competence of the native speaker of a language (that is, the ability to generate an infinite number of sentences and to recognize as correct or incorrect any new sentence encountered). Literary competence is, we admit, different, in that we cannot postulate a "native" reader. But we can all acknowledge that some of us "read" texts better than others do and seem better able to find all of what is there, and only what is there. Acts of performance not only help you to realize more fully whatever text you are performing, but also foster competence in dealing with other texts encountered.

Obviously, performing is a slow process. If you must cover a large body of writing, you could not hope to perform it all. But the competence developed in performing some of it will make you a fuller, more perceptive consumer of the rest. We have no instrument to measure this kind of competence. It is possible to measure knowledge *about* texts and test recall of *information in* texts, but we have as yet no way to measure the full perception and appreciation of a text. Still, our perception of our own experience and that of others does not brook dispute. Performing literature fosters literary competence, which in turn enables us to experience and appreciate literary texts.

We encounter literary texts in many forms. Though the troubadors and bards of earlier years have faded from our tech-

nological world, we still encounter some poems orally—occasionally on television, more often on radio, and increasingly at public performances of literature. The competence required for this kind of transaction with the text is not identical with that of silent reading or of our own oral performances. Even in class you will have already studied and discussed most of the texts other people perform. So how can we become more sophisticated consumers of oral texts that are new to us? Denise Levertov reports on an occasion when that question arose after she, Muriel Rukeyser, and Anthony Hecht had all been reading their poetry at Columbia University:

> A man in, I judge, his late twenties—perhaps older—spoke up. "Maybe this question I'm going to ask will strike you as foolish . . . I'm an engineering student" (idiot laughter from unidentified sources) "but I *am* eager to read poetry . . . . And the question I want to ask is, to get the most out of one's reading, what should one bring to a poem?" . . . Muriel Rukeyser . . . lifted her head and spoke directly to the questioner: "It's *not* a foolish question. It's a question everyone has to ask, all of us. And I think what must be brought to a poem is what must be brought to anything you care about, to anything in life that really matters: ALL of yourself."[1]

Some poems can be grasped on one hearing, but most are more elusive. And despite our best efforts at listening, we are likely to get only some of the poem, probably the intellectual content, because that kind of listening is what we do most often. The poems in which ideas or images are not the most important parts are

[1]Denise Levertov, "An Approach to Public Poetry Listenings," *Virginia Quarterly Review*, XVI (Summer 1965), 424–25.

those we are likely to miss when we hear them. Levertov remarks:

> The poetry I have in mind is rather that in which the sounds—the vowels and consonants, the tone patterns, the currents of rhythm, not the paraphrasable ideas nor yet the visual images (though certainly these are present)—are the chief carriers of content. It is this poetry which is most inaccessible to readers trained to bring, not the whole of themselves, but their wits, to a reading.[2]

One way to get more out of listening is, of course, to practice, and the classroom may be an appropriate place. (Appendix B has a list of sources.) Levertov recommends that in literature class we spend time listening to poets' readings.

> This would by no means substitute for eye-reading; it would complement it. And a generation which at school and college had heard more poetry would tend to make their eye-reading less silent—that is, they would form the good habit of reading not much faster than the voice speaks, because what they were reading with the eye, their inner voice would be sounding out to the alert inner ear.[3]

Any encounter with something new may be exciting, but it may also be unsettling. The familiar is comfortable; we need less adaptation and therefore less energy to accommodate it. Part of our adjustment to life, though, is cultivating ways to deal with the new, and our attitudes in so doing are important. Blind acceptance is hardly better than blind rejection. When we encounter new literary texts—performed or in print—we need an appropriate attitude. Theodore Roethke offers a suggestion:

> A student of mine once wrote in an examination: "I greet a poem, now, like a living person: with curiousity [sic] and respect."

I suggest that if this attitude became habitual with the ordinary reader, or even the professional critic, so often deficient in sensibility, there would be little trouble understanding most modern poetry. For curiosity brings a certain heightening of the attention, an extra awareness of the senses, particularly the eye and ear, an expectancy; and "respect" means, as I take it, that the work will not be cast aside with irritation, or spurned with fear or contempt. For such a reader, the poet will be an honest man who has felt and thought deeply and intensely, or seen something freshly, and who may be lucky enough, on occasion, to create a complete reality in a single poem. Such a reader will be willing to wait for, and cherish, those moments when the poet seems to go beyond himself. Most important of all, such a reader will not be afraid of a reality that is slightly different from his own: He will be willing to step into another world, even if at times it brings him close to the abyss. He will not be afraid of feeling—and this in spite of the deep-rooted fear of emotion existing today, particularly among the half-alive, for whom emotion, even when incorporated into form, becomes a danger, a madness. Poetry is written for the whole [person].[4]

So that's what this book is all about—performing literature to experience it wholly, to foster the capacity to experience it wholly. We want to bring to all texts, not only those we perform but all we may encounter, a competence that will enable us to give them our full attention, what Richard McGuire calls "passionate attention." In the introduction to his book *Passionate Attention: An Introduction to Literary Study,* he explains his use of that phrase from W. H. Auden:

> This book is the explanation of my use of Auden's phrase. I see the acts of living and of reading and studying literature as having value only if they are motivated by love and interest; "passionate attention" is thus the richest short description of literary criticism

[2]*Ibid.*, pp. 426–427.
[3]*Ibid.*, pp. 429–430.

[1]Theodore Roethke, "Five American Poets," *New World Writing* (May, 1953), pp. 83–84.

I know. It represents the two most important human qualities involved in a person's relationships with other persons and with literature.[5]

[5]Richard McGuire, *Passionate Attention: An Introduction to Literary Study* (New York: W. W. Norton, 1973), p. viii.

If we add to his acts "of living . . . reading . . . and studying literature" the acts of attending to performances in and of texts, we may choose to say with him that "passionate attention" is the "richest short description" available for what we do in performance of literature.

WORKSHOP V

Only once in this book, in Workshop II, did we attempt to deal with a whole text by analysis and suggestions for performance. The invited essays in this workshop, however, do just that—not exhaustively, of course, but with attention *to the whole*. The essays that follow offer information about words and thoughts in the texts, external information from the writers and critics, and specific suggestions to help you apply the techniques for study and performance (study through performance) you have learned.

A Primer of the Daily Round
HOWARD NEMEROV

A peels an apple, while B kneels to God,
C telephones to D, who has a hand
On E's knee, F coughs, G turns up the sod
For H's grave, I do not understand
But J is bringing one clay pigeon down
While K brings down a nightstick on L's
    head,
And M takes mustard, N drives into town,
O goes to bed with P, and Q drops dead,
R lies to S, but happens to be heard
By T, who tells U not to fire V
For having to give W the word
That X is now deceiving Y with Z,
    Who happens just now to remember A
    Peeling an apple somewhere far away.

A Completed Round:
Howard Nemerov's
"A Primer of the Daily Round"
by LEE HUDSON[6]

Howard Nemerov's "A Primer of the Daily Round" is an intriguing selection for performance due to the skillfully submerged dramatic situation and the playful but poignant thematic interest neatly enclosed in a traditional sonnet form. Rather than teaching children to read, this alphabetic primer considers the implications of the communal nature of language and society. Language plays as interactive and interdependent a role in our thought as each individual person plays in a social structure. In Nemerov's sonnet, all these threads of social and communicative patterns are artfully woven together.

When we examine the title we discover several important ideas: this is *"a"* primer not "the" only one possible; a *primer* suggests an introduction to language and communication and by derivation echoes primeval, primitive, and primary—all implying a first age or stage in the world; *daily* connotes a day-by-day repetition with a day as the rotation of the earth in orbit—a circular object in circular motion; and *round* reinforces this circular course

[6]Essay used with permission of the author.

and suggests that, as in music, one voice sings a short complete melody followed by a second voice while the first goes on to the next melody. The poem, as we will see, is also a round that returns to its beginning. Beyond these implications, the title also teases the reader or listener with a riddle-like ambiguity that prepares us for a similar spirit in the poem.

The poem's speaker is generalized rather than particularized. Since the poem as a whole testifies to the inseparability of the one from the many, Nemerov elects a more general voice or "poet-voice" instead of a characterized dramatic *persona*. Although not highly defined, we do find that the speaker is more personal than a purely descriptive or detached voice. One of the ways in which Nemerov uses the letters of the alphabet is to reveal this speaker:

> On E's knee, F coughs, G turns up the sod
> For H's grave, I do not understand

A reader or listener at this point notices two characteristics: the more descriptive construction characteristic of the poem is not used, that is, the speaker does not say "I *does* not understand"; and, when the point of view shifts to the first person and the speaker briefly includes himself or herself, the more anonymous voice of the primer abruptly disappears. Unlike the other personified letters whose *external* actions are described (peeling, kneeling, telephoning, grave digging, etc.), this "I" reveals an *internal* state of confusion. This inclusion halts the momentum of events and adds a reflective note. *What* doesn't "I" understand? Neither "I" nor we can stop the flow of events long enough to consider.

In the progression of letters a listener(s) as well as a speaker is also introduced "who tells U." The performer's audience addressed as "you" suddenly becomes involved in the process of events where, in a sense, we have been all along. When the poem is performed the graphic "U" unavoidably becomes "you" aurally and the audience recognizes the pun and their part in it. A performer may reinforce this pun by a gesture and logically would not be very spatially distant from the audience; rather like the speaker, the performer is increasingly involved in the experiences and drawn into the feelings of the poem.

The overall generality of the speaker, lack of definition both physically and attitudinally, and absence of specific spatial or temporal placement cause the prospective performer to focus on more vocal–tonal aspects of the poem. Questions such as the following must be resolved vocally: (1) When does the speaker's confusion become clear? (2) Is this lack of understanding resolved during the poem's final couplet (the last two rhyming lines)? (3) How do you communicate the speaker's apparent knowledge of events simultaneously with an expressed lack of comprehension? and (4) What will be the speaker's tone(s) when describing the various activities? While some of the provocative quality of this poem lies in its ambiguity, we will see that Nemerov's sonnet structure suggests some answers to the questions while demonstrating his *meaning*ful (or organic) use of form.

The fixed form of the sonnet is readily identified by its fourteen lines in iambic pentameter. These lines have varying rhyme patterns depending upon whether the type of sonnet is English (Shakespearean) or Italian (Petrarchan). The sonnet also arranges its thought conventionally by outlining a problem and concluding with a reflection upon the problem or by providing a solution. The terms "problem" and "solution" are used broadly since the sonnet may also divide into description of and commentary upon a subject.

In the English sonnet the first twelve

lines outline the problem and the final two lines produce a solution. Since a convincing resolution is unlikely within the short and usually light-rhyming twenty-syllable couplet, the solution tends to be an epigrammatic, paradoxical, or ironic statement. The Italian sonnet divides more judiciously into an octave (eight lines) setting forth the problem with the final sestet (six lines) to resolve it. These divisions are often visually clear with the twelve–two or eight–six lines in separate stanzas or, in the English version, with the final couplet indented.

Since this poetic structure is so tight, Nemerov's choice of the English sonnet hints at the direction of his logic and rhetoric. The first twelve lines serve to complicate the situation and advance the dilemma that the couplet is to resolve. Although in this sonnet the couplet doesn't literally solve anything, it redirects the question. Significantly, that redirection holds the reader's or listener's focus on the process of thought and action rather than any conclusions drawn from it. In other words, it does not matter what or why the members of a society do what they do but that who they are and what they are doing is directly or indirectly shaped by others. In like cause, they all affect each other.

The sonnet form aids the performer in determining tone and attitude for the speaker by suggesting that at the close of the poem the speaker arrives at an understanding not possessed earlier. The performer may tonally and gesturally reflect some sense of resolution during the final two lines. All that the speaker now understands is not stated as the round is completed but we assume that she or he recognizes a process—the inextricable nature of the course of human events. The earlier confusion indicated by "I do not understand" reaches a form of reconciliation underscored by the anticipated "resolution" of the sonnet structure.

Since poetry presents us with language in an intensified, interesting, and frequently quite unusual way, it reorders the way in which we see things and contemplate ideas. Poetic language becomes in its compression and focus more exciting than the ordinary language we are accustomed to. It will often, as a result, be both highly sensory and mental—stimulating our intellectual energies. While a poet strives to capture a truth in language, the performer must present the poet's "vision" with expressive skill to render it and communicate it to others. Nemerov defines a poem as "a way of getting something right in language."[7] He considers that this rightness is first of all a feeling and "a certain definition to experience."[8] The performance of a poem will, in a very real sense, define your perception and experience of the poem to others.

In "A Primer of the Daily Round" the prospective performer discovers several dimensions to Nemerov's choice of language. Most important is his serviceable and clever use of the alphabet. Besides using the alphabet to introduce a speaker and involve an audience, Nemerov employs it to extend the "primer" concept he mentions in the title. The alphabet becomes a deceptive shield for the levels he is suggesting. Ordinarily we associate the alphabet (root: *alpha* and *beta,* the first two letters of the Greek alphabet) with a series of letters that represent the sounds of language or speech. We view learning the alphabet as rudimentary to using language. Nemerov personifies the letters (i.e., gives inanimate objects animate characteristics) and by so doing links language with individuals and individuals with thought, action, and themselves.

Characteristically in a primer the first letter is A and its example is apple. The

[7]Howard Nemerov, "Poetry and Meaning," *Contemporary Poetry in America,* Robert Boyers, ed. (New York: Schocken Books, 1974), p. 1.

[8]*Ibid.,* p. 9.

alphabet then is revealed in its elementary and inseparable place in the learning process. The action of "A" peeling the apple, or getting under the superficial layer, also implies that a core will never be reached. Even at the core "A" would find seeds—the germinal symbol of the life cycle. The *process* becomes the important thing. With the use of the apple symbol, the "A" looms larger and suggests Adam preparing to sin or perhaps flirting with the idea. Either idea sharply contrasts with its opposite in the second half of the line, "while B kneels to God."

By using the alphabet, Nemerov is additionally able to insert a *catalog* or enumerative rhythm into the poem. Activities are listed passionlessly with no qualifying adjectives or adverbs. This catalog technique incorporates parallel simple syntactical structures that echo a primer while itemizing human action and interaction. When reading the poem aloud, the force of this rhythm will become clear. It moves the poem along quickly as the progression of the alphabet predictably appears.

Also through a deft choice of language, Nemerov manipulates a sense of time to create an illusion of simultaneity and endlessness. All the various activities in the poem appear to be going on and on at the same time. This overlapping is reinforced by the frequent employment of enjambment, or run-on lines, the use of present tense verbs and present participles, and the conjunctive use of pronouns and adverbs:

> *But* J is *bringing* one clay pigeon down
> *While* K *brings down* a nightstick on L's head,
> *And* M *takes* mustard, . . .

Nemerov's syntactical devices create an *immediacy* that prevents us from distancing the poem through historical boundaries. The situation in the poem is an ongoing one and exists in a kind of everpresent time dimension.

The overlapping of "characters" in many of the same activities not only contributes to this simultaneity but also affects the flow and build of the poem. The most intricate situation comes at the close of the alphabet with nine persons implicated:

> R lies to S, but happens to be heard
> By T, who tells U not to fire V
> For having to give W the word
> That X is now deceiving Y with Z,

The poem builds through this sequence to the final couplet with the pause after the twelfth line (reinforced by the comma and end rhyme) identifiable as the *fulcrum* or turning point. The performer would mark this important shift tonally and perhaps gesturally. The open (enjambed) heroic couplet follows linking "A" and "Z":

> Who happens just now to remember A
> Peeling an apple somewhere far away.

The round is completed and begins again as all become part of this life process as effect and cause. In "Primer" the "I"-speaker seeks to understand the fabric of existence in society but cannot interrupt the flow of life to examine it. Only when the pattern is laid forth and the round returns to "A" do we feel that some dimension of knowledge is acquired.

While the interlocked philosophical probes of thought, language, communication, and society provide for an intellectual involvement in the poem, the performance is able to restore sensory responsiveness to the feeling of language and thought. Ultimately the experience of the poem is felt. That experiential knowledge and "rightness" will spark the truth of the poem in performance.

Colette

VLADIMIR NABOKOV

I

In the early years of this century, a travel agency on Nevski Avenue displayed a three-foot-long model of an oak-brown international sleeping car. In delicate verisimilitude it completely outranked the painted tin of my clockwork trains. Unfortunately it was not for sale. One could make out the blue upholstery inside, the embossed leather lining of the compartment walls, their polished panels, inset mirrors, tulip-shaped reading lamps, and other maddening details. Spacious windows alternated with narrower ones, single or geminate, and some of these were of frosted glass. In a few of the compartments, the beds had been made.

The then great and glamorous Nord Express (it was never the same after World War One), consisting solely of such international cars and running but twice a week, connected St. Petersburg with Paris. I would have said: directly with Paris, had passengers not been obliged to change from one train to a superficially similar one at the Russo-German frontier (Verzhbolovo-Eydtkuhnen), where the ample and lazy Russian sixty-and-a-half-inch gauge was replaced by the fifty-six-and-a-half-inch standard of Europe and coal succeeded birch logs.

In the far end of my mind I can unravel, I think, at least five such journeys to Paris, with the Riviera or Biarritz as their ultimate destination. In 1909, the year I now single out, my two small sisters had been left at home with nurses and aunts. Wearing gloves and a traveling cap, my father sat reading a book in the compartment he shared with our tutor. My brother and I were separated from them by a washroom. My mother and her maid occupied a compartment adjacent to ours. The odd one of our party, my father's valet, Osip (whom, a decade later, the pedantic Bolsheviks were to shoot, because he appropriated our bicycles instead of turning them over to the nation), had a stranger for companion.

In April of that year, Peary had reached the North Pole. In May, Chaliapin had sung in Paris. In June, bothered by rumors of new and better Zeppelins, the United States War Department had told reporters of plans for an aërial Navy. In July, Blériot had flown from Calais to Dover (with a little additional loop when he lost his bearings). It was late August now. The firs and marshes of Northwestern Russia sped by, and on the following day gave way to German pine barrens and heather.

At a collapsible table, my mother and I played a card game called *durachki*. Although it was still broad daylight, our cards, a glass and, on a different plane, the locks of a suitcase were reflected in the window. Through forest and field, and in sudden ravines, and among scuttling cottages, those discarnate gamblers kept steadily playing on for steadily sparkling stakes.

"*Ne budet-li, ty ved' ustal* [Haven't you had enough, aren't you tired]?" my mother would ask, and then would be lost in thought as she slowly shuffled the cards. The door of the compartment was open and I could see the corridor window, where the wires—six thin black wires—were doing their best to slant up, to ascend skywards, despite the lightning blows dealt them by one telegraph pole after another; but just as all six, in a triumphant swoop of pathetic elation, were about to reach the top of the window, a particularly vicious blow would bring them down, as low as they had ever been, and they would have to start all over again.

When, on such journeys as these, the train changed its pace to a dignified amble and all but grazed housefronts and shop-signs, as we passed through some big German town, I used to feel a twofold excitement, which terminal stations could not provide. I saw a city, with its toylike trams, linden trees and brick walls, enter the compartment, hobnob with the mirrors, and fill to the brim the windows on the corridor side. This informal contact between train and city was one part of the thrill. The other was putting myself in the place of some passer-by who, I imagined, was moved as I would be moved myself to see the long, romantic, auburn cars, with their intervestibular connecting curtains as black as bat-wings and their metal lettering copper-bright in the low sun, unhurriedly negotiate an iron bridge across an everyday thoroughfare and then turn, with all windows suddenly ablaze, around a last block of houses.

There were drawbacks to those optical amalgamations. The wide-windowed dining car, a vista of chaste bottles of mineral water, miter-folded napkins, and dummy chocolate bars (whose wrappers—Cailler, Kohler, and so forth—enclosed nothing but wood), would be perceived at first as a cool haven beyond a consecution of reeling blue corridors; but as the meal progressed toward its fatal last course, one would keep catching the car in the act of being recklessly sheathed, lurching waiters and all, in the landscape, while the landscape itself went through a complex system of motion, the daytime moon stubbornly keeping abreast of one's plate, the distant meadows opening fanwise, the near trees sweeping up on invisible swings toward the track, a parallel rail line all at once committing suicide by anastomosis, a bank nictitating grass rising, rising, rising, until the little witness of mixed velocities was made to disgorge his portion of *omelette aux confitures de fraises.*

It was at night, however, that the *Compagnie Internationale des Wagons-Lits et des Grands Express Européens* lived up to the magic of its name. From my bed under my brother's bunk (Was he asleep? Was he there at all?), in the semi-darkness of our compartment, I watched things, and parts of things, and shadows, and sections of shadows cautiously moving about and getting nowhere. The woodwork gently creaked and crackled. Near the door that led to the toilet, a dim garment on a peg and, higher up, the tassel of the blue, bivalved night light swung rhythmically. It was hard to correlate those halting approaches, that hooded stealth, with the headlong rush of the outside night, which I knew *was* rushing by, spark-streaked, illegible.

I would put myself to sleep by the simple act of identifying myself with the engine-driver. A sense of drowsy well-being invaded my veins as soon as I had everything nicely arranged—the carefree passengers in their rooms enjoying the ride I was giving them, smoking, exchanging knowing smiles, nodding, dozing; the waiters and cooks and trainguards (whom I had to place somewhere) carousing in the diner; and myself, goggled and begrimed, peering out of the engine-cab at the tapering track, at the ruby or emerald point in the black distance. And then, in my sleep, I would see something totally different—a glass marble rolling under a grand piano or a toy engine lying on its side with its wheels still working gamely.

A change in the speed of the train sometimes interrupted the current of my sleep. Slow lights were stalking by; each, in passing, investigated the same chink, and then a luminous compass measured the shadows. Presently, the train stopped with a long-drawn Westinghousian sigh. Something (my brother's spectacles, as it proved next day) fell from above. It was marvelously exciting to move to the foot of one's bed, with part of the bedclothes following, in order to undo cautiously the catch of the window shade, which could be made to slide only halfway up, impeded as it was by the edge of the upper berth.

Like moons around Jupiter, pale moths revolved about a lone lamp. A dismembered newspaper stirred on a bench. Somewhere on the train one could hear muffled voices, somebody's comfortable cough. There was nothing particularly interesting in the portion of station platform before me, and still I could not tear myself away from it until it departed of its own accord.

Next morning, wet fields with misshappen willows along the radius of a ditch or a row of poplars afar, traversed by a horizontal band of milky-white mist, told one that the train was spinning through Belgium. It reached Paris at 4 P.M., and even if the stay was only an overnnight one, I had always time to purchase something—say, a little brass *Tour Eiffel*, rather roughly coated with silver paint—before we boarded, at noon on the following day, the Sud-Express which, on its way to Madrid, dropped us around 10 P.M. at the La Négresse station of Biarritz, a few miles from the Spanish frontier.

II

Biarritz still retained its quiddity in those days. Dusty blackberry bushes and weedy *terrains à vendre* bordered the road that led to our villa. The Carlton was still being built. Some thirty-six years had to elapse before Brigadier General Samuel McCroskey would occupy the royal suite of the Hotel du Palais, which stands on the site of a former palace, where, in the sixties, that incredibly agile medium, Daniel Home, is said to have been caught stroking with his bare foot (in imitation of a ghost hand) the kind, trustful face of Empress Eugénie. On the promenade near the Casino, an elderly flower-girl, with carbon eyebrows and a painted smile, nimbly slipped the plump torus of a carnation into the button-hole of an intercepted stroller whose left jowl accentuated its royal fold as he glanced down sideways at the coy insertion of the flower.

Along the back line of the *plage,* various seaside chairs and stools supported the parents of straw-hatted children who were playing in front on the sand. I could be seen on my knees trying to set a found comb aflame by means of a magnifying glass. Men sported white trousers that to the eye of to-day would look as if they had comically shrunk in the washing; ladies wore, that particular season, light coats with silk-faced lapels, hats with big crowns and wide brims, dense embroidered white veils, frill-fronted blouses, frills at their wrists, frills on their parasols. The breeze salted one's lips. At a tremendous pace a stray golden-orange butterfly came dashing across the palpitating *plage*.

Additional movement and sound were provided by venders hawking *cacahuètes,* sugared violets, pistachio ice cream of a heavenly green, cachou pellets, and huge convex pieces of dry, gritty, wafer-like stuff that came from a red barrel. With a distinctness that no later superpositions have dimmed, I see that waffleman stomp along through deep mealy sand, with the heavy cask on his bent back. When called, he would sling it off his shoulder by a twist of its strap, bang it down on the sand in a Tower of Pisa position, wipe his face with his sleeve, and proceed to manipulate a kind of arrow-and-dial arrangement with numbers on the lid of the cask. The arrow rasped and whirred around. Luck was supposed to fix the size of a sou's worth of wafer. The bigger the piece, the more I was sorry for him.

The process of bathing took place on another part of the beach. Professional bathers, burly Basques in black bathing suits, were there to help ladies and children enjoy the terrors of the surf. Such a *baigneur* would place you with your back to the incoming wave and hold you by the hand as the rising, rotating mass of foamy, green water violently descended upon you from behind, knocking you off your feet with one mighty wallop. After a dozen of these tumbles, the *baigneur*, glistening like a seal, would lead his panting, shivering, moistly snuffling charge landward, to the flat foreshore, where an unforgettable old woman with grey hairs on her chin promptly chose a bathing-robe from several hanging on a clothes-line. In the security of a little cabin, one would be helped by yet another attendant to peel off one's soggy, sand-heavy bathing suit. It would plop onto the boards, and, still shivering, one would step out of it and trampled on its bluish, diffuse stripes. The cabin smelt of pine. The attendant, a hunchback with beaming wrinkles, brought a basin of steaming-hot water, in which one immersed one's feet. From him I learned, and have preserved ever since in a glass cell of my memory, that "butterfly" in the Basque language is *misericoletea*—or at least it sounded so (among the seven words I have found in dictionaries the closest approach is *micheletea*).

<h1 style="text-align:center">III</h1>

On the browner and wetter part of the *plage*, that part which at low tide yielded the best mud for castles, I found myself digging, one day, side by side with a little French girl called Colette.

She would be ten in November, I had been ten in April. Attention was drawn to a jagged bit of violet mussel shell upon which she had stepped with the bare sole of her narrow long-toed foot. No, I was not English. Her greenish eyes seemed flecked with the overflow of the freckles that covered her sharp-featured face. She wore what might now be termed a playsuit, consisting of a blue jersey with rolled-up sleeves and blue knitted shorts. I had taken her at first for a boy and then had been puzzled by the bracelet on her thin wrist and the corkscrew brown curls dangling from under her sailor cap.

She spoke in birdlike bursts of rapid twitter, mixing governess English and Parisian French. Two years before, on the same *plage*, I had been much attached to the lovely, sun-tanned little daughter of a Serbian physician; but when I met Colette, I knew at once that this was the real thing. Colette seemed to me so much stranger than all my other chance playmates at Biarritz! I somehow acquired the feeling that she was less happy than I, less loved. A bruise on her delicate, downy forearm gave rise to awful conjectures. "He pinches as bad as my mummy," she said, speaking of a crab. I evolved various schemes to save her from her parents, who were *"des bourgeois de Paris"* as I heard somebody tell my mother with a slight shrug. I interpreted the disdain in my own fashion, as I knew that those people had come all the way from Paris in their blue-and-yellow limousine (a fashionable adventure in those days) but had drably sent Colette with her dog and governess by an ordinary coach-train. The dog was a female fox-terrier with bells on her collar and a most waggly behind. From sheer exuberance, she would lap up salt water out of Colette's toy pail. I remember the sail, the sunset and the lighthouse pictured on that pail, but I cannot recall the dog's name, and this bothers me.

During the two months of our stay at Biarritz, my passion for Colette all but surpassed my passion for butterflies. Since my parents were not keen to meet hers, I saw her only on the beach; but I thought of her constantly. If I noticed she had been crying, I felt a surge of helpless anguish that brought tears to my own eyes. I could not destroy the mosquitoes that had left their bites on her frail neck, but I could, and did, have a successful fist fight with a red-haired boy who had been rude to her. She used to give me warm handfuls of hard candy. One day, as we were bending together over a starfish, and Colette's ringlets were tickling my ear, she suddenly turned toward me and kissed me on the cheek. So great was my emotion that all I could think of saying was, "You little monkey."

I had a gold coin that I assumed would pay for our elopement. Where did I want to take her? Spain? America? The mountains above Pau? *Là-bas, là-bas, dans la montagne,* as I had heard Carmen sing at the opera. One strange night, I lay awake, listening to the recurrent thud of the ocean and planning our flight. The ocean seemed to rise and grope in the darkness and then heavily fall on its face.

Of our actual get-away, I have little to report. My memory retains a glimpse of her obediently putting on rope-soled canvas shoes, on the lee side of a flapping tent, while I stuffed a folding butterfly net into a brown-paper bag. The next glimpse is of our evading pursuit by entering a pitch-dark *cinéma* near the Casino (which, of course, was absolutely out of bounds). There we sat, holding hands across the dog, which now and then gently jingled in Colette's lap, and were shown a jerky, drizzly, but highly exciting bull-fight at St. Sebástian. My final glimpse is of myself being led along the promenade by my tutor. His long legs moved with a kind of ominous briskness and I can see the muscles of his grimly set jaw working under the tight skin. My bespectacled brother, aged nine, whom he happens to hold with his other hand, keeps trotting out forward to peer at me with awed curiosity, like a little owl.

Among the trivial souvenirs acquired at Biarritz before leaving, my favorite was not the small bull of black stone and not the sonorous seashell but something which now seems almost symbolic—a meerschaum penholder with a tiny peephole of crystal in its ornamental part. One held it quite close to one's eye, screwing up the other, and when one had got rid of the shimmer of one's own lashes, a miraculous photographic view of the bay and of the line of cliffs ending in a lighthouse could be seen inside.

And now a delightful thing happens. The process of re-creating that penholder and the microcosm in its eyelet, stimulates my memory to a last effort. I try again to recall the name of Colette's dog—and, sure enough, along those remote beaches, over the glossy evening sands of the past, where each footprint slowly fills up with sunset water, here it comes, here it comes, echoing and vibrating: Floss, Floss, Floss!

Colette was back in Paris by the time we stopped there for a day before continuing our homeward journey; and there, in a fawn park under a cold blue sky, I saw her (by arrangement between our mentors, I believe) for the last time. She carried a hoop and a short stick to drive it with, and everything about her was extremely proper and stylish in an autumnal, Parisian, *tenue-de-ville-pour-fillettes* way. She took from her governess and slipped into my brother's hand a farewell present, a box of sugar-coated almonds, meant, I knew, solely for me; and instantly she was off, tap-tapping her glinting hoop through light and shade, around and around a fountain choked with dead leaves, near which I stood. The leaves mingle in my memory with the leather of her shoes and gloves, and there was, I remember, some detail in her attire (perhaps a ribbon on her Scottish cap, or the pattern of her stockings) that reminded me then of the rainbow spiral in a glass marble. I still seem to be holding that wisp of iridescence, not knowing exactly where to fit it, while she runs with her hoop ever faster around me and finally dissolves among the slender shadows cast on the graveled path by the interlaced arches of its low looped fence.

Speak, Memory: An Exercise In Perceiving and Evoking the Text
by PHILLIS RIENSTRA JEFFREY[9]

In his "Foreword" to *Speak, Memory,* Vladimir Nabokov refers to the final edition of this "autobiography revisited" as a "re-Englishing of a Russian re-version of what had been an English re-telling of Russian memories."[10] His emphatic usage of the compound, hyphenated "re" directs our attention to the speaker's effort to turn back to or to look backward at an earlier experience and to renew or restore that previous condition. He creates anew and brings into reality the *plage* (beach) at Biarritz and Colette. In the process of resurrecting these "memorabilia of his mind" the speaker must grasp his reality and his own existence in terms of those things his memory contains. It is not by accident that Nabokov's original title and that of the first edition of *Speak, Memory* was *Conclusive Evidence.* He explains that the title referred to "evidence" of his existence.[11]

At times he recalls this evidence quite effortlessly; at other times he struggles. At yet other moments the vision has become so crystallized that the speaker seems to be almost immersed in the experience he remembers.

What does he actually "do" when, for instance, he finally recalls the name of Colette's dog?

> I try again to recall the name of Colette's dog—and, sure enough, along those remote beaches, over the glossy evening sands of the past, where each footprint slowly fills up with sunset water, here it comes, here it comes, echoing and vibrating: Floss, Floss, Floss!

We would probably agree that when the mind struggles so does the body and that the entire body responds to both the effort and the revelation as the words register them. Note the phrases and their affective effects: (1) "I try again to recall the name of Colette's dog"—The speaker experiences a muscular tension created by the energy he expends in trying to re-

[9]Essay used by permission of the author.

[10]Vladimir Nabokov, *Speak, Memory* (New York: Capricorn Books, 1970), p. 12. Originally appeared in *The New Yorker,* July 31, 1948.

[11]*Ibid.,* p. 13.

member. Any number of gestures could accompany the effort. The hand might, for example, attempt to "aid" the head (mind) in its chore. As the mind and body grope for an answer so does his speech. (2) ". . . and, triumphantly, . . ." —The speaker experiences a momentary acceleration of muscular tensiveness and heightened energy followed immediately by sense imaging and a release of muscular tension as he "sees" the objects associated with the dog's name: ". . . along those remote beaches, over the glossy evening sands of the past, where each footprint fills up with sunset water, . . .". (3) ". . . here it comes, here it comes, echoing and vibrating: Floss, Floss, Floss!"—Here the speaker resumes an intensity of muscular discovery, like a rubber band pulled taut. Additionally, he might suggest a movement toward the scene he envisions as he almost gleefully remembers the dog's name. (Be careful not to *over*interpret his behaviors, misconstruing, say, ecstasy for pleasure.)

Is the speaker alone with these thoughts or does he share them with some one or some other presences? Or does he move rather freely between these extremes? We can assume that the "speaking" of this narrative is important to him and that it suggests, at least some of the time, the presence of a general though sympathetic and interested audience. However, when he is in the process of capturing a "moment of being" as when he feels the name "Floss" coming to him and voices it, he seems to be so immersed in reseeing and participating in the moment as it happens that he speaks more to himself and his vision than to an "other" audience.

When the speaker directly addresses the audience, he or she might well stand and walk and/or point and nod, pace and halt, retreat and confront. Or the speaker might remain seated, though not inert, during much of the narrative. Or these movements and behaviors might be combined as each promotes or demotes, reinforces or minimizes what he wishes to convey.

There is perhaps yet another motivation for the speaker's journeys into the interior of his past. In Chapter Eleven of *Speak, Memory* Nabokov suggests that our memory perfects the things it contains when we resurrect them. He describes a certain pavilion in which he took refuge from a thunderstorm some four years after his encounter with Colette. He reports that the pavilion recurs in his dreams at least twice a year and he remembers it as an exquisitely beautiful structure. He confides that in his memory it is ". . . perhaps a little more perfect," admitting moments later that in reality some of the glass was missing and debris cluttered the entrance.[12]

Nabokov's "technique" is consistent with or an extension of the prose content and resembles that of the photographer who "zooms" in on and magnifies small things or "focuses out" and reduces large ones. Just as the camera selects and reproduces those things its operator sees and wishes to preserve, so the memory retains and reconstitutes in its own way those things significant to its possessor. The memory, too, like the camera, sometimes reproduces a sharp, detailed image of its subject and sometimes only a vague or shadowy one, for example, a sharp, clear image of the picture he and Colette viewed in the forbidden cinema but, as he admits, "Of our actual getaway, I have little to report." Later, he explains of their last meeting that "she runs with her hoop ever faster around me and finally dissolves among the slender shadows cast on the graveled path." His language often, as in this instance, is reminiscent of the photographer's "dissolves" and "shadows." The camera metaphor seems appropriate, too, in exploring the speaker-performer's

[12]*Ibid.,* pp. 215–16.

behaviors. As his memory and its contents fade, his mind's eye sees less clearly the images it strains to bring into focus. The body, too, would suggest this laboring to "see," straining toward the object and looking beyond, not at, the audience, as he images a scene that is removed temporally and spatially from his listeners.

The contents of the speaker's memory are associated with sensations rather than with logic and therefore the personal landscape he revisits is an imagistic–sensual one. In the first three paragraphs of this recollection he recalls a kaleidoscope of color accompanied by various tactile experiences: the mud is *brown* and *wet;* Colette *stepped* on a *violet* mussel shell; she wears *blue,* has *green* eyes and *brown* curls; Colette's *forearm* is *downy* and *bruised.* Later he recalls the *blue-and-yellow* limousine of Colette's family, a *gold coin,* a *red-haired* boy, and a *brown*-paper bag. He also vividly recalls that Osip's "long *legs* move with a kind of ominous briskness" and that the tutor's muscles of "his grimly set *jaw* [were] working under the tight *skin.*" His sensitivity to these kinds of stimuli as a child account for their dominance in this now adult speaker and may account for what George Steiner describes as a prose of "marvel and surprise which comes with personal discovery"[13] characteristic of Nabokov.

He appears also to be "tuned in" to the attitudes and feelings of others. He says that he "interpreted" the disdain in which his parents and their friends held Colette's "des bourgeois de Paris" (common Parisians) family. He also "felt a surge of helpless anguish that brought tears to [his] own eyes" if he noticed that Colette had been crying. In addition, he perceives that she is less loved than he. While he is unusually perceptive and sympathetic

(noticing, too, that Colette's "frail" neck is mosquito bitten), the speaker also displays a boyish humor. With the innocence and honesty of a child he recalls that, overcome with emotion when Colette kissed him, his only response was "You little monkey"; and that he knew immediately that his feeling for Colette was "the real thing." It is entirely conceivable that the young boy and not the older man speaks such lines. The language is not that of the sophisticated older man who, if actually saying, "You little monkey," might render the line as less than honest. Hearing it from the child self, however, we understand it as a spontaneous and genuine expression of affection.

The child's vivid imagination is ignited by his sensory acuteness. The boy's gold coin prompts him to plan an elopement with Colette (he is ten, she nine) and to imagine that they would perhaps retreat "over there, over there, in the mountain" (*Là-bas, là-bas, dans la montagne*). Nothing more than a piece of gold and a line from Bizet's opera are necessary to spark the speaker's imagination and create a vision of Colette as the desirable Carmen and of him as the romantic Don José. His youthful fantasy points to some similarities in fact however for, while Colette is not a gypsy, she is a Parisian bourgeoisie, and, while he is not a dashing Spanish soldier, he is a member of the Russian nobility. Although the fantasy belonged to the ten-year-old boy as did the objects, people, and events, the memory of these things belong to the older, more mature speaker.

The emotional distance between the older man and the boy is often so minimized that the child is more likely to be speaking and the adult observing. This action of "stealing" the scene from the adult occurs sporadically but systematically even though the man usually controls the scenes. The adult begins the narrative, but only lines later are we aware of a child's presence, a voice other than the

[13]George Steiner, *Language and Silence: Essays on Language, Literature, and the Inhuman* (New York: Atheneum, 1967), p. 283.

adult's that responds "No, I was not English" to Colette's implied question. There is, throughout the excerpt, both submission and verbal competition between the two voices. As the voices submit to but vie with each other there is a corresponding submergence–emergence pattern of personality definition. This quality of verbal submission-competition and personality submergence-emergence is apparent in the following exchange in which the boy's "discourse" appears in italics:

> Two years before, on the same *plage,* I had been much attached to the lovely, suntanned, little daughter of a Serbian physician; but when I met Colette, *I knew at once that this was the real thing.* Colette seemed to me *so much stranger than all my other chance playmates at Biarritz!* I somehow acquired the feeling *that she was less happy than I, less loved.* A bruise on her delicate, downy forearm gave rise to awful conjectures. *"He pinches as bad as my mummy," she said, speaking of a crab.*

It is the child's dilemma and his presence, not the adult's, that we acknowledge when the boy voices his quandary, "Where did I want to take her? Spain? America? The mountains above Pau?" A part of us enjoys too the subtle irony expressed through the adult who immediately signals the ill-fated outcome of the child's fantasy. This wiser, more articulate adult remembers that the dream occurred as the child listened to the "recurrent thud of the ocean" that "seemed to rise and grope in the darkness and then heavily fall on its face."

The contrasts between the past and the present, youth and maturity, the ordinary (playing on the beach with Colette) and the unusual (eloping), and fact and fiction account for the tension in this excerpt and for the rich possibilities for performance. Like most literature that engages us, Nabokov's prose appeals first to our sensibilities and then to our recognition of unity, form, and balance. We are, however, ultimately pleased to discover the varied moments of "being" that exist in this text and that can perhaps emerge in various degrees of intensity, immediacy, and personality definition through performance.

The Feast
DAN WRIGHT

CHARACTERS

BLUE JEANS

OLD MAN

ANGRY YOUNG MAN

ELF WITH CHAMPAGNE (Blue Jeans Disguised)

DROWSY CELLIST (likewise)

The curtains open . . . and . . . it must be some kind of mistake. The stage crew is still putting up sets. But no one seems to be much bothered by the fact. It might be a nice touch, though, to have a director, troubled species, to look up and notice. He might shout some muffled expletive off stage about who was the fool who opened the curtains etc., when they weren't ready. But in any case, the stage work-lights remain on, the stage work continues, somebody's complaining about a costume that doesn't fit, and damnitall if the curtains don't stay open. Now some character in blue jeans and spotted shirt comes out along the front of the stage. He is carrying an easel over his shoulder, a large piece of cardboard in his hand, and a pot of paint. For the sake of somebody's reputation, he might smile an apology to the audience. At any rate, when he gets to the opposite end of the stage, he sets up his easel, places the cardboard upon it facing the audience, and paints—rather scrawls, "THE FEAST." He puts his pot of paint aside and sits down on the stage next to his easel. He looks out at the audience and, twirling his glasses in his hand, begins:

BLUE JEANS: Well, now . . . no one said it was going to be an extraordinary sort of play . . . I mean, as a matter of fact, it's quite an ordinary sort of . . . Believe me, it doesn't deserve much of . . . You know, come to think of it, it's such an ordinary . . . I mean, I, for one, wouldn't feel so bad about dispensing with . . . uh . . . that is, I don't want to bother them for the sake of the feast. After all, you start stomping around on the grounds of every whim and . . . well, people get mad. So, we'll just let them go on working . . . go on, go right on and . . . then we can maybe sneak in this bit . . . *(He saunters back among the stagemen and, in a pantomime, wangles two tin buckets, which he brings forward, arranging them about five feet apart.)* . . . I've got friends . . . or, sometimes I seem to . . . CHARLIE *(Calls over audience.)* hey . . . HEY CHARLIE . . . *(A spot comes on, and* BLUE JEANS *waves it over to where he is standing between the buckets. The stage work-lights remain on.* B.J. *places a can on top of one of the buckets.)* I've got characters too, or sometimes I seem . . . they are supposed to arrive . . . *(Factory whistle.* BLUE JEANS *holds up his hand to the audience, nods his head.)* . . . a whistle, if you hadn't guessed, and it signals the start of this play. It makes a suitable sound to start a play? . . . right? It blows, and people change . . . you know, it toots, and people are possessed by it. It beckons in the harbor, and people look up expectant. Maybe it calls from the factory stacks . . . feet move, sometimes a smile . . . and you know it's our own creation, but we pray in our exertion to . . . A CHERUB OUT THERE perhaps. He looks down and chuckles at our business, but he takes up his horn and sounds pause, "take pause" . . . *(The whistle blows again.* B.J. *is about ready to climb down in the orchestra—but one final word.)* . . . and so on, so forth. *(He makes himself comfortable in the first row.* OLD MAN *is heard humming outside.)*

OLD MAN: *(enters through the audience down the center aisle. He is wearing spotted, baggy work pants supported from the shoulders of a red plaid wool shirt by suspenders. He is characterized by an ambling, joyful gait, and when he speaks, it is with the friendly, booming quality of a man who has found a sense of self-assurance and contentment. Go ahead and ham him up . . . no danger. You might as well. He walks all the way down the center aisle, swinging a lunch pail at his side, singing. He sings to the tune of "Freight train, freight train. . . .")* Lunch hour, lunch hour, goin' so faaaast . . . Lunch hour, lunch hour, goin' so faaast . . . Dum de dum, de dum de donn . . . so they won't know where I've gone . . . *(Climbs stage, eventually sees the tin can on the one bucket.)* . . . AH HA! Miserable tin can of a man that I am . . . counting the minutes till your lunch hour comes . . . *(Kicks the can off the bucket.)* TAKE THAT! . . . *(*OLD MAN *gazes after the can and chuckles contentedly.)*

(Several of the stage crew members are still working on the sets, but they are making less noise now. One of the crew calls "Lights!" off stage, and the stage work-lights go off. The red and white border lights remain on, along with the spot centered on the OLD MAN *and on the two buckets . . .* OLD MAN *puts his lunch pail in front of him, and as he opens it,* ANGRY YOUNG MAN *enters from the side. He is wearing old pants and a denim jacket—on his head a battered tweed golf cap. He sits down on the second bucket and . . . facing the audience like the* OLD MAN, *explores the contents of his paper bag. During the conversation that follows,* OLD MAN *eats his lunch out of his lunch pail,* YOUNG MAN, *out of his paper sack.* OLD MAN *chews his lunch in delight.* YOUNG MAN *rips at his lunch in anger. They are about finished with lunch by the time the "feast" begins.* YOUNG MAN *is characterized by brooding, suspicious expressions of a rebelliousness which, I guess, he considers attractive. Certainly he holds no distinct notions of revolt, because you see, indications are that* YOUNG MAN *isn't all that bright. But anyway,* OLD MAN *hums;* YOUNG MAN *broods, and neither seems conscious of the other until* OLD MAN *glances over at* YOUNG MAN *and says offhandedly:)*

> Ah, you are here too . . . So you have come to join in the Great, Green Lunch Hour—that moment of rapture and dizzy joy, that . . . uh, moment of freedom! and . . . *(No response from* ANGRY YOUNG MAN*).* . . . so you have come too?

YOUNG MAN: *(glances around, realizes that* OLD MAN *has spoken to him.)* Yeah, sure, I mean, what do you mean? . . . of course I am here . . . I mean I DON'T EVEN KNOW YOU, OLD MAN!

OLD MAN: As you wish . . . was just trying to make conversation.

YOUNG MAN: Humph. *(Lights begin to fade.)*

OLD MAN: There's this little game, see, that I know . . . makes new acquaintances come much easier . . .

YOUNG MAN: Humph. *(Spot remains on.)*

OLD MAN: It starts out, you see, by me asking a question . . . I ask you, "What did you have for breakfast this morning, stranger?"

YOUNG MAN: Yeah?

OLD MAN: Well, what did you have for breakfast this morning, stranger?

YOUNG MAN: *(suspiciously)* Well, let me see now . . . I had a big bowl of Sugar Crisp—yes, and a cup of coffee from the machine.

OLD MAN: Now I tell you what I had for breakfast. I had this magnificent combination of Wheat Chex . . . I really like Wheat Chex . . . and orange juice, sausage, eggs—poached with pepper—and toast with plenty of kumquat jam. . .

YOUNG MAN: Look here, what kind of a game is this?

OLD MAN: Why . . . it's called the comparative breakfasts game.

YOUNG MAN: *(throwing his hat to the floor)* LOOK HERE, OLD MAN . . . WHAT DIFFERENCE DOES IT MAKE WHAT I HAD FOR BREAKFAST ANYWAY . . . I mean, A MAN'S BREAKFAST IS HIS OWN BUSINESS . . . *(*Y.M. *sputters, dusts off his hat and goes back to his lunch bag.)*

OLD MAN: Exactly . . . you see, disclosing one's breakfast, a very intimate matter indeed, presumes acquaintance and avoids all sorts of embarrassment. Now if I were to tell you what I'm having for lunch . . . for instance, I say, "Well, lemme see, I've got a boiled egg and a thermos of vegetable beef soup and . . . a salomy 'n' lettuce on rye . . . *(Gleefully exhibits the contents of his lunch pail.)*

YOUNG MAN: LOOK HERE . . . I don't happen to be interested in your breakfast, or your lunch, or even your fridgin' dinner, for that matter . . .

(Long pause.)

OLD MAN: It's such a pleasant day out. I just thought maybe . . .

YOUNG MAN: Hey, Dad . . . So happens I think it's a lousy rotten day, and so happens I don't like eating lunch out here in this lousy, rotten storage lot . . . out of a lousy, rotten paper bag. So happens it's a grubby, lousy city in a grubby, rotten world filled up with a lotta grubby, lousy, rotten people . . . try that out for size on the old wazoo.

(OLD MAN *takes a crunchy bite from an apple.)*

OLD MAN: Why, I'd say you are bitter . . . you are bitter, aren't you?

YOUNG MAN: Yeah . . . I am . . . I'm real bitter *(Throws hat on floor again.)* WHAT'YA MEAN BITTER, ANYWAY? . . . WHAT KIND OF QUESTION'S *THAT*? AND WHAT IF I AM . . . *(Turns his back on* O.M., *who shrugs his shoulder. They go back to their lunch.)*

OLD MAN: Well . . . I was just interested, you know . . . I mean bitter people don't usually . . . don't come here, that is . . .

YOUNG MAN: *(challenged)* What do you mean?

OLD MAN: But . . . come to the feast, of course.

YOUNG MAN: The WHAT?

OLD MAN: . . . the feast . . .

YOUNG MAN: Oh, "the feast" . . . look, if that's some underhanded way of telling me you don't like my company, it don't wash, see Dad . . . I've got as much right to this crummy can as the next Joe . . . and so maybe you don't like me, well that's just tough potatoes.

OLD MAN: Oh, you can do what you like . . . the feast is quite open, you know . . . I don't mean to say you weren't invited, in fact this very moment I ask you to be my special guest.

YOUNG MAN: Guest?

OLD MAN: Yes, at the feast.

YOUNG MAN: Yeah, sure, what feast?

OLD MAN: Right now . . . here.

YOUNG MAN: What the fat kind of a feast you expect to have out in this crummy lot . . . I know about feasts, you think I'm dumb or something? . . . You think I'm dumb? My old lady used to tell me about feasts. She used to work at the Regis, and she used to bring junk back to the place and tell me about all the food and the people getting potted and dancing and smoking big cigars.

OLD MAN: Well, you see, this feast is a little different. I mean, your mother . . .

YOUNG MAN: You can leave her out of this. What gives you the right to sit there and . . .

OLD MAN: Really, I'm sure your mother is a very fine woman. I just want to explain . . .

YOUNG MAN: Well, for your information, so happens the old lady can take it in the ear for all I'm concerned.

(Long pause.)

OLD MAN: Let me explain about the feast.

YOUNG MAN: OK, OK, I'm willing to go along with a gag . . . the feast . . . shoot.

OLD MAN: Well take, for example, that little fellow over there on the corner playing the flute.

YOUNG MAN: Where . . . you mean that corner?

OLD MAN: Yes, over there . . . the little fellow with the flute.

YOUNG MAN: Oh, yeah. You mean the traffic cop—sure, I see the traffic cop.

OLD MAN: NO! NO! Not the traffic cop . . . "traffic cop" . . . the little fellow on the corner with a red bandana on his head playing the *flute!*

YOUNG MAN: The newsboy . . . maybe?

OLD MAN: NO! Not the newsboy . . . you mean to say you don't see a little man wearing a green coat and a red bandana, dancing around the bus stop sign, playing a flute? *(He makes a motion as if playing a flute.)*

YOUNG MAN: LOOK! I don't see any little guy in a green coat and a red bandana dancing around any bus stop sign, playing any fridgin' flute on THAT CORNER!

OLD MAN: Well, I supposed that's understandable.

YOUNG MAN: OK. What's the catch?

OLD MAN: My fine young man, any fool, if he uses his eyes, can plainly see that there is no little man with a flute and a bandana . . . quite obviously, he is not there.

YOUNG MAN: *(pause, nods his head, barely restraining his impulse to throw his hat on the floor).* Yes, I . . . I see . . . yes, that . . . come to think of it . . . that's surely the reason why I couldn't see the guy with the flute.

OLD MAN: Now, the feast is about the same as the little man with the flute, you know.

YOUNG MAN: Yeah, I get it, you mean I'm not going to be able to see the feast either . . . well, you didn't have to tell me that!

OLD MAN: NO, NO . . . not in the least . . . you see the feast is like the little man because it is not . . . for the most part, essentially and in *factum* . . . there.

YOUNG MAN: Yeah, sure . . . but, uh . . . how we going to have the feast if it is not there? . . . or here?

OLD MAN: Ah . . . no more time to explain . . . the feast is about to begin. But there's one small matter to settle first.

YOUNG MAN: And what's that?

OLD MAN: Why, the sort of feast that you prefer, of course.

YOUNG MAN: Now, don't tell me we have a choice even . . . of feasts, that is.

OLD MAN: Absolutely! You have the broadest choice of all the choices, so you just say which it is that you prefer, and we will see what we can do.

YOUNG MAN: Yes, well . . . I'm not exactly up on this feast jazz. What sort of choices do I have?

OLD MAN: GREAT SCOTT! Let's see . . . you have wedding feasts, birthday feasts, feasts for coronation celebrations, vengeance feasts, mercy feasts and . . . funeral feasts, war feasts, peace feasts . . . whether you win or lose, you always have a feast . . . and you have feasts for kings, feasts for thieves, demagogues, churchmen, salesmen, boatmen, law men, small men . . . let's see, there are New Year feasts, Easter feasts, Christmas, Halloween, Arbor Day, Ground Hog's Day . . .

YOUNG MAN: Yes, but there's really no fridgin' reason to have a feast, come right down to it.

OLD MAN: I was hoping you'd say that, because you see, that's the best sort of feast to have.

YOUNG MAN: Sure . . . what's that?

OLD MAN: Why, the feast for no fridgin' . . . er, Phrygian reason, as you put it.

YOUNG MAN: Yeah, sure . . . that's bound to be the best . . . uh, feast.

OLD MAN: Certainly the best . . . no red tape of emotion to tangle up the revelry, no sticky cause, you see . . . no cloud of duty hanging overhead . . . yes, the feast for feast's sake is, without a doubt, the best.

YOUNG MAN: Anything you say, Dad . . . it's your show, but seriously, how're you going to have any kind of a feast when all you've got left is half a salomy 'n' lettuce, and me . . . *(Holding up his sandwich fragment.)* . . .

OLD MAN: Come, lad . . . the feast is not essentially a matter for eating. Food is but a key to the door where most any key will fit, you see . . . It is that moment when the appetite is satisfied, when hunger is bubbled away *(Slaps his stomach.)*, and the door opens on the magical landscape of the FEAST! (OLD MAN *strikes a dramatic pose and slowly lifts his hands to the ceiling.* YOUNG MAN *sits awed at the* OLD MAN's *invocation. The spotlight is by now the only light on the stage.)* OH, BACCHUS! SPIRIT OF MIRTH! SPIRIT OF SONG! LOOK DOWN WITH FAVOR UPON US . . . SMILE THE SMILE OF MERRIMENT, for why have we come but for the sake of merriment? Do we come to honor the living or the dead? Do we come to goad ourselves to victory or to cheer the victory already won? NO! Do we come in the guise of charity and pity? Or do we come in the guise of business and serious matters? NO! NONE OF THESE! WE HAVE COME TO THIS GRAND FEAST FOR NO FRIDGING . . . er, PHRYGIAN REASON AT ALL! . . . so to speak-but for the sake of merriment. Let us, oh Bacchus, celebrate this moment.

YOUNG MAN: *(whispering to* OLD MAN*)*. Hey, cut it out! You want somebody to see us and think we're nuts? You want to be shipped off to the booby hatch or something?

OLD MAN: . . . I look upon the vaulted hall, the ranks of bountiful tables smiling in their candlelight. I see kindred faces, expectant faces . . . How best to celebrate this occasion which is, of course, no occasion, we ask. I present to you our special guest (OLD MAN *waves an arm in* YOUNG MAN's *direction.* YOUNG MAN *shrinks back.*) Here is a mind of vigor and youth. He represents a promise for our age . . .

YOUNG MAN: *(whispering). Look here, Old Man,* I don't know what you're up to, but I sure as fat don't like it. I didn't ask to get into this. I . . . I was sucked into this flaming feast, you know damn well I was . . . come on now.

OLD MAN: Ladies and gentlemen, I present to you a young man with depth of spirit, breadth of heart, and fullness of imagination . . .

YOUNG MAN: *(still whispering).* This is no fair, you tricked me . . . you trapped me . . . you . . . *(Shouts in* OLD MAN's *ear.)* . . . FRUITCAKE! (OLD MAN *not fazed.* YOUNG MAN *hastily stoops to pick up his bag and lunch papers, puts on his cap in preparation for flight.)*

OLD MAN: . . . . in short, I present to you the Angry Young Man. (OLD MAN *catches* YOUNG MAN *by the sleeve and leads him into the spotlight.)*

YOUNG MAN: Look here, this gag of yours has gone far enough . . . go right ahead and spout off if you want, just leave me out of it . . . uh, just feast it by yourself, why don't you?

OLD MAN: *(whispering).* Don't spoil it all . . . this is part of the bit. There always has to be some sort of a keynote speech at every feast.

YOUNG MAN: But really, Dad. This is ridiculous . . . I mean, really.

OLD MAN: I don't know what you're so worried about. All you have to do is to say a few words to them . . .

YOUNG MAN: To WHO?

OLD MAN: To them . . . *(Indicates the audience.)* It's just part of the bit, you know.

YOUNG MAN: OK, OK. Nobody's going to say I'm not a good sport, a good Joe, an allright guy . . . just so long as you agree that if someone happens to come by, it's all a joke, see . . . Let's make this short . . . what am I supposed to say?

OLD MAN: Well, let me see . . . you ought to say something about the reason for the feast which, of course, will be a hard part . . . you just say what you like. Yes, and add something about how distinguished the audience is . . . appeal to the emotions, their pity, amuse them, flatter them, agree with them . . .

YOUNG MAN: OK, anything you say. Remember, I'm just going along with the gag. *(Takes off his hat and faces the audience with an embarrassed smile, then turns towards the* OLD MAN *again.)* Aw, come on. This is crazy.

OLD MAN: *(whispering).* Go on, go on . . .

YOUNG MAN: *(turns to the audience, smiling again).* Ladies and gentlemen . . . I'm not much on speeches really . . . *(Turns.)* How's that?

OLD MAN: Fine, fine. Their sympathy is already with you.

YOUNG MAN: *(facing the audience again).* . . . and believe me, it's like a great honor to be here at this moment before you. Now let me tell you about a funny thing that happened to me during my lunch hour. I was sitting there, see, and this old geezer invites me to this feast, just for a gag *(Glances at* OLD MAN.) and so . . . uh, here I am. And the introduction that the Old Man gave me was way out . . . I mean it was too much. But, consider the reason why we are all here . . . What is the reason we're all here, after all? . . . Damned if I know. Man, the whole things is really . . . uh, crazy. *(Glances at* OLD MAN.) Well, there doesn't seem to be any reason for being here—how about all the reasons for not being here? Just put that in your pipe and smoke it. Just think of all the things you might be doing instead of wasting your time at this, uh . . . feast. You could be putting the garbage out. You could be running over rabbits in your car *(Whispers* "Pity" *to* OLD MAN, *who nods his head in approval.)* . . . you could be shoplifting in a super-market or thinking up nasty comments to make to your mother-in-law. Just THINK of all the temptations you might be yielding to if you weren't wasting your time here, feasting it up . . . It's great to have you here and . . . So go right ahead and feast it up because it's great to be here *(Glances at* OLD MAN *for approval.)* and besides that, you are all really great people, and I really agree with you about everything . . . thank you. *(Turns to* OLD MAN.) How was that?

OLD MAN: That was great, just great . . . but wait, you may be called on to make a few toasts.

YOUNG MAN: *(brow-beaten and confused).* Just give the word, Dad . . . I can't make any more a fool of myself. *(He sits down, shaking his head.)*

OLD MAN: We thank the Angry Young Man for his remarks, always apt, well-chosen, short, and to the point. But the time for invocation has passed; the moment of preparation is accomplished . . . Therefore, GIVE US WINE! Let us lift up our glasses and so lift up our hearts. (OLD MAN *looks down at the front row seat where* BLUE JEANS *is sitting.)* PSSSSST! That's your cue . . . the wine . . . (BLUE JEANS *gets up from his seat, goes back up the ladder, and is to be seen at one end of the stage, putting on a short green coat and wrapping a red bandana around his head, both of which were handed out to him from the wings.)*

YOUNG MAN: Wine?

OLD MAN: Of course. How can you drink a toast without wine?

YOUNG MAN: Yeah, sure. This I gotta see. *(Follows* BLUE JEANS *off stage in amazement.)*

OLD MAN: . . . . Bring blushes to our cheeks and so flush the general spirit with unencumbered mirth. *(A cart is pushed out onto the stage, and* BLUE JEANS *trundles it out towards the spotlight. The cart holds a bucket of ice with a bottle of champagne and several glasses.)* Sniff gently the wine's bouquet and rejoice in its sweet vapor. Smile, laugh . . . feel warmth. (ELF *with champagne, i.e.,* BLUE JEANS, *rolls the cart into the spotlight.* YOUNG MAN *stares at him wide-eyed.* BLUE JEANS *answers the stare with an embarrassed shrug.* B.J. *pours out two glasses and hands one to* OLD MAN, *one to* YOUNG MAN.) I PROPOSE A TOAST . . . *(Lifts up his glass)* . . . TO THE FEAST . . . THE FEAST FOR NO FRIDGIN' . . . PHRYGIAN REASON, so the expression goes. *(Drinks, motioning to* YOUNG MAN *to do the same.)*

YOUNG MAN: *(after lowering his glass)* This is ridiculous . . .

OLD MAN: TO THE RIDICULOUS, THEN! *(They drink.)*

YOUNG MAN: This is UNREAL!

OLD MAN: TO THE UNREAL, IF YOU LIKE! *(They drink again.)*

YOUNG MAN: But I mean . . . really . . .

OLD MAN: DRINK! *(Drinks again. As* BLUE JEANS *refills the glasses,* OLD MAN *whis-*

pers to YOUNG MAN.) Now it's your turn to make the toast . . . (YOUNG MAN *hesitates*.) Go on, go on.

YOUNG MAN: Well, OK . . . I propose a toast to, uh . . .

OLD MAN: WHY NOT?!

YOUNG MAN: *(slumping down on the bucket)*. This is too much . . . (BLUE JEANS *has been sneaking a few drinks himself*.)

OLD MAN: All right, all right. So much for the toasts. *(Smacks his lips.)* Let's on to the reading of the ode.

YOUNG MAN: Yeah, sure, "The Ode"!

OLD MAN: Any kind of feast that's worth its salt has a reading of a commemorative ode . . . *(Takes a piece of paper from his shirt pocket and unfolds it.)* . . . You don't want to read the ode, do you? Some people say the special guest should always read the ode.

YOUNG MAN: Oh, no . . . uh, you just go right ahead, and I'll just sort of sit here and listen.

OLD MAN: As you prefer. *(During this time,* BLUE JEANS *has taken off his green coat and bandana, handing them off stage. He runs to the other side of the stage and slips into a tails coat and buttons on a white tie. He carries a cello and a small stool out to the edge of the spotlight, sits down and prepares to play. He yawns and stretches, waiting for* OLD MAN *to begin the reading of the ode.)* I present to you the ODE, forever commemorating this feast . . . our feast without reason or occasion.

(OLD MAN *motions for the* CELLIST *to begin his background music, waits a moment, then sighing, begins. As the ode progresses,* CELLIST *falls almost asleep, bowing of cello is spasmodic, but recorded music plays on.)*

OLD MAN'S ODE

Oh Bacchus, look this way!
See the anger mapping lines upon our brow, trace the print
of trouble's foot around our eyes—
Dismal creatures we must seem, cowering behind the day's
affairs,
Grasping tight to tin toy soldiers of our objective lives,
staring, as imagination dies;
See our mental siege and send down laughing legions to set
us free.

Thus did we call out to Bacchus, and he raised a drunken
eyebrow to our plea.
He sent to us, not legions, but a Cherub from his troop,
One small, fat, sodden Cherub *(Looks at* BLUE JEANS.)
from his troop.

Oh Cherub, harken to our woe!
Listen, minor spirit of the feast, fledgling sent by Bacchus
giving answer to our plea,
Thou, who now would far rather be thronged among thy
master's ranks,

Voicing his choral praise, or tipping the Olympian cup
       upon your lip to drain his liquid revelry,
Listen to our labor's chant, and grant, at least, a momen-
                                  tary feast!
Thus, did we call out to the Cherub Bacchus sent, still
                    pouting from his journey,
He blinked his eyes, and then his pudgy mouth gaped
                         open in a yawn,
But he gave us music, and he gave us wine before our time
                         was up.

(Factory whistle blows. All characters look up. The lights begin to fade on again. BLUE
JEANS *takes his cello and stool off stage, along with his costume. He comes back out and
grabs the glasses away from* YOUNG MAN, *who resists, and from* OLD MAN, *who is resigned.* BLUE JEANS *trundles the champagne cart off stage. The lights come up quickly
now. The stage work-lights are flipped on. The stage crew members begin to return to
their task of putting up sets.)*

YOUNG MAN: *(looking around him, bewildered)* The wine . . . the guy with the
    . . . uh, violin? Where have they gone? The feast . . . what happened?
OLD MAN: Time was up, that's all.
YOUNG MAN: What do you mean, the time was up . . . I mean they were all
    here . . . and your ode? Where's your ode?
OLD MAN: *(checking through his pockets)* I guess I lost it . . . *(He had set it down
    on the cart.)* . . . anyway, you heard the whistle, didn't you . . . back to
    work, you know. *(Cheerful.)*
YOUNG MAN: I guess so . . . (OLD MAN *climbs down the ladder after gathering up
    his things.* YOUNG MAN *puts his lunch papers in the paper bag and crumples it
    up. He gazes up the aisle as* OLD MAN *leaves.)*
OLD MAN: *(turns somewhere up the aisle)* So long, Young Man . . .
YOUNG MAN: So long, Old Man . . . *(Turns and walks slowly off stage pondering
    something. As he goes,* BLUE JEANS *bustles out from the wings, gathers up his easel
    and cardboard and ladder. In this rush he bumps into* YOUNG MAN, *says, "Excuse
    me . . .".* YOUNG MAN *barely notices.)* (BLUE JEANS *bustles off the other side of the
    stage; someone among the stage crew looks up, and noticing that some damn fool
    has opened the curtain when they weren't ready, shouts some expletive off stage.)*
    (The curtains close hurriedly.)

Performance and Analysis of
"The Feast"
by PAUL AND CAROLYN GRAY[14]

In the following discussion of Dan
Wright's "The Feast", though we shall be
neat and tidy about separating analysis
from rehearsal, keep in mind that our
own interpretation derived from both
analysis and rehearsal simultaneously and

that you will correct, amend, and adapt
our analysis as a result of your own experience during rehearsal.

Analysis: Theme and Thesis

All drama is about people in trouble.
Dan Wright's play belongs in the category
of "abstract trouble." In fact, the "trou-

[14]Essay used by permission of the authors.

ble" is so vague that we can't describe it much more precisely than the Angry Young Man when he says, "It's a grubby, lousy city in a grubby, rotten world filled up with a lotta grubby, lousy, rotten people. . .".

"The Feast" explores solutions to this vague trouble. To put the matter simply, this play is about how to cope with a "grubby, rotten world." Two nameless characters, an old man and an angry young man, much alike, must function in this world as best they can. But there is one notable distinction between the two. Unlike the young man, the old man manages to cope with the world by means of something the playwright calls "imaginative reconciliation." On its rational level, "The Feast" explores the nature of imaginative reconciliation. This rational level is organized around three points: first, an exploration of what imaginative reconciliation is *not;* second, a demonstration of how it operates; and third, its effect on those who use it.

First, the old man's imaginative reconciliation is more than pretending, for the young man pretends every bit as much as the old man. He pretends that he is angry, or, as Wright puts it, he is characterized by "brooding, suspicious expressions of a rebelliousness which, I guess, he considers attractive." Furthermore, he pretends not to care about the world that is indifferent to him. His own feigned indifference includes even his mother: "Well, for your information, so happens the old lady can take it in the ear for all I'm concerned." But the young man's pretensions are ironic. Intending to deceive others, he succeeds only in deceiving himself.

The old man's pretensions are of quite a different order. Although far more elaborate than the young man's, they deceive no one—not even the old man himself. Early in the play he asks the young man to see "a little man wearing a green coat and a red bandana, dancing around the bus stop sign, playing a flute." When the young man objects that no such being exists, the old man retorts, "Any fool, if he uses his eyes, can plainly see that there is no little man with a flute and a bandana . . . quite obviously, he is not there."

Once the old man establishes that imaginative reconciliation involves pretending but not deception, he shows how it operates: *participation* (the young man cannot remain passive but must actively engage in the feast) and *ritual* (invocation, speech, toast, and ode of commemoration) result in *transformation* (an empty storage lot becomes a banquet hall and a meal out of a lunch pail becomes a feast).

Finally this imaginative reconciliation changes the young man during the play. At first he is hostile toward any sort of contact with the old man. Then suddenly, without being aware of it, he comes to experience the old man's pretendings as real. The old man no sooner introduces the young man to the imaginary banqueters than the young man starts *whispering.* His common sense tells him that he and the old man are alone, but almost against his will his imaginative self takes over. The final turning point comes in his banquet speech. That he even makes a speech is significant evidence of his growing participation. The feast, he says, is really just a waste of time, but then he thinks of how that time would probably be spent otherwise: "You could be putting the garbage out. You could be running over rabbits in your car . . . you could be shoplifting in a super-market or thinking up nasty comments to make to your mother-in-law." Ironically, the young man's arguments against the feast convince him of its value, until at the end of his speech he can say, "It's great to have you here . . . and it's great to be here."

Now the young man's power of imaginative reconciliation takes over. His dreary common sense is silenced. When the wine is called for, it is real wine, brought by that man in the green coat and bandana the young man could not see before, and the music is actually heard, not pretended.

With the reading of the ode, the factory whistle blows and the reality of the feast ends. The young man, stunned by the extent of his imagination, now finds the everyday world as unreal as he had initially found the feast. One small incident at the end of the play however, suggests that imaginative reconciliation has already begun to change his outlook on the world. When someone accidentally bumps into him, his response is neither the aggression nor anger we might expect. Instead, he "barely notices."

Naturally, Wright's play suggests a significance, or perhaps "significances," beyond its specific subject. The playwright himself encourages us to find these significances. He titles his play "The Feast" and then has the old man point out how much this event should suggest: "Come lad," he says, "the feast is not essentially a matter for eating. Food is but a key to the door where most any key will fit, you see . . . . It is that moment when the appetite is satisfied, when hunger is bubbled away *(Slaps his stomach.)* and the door opens on the magical landscape of the FEAST!"

Imaginative reconciliation, with its ritual and transformation, so necessary to the old man and the young one, is equally necessary for us all. Readers familiar with the Communion service (also based on the feast metaphor) will note how closely the structure of the old man's feast resembles the order of the Eucharist, with one proceeding from invocation, speech, toast and drinking, to ode and the other from invocation, sermon, blessing of the wine and communion, to the benediction.

The play also seems to comment on the nature of drama itself. For drama, and indeed all art, is another form of feast, or imaginative reconciliation. We may begin watching the drama as reluctantly as the young man watches the feast, but gradually, like him, we move from passive observation to active participation, and because the play has significance for us, we, like the angry young man, emerge somehow changed. For all its unreality (and the play, like the old man, never tries to deceive us that its events are real), we experience it as real. Perhaps, Wright hints, this ability to make us experience the unreal as real, by itself justifies art. Plays may be written to support causes and protest wrongs, but at heart they exist because they are necessary. Or, as the old man says of feasts, "the best" are those with "no sticky cause, you see . . . no cloud of duty hanging overhead . . . yes, the feast for feast's sake is, without a doubt, the best."

Analysis: Major Characters

Because the old man copes well, he is assured and confident throughout the play. Notice the language of each character: where the style of Blue Jeans and the angry young man is characterized by halting, uncertain construction, the old man's language has none of the "er," "uh" and incomplete sentences of the other two. We also know that the old man is friendly and happy. Wright's note to the performer is revealing: "He [the old man] is characterized by an ambling, joyful gait, and when he speaks, it is with the friendly booming quality of a man who has found a sense of self-assurance and contentment." Nor does the old man change during the play; he is the same at the end—cheerful.

The angry young man, however, does change. We have pointed earlier to his gradual participation in the feast. Furthermore, he is changed by his experience. When the feast ends, he is not only stunned but sorry that it is over. We know that he has really experienced the feast because he asks of the wine and the violinist, "Where have they gone?" We also realize that he has been changed by the experience, first, because he no longer seems angry (note also that the old man addresses him as "Angry Young Man" during the feast, but simply as "Young Man" at the end) and, second, because Wright tells us that, as the young man leaves the stage, he is "pondering something." So affected has he been by the feast that for once his response is not to scoff or sneer, but to ponder.

When Blue Jeans tells us in his opening speech, "I've got characters," we know that he serves as spokesperson for the playwright. He begins the play with a rather awkward address to the audience. He is embarrassed about the quality of the experience he offers: "no one said it was going to be an extraordinary sort of play . . . I mean, as a matter of fact, it's quite an ordinary sort of . . . ." He then steps aside and acts only as an assistant to the old man. While he refuses to comment on the feast, he does actively participate in its creation.

Since the action of the play could easily begin with the old man's entrance, why is Blue Jeans necessary? Perhaps because although Wright has a thesis, he wishes to present it tentatively, as a possibility, a suggestion. Through Blue Jeans, Wright can communicate his own hesitancy and diffidence. This, we believe, explains why Blue Jeans seems so uncomfortable over demanding the audience's time and attention. In short, where the old man and the angry young man embody the message of the play, Blue Jeans puts the audience in the right mood to receive that message.

Rehearsals

Your first rehearsals should focus on developing a clear image of the characters and their actions. We suggest that you start by working on the whole character rather than on individual speeches. Many successful performers begin with the character's body and how it moves through space. Without worrying about the words, practice the old man's entrance. Visualize clearly how he walks "through the audience down the center aisle." The play-

wright tells us he does this with "an ambling, joyful gait." Remembering his age, practice this gait, visualizing his baggy pants, red plaid shirt, and his suspenders. If you can find suspenders, wear them. What is the old man thinking as he walks down the aisle? Is he lost in thought, or does he see where he is, and is he delighted to be there? Keep in mind why he has come here, for his lunch, which to him will be a feast. When this entrance is easy for you, rehearse it singing "freight train, freight train," in the old man's "friendly, booming" voice.

Now practice the young man's walk. Although he "enters from the side," we suggest that at first you make him enter from the same place as the old man, but in his own unique way. He is not delighted to be there; he is defensive; he is young. Carry your body as if you were expecting someone to hit you unexpectedly. Remember that the young man comes for his lunch, which for him is simply a physical necessity. Improvise a monologue the young man might mutter to himself on his way down the aisle.

As you have probably noticed, in our list of characteristics we have not indicated any age for Blue Jeans. Since the text itself makes no mention of it, this is one of many decisions performers must make for themselves. Keep two things in mind as you make your decision. First, this is a *definite character,* so whatever age you decide on must be specific. You cannot play him as twenty one minute and as seventy the next. Second, the age you pick must "feel right" for you. That is, the age you decide upon must allow him to say what he says and do what he does in the play naturally. The text itself suggests that Blue Jeans is a curious combination of the two main characters. Like the young man, he is awkward and self-conscious and he stammers. At other times he sounds like the old man. In his opening speech, for instance, he says of the factory whistle, "It blows, and people change . . .

you know, it toots, and people are possessed by it. It beckons in the harbor, and people look up expectant." Once you have decided the best age for you and the character, paraphrase his opening speech and move about the stage as Blue Jeans would, talking to the audience as you do so.

Using Properties

Another technique for getting the feel of the whole character is to handle objects, or properties, as the character would. Three easily found properties featured in this play are Blue Jeans's glasses, the old man's lunch pail, and the young man's lunch bag. Go through Blue Jeans's first speech using the glasses to gesture, to emphasize a point, and to reflect the character's awkwardness. Improvise a scene in which the old man packs his lunch pail. Be sure to keep in mind that he is packing not a lunch but a feast. Again, practice his entrance and use the lunch pail to underscore his characteristics. Work through the same improvisation with the young man and his lunch bag. You should run through these physical exercises and others that occur to you not only in early rehearsals but throughout your preparation for performance.

Rehearsing Dialogue

After these exercises, we are now ready to work on a specific scene. For our purposes, we select a brief dialogue exchange, that moment in the play when the old and the young man meet, beginning with old man's "Ah, you are here too ..." and ending with the young man's first "Humph."

Get someone else to read the lines of the young man while you work exclusively on the old man. Pretend that the old man enters the auditorium, sees the young man on stage, and delivers his opening lines of this exchange as he comes down the aisle. This will allow your voice to build on the physical conception you have of the character. Next practice the line with the old man seated as described in the play, concentrating on the shift in tone in the speech. Try to find verbs that describe how the old man says each sentence. We would suggest something like the following: "Oh, you are here too," he noticed. "So you have come to join in the Great, Green Lunch Hour—that moment of rapture and dizzy joy, that ... uh, moment of freedom," he rhapsodized. "So you have come too?" he inquired. As you practice performing these verbs, remember what the feast symbolizes for the old man. Be sure you understand why his description of it climaxes with the phrase "moment of freedom." Practice going from this rhapsody to the more muted last question. The young man clearly has been unresponsive to the old man's enthusiasm. But remember the old man is not threatened by the hostility of the world around him; he is simply responsive to others' moods. This will make it easier to deliver the old man's second speech, "as you wish ... was just trying to make conversation." He does not stop being friendly.

If possible, have some other person read the old man's lines while you rehearse the young man. His opening line also shifts in tone. Although the stage directions say he "realizes that OLD MAN has spoken to him," it takes the whole speech for him to fully comprehend this (he's not very quick). "Yeah, sure," he responds, caught off guard. "I mean, what do you mean?" he parries, putting up his guard. "Of course, I am here," he snaps. "I mean I DON'T EVEN KNOW YOU, OLD MAN," he attacks.

Although the young man is now prepared for a confrontation, the old man's response offers him no excuse for one. Not knowing what to say, but wanting the last word he makes a sound, and any incoherent noise will do, as long as it expresses the young man's annoyance and guarded uneasiness. Again, we recommend that you practice his lines as the young man enters so that you can build on those walking exercises. You should also use properties through the rehearsal of this dialogue.

When you feel comfortable with these characters separately, practice taking both roles. Here the challenge will be to make the physical shifts necessary in going from one speech to another. At first, give yourself plenty of time between speeches. As the shifts become easier, you should be able to eliminate much, if not all, of the physical movement. What you should never eliminate is the bodily tone, the physical set, appropriate for each character.

Throughout the rehearsal process get into the habit of constantly moving back and forth between your initial analysis and your performance. You will find that as you perform the play you will want to correct your analysis, while at the same time your analysis will serve to correct your performance. We end, therefore, as we began—with our belief that understanding and performing literature go hand in hand.

ANTHOLOGY V

Wait
GALWAY KINNELL

Wait, for now.
Distrust everything if you have to.
But trust the hours. Haven't they
carried you everywhere, up to now?
Personal events will become interesting again.
Hair will become interesting.
Pain will become interesting.
Buds that open out of season will become interesting.
Second-hand gloves will become lovely again;
their memories are what give them
the need for other hands. And the desolation
of lovers is the same: that enormous emptiness
carved out of such tiny beings as we are
asks to be filled; the need
for the new love *is* faithfulness to the old.

Wait.
Don't go too early.
You're tired. But everyone's tired.
But no one is tired enough.

Only wait a little and listen:
music of hair,
music of pain,
music of looms weaving all our loves again.

Be there to hear it, it will be the only time,
most of all to hear
the flute of your whole existence,
rehearsed by the sorrows, play itself into total exhaustion.

The School
DONALD BARTHELME

Well, we had all these children out planting trees, see, because we figured
that . . . that was part of their education, to see how, you know, the root sys-
tems . . . and also the sense of responsibility, taking care of things, being indi-
vidually responsible. You know what I mean. And the trees all died. They were
orange trees. I don't know why they died, they just died. Somthing wrong with
the soil possibly or maybe the stuff we got from the nursery wasn't the best.
We complained about it. So we've got thirty kids there, each kid had his or her
own little tree to plant, and we've got these thirty dead trees. All these kids
looking at these little brown sticks, it was depressing.

It wouldn't have been so bad except that just a couple of weeks before the
thing with the trees, the snakes all died. But I think that the snakes—well, the
reason that the snakes kicked off was that . . . you remember, the boiler was
shut off for four days because of the strike, and that was explicable. It was
something you could explain to the kids because of the strike. I mean, none of
their parents would let them cross the picket line and they knew there was a
strike going on and what it meant. So when things got started up again and we
found the snakes they weren't too disturbed.

With the herb gardens it was probably a case of overwatering, and at least
now they know not to overwater. The children were very conscientious with
the herb gardens and some of them probably . . . you know, slipped them a
little extra water when we weren't looking. Or maybe . . . well, I don't like to
think about sabotage, although it did occur to us. I mean, it was something that
crossed our minds. We were thinking that way probably because before that
the gerbils had died, and the white mice had died, and the salamander . . .
well, now they know not to carry them around in plastic bags.

Of course we *expected* the tropical fish to die, that was no surprise. Those
numbers, you look at them crooked and they're belly-up on the surface. But
the lesson plan called for a tropical-fish input at that point, there was nothing
we could do, it happens every year, you just have to hurry past it.

We weren't even supposed to have a puppy.

We weren't even supposed to have one, it was just a puppy the Murdoch
girl found under a Gristede's truck one day and she was afraid the truck would
run over it when the driver had finished making his delivery, so she stuck it in
her knapsack and brought it to school with her. So we had this puppy. As soon
as I saw the puppy I thought, Oh Christ, I bet it will live for about two weeks
and then . . . And that's what it did. It wasn't supposed to be in the classroom
at all, there's some kind of regulation about it, but you can't tell them they can't
have a puppy when the puppy is already there, right in front of them, running
around on the floor and yap yap yapping. They named it Edgar—that is, they
named it after me. They had a lot of fun running after it and yelling, "Here,
Edgar! Nice Edgar!" Then they'd laugh like hell. They enjoyed the ambiguity.

I enjoyed it myself. I don't mind being kidded. They made a little house for it in the supply closet and all that. I don't know what it died of. Distemper, I guess. It probably hadn't had any shots. I got it out of there before the kids got to school. I checked the supply closet each morning, routinely, because I knew what was going to happen. I gave it to the custodian.

And then there was this Korean orphan that the class adopted through the Help the Children program, all the kids brought in a quarter a month, that was the idea. It was an unfortunate thing, the kid's name was Kim and maybe we adopted him too late or something. The cause of death was not stated in the letter we got, they suggested we adopt another child instead and sent us some interesting case histories, but we didn't have the heart. The class took it pretty hard, they began (I think; nobody ever said anything to me directly) to feel that maybe there was something wrong with the school. But I don't think there's anything wrong with the school, particularly, I've seen better and I've seen worse. It was just a run of bad luck. We had an extraordinary number of parents passing away, for instance. There were I think two heart attacks and two suicides, one drowning, and four killed together in a car accident. One stroke. And we had the usual heavy mortality rate among the grandparents, or maybe it was heavier this year, it seemed so. And finally the tragedy.

The tragedy occurred when Matthew Wein and Tony Mavrogordo were playing over where they're excavating for the new federal office building. There were all these big wooden beams stacked, you know, at the edge of the excavation. There's a court case coming out of that, the parents are claiming that the beams were poorly stacked. I don't know what's true and what's not. It's been a strange year.

I forgot to mention Billy Brandt's father, who was knifed fatally when he grappled with a masked intruder in his home.

One day, we had a discussion in class. They asked me, where did they go? The trees, the salamander, the tropical fish, Edgar, the poppas and mommas, Matthew and Tony, where did they go? And I said, I don't know, I don't know. And they said, who knows? and I said, nobody knows. And they said, is death that which gives meaning to life? And I said, no, life is that which gives meaning to life. Then they said, but isn't death, considered as a fundamental datum, the means by which the taken-for-granted mundanity of the everyday may be transcended in the direction of—

I said, yes, maybe.

They said, we don't like it.

I said, that's sound.

They said, it's a bloody shame!

I said, it is.

They said, will you make love now with Helen (our teaching assistant) so that we can see how it is done? We know you like Helen.

I do like Helen but I said that I would not.

We've heard so much about it, they said, but we've never seen it.

I said I would be fired and that it was never, or almost never, done as a demonstration. Helen looked out of the window.

They said, please, please make love with Helen, we require an assertion of value, we are frightened.

I said that they shouldn't be frightened (although I am often frightened) and that there was value everywhere. Helen came and embraced me. I kissed her a few times on the brow. We held each other. The children were excited. Then there was a knock on the door, I opened the door, and the new gerbil walked in. The children cheered wildly.

The Married Man
ROBERT PHILLIPS

I was cut in two.
Two halves separated
cleanly between the eyes.
Half a nose and mouth on one
side, ditto on the other.
The split opened my chest
like a chrysalis, a part
neat in the hair.
Some guillotine slammed
through skull, neck, cage,
spine, pelvis, behind,
like a butcher splits a chicken breast.

I never knew which side my heart
was on. Half of me sat happy
in a chair, stared at the other
lying sad on the floor. Half wanted
to live in clover, half to breathe
the city air. One longed to live
Onassis-like, one aspired to poverty.
The split was red and raw.

I waited for someone to unite me.
My mother couldn't do it. She claimed
the sissy side and dressed it like a doll.
My father couldn't do it. He glared
at both sides and didn't see a one.
My teachers couldn't do it. They stuck
a gold star on one forehead,
dunce-capped the other.

So the two halves lived in a funny
    house,
glared at one another through the
    seasons;
one crowed obscenities past midnight,
the other sat still, empty as a cup.
One's eye roadmapped red from tears,
the other, clear and water-bright.
Stupid halves of me! They couldn't
    even
decide between meat and fish on
    Fridays.
Then one began to die. It turned
    grey as old meat.

Until you entered the room
of my life. You took the hand of one
and the hand of the other
and clasped them in the hands of you.
The two of me and the one of you
joined hands and danced about the room,
and you said, "You've got to pull yourself
together!", and I did, and we are two-
stepping our lives together still,

And it is only when I study hard
the looking-glass I see that one
eye is slightly higher, one corner
of my mouth twitches—a fish on a
    hook!—
whenever you abandon me.

Auto Wreck
KARL SHAPIRO

Its quick soft silver bell beating, beating,
And down the dark one ruby flare
Pulsing out red light like an artery,
The ambulance at top speed floating
    down

Past beacons and illuminated clocks
Wings in a heavy curve, dips down,
And brakes speed, entering the crowd.
The doors leap open, emptying light;
Stretchers are laid out, the mangled lifted

And stowed into the little hospital.
Then the bell, breaking the hush, tolls
    once,
And the ambulance with its terrible cargo
Rocking, slightly rocking, moves away,
As the doors, an afterthought, are closed.

We are deranged, walking among the cops
Who sweep glass and are large and
    composed.
One is still making notes under the light.
One with a bucket douches ponds of
    blood
Into the street and gutter.
One hangs lanterns on the wrecks that
    cling,
Empty husks of locusts, to iron poles.

Our throats were tight as tourniquets,

Our feet were bound with splints, but
    now
Like convalescents intimate and gauche,
We speak through sickly smiles and warn
With the stubborn saw of common sense,
The grim joke and the banal resolution.
The traffic moves around with care,
But we remain, touching a wound
That opens to our richest horror.
Already old, the question Who shall die?
Becomes unspoken Who is innocent?

For death in war is done by hands;
Suicide has cause and stillbirth, logic;
And cancer, simple as a flower, blooms.
But this invites the occult mind,
Cancels our physics with a sneer,
And spatters all we know of denouement
Across the expedient and wicked stones.

From a Survivor
ADRIENNE RICH

The pact that we made was the ordinary pact
of men & women in those days

I don't know who we thought we were
that our personalities
could resist the failures of the race

Lucky or unlucky, we didn't know
the race had failures of that order
and that we were going to share them

Like everybody else, we thought of ourselves as special

Your body is as vivid to me
as it ever was: even more

since my feeling for it is clearer:
I know what it could do and could not do

it is no longer
the body of a god
or anything with power over my life

Next year it would have been 20 years
and you are wastefully dead
who might have made the leap
we talked, too late, of making

which I live now
not as a leap
but a succession of brief, amazing movements

each one making possible the next

Weathering
ALASTAIR REID

I am old enough now for a tree
once planted, knee-high, to have grown to be
twenty times me,

and to have seen babies marry, and heroes grow deaf—
but that's enough meaning-of-life
It's living through time we ought to be connoisseurs of.

From wearing a face all this time, I am made aware
of the maps faces are, of the inside wear and tear.
I take to faces that have come far.

In my father's carved face, the bright eye
he sometimes would look out of, seeing a long way
through all the tree rings of his history.

I am awed by how things weather: the oak mantel
in the house in Spain, fingered to a sheen.
The mark of hands leaned into the lintel,

the tokens in the drawer I sometimes touch—
a crystal lived in on a trip, the watch
my father's wrist wore to a thin gold sandwich.

It is an equilibrium
that wears the cresting seasons but still stays calm
and keeps warm. It deserves a good name.

Weathering. Patina, gloss and whorl.
The trunk of the almond tree, gnarled but still fruitful.
Weathering is what I would like to do well.

Hardweed Path Going
A. R. AMMONS

Every evening, down into the hardweed
going,
the slop bucket heavy, held-out, wire handle
freezing in the hand, put it down a minute, the jerky
smooth unspilling levelness of the knees,
         meditation of a bucket rim,
lest the wheat meal,
floating on clear greasewater, spill,
down the grown-up path:

         don't forget to slop the hogs,
         feed the chickens,
         water the mule,
         cut the kindling,
         build the fire,
         call up the cow:

         supper is over, it's starting to get
dark early,
better get the scraps together, mix a little meal in,
nothing but swill.

         The dead-purple woods hover on the west.
I know those woods.
Under the tall, ceiling-solid pines, beyond the edge of
field and brush, where the wild myrtle grows,
         I let my jo-reet loose.
A jo-reet is a bird. Nine weeks of summer he
sat on the well bench in a screened box,
a stick inside to walk on,
         "jo-reet," he said, "jo-reet."
         and I
would come up to the well and draw the bucket down
deep into the cold place where red and white marbled
clay oozed the purest water, water celebrated
throughout the county:
         "Grits all gone?"
         "jo-reet."
Throw a dipper of cold water on him. Reddish-black
flutter.
         "reet, reet, reet!"

         Better turn him loose before
cold weather comes on.

Doom caving in
inside
any pleasure, pure
attachment
of love.

Beyond the wild myrtle away from cats I turned him loose
and his eye asked me what to do, where to go;
he hopped around, scratched a little, but looked up at me.
Don't look at me. Winter is coming.
Disappear in the bushes. I'm tired of you and will
be alone hereafter. I will go dry in my well.
        I will turn still.
Go south. Grits is not available in any natural form.
Look under leaves, try mushy logs, the floors of pinywoods.
South into the dominion of bugs.

        They're good woods.
But lay me out if a mourning dove far off in the dusky pines
        starts.

        Down the hardweed path going,
leaning, balancing, away from the bucket, to
Sparkle, my favorite hog, sparse, fine black hair,
grunted while feeding if rubbed,
scratched against the hair, or if talked to gently:
got the bottom of the slop bucket:
        "Sparkle . . .
        You hungry?
        Hungry, girly?"
blowing, bubbling in the trough.

        Waiting for the first freeze:
"Think it's going to freeze tonight?" say the neighbors,
the neighbors, going by.

        Hog-killing.

Oh, Sparkle, when the axe tomorrow morning falls
and the rush is made to open your throat,
I will sing, watching dry-eyed as a man, sing my
        love for you in the tender feedings.

        She's nothing but a hog, boy.

Bleed out, Sparkle, the moon-chilled bleaches
        of your body hanging upside-down
hardening through the mind and night of the first freeze.

The Lunatic's Tale
WOODY ALLEN

Madness is a relative state. Who can say which of us is truly insane? And while I roam through Central Park wearing moth-eaten clothes and a surgical mask, screaming revolutionary slogans and laughing hysterically, I wonder even now if what I did was really so irrational. For, dear reader, I was not always what is popularly referred to as "a New York street crazy," pausing at trash cans to fill my shopping bags with bits of string and bottle caps. No, I was once a highly successful doctor living on the upper East Side, gadding about town in a brown Mercedes, and bedecked dashingly in a varied array of Ralph Lauren tweeds. Hard to believe that I, Dr. Ossip Farkis, once a familiar face at theatre openings, Sardi's, Lincoln Center, and the Hamptons, where I boasted great wit and a formidable backhand, am now sometimes seen roller skating unshaven down Broadway wearing a knapsack and a pinwheel hat.

The dilemma that precipitated this catastrophic fall from grace was simply this. I was living with a woman whom I cared for very deeply and who had a winning and delightful personality and mind; rich in culture and humor and a joy to spend time with. But (and I curse Fate for this) she did not turn me on sexually. Concurrently, I was sneaking crosstown nightly to rendezvous with a photographer's model called Tiffany Schmeederer, whose blood-curdling mentality was in direct inverse proportion to the erotic radiation that oozed from her every pore. Undoubtedly, dear reader, you have heard the expression, "a body that wouldn't quit." Well Tiffany's body would not only not quit, it wouldn't take five minutes off for a coffee break. Skin like satin, or should I say like the finest of Zabar's novy, a leonine mane of chestnut hair, long willowy legs and a shape so curvacious that to run one's hands over any portion of it was like a ride on the Cyclone. This not to say the one I roomed with, the scintillating and even profound Olive Chomsky was a slouch physiognomywise. Not at all. In fact she was a handsome woman with all the attendant perquisites of a charming and witty culture vulture and, crudely put, a mechanic in the sack. Perhaps it was the fact that when the light hit Olive at a certain angle she inexplicably resembled my Aunt Rifka. Not that Olive actually *looked* like my mother's sister. (Rifka had the appearance of a character in Yiddish folklore called the Golem.) It was just that some vague similarity existed around the eyes, and then only if the shadows fell properly. Perhaps it was the incest taboo or perhaps it was just that a face and body like Tiffany Schmeederer's comes along every few million years and usually heralds an ice age or the destruction of the world by fire. The point is, my needs required the best of two women.

It was Olive I met first. And this after an endless string of relationships wherein my partner invariably left something to be desired. My first wife was brilliant, but had no sense of humor. Of the Marx Brothers, she was convinced the amusing one was Zeppo. My second wife was beautiful, but lacked real passion. I recall once, while we were making love, a curious optical illusion occurred and for a split second it almost looked as though she was moving. Sharon Pflug, whom I lived with for three months, was too hostile. Whitney Weisglass was too accommodating. Pippa Mondale, a cheerful divorcee, made the fatal mistake of defending candles shaped like Laurel and Hardy.

Well-meaning friends fixed me up with a relentless spate of blind dates, all unerringly from the pages of H. P. Lovecraft. Ads, answered out of desperation, in the *New York Review of Books,* proved equally futile as the "thirtyish poetess" was sixtyish, the "coed who enjoys Bach and Beowulf" looked like Grendel, and the "Bay Area bisexual" told me I didn't quite coincide with either of her desires. This is not to imply that now and again an apparent plum would not somehow emerge: a beautiful woman, sensual and wise with impressive credentials and winning ways. But, obeying some age-old law, perhaps from the Old Testament or Egyptian *Book of the Dead, she* would reject *me.* And so it was that I was the most miserable of men. On the surface, apparently blessed with all the necessities for the good life. Underneath, desperately in search of a fulfilling love.

Nights of loneliness led me to ponder the esthetics of perfection. Is anything in nature actually "perfect" with the exception of my Uncle Hyman's stupidity? Who am I to demand perfection? I, with my myriad faults. I made a list of my faults, but could not get past: 1) Sometimes forgets his hat.

Did anyone I know have a "meaningful relationship"? My parents stayed together 40 years, but that was out of spite. Greenglass, another doctor at the hospital, married a woman who looked like a Feta cheese "because she's kind." Iris Merman cheated with any man who was registered to vote in the tri-state area. Nobody's relationship could actually be called happy. Soon I began to have nightmares.

I dreamed I visited a singles bar where I was attacked by a gang of roving secretaries. They brandished knives and forced me to say favorable things about the borough of Queens. My analyst counseled compromise. My rabbi said, "Settle, settle. What about a woman like Mrs. Blitzstein? She may not be a great beauty, but nobody is better at smuggling food and light firearms in and out of a ghetto." An actress I met, who assured me her real ambition was to be a waitress at a coffee house, seemed promising, but during one brief dinner her single response to everything I said was, "Oh, wow." Then one evening, in an effort to unwind after a particularly trying day at the hospital, I attended a Stravinsky concert alone. During intermission I met Olive Chomsky and my life changed.

Olive Chomsky, literate and wry, who quoted Eliot and played tennis and also Bach's "Two Part Inventions" on the piano. And who never said, "Oh, wow," or wore anything marked Pucci or Gucci or listened to country and western music or dialogue radio. And incidentally, who was always willing at the drop of a hat to do the unspeakable and even initiate it. What joyful months spent with her till my sex drive (listed, I believe, in the *Guinness Book of World Records*) waned. Concerts, movies, dinners, weekends, endless wonderful discussions of everything from Pogo to Rig-Vheda. And never a gaffe from her lips. Insights only. Wit too! And of course the appropriate hostility toward all deserving targets: politicians, television, facelifts, the architecture of housing projects, men in leisure suits, film courses, and people who begin sentences with "basically."

Oh, curse the day that a wanton ray of light coaxed forth those ineffable facial lines bringing to mind Aunt Rifka's stolid visage. And curse the day also that at a loft party in Soho, an erotic archetype with the unlikely name of Tiffany Schmeederer adjusted the top of her plaid wool kneesock and said to me with a voice resembling that of a mouse in the animated cartoons, "What sign are you?" Hair and fangs audibly rising on my face in the manner of the classic lycanthropic, I felt compelled to oblige her with a brief discussion of astrology, a subject rivaling my intellectual interest with such heavy issues as est, alpha waves, and the ability of leprechauns to locate gold.

Hours later I found myself in a state of waxy flexibility as the last piece of bikini underpants slid noiselessly to the floor around her ankles while I lapsed inexplicably into the Dutch National Anthem. We proceeded to make love in the manner of The Flying Wallendas. And so it began.

Alibis to Olive. Furtive meetings with Tiffany. Excuses for the woman I loved while my lust was spent elsewhere. Spent, in fact, on an empty little yo-yo whose touch and wiggle caused the top of my head to dislodge like a frisbee and hover in space like a flying saucer. I was forsaking my responsibility to the woman of my dreams for a physical obsession not unlike the one Emil Jannings experienced in *The Blue Angel*. Once I feigned illness, asking Olive to attend a Brahms Symphony with her mother so that I could satisfy the moronic whims of my sensual goddess who insisted I drop over to watch "This Is Your Life" on television, "because they're doing Johnny Cash!" Yet, after I paid my dues by sitting through the show, she rewarded me by dimming the rheostats and transporting my libido to the planet Neptune. Another time I casually told Olive I was going out to buy the papers. Then I raced seven blocks to Tiffany's, took the elevator up to her floor, but, as luck would have it, the infernal lift stuck. I paced like a caged cougar between floors, unable to satisfy my flaming desires and also unable to return home by a credible time. Released at last by some firemen, I hysterically concocted a tale for Olive featuring myself, two muggers and the Loch Ness monster.

Fortunately, luck was on my side and she was sleeping when I returned home. Olive's own innate decency made it unthinkable to her that I would deceive her with another woman, and while the frequency of our physical relations had fallen off, I husbanded my stamina in such a manner as to at least partially satisfy her. Constantly ridden with guilt, I offered flimsy alibis about fatigue from overwork, which she bought with the guilessness of an angel. In truth, the whole ordeal was taking its toll on me as the months went by. I grew to look more and more like the figure in Edward Munch's "The Scream."

Pity my dilemma, dear reader! This maddening predicament that afflicts perhaps a good many of my contemporaries. Never to find all the requirements one needs in a single member of the opposite sex. On one hand, the yawning abyss of compromise. On the other, the enervating and reprehensible existence of the amorous cheat. Were the French right? Was the trick to have a wife and also a mistress, thereby delegating responsibility for varied needs between two parties? I knew that if I proposed this arrangement openly to Olive, understanding as she was, the chances were very good I would wind up impaled on her British umbrella. I grew weary and depressed and contemplated suicide. I held a pistol to my head, but at the last moment lost my nerve and fired in the air. The bullet passed through my ceiling, causing Mrs. Fitelson in the apartment overhead to leap straight upward on to her bookshelf and remain perched there throughout the high holidays.

Then one night it all cleared up. Suddenly, and with a clarity one usually associates with LSD, my course of action became apparent. I had taken Olive to see a revival of a Bela Lugosi film at the Elgin. In the crucial scene, Lugosi, a mad scientist, switches the brain of some unlucky victim with that of a gorilla, both being strapped to operating tables during an electrical storm. If such a thing could be devised by a screenwriter in the world of fiction, surely a surgeon of my ability could, in real life, accomplish the same thing.

Well, dear reader, I won't bore you with the details which are highly technical and not easily understood by the lay mentality. Suffice it to say that one dark and stormy night a shadowy figure might have been observed smuggling two drugged women (one with a shape that caused men to drive their cars up on the sidewalk) into an unused operating room at Flower Fifth Avenue. There, as bolts of lightning crackled jaggedly through the sky, he performed an operation done before only in the world of celluloid fantasy, and then by a Hungarian actor who would one day turn the hickey into an art form.

The result? Tiffany Schmeederer, her mind now existing in the less spectacular body of Olive Chomsky, found herself delightfully free from the curse of being a sex object. As Darwin taught us, she soon developed a keen intelligence, and while not perhaps the equal of Hannah Arendt's, it did permit her to recognize the follies of astrology and marry happily. Olive Chomsky, suddenly the possessor of a cosmic topography to go with her other superb gifts, became my wife as I became the envy of all around me.

The only hitch was that after several months of bliss with Olive that was the equal of anything in the *Arabian Nights,* I inexplicably grew dissatisfied with this dream woman and developed instead a crush on Billie Jean Zapruder, an airline stewardess whose boyish, flat figure and Alabama twang caused my heart to do flip-flops. It was at this point that I resigned my position at the hospital, donned my pinwheel hat and knapsack and began skating down Broadway.

from *Letters To a Young Poet*
RAINER MARIA RILKE
Translated by M. D. Herter Norton

Paris, February 17th, 1903

My Dear Sir,
Your letter only reached me a few days ago. I want to thank you for its great and kind confidence. I can hardly do more. I cannot go into the nature of your verses; for all critical intention is too far from me. With nothing can one approach a work of art so little as with critical words: they always come down to more or less happy misunderstandings. Things are not all so comprehensible and expressible as one would mostly have us believe; most events are inexpressible, taking place in a realm which no word has ever entered, and more inexpressible than all else are works of art, mysterious existences, the life of which, while ours passes away, endures.

After these prefatory remarks, let me only tell you further that your verses have no individual style, although they do show quiet and hidden beginnings of something personal. I feel this most clearly in the last poem, "My Soul." There something of your own wants to come through to word and melody. And in the lovely poem "To Leopardi" there does perhaps grow up a sort of kinship with the great solitary man. Nevertheless the poems are not yet anything on their own account, nothing independent, even the last and the one to Leopardi. Your kind letter, which accompanied them, does not fail to make clear to me various shortcomings which I felt in reading your verses without however being able specifically to name them.

You ask whether your verses are good. You ask me. You have asked others before. You send them to magazines. You compare them with other poems, and you are disturbed when certain editors reject your efforts. Now (since you have allowed me to advise you) I beg you to give up all that. You are looking outward, and that above all you should not do now. Nobody can counsel and help you, nobody. There is only one single way. Go into yourself. Search for the reason that bids you write; find out whether it is spreading out its roots in the deepest places of your heart, acknowledge to yourself whether you would have to die if it were denied you to write. This above all—ask yourself in the stillest hour of your night: *must* I write? Delve into yourself for a deep answer. And if this should be affirmative, if you may meet this earnest question with a strong and simple *"I must,"* then build your life according to this necessity; your life even into its most indifferent and slightest hour must be a sign of this urge and a testimony to it. Then draw near to Nature. Then try, like some first human being, to say what you see and experience and love and lose. Do not write love-poems; avoid at first those forms that are too facile and common-place: they are the most difficult, for it takes a great, fully matured power to give something of your own where good and even excellent traditions come to mind in quantity. Therefore save yourself from these general themes and seek those which your own everyday life offers you; describe your sorrows and desires, passing thoughts and the belief in some sort of beauty—describe all these with loving, quiet, humble sincerity, and use, to express yourself, the things in your environment, the images from your dreams, and the objects of your memory. If your daily life seems poor, do not blame it; blame yourself, tell yourself that you are not poet enough to call forth its riches; for to the creator there is no poverty and no poor indifferent place. And even if you were in some prison the walls of which let none of the sounds of the world come to your senses—would you not then still have your childhood, that precious, kingly possession, that treasure-house of memories? Turn your attention thither. Try to raise the submerged sensations of that ample past; your personality will grow more firm, your solitude will widen and will become a dusky dwelling past which the noise of others goes by far away.—And if out of this turning inward, out of this absorption into your own world *verses* come, then it will not occur to you to ask anyone whether they are good *verses*. Nor will you try to interest magazines in your poems: for you will see in them your fond natural possession, a fragment and a voice of your life. A work of art is good if it has sprung from necessity. In this nature of its origin lies the judgment of it: there is no other. Therefore, my dear sir, I know no advice for you save this: to go into yourself and test the deeps in which your life takes rise; at its source you will find the answer to the question whether you *must* create. Accept it, just as it sounds, without inquiring into it. Perhaps it will turn out that you are called to be an aritst. Then take that destiny upon yourself and bear it, its burden and its greatness, without ever asking what recompense might come from outside. For the creator must be a world for himself and find everything in himself and in Nature to whom he has attached himself.

But perhaps after this descent into yourself and into your inner solitude you will have to give up becoming a poet; (it is enough, as I have said, to feel that one could live without writing: then one must not attempt it at all). But even then this inward searching which I ask of you will not have been in vain. Your life will in any case find its own ways thence, and that they may be good, rich and wide I wish you more than I can say.

What more shall I say to you? Everything seems to me to have its just emphasis; and after all I do only want to advise you to keep growing quietly and seriously throughout your whole development; you cannot disturb it more rudely than by looking outward and expecting from outside replies to questions that only your inmost feeling in your most hushed hour can perhaps answer.

It was a pleasure to me to find in your letter the name of Professor Horaček; I keep for that lovable and learned man a great veneration and a gratitude that endures through the years. Will you, please, tell him how I feel; it is very good of him still to think of me, and I know how to appreciate it.

The verses which you kindly entrusted to me I am returning at the same time. And I thank you once more for your great and sincere confidence, of which I have tried, through this honest answer given to the best of my knowledge, to make myself a little worthier than, as a stranger, I really am.

Yours faithfully and with all sympathy:
RAINER MARIA RILKE

Accomplishments
CYNTHIA MACDONALD

I painted a picture—green sky—and showed it to my mother.
She said that's nice, I guess.
So I painted another holding the paintbrush in my teeth,
Look, Ma, no hands. And she said
I guess someone would admire that if they knew
How you did it and they were interested in painting which I am not.

I played clarinet solo in Gounod's Clarinet Concerto
With the Buffalo Philharmonic. Mother came to listen and said
That's nice, I guess.
So I played it with the Boston Symphony,
Lying on my back and using my toes,
Look, Ma, no hands. And she said
I guess someone would admire that if they knew
How you did it and they were interested in music which I am not.

I made an almond soufflé and served it to my mother.
She said, that's nice, I guess.
So I made another, beating it with my breath,
Serving it with my elbows,
Look, Ma, no hands. And she said

I guess someone would admire that if they knew
How you did it and they were interested in eating which I am not.

So I sterilized my wrists, performed the amputation, threw away
My hands and went to my mother, but before I could say
Look, Ma, no hands, she said
I have a present for you and insisted I try on
The blue kid gloves to make sure they were the right size.

Staying Alive
DAVID WAGONER

Staying alive in the woods is a matter of calming down
At first and deciding whether to wait for rescue,
Trusting to others,
Or simply to start walking and walking in one direction
Till you come out—or something happens to stop you.
By far the safer choice
Is to settle down where you are, and try to make a living
Off the land, camping near water, away from shadows.
Eat no white berries;
Spit out all bitterness. Shooting at anything
Means hiking further and further every day
To hunt survivors;
It may be best to learn what you have to learn without a gun,
Not killing but watching birds and animals go
In and out of shelter
At will. Following their example, build for a whole season:
Facing across the wind in your lean-to,
You may feel wilder,
But nothing, not even you, will have to stay in hiding.
If you have no matches, a stick and a fire-bow
Will keep you warmer,
Or the crystal of your watch, filled with water, held up to the sun
Will do the same in time. In case of snow
Drifting toward winter,
Don't try to stay awake through the night, afraid of freezing—
The bottom of your mind knows all about zero;
It will turn you over
And shake you till you waken. If you have trouble sleeping
Even in the best of weather, jumping to follow
With eyes strained to their corners
The unidentifiable noises of the night and feeling
Bears and packs of wolves nuzzling your elbow,
Remember the trappers
Who treated them indifferently and were left alone.
If you hurt yourself, no one will comfort you

Or take your temperature,
So stumbling, wading, and climbing are as dangerous as flying.
But if you decide, at last, you must break through
In spite of all danger,
Think of yourself by time and not by distance, counting
Where ever you're going by how long it takes you;
No other measure
Will bring you safe to nightfall. Follow no streams; they run
Under the ground or fall into wilder country.
Remember the stars
And moss when your mind runs into circles. If it should rain
Or the fog should roll the horizon in around you,
Hold still for hours
Or days if you must, or weeks, for seeing is believing
In the wilderness. And if you find a pathway,
Wheel-rut, or fence-wire,
Retrace it left or right: someone knew where he was going
Once upon a time, and you can follow
Hopefully, somewhere,
Just in case. There may even come, on some uncanny evening,
A time when you're warm and dry, well fed, not thirsty,
Uninjured, without fear,
When nothing, either good or bad, is happening.
This is called staying alive. It's temporary.
What occurs after
Is doubtful. You must always be ready for something to come bursting
Through the far edge of a clearing, running toward you,
Grinning from ear to ear
And hoarse with welcome. Or something crossing and hovering
Overhead, as light as air, like a break in the sky,
Wondering what you are.
Here you are face to face with the problem of recognition.
Having no time to make smoke, too much to say,
You should have a mirror
With a tiny hole in the back for better aiming, for reflecting
Whatever disaster you can think of, to show
The way you suffer.
These body signals have universal meaning: If you are lying
Flat on your back with arms outstretched behind you,
You say you require
Emergency treatment; if you are standing erect and holding
Arms horizontal, you mean you are not ready;
If you hold them over
Your head, you want to be picked up. Three of anything
Is a sign of distress. Afterward, if you see
No ropes, no ladders,
No maps or messages falling, no searchlights or trails blazing.
Then, chances are, you should be prepared to burrow
Deep for a deep winter.

The Public Library
ISAAC BABEL

You can feel straightaway that The Book reigns supreme here. All the people who work in the library have entered into communion with The Book, with life at second-hand, and have themselves become, as it were, a mere reflection of the living.

Even the attendants in the cloakroom are hushed and enigmatic, full of inward-looking calm, and their hair is neither dark nor fair, but something in between.

It is quite possible that at home they drink methylated spirits on Saturday nights and systematically beat their wives. But in the library they are as quiet as mice, self-effacing, withdrawn, and somber.

Then there is the cloakroom attendant who draws. His eyes are kind and woebegone. Once every two weeks, helping a fat man in a black jacket to take off his coat, he murmurs that "Nikolai Sergeyevich likes my drawings, and so does Konstantin Vasilyevich. I've only had elementary schooling, and where I go from here I really don't know."

The fat man listens. He is a reporter, a married man, fond of his food and overworked. Once every two weeks he goes to the library to rest—he reads about some trial or other, carefully copies out the plan of the building where the murder took place, is perfectly happy and forgets that he's married and overworked.

He listens to the attendant in anxious bewilderment and wonders how he should deal with someone like this. If he gives him a tip when he leaves, the man might be offended—he's an artist, after all. If he doesn't give him anything, he might still be offended—after all, he's an attendant.

In the reading room there are the more exalted members of the staff: the assistants. Some of them stand out by virtue of a pronounced physical defect—one has his fingers all curled up and another has a head which has dropped over on one side and got stuck there. They are dowdily dressed and extremely thin. They look as though they are possessed of some idea unknown to the world at large.

Gogol would have described them well!

Those assistants who don't "stand out" have gentle balding patches, neat gray suits, a prim look in their eyes, and a painful slowness of movement. They are always chewing something and moving their jaws, although they have nothing in their mouths, and they talk in a practiced whisper. Altogether, they have been debilitated by books, by not being able to have a good yawn every now and then.

Nowadays, during the war, the readers have changed. There are fewer students—scarcely any, indeed. Once in a blue moon you may see one pining away, without undue hardship, in a corner. He will be on a "white ticket," that is, will have a military exemption on grounds of health. He will wear horn-rimmed spectacles or cultivate a slight limp. There are also, however, those on state scholarships and hence temporarily exempted. They have a hangdog look, wear drooping mustaches, appear tired of life and very introspective: they keep reading a little, thinking a little, looking at the pattern of the reading lamp and burying themselves in a book again. They're supposed to graduate and go into the army, but they're in no hurry. Everything in its time.

Here's a former student who has come back in the shape of a wounded officer, with a black sling. His wound is healing. He is young and rosy-cheeked. He has had his dinner and taken a stroll down the Nevsky. The Nevsky is already lit up. The evening edition of the *Stock Exchange News* is already making its triumphal rounds. In Yeliseyev's there are grapes cradled in millet seed. He's early for his evening engagement, so the officer, just for old times' sake, goes to the library. He stretches out his long legs under the table at which he is sitting and reads the *Apollon*. It's a little boring. Opposite sits a girl student. She is studying anatomy and copying a drawing of the stomach into her notebook. She looks as though she's from Kaluga or thereabouts—broad-faced, big-boned, rosy-cheeked, thoroughgoing, and tough. If she has a boyfriend, then that's the best thing for her: she's made for love.

Next to her is a picturesque tableau, an inevitable feature of any public library in the Russian Empire: a sleeping Jew. He is worn out. His hair is a burnished black. His cheeks are sunken. His forehead is bruised and his mouth is half open. He makes wheezing noises. Goodness knows where he comes from, or whether he has a residence permit. He reads every day, and he also sleeps every day. His face is a picture of overwhelming weariness and near-madness. He is a martyr to the book, peculiarly Jewish, an inextinguishable martyr.

Next to the assistants' counter there sits reading a large, broad-chested woman in a gray jumper. She is the sort who talks in the library in unexpectedly loud tones, frankly and ecstatically voicing her astonishment at the printed word and engaging her neighbors in conversation. Her reason for coming here is to find a way of making soap at home. She is about forty-five years old. Is she right in the head, they wonder.

Another regular reader is a lean little colonel in a loose-fitting tunic, wide breeches, and brightly polished boots. He has short legs and his mustaches are the color of cigar ash. He dresses them with brilliantine, as a result of which they run to all shades of dark gray. In days of yore he was so dumb he couldn't even make the rank of colonel and hence be retired as a major general. In retirement he has been an infernal nuisance to the gardener, the servants, and his grandson. At the age of seventy-three he took it into his head to write a history of his regiment. He writes surrounded by a mountain of materials. He is liked by the assistants, whom he greets with exquisite courtesy. He no longer gets on his family's nerves. The servant gladly polishes his boots.

There are all kinds of other people in the public library—too many to be described.

It is evening. The reading room is almost dark. The silent figures at the tables are a study in weariness, thirst for knowledge, ambition. . . .

Soft snow weaves its weft behind the large windows. Nearby, on the Nevsky, there is teeming life. Far away, in the Carpathians, blood is flowing. *C'est la vie.*

Some Foreign Letters
ANNE SEXTON

I knew you forever and you were always old,
soft white lady of my heart. Surely you would scold
me for sitting up late, reading your letters,
as if these foreign postmarks were meant for me.

You posted them first in London, wearing furs
and a new dress in the winter of eighteen-ninety.
I read how London is dull on Lord Mayor's Day,
where you guided past groups of robbers, the sad holes
of Whitechapel, clutching your pocketbook, on the way
to Jack the Ripper dissecting his famous bones.
This Wednesday in Berlin, you say, you will
go to a bazaar at Bismarck's house. And I
see you as a young girl in a good world still,
writing three generations before mine. I try
to reach into your page and breathe it back . . .
but life is a trick, life is a kitten in a sack.

This is the sack of time your death vacates.
How distant you are on your nickel-plated skates
in the skating park in Berlin, gliding past
me with your Count, while a military band
plays a Strauss waltz. I loved you last,
a pleated old lady with a crooked hand.
Once you read *Lohengrin* and every goose
hung high while you practiced castle life
in Hanover. Tonight your letters reduce
history to a guess. The Count had a wife.
You were the old maid aunt who lived with us.
Tonight I read how the winter howled around
the towers of Schloss Schwöbber, how the tedious
language grew in your jaw, how you loved the sound
of the music of the rats tapping on the stone
floors. When you were mine you wore an earphone.

This is Wednesday, May 9th, near Lucerne,
Switzerland, sixty-nine years ago. I learn
your first climb up Mount San Salvatore;
this is the rocky path, the hole in your shoes,
the yankee girl, the iron interior
of her sweet body. You let the Count choose
your next climb. You went together, armed
with alpine stocks, with ham sandwiches
and *seltzer wasser*. You were not alarmed
by the thick woods of briars and bushes,
nor the rugged cliff, nor the first vertigo
up over Lake Lucerne. The Count sweated
with his coat off as you waded through top snow.
He held your hand and kissed you. You rattled
down on the train to catch a steamboat for home;
or other postmarks: Paris, Verona, Rome.

This is Italy. You learn its mother tongue.
I read how you walked on the Palatine among

the ruins of the palaces of the Caesars;
alone in the Roman autumn, alone since July.
When you were mine they wrapped you out of here
with your best hat over your face. I cried
because I was seventeen. I am older now.
I read how your student ticket admitted you
into the private chapel of the Vatican and how
you cheered with the others, as we used to do
on the Fourth of July. On Wednesday in November
you watched a balloon, painted like a silver ball,
float up over the Forum, up over the lost emperors,
to shiver its little modern cage in an occasional
breeze. You worked your New England conscience out
beside artisans, chestnut vendors and the devout.

Tonight I will learn to love you twice;
learn your first days, your mid-Victorian face.
Tonight I will speak up and interrupt
your letters, warning you that wars are coming,
that the Count will die, that you will accept
your America back to live like a prim thing
on the farm in Maine. I tell you, you will come
here, to the suburbs of Boston, to see the blue-nose
world go drunk each night, to see the handsome
children jitterbug, to feel your left ear close
one Friday at Symphony. And I tell you,
you will tip your boot feet out of that hall,
rocking from its sour sound, out onto
the crowded street, letting your spectacles fall
and your hair net tangle as you stop passers-by
to mumble your guilty love while your ears die.

Emma Zunz
JORGE LOUIS BORGES
Translated by Donald A. Yates

Returning home from the Tarbuch and Loewenthal textile mills on the 14th of January, 1922, Emma Zunz discovered in the rear of the entrance hall a letter, posted in Brazil, which informed her that her father had died. The stamp and the envelope deceived her at first; then the unfamiliar handwriting made her uneasy. Nine or ten lines tried to fill up the page; Emma read that Mr. Maier had taken by mistake a large dose of veronal and had died on the third of the month in the hospital of Bagé. A boardinghouse friend of her father had signed the letter, some Fein or Fain from Río Grande, with no way of knowing that he was addressing the deceased's daughter.

Emma dropped the paper. Her first impression was of a weak feeling in her stomach and in her knees; then of blind guilt, of unreality, of coldness, of fear; then she wished that it were already the next day. Immediately afterward she realized that that wish was futile because the death of her father was the only thing that had happened in the world, and it would go on happening endlessly. She picked up the piece of paper and went to her room. Furtively, she hid it in a drawer, as if somehow she already knew the ulterior facts. She had already begun to suspect them, perhaps; she had already become the person she would be.

In the growing darkness, Emma wept until the end of that day for the suicide of Manuel Maier, who in the old happy days was Emmanuel Zunz. She remembered summer vacations at a little farm near Gualeguay, she remembered (tried to remember) her mother, she remembered the little house at Lanús which had been auctioned off, she remembered the yellow lozenges of a window, she remembered the warrant for arrest, the ignominy, she remembered the poison-pen letters with the newspaper's account of "the cashier's embezzlement," she remembered (but this she never forgot) that her father, on the last night, had sworn to her that the thief was Loewenthal. Loewenthal, Aaron Loewenthal, formerly the manager of the factory and now one of the owners. Since 1916 Emma had guarded the secret. She had revealed it to no one, not even to her best friend, Elsa Urstein. Perhaps she was shunning profane incredulity; perhaps she believed that the secret was a link between herself and the absent parent. Loewenthal did not know that she knew; Emma Zunz derived from this slight fact a feeling of power.

She did not sleep that night and when the first light of dawn defined the rectangle of the window, her plan was already perfected. She tried to make the day, which seemed interminable to her, like any other. At the factory there were rumors of a strike. Emma declared herself, as usual, against all violence. At six o'clock, with work over, she went with Elsa to a women's club that had a gymnasium and a swimming pool. They signed their names; she had to repeat and spell out her first and her last name, she had to respond to the vulgar jokes that accompanied the medical examination. With Elsa and with the youngest of the Kronfuss girls she discussed what movie they would go to Sunday afternoon. Then they talked about boyfriends and no one expected Emma to speak. In April she would be nineteen years old, but men inspired in her, still, an almost pathological fear . . . Having returned home, she prepared a tapioca soup and a few vegetables, ate early, went to bed and forced herself to sleep. In this way, laborious and trivial, Friday the fifteenth, the day before, elapsed.

Impatience awoke her on Saturday. Impatience it was, not uneasiness, and the special relief of it being that day at last. No longer did she have to plan and imagine; within a few hours the simplicity of the facts would suffice. She read in *La Prensa* that the *Nordstjärnan*, out of Malmö, would sail that evening from Pier 3. She phoned Loewenthal, insinuated that she wanted to confide in him, without the other girls knowing, something pertaining to the strike; and she promised to stop by at his office at nightfall. Her voice trembled; the tremor was suitable to an informer. Nothing else of note happened that morning. Emma worked until twelve o'clock and then settled with Elsa and Perla Kronfuss the details of their Sunday stroll. She lay down after lunch and reviewed, with her eyes closed, the plan she had devised. She thought that the final step would be less horrible than the first and that it would doubtlessly afford her the taste of victory and justice. Suddenly, alarmed, she got up and ran to the dresser drawer. She opened it; beneath the picture of Milton Sills, where she had left it the night before, was Fain's letter. No one could have seen it; she began to read it and tore it up.

To relate with some reality the events of that afternoon would be difficult and perhaps unrighteous. One attribute of a hellish experience is unreality, an attribute that seems to allay its terrors and which aggravates them perhaps. How could one make credible an action which was scarcely believed in by the person who executed it, how to recover that brief chaos which today the memory of Emma Zunz repudiates and confuses? Emma lived in Almagro, on Liniers Street: we are certain that in the afternoon she went down to the water-front. Perhaps on the infamous Paseo de Julio she saw herself multiplied in mirrors, revealed by lights and denuded by hungry eyes, but it is more reasonable to suppose that at first she wandered, unnoticed, through the indifferent portico . . . She entered two or three bars, noted the routine or technique of the other women. Finally she came across men from the *Nordstjärnan*. One of them, very young, she feared might inspire some tenderness in her and she chose instead another, perhaps shorter than she and coarse, in order that the purity of the horror might not be mitigated. The man led her to a door, then to a murky entrance hall and afterwards to a narrow stairway and then a vestibule (in which there was a window with lozenges identical to those in the house at Lanús) and then to a passageway and then to a door which was closed behind her. The arduous events are outside of time, either because the immediate past is as if disconnected from the future, or because the parts which form these events do not seem to be consecutive.

During that time outside of time, in that perplexing disorder of disconnected and atrocious sensations, did Emma Zunz think *once* about the dead man who motivated the sacrifice? It is my belief that she did think once, and in that moment she endangered her desperate undertaking. She thought (she was unable not to think) that her father had done to her mother the hideous thing that was being done to her now. She thought of it with weak amazement and took refuge, quickly, in vertigo. The man, a Swede or Finn, did not speak Spanish. He was a tool for Emma, as she was for him, but she served him for pleasure whereas he served her for justice.

When she was alone, Emma did not open her eyes immediately. On the little night table was the money that the man had left; Emma sat up and tore it to pieces as before she had torn the letter. Tearing money is an impiety, like throwing away bread; Emma repented the moment after she did it. An act of pride and on that day . . . Her fear was lost in the grief of her body, in her disgust. The grief and the nausea were chaining her, but Emma got up slowly and proceeded to dress herself. In the room there were no longer any bright colors; the last light of dusk was weakening. Emma was able to leave without anyone seeing her; at the corner she got on a Lacroze streetcar heading west. She selected, in keeping with her plan, the seat farthest toward the front, so that her face would not be seen. Perhaps it comforted her to verify in the insipid movement along the streets that what had happened had not contaminated things. She rode through the diminishing opaque suburbs, seeing them and forgetting them at the same instant, and got off on one of the side streets of Warnes. Paradoxically her fatigue was turning out to be a strength, since it obligated her to concentrate on the details of the adventure and concealed from her the background and the objective.

Aaron Loewenthal was to all persons a serious man, to his intimate friends a miser. He lived above the factory, alone. Situated in the barren outskirts of the town, he feared thieves; in the patio of the factory there was a large dog and in the drawer of his desk, everyone knew, a revolver. He had mourned with gravity, the year before, the unexpected death of his wife—a Gauss who had brought him a fine dowry—but money was his real passion. With intimate embarrassment, he knew himself to be less apt at earning it than at saving it. He was very religious; he believed he had a secret pact with God which exempted him from doing good in exchange for prayers and piety. Bald, fat, wearing the band of mourning, with smoked glasses and blond beard, he was standing next to the window awaiting the confidential report of worker Zunz.

He saw her push the iron gate (which he had left open for her) and cross the gloomy patio. He saw her make a little detour when the chained dog barked. Emma's lips were moving rapidly, like those of someone praying in a low voice; weary, they were repeating the sentence which Mr. Loewenthal would hear before dying.

Things did not happen as Emma Zunz had anticipated. Ever since the morning before she had imagined herself wielding the firm revolver, forcing the wretched creature to confess his wretched guilt and exposing the daring stratagem which would permit the Justice of God to triumph over human justice. (Not out of fear but because of being an instrument of Justice she did not want to be punished.) Then, one single shot in the center of his chest would seal Loewenthal's fate. But things did not happen that way.

In Aaron Loewenthal's presence, more than the urgency of avenging her father, Emma felt the need of inflicting punishment for the outrage she had suffered. She was unable not to kill him after that thorough dishonor. Nor did she have time for theatrics. Seated, timid, she made excuses to Loewenthal, she invoked (as a privilege of the informer) the obligation of loyalty, uttered a few names, inferred others and broke off as if fear had conquered her. She managed to have Loewenthal leave to get a glass of water for her. When the former, unconvinced by such a fuss but indulgent, returned from the dining room, Emma had already taken the heavy revolver out of the drawer. She squeezed the trigger twice. The large body collapsed as if the reports and the smoke had shattered it, the glass of water smashed, the face looked at her with amazement and anger, the mouth of the face swore at her in Spanish and Yiddish. The evil words did not slacken; Emma had to fire again. In the patio the chained dog broke out barking, and a gush of rude blood flowed from the obscene lips and soiled the beard and the clothing. Emma began the accusation she had prepared ("I have avenged my father and they will not be able to punish me . . ."), but she did not finish it, because Mr. Lowewenthal had already died. She never knew if he managed to understand.

The straining barks reminded her that she could not, yet, rest. She disarranged the divan, unbuttoned the dead man's jacket, took off the bespattered glasses and left them on the filing cabinet. Then she picked up the telephone and repeated what she would repeat so many times again, with these and with other words: *Something incredible has happened . . . Mr. Loewenthal had me come over on the pretext of the strike . . . He abused me, I killed him . . .*

Actually, the story *was* incredible, but it impressed everyone because substantially it was true. True was Emma Zunz's tone, true was her shame, true was her hate. True also was the outrage she had suffered: only the circumstances were false, the time, and one or two proper names.

Las Dos Caras del Patroncito
LUIS VALDEZ

CHARACTERS

ESQUIROL

PATRONCITO

ARMED GUARD

In September, 1965, six thousand farmworkers went on strike in the grape fields of De-lano. During the first months of the ensuing Huelga, the growers tried to intimidate the struggling workers to return to the vineyards. They mounted shotguns in their pickups, prominently displayed in the rear windows of the cab; they hired armed guards; they roared by in their huge caruchas, etc. It seemed that they were trying to destroy the spirit of the strikers with mere materialistic evidence of their power. Too poor to afford La Causa, many of the huelgistas left Delano to work in other areas; most of them stayed behind to picket through the winter; and a few returned to the fields to scab, pruning vines. The growers started trucking in more esquiroles from Texas and Mexico.

In response to this situation—especially the phoney "scary" front of the rancheros, we created Dos Caras. *It grew out of an improvisation in the old pink house behind the Huelga office in Delano. It was intended to show the "two faces of the boss."*

(A FARMWORKER *enters, carrying a pair of pruning shears.)*

FARMWORKER: *(To audience.)* Buenos días! This is the ranch of my patroncito, and I come here to prune grape vines. My patrón bring me all the way from Mexico here to California—the land of sun and money! More sun than money. But I better get to jalar now because my patroncito he don't like to see me talking to strangers. *(There is a roar backstage.)* Ay, here he comes in his big car! I better get to work. *(He prunes.)*

(The PATRONCITO *enters, wearing a yellow pig face mask. He is driving an imaginary limousine, making the roaring sound of the motor.)*

PATRONCITO: Good morning, boy!

FARMWORKER: Buenos días, patroncito. *(His hat in his hands.)*

PATRONCITO: You working hard, boy?

FARMWORKER: Oh, sí, patrón! Muy hard! *(He starts working furiously.)*

PATRONCITO: Oh, you can work harder than that, boy. *(He works harder.)* Harder! *(He works harder.)* Harder! *(He works still harder.)* HARDER!

FARMWORKER: Ay, that's too hard, patrón!

(The PATRONCITO *looks downstage then upstage along the imaginary row of vines, with the* FARMWORKER'S *head alongside his, following his movement.)*

PATRONCITO: How come you cutting all the wires instead of the vines, boy? *(The* FARMWORKER *shrugs helplessly, frightened and defenseless.)* Look, lemme show you something. Cut this vine here. *(Points to a vine.)* Now this one. *(*FARMWORKER *cuts.)* Now this one. *(*FARMWORKER *cuts.)* Now this one. *(The* FARMWORKER *almost cuts the* PATRONCITO'S *extended finger.)* HEH!

FARMWORKER: *(Jumps back.)* Ay!

PATRONCITO: Ain't you scared of me, boy? *(*FARMWORKER *nods.)* Huh, boy? *(*FARMWORKER *nods and makes a grunt signifying yes.)* What, boy? You don't have to be scared of me! I love my Mexicans. You're one of the new ones, huh? Com in from . . .

FARMWORKER: México, señor.

PATRONCITO: Did you like the truck ride, boy? *(*FARMWORKER *shakes head indicating no.)* What?!

FARMWORKER: I loved it, señor!

PATRONCITO: Of course you did. All my Mexicans love to ride in trucks! Just the sight of them barreling down the freeway makes my heart feel good; hands on their sombreros, hair flying in the wind, bouncing along happy as babies. Yes siree, I sure love my Mexicans, boy!

FARMWORKER: *(Puts his arm around* PATRONCITO.*)* Oh, Patrón.

PATRONCITO: *(Pushing him away.)* I love 'em about ten feet away from me, boy. Why, there ain't another grower in this whole damn valley that treats you like I do. Some growers got Filipinos, others got Arabs, me I prefer Mexicans. That's why I come down here to visit you, here in the field. I'm an important man, boy! Bank of America, University of California, Safeway stores—I got a hand in all of 'em. But look, I don't even have my shoes shined.

FARMWORKER: Oh, patrón, I'll shine your shoes! *(He gets down to shine* PATRONCITO'S *shoes.)*

PATRONCITO: Nevermind, get back to work. Up, boy, up I say! *(The* FARMWORKER *keeps trying to shine his shoes.)* Come on, stop it. STOP IT!

*(*CHARLIE *"La Jura" or "Rent-a-Fuzz" enters like an ape. He immediately lunges for the* FARMWORKER.*)*

PATRONCITO: Charlie! Charlie! no! It's okay, boy. This is one of MY Mexicans! He was only trying to shine my shoes.

CHARLIE: You sure?

PATRONCITO: Of course! Now you go back to the road and watch for union organizers.

CHARLIE: Okay.

*(*CHARLIE *exits like an ape. The* FARMWORKER *is off to one side, trembling with fear.)*

PATRONCITO: *(To* FARMWORKER.*)* Scared you, huh boy? Well lemme tell you, you don't have to be afraid of him, AS LONG AS YOU'RE WITH ME, comprende? I got him around to keep an eye on them huelguistas. You ever heard of them, son? Ever heard of Huelga? Or Cesar Ch'vez?

FARMWORKER: Oh sí, patrón!

PATRONCITO: What?

FARMWORKER: Oh no, señor! Es comunista! Y la huelga es puro pedo. Bola de colorados, arrastrados, huevones! No trabajan porque no quieren!

PATRONCITO: That's right, son. Sic'em Sic'em, boy!

FARMWORKER: *(Really getting into it.)* Comunistas! Desgraciados! Mendigos huevones!

PATRONCITO: Good boy! (FARMWORKER *falls to his knees, hands in front of his chest like a docile dog; his tongue hangs out.* PATRONCITO *pats him on the head.)* Good boy.

(The PATRONCITO *steps to one side and leans over:* FARMWORKER *kisses his ass.* PATRONCITO *snaps up triumphantly.)*

PATRONCITO: Atta' baby! You're OK, Pancho.

FARMWORKER: *(Smiling.)* Pedro.

PATRONCITO: Of course you are. Hell, you got it good here!

FARMWORKER: Me?

PATRONCITO: Damn right! You sure as hell ain't got my problems, I'll tell you that. Taxes, insurance, supporting all them bums on welfare. You don't have to worry about none of that. Like housing: don't I let you live in my labor camp—nice, rent-free cabins, air-conditioned?

FARMWORKER: Sí señor, ayer se cayó la puerta.

PATRONCITO: What was that? ENGLISH.

FARMWORKER: Yesterday, the door fell off, señor. And there's rats también. Y los escusados, the restrooms—ay, señor, fuchi! *(Holds fingers to his nose.)*

PATRONCITO: AWRIGHT! (FARMWORKER *shuts up.*) So you gotta rough it a little—I do that every time I go hunting in the mountains, Why, it's almost like camping out, boy. A free vacation!

FARMWORKER: Vacation?

PATRONCITO: Free!

FARMWORKER: Qué bueno. Thank you, patrón!

PATRONCITO: Don't mention it. So what do you pay for housing, boy?

FARMWORKER: NOthing! *(Pronounced "naw-thing.")*

PATRONCITO: Nothing, right! Now what about transportation? Don't I let you ride free in my trucks? To and from the fields?

FARMWORKER: Sí, señor.

PATRONCITO: What do you pay for transportation boy?

FARMWORKER: NOthing!

PATRONCITO: *(With* FARMWORKER.*)* Nothing! What about food? What do you eat, boy?

FARMWORKER: Tortillas y frijoles con chile.

PATRONCITO: Beans and tortillas. What's beans and tortillas cost, boy?

FARMWORKER: *(Together with* PATRÓN.*)* Nothing!

PATRONCITO: Okay! So what you got to complain about?

FARMWORKER: Nothing?

PATRONCITO: Exactly. You got it good! Now look at me: they say I'm greedy, that I'm rich. Well, let me tell you, boy, I got problems. No free housing for me, Pancho. I gotta pay for what I got. You see that car? How much you think a Lincoln Continental like that costs? Cash! $12,000! Ever write out a check for $12,000, boy?

FARMWORKER: No señor.

PATRONCITO: Well, lemme tell you, it hurts. It hurts right here! (*Slaps his wallet in his hind pocket.*) And what for? I don't NEED a car like that. I could throw it away!

FARMWORKER: (*Quickly.*) I'll take it, patrón.

PATRONCITO: GIT YOUR GREASY HANDS OFFA IT! (*Pause.*) Now, let's take a look at my housing. No free air-conditioned mountain cabin for me. No sir! You see that LBJ Ranch Style house up there, boy? How much you think a house like that costs? Together with the hill, which I built? $350,000!

FARMWORKER: (*Whistles.*) That's a lot of frijoles, patrón.

PATRONCITO: You're tellin' me! (*Stops, looks toward house.*) Oh yeah, and look at that, boy! You see her coming out of the house, onto the patio by the pool? The blonde with the mink bikini?

FARMWORKER: What bikini?

PATRONCITO: Well, it's small but it's there. I oughta know—it cost me $5,000! And every weekend she wants to take trips—trips to L.A., San Francisco, Chicago, New York. That woman hurts. It all costs money! You don't have problems like that, muchacho—that's why you're so lucky. Me, all I got is the woman, the house, the hill, the land. (*Starts to get emotional.*) Those commie bastards say I don't know what hard work is, that I exploit my workers. But look at all them vines, boy! (*Waves an arm toward the audience.*) Who the hell do they think planted all them vines with his own bare hands? Working from sun-up to sunset! Shoving vine shoots into the ground! With blood pouring out of his fingernails. Working in the heat, the frost, the fog, the sleet! (FARMWORKER *has been jumping up and down trying to answer him.*)

FARMWORKER: You, patrón, you!

PATRONCITO: (*Matter of factly.*) Naw, my grandfather, he worked his ass off out here. BUT I inherited, and it's all mine!

FARMWORKER: You sure work hard, boss.

PATRONCITO: Juan . . . ?

FARMWORKER: Pedro.

PATRONCITO: I'm going to let you in on a little secret. Sometimes I sit up there in my office and think to myself: I wish I was a Mexican.

FARMWORKER: You?

PATRONCITO: Just one of my own boys. Riding in the trucks, hair flying in the wind, feeling all that freedom, coming out here to the fields, working under the green vines, smoking a cigarette, my hands in the cool soft earth, underneath the blue skies, with white clouds drifting by, looking at the mountains, listening to the birdies sing.

FARMWORKER: (*Entranced.*) I got it good.

PATRONCITO: What you want a union for, boy?

FARMWORKER: I don't want no union, patrón.

PATRONCITO: What you want more money for?

FARMWORKER: I don't want—I want more money!

PATRONCITO: Shut up! You want my problems, is that it? After all I explained to you? Listen to me, son, if I had the power, if I had the POWER . . . wait a minute, I got the power! *(Turns toward* FARMWORKER, *frightening him.)* Boy!

FARMWORKER: I din't do it, patrón.

PATRONCITO: How would you like to be a Rancher for a day?

FARMWORKER: Who me? Oh no, señor. I can't do that.

PATRONCITO: Shut up. Gimme that. *(Takes his hat, shears, sign.)*

FARMWORKER: No, patrón, por favor, señor! Patroncito!

PATRONCITO: *(Takes off his own sign & puts it on* FARMWORKER.) Here!

FARMWORKER: Patrón . . . cito. *(He looks down at "patroncito" sign.)*

PATRONCITO: Alright, now take the cigar. *(*FARMWORKER *takes cigar.)* And the whip. *(*FARMWORKER *takes whip.)* Now look tough, boy. Act like you're the boss.

FARMWORKER: Sí, señor. *(He cracks the whip & almost hits his foot.)*

PATRONCITO: Come on, boy! Head up, chin out! Look tough, look mean. *(*FARM-WORKER *looks tough & mean.)* Act like you can walk into the governor's office and tell him off!

FARMWORKER: *(With unexpected force & power.)* Now, look here, Ronnie! *(*FARM-WORKER *scares himself.)*

PATRONCITO: That's good. But it's still not good enough. Let's see. Here take my coat.

FARMWORKER: Oh no, patrón, I can't.

PATRONCITO: Take it!

FARMWORKER: No, señor.

PATRONCITO: Come on!

FARMWORKER: Chale.

*(*PATRONCITO *backs away from* FARMWORKER. *He takes his coat and holds it out like a bullfighter's cape, assuming the bullfighting position.)*

PATRONCITO: Uh-huh, toro.

FARMWORKER: Ay! *(He turns toward the coat and snags it with an extended arm like a horn.)*

PATRONCITO: Ole! Okay, now let's have a look at you. *(*FARMWORKER *puts on coat.)* Naw, you're still missing something! You need something!

FARMWORKER: Maybe a new pair of pants?

PATRONCITO: *(A sudden flash.)* Wait a minute! *(He touches his pig mask.)*

FARMWORKER: Oh, no! Patrón, not that! *(He hides his face.)*

*(*PATRONCITO *removes his mask with a big grunt.* FARMWORKER *looks up cautiously, sees the* PATRÓN's *real face & cracks up laughing.)*

FARMWORKER: Patrón, you look like me!

PATRONCITO: You mean . . . I . . . look like a Mexican?

FARMWORKER: Sí, señor!

(FARMWORKER *turns to put on the mask, and* PATRONCITO *starts picking up* FARM-WORKER's *hat, sign, etc., and putting them on.*)

PATRONCITO: I'm going to be one of my own boys.

(FARMWORKER, *who has his back to the audience, jerks suddenly as he puts on "patron-cito" mask. He stands tall and turns slowly, now looking very much like a patrón.*)

PATRONCITO: (*Suddenly fearful, but playing along.*) Oh, that's good! That's . . . great.

FARMWORKER: (*Booming, brusque, patrón-like.*) Shut up and get to work, boy!

PATRONCITO: Hey, now that's more like it!

FARMWORKER: I said get to work! (*He kicks* PATRONCITO.)

PATRONCITO: Heh, why did you do that for?

FARMWORKER: Because I felt like it, boy! You hear me, boy? I like your name, boy! I think I'll call you boy boy!

PATRONCITO: You sure learn fast, boy.

FARMWORKER: I said SHUT UP!

PATRONCITO: What an actor. (*To audience.*) He's good, isn't he?

FARMWORKER: Come 'ere boy.

PATRONCITO: (*His idea of a Mexican.*) Sí, señor, I theeenk.

FARMWORKER: I don't pay you to think, son. I pay you to work. Now look here—see that car? It's mine.

PATRONCITO: My Lincoln Conti- Oh, you're acting. Sure.

FARMWORKER: And that LBJ Ranch Style house, with the hill? That's mine too.

PATRONCITO: The house too?

FARMWORKER: All mine.

PATRONCITO: (*More & more uneasy.*) What a joker.

FARMWORKER: Oh, wait a minute. Respect, boy! (*He pulls off* PATRONCITO's *farmworker hat.*) Do you see her? Coming out of *my* house, onto *my* patio by *my* pool? The blonde in the bikini? Well, she's mine too!

PATRONCITO: But that's my wife!

FAMRWORKER: Tough luck, son. You see this land, all these vines? They're mine.

PATRONCITO: Just a damn minute here. The land, the car, the house, hill, and the cherry on top too? You're crazy! Where am I going to live?

FARMWORKER: I got a nice, air-conditioned cabin down in the labor camp. Free housing, free transportation—

PATRONCITO: You're nuts! I can't live in those shacks! They got rats, cock-roaches. And those trucks are unsafe. You want me to get killed?

FARMWORKER: Then buy a car.

PATRONCITO: With what? How much you paying me here anyway?

FARMWORKER: Eighty-five cents an hour.

PATRONCITO: I was paying you a buck twenty-five!

FARMWORKER: I got problems, boy! Go on welfare!

PATRONCITO: Oh no, this is too much. You've gone too far, boy. I think you better gimme back my things. (*He takes off farmworker sign & hat, throws down shears, and tells the audience*) You know that damn Cesar Chavez is right? You can't do this work for less than two dollars an hour. No, boy, I think we've played enough. Give me back—

FARMWORKER: GIT YOUR HANDS OFFA ME, SPIC!

PATRONCITO: Now stop it, boy!

FARMWORKER: Get away from me, greaseball! (PATRONCITO *tries to grab mask.*) Charlie! Charlie!

(CHARLIE *the Rent-a-Fuzz comes bouncing in.* PATRONCITO *tries to talk to him.*)

PATRONCITO: Now listen, Charlie, I—

CHARLIE: (*Pushing him aside.*) Out of my way, Mex! (*He goes over to* FARM-WORKER.) Yeah, boss?

PATRONCITO: This union commie bastard is giving me trouble. He's trying to steal my car, my land, my ranch, and he even tried to rape my wife!

CHARLIE: (*Turning around, an infuriated ape.*) You touched a white woman, boy?

PATRONCITO: Charlie, you idiot, it's me! Your boss!

CHARLIE: Shut up!

PATRONCITO: Charlie! It's me!

CHARLIE: I'm gonna whup you good, boy! (*He grabs him.*)

PATRONCITO: (CHARLIE *starts dragging him out.*) Charlie! Stop it! Somebody help me! Help! Where's those damn union organizers? Where's Cesar Chavez? Help! Huelga! HUELGAAAAAA!

(CHARLIE *drags out the* PATRONCITO. *The* FARMWORKER *takes off the pig mask and turns toward the audience.*)

FARMWORKER: Bueno, so much for the patrón. I got his house, his land, his car—only I'm not going to keep 'em. He can have them. But I'm taking the cigar. Ay los watcho. (*Exit.*)

Vacation
WILLIAM STAFFORD

One scene as I bow to pour her coffee:—

> Three Indians in the scouring drouth
> huddle at a grave scooped in the gravel,
> lean to the wind as our train goes by.
> Someone is gone.
> There is dust on everything in Nevada.

I pour the cream.

Autobiographical Notes
JAMES BALDWIN

I was born in Harlem thirty-one years ago. I began plotting novels at about the time I learned to read. The story of my childhood is the usual bleak fantasy, and we can dismiss it with the restrained observation that I certainly would not consider living it again. In those days my mother was given to the exasperating and mysterious habit of having babies. As they were born, I took them over with one hand and held a book with the other. The children probably suffered, though they have since been kind enough to deny it, and in this way I read *Uncle Tom's Cabin* and *A Tale of Two Cities* over and over again; in this way, in fact, I read just about everything I could get my hands on—except the Bible, probably because it was the only book I was encouraged to read. I must also confess that I wrote—a great deal—and my first professional triumph, in any case, the first effort of mine to be seen in print, occurred at the age of twelve or thereabouts, when a short story I had written about the Spanish revolution won some sort of prize in an extremely short-lived church newspaper. I remember the story was censored by the lady editor, though I don't remember why, and I was outraged.

Also wrote plays, and songs, for one of which I received a letter of congratulations from Mayor La Guardia, and poetry, about which the less said, the better. My mother was delighted by all these goings-on, but my father wasn't; he wanted me to be a preacher. When I was fourteen I became a preacher, and when I was seventeen I stopped. Very shortly thereafter I left home. For God knows how long I struggled with the world of commerce and industry—I guess they would say they struggled with *me*—and when I was about twenty-one I had enough done of a novel to get a Saxton Fellowship. When I was twenty-two the fellowship was over, the novel turned out to be unsalable, and I started waiting on tables in a Village restaurant and writing book reviews—mostly, as it turned out, about the Negro problem, concerning which the color of my skin made me automatically an expert. Did another book, in company with photographer Theodore Pelatowski, about the store-front churches in Harlem. This book met exactly the same fate as my first—fellowship, but no sale. (It was a Rosenwald Fellowship.) By the time I was twenty-four I had decided to stop reviewing books about the Negro problem—which, by this time, was only slightly less horrible in print than it was in life—and I packed my bags and went to France, where I finished, God knows how, *Go Tell It on the Mountain.*

Any writer, I suppose, feels that the world into which he was born is nothing less than a conspiracy against the cultivation of his talent—which attitude certainly has a great deal to support it. On the other hand, it is only because the world looks on his talent with such a frightening indifference that the artist is compelled to make his talent important. So that any writer, looking back over even so short a span of time as I am here forced to assess, finds that the things which hurt him and the things which helped him cannot be divorced from each other; he could be helped in a certain way only because he was hurt in a certain way; and his help is simply to be enabled to move from one conundrum to the next—one is tempted to say that he moves from one disaster to the next. When one begins looking for influences one finds them by the score. I haven't thought much about my own, not enough anyway; I hazard that the King James Bible, the rhetoric of the store-front church, something ironic and violent and perpetually understated in Negro speech—and something of Dickens' love for bravura—have something to do with me today; but I wouldn't stake my life on it. Likewise, innumerable people have helped me in many ways; but finally, I suppose, the most difficult (and most rewarding) thing in my life has been the fact that I was born a Negro and was forced, therefore, to effect some kind of truce with this reality. (Truce, by the way, is the best one can hope for.)

One of the difficulties about being a Negro writer (and this is not special pleading, since I don't mean to suggest that he has it worse than anybody else) is that the Negro problem is written about so widely. The bookshelves groan under the weight of information, and everyone therefore considers himself informed. And this information, furthermore, operates usually (generally, popularly) to reinforce traditional attitudes. Of traditional attitudes there are only two—For or Against—and I, personally, find it difficult to say which attitude has caused me the most pain. I am speaking as a writer; from a social point of view I am perfectly aware that the change from ill-will to good-will, however motivated, however imperfect, however expressed, is better than no change at all.

But it is part of the business of the writer—as I see it—to examine attitudes, to go beneath the surface, to tap the source. From this point of view the Negro problem is nearly inaccessible. It is not only written about so widely; it is written about so badly. It is quite possible to say that the price a Negro pays for becoming articulate is to find himself, at length, with nothing to be articulate about. ("You taught me language," says Caliban to Prospero, "and my profit on't is I know how to curse.") Consider: the tremendous social activity that this problem generates imposes on whites and Negroes alike the necessity of looking forward, of working to bring about a better day. This is fine, it keeps the waters troubled; it is all, indeed, that has made possible the Negro's progress. Nevertheless, social affairs are not generally speaking the writer's prime concern, whether they ought to be or not; it is absolutely necessary that he establish between himself and these affairs a distance which will allow, at least, for clarity, so that before he can look forward in any meaningful sense, he must first be allowed to take a long look back. In the context of the Negro problem neither whites nor blacks, for excellent reasons of their own, have the faintest desire to look back; but I think that the past is all that makes the present coherent, and further, that the past will remain horrible for exactly as long as we refuse to assess it honestly.

I know, in any case, that the most crucial time in my own development came when I was forced to recognize that I was a kind of bastard of the West; when I followed the line of my past, I did not find myself in Europe but in Africa. And this meant that in some subtle way, in a really profound way, I brought to Shakespeare, Bach, Rembrandt, to the stones of Paris, to the cathedral at Chartres, and to the Empire State Building, a special attitude. These were not really my creations, they did not contain my history; I might search in them in vain forever for any reflection of myself. I was an interloper; this was not my heritage. At the same time I had no other heritage which I could possibly hope to use—I had certainly been unfitted for the jungle or the tribe. I would have to appropriate these white centuries, I would have to make them mine—I would have to accept my special attitude, my special place in this scheme—otherwise I would have no place in *any* scheme. What was the most difficult was the fact that I was forced to admit something I had always hidden from myself, which the American Negro has had to hide from himself as the price of his public progress; that I hated and feared white people. This did not mean that I loved black people; on the contrary, I despised them, possibly because they failed to produce Rembrandt. In effect, I hated and feared the world. And this meant, not only that I thus gave the world an altogether murderous power over me, but also that in such a self-destroying limbo I could never hope to write.

One writes out of one thing only—one's own experience. Everything depends on how relentlessly one forces from this experience the last drop, sweet or bitter, it can possibly give. This is the only real concern of the artist, to re-create out of the disorder of life that order which is art. The difficulty then, for me, of being a Negro writer was the fact that I was, in effect, prohibited from examining my own experience too closely by the tremendous demands and the very real dangers of my social situation.

I don't think the dilemma outlined above is uncommon. I do think, since writers work in the disastrously explicit medium of language, that it goes a little way towards explaining why, out of the enormous resources of Negro speech and life, and despite the example of Negro music, prose written by Negroes has been generally speaking so pallid and so harsh. I have not written about being a Negro at such length because I expect that to be my only subject, but only because it was the gate I had to unlock before I could hope to write about anything else. I don't think that the Negro problem in America can be even discussed coherently without bearing in mind its context; its context being the history, traditions, customs, the moral assumptions and preoccupations of the country; in short, the general social fabric. Appearances to the contrary, no one in America escapes its effects and everyone in America bears some responsibility for it. I believe this the more firmly because it is the overwhelming tendency to speak of this problem as though it were a thing apart. But in the work of Faulkner, in the general attitude and certain specific passages in Robert Penn Warren, and, most significantly, in the advent of Ralph Ellison, one sees the beginnings—at least—of a more genuinely penetrating search. Mr. Ellison, by the way, is the first Negro novelist I have ever read to utilize in language, and brilliantly, some of the ambiguity and irony of Negro life.

About my interests: I don't know if I have any, unless the morbid desire to own a sixteen-millimeter camera and make experimental movies can be so classified. Otherwise, I love to eat and drink—it's my melancholy conviction that I've scarcely ever had enough to eat (this is because it's *impossible* to eat enough if you're worried about the next meal)—and I love to argue with people who do not disagree with me too profoundly, and I love to laugh. I do *not* like bohemia, or bohemians, I do not like people whose principal aim is pleasure, and I do not like people who are *earnest* about anything. I don't like people who like me because I'm a Negro; neither do I like people who find in the same accident grounds for contempt. I love America more than any other country in the world, and, exactly for this reason, I insist on the right to criticize her perpetually. I think all theories are suspect, that the finest principles may have to be modified, or may even be pulverized by the demands of life, and that one must find, therefore, one's own moral center and move through the world hoping that this center will guide one aright. I consider that I have many responsibilities, but none greater than this: to last, as Hemingway says, and get my work done.

I want to be an honest man and a good writer.

Acquainted with the Night
ROBERT FROST

I have been one acquainted with the night.
I have walked out in rain—and back in rain.
I have outwalked the furthest city light.

I have looked down the saddest city lane.
I have passed by the watchman on his beat
And dropped my eyes, unwilling to explain.

I have stood still and stopped the sound of feet
When far away an interrupted cry
Came over houses from another street,

But not to call me back or say good-by;
And further still at an unearthly height,
One luminary clock against the sky

Proclaimed the time was neither wrong nor right.
I have been one acquainted with the night.

The Man from Washington
JAMES WELCH

The end came easy for most of us.
Packed away in our crude beginnings
in some far corner of a flat world,
we didn't expect much more
than firewood and buffalo robes
to keep us warm. The man came down,
a slouching dwarf with rainwater eyes,
and spoke to us. He promised
that life would go on as usual,
that treaties would be signed, and everyone—
man, woman and child—would be inoculated
against a world in which we had no part,
a world of money, promise and disease.

Her Wisdom
W. S. MERWIN

So is she with love's tenderness
Made tender—and touched tenderness is pain;
Pain in fit subject distorts or burns into wisdom—

That she both by usual things and presences
Too delicate for usual ears and eyes
At all hands is touched and made wise,

Being instructed by stones of their rough childhoods,
In the migratory tides of birds seeing the cold
Hand of the moon and the shape of their shore;

She suffers too the noise of night's shadow flexing
Invisible in the unrustling air of noon,
With a sound between parchment stretched and a bat's squeak;

Is aware at all hours of the scream and sigh
Of shadows, of each moment: things forever violated,
Forever virgin; hears sleep falling wherever it falls.

Such understanding, uncommunicable
To other senses, and seeming so simple,
Is more a mystery than things not known at all;

For pain is common, but learned of not often,
Taught never; and who, could she speak it,
Would have ears to hear? She would not if she could,

Because of her tenderness. But should
Love's wisdom so wound her that she die
Would the knowledge then to which she succumbed

Most resemble the fear which we hear in the leaves' falling,
Hope as it falters in our failing questions,
Or joy as it overtakes us even in pain?

The Widower
FERRIS TAKAHASHI

"Partake of a little nourishment, Sato-san," they said to him, offering tea.
Why did they not prepare some rice and serve him strength-building soup?
Emi would have had soup for him. Emi would let no person, least of all her
husband, rise hungry from table. And he was hungry, he was not sick. He had
not eaten since the night before the funeral . . . Why did not Emi hurry in
from the kitchen, her white skin flushed pink, her long, narrow eyes bright

with pleasure and the mist from a dish of hot food beading her smooth hair? Why should Emi not be here when all these friends and neighbors filled their house with such a pulse of abundant life?

All day there had been such a crush of people in the rooms. He felt like a drunken man, sick-brained and giddy. All did the same things, the proper things. They came to him whispering or in silence. His hands ached with pattings and pressings and squeezings. Then, after a while, the women, crowded together, twittered softly and the close air of the stuffy rooms vibrated like a gong. The men remained subdued—when, at last, the funeral was over and the last "Amen" raggedly repeated, it was the men who led him away.

To see a coffin let down into the ground was a terrible thing. Thinking of this, he had asked that the two children be taken to a neighbor's house. Himself, as the men turned him away from the grave where floral pieces were quickly set across tumbled earth, he had struggled. It was very necessary to wait and watch for a while in case the quiet one below should rouse and want to move . . . there had been such cases. He could see Emi now, half-laughing, half-angry, trying to make these men who called themselves his friends let go of his arms . . .

In the old land, in Japan, it was customary to cremate, but he had rejected cremation. He could not tell any of them that he wanted her secret body kept as it had been, as only he had known it. So soft, cushioning, smooth-skinned . . .

As he sat among the people on an uncomfortable chair which was American, just as all the conditions of the funeral were properly Christian and American, he found himself crying. This he had promised himself he would not do. He did not feel like crying. But as he looked down at his hands, they were wet . . . he saw the heave of his own chest and belly.

An eager response went through the room. The people, up to now so careful of decorum, seemed to have been waiting for this. The paroxysm of lament crackled from body to body. Everyone was sobbing softly.

Then the children were brought to him, one on either side of a neighbor whose face he had suddenly forgotten. He could not remember whom she was nor why she was there. This was a bad thing, to bring the children at this time. They would remember this.

He put his arms around them. They stared at him, shaken, waiting to take their cue from him.

"These are my children," he said. "Ken and Lily. Now I am going to be father and mother to them. Mother is not really gone. She has only given me part of her work to do."

"Partake of a little nourishment, Sato-san," they said to him and Mrs. Shio offered him hot rice wine in the formal way. This *sake* was best quality, no doubt, but he had become middle-aged, it no longer warmed his blood. The Shio family seemed to wait for him to speak. He could not understand why they had brought him to their house to meet a *baishakunin*. Surely they remembered how often Emi had visited here with Mrs. Shio, borrowed back and forth, come in and out . . .

"Kano-san was greatly respected in Nagoya," Mr. Shio said proudly. "He has assisted many families even here in the new country. He sees the grandchildren growing up and flourishing."

"Even some of this younger generation grow up to respect what they scoffed at in their unripeness," the marriage broker said. "In my village near Nagoya, the making of the whole community's future was in my hands. Did a marriage broker not consider the social good, what disaster! Believe me, it is no easy work."

He spoke mincingly and made an elaborate gesture with the wine cup in his broad peasant hand.

"We have told you something about Sato-san, our life-long friend," Mr. Shio began. "—How he came young from the homeland, having already chosen his life-partner. Together they made a little business, a nursery of green plants. Together we became brothers in Christ when we joined the Church. But God willed to take away this good-life-partner from our friend too soon. His children, Ken and Lily, will soon go to the high school. He has worked as one does not think of a man working—cooking, washing the clothes. He had no time to meet the widow ladies whom we knew around the Church . . . Why! He even used to carry his little girl on his back when he had to go out at night and would lead his boy by the hand rather than leave them alone . . . my wife has done all she could and his children have been to us as our own. But one must think of the future."

"All his friends have done what they could," Mrs. Shio put in. "But there is no substitute for a woman in the home. Only when she is finally gone, does a man realize what he lacks."

Mr. Sato looked down at his cup. Emi and he had married in a Western way, a bold way, choosing each other without the direction of parents or marriage-brokers.

"Thank you most abundantly," he said at last. "You are kind to feel a concern for me, unimportant as I am. When my children were young, I tried to be father and mother to them. I did not wish them to forget their mother, who loved them so. I wanted them to grow up as *her* children, not the children of another woman . . . but I see my words are becoming confusing to you . . . So now my children, Ken and Lily, will soon go to the high school. My boy will go to college, where he can increase his ability to follow a profession. My children will then begin to care for me in turn. . . . How could I presume . . . (he decided to use smooth words to soothe their feelings) . . . how could I presume to offer some worthy woman a struggling existence? For all I earn shall go to take care of my children. Your kindness is, nonetheless, most appreciated."

Again it was that day of the year which the old custom called the Day of the Dead, and in accord with his practice he brought potted plants from the nursery to Emi's grave, set them, tended the plot and cultivated the borders on the surrounding plots which had become as familiar as his own. His corner of the cemetery was no longer used and not often visited. He had much work to do to keep the area as it should be, for the custodians were glad to have him do their work and left him quite alone.

He knew the years had made him grey and silent. There had been a long time of war, during which he and everyone he knew had been taken away and put in a kind of family prison for no reason and then, with as little reason, released and set adrift. And coming back, he found that he had the work of his youth to re-do: the shattered greenhouse to repair, the growing plants to renew, even the corner of the cemetery to restore from wilderness.

Ken was now a college graduate. How proud a thing it had been to see him, how clutching a surprise to hear on that very day of achievement that Ken planned to marry, even before he had found the architectural job of which he dreamed.

Now Ken worked for a construction company and the babies had come fast, one and two, and were soon little children who lived the life of adults: they visited and had parties with their playmates and were so busy that they could not often travel across the city to see their grandfather. And Ken's wife was a modern girl who could cause a husband much anxiety with talk of nerves and uncertain health.

When Mr. Sato was making himself supper on the kerosene stove in the room back of the greenhouse, he liked to talk aloud to Ken and Lily as though they were still little, telling them not to wriggle and jump about so much, not to be always asking for candy and "cokes" but to eat the good food so that they would be tall and strong . . . And they had grown tall, much taller than their parents and Lily had written from the East Coast city where she worked, that she would soon be married to a fine young man, with a good job, a church member, too.

To the wedding he would go, if they should send for him, yes, he lived on the hope of it, but Lily had not written that there was room for him in the new life ahead. Indeed, a short, grey dull father in the young, bright apartment of the newly-weds! Indeed, such a father would have to hide himself when their friends came for very shame.

He wandered about his narrow room, touching the things which were always placed where he could be close to them: photographs of Ken and Lily through the years, a bowl from the homeland, a scroll of calligraphy Emi had given him long ago, being unable to read but dreaming even then of children more able than their parents.

Long, so long ago, he had begun to rebuild Emi's presence by a clever device:

"Ai, my back aches so, *mamma-san*," he would say. "Rub it for me—" and then feel the quick, strong hands at the small of his back and the downy pressure of her breast against his shoulder. He told her all the news of Ken and read Lily's letters over and over and together they marveled at these children who walked now in the sun of success.

There came a certain night of the Day of the Dead when all these small satisfactions were strangely, suddenly brought to nothing, and the nearness of Emi herself ceased to be. How often he had been able to remember the sound of her feet pattering towards the bed! He heard no sound as he groped around in the dark, looking for matches so that he might light the stove and make tea. Suddenly he began to sob, clumsy sobs, old man's crying. Then, without matches, without jacket, still in his house slippers, he went unsteadily out on the street, down to the phone booth on the corner.

He would call the Shios. He did not see them very often, for they too had moved across town and lived with Shizuo, their married son. But they would remember, of course they would remember.

"Shio-san? Here Sato. Yes, Sato. . . How goes it with you, with your son, your wife? My wife thinks of her so often.—No, no, I am quite well. I am quite well. I am in good health. . . . We thought that in spite of the hour you would come over to visit us. . . . In bed? It is then so late? . . . No, no, I am not sick.

I can call my son, Ken, if I need anything. Thank you. I am sorry. Excuse me, please, for troubling you. . . ."

Across the city, the alert of the phone rang in the apartment of Ken Sato.

"Ken, is this you? Yeah, this is Shiz Shio. Hate to bother you this time of night, but look, it's something about your dad.—Yeah, sure, I know it's 2:30 in the morning; our whole family is up with *this* call from your dad. He just called up and my parents sleep in the living room beside the phone.

"He wanted them to come over and see him, just like that, middle of the night, and my dad worries and says I've got to call you right away. He was goin' to call you but I did it for him, he don't speak English so good, y'know.— No, not sick, more like raving. Out of his mind, talking like your Mom was there with him.

"Y'know, Ken, he oughtn't be living alone like he does. It's an unkindness to the old man—Naw, Ken, I din' mean it that way, I know you do all you can—Sure, Ken, you know what Alice and I been through, the old folks underfoot every minute and telling her how to bring up her kids. . . . Here's my mother right now yakking about how she tried her best to help with the marriage-broker, it's Sato-san's own fault, I dunno what she means. Old folks, they get mixed up. It's a burden.—Sure, Ken, I know what you go through with your wife's nerves. Here's *my* ole lady now, says to cut out the jawin' and le's all get some sleep.—I din' wanna wake you up but nothing else would satisfy my dad but I call you right away. Maybe you can run over tomorrow and see what's going on.

"Have a little orange juice, Papa—" Ken said, holding out a tumbler of the bitter fluid.

Here in this "nursing-home," tea was only to be had at mealtime. Not even always then, for the others who came to table were *hakujin* and to them were served milk, coffee and on the Sundays, cocoa. Why could there not be tea for an old man who could not digest these other beverages? Why did Ken press the glass of bitter juice into his hand although he had already sipped and put it away? Why did the *hakujin* woman in the white dress look in through the door so impatiently? Ken had just been telling Mr. Sato of the expense of this place, expense which paid for good food and a clean, healthful room. But the room behind the greenhouse was healthful, fresh with the woodsy odor of potting plants and running water. There was a strange smell in this place.

But Father was not to worry about expense, Ken was repeating in his grammar-school Japanese, mixed with many English words. Expense is nothing when a man wishes to care for his father. This is a fine place. The *hakujin* people here are kind and well-mannered, both the guests and those who attend to them. True, there is a home for elderly Japanese men in the city but it is much too crowded. It would not do in any case. The men there are indigent. What would the people say if Ken Sato's father were in a pauper's home?—Better to rest here—and it is only for a short time—in this fine, costly nursing home till health and strength return and no voices are heard which others cannot hear . . . until the wife of Ken is a little less nervous after the expected new baby and a house can be found where all the Sato family will be together.

Ken's eyeglasses rode up on the wrinkles of his forehead and a little dampness appeared in the creases of his nose. This was a grown man facing him, Mr. Sato realized, a man showing already the marks of middle age as he pushed his shoulders forward eagerly and rubbed with his forefinger nervously, tensely across his dry upper lip.

"You *are* comfortable here, Papa, aren't you? You *do* see that it's the best thing till things get straightened out—only till then?"

"Yes," Mr. Sato said. He did not want to say the word at all but Ken's lips seemed to shape it for him unconsciously; Ken's forehead wrinkled as though it could not relax unless the word was said: "It is very well here. Oh yes, yes, yes."

"The Christ" and His Teachings
ELDRIDGE CLEAVER

Folsom Prison,
September 10, 1965

My first awareness of Thomas Merton came in San Quentin, back in (I believe) 1959–60. During that time, a saint walked the earth in the person of one Chris Lovdjieff. He was a teacher at San Quentin and guru to all who came to him. What did he teach? Everything. It is easier just to say he taught Lovdjieff and let it go at that. He himself claimed to be sort of a disciple of Alan W. Watts, whom he used to bring over to Q to lecture us now and then in Hinduism, Zen Buddhism, and on the ways the peoples of Asia view the universe. I never understood how "The Christ" (as I used to call Lovdjieff, to his great sorrow and pain) could sit at Watts' feet, because he always seemed to me more warm, more human, and possessed of greater wisdom than Watts displayed either in his lectures or his books. It may be that I received this impression from having been exposed more to Lovdjieff than to Watts. Yet there was something about Watts that reminded me of a slick advertisement for a labor-saving device, aimed at the American housewife, out of the center page of *Life* magazine; while Lovdjieff's central quality seemed to be pain, suffering, and a peculiar strength based on his understanding of his own helplessness, weakness, and need. Under Lovdjieff I studied world history, Oriental philosophy, Occidental philosophy, comparative religion, and economics. I could not tell one class from the other—neither could the other students and neither, I believe, could Lovdjieff. It was all Lovdjieff.

The walls of his classrooms were covered with cardboard placards which bore quotations from the world's great thinkers. There were quotes from Japanese, Eskimos, Africans, Hopi Indians, Peruvians, Voltaire, Confucius, Lao-tse, Jesus Christ, Moses, Mohammed, Buddha, Rabbi Hillel, Plato, Aristotle, Marx, Lenin, Mao Tse-tung, Zoroaster—and Thomas Merton, among others. Once Lovdjieff gave a lecture on Merton, reading from his works and trying to put the man's life and work in context. He seemed desperately to want us to respect Merton's vocation and choice of the contemplative life. It was an uphill battle because a prison is in many ways like a monastery. The convicts in Lovdjieff's class hated prison. We were appalled that a free man would voluntarily enter prison—or a monastery. Let me say it right out: we thought Merton was some kind of nut. We thought the same thing about Lovdjieff. My secret disgust was that in many ways I was nothing but a monk, and how I loathed that view of myself!

I was mystified by Merton and I could not believe in his passionate defense of monkhood. I distrusted Lovdjieff on the subject of Thomas Merton. My mind heard a special pleading in his voice. In his ardent defense of Merton, Lovdjieff seemed to be defending himself, even trying to convince himself. One day Lovdjieff confided to us that he had tried to be a monk but couldn't make it. He made it, all right, without even realizing it. San Quentin was his monastery. He busied himself about the prison as though he had a special calling to minister to the prisoners. He was there day and night and on Saturdays, without fail. The officials would sometimes have to send a guard to his class to make him stop teaching, so the inmates could be locked up for the night. He was horror-stricken that they could make such a demand of him. Reluctantly, he'd sit down heavily in his seat, burdened by defeat and tell us to go to our cells. Part of the power we gave him was that we would never leave his class unless he himself dismissed us. If a guard came and told us to leave, he got only cold stares; we would not move until Lovdjieff gave the word. He got a secret kick out of this little victory over his tormentors. If, as happened once, he was unable to make it to the prison because his car had a blowout, he'd be full of apologies and pain next day.

Lovdjieff had extracted from me my word that I would some day read Merton for myself—he did not insist upon any particular time, just "some day." Easy enough. I gave my promise. In 1963, when I was transferred from San Quentin to Folsom for being an agitator, they put me in solitary confinement. The officials did not deem it wise, at that time, to allow me to circulate among the general inmate population. I had evolved a crash program which I would immediately activate whenever I was placed in solitary: stock up on books and read, read, read; do calisthenics and forget about the rest of the world. I had learned the waste and futility of worry. (Years ago, I had stopped being one of those convicts who take a little calendar and mark off each day.) When I asked for books to read in this particular hole, a trustee brought me a list from which to make selections. On the list I was delighted to see Merton's *The Seven Storey Moutain,* his autobiography. I thought of Lovdjieff. Here was a chance to fulfill my promise.

I was tortured by that book because Merton's suffering, in his quest for God, seemed all in vain to me. At the time, I was a Black Muslim chained in the bottom of a pit by the Devil. Did I expect Allah to tear down the walls and set me free? To me, the language and symbols of religion were nothing but weapons of war. I had no other purpose for them. All the gods are dead except the god of war. I wished that Merton had stated in secular terms the reasons he withdrew from the political, economic, military, and social system into which he was born, seeking refuge in a monastery.

Despite my rejection of Merton's theistic world view, I could not keep him out of the room. He shouldered his way through the door. Welcome, Brother Merton. I give him a bear hug. Most impressive of all to me was Merton's description of New York's black ghetto—Harlem. I liked it so much I copied out the heart of it in longhand. Later, after getting out of solitary, I used to keep this passage in mind when delivering Black Muslim lectures to other prisoners. Here is an excerpt:

Here in this huge, dark, steaming slum, hundreds of thousands of Negroes are herded together like cattle, most of them with nothing to eat and nothing to do. All the senses and imagination and sensibilities and emotions and sorrows and desires and hopes and ideas of a race with vivid feelings and deep emotional reactions are forced in upon themselves, bound inward by an iron ring of frustration: the prejudice that hems them in with its four insurmountable walls. In this huge cauldron, inestimable natural gifts, wisdom, love, music, science, poetry are stamped down and left to boil with the dregs of an elementally corrupted nature, and thousands upon thousands of souls are destroyed by vice and misery and degradation, obliterated, wiped out, washed from the register of the living, dehumanized.

What has not been devoured, in your dark furnace, Harlem, by marijuana, by gin, by insanity, hysteria, syphilis?

For a while, whenever I felt myself softening, relaxing, I had only to read that passage to become once more a rigid flame of indignation. It had precisely the same effect on me that Elijah Muhammad's writings used to have, or the words of Malcolm X, or the words of any spokesman of the oppressed in any land. I vibrate sympathetically to any protest against tyranny.

But I want to tell more about Lovdjieff—The Christ.

Chris Lovdjieff had a profound mind and an ecumenical education. I got the impression that the carnage of World War II, particularly the scientific, systematic approach to genocide of the Nazi regime, had been a traumatic experience from which it was impossible for him to recover. It was as if he had seen or experienced something which had changed him forever, sickened his soul, overwhelmed him with sympathy and love for all mankind. He hated all restraints upon the human mind, the human spirit, all blind believing, all dogmatic assertion. He questioned everything.

I was never sure of just what was driving him. That he was driven there could be no doubt. There was a sense of unreality about him. It seemed that he moved about in a mist. The atmosphere he created was like the mystic spell of Kahlil Gibran's poetry. He seemed always to be listening to distant music, or silent voices, or to be talking in a whisper to himself. He loved silence and said that it should only be broken for important communications, and he would expel students from his classes for distracting the others by chatting idly in the back rows. In his classes he was a dictator. He enforced certain rules which brooked no deviation—no smoking in his classroom at any time, before class, during class, at recess, or even when school was out; no talking in Lovdjieff's class unless it was pertinent to the subject at hand; no eating or chewing gum in his classroom; no profanity. Simple rules, perhaps, but in San Quentin they were visionary, adventurous, audacious. The Christ enforced them strictly. The other teachers and the guards wondered how he got away with it. We students wondered why we enthusiastically submitted to it. The Christ would look surprised, as if he did not understand, if you asked him about it. If one of the other teachers forgot and came into Lovdjieff's classroom smoking, he was sent hopping. The same went for prison guards. I can still see the shocked expression of a substitute teacher who, coming into Lovdjieff's room during recess smoking a pipe, was told: "Leave this room!"

When you came to Lovdjieff's classes, you came to learn. If you betrayed other motives, "Get out of here this minute!"—without malice but without equivocation. He was a magnet, an institution. He worked indefatigably. His day started when the school bell rang at 8 A.M. Often he would forego lunch to interview a few students to help them along with their schoolwork or personal problems. He never ceased complaining because the officials refused to allow him to eat lunch in the mess hall with the prisoners. Had they given him a cell he would have taken it. After lunch, he'd teach until 3 P.M. When night school convened at 6 P.M., The Christ would be there, beaming, radiating, and he'd teach passionately until 10 P.M. Then, reluctantly, he'd go home to suffer in exile until school opened next day. On Saturdays he'd be there bright and early to teach—Lovdjieff. He would have come on Sundays too, only the officials put their foot down and refused to hear of it. The Christ settled for a Sunday evening radio program of two hours which he taped for broadcast to the prisoners.

His classes were works of art. He made ancient history contemporary by evoking the total environment—intellectual, social, political, economic—of an era. He breathed life into the shattered ruins of the past. Students sat entranced while The Christ performed, his silver-rimmed glasses reflecting the light in eye-twinkling flashes.

He dressed like a college boy, betraying a penchant for simple sweaters and plain slacks of no particular distinction. He burned incense in his classroom when he lectured on religion, to evoke a certain mood. He was drawn to those students who seemed most impossible to teach—old men who had been illiterate all their lives and set in their ways. Lovdjieff didn't believe that anyone or anything in the universe was "set in its ways." Those students who were intelligent and quickest to learn he seemed reluctant to bother with, almost as if to say, pointing at the illiterates and speaking to the bright ones: "Go away. Leave me. You don't need me. These others do."

Jesus wept. Lovdjieff would weep over a tragic event that had taken place ten thousand years ago in some forgotten byway in the Fertile Crescent. Once he was lecturing on the ancient Hebrews. He was angry with them for choosing to settle along the trade routes between Egypt and Mesopotamia. He showed how, over the centuries, time and time again, these people had been invaded, slaughtered, driven out, captured, but always to return.

"What is it that keeps pulling them back to this spot!" he exclaimed. He lost his breath. His face crumbled, and he broke down and wept. "Why do they insist on living in the middle of that—that [for once, I thought meanly, The Christ couldn't find a word] that—that—Freeway! They have to sit down in the center of the Freeway! That's all it is—look!" He pointed out the trade routes on the map behind his desk, then he sat down and cried uncontrollably for several minutes.

Another time, he brought tape-recorded selections from Thomas Wolfe's *Look Homeward Angel*. The Christ wept all through the tape.

The Christ could weep over a line of poetry, over a single image in a poem, over the beauty of a poem's music, over the fact that man can talk, read, write, walk, reproduce, die, eat, eliminate—over the fact that a chicken can lay an egg.

Once he lectured us all week on Love. He quoted what poets had said of Love, what novelists had said of Love, what playwrights had said of Love. He played tapes of Ashley Montagu on Love. Over the weekend, each student was to write an essay on his own conception of Love, mindful to have been influenced by what he had been listening to all week long. In my essay I explained that I did not love white people. I quoted Malcolm X:

> How can I love the man who raped my mother, killed my father, enslaved my ancestors, dropped atomic bombs on Japan, killed off the Indians and keeps me cooped up in the slums? I'd rather be tied up in a sack and tossed into the Harlem River first.

Lovdjieff refused to grade my paper. He returned it to me. I protested that he was being narrow-minded and dogmatic in not understanding why I did not love white people simply because he himself was white. He told me to talk with him after class.

"How can you do this to me?" he asked.

"I've only written the way I feel," I said.

Instead of answering, he cried.

"Jesus wept," I told him and walked out.

Two days later, he returned my essay—ungraded. There were instead spots on it which I realized to be his tears.

Although Lovdjieff's popularity among the prisoners continued to soar and the waiting lists for his classes grew longer and longer, prison authorities banned his radio program. Then they stopped him from coming in on Saturdays. Then they stopped him from teaching night school. Then they took away his pass and barred him from San Quentin.

I must say that this man has not been adequately described. Certain things I hold back on purpose, others I don't know how to say. Until I began writing this, I did not know that I had a vivid memory of him. But now I can close my eyes and relive many scenes in which he goes into his act.

Alone, Like a Window Washer at the 50th Story
DIANE WAKOSKI

Now I know
that you must
depend on
some
things.
    A sturdy scaffold,
    a strong harness,
    and your own sense of balance
when you reach the high places.

Do not ever let
anyone hold
these things for you;
do not assume that you will ever
learn to look down
with equanimity.

Do not ask
what others think,
for they are not
doing your job.

I wash the windows,
they sparkle
like the eyes of a snake.

I know challenges,
even when they are not hissing
under my foot.
Now I know that you must
depend
on some things
and I also know

what it is that you have to do
strictly
alone.
All those years
when I was confused
and longed for company,
I was not looking
through the glittering glass,
not knowing the satisfaction
of singular accomplishments,
that windows which are not cleaned

on the 50th floor
look particularly grim,
the grime magnified
by the height;
I alone
restore the beauty, the light.
I am proud,
pleased
to do that
alone.

Dancing on the Grave of a Son of a Bitch
DIANE WAKOSKI

Foreword

This poem is more properly a "dance poem" than a song or chant because the element of repetition is created by movements of language rather than duplicating words and sounds. However, it is in the spirit of ritual recitation that I wrote it / a performance to drive away bad spirits perhaps.

The story behind the poem is this: a man and woman who have been living together for some time separate. Part of the pain of separation involves possessions which they had shared. They both angrily believe they should have what they want. She asks for some possession and he denies her right to it. She replies that she gave him money for a possession which he has and therefore should have what she wants now. He replies that she has forgotten that for the number of years they lived together he never charged her rent and if he had she would now owe him $7,000.

She is appalled that he equates their history with a sum of money. She is even more furious to realize that this sum of money represents the entire rent on the apartment and implies that he should not have paid anything at all. She is furious. She kills him mentally. Once and for all she decides she is well rid of this man and that she shouldn't feel sad at their parting. She decides to prove to herself that she's glad he's gone from her life. With joy she will dance on all the bad memories of their life together.

for my motorcycle betrayer

God damn it,
at last I am going to dance on your grave,
old man;
          you've stepped on my shadow once too often,
you've been unfaithful to me with other women,
women so cheap and insipid it psychs me out to think I might
ever
be put

in the same category with them;
you've left me alone so often that I might as well have been
a homesteader in Alaska
these past years;
and you've left me, thrown me out of your life
often enough
that I might as well be a newspaper,
differently discarded each day.
Now you're gone for good
and I dont know why
but your leaving actually made me as miserable
as an earthworm with no
earth,
but now I've crawled out of the ground where you stomped me
and I gradually stand taller and taller each
day.
I have learned to sing new songs,
and as I sing,
I'm going to dance on your grave
because you are
        dead
        dead
        dead
under the earth with the rest of the shit,
I'm going to plant deadly nightshade
on your grassy mound
and make sure a hemlock tree starts growing there.
Henbane is too good for you,
but I'll let a bit grow there for good measure
because we want to dance,
we want to sing,
we want to throw this old man
to the wolves,
but they are too beautiful for him, singing in harmony
with each other.   So some white wolves and I
will sing on your grave, old man
and dance for the joy of your death.
"Is this an angry statement?"
               "No, it is a statement of joy."
"Will the sun shine again?"
               "Yes,
               yes,
               yes,"
               because I'm going to dance dance dance
Duncan's measure, and Pindar's tune,
Lorca's cadence, and Creeley's hum,
Stevens' sirens and Williams' little Morris dance,
oh, the poets will call the tune,

and I will dance, dance, dance
on your grave, grave, grave,
because you're a sonofabitch, a sonofabitch,
and you tried to do me in,
but you cant cant cant.
You were a liar in a way that only I know:
            You ride a broken motorcycle,
            You speak a dead language
            You are a bad plumber,
            And you write with an inkless pen.
You were mean to me,
and I've survived,
God damn you,
at last I am going to dance on your grave,
old man,
I'm going to learn every traditional dance,
every measure,
and dance dance dance on your grave
                                one step
for every time
you done me wrong.

Map of My Country
JOHN HOLMES

A map of my native country is all edges,
The shore touching sea, the easy impartial rivers
Splitting the local boundary lines, round hills in two townships,
Blue ponds interrupting the careful county shapes.
The Mississippi runs down the middle. Cape Cod. The Gulf.
Nebraska is on latitude forty. Kansas is west of Missouri.

When I was a child, I drew it, from memory,
A game in the schoolroom, naming the big cities right.

Cloud shadows were not shown, nor where winter whitens,
Nor the wide road the day's wind takes.
None of the ten letters told my grandfather's name.
Nothing said, Here they see in clear air a hundred miles.
Here they go to bed early. They fear snow here.
Oak trees and maple boughs I had seen on the long hillsides
Changing color, and laurel, and bayberry, were never mapped.
Geography told only capitals and state lines.

I have come a long way using other men's maps for the turnings.
I have a long way to go.
It is time I drew the map again,

Spread with the broad colors of life, and words of my own
Saying, Here the people worked hard, and died for the wrong reasons.
Here wild strawberries tell the time of year.
I could not sleep, here, while bell-buoys beyond the surf rang.
Here trains passed in the night, crying of distance,
Calling to cities far away, listening for an answer.

On my own map of my own country
I shall show where there were never wars,
And plot the changed way I hear men speak in the west,
Words in the south slower, and food different.
Not the court-houses seen floodlighted at night from trains,
But the local stone built into housewalls,
And barns telling the traveler where he is
By the slant of the roof, the color of the paint.
Not monuments. Not the battlefields famous in school.
But Thoreau's pond, and Huckleberry Finn's island.
I shall name an unhistorical hill three boys climbed one morning.
Lines indicate my few journeys,
And the long way letters come from absent friends.

Forest is where green fern cooled me under the big trees.
Ocean is where I ran in the white drag of waves on white sand.
Music is what I heard in a country house while hearts broke,
Not knowing they were breaking, and Brahms wrote it.

All that I remember happened to me here.
This is the known world.
I shall make a star here for a man who died too young.
Here, and here, in gold, I shall mark two towns
Famous for nothing, except that I have been happy in them.

my father moved through dooms of love
E.E. CUMMINGS

my father moved through dooms of love
through sames of am through haves of
   give,
singing each morning out of each night
my father moved through depths of
   height

this motionless forgetful where
turned at his glance to shining here;
that if (so timid air is firm)
under his eyes would stir and squirm

newly as from unburied which
floats the first who, his april touch
drove sleeping selves to swarm their fates
woke dreamers to their ghostly roots

and should some why completely weep
my father's fingers brought her sleep:
vainly no smallest voice might cry
for he could feel the mountains grow.

Lifting the valleys of the sea
my father moved through griefs of joy;

praising a forehead called the moon
singing desire into begin

joy was his song and joy so pure
a heart of star by him could steer
and pure so now and now so yes
the wrists of twilight would rejoice

keen as midsummer's keen beyond
conceiving mind of sun will stand,
so strictly (over utmost him
so hugely) stood my father's dream

his flesh was flesh his blood was blood:
no hungry man but wished him food;
no cripple wouldn't creep one mile
uphill to only see him smile.

Scorning the pomp of must and shall
my father moved through dooms of feel;
his anger was as right as rain
his pity was as green as grain

septembering arms of year extend
less humbly wealth to foe and friend
than he to foolish and to wise
offered immeasurable is

proudly and (by octobering flame
beckoned) as earth will downward climb,
so naked for immortal work
his shoulders marched against the dark

his sorrow was as true as bread:
no liar looked him in the head;
if every friend became his foe
he'd laugh and build a world with snow.

My father moved through theys of we,
singing each new leaf out of each tree
(and every child was sure that spring
danced when she heard my father sing)

then let men kill which cannot share,
let blood and flesh be mud and mire,
scheming imagine, passion willed,
freedom a drug that's bought and sold

giving to steal and cruel kind,
a heart to fear, to doubt a mind,
to differ a disease of same,
conform the pinnacle of am

though dull were all we taste as bright,
bitter all utterly things sweet,
maggoty minus and dumb death
all we inherit, all bequeath

and nothing quite so least as truth
—i say though hate were why men
        breathe—
because my father lived his soul
love is the whole and more than all

Canadian Gothic
JOANNA GLASS

CHARACTERS
FATHER   JEAN
MOTHER   BEN REDLEAF

Scene: A small town on the Saskatchewan prairie in the 1950s.
*There are three wooden chairs onstage, approximately three yards apart. The middle
chair is not on a parallel with the other two, but is slightly to the back of them. The
Father is seated in the chair down right. He is blind, and wears dark glasses. He is
dressed in a business suit. He is in his early sixties. The Mother is seated in the chair
down left. She is thirty years old. The Daughter is not present at the opening. When she
enters, she sits in the middle chair. She, also, is thirty. There may be, suspended at the
rear, a large window with a plain, slightly warped wooden frame.*

FATHER: After all's said and done, the town of Cardigan's been good to me. I was born here, in the year 1910. My father was a shoemaker who'd emigrated from the Highlands. I never had any complaints against this town. Pioneers of hardy stock built it in the middle of the prairie. Built the schools and hospitals, the stores and libraries, and finally, the university. Civilized institutions for civilized people. I received my degree in dentistry from the university in 1932.

MOTHER: Rare he was, in 1932, having a degree in dentistry. The university was mostly an agriculture school at the time, being, as we were, in the heart of the wheat country. A little prim he was, and I knew he'd never known a woman. I knew he'd never visited that famous clapboard house on the outskirts of town. I knew he didn't get drunk in the beer parlour, and his conduct was never disorderly at hockey games. After our wedding I knew, and it nearly killed me at the time. I knew the routine we'd set that first week of marriage was the one we'd follow for the rest of our lives.

FATHER: In choosing a wife I looked for a woman with spirit. When I met Natalie, I walked her down by the river—that shady spot there by Grant Island. I put my hands on her breasts. She said, "Tut, tut, Jack, don't you know? God made those for babies!" And off she ran, laughing, a fine filly of a lass.

MOTHER: *(Sighing deeply)* So many things I never understood. What was most attractive became a bone of contention. The spirit he admired before we wed became a thorn in his side by the first anniversary. And I knew the thorn would fester there for the rest of our lives. Both of us helpless, in our natures, to either remove it, or ignore it.

FATHER: She never did the things that other women did! The house was put to rights by noon. She could hoe and weed the garden quick as you could say Jack Robinson. Spring cleaning in every other house took a full week. In ours, one frantic day. All the curtains, all the rugs—shazaam!—down before breakfast, up again by dinnertime. "Busy work," she'd say, and bring down the wrath of the neighborhood with those two words.

MOTHER: "Too much idle time," he'd say. I liked to do charcoal drawings. I went to the river almost every afternoon, summer and winter, ninety above and thirty below. It gave me great pleasure to sketch and draw there, and try to master the arcs of our two bridges, spanning the river. The arcs were so hard to get right! I worked like a demon on them, but never did master the exact geometry of those two bridges. *(The Father opens his mouth to speak, the Mother interrupts and continues)* I'd get the one in the foreground *just right,* but the one upriver, behind the first, escaped me.

FATHER: Her little fingers, at dinnertime, were blue at first, and then beet red. Thirty below she'd go down to the riverbank with her pieces of charcoal and pad of paper. She never learned to sketch with gloves on, although you'd think that would have been the first order of business. I remember frost-bite on at least three occasions. All because she couldn't get that second bridge right. My God, what a lot of effort, day after day! The truth was, I was ready to go down there and dynamite that damned second bridge. But amazingly, one day she said:

MOTHER: All right, Jack. I guess the time has come to settle for the one.

FATHER: And damned if she didn't sell that first picture right off, for thirty dollars. Back in those days I used to work a whole week for thirty dollars.

MOTHER: The Mayor bought my first completed picture. I said, "Mr. Mayor, don't you notice the absence of something in that picture?" "No," he said. "There's great technique in that one bridge—at least thirty dollars worth, I don't mind telling you." I said, "But Mr. Mayor, from that spot on the bank you can see the Fulton Bridge." "Yes, I know," he said, "and thanks for leaving it out. I expect you'd make me pay sixty for two of 'em."

FATHER: *(Shifting in his chair)* They say in every person's life there comes a time when we're faced with a fork in the road. We stop, we consider the two choices, we make our decision. In the third year of our marriage it happened to us. Nothing monumental caused it. We had a simple conversation. And after that she went one way, and I went the other.

MOTHER: There was a polio epidemic in Cardigan. It was a terrible time. There was fear, and panic, and endless prayer. For nearly a year, everyone's conversation was the same:
Didja hear? Didja hear? The Ferguson boy's in a brace for life!
Didja hear? Didja hear? It's hit poor Mr. Jamison. He's in a brace for the rest of his life.
I had no stomach at all for sick or crippled people. I went to pieces whenever I had to be around them. Every morning during the epidemic I'd cry into my coffee and tell Jack the news from the day before. *(They turn, slightly, toward each other)*

FATHER: Really, Natalie! Must I face this waterfall every morning at breakfast?

MOTHER: Yes, you must. *(Quietly)* Unless you choose to eat somewhere else.

FATHER: *(Resigned)* Well, who is it now?

MOTHER: The Ferguson boy.

FATHER: *Which* Ferguson boy? The town's full of Fergusons.

MOTHER: You wouldn't want to waste sympathy on one you didn't know. *(Pause)* Dougie Ferguson. He's in a brace for the rest of his life.

FATHER: Dougie Ferguson . . .

MOTHER: He's a *patient* of yours, Jack! And he's—he *was*—goalie on the Pee-Wee team! We've watched him many times.

FATHER: Oh, yes, little Dougie. Yes. Too bad.

MOTHER: Jack, *listen* to me! I'm losing my mind! How can I *face* Mrs. Ferguson? What can I *say* to Mrs. Ferguson?

FATHER: The less said, the better. Things are easier dealt with when they're not put into words.

MOTHER: He reached for the marmalade and spread it on his toast. *(Pause)* I began to get a fixed image of Jack in my mind. I thought of him as a man in a brace—a mechanical man. There was no way to penetrate this thing that he wore. I asked him. I said, "Jack, tell me. What is it that makes you harness yourself against life like this?"

FATHER: I wanted to answer as best I could, because I never, ever, wanted it asked again. *(Pause)* An awareness, I guess, of the softness at the middle.

MOTHER: I don't understand that, Jack.

FATHER: Natalie, a man needs a crust. This bread has a crust. The earth has a crust. That maple there, out the window—its bark is its crust. It's all protection for the softness at the middle. *(He turns away, in his chair)* Natalie, we're unequal partners. Accept it, and leave me be.

MOTHER: We never talked of it again. I let him be. *(She frowns)* As far as a woman's able.

(The Daughter, Jean, enters youthfully. She sits in the middle chair)

FATHER: I was very happy when our daughter, Jean, was born. I remember thinking this new child would fill her afternoons for twenty years to come. That just goes to show you how much I knew. I said, "Natalie, this'll take up the slack of all those afternoons." And she said:

MOTHER: There's no slack! There's no slack anywhere. Every hour is taut and I mean to keep it that way.

FATHER: So, the house, and the garden, and the *baby* were put to rights by noon. *(Pause)* God in Heaven, why did I let it gall me so? I wasted myself on petty victories—a speck of dust on the sideboard, a dandelion among the iris, a wet diaper, the beginnings of a rash. "Neglect," I'd say. "Too much idle time." "Busy work," she'd say, and thereby lost her last remaining female friend in Cardigan. *(Pause)* As time went on, she befriended Jean.

JEAN: Every day, before I started school, my mother took me past the city limits, to the fields around Cardigan. In the spring we collected wild prairie crocus. I wore dirndl skirts then. I'd lift the whole front of my skirt and fill it with stubby mauve crocus. When the skirt was full, and I couldn't bend down any more without the flowers spilling out, I stopped. She always hummed one song: *I Dream of Jeannie With the Light Brown Hair.* When I couldn't hear it, I knew I'd strayed too far. We did the same thing with tiger lilies in the summer, bringing them home and stuffing them into old honey cans and pickle jars. I never believed when they closed at night they'd open again in the morning. *(Pause)* Why do they do that, Mama?

MOTHER: It's magic. Nature's magic.

JEAN: Daddy says there's no magic. He says all magic is tricks.

MOTHER: Then maybe you'd better ask your Daddy.

JEAN: I already did.

MOTHER: And what did he say?

JEAN: I forget.

MOTHER: Well, until you remember, let's just call it nature's magic. *(Pause, the Mother shifts back to the audience)* In the fall we went into the fields to watch the mallards. The fields were one big sanctuary then, before the bricks and lumber got that far. "Isn't it a miracle," I'd say, "the way they inform each other when it's time to take wing and fly south. I wonder how they know?"

JEAN: Daddy says it's the most spectacular phenomenon in the world. He says there's vertical migration, when they move down the mountains to the valleys, and there's long migration, when they move from here to South America. They move on the Atlantic flyway and the Mississippi flyway, and they mostly move nocturnally. We know about their routes because of bird banding.

MOTHER: Oh? My, my, my.

JEAN: Yes. Scientists put numbered aluminum bands around their legs and make records of the flights.

MOTHER: But I wonder how so many millions of them can agree on the *exact time* to go?

JEAN: Personally, I think it's nature's magic.

FATHER: They went in the spring and the summer and the fall, frittering away whole seasons. And damned if they didn't go out there and skate on the frozen sloughs in January! A block away from our house there was a spanking new rink my taxes helped to build. You could open the front door of a winter's evening and hear "The Skater's Waltz" wafting up our street. Do you think they'd go to that rink? No, sir! Oh, it was picturesque on the sloughs, all right, but it wasn't safe. Fell in, both of 'em, ass over teakettle, several times. I remember them coming home drenched, with purple lips, and joints so stiff they wouldn't move. *(Pause)* I remember the stink of wet wool as it dried on the radiator. *(The Mother rises, touches Jean, and exits. The Father and Jean slouch over, heads hanging down. There is a brief pause)* Well, they didn't have much in the way of medications back in those days. Hell, one way or another it didn't matter. I'd bawled her out for falling in, and she wouldn't have the doctor after that. I told her if she ever went again I'd break her bloody neck. She said, "Let's wait till *then* for the doctor, Jack. They're best at mending broken bones." We got to the hospital on the heels of her last breath. She died the minute they put her under the oxygen tent. *(Pause)* I remember thinking that tent was like old snuffers we used to use to put out candles. *(Jean rises, moves down left, and sits in the Mother's chair. Her voice is harder, more mature, in the following segments)*

JEAN: Fortunately, there's gold in dentistry. My father wouldn't have live-in help under foot in the evenings so we hired a woman to do the washing, and we hired a woman to do the cooking. In accordance with his nature, we took care of these things first, and then we mourned.

FATHER: And we hired a woman to come in and do the spring cleaning. What took Natalie one frantic day, and the neighbor ladies one full week, took that hired woman two full weeks. At a dollar an hour, I remember. I mourned, publicly, for half a year. I will mourn, privately, for the rest of my life. But even in that mourning there's bitterness and rancor. For she had handed down that temperament intact. No, not intact. Threefold. And if I couldn't cope with it in the adult, God knows: spirit in a child is a terrible thing!

JEAN: There was no time when I could look across a room and say, "He's lonely now. He misses her." He went about his business, his grief was private. And I resented that. It seemed to me that he was free at last, free from a voice that once asked for his time, his ear, his company, his heart.
    The wonder of my mother's voice was this: it asked, it was refused, it

never asked again. It found some other place to sing its song. It didn't seek its answers in other men, clubs, church, civic activities. It never aired its tale of woe over any neighbor's back fence. Once refused, it was forever silent.

   She was just thirty when she died. I knew that in the fields around Cardigan there was still stubby crocus. There were lilies and mallards. Only her song was gone.

FATHER: Well, that's her side of the story. What she didn't know, and what her mother knew too well, was that in her silence she could mock me, accuse me, deny me, defy me. But Jean was artless. It took her years to learn those skills. *(Short pause)* And so she asked, and asked, and asked again. No soul on earth petitions like a child.

JEAN: I defied him every inch of the way. When he sent me to my room, I made him haul me there, kicking and screaming until we both were bruised. In school I was called an imaginative child. I loved to read horror stories. *(She smiles)* Late one night, when I was nine, I attached two cardboard fangs to my eye teeth, and went into his room. I woke him up and grinned a fangy grin. *(She does so)*

FATHER: For *Christsake!* What do you *want?*

JEAN: *I vant to bite your neck!!*

FATHER: Ketchup sandwiches! I always thought a sandwich was two pieces of bread with a slice of meat in between. No, sir! Ketchup sandwiches. She had a two hundred dollar solid mahogany dresser in her bedroom. Wouldn't use it. Ugly as sin, she said. She went to the store and got some orange crates and built herself a thing with a big organdy skirt around it. *"Vanity,"* she said. "You're damned *right,"* I said. "In no small measure!" At fourteen she was five feet eight inches tall. She took the heels off every pair of shoes I bought her. I took them to the shoemaker and had the heels put back. She refused to leave the house until those heels came off again. She missed three whole days of school one week, on account of that. *(Pause)* At fifteen, on the eighth anniversary of her mother's death, she started going out to the fields again.

(A young man enters. He is darkskinned; a full-blooded Cree Indian. He wears a pale blue shirt, open at the neck, and jeans. He sits in the middle chair)

JEAN: One day in late June, I saw him at the edge of a slough, crouching down, fiddling with something. His hair was jet black—blue in the sunlight. Hair like that on the prairie could only belong to an Indian.

BEN: They called us all half-breeds, whether we were or not. I was not. I was full-blooded Cree. On the farms they said one thing: they said we stole their chickens. In the cities they said another: they said we could be found, lurking, in the back seats of white women's cars. *(He shrugs, and smiles)* I paid no attention. That day I was setting a trap. She was very young. She had light brown hair. I thought she'd go away when she saw me.

JEAN: Are you setting a trap?

BEN: That's right.

JEAN: What for?

BEN.   Oh, I dunno. Jackrabbit, I guess.

JEAN: What for?

BEN: Oh, I dunno. It's what I do in June.

JEAN: I mean—for fun, for food, for recreation?

BEN: Geez, I dunno. Something to do.

JEAN: Well, I guess I have to say I don't like you much for that.

BEN: Well, paleface, I guess I have to say I don't give a damn one way or the other.

JEAN: Sassy Indian!

BEN: Yessiree!! Getting sassier every day. G'wan home and tell your Maw you met a sassy Indian.

JEAN: I told him my mother died when I was seven. He said he was sorry. He said his name was Ben Redleaf. I told him mine was Jean MacPherson. "Well, there you are," he said. He smiled, and said . . .

BEN: I'll bet they call you bonnie Jean. *(Pause)* I told her about the time my brother set a trap for jackrabbit, and when he got there to check it one day, he couldn't believe his eyes. There was a bloody rabbit's foot in the trap, but the animal was gone. That rabbit chewed off his foot and part of his leg in order to get away. I made it as bloody as I could—and I watched that white girl. I told her the blue veins were hanging off the foot—*dangling*—*glistening* in the sun. Crazy white girl. When I finished, her eyes filled with tears and she said, "Oh, Ben, that's a beautiful story!"

JEAN: I met him in the fields every day all that summer, sunshine or rain. I knew he came into the city sometimes, and one day I persuaded him to have a Coke with me at the Sunset Cafe. I don't know what was in my head, thinking he and I could sit and have a Coke in the Sunset Cafe, plain as day. When we were finished, and out on the sidewalk, he turned to me and said, "Well, Jeannie, I guess we'll never do that again." "No," I said, "I guess we won't."

BEN: Just for the hell of it, I walked down Third Street one day and stopped in front of her Dad's practice. I wanted to get a look at the old buzzard. I was hanging around there, waiting for a glimpse of him, when I could see the nurse at the desk getting all upset. Suddenly, there he was, right beside me in front of the window.

FATHER: Can I do something for you, boy?

BEN: No, thanks. Nothing.

FATHER: Got a toothache, have you?

BEN: No, sir. Just wanted to see how the other half lives.

FATHER: Well, I'll tell you. You g'wan down to Eighth Street there and see Dr. Lutz. He's the one they all go to when they've got a toothache.

BEN: *(To audience)* I didn't have a toothache. As a matter of fact, I'd *never* had a toothache. My mother used to say we had strong teeth from chewing buffalo hide. I used to say, "Yeah, that accounts for the women. They did all the chewing. What about the men?" To that she'd say, "God takes care of Indians in small ways." Then my father would chime in. "Yeah," he'd say, "in ways so small nobody's ever noticed."

   All the kids in town went to dances every Saturday night, and guzzled beer in some back room. The Indian kids did the same at a place out on

Willow Road. I couldn't take her; she couldn't take me. One day I got a bottle of wine and met her in the fields *(He takes Jean's hand)* Guess what we're going to do today?

JEAN: How many guesses do I get?

BEN: Two.

JEAN: We're going to make love.

BEN: Right, that's one. What's the other?

JEAN: We're going to make love again.

BEN: That's a possible *third.* What's the second?

JEAN: Geez, I dunno. I give up.

BEN: We're going to dance.

JEAN: *Dance?*

BEN: Yeah.

JEAN: *(After a moment) Rain* dance?

BEN: How'dja like a fat lip? We're gonna drink some wine and we're gonna dance.

JEAN: To the music of whom?

BEN: I brought the wine. I guess you'll have to sing.

JEAN: O.K. What'll I sing?

BEN: I dunno. It's up to you.

JEAN: How about *Rose Marie?*

BEN: Nah.

JEAN: How about *Ramona?*

BEN: Don't think so.

JEAN: How about: *(She sings)* "One little, two little, three little—"

BEN: *(Holding up his fist)* How about a *big, fat, lip?*

JEAN: O.K. How about *Stardust?*

BEN: Yeah! How about that?

(There is a pause. Jean turns away from Ben and faces front)

JEAN: There is, among friends, a catalogue of virgin crossings. They like to relate, with grins and hindsight, first gropings, adolescent clumsiness. *(Pause)* Doris Meyers lost her virginity at noon one day in her uncle's hayloft, and broke out in hives immediately afterward. Sheila Fraser lost hers in a canoe at Waskesui. Evelyn Davidson lost hers in the boiler room of the Biology Lab. They say, "Come on, Jean, tell us yours!" I am, after all's said and done, my father's daughter. Things are easier dealt with when they're not put into words.
    We would lie in the fields for hours and look at the sky till it nearly hypnotized us.

(They lean back in their chairs and stretch out their legs. They fold their arms over their eyes, as if to provide protection from a blinding sun)

BEN: Tell me about your Dad.

JEAN: What's to tell? A dad's a dad.

BEN: Has he got a girlfriend?

JEAN: Are you kidding?

BEN: He's not that old. I'll bet he's hiding a lady friend somewhere.

JEAN: He wouldn't know what to *do* with a lady friend.

BEN: He knew what to do with your mother.

JEAN: I doubt it.

BEN: Aw, come on. You're the proof of it.

JEAN: I look at him, and I look at her picture, and I just can't imagine them doing it. You know? Maybe it's always that way with parents.

BEN: I can sure as hell imagine *my* Dad doing it.

JEAN: Has he got a lady friend?

BEN: Always. Always has, always will. He's a real horny old bugger. And he's always promising to turn over a new leaf. And he never does. *(Pause)* I made up a limerick about him once.

JEAN: Tell me.

BEN: Nah. It's dirty.

JEAN: How dirty?

BEN: Real dirty.

JEAN: That's the way I like 'em.

BEN: Jeannie, you're a raunchy little girl.

JEAN: I know I am. But it's normal.

BEN: Who says?

JEAN: I've got a book about teenage behavior. My Dad bought it for me. He's like that, you know. Whenever there's something he'd rather not talk about, he writes to Toronto for a book. Anyway, this book says fifteen's a raunchy age. Come on, tell me your limerick.

BEN: Oh, O.K.
There was an Old Injun from Cardigan
Who promised to make a clean start again
He said that he would
We hoped that he could
But each squaw that he saw made it hard again

(They both laugh. Jean faces front, Ben sits upright in his chair)

JEAN: I spent each afternoon alone with Ben, and I spent each evening alone in my room. I could hear my father downstairs, fixing tea, listening to the radio, taking the newspaper out to the porch. I sat up there, and it struck me that we were more than a flight of stairs apart. In our minds, he was my old man, downstairs; I was his little girl, upstairs. I remembered the events of the afternoon and I thought how innocent he was, really, sitting in the kitchen, waiting for the kettle to whistle. Sometimes I wondered if Ben Redleaf fit into the picture at all.

BEN: I was not alone in my room all that often. I shared a room with my older brother, and my younger brother. Our house was one of those concrete block things—my brother called them "urban igloos." Anyway, when I was alone in my room those summer evenings, strange things began to happen in my mind. I started thinking about my future. I'd been drifting along, thinking the future was something you worried about when you were thirty. I began to think I'd better look into some kind of government aid, and get myself into a trade school. I could take apart a V8 engine and put it back together again blindfolded. So I thought maybe I'd make a good mechanic. But as the summer went on, I really went off the deep end. I began to have all kinds of pipe dreams. I imagined myself as a lab technician. I wore a white coat and I carried around trays of test tubes. And I always had a book of litmus paper in my pocket. I imagined all this because I'd convinced myself that this girl was in my league. That just goes to show you what a really screwy summer it was. Sky and sun and tiger lilies, and white people's pipe dreams. *(Pause, and transition)* On Friday, October 14th, she came to the fields and told me. On Saturday, October 15th, at breakfast, she told her father. On Sunday, October 16th, she boarded the train for Winnipeg.

JEAN: Dad, I'm going to have a baby. *(There is no reaction)* I thought he'd fly off in a fit and call me names. I thought he'd leap up, wail, berate me. I thought he'd at least turn ashen gray. No, sir! He reached for the marmalade.

FATHER: I think you're overstating the case. I think you misunderstand.

JEAN: No, Dad! *You* misunderstand. I'm going to have a baby.

FATHER: Jean, you're fifteen years old. You are not going to *have* a baby. If you are carrying a child you'll go to Winnipeg and leave it there in a doctor's pail.

JEAN: I watched him spread the marmalade on his toast. I marvelled at his steady hand. He didn't look at me, but then, he never did. I should have let it go at that. I thought of my mother. I thought of all the times she'd watched his steady hand. I had a trump card. I decided to play it.
Whose do you think it is?

FATHER: I bit my tongue. I tried to count to ten. I didn't make it. "The better question *is*," I said, "whose do *you* think it is?" She didn't answer. She tapped her finger, nonchalantly, on the chair. "How far along?" I said.

JEAN: About two months.

FATHER: Well, they're not really *babies* at that stage.

JEAN: Oh, Jack! I've got a punchline! This one isn't a *baby,* this one's a *papoose*! *(Pause)* It was not his nature to fly off in a fit. He didn't wail, he didn't berate me. He did turn ashen gray. In retrospect, it was a petty victory.

BEN: We'd decided, the day before, that I was to come by around eleven. I don't know what was in our heads even to consider such a meeting. Oh, I guess I know. She was fifteen, I was twenty. We were going to stand together, heads erect, a united front. We were going to deliver our message and let the chips fall where they may. That worn out, threadbare message. We were going to tell him that we loved each other. *(Pause. Tension)* Did you tell him?

JEAN: I told him.

BEN: What'd he say?

JEAN: He already made a phone call. Long distance. I'm to go to some doctor in Winnipeg and leave it there. *(Pause)* Imagine him even knowing where to call!

BEN: Over my dead body!

JEAN: I don't know, Ben. It's a closed subject.

BEN: Where is he?

JEAN: In the basement. Doing something at his workbench. He made the call and went right down.

BEN: She nodded toward the door that led to the basement. I went down the stairs, having to grope, because he hadn't turned the light on. He wasn't doing anything, just standing there, hunched over his workbench. He squinted at me for a minute. Then he began to mumble.

FATHER: You—bastard! You—fucking Indian!

BEN: *(Incredulous) Fucking Indian?* What could I do? I laughed.

FATHER: That red-skinned bastard laughed at me! Jean was standing at the top of the stairs. It was like an echo, reverberating through the basement. "Fucking Indian?" she said, and threw her head back and laughed. Their laughter was—arrogant. It was the most arrogant laughter I'd ever heard. I picked up the nearest thing to me, a hammer. I threw it at him. It missed him by an inch and hit the water meter. I remember the crash and the broken glass from the water meter falling on the floor. I picked up a wrench—

BEN: I picked up the nearest thing to me and threw it at him. It was metal and round. It hit him in the face. It was a can of lye.

(All three slouch over in their chairs, elbows on knees, heads hanging down)

JEAN: An ambulance, sirens, howling neighbors, two police cars, and for some reason, the Fire Chief came too. My father was put into the back of the ambulance. Ben was handcuffed and put into the police car. Fifteen years have passed since then, and a thousand nightmares. The nightmare is always the same. There is a miniature police car and a miniature ambulance. There are infinite miniature doors hanging open on each. They hang there, gaping. They beckon to me. A stranger pushes my shoulder and says, "Go, child, go!" I wear metal shoes and there are magnets under the sidewalk. I'm held there, straining but powerless, until dawn. In actual fact I was pushed, and I went. In the back of the ambulance I was grateful that they'd covered my father's face. *(Ben rises, and exits)* That evening in the hospital, I sat on his bed and held his hand.

FATHER: Is it still Saturday?

JEAN: Yes. Eight o'clock.

FATHER: Are you crying?

JEAN: Yes.

FATHER: I wonder—for whom?

JEAN: All of us. *(Pause)* Why did we have lye in the basement?

FATHER: You have an appointment in Winnipeg.

JEAN: Dad, he grabbed the nearest thing! What were we doing with lye in the basement?

FATHER: The sight is gone, Jeannie, but the child is growing. First things first. Get rid of that papoose.

(There is a pause. Jean leans forward and cups her hands over her mouth)

JEAN: Didja hear? Didja hear? She's up and going to Winnipeg and leaving her blind father! Doctor ordered it, they say. Terrible state of shock she's in. And Lord knows, wouldn't it be? Finding an Indian in your basement? Who was he, anyway? Paper says some half-breed from Willow Road. It's a blessing her mother's gone. Did you know her mother? Strange woman. Artistic. Never did a lick of work, I knew of.

FATHER: Ben Redleaf was accused of assault with intent to kill. He was sentenced to four years in the Provincial Penitentiary.

JEAN: Didja hear? Didja hear? Four bloody years is all that savage got! He'll come out again and do the same. It's the courts, y'know, the judges. They're a bunch of bleeding hearts where the Indians are concerned. My father sold his practice. It seemed he had to sign a hundred papers to complete that transaction. The lawyers were amazing. They'd hand him a sheet and say, "Sign right there, please." "Oh, yes," he'd say, and scribble his name across the middle. Finally, he let me guide his hand.

FATHER: The sight was gone, the child was gone, the pride remained a problem.

JEAN: He put salt in his tea for the first few days. He put lard on his bread. His meat ended up in his lap until he let me cut it for him. The part in his hair was never straight. He socks were never the same color. Our first caller was the paper boy.
      Collecting, sir. Three dollars, please.

FATHER: Oh, yes. Yes. Right here. Just a minute now. Yes. There you are.

JEAN: That's a five and two ones, sir. Do you have three ones?

FATHER: Oh, yes, just a minute. I'm sure I—yes, I think I can—

JEAN: No, sir, you haven't got it. *(She leans forward)* Here, I'll take this five and change it—

FATHER: *(Bellowing)* Get your damned hands off my money! *(He calls)* Jean? Jean? Jeannie, will you come help me?

JEAN: We tried going for walks together during the day, but he wouldn't let me guide him.

FATHER: *(With a small smile)* She had a running commentary that drove me crazy. This is Mrs. Bradley's house—remember, they have nasturtiums up their walk. It's a very pungent smell. You'll always know the Bradleys' by that smell. There's a crack in the walk, there, where it's buckled. If you veer too far to the right you'll hit the fire hydrant. Watch it! Some kid's left a tricycle here! Hold it! Oh, *damn.* You've stepped in a big wet dog mess. *(Pause)* After that we walked at night, and I held her arm.

JEAN: He'd feathered his nest very nicely over the years. We hired whatever help we needed. We took the train to Banff every summer. We never, ever, spoke of Ben Redleaf. I have four Christmas cards in a box upstairs. None is signed. They say, "Merry Christmas, bonnie Jean, four to go. Merry Christmas, bonnie Jean, three to go. Merry Christmas, bonnie Jean, two to go. Merry Christmas, bonnie Jean, one to go." *(Pause)* He came to see me when he got out of jail. We talked for about five minutes. It was around ten o'clock at night. It was twelve years ago. *(She suddenly claps her hands, twice, sharply and quickly)*

FATHER: *(Calling)* What's that noise on the porch, Jean?

JEAN: *(Calling)* Just the screen door, Dad. It bangs in the wind.

FATHER: Oh, yes. Have to get somebody in to fix that.

JEAN: Yes. One of these days. *(She turns, and whispers)* Ben? Ben Redleaf, is that you? *(Ben enters, as described in the following, but for hat and blade of grass. He stands behind the middle chair)* His face, in the half-light, had changed. He'd matured. He looked like a real Indian now—pronounced cheek bones, a black felt cowboy hat, a blade of grass sticking out of his mouth. His eyes were sly, his expression cocky. He leaned against our porch rail and spat, over the edge, on our honeysuckle bush.

BEN: Hiya, Jeannie.

JEAN: Hello, Ben. *(Pause. Ben nods to the right)*

BEN: Is he in there?

JEAN: Yes.

BEN: How's he doing?

JEAN: Pretty well. He's learned braille. He still has pains in his forehead.

BEN: Watcha been doing with yourself?

JEAN: I'm in my second year at the university. How about you?

BEN: *(Broad smile)* Just can't make up my mind, got so many offers. Royal Bank of Canada, Richardson and Sons—they all want me real bad.

JEAN: Ben, what did you do there all those years?

BEN: Swung a pick-ax every day. Kept my back against the wall at night.

JEAN: Oh?

BEN: Yeah.

JEAN: He turned and spat on the honeysuckle bush a second time. He was lean and hard. Oh, my God, he was lean and hard. I didn't dare touch him.

FATHER: Jean? I'm just damned sure I hear something out on that porch!

JEAN: No, Dad. Just me. Nothing to fret about. *(Turning to Ben)* What are you going to do, Ben?

BEN: Got to get off this prairie, that's for sure. Lot of talk around the pen about some white man in northern British Columbia. He owns a big lumber camp. Seems he only hires Indian ex-cons. Doesn't pay anything at all, but I hear the food is good. And the quarters fair. Guess I'll get my ass up there for awhile.

JEAN: And then my father came out to the porch.

(The Father moves down left. He stands between Jean and Ben)

FATHER: Jean? Sure you're all right out here alone?

JEAN: Just fine, Dad, really. There's a chill tonight. You'd better stay inside.

FATHER: Oh, you're such an old granny! There's no chill. It's a very pleasant night. *(He sniffs at the air, and sighs)* Come what may that honeysuckle bush just keeps on blooming. Full bloom now?

JEAN: Not quite yet. Another day or two. *(Pause)* Ben stood so still—I never saw a man stand so still. Then, suddenly *(She claps her hands again)* the screen door banged in the wind. It startled my father and he jumped slightly.

FATHER: That's a hell of a nuisance! Have to get somebody in here to fix that one of these days.

JEAN: Ben Redleaf tipped his hat, and crept away. *(There is a tableau for a moment)* It's habit now to look for him wherever they gather in groups. Saturday afternoons we often drive to Grant Island. I see them crouched along the road, selling beads, moccasins, toy wig-wams. I see them on the bus late at night, drunk and mumbling to themselves. I've looked up alleys along Eighth Street and seen them huddled there with cheap wine, vanilla extract, canned heat. Sunday mornings I've seen them vomiting in the park.

FATHER: She's moody and depressed when she sees these things. Nothing I could say would comfort her. I know, and I knew, that her contribution to that scene was better left in Winnipeg.

JEAN: I've looked for him riding at fairs and rodeos. I've looked for him climbing oil rigs in Alberta. I've looked for him picking sugar beets, near Lethbridge; cherries in the Okanogan. I've looked for him posing for pictures, in borrowed regalia, at Lake Louise. The slant of a forehead, the nape of a neck can make my palms grow wet, can make me ache. There are a thousand dead ringers for Ben Redleaf, but he's gone. *(She rises, and moves behind her chair, in reverie)* It's a shame, in a way, that I have so little tangible evidence of him. There are the four Christmas cards, but there are none of the ordinary mementos. No snapshots, no dried orchid from any high school prom. There is one piece of paper. The receipt from the doctor in Winnipeg. My father keeps it in his strongbox, upstairs. For some reason, he used my mother's maiden name when he made the call. So the receipt is made out to Miss Natalie Duncan. And it is stamped in purple ink—*Paid in Full.* I have very little evidence of my mother, either. Her spirit, her vitality, have become dimmed by time. My memory of her is like a rumor I once heard, and can't quite remember, and can't quite forget. Once a year I go down to City Hall to pay our taxes. I always pause at the Mayor's office. The Mayors have changed several times, but the receptionist is always the same, and she expects me. Mother's picture still hangs there. The riverbank, the water, the one perfect bridge.

(Jean and the Father sigh, exhale, touch their foreheads. The Father loosens his tie. He moves the middle chair down, closer to Jean's. Gradually, they settle into the chairs)

FATHER: That damned thing they call spring comes and goes before you notice it. Then it's heat, heat, heat.

JEAN: Yes, with no let-up in sight. Not much better out here than in the house.

FATHER: Not much. Don't hear a single leaf moving. *(Pause)* I've been thinking about this summer. We've gone to Banff for fourteen years now. Seems to me we're in a helluva rut.

JEAN: I'd just as soon stay here, if you would.

FATHER: Oh, I don't know. The mountains, the Maritimes—it's all the same to me. Just a different smell, s'all, hotel to hotel. It's you I think about.

JEAN: It's all the same to me, too, Dad.

FATHER: I used to think you'd find a beau on one of those holidays.

JEAN: If you look for a beau, I guess you can find one.

FATHER: Yep, I guess so. *(Pause)* I used to think about moving, too.

JEAN: So did I. I think the time has come, Dad, to settle for Cardigan.

FATHER: Yep. After all's said and done, Cardigan's been good to us. Everything's changing, though. I heard on the radio families move an average of once every four years nowadays.

JEAN: Mobile Society.

FATHER: I wonder if it stacks up any different in the long run.

JEAN: How so?

FATHER: Well, it might be easier, making your mistakes and leaving them behind. In the old days we just piled 'em up in one place and scratched a living off the top.

JEAN: Don't you think you do that whether you move or not?

FATHER: I guess so. *(He groans, and puts his palm to his head)*

JEAN: Got some pain tonight?

FATHER: Just a tad. Guess I'll take a couple of those new pills and go to bed.

JEAN: Get the right bottle now. Here, I'd better—*(She begins to rise)*

FATHER: Never mind, never mind! I know which ones. It's all *aspirin,* anyway.

JEAN: No, Dad. These new ones are pink.

FATHER: *Pink, yellow, red, green.* The pharmacist's artistry. It's wasted on me.

JEAN: Dad, I taped a safety pin on the lid.

FATHER: All right, I'll feel for it. *(Muttering, as he exits)* They play their little games. My gullet knows it's all aspirin. Will you lock up?

JEAN: Yes.

FATHER: And you'd better check the windows. You never know, it might—

JEAN: I don't think so—

FATHER: I don't think so, either. But you never know. Better to be safe than—

JEAN: Right. I'll close them. Good night, Dad.

FATHER: Good night, Jeannie.

BLACKOUT

Birthday Card for a Psychiatrist
MONA VAN DUYN

Your friends come fondly to your living room
believing, my dear, that the occasion's mild.
Who still feels forty as a moral *crise*
in this, the Century of the Common Child?

Uncommon gifts, brought to mid-life in pain,
are not a prize. The age demands a cure
for tragedy and gives us brand-new charts
for taking down our psychic temperature.

Othello, of course, regrets having been aggressive,
Hamlet feels pretty silly to think he trusted
terms such as "art" and "honor" instead of "projection,"
and out on the moor King Lear feels maladjusted.

An arrogant richness of the human stuff
is not a value. Nobody wants to be
left holding the bag of himself when all the others
are a democratic homogeneity.

Prospero strips down to his underpants
to teach Miranda that fathers can be informal,
while Cleopatra, Juliet, Rosalind, Kate
fight for the golden apple labelled NORMAL.

In such a state, what laurels can poems bring,
what consolation, what wishes, what advice?
May your conflicts thin out with your hair? BE HAPPY?
We hope you're feeling well? We think you're nice?

Till Burnam Wood shall come to Dunsinane,
till time shall tell us what we really are,
till Responsibility, not Health, defines
the terms of living on this serious star.

To receive the trauma of birth and pass it on
is all we're here for. Yet we hope you realize
we're glad that forty years ago you came
to join in our neurotic enterprise.

Villanelle
W. H. AUDEN

Time can say nothing but I told you so,
Time only knows the price we have to pay;
If I could tell you, I would let you know.

If we should weep when clowns put on their show,
If we should stumble when musicians play,
Time can say nothing but I told you so.

There are no fortunes to be told, although
Because I love you more than I can say,
If I could tell you, I would let you know.

The winds must come from somewhere when they blow,
There must be reasons why the leaves decay;
Time can say nothing but I told you so.

Perhaps the roses really want to grow,
The vision seriously intends to stay;
If I could tell you, I would let you know.

Suppose the lions all get up and go,
And all the brooks and soldiers run away?
Time can say nothing but I told you so;
If I could tell you, I would let you know.

A Couple of Hamburgers
JAMES THURBER

It had been raining for a long time, a slow, cold rain falling out of iron-colored clouds. They had been driving since morning and they still had a hundred and thirty miles to go. It was about three o'clock in the afternoon. "I'm getting hungry," she said. He took his eyes off the wet, winding road for a fraction of a second and said, "We'll stop at a dog-wagon." She shifted her position irritably. "I wish you wouldn't call them *dog*-wagons," she said. He pressed the klaxon button and went around a slow car. "That's what they are," he said. "Dogwagons." She waited a few seconds. "*Decent* people call them *diners*," she told him, and added, "Even if you call them diners, I don't like them." He speeded up a hill. "They have better stuff than most restaurants," he said. "Anyway, I want to get home before dark and it takes too long in a restaurant. We can stay our stomachs with a couple hamburgers." She lighted a cigarette and he asked her to light one for him. She lighted one deliberately and handed it to him. "I wish you wouldn't say 'stay our stomachs,' " she said. "You know I hate that. It's like 'sticking to your ribs.' You say that all the time." He grinned. "Good old American expressions, both of them," he said. "Like sow belly. Old pioneer term, sow belly." She sniffed. "My ancestors were pioneers, too. You don't have to be vulgar just because you were a pioneer." "Your ancestors never got as far west as mine did," he said. "The real pioneers travelled on their sow belly and got somewhere." He laughed loudly at that. She looked out at the wet trees and signs and telephone poles going by. They drove on for several miles without a word; he kept chortling every now and then.

"What's that funny sound?" she asked, suddenly. It invariably made him angry when she heard a funny sound. "What funny sound?" he demanded. "You're always hearing funny sounds." She laughed briefly. "That's what you said when the bearing burned out," she reminded him. "You'd never have noticed it if it hadn't been for me." "I noticed it, all right," he said. "Yes," she said. "When it was too late." She enjoyed bringing up the subject of the burned-out bearing whenever he got to chortling. "It was too late when *you* noticed it, as far as that goes," he said. Then, after a pause, "Well, what does it sound like *this* time? All engines make a noise running, you know." "I know all about that," she answered. "It sounds like—it sounds like a lot of safety pins being jiggled around in a tumbler." He snorted. "That's your imagination. Nothing gets the matter with a car that sounds like a lot of safety pins. I happen to know that." She tossed away her cigarette. "Oh, sure," she said. "You always happen to know everything." They drove on in silence.

"I want to stop somewhere and get something to *eat!*" she said loudly. "All right, all right!" he said. "I been watching for a dog-wagon, haven't I? There hasn't been any. I can't make you a dog-wagon." The wind blew rain in on her and she put up the window on her side all the way. "I won't stop at just any old diner," she said. "I won't stop unless it's a cute one." He looked around at her. "Unless it's a *what* one?" he shouted. "You know what I mean," she said. "I mean a decent, clean one where they don't slosh things at you. I hate to have a lot of milky coffee sloshed at me." "All right," he said. "We'll find a cute one, then. You pick it out. I wouldn't know. I might find one that was cunning but not cute." That struck him as funny and he began to chortle again. "Oh, shut up," she said.

Five miles farther along they came to a place called Sam's Diner. "Here's one," he said, slowing down. She looked it over. "I don't want to stop there," she said. "I don't like the ones that have nicknames." He brought the car to a stop at one side of the road. "Just what's the matter with the ones that have nicknames?" he asked with edgy, mock interest. "They're always Greek ones," she told him. "They're always Greek ones," he repeated after her. He set his teeth firmly together and started up again. After a time, "Good old Sam, the Greek," he said, in a singsong. "Good old Connecticut Sam Beardsley, the Greek." "You didn't see his name," she snapped. "Winthrop, then," he said. "Old Samuel Cabot Winthrop, the Greek dog-wagon man." He was getting hungry.

On the outskirts of the next town she said, as he slowed down, "It looks like a factory kind of town." He knew that she meant she wouldn't stop there. He drove on through the place. She lighted a cigarette as they pulled out into the open again. He slowed down and lighted a cigarette for himself. "Factory kind of town than *I* am!" he snarled. It was ten miles before they came to another town. "Torrington," he growled. "Happen to know there's a dog-wagon here because I stopped in it once with Bob Combs. Damn cute place, too, if you ask me." "I'm not asking you anything," she said, coldly. "You think you're *so* funny. I think I know the one you mean," she said, after a moment. "It's right in the town and it sits at an angle from the road. They're never so good, for some reason." He glared at her and almost ran up against the curb. "What the hell do you mean 'sits at an angle from the road'?" he cried. He was very hungry now. "Well, it isn't silly," she said, calmly. "I've noticed the ones that sit at an angle. They're cheaper, because they fitted them into funny little pieces of ground. The big ones parallel to the road are the best." He drove right through Torrington, his lips compressed. "Angle from the road, for God's sake!" he snarled, finally. She was looking out her window.

On the outskirts of the next town there was a diner called The Elite Diner. "This looks—" she began. "I see it, I see it!" he said. "It doesn't happen to look any cuter to me than any goddam—" she cut him off. "Don't be such a sorehead, for Lord's sake," she said. He pulled up and stopped beside the diner, and turned on her. "Listen," he said, grittingly, "I'm going to put down a couple of hamburgers in this place even if there isn't one single inch of chintz or cretonne in the whole—" "Oh, be still," she said. "You're just hungry and mean like a child. Eat your old hamburgers, what do I care?" Inside the place they sat down on stools and the counterman walked over to them, wiping up the counter top with a cloth as he did so. "What'll it be, folks?" he said. "Bad day, ain't it? Except for ducks." "I'll have a couple of—" began the husband, but his wife cut in. "I just want a pack of cigarettes," she said. He turned around slowly on his stool and stared at her as she put a dime and a nickel in the cigarette machine and ejected a package of Lucky Strikes. He turned to the counterman again. "I want a couple of hamburgers," he said. "With mustard and lots of onion. *Lots* of onion!" She hated onions. "I'll wait for you in the car," she said. He didn't answer and she went out.

He finished his hamburgers and his coffee slowly. It was terrible coffee. Then he went out to the car and got in and drove off, slowly humming "Who's Afraid of the Big Bad Wolf?" After a mile or so, "Well," he said, "what was the matter with the Elite Diner, milady?" "Didn't you *see* that cloth the man was wiping the counter with?" she demanded. "Ugh!" She shuddered. "I didn't happen to want to eat any of the counter," he said. He laughed at that comeback. "You didn't even notice it," she said. "You never notice anything. It was filthy." "I noticed they had some damn fine coffee in there," he said. "It was swell." He knew she loved good coffee. He began to hum his tune again; then he whistled it; then he began to sing it. She did not show her annoyance, but she knew that he knew she was annoyed. "Will you be kind enough to tell me what time it is?" she asked. "Big *bad* wolf, big *bad* wolf—five minutes o' five— tum-dee-*doo*-dee-dum-m-m." She settled back in her seat and took a cigarette from her case and tapped it on the case. "I'll wait till we get home," she said. "If you'll be kind enough to speed up a little." He drove on at the same speed. After a time he gave up the "Big Bad Wolf" and there was deep silence for two miles. Then suddenly he began to sing, very loudly, *H*-A-double-R-*I*-G-A-N *spells Harr*-i-gan—" She gritted her teeth. She hated that worse than any of his songs except "Barney Google." He would go on to "Barney Google" pretty soon, she knew. Suddenly she leaned slightly forward. The straight line of her lips began to curve up ever so slightly. She heard the safety pins in the tumbler again. Only now they were louder, more insistent, ominous. He was singing too loud to hear them. "Is a *name* that *shame* has never been con-*nec*-ted with— *Harr*-i-gan, that's *me*!" She relaxed against the back of the seat content to wait.

Ars Poetica?
CZESLAW MILOSZ
Translated by the Author and Lillian Vallee

I have always aspired to a more spacious form
that would be free from the claims of poetry or prose
and would let us understand each other without exposing
the author or reader to sublime agonies.

In the very essence of poetry there is something indecent:
a thing is brought forth which we didn't know we had in us,
so we blink our eyes, as if a tiger had sprung out
and stood in the light, lashing his tail.

That's why poetry is rightly said to be dictated by a daimonion,
though it's an exaggeration to maintain that he must be an angel.
It's hard to guess where that pride of poets comes from,
when so often they're put to shame by the disclosure of their frailty.

What reasonable man would like to be a city of demons,
who behave as if they were at home, speak in many tongues,
and who, not satisfied with stealing his lips or hand,
work at changing his destiny for their convenience?

It's true that what is morbid is highly valued today,
and so you may think that I am only joking
or that I've devised just one more means
of praising Art with the help of irony.

There was a time when only wise books were read
helping us to bear our pain and misery.
This, after all, is not quite the same
as leafing through a thousand words fresh from psychiatric clinics.

And yet the world is different from what it seems to be
and we are other than how we see ourselves in our ravings.
People therefore preserve silent integrity
thus earning the respect of their relatives and neighbors.

The purpose of poetry is to remind us
how difficult it is to remain just one person,
for our house is open, there are no keys in the doors,
and invisible guests come in and out at will.

What I'm saying here is not, I agree, poetry,
as poems should be written rarely and reluctantly,
under unbearable duress and only with the hope
that good spirits, not evil ones, choose us for their instrument.

Selected Bibliography

Items cited elsewhere in the book are not included in this section.

Performing Literature

Bacon, Wallace A., "An Aesthetics of Performance," *Literature in Performance,* 1 (November 1980), 1–9.

———, *The Art of Interpretation,* 3rd ed. New York: Holt, Rinehart and Winston, 1979.

———, and Robert Breen, *Literature as Experience.* New York: McGraw-Hill, 1959.

Bahn, Eugene, and Margaret L. Bahn, *A History of Oral Interpretation.* Minneapolis: Burgess, 1970.

Beardsley, Monroe C., "Right Readings and Good Readings," *Literature in Performance,* 1 (November 1980), 10–22.

Berleant, Arnold, "The Verbal Presence: An Aesthetics of Literary Performance," *Journal of Aesthetics and Art Criticism,* 31 (Spring 1973), 339–346.

Campbell, Paul, "Communication Aesthetics," *Today's Speech,* 19 (Summer 1971), 134–139.

Cohen, Robert, *Acting Power.* Palo Alto, Calif.: Mayfield, 1978.

Fernandez, Thomas L., ed., *Oral Interpretation and the Teaching of English: A Collection of Readings.* Champaign, Ill.: National Council of Teachers of English, 1969.

Fine, Elizabeth C., and Jean Haskell Speer, "A New Look at Performance," *Communication Monographs,* 44 (November 1977), 374–389.

Forrest, William Craig, "Literature as Aesthetic Object: The Kinesthetic Stratum," *Journal of Aesthetics and Art Criticism,* 27 (Summer 1969), 455–459.

———, "The Kinesthetic Feel of Literature," *Bucknell Review,* 16 (December 1968), 91–106.

———, "The Poem as a Summons to Performance," *British Journal of Aesthetics,* 9 (April 1969), 298–305.

Geiger, Don, "Performance as the Act of Understanding Literature," *Oral English,* 1 (Winter 1972), 3–6.

———, "Poetic Realizing as Knowing," *Quarterly Journal of Speech,* 59 (October 1973), 311–318.

Gray, Paul H., "Strange Bedfellows: My Life and Hard Times in a Speech Communication Department," *Southern Speech Communication Journal,* 44 (Winter 1979), 159–166.

Haas, Richard and David A. Williams, eds., *The Study of Oral Interpretation: Theory and Comment.* Indianapolis: The Bobbs-Merrill Co., 1975.

Hein, Hilde, "Performance as an Aesthetic Category," *Journal of Aesthetics and Art Criticism,* 28 (Spring 1970), 381–386.

Henning, W. Keith, "Interpretation as a Revelatory Act: A Wheelwrightean Perspective," *Studies in Interpretation, II,* eds. Esther M. Doyle and Virginia Hastings Floyd. Amsterdam: Rodopi, 1977, pp. 167–182.

Hornby, Richard, *Script into Performance: A Structuralist View of Play Production.* Austin: University of Texas Press, 1977.

Hudson, Lee, "Oral Interpretation as Metaphorical Expression," *Speech Teacher,* 22 (January 1973), 27–31.

Loesch, Katharine T., "Towards an Ontology of Literature in Performance," *Oral English,* 1 (Fall 1972), 8–14.

Long, Chester C., *The Liberal Art of Interpretation.* New York: Harper & Row, 1974.

Macksoud, S. John, "Anyone's How Town: Interpretation as Rhetorical Discipline," *Speech Monographs,* 35 (March 1968), 70–76.

Maher, Mary Z., "Internal Rhetorical Analysis and the Interpretation of Drama," *Central States Speech Journal,* 26 (Winter 1975), 267–273.

McGaw, Charles, *Acting is Believing,* 4th ed. New York: Holt, Rinehart & Winston, 1980.

PEARSE, JAMES A., "Beyond the Narrational Frame: Interpretation and Metafiction," *Quarterly Journal of Speech*, 66 (February 1980), 73–84.

POST, ROBERT M., "Oral Interpretation and the Stanislavski Method," *Southern Speech Journal*, 32 (Spring 1967), 180–187.

——, "Perception Through Performance of Literature," *Speech Teacher*, 19 (September 1970), 168–172.

RICKERT, WILLIAM E., "Structural Functions of Rhyme and the Performance of Poetry," *Quarterly Journal of Speech*, 62 (October 1976), 250–255.

ROLOFF, LELAND, H. *The Perception and Evocation of Literature*. Glenview, Ill.: Scott, Foresman, 1973.

SALPER, DONALD R., "The 'Sounding' of a Poem," *Quarterly Journal of Speech*, 57 (April 1971), 129–133.

SCHNEIDER, RAYMOND, "The Visible Metaphor," *Communication Education*, 25 (March 1976), 121–126.

SHATTUCK, ROGER, "How to Rescue Literature," *The New York Review of Books*, 27 (April 17, 1980), 29–35.

SLOAN, THOMAS O., ed., *The Oral Study of Literature*. New York: Random House, 1966.

——, "Speaking Literature," *Studies in Interpretation*, eds. Esther M. Doyle and Virginia Hastings Floyd. Amsterdam: Rodopi, 1972, pp. 341–362.

SMITH, ROBERT E., JR., *Fundamentals of Oral Interpretation: Modules in Speech Communication*. Chicago: Science Research Associates-IBM, 1978.

SPOLIN, VIOLA, *Improvisation for the Theater*. Evanston: Northwestern University Press, 1963.

VEILLEUX, JERÉ, "Toward a Theory of Interpretation," *Quarterly Journal of Speech*, 55 (April 1969), 105–115.

WILLIAMS, DAVID A., "Audience Response and the Interpreter," *Studies in Interpretation, II*, eds. Esther M. Doyle and Virginia Hastings Floyd. Amsterdam: Rodopi, 1977, pp. 199–206.

Dramatic Analysis

ADAIR, SUZANNE, MARGARET DAVIDSON, and ELIZABETH FINE, "Behavioral Objectives for an Introductory Course in Oral Interpretation," *Communication Education*, 27 (January 1978), 68–70.

CAMPBELL, PAUL, *The Speaking and the Speakers of Literature*. Belmont, Calif.: Dickenson, 1967.

EATON, MARCIA M., "Liars, Ranters, and Dramatic Speakers," in *Language and Aesthetics*, ed. Benjamin R. Tilghman. Lawrence: The University Press of Kansas, 1973, pp. 43–63.

GEIGER, DON, *The Sound, Sense, and Performance of Literature*. Glenview, Ill.: Scott, Foresman, 1963.

——, *The Dramatic Impulse in Modern Poetics*. Baton Rouge: Louisiana State University Press, 1967.

MACLAY, JOANNA H., and THOMAS O. SLOAN. *Interpretation: An Approach to the Study of Literature*. New York: Random House, 1972.

THOMPSON DAVID W., and VIRGINIA FREDERICKS, *Oral Interpretation of Fiction: A Dramatistic Approach*. Minneapolis: Burgess, 1967.

VALENTINE, K. B., *Interlocking Pieces: Twenty Questions for Understanding Literature*. Dubuque, Iowa: Kendall/Hunt, 1977.

Speaker: Character, Narrator, Persona

ALLEN, WALTER, "Narrative Distance, Tone, and Character," *The Theory of the Novel: New Essays*, ed. John Halperin. New York: Oxford University Press, 1974, pp. 323–337.

BENNETT, SUZANNE, "Lyric Fiction: The 'Semi-Transparent' Narrative Mode," *Literature in Performance*, I (April 1981), 36–44.

BOOTH, WAYNE C., *The Rhetoric of Fiction*. Chicago: University of Chicago Press, 1961.

CARLSEN, JAMES W., "Persona, Personality, and Performance," *Studies in Interpretation, II*, eds. Esther M. Doyle and Virginia Hastings Floyd. Amsterdam: Rodopi, 1977, pp. 221–232.

CIXIOUS, HÉLÉNE, "The Character of 'Character'," *New Literary History*, trans. Keith Cohen, 5 (Winter 1974), 383–402.

COHN, DORRIT, *Transparent Minds: Narrative Modes for Presenting Consciousness in Fiction*. Princeton, N.J.: Princeton University Press, 1978.

EATON, MARCIA M., "On Being a Character," *British Journal of Aesthetics*, 16 (Winter 1976), 24–31.

ESPINOLA, JUDITH, "Narrative Discourse in Virginia Woolf's *To the Lighthouse*," *Studies in Interpretation, II,* pp. 29–43.

———, "The Nature, Function, and Performance of Indirect Discourse in Prose Fiction," *Speech Monographs*, 41 (August 1974), 193–204

FLOYD, VIRGINIA HASTINGS, "Point of View in Modern Drama," *Studies in Interpretation, II*, pp. 13–27.

FRIEDMAN, NORMAN, "Point of View in Fiction: The Development of a Critical Concept," *Publications of the Modern Language Association,* 70 (December, 1955), 1160–1184.

GUDAS, FABIAN, "Persona," *Princeton Encyclopedia of Poetry and Poetics* (enl. ed.), eds. Alex Preminger, Frank J. Warnke, O. B. Hardison, Jr. Princeton, N.J.: Princeton, University Press, 1974, pp. 959–961.

GURA, TIMOTHY J., "The Solo Performer and Drama," *Speech Teacher*, 24 (September 1975), 278–281.

HAAS, RICHARD, "Oral Interpretation as Discovery Through Persona," *Oral English*, 1 (Spring 1972), 13–14.

HARVEY, W. H. *Character and the Novel*. Ithaca, N.Y.: Cornell University Press, 1965.

HELLER, L. G., "The Structural Relationship Between Theme and Characterization," *Language and Style*, 4 (Spring 1971), pp. 123–130.

HESTON, LILLA A., "The Interpreter and the Structure of the Novel," *Studies in Interpretation*, pp. 137–154.

———, "The Solo Performance of Prose Fiction," *Speech Teacher*, 24 (September 1975), 269–277.

HRUSHOVSKI, BENJAMIN, ed., "Narratology III: Narration and Perspective in Fiction," *Poetics Today*, II (Winter 1981), 5–156.

IRVINE, PETER L., "The 'Witness' Point of View in Fiction," *South Atlantic Quarterly*, 69, (Spring 1970), pp. 217–225.

JORDAN, RICHARD DOUGLAS, "Persona: The Dancer and the Dance," *Quadrant*, 20 (January 1976), pp. 77–79.

KUMIN, MAXINE, "Four Kinds of *I*," *To Make a Prairie: Essays on Poets, Poetry, and Country Living*. Ann Arbor: University of Michigan Press, 1979, pp. 147–54.

LANGBAUM, ROBERT, *The Poetry of Experience: The Dramatic Monologue in Modern Literary Tradition*. New York: Random House, 1957.

LENTZ, TONY M., ed., "The Issue: A Performance," *Issues in Interpretation*, IV (Spring 1980), 2–18.

MACLAY, JOANNA HAWKINS, "The Interpreter and Modern Fiction: Problems of Point of View and Structural Tensiveness," *Studies in Interpretation*, I, pp. 155–169.

MENDELSOHN, LEONARD R., "The Player as Director: An Approach to Character," *Comparative Drama*, 6 (Summer 1972), pp. 115–124.

NADIN, MIHAI, "Text and Character," *Poetics: International Review for the Theory of Literature*, 6 (December 1977), pp. 255–286.

ONG, WALTER J., "A Dialectic of Aural and Objective Correlatives," *Essays in Criticism*, 8 (April 1958), pp. 166–181.

PARRELLA, GILDA, "Through the 'I' of the Beholder: A Rationale for Physicalization in the Performance of Narratives," *Central States Speech Journal*, 25 (Winter 1974), 296–302.

ROLOFF, LELAND, H. "The Roles of the Interpreter and the Actor," *Speech Teacher*, 22 (March 1973), 144–147.

ROMBERG, BERTIL, *Studies in the Narrative Technique of the First-Person Novel*. Stockholm: Almkvist and Wiksell, 1962.

ROSS, STEPHEN M., " 'Voice' in Narrative Texts: The Example of *As I Lay Dying*," *Publications of the Modern Language Association*, 94 (March 1979), 300–310.

SCHULZ, MAX F., "Characters (Contra Characterization) in the Contemporary Novel," *The Theory of the Novel: New Essays*, ed., John Halperin. New York: Oxford University Press, 1974, pp. 141–154.

SHARP, WILLIAM L., *Language in Drama: Meanings for the Director and the Actor*, San Francisco: Chandler, 1970.

SINFIELD, ALAN, *Dramatic Monologue.* New York: Barnes & Noble, 1977.

SPRINGER, MARY DOYLE, *A Rhetoric of Literary Character: Some Women of Henry James.* Chicago: University of Chicago Press, 1979.

STRINE, MARY S., "Narrative Strategy and Communicative Design in Flannery O'Connor's *The Violent Bear It Away,*" *Studies in Interpretation, II,* pp. 45–57.

STYAN, J. L., *The Elements of Drama.* London: Cambridge University Press, 1963.

WALCUTT, CHARLES CHILD, *Man's Changing Mask: Modes and Methods of Characterization.* Minneapolis: Minnesota Press, 1966.

WOOD, JAMES, *Poetry Is: Thoughts About the What, Why, and Who of Poetry.* Boston: Houghton Mifflin, 1972.

Writers as Readers of Their Own Works

Appendix B contains a list of several companies from whom you can secure recordings, cassettes, video tapes, and filmstrips of literature in performance—and most of it by the writers themselves. In addition to providing pleasure, performances by writers are typically instructive about the literature performed. Each of the following sources deals with the widespread practice of writers reading their own works.

CIARDI, JOHN, "Writers as Readers of Poetry," *Saturday Review,* November 23, 1957; "Seniors and Juniors," *Saturday Review,* June 11, 1960; "The Poet as a Reader," *Saturday Review,* December 29, 1962.

FLEISCHMANN, WOLFGANG BERNARD, "Poetry Reading," *Princeton Encyclopedia of Poetry and Poetics,* enl. ed., eds. Alex Preminger, Frank J. Warnke, and O. B. Hardison, Jr. Princeton, N.J.: Princeton University Press, 1974, pp. 967–970.

GEIGER, DON, "Note on Poets' Recorded Readings of Their Works," *The Sound, Sense, and Performance of Literature.* Glenview, Ill.: Scott, Foresman, Company, 1963, pp. 55–60.

HALL, DONALD, *Remembering Poets: Reminiscences and Opinions.* New York: Harper & Row, 1978. (Although this book is not primarily about poets reading, Hall does comment on performance in his discussion of Dylan Thomas, Robert Frost, T. S. Eliot, and Ezra Pound.)

HART, M. BLAIR, "The Writer: Poet's Thoughts on Oral Interpretation," *Perspectives on Oral Interpretation: Essays and Readings,* ed. John W. Gray. Minneapolis: Burgess, 1968, pp. 31–44.

HOPKINS, MARY FRANCES, "Sincerity and the Performing Artist: An Old Critical Concept Reestablished," *Studies in Interpretation, II,* eds. Esther M. Doyle and Virginia Hastings Floyd. Amsterdam: Rodopi, 1977, pp. 207–219.

HUDSON, LEE, "Poetics in Performance: The Beat Generation," *Studies in Interpretation, II,* pp. 59–76.

"Stirring Times," *Times Literary Supplement,* June 17, 1965. (A reply to this editorial appeared July 15, 1965.)

WEALES, GERALD, "The Poet as Player," *New World Writing* (May 1957), pp. 231–43.

WHITAKER, BEVERLY, "John Ciardi on Poets' Recorded Readings," *Southern Speech Journal,* 29 (Spring 1964), 209–213.

WILLIAMS, HUGO, "Poetry, Sold Out," *London Magazine,* 5 (August 1965), 95–102.

WRAY, JUDITH EDWORTHY, "Theories and Methods of Representative Contemporary Poets as Readers of Their Own Poetry." Unpublished Ph.D. Dissertation, University of Wisconsin at Madison, 1961.

Appendix A:
Advanced Assignments

Space does not permit us to consider any of these advanced assignments in detail, but we will mention three briefly and include several sources that can be of assistance.

1. An *author-centered program* asks you to select several works by and about one writer for a class presentation. While you will need some kind of focus for your program, you will probably want to "show off" the writer as much as possible. Most of the writers included in this book have published widely, and for transitional purposes in your program, most have been the subject of diverse critical commentaries. The sources listed in the bibliography contain more explicit suggestions.

2. A *theme- or subject-centered program* asks you to select works by any number of writers concerned with the same topic for class presentation. Those themes range almost indefinitely—from initiation to death and love to alienation. As with the author-centered program, you will want to give your presentation some kind of "shape" while treating each selection of literature fairly and fully.

3. Particularly if the members of your class are able to work together as a unit, you may be asked to present a *group performance of one or more literary texts*. The project might involve the works of one author, as in assignment 1, or the works of several writers about a related subject, as in 2. Your plan for the project will probably evolve from the belief that a group of persons can better show these particular literary texts than can a lone individual. Again, we cannot be more specific here, but the suggested readings—though they are certainly not all in agreement—should prove helpful and directive.

Programming

BOWEN, ELBERT R., OTIS J. AGGERTT, and WILLIAM E. RICKERT, *Communicative Reading*, 4th ed. New York: Macmillan, 1978, pp. 387–391. Short program on poetry of John Ciardi.

COHEN, EDWIN, *Oral Interpretation: The Communication of Literature*. Chicago: Science Research Associates, 1977. Section on programming and cutting. Sample program is theme centered: "The Athlete as Symbol: Hero with Feet of Clay," which includes poetry and nonfiction.

GILBERT, CAROLYN A., *Communicative Performance of Literature*. New York: Macmillan, 1977, pp. 78–89. In section on lecture recital, considers unifying devices, transitions. Full sample of "Around the World," a theme-centered program of poetry and prose.

LEE CHARLOTTE, and FRANK GALATI, *Oral Interpretation*, 5th ed. Boston: Houghton Mifflin, 1977, pp. 542–554. Considers selecting material, theme, transitions, adapting to the audience. No full examples but an extensive description of possibilities for a program on D. H. Lawrence.

LOWREY, SARA, and GERTUDE E. JOHNSON, *Interpretative Reading: Techniques and Selections*, rev. ed. New York: Appleton-Century-Crofts, 1953, pp. 243–253. Programs and lecture recitals. Program example is "Recital from the Poetry of John Masefield." Also includes complete text of "Love's Courage," a lecture recital based on the poetry and letters of Robert and Elizabeth Barrett Browning (pp. 447–476).

MATTINGLY, ALETHEA SMITH, and WILMA H. GRIMES, *Interpretation: Writer, Reader, Au-*

dience, 2nd ed. Belmont, Calif.: Wadsworth, 1970, pp. 306–325. Discussion of selection, arrangement, and transitions. Includes sample program selections, both author centered and theme centered: "The Winter Poetry of Robert Frost," "Man Looks at Woman," "The Other Side of Love in the Spring," "Black Man Looks at Black Man," "The Dry Mock," "A Beastly Reading Hour."

MERRITT, FRANCINE, "Teaching Interpretation," *Speech Methods and Resources*, ed. Waldo W. Braden, pp. 307–310. New York: Harper & Brothers, 1961. Discussion of both author-centered and theme-centered programs. Includes outline by which students can report their steps in preparing the program.

Group Performance

BREEN, ROBERT S., *Chamber Theatre*. Englewood Cliffs, N.J.: Prentice-Hall, 1978. Rich treatment of Chamber Theatre productions of prose fiction, adaptations and staging that are dramatic and also preserve the narrative structure, particularly point of view.

COGER, LESLIE IRENE, and MELVIN R. WHITE, *Readers Theatre Handbook: A Dramatic Approach to Literature,* rev. ed. Glenview, Ill.: Scott, Foresman, 1973. First full treatment of the subject. Includes sections on selection, adaptation, rehearsal, and staging. Scripts, illustrations, and extensive bibliography.

IZ CRANE, ed. *Readers Theatre News.* Periodical published since 1973 by the Institute for Readers Theatre, P.O. Box 15847, San Diego, CA 92115. Articles, interviews, scripts, news, photographs.

HAAS, RICHARD, *Theatres of Interpretation.* Ann Arbor, Mich.: Roberts-Burton, 1976. Lively, nonprescriptive consideration of some of the aims and possibilities of group performance. Includes one script.

KLEINAU, MARION L. and JANET LARSEN McHUGHES, *Theatres for Literature.* Sherman Oaks, California: Alfred Publishing, 1980. Extensive coverage of presentational form in group performance. Includes steps in analysis, script construction, staging, direction and production, with several scripts.

LONG, BEVERLY WHITAKER, LEE HUDSON, and PHILLIS RIENSTRA JEFFREY, *Group Performance of Literature.* Englewood Cliffs, N.J.: Prentice-Hall, 1977. Considers basic principles of analysis, adaptation, rehearsal, and production of several genres. Contains sixteen scripts adapted for group performance, together with adaptor's comments.

MACLAY, JOANNA HAWKINS, *Readers Theatre: Toward a Grammar of Practice.* New York: Random House, Inc., 1971. Clear discussion of principles of casting and staging in group performances intended to "feature the text." Includes a script based on works of Laurence Durrell.

Appendix B: Sources for Audio and Video Recordings of Performed Literature

The following companies provide catalogs of their holdings and sell or rent audio or video recordings—and sometimes both—of works by most of the authors represented in this book. Sometimes actors do the performance, occasionally critics, but most often the writers themselves perform. The prices for these resources range from under ten dollars to several hundred dollars. However, the rental fee for many of the half-hour video tapes is under fifteen dollars. Many libraries are developing nonprint holdings and will purchase or jointly purchase items such as these. Your experiences with these materials can be both pleasurable and instructive.

A more extensive list of publishers and works is available in *Schwann 2*, released semiannually from 137 Newbury Street, Boston, Mass. 02116.

American Poetry Archive, The Poetry Center, San Francisco State University, San Francisco, Calif. 94132

Argo, Houghton-Mifflin, Dept. M-70, One Beacon St., Boston, Mass. 02107

Audio Brandon Films, 3910 Harlem Road, Buffalo, N.Y. 14226

Audio-Text, 8110 Webb Avenue, N. Hollywood, Calif. 91605

Black Box, P.O. Box 4174, Washington, D.C. 20015

Broadside Press, 47 Glendale Hi Park, Detroit, Mich. 48203

Caedmon, 1995 Broadway, New York, N.Y. 10023

Contemporary Films, McGraw-Hill, 1221 Avenue of the Americas, New York, N.Y. 10020

Coronet Films, Inc., 65 E. South Water Street, Chicago, Ill. 60601

Educational Audio Visual, Inc., 29 Marble Ave., Pleasantville, N.Y. 10570

Encyclopaedia Britannica Education Co., 425 N. Michigan Ave., Chicago, Ill. 60611

Everett/Edwards, Inc., P.O. Box 1060, Deland, Fla. 32720

Films for the Humanities, P.O. Box 2053, Princeton, N.J. 08540

Folkway Records, 43 W. 61st St., New York, N.Y. 10023

Learning Arts, P.O. Box 179, Wichita, Kans. 67201

The Library of Congress, Recorded Sound Section, Washington, D.C. 20540

National Council of Teachers of English, 1111 Kenyon Rd., Champaign, Ill. 61820

NET Film Service, Indiana University, Audio-Visual-Center, Bloomington, Ind. 47405

Northwestern University, Film Library, P.O. Box 1665, Evanston, Ill. 60204

Profiles in Literature, Temple University, Office of Television Services, Tomlinson Hall 214, Philadelphia, Pa. 19122

Spoken Arts, 310 North Avenue, New Rochelle, N.Y. 10801

Time-Life Video, Inc., 1271 Avenue of the Americas, New York, N.Y. 10020

WCBS-TV, 51 West 57th St., New York, N.Y. 10019

A good source of information about new and developing outlets for audio and video recordings is *Coda,* published by Poets & Writers, Inc., 201 West 54th St., New York, N.Y. 10019.

Acknowledgments

Poetry

CONRAD AIKEN, "South End"
From *Collected Poems*, second edition, by Conrad Aiken. © 1953, 1970 by Conrad Aiken. Reprinted by permission of Oxford University Press, Inc.

ALURISTA, "What's Happening"
From *Floricanto en Aztlan.* © 1971 by the Regents of the University of California; published by the Chicano Studies Center Publications, University of California, 405 Hilgard Avenue, Los Angeles, Calif. 90024.

A.R. AMMONS, "Hardweed Path Going"
From *Collected Poems, 1951–1971*, by A.R. Ammons, with the permission of W.W. Norton & Company, Inc. © 1972 by A.R. Ammons.

W.H. AUDEN, "If I Could Tell You" ("Villanelle")
Reprinted from *Collected Poems*, by W.H. AUDEN, ed. Edward Mendelson. By permission of Random House, Inc., and Faber & Faber Limited, London. © 1945 by W.H. Auden.

LEONARD BACON, "An Afternoon in Artillery Walk"
From *Guinea-Fowl and Other Poultry* by Leonard Bacon. By permission of Harper & Row Publishers, Inc. © 1927 by Harper & Row, Publishers, Inc.; renewed 1955 by Martha Sherman Stringham Bacon.

MICHAEL BENEDIKT, "The Meat Epitaph"
Reprinted from *Night Cries*. By permission of Wesleyan University Press. © 1975 by Michael Benedikt.

JOHN BETJEMAN, "In Westminster Abbey"
From *Collected Poems*. Reprinted by permission of Houghton Mifflin Co. and John Murray Publishers, Ltd. © 1959 by John Betjeman.

ELIZABETH BISHOP, "House Guest"
From *The Complete Poems* by Elizabeth Bishop. Reprinted with the permission of Farrar, Straus & Giroux, Inc. © 1968 by Elizabeth Bishop. Originally appeared in *The New Yorker*.

CLAUS BREMER, "Participate"
From *Ideogramme* (Frauenfeld, 1964). Reprinted in *Open Poetry: Four Anthologies of Expanded Poems*, eds. Ronald Gross, George Quasha, Emmett Williams, John Robert Colombo & Walter Lowenfels. Simon & Schuster, 1973. Reprinted by permission of the author.

GWENDOLYN BROOKS, "To Be in Love"
From *Selected Poems* by Gwendolyn Brooks. By permission of Harper & Row, Publishers, Inc. © 1963 by Gwendolyn Brooks Blakely.

GWENDOLYN BROOKS, "The Mother"
From *The World of Gwendolyn Brooks*. By permission of Harper and Row, Publishers, Inc. © 1945 by Gwendolyn Brooks Blakely.

CONSTANTINE CAVAFY, "Nero's Term"
Reprinted by permission of Harcourt Brace Jovanovich, Inc., from *The Complete Poems of Cavafy*, trans. Rae Dalven. © 1961 by Rae Dalven.

All rights, including professional, amateur, motion picture, recitation, lecturing, public reading, radio broadcasting, and television are strictly reserved. Inquiries on all rights should be addressed to Harcourt Brace Jovanovich, Inc., 757 Third Avenue, New York, New York 10017

FRED CHAPPELL, "My Father Burns Washington"
Reprinted by permission of Louisiana State University Press from *Bloodfire*. © 1978 by Fred Chappell.

JOHN CIARDI, "A Sentiment for December 25"
From *Person to Person* by John Ciardi. © Rutgers, The State University, 1964. Reprinted by permission of the author.

VICTOR HERNANDEZ CRUZ, "today is a day of great joy"
From *Snaps*, by Victor Hernandez Cruz. © 1968, 1969 by Victor Hernandez Cruz. Reprinted by permission of Random House, Inc.

E.E. CUMMINGS, "my father moved through dooms of love"
Reprinted from *Complete Poems 1913–1962* by e. e. cummings. By permission of Harcourt Brace Jovanovich, Inc. Copyright 1940 by e. e. cummings; renewed 1968 by Marion Morehouse Cummings.

All rights, including professional, amateur, motion picture, recitation, lecturing, public reading, radio broadcasting, and television are strictly reserved. Inquiries on all rights should be addressed to Harcourt Brace Jovanovich, Inc., 757 Third Avenue, New York, New York 10017

J.V. CUNNINGHAM, "And What is Love?" ("Epigram")
From *The Exclusions of a Rhyme*, "Poems and Epigrams" by J.V. Cunningham, 1960. Reprinted by permission of the author.

JAMES DICKEY, "The Bee"
Reprinted from *Poems 1957–1967*. By permission of Wesleyan University Press. © 1966 by James Dickey.

RICHARD EBERHART, "The Fury of Aerial Bombardment"
From *Collected Poems 1930–1976* by Richard Eberhart. Reprinted by permission of Oxford University Press, Inc., and Chatto & Windus. © 1976 by Richard Eberhart.

RICHARD EBERHART, "Am I My Neighbor's Keeper?"
From *The Quarry* by Richard Eberhart. Reprinted by permission of Oxford University Press, Inc. © 1964 by Richard Eberhart.

RUSSELL EDSON, "Because Things Get Sad, Father"
From *The Very Thing That Happens.* Reprinted by permission of New Directions Publishing Corporation. © 1964 by Russell Edson.

T.S. ELIOT, "Journey of the Magi"
From *Collected Poems 1909–1962* by T. S. Eliot. Reprinted by permission of the publishers and Faber and Faber Ltd. Copyright 1936 by Harcourt Brace Jovanovich, Inc.; © 1963, 1964 by T. S. Eliot. CAUTION: All rights, including professional, amateur, motion picture, recitation, lecturing, public reading, radio broadcasting, and television are strictly reserved. Inquiries on all rights should be addressed to Harcourt Brace Jovanovich, Inc., 757 Third Avenue, New York, New York 10017

PAUL ENGLE, "Together"
Reprinted from *Embrace: Selected Love Poems* by Paul Engle. By permission of Random House, Inc. © 1969 by Paul Engle.

MARI EVANS, "Vive Noir" and "When In Rome"
From *I Am a Black Woman.* Published by William Morrow & Company, 1970, and reprinted by permission of the author.

LAWRENCE FERLINGHETTI, "Dog"
From a *Coney Island of the Mind* by Lawrence Ferlinghetti. Reprinted by permission of New Directions Publishing Corporation. © 1958 by Lawrence Ferlinghetti.

EDWARD FIELD, "Unwanted"
From *Stand Up Friend With Me* by Edward Field. Reprinted by permission of Grove Press, Inc. © 1963 by Edward Field.

ROBERT FRANCIS, "The Base Stealer"
Reprinted from *The Orb Weaver.* By permission of Wesleyan University Press. © 1948 by Robert Francis.

ROBERT FROST, "Acquainted with the Night"
From *The Poetry of Robert Frost,* ed. Edward Connery Lathem. Reprinted by permission of Holt, Rinehart, & Winston, Publishers. © 1928, 1969 by Holt, Rinehart, & Winston. © 1956 by Robert Frost.

ISABELLA GARDNER, "Summer Remembered"
Reprinted from *The Looking Glass* by Isabella Gardner. By permission of the University of Chicago Press.

NIKKI GIOVANNI, "Nikki-Rosa"

From *Black Judgement.* Reprinted by permission of the Broadside Press. © 1968 by Nikki Giovanni.

AMBROSE GORDON, JR., "Departures"
From *Thicket,* Vol. 1. Lucille Press, 1975. Reprinted by permission of the author.

ROBERT GRAVES, "Semidetached"
Published in *New American Review,* no. 9. Reprinted by permission of Curtis Brown, Ltd. © 1970 by Robert Graves.

RONALD GROSS, "Sonnet"
From *Pop Poems,* by Ronald Gross. Reprinted by permission of Simon & Schuster, a division of Gulf & Western Corporation. © 1967 by Ronald Gross.

WOODY GUTHRIE, "Plane Wreck at Los Gatos (Deportee)"
Lyric by Woody Guthrie; music by Martin Hoffman, TRO. © 1961 and 1963 Ludlow Music, Inc., New York, NY. Used by permission.

EDWIN A. HOOEY, "Foul Shot"
Special permission granted by *Read Magazine.* Published by Xerox Educational Publications. © Xerox Corporation, 1962.

JOHN HOLMES, "Map of My Country"
From *Map of My Country.* Duell, Sloan, & Pearce, 1943.

RICHARD HOWARD, "One More Eyewitness"
Reprinted by permission of the author; appeared in *Chelsea* 24/25, October, 1968.

LANGSTON HUGHES, "Making Poetry Pay"
"Dressed Up." Reprinted from *The Dream Keeper and Other Poems,* by Langston Hughes. By permission of Alfred A. Knopf, Inc. © 1927 by Alfred A. Knopf, Inc., and renewed 1955 by Langston Hughes.
"Porter." Reprinted from *Selected Poems of Langston Hughes.* By permission of Alfred A. Knopf, Inc. © 1927 by Alfred A. Knopf, Inc., and renewed 1955 by Langston Hughes.
Excerpt from "Sharecroppers." Reprinted from *Selected Poems of Langston Hughes.* By permission of Alfred A. Knopf, Inc. © 1942 by Alfred A. Knopf, Inc., and renewed 1970 by Arna Bontemps and George Houston Bass.
"Justice." Reprinted from *The Panther and the Lash: Poems of Our Times,* by Langston Hughes. By permission of Alfred A. Knopf, Inc. © 1967 by Arna Bontemps and George Houston Bass.
"Cross." Reprinted from *Selected Poems of Langston Hughes.* By permission of Alfred A. Knopf, Inc. © 1927 by Alfred A. Knopf, Inc., and renewed 1954 by Langston Hughes.
"I, Too." Reprinted from *Selected Poems of Langston Hughes.* By permission of Alfred A. Knopf, Inc. © 1926 by Alfred A. Knopf, Inc., and renewed 1954 by Langston Hughes.

LANGSTON HUGHES, "Theme for English B"
From *Montage of a Dream Deferred.* Reprinted by per-

mission of Harold Ober Association, Inc. © 1951 by Langston Hughes.

DAVID IGNATOW, "All Quiet"
Reprinted from *Rescue the Dead.* By permission of Wesleyan University Press. "All Quiet" originally appeared in *Poetry.* Copyright 1966 by David Ignatow.

LUCILLE IVERSON, "Outrage"
From *Outrage, Poems 1971–1974* by Lucille Iverson. Published by Know, Inc., of Pittsburgh. © 1974 by Lucille Iverson.

RANDALL JARRELL, "Next Day"
From *The Lost World* by Randall Jarrell. Reprinted with permission of Macmillan Publishing Co., Inc. © Randall Jarrell 1963, 1965. Originally appeared in *The New Yorker.*

ROBINSON JEFFERS, "Divinely Superfluous Beauty"
Reprinted from *Selected Poetry of Robinson Jeffers.* By permission of Random House, Inc. © 1924, 1952 by Robinson Jeffers.

JAMES WELDON JOHNSON, "The Judgment Day"
From *God's Trombones* by James Weldon Johnson. Reprinted by permission of Viking Penguin, Inc. Copyright 1927; © renewed 1955 by Grace Nail Johnson. All rights reserved.

LEROI JONES, "A Poem for Black Hearts"
From *Black Magic Poetry.* Reprinted by permission of the Sterling Lord Agency, Inc. © 1969 by LeRoi Jones.

ERICA JONG, "The Man Under the Bed"
From *Fruits and Vegetables* by Erica Jong. Reprinted by permission of Holt, Rinehart and Winston, Publishers. © 1968, 1970, 1971 by Erica Mann Jong.

GALWAY KINNELL, "Wait"
Reprinted by permission. © 1975 *The New Yorker* Magazine, Inc.

ETHERIDGE KNIGHT, "For Malcolm, A Year After"
From *Poems from Prison.* Reprinted by permission of Broadside Press. © 1968 by Etheridge Knight.

KENNETH KOCH, "Variations on a Theme by William Carlos Williams"
From *Thank You & Other Poems.* Reprinted by permission of Grove Press. Copyright 1962.

MAXINE KUMIN, "A Family Man"
From *The Nightmare Factory* by Maxine Kumin. By permission of Harper & Row, Publishers, Inc. © 1970 by Maxine Kumin.

JOSEPH LANGLAND, "War"
From *The Green Town (Poets of Today III).* Scribner's, 1956. First appeared in *The New Orleans Poetry Journal.* Reprinted by permission of the author. Copyright, Joseph Langland.

D.H. LAWRENCE, "Piano"
From *The Complete Poems of D.H. Lawrence,* eds. Vivian de Sola and F. Warren Roberts. Reprinted by permission of Viking, Inc. © 1964,

1971 by Angelo Ravagli and C. M. Weekley, Executors of the Estate of Frieda Lawrence Ravagli. All rights reserved.

NAOMI LAZARD, "Ordinance on Enrollment"
Reprinted from *Harper's Magazine,* September 1976. By permission of the author. © 1976 by *Harper's Magazine.* All rights reserved.

DENISE LEVERTOV, "The Day the Audience Walked Out on Me, and Why"
From *Footprints* by Denise Levertov. Reprinted by permission of New Directions Publishing Corporation. © 1972 by Denise Levertov.

ETHEL LIVINGSTON, "Somehow you know when it arrives,"
From *31 New American Poets,* ed. Ron Schreiber. Hill and Wang, 1969. Reprinted by permission of the author.

ROBERT LOWELL, "For Sale"
From *Life Studies* by Robert Lowell. Reprinted by permission of Farrar, Straus & Giroux, Inc. © 1956, 1959 by Robert Lowell.

CYNTHIA MACDONALD, "Accomplishments"
From *Transplants* by Cynthia Macdonald. Reprinted by permission of George Braziller, Inc. © 1976.

ARCHIBALD MACLEISH, "The Old Gray Couple (1)" and "The Old Gray Couple (2)"
From *New and Collected Poems: 1917–1976.* By permission of Houghton Mifflin Company. © 1976 by Archibald MacLeish.

NAOMI LONG MADGETT, "Her Story"
From *Star by Star* by Naomi Long Madgett. Detroit: Lotus Press, 1970. By permission of the author.

EDGAR LEE MASTERS, from *Spoon River Anthology:*
"Anne Rutledge"   "Mrs. Meyers"
"Hannah Armstrong"   "Mrs. Charles Bliss"
"Roscoe Purkapile"   "Rev. Lemuel Wiley"
"Mrs. Purkapile"   "Yee Bow"
"Albert Sherding"   "Judge Somers"
"Jonas Keene"   "Chase Henry"
"Minerva Jones"   "Elsa Wertman"
"Doctor Meyers"   "Hamilton Greene"
From *Spoon River Anthology,* by Edgar Lee Masters. Published 1916 by the Macmillan Company. By permission of Mrs. Ellen C. Masters.

EVE MERRIAM, "How to Eat a Poem"
From *It Doesn't Always Have to Rhyme.* By permission of Atheneum Publishers. © 1964 by Eve Merriam.

W.S. MERWIN, "Her Wisdom"
From *The First Four Books of Poems* by W. S. Merwin. These poems appeared originally in W. S. Merwin's *Green with Beasts.* Reprinted by permission of Atheneum Publishers. © 1955, 1956, 1975 by W. S. Merwin.

JOSEPHINE MILES, "Reason"
From *Poems 1930–1960* by Josephine Miles. Re-

printed by permission of Indiana University Press. © 1960.

CZESLAW MILOSZ, "Ars Poetica?"
From *Bells in Winter*. The Ecco Press. Reprinted by permission. © 1978 by Czeslaw Milosz.

JOHN MOFFITT, "To Look at Any Thing"
Reprinted from *The Living Seed*. By permission of Harcourt Brace Jovanovich, Inc. © 1961 by John Moffitt.
    All rights, including professional, amateur, motion picture, recitation, lecturing, public reading, radio broadcasting, and television are strictly reserved. Inquiries on all rights should be addressed to Harcourt Brace Jovanovich, Inc., 757 Third Avenue, New York, New York 10017

MARIANNE MOORE, "A Face"
From *Collected Poems* by Marianne Moore. Reprinted with permission of Macmillan Publishing Co., Inc. © 1951 by Marianne Moore.

OGDEN NASH, "The Private Dining Room"
From *Verses from 1929 On* by Ogden Nash. By permission of Little, Brown, and Company. First appeared in *The New Yorker*. © 1951 by Ogden Nash.

HOWARD NEMEROV, "A Primer of the Daily Round"
From *New and Selected Poems* by Howard Nemerov. The University of Chicago Press, 1960. Copyright by the author.

JOHN FREDERICK NIMS, "Love Poem"
From *The Iron Pastoral* by John Frederick Nims. Reprinted by permission of William Morrow & Company, Inc. © 1947 by John Frederick Nims.

ROBERT PACK, "Love"
From *Home from the Cemetery* by Robert Pack. Reprinted by permission of Rutgers University Press. © 1969 by Rutgers University, The State University of New Jersey.

ROBERT PHILLIPS, "The Married Man"
From *The Pregnant Man* by Robert Phillips. Reprinted by permission of Doubleday & Co., Inc. © 1972 by Choice Magazine, Inc.

FELIX POLLAK, "Speaking: The Hero"
From *Ginkgo*, by Felix Pollak. New Rochelle, N.Y.: Elizabeth Press, 1973. Reprinted by permission of the author.

JOHN CROWE RANSOM, "Piazza Piece"
Reprinted from *Selected Poems*, 3rd ed., revised and enlarged, by John Crowe Ransom. By permission of Alfred A. Knopf, Inc. Copyright 1927 by Alfred A. Knopf, Inc. and renewed 1955 by John Crowe Ransom.

ISHMAEL REED, ".05"
From *Chattanooga*, by Ishmael Reed. Reprinted by permission of Random House, Inc. © 1973 by Ishmael Reed.

ALASTAIR REID, "Weathering"
Reprinted by permission of *The New Republic* © 1978, The New Republic, Inc.

ADRIENNE RICH, "From a Survivor" and "Rape"
Reprinted from *Poems, Selected and New, 1950–1974* by Adrienne Rich. By permission of W.W. Norton & Company, Inc. © 1975, 1973, 1971, 1969, 1966 by W. W. Norton & Co., Inc. © 1967, 1963, 1962, 1961, 1960, 1959, 1958, 1957, 1956, 1955, 1954, 1953, 1952, 1951 by Adrienne Rich.

RAINER MARIA RILKE, "Loneliness"
From *Modern European Poetry*, ed. Willis Barnstone, trans. Edwin Morgan. Bantam, 1966. Reprinted by permission of Edwin Morgan.

EDWARD ARLINGTON ROBINSON, "How Annandale Went Out"
Originally published in *The Children of the Night*. Charles Scribner's Sons, 1897.

THEODORE ROETHKE, "The Serpent"
Reprinted from *The Collected Poems of Theodore Roethke*. By permission of Doubleday & Co., Inc. Copyright 1950 by Theodore Roethke.

THEODORE ROETHKE, "Otto"
From *The Collected Poems of Theodore Roethke*. By permission of Doubleday & Company, Inc. © 1963 by Beatrice Roethke, Administratix of the Estate of Theodore Roethke.

MURIEL RUKEYSER, "Ballad of Orange and Grape" and "Myth"
From *Breaking Open* by Muriel Rukeyser. Reprinted by permission of Monica McCall, International Creative Management. © 1973 by Muriel Rukeyser.

LOUIS B. SALOMON, "Univac to Univac"
Reprinted by permission of the author. © 1958 by *Harper's Magazine*.

SONIA SANCHEZ, "small comment"
From *Home Coming* by Sonia Sanchez. Reprinted by permission of Broadside Press. © 1969 by Sonia Sanchez.

JAMES SEAY, "Let Not Your Hart be Truble"
Reprinted from *Let Not Your Hart*. By permission of Wesleyan University Press. © 1968 by James Seay.

ANNE SEXTON, "Some Foreign Letters"
From *To Bedlam and Part Way Back* by Anne Sexton. Reprinted by permission of Houghton Mifflin Company. © 1960 by Anne Sexton.

NTOZAKE SHANGE, "no assistance"
Reprinted with permission of Macmillan Publishing Co., Inc. from *For Colored Girls Who Have Considered Suicide/When the Rainbow Is Enuf* by Ntozake Shange. © 1975, 1976, 1977 by Ntozake Shange.

KARL SHAPIRO, "Auto Wreck"
Reprinted from *Collected Poems 1940–1978*, by Karl Shapiro. By permission of Random House,

Inc. Copyright 1942 and renewed 1970 by Karl Shapiro.

W. D. Snodgrass, #7 of *Heart's Needle*
Reprinted from *Heart's Needle* by W. D. Snodgrass. By permission of Alfred A. Knopf, Inc. © 1959 by W. D. Snodgrass.

Alexander Solzhenitsyn, "Freedom to Breathe"
From *Stories and Prose Poems* by Alexander Solzhenitsyn, trans. Michael Glenny. Reprinted with the permission of Farrar, Straus & Giroux, Inc., and the Bodley Head. © 1961 by Farrar, Straus & Cudahy, Inc. (now Farrar, Straus & Giroux, Inc.). © 1970, 1971 by Michael Glenny.

Raymond Souster, "Get the Poem Outdoors"
From *So Far So Good* by Raymond Souster. By permission of Oberon Press.

Wole Soyinka, "Telephone Conversation"
From *A Book of African Verse*, ed. Reed & Wake, 1964. Reprinted by permission of the author.

Barry Spacks, "Freshmen"
From *The Company of Children* by Barry Spacks. Reprinted by permission of Doubleday & Company, Inc. Originally appeared in *The New Yorker*. © 1966 by Barry Spacks.

William Stafford, "A Tentative Welcome to Readers"
First appeared in *Poetry*. Reprinted by permission of the Editor of *Poetry* and William Stafford. © 1980 by the Modern Poetry Association.

William Stafford, "Vacation"
From *The Rescued Year* by William Stafford. Reprinted by permission of Harper & Row, Publishers, Inc. © 1960 by William E. Stafford.

James Stephens, "What Thomas an Buile Said in a Pub"
From *Collected Poems* by James Stephens. New York: Macmillan, 1954. Reprinted by permission of Mrs. Iris Wise and Macmillan, London and Basingstoke.

Wallace Stevens, "The Motive for Metaphor"
Reprinted from *The Collected Poems of Wallace Stevens* by Wallace Stevens. By permission of Alfred A. Knopf, Inc. Copyright 1947 by Wallace Stevens.

Leon Stokesbury, "To Laura Phelan: 1880–1906"
First appeared in *Southern Poetry Review*, Fall 1971. Reprinted by permission of the Editor.

May Swenson, "After the Dentist" and "Of Rounds"
From *Half Sun Half Sleep*. Reprinted by permission of the author. © 1967 by May Swenson.

Sara Teasdale, "Water Lilies"
Reprinted with permission of Macmillan Publishing Co., Inc., from *Collected Poems* by Sara Teasdale. Copyright 1920 by Macmillan Publishing Co., Inc.; renewed 1948 by Mamie T. Wheless.

Dylan Thomas, "Do Not Go Gentle Into That Good Night"

From *The Poems of Dylan Thomas*. Reprinted by permission of New Directions Publishing Corporation, J.M. Dent & Sons, Ltd., and Trustees for the copyrights of the late Dylan Thomas. Copyright 1952 by Dylan Thomas.

Mona Van Duyn, "Birthday Card for a Psychiatrist"
From *To See, To Take* by Mona Van Duyn. Reprinted by permission of Atheneum Publishers. Appeared originally in *Poetry*. © 1969, 1970 Mona Van Duyn.

Andrei Voznesensky, "Someone Is Beating a Woman"
From *Antiworlds and The Fifth Ace*, by Andrei Voznesensky, eds. Patricia Blake and Max Hayward. © 1966, 1967 by Basic Books, Inc., Publishers, New York. © 1963 by Encounter Ltd.

David Wagoner, "Staying Alive"
From *New and Selected Poems* by David Wagoner. Reprinted by permission of the publisher. © 1969 by Indiana University Press.

Diane Wakoski, "Dancing on the Grave of a Son of a Bitch"
Published in *Dancing on the Grave of a Son of a Bitch* by Black Sparrow Press. © 1973 by Diane Wakoski.

Diane Wakoski, "Alone Like a Window Washer at the 50th Story"
From *Virtuoso Literature for Two and Four Hands* by Diane Wakoski. Reprinted by permission of Doubleday and Company, Inc. © 1973, 1975, by Diane Wakoski.

Anne Waldman, "Things that go away and come back again"
From *The World Anthology*. Bobbs-Merrill, 1969. By permission of the author.

Anne Waldman, "Lady Tactics"
From *Fast Talking Woman*. © 1975, City Lights Pocket Poet Series 33.

Robert Penn Warren, "School Lesson Based on Word of Tragic Death of Entire Gillum Family"
From *Selected Poems 1923–1975*, by Robert Penn Warren. Reprinted by permission of Random House, Inc. © 1966 by Robert Penn Warren.

James Welch, "The Man From Washington"
Published in *Riding the Earthboy*, 40, revised ed., by James Welch. Reprinted by permission of Harper & Row, Publishers, Inc. © 1971, 1976 by James Welch.

Ruth Whitman, "Listening to grownups quarreling"
From *The Passion of Lizzie Borden: New and Selected Poems*. October House, 1973). © 1973 by Ruth Whitman.

Reed Whittemore, "The Bad Daddy"
From *Poems: New and Selected*. University of Minnesota Press, Minneapolis, © 1967 by Reed Whittemore.

RICHARD WILBUR, "The Pardon"
From *Ceremony and Other Poems*. Reprinted by permission of Harcourt Brace Jovanovich, Inc. Copyright 1950, 1978 by Richard Wilbur.

    All rights, including professional, amateur, motion picture, recitation, lecturing, public reading, radio broadcasting, and television are strictly reserved. Inquiries on all rights should be addressed to Harcourt Brace Jovanovich, Inc., 757 Third Avenue, New York, New York 10017

RICHARD WILBUR, "The Writer"
Reprinted from *The Mind-Reader*. By permission of Harcourt Brace Jovanovich, Inc. © 1971 by Richard Wilbur.

    All rights, including professional, amateur, motion picture, recitation, lecturing, public reading, radio broadcasting, and television are strictly reserved. Inquiries on all rights should be addressed to Harcourt Brace Jovanovich, Inc., 757 Third Avenue, New York, New York 10017

PETER WILD, "An Apology for Wolves"
From *The Afternoon in Dismay, 1968*. Art Association of Cincinnati. Reprinted by permission of the author. © Peter Wild, 1968.

WILLIAM CARLOS WILLIAMS, "This is Just to Say"
From *Collected Earlier Poems of William Carlos Williams*. Reprinted by permission of New Directions. Copyright 1938 by New Directions Publishing Corporation.

WILLIAM CARLOS WILLIAMS, "Dedication for a Plot of Ground"
From *Collected Earlier Poems*. Reprinted by permission of New Directions Publishing Corporation. Copyright 1938 by William Carlos Williams.

Prose

WOODY ALLEN, "The Lunatic's Tale"
From *The New Republic,* April 23, 1977. Reprinted by permission of the author. © 1977 by Woody Allen.

SHERWOOD ANDERSON, "Hands"
From *Winesburg, Ohio* by Sherwood Anderson. Reprinted by permission of the Viking Press. © 1919 by B. W. Huebsch, © 1947 by Eleanor Copenhaver Anderson.

ISAAC BABEL, "The Public Library"
From *You Must Know Everything* by Isaac Babel, trans. from the Russian by Max Hayward, ed. and with notes by Nathalie Babel. Reprinted with the permission of Farrar, Straus & Giroux, Inc. © 1967, 1968, 1969 by Nathalie Babel.

JAMES BALDWIN, "Autobiographical Notes"
From *Notes of a Native Son* by James Baldwin. Reprinted by permission of Beacon Press. © 1955 by James Baldwin.

DONALD BARTHELME, "The School"
From *Amateurs* by Donald Barthelme. Originally appeared in *The New Yorker*. Reprinted by permission of Farrar, Straus & Giroux, Inc. © 1974 by Donald Barthelme.

JORGE LUIS BORGES, "Emma Zunz"
From *Labyrinths* by Jorge Luis Borges, trans. by Donald A. Yates. Reprinted by permission of New Directions Publishing Corporation. © 1962 by New Directions Publishing Corporation.

WILLA CATHER, "A Wagner Matinée"
From *Youth and the Bright Medusa* by Willa Cather. Courtesy of Alfred A. Knopf, Inc.

ELDRIDGE CLEAVER, " 'The Christ' and His Teachings"
From *Soul on Ice* by Eldridge Cleaver. By permission of McGraw-Hill Book Co. © 1968 by Eldridge Cleaver.

JOHN COLLIER, "The Chaser"
From *Fancies and Goodnights* by John Collier. Reprinted by permission of The Harold Matson Co., Inc. © 1940, 1968 by John Collier.

WILLIAM L. COPITHORNE, "From Us To You"
Reprinted with permission. © 1954 by The Atlantic Monthly Company, Boston, Mass.

WILLIAM FAULKNER, "A Rose for Emily"
From *Selected Short Stories of William Faulkner* by William Faulkner. By permission of Random House, Inc. © 1930, 1958 by William Faulkner.

ANNE FRANK, from *The Diary of a Young Girl*
Published 1947 and reprinted by permission of Vallentine, Mitchell, & Co., Ltd., London.

ANGELICA GIBBS, "The Test"
Reprinted with permission from *The New Yorker,* June 15, 1940.

JOSEPH HELLER, "Love, Dad"
Published in *Playboy Magazine,* November, 1969. Reprinted by permission of Candida Donadio & Associates, Inc. © 1969 by Joseph Heller.

LANGSTON HUGHES, "Making Poetry Pay"
From *I Wonder as I Wander* by Langston Hughes. Reprinted by permission of Farrar, Straus, & Giroux, Inc. © 1956 by Langston Hughes.

JAMES JOYCE, "Araby"
From *Dubliners* by James Joyce. Reprinted by permission of Viking Penguin, Inc. © 1967 by the Estate of James Joyce.

WILLIAM MELVIN KELLEY, "Not Exactly Lena Horne"
From *Dancers on the Shore* by William Melvin Kelley. By permission of Doubleday & Company, Inc. © 1964 by William Melvin Kelley.

JOHN LENNON, "Randolf's Party"
From *In His Own Write*. Jonathon Cape Ltd., 1964. Reprinted by permission of the author.

BERNARD MALAMUD, "The Jewbird"
From *Idiots First* by Bernard Malamud. Reprinted with the permission of Farrar, Straus, & Giroux, Inc. © 1963 by Bernard Malamud.

KATHERINE MANSFIELD, "Miss Brill"
From *The Short Stories of Katherine Mansfield* by Katherine Mansfield. By permission of Alfred A. Knopf, Inc. © 1922 by Alfred A. Knopf, Inc., and renewed 1950 by John Middleton Murry.

ARCHIBALD MARSHALL, "The Ancient Roman"
From *Simple Stories* by Archibald Marshall. © 1968 by Elizabeth Lawrence Potts, Pantheon Books.

CARSON MCCULLERS, "Madame Zilensky and the King of Finland"
From *The Ballad of the Sad Cafe and Other Stories*. By permission of Houghton Mifflin Company. © 1955 by Carson McCullers.

VLADIMIR NABOKOV, "Collette"
Originally published under the title "First Love." From *Nabokov's Dozen* by Vladimir Nabokov. Originally appeared in *The New Yorker*, July 31, 1948. Reprinted by permission of Doubleday & Co., Inc., and *The New Yorker*. © 1948 by Vladimir Nabokov.

FLANNERY O'CONNER, "The Crop"
From *The Complete Stories* by Flannery O'Conner. Reprinted with permission of Farrar, Straus, & Giroux, Inc. © 1971 by the Estate of Mary Flannery O'Conner.

FLANNERY O'CONNOR, "A Good Man Is Hard to Find"
From *A Good Man Is Hard to Find and Other Stories*. By permission of Harcourt Brace Jovanovich, Inc. © 1953 by Flannery O'Connor.
All rights, including professional, amateur, motion picture, recitation, lecturing, public reading, radio broadcasting, and television are strictly reserved. Inquiries on all rights should be addressed to Harcourt Brace Jovanovich, Inc., 757 Third Avenue, New York, New York 10017

TILLIE OLSEN, "I Stand Here Ironing"
Excerpted from *Tell Me a Riddle* by Tillie Olsen. Originally appeared in *Pacific Spectator*. Reprinted by permission of Delacorte Press/Seymour Lawrence. © 1956 by Tillie Olsen.

KATHARINE ANNE PORTER, "Rope"
From *Flowering Judas and Other Stories*. By permission of Harcourt Brace Jovanovich, Inc. © 1930, 1958 by Katherine Anne Porter.
All rights, including professional, amateur, motion picture, recitation, lecturing, public reading, radio broadcasting, and television are strictly reserved. Inquiries on all rights should be addressed to Harcourt Brace Jovanovich, Inc., 757 Third Avenue, New York, New York 10017

ERNIE PYLE, "The Movies"
From *The Home Country*. Reprinted with permission of The Scripps-Howard Foundation.

CYNTHIA RICH, "My Sister's Marriage"
First published in *Mademoiselle*. Reprinted by permission of the author. © 1955 by Cynthia Marshall Rich.

RAINER MARIA RILKE, from *Letters to a Young Poet*
From *Letters to a Young Poet* by Rainer Maria Rilke, trans. M. D. Herter Norton. By permission of W. W. Norton & Company, Inc. © 1934 by W. W. Norton & Company, Inc. © renewed by M. D. Herter Norton. © Revised Edition 1954 by W. W. Norton & Company, Inc.

LEONARD Q. ROSS, "The Rather Difficult Case of Mr. K*A*P*L*A*N"
From *The Education of Hyman Kaplan* by Leonard Q. Ross. Reprinted by permission of the publisher. © 1937 by Harcourt Brace Jovanovich, Inc.; renewed, 1965, by Leo C. Rosten.
All rights, including professional, amateur, motion picture, recitation, lecturing, public reading, radio broadcasting, and television are strictly reserved. Inquiries on all rights should be addressed to Harcourt Brace Jovanovich, Inc., 757 Third Avenue, New York, New York 10017

BEVERLY SILLS, from *Bubbles*
From *Bubbles* by Beverly Sills. Reprinted by permission of the Bobbs-Merrill Co., Inc. © 1976 by Meredith Enterprises.

LEE SMITH, "Between the Lines"
From *Carolina Quarterly*, Winter 1980. By permission of Lee Smith Seay.

MARGARET CHASE SMITH, "Declaration of Conscience I"
From *Declaration of Conscience* by Margaret Chase Smith. By permission of Doubleday & Company, Inc. © 1972 by Margaret Chase Smith.

MURIEL SPARK, "Miss Pinkerton's Apocalypse"
From *The Go-Away Bird and Other Stories* by Muriel Spark. Reprinted by permission of Harold Ober Associates Incorporated. © 1958 by Muriel Spark.

JEAN STAFFORD, "The Hope Chest"
From *The Collected Stories of Jean Stafford*. Reprinted by permission of Farrar, Straus & Giroux, Inc. © 1946, 1974, by Jean Stafford.

GERTRUDE STEIN, "Saving the Sentence"
From *Storytellers and Their Art*, eds. Georgianne Trask & Charles Burkhart. Reprinted by permission of Doubleday & Company, Inc. © 1963 by Charles Burkhart.

FERRIS TAKAHASHI, "The Widower"
From *The Pacific Citizen*, December 21, 1956. Reprinted by permission of the author.

STUDS TERKEL, "Roger" and "Cesar Chavez"
From *Hard Times: An Oral History of the Great Depression* by Studs Terkel. Reprinted by permission of Pantheon Books, a Division of Random House, Inc. © 1970 by Studs Terkel.

JAMES THURBER, "The Very Proper Gander"
From *Fables for Our Time*. Published by Harper &

Row. Originally printed in *The New Yorker*. ©
1940 by James Thurber. © 1968 by Helen
Thurber.

JAMES THURBER, "Which"
From *The Owl in the Attic*. Published by Harper &
Row. Originally printed in *The New Yorker*. ©
1931, 1959 by James Thurber.

JAMES THURBER, "A Couple of Hamburgers"
From *Let Your Mind Alone*. Published by Harper and
Row. Originally printed in *The New Yorker*. ©
1937 James Thurber.

KURT VONNEGUT, JR., "Who Am I This Time?"
Welcome to the Monkey House by Kurt Vonnegut, Jr.
Originally published in *The Saturday Evening
Post* as "My Name Is Everyone." Reprinted by
permission of Delacorte Press/Seymour Law-
rence. © 1961 by Kurt Vonnegut, Jr.

EUDORA WELTY, "A Worn Path"
From *A Curtain of Green and Other Stories*. By permission of Harcourt Brace Jovanovich, Inc. ©
1941, 1969, by Eudora Welty.
    All rights, including professional, amateur,
motion picture, recitation, lecturing, public
reading, radio broadcasting, and television are
strictly reserved. Inquiries on all rights should
be addressed to Harcourt Brace Jovanovich,
Inc., 757 Third Avenue, New York, New
York 10017

E. B. WHITE, "The Hour of Letdown"
From *The Second Tree from the Corner* by E. B. White.
Originally appeared in *The New Yorker*. Reprinted by permission of Harper & Row, Publishers, Inc. © 1951 by E. B. White.

Drama

JOANNA M. GLASS, "Canadian Gothic"
Canadian Gothic is fully protected under the copyright laws of the United States of America,
and of all countries covered by the International Copyright Union (including the Dominion of Canada and the rest of the British
Commonwealth), and of all countries covered
by the Universal Copyright Convention, and
of all countries with which the United States
has reciprocal copyright relations. All rights,
including professional, amateur, motion picture, recitation, lecturing, public reading, radio broadcasting, television, and the rights of
translation into foreign languages, are strictly
reserved. Particular emphasis is laid on the
question of readings, permission for which
must be secured from the author's agent in
writing. All inquiries (except for amateur
rights) should be addressed to the Lucy Kroll
Agency, 390 West End Avenue, New York,
N.Y. 10024.
    The amateur production rights in *Canadian
Gothic* are controlled exclusively by the

Dramatists Play Service, Inc., 440 Park South,
New York, N.Y. 10016. No amateur performance of either play may be given without ob-
taining in advance the written permission of
the Dramatists Play Service, Inc., and paying
the requisite fee.

HELEN HAYES, from "Favorite Scenes"
From *A Gift of Joy* by Helen Hayes with Lewis Funke.
Reprinted by permission of the publisher, M.
Evans and Company, Inc., New York. © 1965
by Helen Hayes and Lewis Funke.

WILLIAM INGE, "To Bobolink, For Her Spirit"
Reprinted from *Summer Brave and Eleven Short Plays*
by William Inge. By permission of Random
House, Inc. © 1950 by William Inge.

EUGENE O'NEILL, "Before Breakfast"
From *The Plays of Eugene O'Neill*, by Eugene O'Neill.
By permission of Random House, Inc. © 1924
by Boni and Liveright, Inc.

EUGENE O'NEILL, "Ile"
From *The Plays of Eugene O'Neill* by Eugene O'Neill.
By permission of Random House, Inc. © 1919
and 1947 by Eugene O'Neill.

HAROLD PINTER, "Trouble in the Works"
From *Revue Sketches*. By permission of Grove Press,
Inc. © 1961 by Harold Pinter.

LUIGI PIRANDELLO, "The Man with the Flower in His
Mouth"
Translated by Eric Bently. Reprinted by permission
of Toby Cole, agent for the Pirandello Estate.
© Grove Press, 1961.

MURRAY SCHISGAL, "Memorial Day"
From *Fragments, Windows, and Other Plays*. Reprinted
by permission of International Creative Management. © 1965 by Murray Schisgal.

GEORGE BERNARD SHAW, from *Androcles and the Lion*
From *Complete Plays with Prefaces, Vol. V*. By permission of The Society of Authors, on behalf of
the Bernard Shaw Estate.

JOHN M. SYNGE, "Riders to the Sea"
From *The Complete Works of John M. Synge*. Random
House, Inc.

LUIS VALDEZ, "Las Dos Caras del Patroncito"
From *Speaking for Ourselves: American Ethnic Writing*,
eds. Lillian Faderman and Barbara Bradshaw.
Reprinted by permission of Menyah Productions. © 1975.

TENNESSEE WILLIAMS, "This Property Is Condemned"
From *Twenty-seven Wagons Full of Cotton*. Reprinted
by permission of New Directions Publishing
Corporation. © 1945 by Tennessee Williams.

DANIEL WRIGHT, "The Feast"
From *Ten Great One-Act Plays*, ed. Morris Sweetkind.
Published by Bantam Books, Inc. By permis-
sion of the publisher. © 1966 by Daniel
Wright.

Index